■ Beating the Odds

Beating the Odds

A Teen Guide to 75 Superstars Who Overcame Adversity

Mary Ellen Snodgrass

GREENWOOD PRESS
Westport, Connecticut • London

Library of Congress Cataloging-in-Publication Data

Snodgrass, Mary Ellen.
  Beating the odds : a teen guide to 75 superstars who overcame adversity / Mary Ellen Snodgrass.
      p.   cm.
  Includes bibliographical references and index.
  ISBN: 978–0–313–34564–7 (alk. paper)
    1. People with disabilities—Biography.   2. People with mental disabilities—Biography.
3. People with social disabilities—Biography.   4. Celebrities—Biography.   5. Courage—Case studies.
6. Character—Case studies.   I. Title.
  HV1552.3.S67   2008
  362.4092′2—dc22   2008016572

British Library Cataloguing in Publication Data is available.

Library of Congress Catalog Card Number: 2008016572
ISBN: 978–0–313–34564–7

First published in 2008

Greenwood Press, 88 Post Road West, Westport, CT 06881
An imprint of Greenwood Publishing Group, Inc.
www.greenwood.com

Printed in the United States of America

The paper used in this book complies with the
Permanent Paper Standard issued by the National
Information Standards Organization (Z39.48–1984).

10 9 8 7 6 5 4 3 2 1

For Jacob and Tom

Lord, make me to know the measure of my days on earth,
to consider my frailties, that I must perish.

—Johannes Brahms, *Requiem Mass* (1868)

■ Contents

■ Preface

Survival is part inborn, part learned. People who refuse to be cowed by political situations, disease, or personal calamity serve others as standards. They rise above the ordinary, not for purity of motive or exemplary behavior, but for the quality that Ernest Hemingway identified as grace under pressure. To foster human resilience, this work assembles 75 biographies to impress on readers unique means of fighting adversity, from survival in an iron lung to publishing a controversial religious view, from escaping gangs, stalkers, and ghettos to confronting racism, sexism, death of a loved one, or long-term physical and emotional abuse. Paragons of strength and ingenuity come from a variety of backgrounds—athletics, business, child advocacy, film, fine arts, law, medicine, politics, religion, royalty, scientific research, the stage, and television. Individual examples juxtapose character vigor alongside a panorama of human weaknesses—alcoholism, adultery, self-pity, overconfidence, eating disorders, and vengeance. Along the way to triumph, some of the winners detoured to private lairs of substance abuse, solitude, workaholism, and mental terrors before emerging to face deprivation, persecution, hurt, or loss. Whatever the cost of personal growth to each, the reward to the self is a measure of contentment seized from struggle. Those who admire and emulate the success stories share the winners' rewards and store up like windfalls glimmers of wisdom and inklings of compassion.

Beating the Odds: A Teen Guide to 75 Superstars Who Overcame Adversity offers the reader, researcher, teacher, counselor, platform or pulpit speaker, and therapist a cornucopia of success stories. The text orders examples alphabetically by struggle—HIV, whistle-blowing, speech defect, gender misidentification, and bipolarity, among others—to set in context signal acts of self-rescue. Entries summarize the resolve of individuals to elude failure, pain, or death by unique strategies. Enhancing biographical data are quotations that capture the spirit of Olympians Jackie Joyner-Kersee and Greg Louganis, the commitment to civil disobedience of the Berrigan brothers and Jane Fonda, the self-empowerment of Oprah Winfrey and John Bul Dau, and the parental risk-taking of Betty Mahmoody and Jane Seymour. Details place subjects alongside period struggles, including school integration in Little Rock, the Vietnam War, the Native American seizure of Alcatraz, and protests of the Iraq War and the American prison in Guantanamo, Cuba.

Research materials derive from various sources—memoirs, author and press interviews, career commentaries, biographical videos and DVDs, news headlines, and overviews of epidemics and political dissent. Rounding out the text, additional aids particularize people, physical limitations, and public response to triumphs:

- Entry bibliographies present primary and secondary sources for additional perusal, including Queen Noor's *Leap of Faith: Memoirs of an Unexpected Life*, Jane Fonda's *My Life So Far*, Mitch Albom's *Tuesdays with Morrie*, Paula Deen's *It Ain't All About the Cookin'*, and Luis J. Rodriguez's *Always Running: La Vida Loca: Gang Days in L. A.*

- A glossary of 67 medical terms provides definitions and symptoms of painful or crippling mental and physical traumas, for example, survivor guilt in Nazi survivor

Johanna Reiss, ptosis in the eyelids of condemned author Salman Rushdie, anorexia in prima ballerina Gelsey Kirkland, hydrocephalus in author Alexie Sherman, myasthenia gravis in Cherokee Chief Wilma Mankiller, Lyme disease in novelist Amy Tan, and adrenoleukodystrophy, a catastrophic genetic disorder in boys like Lorenzo Odone.

- A filmography suggests video and DVD biographies for further study of such public figures as Caroline Kennedy, Patricia Neal, Ron Kovic, Magic Johnson, Jessica Lynch, Pete Seeger, Oprah Winfrey, Ben Carson, and Jeanne Wakatsuki Houston.

- An exhaustive index lists biographical entries (like Toni Morrison, Joseph Bruchac, Sean Covey, and Stephen King) and major struggles (like tyranny, public ridicule, Third World poverty, and capture). Key to understanding are references to secondary terms:

  People—Janet Reno, George H. W. Bush, Raphael Trujillo, Ojibway, Max Cleland, Cesar Chavez, Cindy Sheehan, Susan Sarandon, John W. Hinckley, Jr.

  Institutions—FBI, Red Cross, School of the Americas, House Un-American Activities Committee, Immigration and Naturalization Service, U.S. Supreme Court.

  Places—Vietnam Memorial, Sudan, concentration camp, Siberia, Korea, The Citadel, India, Mount Everest, Harlem, Vieques, Puerto Rico.

  Events—folk music revival, *Brown v. the Board of Education* (1954), Japanese internment, assassination, civil war, Sino-Japanese War, Native American Renaissance, Tour de France.

  Goals—Booker Prize, diet, microfinancing, Olympics, multiculturalism, Academy Award, presidency, self-help, child advocacy, Golden Globe, immigration, rehabilitation, Nobel Prize.

  Self-Expression—mountain climbing, writing, bodybuilding, *The Nutcracker*, cooking, flying, design, reading, advertising, storytelling, guitar, lecturing, medicine, sports.

  Issues—kidnap, rape, reservation life, censorship, plastic surgery, adoption, sex scandal, bullying, child neglect, delinquency, gun-related crime, eugenics, tribal relocation.

  Beliefs—atheism, Judaism, Islam, Catholicism, pacifism, Buddhism, Communism, proactivism, Marxism.

  Concepts—First Amendment rights, colonialism, slavery, civil disobedience, abstinence, Jim Crow, Taliban.

  Social Movements—United Farm Workers, Feminist Movement, gangs, Catholic Workers Movement, pacifism.

  Punishments—police brutality, poverty, suicide, terrorism, female silencing, confiscation, sexual harassment, bombing, exile, fatwa.

The completed volume promises an uplifting read about icons like Elie Wiesel, Muhammad Yunus, Martin Sheen, Caroline Kennedy, Maya Lin, Ben Carson, and Dolores Hurerta alongside controversial figures Roseanne Barr, Hillary Clinton, Jamie Koufman, Francine Moran Hughes, and Angela Davis. In each life, there is much to respect.

N.B. During the processing of this work, two of the subjects died. Dianne O'Dell of Jackson, Tennessee, the longest surviving polio patient confined to an iron lung, died on May 28, 2008, at age 61 of asphyxiation after a power outage shut down her life support system. Lorenzo Odone of Fairfax, Virginia, a victim of degeneration in the myelin sheath of nerve cells, died of pneumonia on May 30, 2008, the day after his thirtieth birthday.

■ Acknowledgments

Katherine Balkin, literary agent, New York City

Joseph Bruchac, author, Saratoga, New York

Frank Collerius, librarian, Jefferson Market Library, Greenwich Village, New York

Pat Conroy, author, Beaufort, South Carolina

Rena Coughlin, retired executive assistant, Virginia Beach, Virginia

Kaye Gibbons, author, Raleigh, North Carolina

James D. Houston and Jeanne Wakatsuki Houston, authors, Santa Clara, California

Hannah Owen, deputy director, Hickory Public Library, Hickory, North Carolina

Dayle Reilly, coordinator, Sonoma State University Library, Rohnert Park, California

Yoko Kawashima Watkins, author, Brewster, Massachusetts

■ Accident
Stephen King

Stephen King, an international icon of fantasy and gothic fiction, mounted a vigorous career until a one-car accident compromised his stamina and concentration. Born on September 21, 1947, in Portland, Maine, he was a sickly child troubled by earaches and strep throat. His mother, Nellie Ruth Pillsbury King, reared Stephen and his adopted older brother David after the abandonment by their father, lumberman and amateur fantasy writer Donald Edwin King. Without an explanation, the father slipped away in 1949 under the ruse of going out for cigarettes. A search for family security took the mother and two sons from Durham, Maine, to Fort Wayne, Indiana, to Stratford, Connecticut. While the "latchkey" boys cared for themselves after school, Nellie King worked as a doughnut maker, store clerk, laundry presser, retirement home cook, and caretaker for the elderly. Her devotion to the fatherless boys launched King's liberal conscientiousness and his sympathy for the lone female and the outsider, a label he applied to himself.

King's childhood dreams were vivid, but his experiences with terror were unremarkable. He loved baseball games, live or on the radio. A bibliophile from preschool days, he listened to his brother read aloud and later to his mother's chapter-by-chapter reading of Robert Louis Stevenson's *Treasure Island* and *Dr. Jekyll and Mr. Hyde*. Alone by night at the radio, Stephen comforted his fears by the light from the bathroom while listening to a broadcast of Ray Bradbury's *Mars Is Heaven* (1950). At the cinema, he saw *Creature from the Black Lagoon* (1954), *Earth vs. the Flying Saucers* (1956), *Attack of the Giant Leeches* (1959), and *The Pit and the Pendulum* (1961). From the mailman, Steven grabbed the family's copy of the *Saturday Evening Post* and devoured an installment of the latest serial. In Sunday school, he pondered the biblical terrors of God's mark on Cain, Noah's Ark rumbling through the flood, Jonah in the whale's belly, and the scourging and crucifixion of Jesus. During a physical terror, King suffered stings after he stirred a nest of wasps from a cinder block. On a visit to a doctor, he endured without anesthetic the puncture of his infected eardrum, a procedure that required three repetitions. He later longed to have the doctor imprisoned for lying about the "painless" treatment. King claimed, "I think that in some deep valley of my head, that last scream is still echoing" (Whitelaw, 2006, 13).

Learning from the Masters

Stephen refined his interest in horror through readings from the *Tales from the Crypt* comic book series and from works by Isaac Asimov, William Golding, Robert Heinlein, Shirley Jackson, H. P. Lovecraft, Richard Matheson, Edgar Allan Poe, J. R. R. Tolkien, and Daphne du Maurier. Ignoring the admonitions of his teachers, in boyhood, he composed supernatural stories and screenplays. His brother mimeographed them in the two-man newspaper, *Dave's Rag*, which sold for 30 cents each to a 20-household circulation list. With friend Christopher Chesley, Stephen composed round-robin stories, alternating chapters with Chris as the tales took shape. In addition, Stephen worked as a stringer for the *Lisbon Enterprise* and distributed an illegal underground high school satire, the *Village Vomit*, for which he served 2 weeks in detention and apologized to all the teachers he ridiculed in print. Derived from his part-time job as a gravedigger, his first published work, "I Was a Teen-Age Grave-Robber" (1965), appeared in *Comics Review*, a horror magazine issued in Birmingham, Alabama. The triumph boosted his self-esteem. Although relegated to the classroom losers, before his teens, King could call himself an author.

On a scholarship and the wages of an industrial laundryman, King entered the University of Maine at Orono in 1966 to study American and British literature and speech with a minor in education. For the student paper, *Maine Campus*, he penned the column "King's Garbage Truck," a roving satire on college snobbery and cliques. In 1967, he sold "The Glass Floor" to *Startling Mystery Stories*. At age 21, he became the first nondegreed person at the university to team-teach a college course, "Popular Literature and Culture," which he designed to broaden the curriculum. Influenced by English writer Robert Browning's poem on Childe Roland, King wrote *Sword in the Darkness* (2006) and *Dark Tower* (2004), which remained unpublished until late in his career. He had earned five checks for stories he submitted to *Magazine of Fantasy and Science Fiction* by the time he graduated college in 1970.

In an era of social turmoil and civil disobedience, King joined the counterculture. He challenged the draft during the Vietnam War and received a 4-F classification because of his limited vision and pierced eardrum. On January 2, 1971, he married Tabitha "Tabby" Spruce, a fellow writer, history student, and poetry lover whom he met while working at the college library. He later compared her to the "pearl of great price," a tender image from a parable that Jesus told (Matthew 13: 45–46). The couple rented a double-wide trailer and made a home for their family of three, Naomi Rachel, now a Unitarian minister, and Joseph Hillstrom and Owen Phillip, both authors. At Hampden Academy, a public high school in Hampden, Maine, Stephen joined the English staff and taught creative writing and literature. He supplemented a teacher's salary with proceeds from pumping gas, cleaning a girls' locker room, and selling horror tales that he pecked out on Tabby's Olivetti typewriter.

A Solid Career

Like his hardworking mother Nellie Ruth, King persevered at his profession. He wrote some 200 stories for *Adam*, *Cavalier*, *Dark Forces*, *Gent*, *New Yorker*, *Penthouse*, *Playboy*, *Twilight Zone Magazine*, and *Whispers* but clipped out erotic sections before he sent them to her to read. His style featured his concept of "phobic pressure points," his term for the breaking points in human courage (King, 1981, 2). He achieved stardom for a classic horror novella, *Carrie* (1973), a tale of vengeance and telekinesis that Tabby rescued from the scrap heap and urged him to finish. The story featured the type of alienated teen that King had been in high school. He developed the narrative in his idiosyncratic style—by placing himself in a "what if" situation and imagining how Carrie would get even with her tormentors. In late December 1973, during his 59-year-old mother's last days fighting uterine cancer, King's Aunt Emma read the novel aloud to her. With a $2,500 advance from Doubleday, King replaced his ramshackle car, pulled his family out of poverty, and moved them from a trailer to an apartment.

Good times seemed unending for King. By spring 1973, on the $400,000 advance for paperback rights to *Carrie*, he quit the classroom to write full time, even though he was fond of teaching teenagers. After spending a year in Boulder, Colorado, where Stephen researched another horror novel, the King family settled in western Maine in the summer of 1975. Brian de Palma filmed *Carrie* in 1976, featuring Piper Laurie and child star Sissy Spacek as a dysfunctional mother and daughter, Margaret and Carrie White. Both actors earned

Oscar nominations for their performances. Under the pen name Richard Bachman, Stephen King doubled his production and published *Rage* (1977), *The Long Walk* (1979), *Road Work* (1981), *The Running Man* (1982), and *Thinner* (1984). In 1978, while completing *The Stand*, King taught creative writing at his alma mater. Pressures worsened his habitual drinking and abuse of cigarettes and marijuana, NyQuil and cough medicine, Xanax, Valium, and cocaine. He took a break from intrusive fans by moving to Fleet, England, 40 miles southwest of London, but the move did little to advance his career.

More Fame, More Movies

After returning to Maine, King killed off Richard Bachman with a witty disease, "cancer of the pseudonym, a rare form of schizonomia." King returned to his real identity with a first *New York Times* bestseller, *The Dead Zone* (1979), a tale of time travel that the author lauded as one of his best for its tightly constructed plot. Proclaimed as America's most popular author by *People* magazine, he issued a study of pyromania and government-sponsored experiments on children in *Firestarter* (1980). Within months, he finished *Danse Macabre* (1980), a horror handbook compiled from lectures at the University of Maine on the supernatural; a killer St. Bernard story in *Cujo* (1981); and the short story "Shawshank Redemption" (1981), a film vehicle for Tim Robbins and Morgan Freeman. King created a new alter ego, John Swithen, as author of "The Fifth Quarter," issued in *Cavalier* magazine and collected in a fiction anthology, *Nightmares & Dreamscapes* (1993), the sources of a Turner Network Television miniseries. Another of King's eerie classics, the serial novel *The Green Mile* (1996), a slang term for death row, was the vehicle for a Tom Hanks film about faith healing, produced by Frank Darabont 3 years later. The film won four Oscar nominations, a Blockbuster Entertainment Award, two Critics Choice Awards, a Reader's Choice citation, and a First Americans in the Arts award for actor Graham Greene, who played the part of condemned prisoner Arlen Bitterbuck.

Although bypassed for serious literary awards early in his career, King won a series of recognitions from fellow gothic authors and fans of horror fiction. He achieved a first Nebula Award, the first two of six Bram Stoker Awards, the first two of four Locus Awards, the first of four Horror Guild citations, a Hugo Award, a World Fantasy Award, and a British Fantasy Award. He earned the 1996 O. Henry Award for a satanic fable, "The Man in the Black Suit." In 1997, novelist Joyce Carol Oates introduced King to an audience at Princeton University and chose her favorites from his inventive corpus: *Salem's Lot* (1976), *Misery* (1987), *Pet Sematary* (1988), and *Dolores Claiborne* (1992), each the source of a popular film. In another of her picks, *The Shining* (1977), King wrote about a weekend he spent with Tabby as the only guests at the Stanley Hotel in Estes Park, Colorado. In 1996, he achieved a signal honor based on popular appeal, a mention in the *Guinness Book of World Records* for the only author with six titles on the bestseller list at one time.

Broken Bones

Three months before his 50th birthday, King made his afternoon 4-mile jog along Route Five in Center Lovell, Maine, when the Dodge Caravan of a drunk driver swerved and struck him from behind. The collision threw King 14 feet, breaking his right hip and four ribs, crushing his right leg and splitting the knee, chipping his spine, and puncturing his right lung. The rescue crew predicted that he would survive. After an emergency room physician dispatched King by helicopter to Central Maine Medical Center in Lewiston, he required a 3-week recuperation from five surgeries. While his "hardware-encumbered leg" progressed from wheelchair to walker to crutches and a cane, he took "enough painkillers to levitate a horse" (King, 2000, 13). Hobbling about at home, he occupied himself reading J. K. Rowling's Harry Potter series, which he critiqued for the *New York Times* book review, and "found [himself] a lot more than moderately wowed" by the popular metaphysical novels (Ibid.). Although he remained hopeful and optimistic about his recovery, the agony of a splintered hip, pins in his leg, and repeated infections inhibited his sitting at a computer keyboard to write.

In addition to Tabby's encouragement, King needed the rigor of his profession to guard him from a new addiction to painkillers. He completed an autobiography and succinct guide to authors, *On Writing: A Memoir of the Craft* (2000). He chose the accident as a source of plot for the *Dark Tower* series and inserted himself as protagonist Jake Chambers. During recuperation, King used pen and notebook to draft *Dreamcatcher* (2001). In a nod toward electronic publishing, in 2000, he serialized "Riding the Bullet" and the novel *The Plant* on the Internet—but found the outreach limited. In 2002, his daily struggle with posttraumatic pain forced him to cease writing. Still infused with creativity, in 2003, the year of his Horror Writers' Association Lifetime Achievement citation, he produced a column for *Entertainment Weekly* entitled "The Pop of King." For publishing 50 works selling over 250 million copies, on November 19, 2003, he received a National Book Foundation medal at a time when his health was still compromised by 25 percent. For his contributions to metaphysical fiction, in 2004, he accepted the World Fantasy lifetime achievement award.

Recovery

King asserts his ongoing ambition to be a storyteller. His method remains unchanged: he plants a narrative seed and lets it develop on its own, sometimes surprising him at its conclusion. He explained in an essay on J. K. Rowling, "The fantasy writer's job is to conduct the willing reader from mundanity to magic" (King, 2000, 14). In a subsequent essay for the *Washington Post*, "Watching a Writer Write Is About as Interesting as Watching Paint Dry," King warns the curious that "[t]here is little mystery or tragic romance" about the profession (King, 2006, T10).

Still walking $3^1/_2$ miles per day, King refuses to be sidelined by the accident. His most recent projects tend to be minimalist works readily accessible to young readers. In October 2005, he began writing in collaboration with Marvel Comics. In June 2006, he joined a live Webcast called *Amazon Fishbowl*. Under the pen name Richard Bachman, King issued *Blaze* (2007), a trunk novel, a slang term for a work that remains unfinished or unpublished over a long time span. Wealthy beyond his expectations, he earned more from the horror genre than any author. He owns a Gulf-side summer home in Sarasota, Florida, and donates to children's athletics, the University of Maine, the YMCA and YWCA, and scholarship programs. As a promoter of civil liberties, he supports independent booksellers and an end to censorship.

Sources

King, Stephen. *Danse Macabre*. New York: Everest House, 1981.
———. *Nightmares & Dreamscapes*. New York: Viking, 1993.
———. "Watching a Writer Write Is About as Interesting as Watching Paint Dry." *Washington Post*, October 1, 2006, T10.

———. "Wild About Harry." *New York Times* Sunday Book Review, July 23, 2000, 13–14.

Oates, Joyce Carol. *Telling Stories*. New York: W. W. Norton, 1998.

Smith, Greg, "The Literary Equivalent of a Big Mac and Fries? Academics, Moralists, and the Stephen King Phenomenon." *Midwest Quarterly* 43(4) (Summer 2002): 329–346.

Whitelaw, Nancy. *Dark Dreams: The Story of Stephen King*. Greensboro, NC: Morgan Reynolds, 2006.

■ Adultery
Hillary Clinton

Hillary Diane Rodham Clinton, a rising political power and crusader for child welfare and literacy, endured the public shame of her husband's adultery. A brilliant and innovative First Lady, she was born in Chicago on October 26, 1947, and spent her childhood in suburban Park Ridge, Illinois. Her parents, Dorothy Emma Howell and Hugh Ellsworth Rodham, a textile manufacturer and veteran of World War II, produced two more children, sons Hugh and Tony. Hillary enjoyed a typical American upbringing—activities at the Methodist Church, Girl Scouts, debating, honor society, and student council at Maine East High School—as well as encouragement to pursue excellence.

Dorothy and Hugh Rodham supported their daughter's aspirations. In junior high, she pondered a career as an astronaut until she learned that the National Aeronautics and Space Administration hired only males; she later considered joining the U.S. Marines. A National Merit Scholarship finalist, she majored in political science at Wellesley College in Wellesley, Massachusetts, where the liberal causes of the mid-1960s seized her imagination. She championed the Civil Rights Movement, studied the speeches of Martin Luther King, Jr., and promoted the presidential campaign of Democrat Eugene McCarthy, a vocal warrior against the Vietnam War. On summer break, while interning at the House Republican Conference, she abandoned the conservatism of her parents. Her graduation address brought national attention for its keen political perceptions and for a frontal assault on the "good old boy" political mindset of keynote speaker U.S. Senator Edward Brooke.

During a summer working as a salmon canner in Valdez, Alaska, and a dishwasher at Mount McKinley National Park, Hillary Clinton lost the first job by protesting unsanitary work conditions. She enrolled at Yale Law School in New Haven, Connecticut, and sharpened her understanding of public policy, power, and progressive ideals. As a sophomore, she exhibited social consciousness during her research into child abuse for Yale New Haven Hospital and at the Yale Child Study Center and offered pro bono assistance to the indigent for New Haven Legal Services. At age 23, on a grant to foster Marian Wright Edelman's Washington Research Project, Hillary clerked for Senator Walter Mondale as an analyst of migrant labor privations, particularly those relegating children to physical, emotional, and educational invisibility. For statistical grounding, she took courses in psychology and child development and voiced concern for the voiceless. Her dedication to child welfare, due process for minors, and family law continued in 1971, when she worked for the law firm of Treuhaft, Walker, and Burnstein in Oakland, California. Her last year of professional study included stumping for Democratic presidential candidate George McGovern and postgraduate surveys of pediatric medical care at the Yale Child Study Center. In 1973, she published "Children under the Law" in the *Harvard Educational Review*.

Child Advocate Turned Parent

Into her late 20s, Hillary Clinton followed profound inclinations toward child protection, which became the thrust of her political life. While providing legal counsel during the Watergate and impeachment hearings, she experienced a thrill of accomplishment: "What a gift! I was 26 years old. I felt like I was walking around with my mouth open all the time" (Caroli, 2003, 296). Simultaneous with her service to the House Judiciary Committee, she argued cases for the Children's Defense Fund in Cambridge, Massachusetts, and advised the Carnegie Council on Children. After 4 years of courtship, on October 11, 1975, she married law instructor Bill Clinton, an Arkansas candidate for the U.S. House of Representatives. To maintain a separate career, she kept her maiden name. The couple settled in Little Rock after Bill won election to state attorney general. As the first female at the Rose Law Firm, the oldest west of the Mississippi River, Hillary handled patent and property cases and continued donating expertise to child protection through the Arkansas Advocates for Children and Families, which she cofounded. She also directed the New World Foundation, a community development fund that promoted women's rights. For President Jimmy Carter, she chaired the Legal Services Corporation, a post that demanded her attention after Bill's election to state governor. Her husband chose her to head the Rural Health Advisory Committee, which secured funding for medical care for the poor.

After the birth of their daughter, Chelsea Victoria Clinton, on February 27, 1980, Hillary adopted her husband's surname and returned to the post of state First Lady in 1982. Her busy schedule included director of the boards of Lafarge, Wal-Mart, and TCBY as well as breastfeeding Chelsea. She led a reform effort of the Arkansas Educational Standards Committee to lower class size, lengthen the school calendar, and upgrade teacher testing and curriculum. To advance pupil readiness, she initiated the Home Instruction Program for Preschool Youngsters. As a full partner of the Rose law firm, she battled gender prejudice for the Commission on Women in the Profession. For her feminist advances for the American Bar Association, the *National Law Journal* twice selected her one of America's most influential attorneys. Although Bill admitted that she knew more about domestic and education policy than most aides, in 1990, she jettisoned thoughts of running for governor and again served Arkansas as First Lady after Bill began another term.

Wife in the White House

Hillary Clinton's rise to First Lady coincided with the upsurge in women's political and economic clout in American society. Bill's run for U.S. president forced her into the spotlight to defend their marriage. In 1992, after listening to tapes proving Bill's infidelity, she spoke on *60 Minutes* of charges that he had romanced Gennifer Flowers, an Arkansas lounge singer who aired in *Star* magazine an embroidered claim of a 12-year affair. Rather than sit quietly during allegations, Hillary admitted to knowing about the involvement. She revealed, "Bill talked to this woman every time she called distraught, saying her life was going to be ruined, and he'd get off the phone and tell me that she said sort of wacky things" (Conason and Lyons, 2000, 24). Hillary accepted Bill's conclusions that Flowers demanded attention because she was terrified and charged voters to make up their own minds about his character. Nonetheless, scandalmongers delved into interviews, love letters, motel records, and photos in search of hard evidence of Bill's sexual indiscretions.

Bill Clinton touted his candidacy by promising the American voter the services of his wife and himself as tandem politicos, which critics stigmatized as "copresidents." Their 8 years as the "First Couple" began in January 1993. She contributed to American history as the first presidential wife to hold a doctorate and to pursue a career that made more salary than the president made. She set up office in the West Wing, caucused on Capitol Hill, and, in the style of Eleanor Roosevelt, influenced presidential policy. Her controversial take-charge attitude aroused anger after she led the Task Force on National Health Care Reform. The complex issue brought out her inexperience in policy making for the entire nation. One critic labeled Hillary's reform plan naive and coercive to drug firms, physicians, hospitals, employers, and state governments. As her approval rating plunged, she wore a bulletproof vest in public during a bus tour to sample citizen opinions. Her domestic troubles turned critics toward a new enemy, Paula Corbin Jones, an Arkansas civil servant who, on May 6, 1994, sued Bill for sexual harassment. The case opened the president to charges of serial skirt chasing and subjected his daughter Chelsea to humiliation during her first year on the West Coast as a freshman at Stanford University.

Survivor in the White House

Hillary Clinton resurged from rumor and smear campaigns to become the most traveled First Lady and a voice for global cooperation. She advocated children's health insurance, nationwide immunization, research into asthma and prostate cancer, and Medicare coverage of mammograms for older women. For veterans and women, she investigated Gulf War syndrome and Taliban torture of women in Afghanistan and increased the outreach of the justice department by fostering the Office on Violence Against Women. She admitted her polarizing effect on the most conservative voters: "For many of these wounded men, I'm the boss they never wanted. . . . the daughter who they never wanted to turn out to be so independent" (Caroli, 2003, 207). She added in self-defense, "It's not me personally they hate—it's the changes I represent" (Ibid.). In 1995, she addressed the Fourth World Conference on Women in Beijing on the subject of spousal abuse. Within months, conservative forces demeaned the First Lady by perusing financial records concerning her involvement in the Whitewater Development Corporation. She became the first presidential wife subpoenaed by a grand jury—but incurred no charges of wrongdoing. Independent Counsel Kenneth Starr extended the investigation by accusing her of masterminding firings at the White House and of abusing privileged information from FBI files.

The conservative battery of insinuations against the Clintons reached a peak on January 17, 1998, when the press broke the Monica Lewinsky scandal. On *The Today Show* 10 days later, Hillary Clinton dismissed the seamy reports as a conservative conspiracy to keep the couple perpetually on the defensive. She took another tack in blaming prejudice against citizens of Arkansas, but persistent probings resulted in the president's admission of infidelity on August 17, 1998. Talk shows and glib tabloids derided thong underwear and the Monica beret, which appeared in TV replays around the globe. Amid daily grilling and public ridicule, the First Lady flourished in crisis management with the aid of spiritual counselor Jesse Jackson. She maintained composure and continued issuing her column, "Talking It Over," a reprise of domestic conversations with women and children worldwide. During her much publicized walk to the Marine One helicopter for a family vacation on Martha's Vineyard, Massachusetts, her facial expression and posture revealed the success of hurtful gossip. Prolonging the trauma, from December 18, 1998, to February 12, 1999, impeachment proceedings censured the president's peccadilloes but exonerated him of perjury and obstruction of justice. Badly shaken, Hillary agreed to weekly marital counseling, which extended over a year. The public rose to her support, but extremes of controversy both praised and maligned her for standing by her man. Bill confessed, "I was grateful that she was brave enough to participate in the counseling. We were still each other's best friend, and I hoped we could save our marriage" (Clinton, 2005, 1329).

The fallout of the Lewinsky affair pushed Hillary Clinton into greater commitment to motherhood and advocacy. She voiced concern for violent video games, afterschool neglect, the targeting of young audiences by commercial television and gun sellers, criminalization of homeless families, and the overdosing of problem learners with Ritalin. She published a child-positive bestseller, *It Takes a Village: And Other Lessons Children Teach Us* (1996), a White House memoir in *Dear Socks, Dear Buddy: Kids' Letters to the First Pets* (1998), and *An Invitation to the White House: At Home with History* (2000), a lavishly illustrated coffee table book on the presidential manse. She launched the Save America's Treasures project, exhibited glass and pottery in the White House, opened a sculpture display in the Jacqueline Kennedy Garden, and redecorated the Blue Room, Map Room, and Treaty Room. In 2000, she hosted a bicentennial celebration of the White House. She posed for an official portrait and issued an autobiography, *Living History* (2003), which described the Lewinsky sex scandal and the president's lies as the most shocking and painful ordeal of her life. She described the intersection of loyalties: "As his wife, I wanted to wring Bill's neck. But he was not only my husband, he was also my president, and I thought that, in spite of everything, Bill led America and the world in a way that I continued to support" (Clinton, 2003).

A Political Career

At age 53, Hillary Clinton reignited her political ambitions with a run for the seat of retiring U.S. Senator Daniel Patrick Moynihan of New York. The campaign required their move to a residence, which they bought in Chappaqua, New York. She sought input from voters in each county and built a platform on bolstering the economy through tax credits, business incentives, full employment, and tax cuts for college tuition and long-term care during catastrophic illness. With 55 percent of the vote, she entered the senate on January 3, 2001, and made a slow advance based on her own record rather than as former First Lady. Committee work in budget, education, medical care, and the military preceded her national security and first responders health initiatives following the 9/11 destruction of the World Trade Center. She supported civil rights and military action against the Taliban and Saddam Hussein, but she challenged the Bush administration's mismanaged war in Iraq. Her middle-of-the-road stance sanctioned same-sex marriage and promoted child protection from sexually explicit electronic amusements. In her second senate term, she opposed escalation of the Iraq War by demanding troop reduction.

From 2002, Senator Hillary Clinton shaped a run for the White House, making her the first former First Lady to aspire to the highest office in the land. She gravitated toward women's issues—breast cancer research, health care, and reproductive freedom—as well as denunciation of the George Bush administration for its war record. Her plan immediately divided voters and parties on issues of Hillary's electability and on the nation's readiness for its first female leader. Facing off against former Senator John Edwards of North Carolina and Senator Barack Obama of Illinois, she amassed a record-setting campaign chest. Backing her liberal stance were the American Civil Liberties Union, NARAL Pro-Choice America, and her politically savvy husband. Bill admitted in his autobiography, *My Life* (2005), "What I had done with Monica Lewinsky was immoral and foolish. I was deeply ashamed of it" (Clinton, 2005, 1268). Pundits described his campaign fervor as penance for the pain his extramarital liaisons caused his life partner.

Sources

Caroli, Betty Boyd. *First Ladies: From Martha Washington to Laura Bush*. Oxford: Oxford University Press, 2003.

Clinton, Bill. *My Life*. New York: Vintage Books, 2005.

Clinton, Hillary. *Living History*. New York: Simon & Schuster, 2003.

Conason, Joe, and Gene Lyons. *The Hunting of the President: The Ten-Year Campaign to Destroy Bill and Hillary Clinton*. New York: St. Martin's Press, 2000.

Estrich, Susan. *The Case for Hillary Clinton*. New York: HarperCollins, 2005.

Kelley, Colleen E. *The Rhetoric of First Lady Hillary Rodham Clinton: Crisis Management Discourse*. Westport, CT: Greenwood, 2001.

■ Ageism
Maya Lin

An unusual model of struggle against ageism, landscape artist and sculptor Maya Ying Lin epitomized a nation's grief for the fallen warriors of the Vietnam War. A native of Athens, Ohio, she was born in October 5, 1959, to ceramist Henry Huan-Lin, the dean of the Ohio University College of Fine Arts, and Julia Chang Lin, a poet and literature teacher at Ohio University. From family stories, Lin learned about the work of her aunt and uncle, Lin Hui-Yin and Liang Si Cheng, designers of Tiananmen Square and documenters of China's architectural history. The turmoil of the 1960s marked Lin's earliest years, when she and her older brother, Tan Lin, were too young and too involved in studies to form an opinion of hawks and doves. A shy loner in childhood, she stuck close to home and campus, played in the surrounding woods, and dined each evening with the family. She noted, "Kent State, the war in Vietnam, and civil rights struggles didn't have any bearing on me" (Lin, 2006, 60).

Lin acquired respect for scholarship while she and her brother lived for several months at the University of Washington in Seattle, where their mother completed a doctoral dissertation. Lin satisfied her own intellectual curiosity by taking courses at Ohio University, visiting her father's ceramics studio, studying the lost wax method of bronze sculpting, and casting pieces at the campus foundry. For hobbies, she ventured from clay and macramé to silversmithing. She explained, "Creativity and my artistic drive emanate from that childhood. In a way I didn't have anyone to play with so I made up my own world" ("Interview," 2000). She developed regard for ethnic spaces in America, particularly Hopewell Indian mound culture, Adena Indian berms, Shaker designs, and the raked stones of Japanese gardens and temple compounds. Among college professors, she learned to question tradition and standards and retained a graceful, open-ended view of art and buildings that marked her life's work. From these influences on her evolution as a designer came her perception of monuments as hybrids linking artistic principles with architectural structure.

Designing the Wall

The 21-year-old undergraduate won a competition established by Jan Scruggs and the Vietnam Veterans Memorial Fund (VVMF) to design a monument for Washington, D.C. To encourage participation, the VVMF distributed posters. By involving the public, the VVMF hoped to arouse national support as well as sympathy for survivors of an unpopular military clash. The finished work had one overriding requirement—to honor by name some 58,000 American soldiers lost or killed during the Vietnam War. With five classmates, she entered the contest as part of a senior requirement to complete a thesis. She explained the classroom style of the collaboration: "We found an adviser, Professor Andy Burr, who agrees to be our professor" for the completion of a project on funerary architecture (Lin, 2005, 315). To suit design to site, she visited the plot set aside in a park along Constitution Avenue during Thanksgiving break. She set her sights on a memorial that would invite visitation by pedestrians and encourage individual thought on the Vietnam War. She maintained an objective attitude to a "formalistically [sic] extremely different" design and described herself as "someone who never counts on anything until it's real" (Lin, 2005, 316).

Lin flew to Washington to meet the VVMF committee and imagined their response to her: "You're just a kid" (Lin, 2005, 317). To their surprise, she insisted on remaining directly involved in details of construction. After determining the purpose of a combat memorial, she focused on combatants and the exclusion of the politics that launched and judged the war. She was unprepared for complaints that so young a girl could immortalize a conflict she didn't remember. After the *Washington Post* referred to her work as "an Asian Memorial for an Asian War," she was also shocked to hear remarks about "a 'gook' designing the memorial" (Lin, 2006, 96). Judged by professional architects and artists, her V-shaped funerary design mirrored the incisive edges of a geode while suggesting the intimate rites of mourning. Her blueprint, along with 1,420 other proposals, came under consideration in March 31, 1981, when a selection committee mounted each unsigned scale drawing in a hangar at Andrews Air Force Base outside Washington, D.C. For the gravity, integrity, and egalitarianism of the Wall, on May 6, nine panelists awarded the $50,000 prize to Lin. She intended to finance future study in her chosen field with the money.

Controversy arose over her gender and Asian ethnicity but primarily over her age, limited education, and inexperience at creating public art. She was not only a student but also an undergraduate. She was inured to discounting from girlhood because of her petite size, which encouraged a "porcelain doll" syndrome for her diminution by peers. More surprising was the perception of veterans that the designer was a long-haired Chinese hippie coed from a liberal Ivy League university who lived disconnected from the Vietnam combat and its divisive aftermath. In 2006, she admitted, "It was extremely naive of me to think that I could produce a neutral statement that would not become politically controversial simply because it chose not to take sides" (Lin, 2006, 94). She steeled herself for tense negotiations amid distrust and ill will.

A Clash of Viewpoints

Detractors of Lin's austere, contemplative gash in the terrain preferred traditional war memorabilia, particularly weaponry, vertical columns, patriotic and heroic symbolism, flags, and identifiable figures in white marble or bronze, the usual colors and minerals of monuments. More traditional Vietnam vets demanded an epic quality conveying grandeur and sacrifice. Some saw the waning height of the final two panels that support the wall as efforts to hide the war below the gradient. More positive spectators looked to the rise at center as Lin's apolitical gesture affirming a cathartic glimpse of the national spirit. She recalled, "I played it extremely naive about politics, instead turning the issue into a strictly aesthetic one" (Lin, 2006, 17). A few conservationists recognized Lin's intent to blend art with nature rather than reshape the park into a showy exaltation of war. Secretary of the Interior

James Watt negotiated a compromise to variant expectations by appending bronze figures of American soldiers flanking an American flag on a 60-foot pole.

The uproar disillusioned Lin, who faced daily personal, official, and media challenge to the Wall's nonreferential integrity and significance. She defended the minimalist design before the U.S. Congress as facing pages of a stone history book conveying the names of the fallen. She summarized a straightforward gesture to the dead: "I allowed the names to be the memorial. That's it" (Lin, 2005, 318). Lin's uncompromising chevron suggested the outlines of a pure elemental form arising from the earth. She pictured grasping a blade and slicing into the turf, "an initial violence and pain that in time would heal" (Lin, 2006, 21). Like a scar, the dark surface mirrored the inevitability of death as well as the stigma of a failed war and the disgrace that soldiers returned to. Legislators admired the peace of the cloistered space and recognized the wisdom of allowing casualties' names to speak for themselves the cost of war.

While opinions clashed, the Congress set aside 3 acres for development. On March 26, 1982, at the unveiling of the site, in the Constitution Gardens alongside the National Mall, Lin's name was left off the program. During the dedication, John Devitt, a veteran from Stockton, California, formed an opinion that Lin's work could heal more people if it were replicated as a traveling monument identifying individual soldiers with their hometowns. He established the Vietnam Combat Veterans, source of the Moving Wall, a half-size replica that first touched viewers in Tyler, Texas, in 1984. His model wall was so popular that two more replicas began touring the country to shape the thoughts of some 10 million spectators on Lin's creation.

The Finished Site

Workers under direction of the Cooper-Lecky architectural firm and the U.S. National Park Service began erecting the Vietnam War Memorial in three stages: Lin's Wall, a Three Soldiers statue, and a Vietnam Women's Memorial. The focus took shape as two black stone ramparts 75 meters long that rise to 3 meters at the joint. Parting at an angle of 125 degrees, 20 minutes, the monoliths gradually disappear into the ground at a height of 8 inches. For material, builders cut 72 panels into lustrous granite from Bangalore, India. Their choice was politically motivated—they couldn't patronize quarries in Canada or Sweden because of the perception of those countries as shelters for draft evaders. Specialists polished the surfaces in Barre, Vermont, to blend the $\frac{1}{2}$-inch high lettering with the reflection of viewers' faces and the trees and historic buildings of the nation's capital.

In Memphis, Tennessee, stonecutters at Glass Craft etched the names of casualties on seventy of the panels with a process that merged sandblasting with photo emulsion, which hardened the surface under ultraviolet rays. The names, cut in a sans serif Optima font from left to right, appear in chronological order from July 8, 1959, to war's end on May 25, 1968. The roster begins with the sniper killings of two military advisers, Dale Rirchard Buis of Pender, Nebraska, and Chester Melvin Ovnand of Copperas Cove, Texas. The two men died while watching a movie in Bien Hoa, 20 miles northeast of Saigon. Pointing in opposite directions to the Washington Monument, an emblem of the American Revolution, and to the Lincoln Memorial, a reminder of civil disjunction during the Civil War, Lin's design treats each casualty as an individual human being stripped of rank and details of service. Of the 58,256 entries to date, eight are female. A diamond marks each death; a cross indicates a casualty missing in action or imprisoned. If any death is incorrect, the return of the soldier will be marked with a diamond overlaying the cross.

Viewer Contemplates Wall

Lin intended the Wall to be interactive, with individuals completing the communication of finality and loss. After the formal opening on Veterans' Day, November 11, 1982, a deluge of veteran and civilian visitors swelled to 100,000 a day, nearly 4 million per year. Fascination with the Wall produced a steady stream of viewers who prayed, admired, and contemplated an abstract monument listed as a national historic place. Attendants guided the curious to print catalogs of casualties.

Moved by Lin's stark, unemotional stone scroll, the most involved wept for combat losses and hurts and eased finger pads over familiar names sunk crisply in granite. The park service began collecting memorial flags and stones, holiday tokens, letters, and sentimental offerings left by people grieving for fallen soldiers. At the Museum and Archaeological Regional Storage facility, boxes of uniform jackets and caps, boots, medals, and insignia attest to Lin's effective strategy to cleanse viewers of pain and acrimony over the controversial Southeast Asian war. At the American History Museum of the Smithsonian Institution, a display of selected items revealed the extremes of reactions to the Wall.

Post-Wall Projects

After Lin's graduation with a degree in architecture from Saybrook College at Yale, in 1987, the university awarded her an honorary degree in fine arts. She experienced a sense of withdrawal from a campus setting, a milieu she had always loved for its intellectual stimulus. She wed photographer Daniel Wolf, the father of their two daughters, and opened Maya Lin Studios in New York City. The family split residence in New York with time in Colorado. Rather than compete with the work of her youth, she set out in a new direction to create innovative ways of enhancing viewers' perceptions of time, environment, and shifts in light.

The Civil Rights Memorial in Montgomery, Alabama, Lin's next endeavor, opened on November 5, 1989, with a moving water table that advances over a horizontal circle to mourn the waste of forty civil rights activists. Like the Wall, the Alabama monument covers a 14-year time frame, from the end of segregation after the *Brown v. Board of Education* decision on May 17, 1954, to the killing of Dr. Martin Luther King, Jr., in Memphis, Tennessee, on April 4, 1968. In a departure from lugubrious subjectives, in 1991, she chose holly bushes to mark the playful "Topo" at the Sports Coliseum in Charlotte, North Carolina. In 1992, she served the Wexner Center at Ohio State University as artist in residence and creator of "Groundswell," an undulating form alternating earth with 43 tons of shattered car safety glass. In 1994, she designed the Weber Residence in Williamstown, Massachusetts, with a free-flowing roofline dramatizing the shape of Berkshire Mountains. Her subsequent monument designs—a spiral of numbers on the "Women's Table" at Yale University in 1993, the "Reading a Garden" centerpiece at a reflecting pool of the Cleveland Public Library, the changing light of "Eclipsed Time" in the ceiling of Pennsylvania Station in New York City in 1995, and the earth sculpture "Wave Field" at the University of Michigan's François Xavier Bagnoud Aerospace Engineering Building in Ann Arbor in 1995—attested her vision and awareness of American tastes and perspectives. In 1999, she coupled an antebellum barn with corncribs to create a civil rights reading room for the Langston Hughes Library at Haley Farm in Clinton, Tennessee.

At age 41, Lin published *Boundaries* (2000) and sculpted on the David Packard Electrical Engineering Building "Timetable," another water table forming a rotating stone clock. She began superintending her most ambitious outdoor work, the Confluence Project, a track followed by the Lewis and Clark expedition along the Columbia River and Snake River in Washington state. In 2003, she joined the panel overseeing the selection of a design to fill the World Trade Center site, destroyed in the 9/11 terrorist attack in 2001. Her preliminary sketches for the *New York Times* influenced Michael Arad's "Reflecting Absence," which filled the gaping block. Her honors include recognition by her alma mater, Smith College, and William College, and election to the American Academy of Arts and Letters and the Women's Hall of Fame.

Sources

"Interview: Maya Lin." *Artist and Architect* http://www.achievement.org/autodoc/printmember/lin0int-1 (last accessed June 16, 2000).

Lashnits, Tom. *Maya Lin*. New York: Chelsea House, 2007.

Lin, Maya. *Boundaries*. New York: Simon & Schuster, 2006.

———. "Creating the Vietnam Veterans Memorial." In *Booknotes on American Character: People, Politics, and Conflict in American History*, ed. Brian Lamb. New York: Perseus, 2005.

■ Agoraphobia
Paula Deen

A familiar face on cooking shows and the covers of regional recipe books, restaurateur Paula Ann Hiers Deen had to overcome fear of leaving home before she could succeed. The daughter of Corrie Paul Hiers and car mechanic Earl Hiers, she was born in Albany, Georgia, on January 19, 1947. While her father ran a gas station, she and brother Earl "Bubba" Hiers grew up in the back room and witnessed the racial strife that brought Dr. Martin Luther King, Jr., to Albany with the Freedom Riders. Grandfather Paul owned a resort at River Bend and ran a restaurant, the White House. Grandmother Paul taught Deen how to bake Japanese fruitcake for Christmas and cook roe, rabbit, and squirrel that Earl Hiers provided fresh. She wilted green beans and flavored them Southern-style with salt pork and bacon grease. Deen's mother—a "beautiful, kind, genteel, and gracious red-haired lady" called "Red"—encouraged creature comforts by making impromptu chocolate-dipped doughnuts and entertaining year round (Deen, 2006, 50). From the Deep South oral tradition, Deen acquired a jaunty storytelling style that was both informative and self-deprecating. At Albany High School, she became a cheerleader and an instant friend maker with a personable, anecdotal style.

Deen was a lackadaisical student who married straight out of high school. She once opined on television, "Love is blind, but marriage is a real eye-opener," a veiled reference to her high school sweetheart, Jimmy Deen, who changed plugs and fixed tires at a filling station (Martin, 2006, 47). He was a heavy drinker and wife controller who was incapable of supporting her. She displayed kitchen talent at age 19, when her mother noted,

"Honey, you're gonna be a better cook than your mother" (Deen, 2006, 50). In 1970, both her parents died. The effect of grief and her husband's move from the area generated severe neurosis that she termed "terror with no name" (Deen, 2007, 5). Because of a racing heart rate and numbness from chronic agoraphobia, in 1978, she suffered public paralysis: "Couldn't breathe, couldn't stop trembling. I felt weak and nauseated and dizzy, and I just knew I was gonna die" (Ibid.). Deen couldn't afford psychiatric care for the panic that forced her to breathe into a paper bag. She gave up driving her boys to afterschool baseball practice, buying groceries, and cruising the mall, where she once collapsed behind a clothes rack at J.C. Penney's. For self-treatment, she depended on the Alcoholics Anonymous Serenity Prayer and swapped dependence on her father with constant attendance by Jimmy. After he settled the family in Savannah, she took to her bed for 8 weeks of crying.

To occupy herself in the safety of home, Deen focused on cooking. She chopped vegetables to bits to introduce celery and onions to her picky sons. She amassed early Southern recipes like lemon chess pie and invented her signature style from easily accessible ingredients. She mastered such regional comfort foods as pan-fried corn and pork chops, ribs, chili, muffuletta, sandwiches, Beaufort shrimp pie, squash casserole, and she-crab soup. After 17 years of virtual house arrest, she worked as a bank teller. In 1988, a thief held a gun to her head, thrusting her once more into panic attacks.

Cooking Up a Business

After divorcing her husband of 27 years, Deen began a 10-year affair with a married electrical engineer who abused her. By night, she lay awake mapping out a kitchen business to support her children. On an investment of $200, in 1989, she established Bag Lady, a catering service featuring light entrees and brown bag sandwiches delivered in baskets to offices and residences by her sons Bobby, a high school senior, and Jamie, a junior college graduate. She incorporated Southern staples, including grits, corn on the cob, Georgia peaches, New Orleans crab and shrimp, Vidalia onions, sweet tea, Tennessee bourbon, and Caribbean rum. She reflected on being "fortunate to get beyond the major obstacles that occur when entrepreneurs begin their dream" (Deen, 2006, 43). For her reputation as a food maven, organizers of baking contests chose her to judge. Because of demand for her specialties, she pondered going public, despite her grandmother's query, "Paula, have you lost your damned mind?" (Deen, 2006). Before investing in real estate, Deen managed an eatery in Savannah's Best Western Hotel. She put in more than sixteen hours a day; her sons scrubbed pots. She characterized the stress with chagrin: "Those years were the hardest years of my life" (Tracy et al., 2007, 241).

On January 8, 1996, Deen and her sons opened The Lady and Sons, on West Congress Street in the downtown area. Jamie helped Deen serve plates while Bobby seated patrons. She admitted to having an eye for male clientele. One of her more famous patrons was Clint Eastwood during the filming of a Savannah murder scandal, John Berendt's *Midnight in the Garden of Good and Evil* (1995). Deen also formulated a sweet potato pie at the request of Sean Jones, a player for the Packers. She issued *The Lady & Sons Savannah Country Cookbook* (1997), the spiral-bound *Favorite Recipes of the Lady & Her Friends* (1997), and *The Lady & Sons Savannah Country Cooking Too* (1997), collections known for "Ooey Gooey Butter Cake" (Deen, 2005, 82). She described such unpretentious kitchen equipment as canning jars and muffin tins and favored cast iron skillets over copper-bottomed cookware. To the uninformed, she explained how to season cast iron by coating it with shortening and baking it upside down in the oven.

National Appeal

Culinary critics bent on promoting voguish cookery tended to force Deen into a stereo-typed peasant food corner. In truth, her versatility produced menus ranging from *brie en croûte*, puttanesca sauce, and steak au poivre to Georgia sugared peanuts and black bottom pie. Of simple fare, she praised buttermilk corn bread and peach pickles and snickered her way through instructions for beer-in-the-rear chicken. A three-ingredient house seasoning—salt, pepper, and garlic powder—supplied readers with a handy shaker topping for most meats. Of satisfying foods, she wrote, "Potato soup is an unsung hero of the soup world; there is just nothing more belly-pleasing" ("Best," 2007, 76). She recommended local ingredients, such as mayhaw jelly "made from the tart red berries of the mayhaw trees that grow only in southwest Georgia" (Deen, 2005, 108).

The author won readers' hearts with shortcuts, like basing sophisticated recipes on Cheez Whiz, Velveeta, condensed milk, canned mushroom soup, Jell-O, and Duncan Hines cake mix. Her sensible approach to kitchen toil offered time-saving steps such as lining a pan with slices of bread before baking meat loaf on top. She tossed the bread after it soaked up the greasy overflow, one of the unaesthetic results of fatty ingredients. She reduced first-timer cooks' insecurities by recommending tossing house clutter into a plastic trash bag in a closet and by serving guests soup in plastic cups. With typical insouciance she declared, "There's no need to get fussy with the napkin fold" (Ibid., 54). She also promoted great-heartedness by listing foods popular with dialysis patients and shut-ins and by claiming the kitchen as the home's heart.

From her starter restaurant, an expanded business headquartered in the city's historic district, Deen offered her customers a buffet. She summarized her working strategy: "I conduct myself the same way now as I did when I was running all over Savannah delivering lunch to business people" (Tracy et al., 2007, ii). At the end of her ability to cope with a nonstop schedule and solitude, she prayed, "God, please send me a neighbor," a cheeky demand that the Almighty end her loneliness (Ibid., 1). She focused on a spread of fried chicken, cheese meatloaf, collards, sweet potatoes, macaroni and cheese, creamed corn, beans, hoecakes, and biscuits, the basics of Southern tables. Diners liked her panache with butter and cream as well as the defiance of upscale eateries featuring nouvelle cuisine, which offered minuscule portions on oversized plates. In 1999, *USA Today* lauded her menu as the "International Meal of the Year."

Broadening the Menu

Deen increased demand for her artistry with audience appeal. Her sparkling style invited kitchen neophytes to try more complex entrees. Her philosophy of inclusion broke culinary and ethnic barriers: "The love and appreciation for our Deep South cookin' knows no geographic boundaries" (Deen, 2005). In 1999, she appeared on *Ready, Set, Cook!* and *Door Knock Dinners*, a series on the Food Network. In 2001, she made a pilot for *After-noon Tea*, which didn't sell. The next year, she found her niche with *Paula's Home Cooking*, which she taped in the kitchen of producer Gordon Elliott in Millbrook, New York. To her bemusement, fans wrote in asking questions and declaring that she seemed more like kin rather than the aproned host of a cooking show. In November 2005, the location shifted south to Deen's home in Savannah. Oprah Winfrey applauded her success with guest invitations in 2002 and 2007. Of her popularity, Deen asserted, "The best people are the ones who are themselves—just the real deal" (Tracy et al., 2007, 153). She likened her personality to the family caretaker, the bulwark often taken for granted in extended households. She aimed to increase the fold by reclaiming a generation lost to junk food.

On March 6, 2004, Deen married a Savannah port tug navigator, Michael Anthony "Mikey" Groover, a flirty 5th-generation Georgian. He shared her delight in family and in cooking for crowds. The network taped their wedding ceremony and reception for airing later in the year. Deen added Groover's children, Michelle and Anthony, to her family. When Anthony returned to a military academy, Deen had already sized up his taste in treats and baked a batch of mint cookies for him to carry along. The two developed a kitchen partnership that turned him into a cook.

The food show hostess added new titles to her résumé, beginning with *Paula Deen's Kitchen Classics: The Lady and Sons Savannah Country Cookbook* (2005) and including a Thanksgiving special that drew the largest audience in Food Network history. For *Paula Deen & Friends: Living It Up Southern Style* (2005), she admitted that menu mapping was her least favorite task. She provided color-coordinated recipes for specific occasions, including a Bridge Club Supper, a low country seafood boil, and a "Georgia Bulldawg Parking Lot Tailgate" picnic (Deen, 2005). As a pictorial reminder of the provenance of entrees, she dotted pages with sketches of magnolia blooms. For Hoffman Media, she initiated the domestic magazine *Cooking with Paula Deen*, which featured photos of her tousled silver hair, blue eyes, and winsome smile above inviting dishes. Deen intended the layout to appeal to all women, not just Southerners. Tips to readers covered decorating, feasting, and partying. She debuted in the movie *Elizabethtown* (2005) as Aunt Dora, a matronly character cast opposite Orlando Bloom and Kirsten Dunst. The Food Network exploited the movie with a TV special, *Paula Deen Does Hollywood* (2005), and, in March 2006, produced a biopic of Deen for *Chefography*.

A Devoted Fan Following

The celebrity chef continued to stretch her ambitions with a new show, *Paula's Party*, shot at a seafood restaurant kitchen in fall 2006, and with recipes featured in *Food & Wine* magazine's "25 Best Cookbooks of the Year." She issued two compendia on entertaining, *The Lady and Sons Just Desserts: More Than 120 Sweet Temptations from Savannah's Favorite Restaurant* (2006) and *Paula Deen Celebrates!: Best Dishes and Best Wishes for the Best Times of Your Life* (2006). The latter covered New Year's Day, Christmas, and Father's Day plus "Movie Watching Pizza Party in Bed" and bashes for Cinco de Mayo and Mardi Gras, a nod to her Southern roots. For Elvis' birthday, she suggested banana and peanut butter sandwiches. She informed readers of the lifestyles of the relatives she loved in childhood. The introduction read like a daytime soap opera with her account of moving herself and dogs Otis and Sam from urban Savannah to a Turner's Creek marsh on Wilmington Island on the Atlantic shore. Contributing serenity to her new home were views of herons stalking tide pools and porpoises leaping through the surf.

At age 60, Deen thrived on writing and collecting culinary treats. Signed first editions of her earlier works demanded prices as high as $1,500. She coauthored *Uncle Bubba's Savannah Seafood: More Than 100 Down-Home Southern Recipes for Good Food and Good Times,* a cookbook featuring the coastal style of her baby brother and partner Earl Hiers, owner of Uncle Bubba's Oyster House. While her sons departed to host their own show, *Road Tasted*, Deen traveled to Paris with Michael for the filming of a special, *Paula Goes to Europe*. She compiled cookie, gift food, and pudding recipes and family photos for *Christmas with Paula Deen: Recipes and Stories from My Favorite Holiday*, a calendar, and *Paula Deen: It Ain't All about the Cookin'*, a memoir coauthored by Sherry Suib Cohen. In taped sessions on Deen's bed, the kitchen diva wept and laughed over memories. The publication coincided with her receipt of two Daytime Emmys and her naming to *Forbes* magazine's most powerful celebrities.

Meanwhile, Deen's schedule filled up with interviews on *Oprah* and *Larry King Live*. Her Christmas guest list swelled to thirty people eager for homey dishes. She adored Jimmy's 2-month-old son Jack and planned to launch a youth cookbook and food products for infants. In 2008, she collaborated with Katie Lee Joel and Miki Duisterhof for a work suited to Deen's style, *The Comfort Table*. In summary of success, Deen mused, "I'm a sixty-year-old, grey-haired, overweight woman and I'm still employed. Life is a beautiful thing" (Dean, 2007, viii).

Sources

Deen, Paula H. *The Lady & Sons Just Desserts: More Than 120 Sweet Temptations from Savannah's Favorite Restaurant*. New York: Simon & Schuster, 2006.

———. *Paula Deen: It Ain't All about the Cookin'*. New York: Simon & Schuster, 2007.

———. *Paula Deen & Friends: Living It Up, Southern Style*. New York: Simon & Schuster, 2005.

Editors of *Food & Wine* magazine. *Best of the Best: The Best Recipes from the 25 Best Cookbooks of the Year*. New York: Sterling, 2006.

Martin, Phyllis, comp. *Quips, Quotes and Savvy Sayings: A Resource for Lovers of the Language*. New York: iUniverse, 2006.

Tracy, Marta, Terence Noonan, Paula Deen, and Karen Kelly. *Starring You!: The Insiders' Guide to Using Television and Media to Launch Your Brand, Your Business and Your Life*. New York: Harper Paperbacks, 2007.

■ AIDS
Greg Louganis

A chipper representative of American Olympic spirit, Greg Louganis abruptly ended a dazzling diving career when he chose to reveal he was infected with the acquired immune deficiency syndrome (AIDS). Born Gregory Efthimios Louganis on January 29, 1960, in El Cajon, California, he claims Samoan-Scandinavian heritage from his parents, who were 15 years old and unmarried when they abandoned him. At age 9 months, he became the son of Greek-American parents, Frances and immigrant dock owner Peter "Pete" Louganis, of San Diego, and the sibling of an older sister, Despina. By a year and a half, Greg was a toddler dancer. In 1963, he began learning the mental rehearsal technique of performance, a mind-over-matter metaphysics similar to an out-of-body experience. He took to the stage to dance and compete in tumbling and gymnastics; at age 9, he trained fellow divers. In summer, under his father's direction, he hauled in tuna nets from buoys and repaired gashes with a needle and marine-weight twine.

Throughout early childhood, Louganis fought internal battles. He withdrew into self while combating prejudice against his Polynesian coloring and ridicule for being dyslexic, a stutterer, adopted, and a male dancer. He felt permanently maligned as a "nigger dummy sissy" (Fensch, 1995, 1000). More troubling was the need to hide his amphetamine and marijuana abuse, alcoholism, and homosexuality, especially from a domineering, judgmental father. His mother, cowed by Pete, slunk away from shielding her only son from his father's macho posturing.

During an assault at the bus stop by school bullies, Greg recalled his father and a cousin in the crowd. He cringed at the implications: "I had this awful feeling that Dad thought I deserved to get beat up, that he thought I was a sissy" (Landrum, 2006, 200). His confidante, Coach Ron O'Brien, recognized signs of insecurity and remarked on Greg's complex neuroses, "He was a scared kid. Scared of so darn many things" (Fensch, 1995, 93). For support in times of guilt and denial, Greg depended on his mother, a lover of theater who watched him perform from the stands and cheered his patriotism. He later mused that she sensed his gay sexual orientation long before he did and that she accepted him without question.

Becoming an Olympian

In 1970, Louganis involved himself in precision diving by visualizing each phase of launching from the board, physical contortion, and contact with the water, a breakdown he mastered in dance class. He explained, "I had the routine so deeply memorized that I could feel it. Dancers call it kinetic memory" (Louganis and Marcus, 1995, 18). In 1972, damage to his knees from 9 years of tumbling and dance lessons precipitated a suicidal bout in despair of losing outlets for self-expression. Fortunately, he failed at swallowing pills and slitting his wrists and succeeded at diving. To Greg, dives were like dance routines—more performance than athletic executions. After 40 repetitions of an aquatic dance sequence, he could compose his mind and face, relax his limbs, and concentrate on performance. Within months, he scored a perfect dive at the Junior Olympics in Colorado Springs. He mused, "The name-calling and the humiliation pushed me to strive to be better than everyone. It made me angry" (Louganis and Marcus, 1995, 38).

Training required relocation. After preparing in Europe in 1973 for world competition, he boarded with a diving family in Arizona the next summer. In 1975, he moved to Decatur, Alabama, to study at Coach O'Brien's camp. During school terms, he managed part-time employment at a recreation center and two clothing shops. As though storing up for his eventual independence from family, he saved cash for a house to give him "a sense of roots" (Fensch, 1995, 99). He boarded with ear, nose, and throat specialist Sammy Lee, a two-time Olympic medalist in diving and the first nonwhite to achieve in international competition. To bolster a sense of home while training, Louganis learned Chinese and Korean cookery from Lee's wife Roz. During classes at a predominantly Chicano high school, he found one answer to a question of ethnicity: "I was a little nervous. But I kind of fit in because I was dark haired and dark complected" (Fensch, 1995, 99).

At age 16, Louganis joined the American diving team at the Summer Olympics in Montreal, where he fell in love for the first time. Other athletes made menacing signs and slurs about gays. The diver acknowledged the source of his isolation: "Secrets really imprison you, so I had to share it" (Bare and Kornegay, 1995, 280). Against top platform diver Klaus Dibiasi of Italy, "Lugo" won silver that year. After a romantic breakup, he sank into another malaise that returned him to the edge of suicide. In 1978, he secured a gold medal and his first world title at the World Aquatic Championship and the U.S. diving competition in 1-meter and 10-meter plunges. He faced a recurring sports and dance problem at his first recital, when he feared rounding out his act just as he doubted his ability to polish off a dive. The next year, he snagged two gold medals at the Pan American Games in San Juan, Puerto Rico. He trained to vie at the 1980 Summer Olympics in Moscow until President Jimmy Carter declared a boycott to protest the seizure of Afghanistan on December 25, 1979, by the Soviet army. The disappointment spread to athletes from a dozen countries.

Two Kinds of Battles

While perfecting his Springfield technique, on a diving scholarship, Louganis majored in theater at the University of Miami, a haven a long way from San Diego. In the anonymity of south Florida, he introduced his mother to gay bars. In the pool, he survived a shoulder dislocation, wrist pain, and a crack on the head at the diving board that knocked him out cold for a quarter hour. A worse wipeout occurred in New Zealand, when a faulty dive impacted his calves and damaged the blood vessels of his back and legs. He downplayed his athletic record while appearing in productions of *Camelot*, *Carousel*, and *Working* and as Nugget and the young rider in a 1980 campus production of *Equus*. While he completed a B.A. degree at the University of California at Irvine, he trained under Coach Ron O'Brien at the Mission Viejo Club outside San Diego. O'Brien taught him a new combination, a three-and-a-half tuck, which requires tight, upside down rotations in space at a speed of 40 miles per hour 33 feet from the water. Despite rebellious bouts of cigarette smoking and beer and wine swilling, he handily swept the 1983 Pan American Games at United Nations Park in Caracas, Venezuela, and, without outside help, gave up smoking, drugs, and booze.

Louganis hired school chum Jim Babbitt as a manager, who helped him achieve top billing as "the Baryshnikov of diving" (Landrum, 2006, 207). While training for meets, he joined the casts of two films, *Dirty Laundry* (1985) and *16 Days of Glory* (1985), played in a 1987 production of *Dance Kaleidoscope*, recapped the 1984 Olympics for ESPN, and took the lead in *Pippin*. While pursuing both athletics and drama, he won two gold medals in 1982 in Guayaquil, Ecuador, and in 1986 in Madrid, Spain. At the 1984 Los Angeles Olympics and 4 years later at the 1988 Seoul Olympics in South Korea, he claimed titles in the 3-meter springboard and 10-meter platform dives. The former Olympiad earned him a record for the first diver to achieve over 700 points and a top Amateur Athletic Union citation, the James E. Sullivan Award for outstanding achievement. At the 1985 Olympic festival in Louisiana, more antigay rhetoric preceded a public snub after Greg "outdived" the competition.

A Bump on the Head

The 1988 Olympiad amazed fans because Louganis achieved a perfect score during qualifying rounds at Chamshil Pool after an injury. He grazed his head on a 3-meter diving board while tucking into a reverse two-and–a-half pike, the legendary "dive of death" that had already killed two competitors. While Dr. James Puffer closed the 3-inch scalp laceration with five sutures, the diver concealed the danger from blood contamination. He weathered the blow to his pride and focused on completing a final dive. Within 35 minutes, he returned from the hospital to the pool. His performance to a mental recording of "If You Believe" from *The Wiz* put him ahead of 35 competitors. For Louganis' perseverance, ABC TV's *Wide World of Sports* named him athlete of the year 1988.

The diver enlarged his fan base with candor. At a difficult pass in his father-son relationship, he cared for his father during 6 weeks of decline from cancer and informed Pete of the AIDS infection. On the advice of his cousin John, a physician, Greg took two AZT tablets every 4 hours. In 1987, *Playgirl* magazine featured a nude pose of Louganis; he starred as the prince in a 1989 Long Beach Civic Light Opera production of *Cinderella* and as Tony in *The Boyfriend*, a 1990 performance of the Sacramento Music Circus. At age 34, on the February 24, 1995, episode of ABC TV's *20/20*, he disclosed to interviewer Barbara Walters his gay sexual orientation. The announcement revealed his quandary over privacy issues and over the advice of his physician and Coach Lee to continue diving. Louganis felt comforted by the fact that chlorinated pool water would kill the virus.

In the aftermath of venting his homosexuality and viral infection, Louganis felt relieved. He reported to an interviewer, "Do I say something, it's . . . you know, this has been an incredibly guarded secret" (Sandomir, 1995). The U.S. Olympic Committee executive director Dr. Harvey Schiller charged Louganis with endangering the health of other contenders at the 1988 Olympic games. Louganis' civil rights attorneys reminded Schiller that, under International Olympic Committee regulations, the diver had no obligation to reveal his condition. The Centers for Disease Control also backed Louganis by informing the public that the burden of health protection lies on medical care providers.

Gay and Proud

After a year of psychotherapy, on June 18, 1994, Louganis competed in New York City at the Gay Games, a sporting event featuring lesbian, gay, bisexual, and transgender athletes. He became an advocate in July at a presentation of the Robert J. Kane Award from the U.S. Olympic Committee when he denounced antigay laws in Cobb County, Georgia. He urged sports officials to move volleyball preliminaries to a more open-minded locale. The next year, author Eric Marcus aided Louganis in composing an autobiography, *Breaking the Surface* (1995), one of the top bestsellers by an athlete. The text detailed infidelity and abuse by his mate Jim over a 6-year period and his blackmail of Louganis to go public with his homosexuality and infection with AIDS. The poignant text described the depression and suicide attempts that accompanied closeted gay lifestyles. Louganis' medical consultant, immunologist Anthony Stephen Fauci, an AIDS specialist at the National Institute of Allergy and Infectious Diseases in Bethesda, Maryland, put to rest fears that bleeding from the head injury could infect other divers. Nonetheless, like other AIDS victims, Louganis found himself isolated by the fearful. Of his sponsors, only Speedo remained loyal. In this same troubled period, he spent half a million dollars on settling a domestic breakup.

In retirement from sports, Louganis settled at his dream house in Malibu, California, and pledged himself to making a difference in the world. One of his kindnesses involved befriending Ryan White, a child pariah with AIDS. Louganis trained harlequin great danes and groomed Jack Russell terrier Nipper for the U.S. Dog Agility Association Grand Prix World Championship. On stage, he played the part of gay dancer Darius in Paul Rudnick's romantic comedy *Jeffrey* (1993), a role that relieved some fears of dying young from a socially loathsome and debilitating disease. At the Actors Playhouse in New York, in 1996, Louganis performed a one-man show, *The Only Thing Worse You Could Have Told Me*, and appeared in the film *It's My Party* (1996). He followed with the role of David in the romantic drama *Touch Me* (1997). On March 19, 1997, the Showtime teleplay *Breaking the Surface: The Greg Louganis Story* cast American actor Mario López as the diver and Louganis as the narrator.

Two years later, Louganis played Junior in *Just Say No* at the Bailiwick Theater in Chicago and as Sister Robert Ann, a street-smart nun in *Nunsense A-Men* in Hollywood, Florida. Aided by writer Betsy Sikora Siino, he compiled *For the Life of Your Dog: A Complete Guide to Having a Dog in Your Life, from Adoption and Birth through Sickness and Health* (1999).

Louganis provided color commentary for Acapulco cliff diving meets and appeared on televised sports specials and, on September 18, 2007, on the *Hollywood Squares* dream team, which featured Olympians Oksana Baiul, Janet Evans, Scott Hamilton, Bruce Jenner, and Jackie Joyner-Kersee. To spare others the pain of domestic violence and AIDS, Louganis became the spokesman for *Muses Legal Guide to Living Together* and expanded his involvement in youth advocacy. In addition to modeling sports excellence worldwide, he lectured at colleges and university diving clinics, addressed dyslexic students at youth enclaves, promoted AIDS charities, and counseled alcohol and substance abusers in rehabilitation groups. He advised gays and lesbians to avoid self-harm from unsafe sex and to escape low self-esteem by letting go of secrets. He expressed his upbeat outlook in a video journal, *Looking to the Light* (1997). In addition to being the only man to win successive double Olympic gold medals, his awards include six world and 47 national championships, the Jesse Owens International Trophy, induction into the Olympic Hall of Fame and International Swimming Hall of Fame, and the 1988 Maxwell House United States Olympic Committee Spirit Award. Of his future, he stated the optimism of the AIDS survivor: "I'm looking forward to the day I am just seen as a man" (Bare and Kornegay, 1995, 281).

Sources

Bare, Kelly, and Michele Kornegay. *The Inside Scoop on College Life*. Lawrenceville, NJ: Peterson's, 1995.

Fensch, Thomas. *The Sports Writing Handbook*. New York: Lawrence Erlbaum Associates, 1995.

Landrum, Gene N. *Empowerment: The Competitive Edge in Sports, Business & Life*. Burlington, ON: Brendan Kelly, 2006.

Louganis, Greg, and Eric Marcus. *Breaking the Surface*. New York: Random House, 1995.

Sandomir, Richard. "Agonizing over Disclosure of AIDS." *New York Times*, February 24, 1995.

■ Anorexia and Bulimia
Gelsey Kirkland

One of the prima ballerinas and dance actors of the late 20th century, Gelsey "Gels" Kirkland fought eating disorders, the dancer's curse. A native of Bethlehem, Pennsylvania, she was born on a Bucks County farm on December 29, 1952, to actor Nancy Hoadley and dramatist and playwright Jack Kirkland, adapter of *Tobacco Road* (1933), *Tortilla Flat* (1938), *Mandingo* (1961), and *Cheyenne Autumn* (1964). Her large family included the parental favorite, her beautiful older sister, Johanna, as well as younger brother Marshall and stepsiblings Christopher, Patricia, and Robin from Jack's previous marriages. Until 1954, Kirkland appeared to be mute when an outburst revealed that she was silent by choice. Despite her mother's tendency to hover and ward off danger, Kirkland pursued horseback riding and ice-skating.

To settle debts, in 1956, the Kirklands gave up their acreage and moved to Central Park West in Manhattan. Nancy developed an interest in Christian Science and enrolled her children in Sunday school. Jack mismanaged his income, drank heavily, and suffered five heart attacks. Fearing for his survival, Gelsey again sank into speechlessness rather than risk his anger by displeasing him. At camp, other girls disparaged her disproportionate body and pear-shaped head. She hid her displeasure in comedy: "I turned my abdominal bulge to advantage by performing a belly dance to amuse those in my cabin" (Kirkland and Lawrence, 1986, 10). She discovered that controlling her body was the only aspect of her world that was truly hers to command.

Dance became Kirkland's outlet for stress, fear, and rage. In 1960, she, like Johanna, began studying ballet, patterning her fantasies of stage fame on the life of diva Margot Fonteyn. Kirkland grew so obsessed that she awakened the household at night by thumping out step combinations in her bedroom. On the basis of musical interpretation, speed, technical geometry, and upper body strength, an audition placed her in the first division of the School of American Ballet. She battered herself with criticism for being only 5 feet 4 inches tall with a tendency toward a rounded torso. To overcome body faults, she quit high school and took modeling jobs to pay for extra lessons under Maggie Black, mime Pilar Garcia, David Howard, and Stanley Williams. The frenzied schedule threatened her with injuries and chronic muscle pain.

A Baby Ballerina

As one of director George Balanchine's young female discoveries, in 1968, Kirkland adopted the famous tyrant as a father figure. She willingly entered a concentration camp atmosphere and condemned herself to bizarre diets that extended to watermelon feasts. She described his control of her dating, his low opinion of female intellect, and his yanks to her leg muscles and admitted, "He was the only teacher at the School of American Ballet whom I could have forgiven for such an offense" (Buonaventura, 2005, 240). Under his mentoring, she developed a reputation for volatility and overachievement. She performed for 6 years with the New York City Ballet in beginning roles as Columbine in *Harlequinade*, *A Midsummer Night's Dream*, and *The Nutcracker*, in which she played the Dew Drop Fairy and, later, the Sugar Plum Fairy. At a workshop in 1968, she danced in a duet from *Flower Festival at Genzano* and a pas de trois from *Paquita*. She characterized these instructive parts as her favorite stage memories.

Within a year, Kirkland soloed in *The Cage*, *Concerto Barocco*, *Dances at a Gathering*, *Irish Fantasy*, *Monumentum Pro Gesualdo*, *Symphony in C*, *La Source*, *Tarantella*, and *Theme and Variations* and paired up with her sister Johanna in John Clifford's *Reveries* (1971). During Gelsey's rise to stardom, Balanchine demanded starvation by groping her skeleton before the whole class: "With his knuckles, he thumped on my sternum and down my rib cage clucking his tongue and remarking 'Must see the bones'" (Kirkland and Lawrence, 1986, 56). At the time, she weighed less than 100 pounds. She described the Balanchine ideal as a defeminization that accentuated the starkness of clavicles and neck. From his excessive ideal grew a fashion trend toward grotesque thinness that suppressed the menstrual cycle because of malnutrition, overtraining, and exhaustion.

The Center of Attention

At an artistic pinnacle at age 17, Kirkland appeared on May 28, 1970, as the title metaphor in Igor Stravinsky's *Firebird*, a dynamic showpiece opposite Jacques d'Amboise as

Prince Ivan that Balanchine choreographed specifically for her. Wearing a red tutu and vibrating like a hummingbird against Marc Chagall's scenery and costumes, she riveted attention to exotic steps and gestures. At age twenty, she became the company's female principal, dominating choreographer John Taras' festival production of *Song of the Nightingale* (1972). She danced ballets that Jerome Robbins designed for her and Icelandic partner Helgi Tomasson. For Robbins's *Four Bagatelles* (1974), she and partner Jean-Pierre Bonnefoux dressed in peasant garb to execute spirited leaps, and the intricate footwork that became her trademark. She starred in Peter Goldberg's *Goldberg Variations* (1971), *Scherzo Fantastique* (1972), and *An Evening's Waltzes* (1973) and in English choreographer Antony Tudor's *The Leaves Are Fading* (1975). Her form produced such a unified impression that one admirer described her as a hologram beamed from outer space.

Kirkland's unique gift for acting set her apart from other women whom Balanchine had goaded into becoming his puppets. She paired with the top males of the era—Cuban-trained dancer Fernando Bujones, Massachusetts-born star Jacques d'Amboise, Hong Kong Ballet Director Stephen Jefferies of West Germany, Danish dancers Peter Martins and Peter Schaufuss, Hungarian star Ivan Nagy, Siberian perfectionist Rudolph Nureyev, and New Yorker Edward Villella. After attempting to learn modern stage humor in Twyla Tharp's witty *Push Comes to Shove* (1976), Kirkland, like her idol Natalia Makarova, abandoned innovative eccentricity for a rededication to classical dance romance and seamless execution. In Tudor's *The Tiller in the Fields* (1978), she played out a Cinderella fantasy in which an awkward teen suffered rejection from her haughty first love.

Starring Roles

Kirkland set her aims on full-length ballet roles from the classical European repertoire. On tour in Russia, Balanchine gave her amphetamines to fuel her drive. On return in September 1974, she paired up with Latvian dancer Mikhail "Misha" Baryshnikov, a recent defector to Toronto, who admired her as the best performer of the period. They debuted with the Royal Winnipeg Ballet Company. For four years, he was her lover. At American Ballet Theatre, she appeared as Kitri to his title role in *Don Quixote*; for John Neumeier's *Hamlet* in 1976, she danced to Aaron Copland's score *The Decline of Ophelia* to Misha's prince of Denmark. Her face and form graced the covers of *Dance and Life* magazine. Her lead parts covered the genre of story ballet—Lise in *La Fille Mal Gardée*, Nikiya in *The Kingdom of the Shades*, the Sleepwalker in *La Sonnambula*, the opposites Odette and Odile in *Swan Lake*, the Sylph in *La Sylphide*, and the Mazurka and pas de deux in *Les Sylphides*. Beginning in September 1975, the two dominated the American Ballet Theatre in poignant dramatic staples—the title character and her deceiver Prince Albrecht in *Giselle* (1976), Shakespeare's tragic figures in *Romeo and Juliet* (1976), and Aurora and Prince Florimund in the ballet pantomime *The Sleeping Beauty* (1976). Baryshnikov's *Live at Wolf Trap* (1976) medley pictured him as Franz opposite Kirkland as Swanilda in *Coppélia*.

In Baryshnikov's own production, on December 21, 1976, the two played Clara Silberhaus and the prince in the fairy tale ballet *The Nutcracker*, which premiered at the Kennedy Center at the height of the ballet season. On public television, it delighted holiday viewers in a December 16, 1977, performance filmed in Toronto. The role on screen, DVD, and video made Kirkland a popular star and won Emmy nominations for programming and for Baryshnikov's artistry. Families chose her first name for their baby girls; Chinese ballerinas viewed videos of her performances for tips on technique. On May 1, 1978, she appeared in costume on the cover of *Time* magazine. Her solos from *Swan Lake* found popular outlets on stage on May 17, 1978, in *Live from Lincoln Center* and on television in 1981 in a dying swan cameo for the *Bell Telephone Hour*.

No Longer Young

After Baryshnikov abandoned Kirkland for actor Jessica Lange and took Balanchine's role at the New York City Ballet, Kirkland moved on. When she resigned from the American Ballet Theatre in January 1980, choreographer Antony Tudor, a solace to her troubles, replied to her letter with a card on which he had drawn a lone red heart. She partnered with the unstable Patrick Bissel, a native of Corpus Christi, Texas, who killed himself by drug overdose at age 30. Under his influence, she grew dissatisfied with her physical appearance: "I wanted to lose my identity. . . . I was able to dream my way into somebody else's body. I was no longer Gelsey" (Kirkland and Lawrence, 1986, 205).

The dreams presaged Kirkland's decline. Like her self-destructive father, she took health risks and rehearsed on cracked bones. Out of a distorted sense of self, she turned to plastic surgery for silicone-enhanced breasts, lopped earlobes, and plumped ankles and nose. Most obvious in camera close-ups was a Hollywood fad for swollen lips resulting from collagen injections. She jeopardized her profession and well-being by indulging in cocaine, which Bissel supplied. The upper controlled her appetite and suppressed weight gain. She described ongoing self-abuse as a form of combat: "In my fanatical pursuit of beauty, I was at war with myself, driven by vanity and mortified by my appearance" (Kirkland and Lawrence, 1986, 35).

Drugs, sex, and food frenzy defined Kirkland's relationship with her partner and threatened her meticulous stage presence. At the same time, cocaine made bearable her intense workouts and performance schedule as well as her strivings for the perfect body. To supply herself with cocaine, she indulged in random sex as an exchange medium. She incurred firings and rehirings for enhancing performances with cocaine and for balancing highs with Valium lows for sleep. At age 32, she collapsed from emotional exhaustion and a potassium deficiency, which threatened her heart, kidneys, and muscles. Austrian psychiatrist Otto F. Kernberg, a specialist in narcissism, admitted her to a Westchester psychiatric ward to treat cocaine seizures, anorexia, bulimia, and a personality disorder. The hospitalization cost her a role in the movie *The Turning Point* (1977), which featured Leslie Brown opposite Baryshnikov, who won an Oscar for his performance.

Teaching and Writing

Upon recovery, Kirkland retired from the stage. In 1985, she married critic and dramaturge Greg Lawrence, who also suffered from depression and cocaine dependence. On November 16, 1986, in an interview with journalist Diane Sawyer for CBS TV's *60 Minutes*, Kirkland summarized the worst of her career lows and accused Balanchine of physical torment and of demanding silence and passivity, the stereotypical male expectations from female dancers. Upon invitation of Queen Elizabeth II to her 60th birthday gala, Kirkland performed at Covent Garden with the Royal Ballet in Sir Kenneth MacMillan's *Romeo and Juliet* and *The Sleeping Beauty*. Her grand moment paired her with Sir Anthony James Dowell of London in the balcony pas de deux. Kirkland stayed on in London with the corps de ballet for 6 years, when an injury shortened her stay. Another reprise of past greatness presented Kirkland with the Stuttgart Ballet in John Cranko's version of *Romeo and Juliet*.

With the aid of her husband, Kirkland revealed emotional torment in a confessional autobiography, the bestselling *Dancing on My Grave* (1986), published by ballet fan Jacqueline Kennedy Onassis. The dancer praised the trio's working relationship: "Jackie believed in us when few others did. . . . She was protective of us and steadfastly loyal" (Kirkland and Lawrence, 1986). The ballerina's candor gripped the dance, film, and fashion spheres for its exposé of dieting and vomiting regimens that exploited the egos of ultraslender divas. Kirkland completed her life study with a sequel, *The Shape of Love* (1990), illustrated with photos of her triumphs. The first volume was a Book of the Month Club selection and a *Cosmopolitan* serial. For criticizing Balanchine for posturing and tyrannizing neophytes, she earned shunning among professionals. The second volume turned to technique with descriptions of such Kirkland innovations as her mental creation of Juliet's ballroom, which was invisible to the audience. As a unit, the two memoirs present a rounded view of Kirkland as a neophyte and as a seasoned veteran.

With second husband Michael Chernov, the dancer settled in a seaside house in Melbourne, Australia, to write and study with Alexandra Lawler, Nina Osipian, and Robert Ray at the Victorian College of the Arts in Australia. Kirkland coached for Adelphi University, the American Ballet Theatre, the Australian Ballet, the English National Ballet, and the Royal Ballet School. To select pupils, she taught the Agrippina Vaganova method, a Russian philosophy of pedagogy based on core dynamics—precision, strength, flexibility, and endurance rather than Italian master Enrico Cecchetti's preference for delicacy, gesture, and illusion.

In 1993, Kirkland collaborated on a picture book, *The Little Ballerina and Her Dancing Horse*, which discloses some of the anticipation that the dancer experienced in girlhood. Her kudos include First Lady Nancy Reagan's invitation to the White House and recognition at the 50th Anniversary Gala for American Ballet Theatre at the Metropolitan Opera House, the Victory of the Spirit Award from the Kennedy Center, national chair for U.S.A. International Ballet Competition, a citation from *Dance* magazine, and the Gerard Manley Hopkins Theatre Award. Grooming new talent took her to teacher-in-residence at the Broadway Dance Center in New York City and as a guest artist and teacher at *STEPS* on Broadway, a prestigious studio founded in 1979. In May 2005, she returned to the American Ballet Theatre and the Jacqueline Kennedy Onassis School to teach. At age 55, she performed the character part of Carabosse in *The Sleeping Beauty*, which she and Chernov choreographed.

Sources

Buonaventura, Wendy. *Something in the Way She Moves: Dancing Women from Salomé to Madonna*. New York: Da Capo, 2005.

Kandall, Stephen R. *Substance and Shadow: Women and Addiction in the United States*. Cambridge, MA: Harvard University Press, 1999.

Kirkland, Gelsey, and Greg Lawrence. *Dancing on My Grave*. New York: Berkley Books, 1986.

———. *The Shape of Love*. New York: Doubleday, 1990.

Lydon, Kate. "Straight from the Heart: Gelsey Kirkland Looks Back . . . and Ahead." *Dance* (September 2005).

Perron, Wendy. "Curtain Up: Gelsey Kirkland." *Dance* 79 (9) (September 12, 2005): 12.

Terry, Walter. "Turning 'The Nutcracker' into a TV Spectacular." *New York Times*, December 11, 1977.

■ Asthma
Jackie Joyner-Kersee

Olympic heptathlon star Jacqueline "Jackie" Joyner-Kersee faced her greatest adversary from exercise-induced asthma. At her birth in East St. Louis, Illinois, on March 3, 1962, to former high school athlete and railroad switchman Alfred "A. J." Joyner and nurse's aide Mary Ruth Gaines Joyner, she was the second of four children, following the arrival of only son Alfredrick "Al" Alphonzo Joyner, a childhood competitor 2 years her senior. Her paternal grandmother, Evelyn Joyner, approved the name "Jacqueline" after the wife of President Jack Kennedy and predicted that the little one would be a First Lady in her own right. In girlhood, Jackie counted stars and climbed trees while battling poverty, racism, and loss. She grew up on Piggott Avenue in the south end ghetto and attended John Robinson Elementary School with sisters Gerald and Sherrell. Her family lived in a poorly heated hovel in sight of a poolroom and liquor store, where a public shooting resulted in a death. On cold nights, they spread blankets on the kitchen linoleum and warmed themselves by the oven. When her father left home frequently in search of work, her mother was the decision maker. In 1973, Jackie lost her grandmother to spousal abuse after her drunken grandfather killed his sleeping wife with a shotgun.

A thin gamine in pigtails nicknamed "Joker," Jackie developed into a competitor and an outstanding student with the support of her mother. Mary limited her preteen daughter to dance and cheerleading but ruled out boyfriends, smoking, drinking, and drugs. In 1971, Jackie and other girls scoured the playground for sand and transported it home in potato chip bags. In front of the porch, they poured enough sand to soften their landings in a long jump pit. Under volunteer coaches Nino Fennoy and George Ward, the girls formed a junior track team named the East St. Louis Railers, who practiced at the Mayor Brown Center. The passage of Title IX in 1972 ensured that schools would equalize sports opportunities for boys and girls. At age 12 at Hughes Quinn Junior High, Jackie vied in basketball and volleyball and discovered her affinity for track and field by entering the long jump competition.

In 1975, Jackie chose as sports examples Olympian Wilma Rudolph and the basketball, golf, and track and field great Mildred "Babe" Didrickson Zaharias, whom Jackie studied in a television biopic. By age 14, Jackie exulted at beating her older brother in a footrace. During bouts of breathing difficulties, doctors misdiagnosed her problem as bronchitis and mononucleosis. Jackie blamed poor performance on lack of workouts and inadequate training and pushed herself harder. Her mother took the pragmatic approach by limiting Jackie to time-out to calm her system from too much exertion. At Lincoln High School, at an adult size of 5 feet 10 inches and 150 pounds, she was an all-American selection in basketball and volleyball and a competitor on the school's cinder track. She contended in the U.S. Junior long jump and 100-meter hurdles against Olympian Carol Lewis.

After graduation, Jackie chose between full basketball and track scholarships to college and opted for the former. She led the University of California, Los Angeles, (UCLA) basketball team, the Bruins, as star forward and, in 1980, competed in the Olympic long jump trials. At the end of her first term, she returned to East St. Louis to confer with Al on the brain death of their 37-year-old mother, who died of spinal meningitis. For solace, Jackie turned to UCLA women's track coach Bob Kersee, a Panamanian-American and fellow perfectionist who guided her to All-America honors. A former U.S. Marine sergeant and compassionate sports mentor, he married her in a Baptist ceremony on January 11, 1986, in Long Beach.

Human Limitations

In 1983, Jackie experienced the onset of exercise-induced asthma (EIA), which she dismissed as a natural result of training. Like a pillow over the face, shortness of breath and tightness in the chest brought on panic and threatened her grace and power. Doctor Rogert Katz deduced that lengthy aerobic exercise, stress, and changing environments brought on bouts of the noninflammatory breathing deficiency, which she concealed from coaches and teammates for 5 years. She explained her aversion to medical care: "I'd hated hospitals ever since my mother died" (Joyner-Kersee and Steptoe, 1997, 154). The disease resulted from nose and mouth breathing of cool air that expanded vessels in the bronchial tract. Edema constricted blood flow and blocked air to her lungs. Attacks caused headache, gasping, coughing, and wheezing and threatened faintness and cyanosis or lack of oxygen to the blood. Her husband convinced her to respect her body's limits. She complied by seeing the disease as a natural part of life: "I started to think of my asthma as part of my training" (Henehan, 2002, 162). To protect her lungs, she masked her face while exercising but still incurred hospitalization because of all-out competition at track and field events. Contributing to the syndrome were her denial of the danger and dismissal of medical regimens to save her life. In addition, athletic rules disallowed prednisone, a stimulant that weakened the muscles.

Jackie's athletic greatness emerged in her twenties, when she set standards of courage and persistence for women's competitions in all sports. She suffered a torn left hamstring and narrow defeat to Australian Olympian Glynis Nunn of Queensland for the heptathlon—a 2-day ordeal comprised of 100-meter hurdles, high jump, shot put, 200-meter dash, long jump, javelin throw, and 800-meter dash—at the 1984 Olympics in Los Angeles, where her brother Al medaled first in triple jump and earned the Jim Thorpe Award. Jackie told a reporter from *Track & Field News* that she blamed her mental attitude for losing by only 5 points. At an outdoor meet in Baton Rouge, Louisiana, on July 7, 1985, she boosted the U.S. team with 6,718 points. The next year, she gave up basketball and achieved a fourth heptathlon victory for UCLA that set a stadium record. On July 7, 1986, she set a women's world record at the Goodwill Games in Moscow by amassing 7,148 points, breaking the 7,000 ceiling set by her idol, Babe Didrikson Zaharias in the triathlon. Jackie's performance earned her the James E. Sullivan Award as the top U.S. amateur heptathlete. She reset the record 4 weeks later in 126-degree heat at the Olympic Festival in Houston, Texas, with 7,158 points and a second time at the 1988 Olympic trials with 7,215 points.

A Female Superstar

With three International Association of Athletics Federations (IAAF) wins in 1987 for long jump, heptathlon, and 60-meter hurdles, Jackie seized the spotlight from dominant male athletes. *Sports Illustrated* featured her as "superwoman" on the cover in 1987 following the world championships in Rome on September 1, when she seized a long jump and two heptathlon titles with a total score of 7,128 points. Her therapist, Bob Forster of Santa Monica, relieved shin pain by lining her shoes with cork orthotics. At the 1988 Olympic trials in Indianapolis, Indiana, she upped her tally to a record 7,215 points, a score that reduced her coach-husband to tears. *New York Times* sports reporter Joe Morgenstern dubbed her a "late 20th-century Atalanta," a reference to the Greek woman who raced against men (Morgenstern, 1988). Her brother Al added, "She's like a computer. You punch the right keys and she's dangerous" (Ibid.). On September 24, at the 1988 games in Seoul, Korea, despite a strained knee, 26-year-old Jackie made her best showing. Against the opinion of sports handicappers, she added two gold medals to the United States total for pushing the long jump to 7.4 meters against German competitor Heike Dreschsler. Jackie totaled 7,291 points, a standing record. The effort produced a signal defeat for East Germany's stars Sabine John and Anke Vater-Behmer.

Jackie's phenomenal performances began to wane in her late 20s. In 1989, she abandoned the heptathlon and long jump for hurdling in the 100- and 400-meter events. Summer of 1990 proved difficult for Jackie and her coach because of her tender groin and hamstring muscles. Travel, pollen, and allergies to dust, grass, seafood, peanuts, almonds, apples, peaches, and plums increased discomfort, which she eased with a Ventolin inhaler. In November 1990, she contracted pneumonia. Four months later, airway constriction twice hospitalized her. She recalled, "Suddenly, there in broad daylight, I saw stars. Then I felt my throat closing" (Joyner-Kersee and Steptoe, 1997, 211). Her brother and husband carried her into the emergency room to seek treatment for an attack that brought her to the edge of consciousness. With 6,783 points, she won the Goodwill Games in Seattle, Washington, on July 7, 1990, but set no records. In New York City the next year on June 13, she edged up her point count to 6,878. Another attack in Eugene, Oregon, occurred after the National Collegiate Athletic Association outdoor championships in June 1991 and required an overnight hospital stay.

In the Global Spotlight

Jackie refused to be sidelined. In Tokyo, Japan, in late August 1991, she added another gold medal for long jump. She despaired of female athletes to compete against. Her expertise roused allegations of steroid use, a violation that ended the career of challenger Larisa Nikitina of the Soviet Union, but no test proved Jackie guilty of breaking the rules. On August 2, 1992, at the Olympics in Barcelona, Spain, in spite of illness and hot weather, she defended her heptathlon record against challenger Sabine Braun of Germany by snagging a third gold medal in heptathlon with 7,044 points, a leap of 166 points. The battle was grueling because of a knee injury, twisted ankle, and Jackie's ongoing spats with the coach. In Stuttgart, Germany, on August 16, 1993, her heptathlon score of 6,837 won another gold following her most lethal asthma attack. At the IAAF Mobil Grand Prix Final in Paris, France, on September 3, 1994, she topped the charts in long jump. After the hurdles at the 1996 Games in Atlanta, Georgia, a right hamstring pull forced her out of the heptathlon after she ran the hurdles in the rain. Her sports therapist treated leg pain with massage, ice packs, and rehabilitation. Six days later, she returned to the field favoring a throbbing right thigh, lost the gold to Kim Blair, and won a bronze medal for the long jump by 1 inch. She took the loss as a reminder that winning is a coordinated effort graced by luck and timing.

As the asthma attacks worsened, Jackie remained competitive to the end of her athletic career. She played briefly for the Richmond Rage in the newly formed American Basketball League. She roused interest in women's teams, but scored 4 points or less in 17 games during a 21–19 win-loss season. At age 36, she retired from track with an enviable Olympic record of three gold, one silver, and two bronze medals, making her the most decorated of U.S. female Olympians. In hot, humid weather at the 1998 Goodwill Games in Uniondale, New York, on July 22, she returned to competition and beat DeDee Nation in the heptathlon with only 6,502 points. In two competitions—on July 25, 1998, at the Grand Prix meet held at Edwardsville, Illinois, and at the 2000 Olympic trials—Jackie placed sixth. She collapsed against Bob and cried for the end of an exemplary career. The year brought sadness to the athletic family in Mission Viejo, California, with the sudden death in sleep from a grand mal seizure of Al's wife, Delorez Florence Griffith "Flo Jo" Joyner, the mother of Jackie's niece Mary Ruth.

A Remarkable Record

A winner of the Jesse Owens Award and three-time recipient of the Track and Field Athlete of the Year, Jackie set records in the National Collegiate Athletic Association, Olympic, U.S., and world heptathlon events. Her awards for college basketball, running, long jump, and indoor and outdoor sprint hurdling placed her among the world's finest and most respected athletes, male and female. Decathlon star Bruce Jenner praised her as the best ever multievent competitor. Sportscasters compared her to skater Sonja Henie and tennis greats Chris Evert, Billie Jean King, and Martina Navratilova. As a beacon to the next generation of women athletes, Jackie shone in the dreams of future greats, soccer player Mia Hamm and track and field contender Marion Jones Thompson. On February 21, 1998, sports fans voted Jackie one of the top 15 players in UCLA women's basketball. She came in sixth at the Olympic trials in 2000. *Sports Illustrated* chose her as the century's greatest female competitor. Another honor awaited her in April 2001, when 976 NCAA schools named her the top female collegiate athlete in the last quarter century.

In retirement, Jackie sponsored a NASCAR team and opened Elite Sports Marketing, a management consortium for athletes, and Gold Medal Rehab, a sports medicine clinic. In 2000, she received a walk of fame star in St. Louis, where a youth center and MetroLink light rail station bear her name. A yearly invitational track meet at her alma mater honors her and alumnus Rafer Johnson, a star decathlete, with competition in discus, hammer throw, high jump, hurling, javelin, long jump, pole vault, relay, shot put, sprints, and triple jump. She and husband Bob established the Jackie Joyner-Kersee Community Foundation, a charity uplifting families at home and worldwide by broadening educational and recreational opportunities and by encouraging children to compete in sports. As a representative of the Asthma All-Stars, a national asthma education program supported by GlaxoSmithKline, she informs children of the severity and threat of chronic lung and breathing disorders in 5,000 U.S. victims annually.

Sources

Henehan, Mary Pat. *Integrating Spirit and Psyche: Using Women's Narratives in Psychotherapy*. Binghamton, NY: Haworth Press, 2002.

Janofsky, Michael. "Track and Field: Still Racing with the Wind." *New York Times*, June 9, 1991.

Joyner-Kersee, Jackie, and Sonja Steptoe. *A Kind of Grace: The Autobiography of the World's Greatest Female Athlete*. New York: Grand Central, 1997.

Morgenstern, Joe. "Worldbeater: Olympic Athlete Jackie Joyner-Kersee." *New York Times*, July 31, 1988.

Rundell, Kenneth W., Randall L. Wilber, and Robert F. Lemanske. *Exercise-Induced Asthma: Pathophysiology and Treatment*. Champaign, IL: Human Kinetics, 2002.

Wiggins, David K., and Patrick B. Miller. *The Unlevel Playing Field: A Documentary History of the African American Experience in Sport*. Champaign, IL: University of Illinois Press, 2003.

Bariatric Surgery
Roseanne Barr

Feminist insult comedian and actor Roseanne Cherrie Barr set standards of self-help by undergoing life-altering elective surgery. A native of Salt Lake City, Utah, she was born on November 3, 1952, to what she terms as working-class Jewish parents who lived in a trailer and later in her maternal grandparents' tenement. Her parents, bookkeeper Helen Davis Barr and blanket salesman Jerome Hershel "Jerry" Barr, were first-generation Orthodox Jewish Americans of Austro-Hungarian and Lithuanian extraction. They lopped the surname "Borisofsky" to a more manageable "Barr." Helen and Jerry kept a low religious profile in Mormon territory while Helen's parents hosted fellow survivors of the Holocaust.

At age 3, Barr entertained her extended family at traditional Friday evening Sabbath meals and dreamed of being a gypsy or of tap-dancing her way to notoriety. The next year, she suffered temporary facial disfigurement from the onset of Bell's palsy, an acute nerve paralysis that causes the muscles to droop. The parents sired three more children—Ben, Geraldine, and Stephanie—and pretended to rear them in the Church of Jesus Christ of Latter-Day Saints, the predominant faith of their neighbors. The peculiar blend of faiths turned Barr to Christianity and to Kabbalah, Jewish mysticism based on numerology as a means of communing directly with God. For childhood comfort and mentoring, she relied on her feisty maternal grandmother, "Bubbe Mary" Butrum Davis. For attention, she directed junior high theatricals and appeared as Ahasuerus, the king of Persia, at her synagogue in a Purim reenactment of Queen Esther's heroism.

Troubled Teen Mother

A car accident on September 17, 1968, tossed Barr into the air. She plummeted headfirst onto a hood ornament, which pierced her skull and plunged her into a coma. The trauma left Barr with limited concentration and short-term amnesia that aroused terrifying nightmares of premature burial. After quitting East High School, she spent 8 months in a Utah state psychiatric ward. She cut her ties with a troubled past and took a bus headed east to a Colorado art colony. While living in Denver, Colorado, in 1973, she waited tables, washed dishes and served cocktails at Bennigan's restaurant, dressed windows at GiGi's, and assisted the French chef at the Silver Queen.

At age 19, Barr rejected the boyfriend who impregnated her and gave birth to daughter Brandi Brown, whom she named Elisa. Barr surrendered the infant for adoption to Salvation Army workers at Booth Memorial Home for Unwed Mothers. Mother and daughter remained apart until their reunion in Los Angeles in 1989. On February 4, 1974, Barr married motel night clerk William "Bill" Pentland, from Georgetown, Colorado, and father of their three children, Jacob, Jennifer, and Jessica Pentland. While the family occupied a trailer, Roseanne nurtured a dream of advancing to clothing buyer for department stores.

Turning Pain into Laughs

Comedy came easily to Barr, who had good reason to defy the patriarchal rules that women be quiet, obedient, and refined. Analyst Yvonne Tasker identified Barr's métier as a pose as a "cynical survivor of heterosexuality . . ., a knowing commentary on the short-comings of conventional behaviors and structures juxtaposed with a celebration of the plea-sures of indulgence" (Tasker, 1998, 167). Barr emulated the self-discipline, candor, and assertiveness of Redd Foxx, Richard Pryor, and Mae West by channeling female rage into a fantasy extreme. She noted, "I had found my voice. . . . I began to speak as a working-class woman who is a mother," a universal language for females (Lavin, 2004, 57). Her style suited motorcycle pubs and punk rock clubs. In 1985, she moved her family to Los Angeles after she landed a contract from Mitzi Shore with the Comedy Store on Sunset Strip.

At age 26, Barr produced *Women, Take Back the Mike*, a stage routine promoting the feminist project "Take Back the Night," a part of the Women Against Violence in Pornography and Media effort at the University of Colorado. The program introduced her as "Person of Ceremonies: an adorably angry/vicious comic, wife of years, mother of three, affectionately referred to as 'castrating bitch' by many male colleagues" (Lavin, 2004, 54). In the 1980s, comic appearances at a Unitarian coffeehouse in Denver began her career in solo feminist humor. She became a regular at the Mercury Café, Muddy's Java Café, and Straight Johnson's and, in 1983, won the Denver Laff-Off competition, which earned her the title "Queen of Denver Comedy."

Boost to Greatness

On August 23, 1985, funnyman Johnny Carson introduced Barr nationwide on *The Tonight Show*, where she raised critical hackles by uttering the word "uterus." Taking comedy as a calling, she built a ribald stand-up routine ridiculing housewifery by creating the "domestic goddess," a tell-all stage persona who freed her from ego restraint. Her one-liners overturned stereotypes about overweight women as complacent and sexually inactive. She gained recognition on a Rodney Dangerfield HBO TV special and in Las Vegas, where she appeared at Caesar's Palace, the Desert Inn, and the Dunes and earned a 1987 Cable Ace Award for funniest female comic. On *Lifetime Salutes Mom* (1987), Barr acknowledged her mother Helen.

By manufacturing a public self, the comic manipulated viewer perceptions in television, on stage, and in the tabloids, which exploited her image from unconventional to monstrous. In 1988, Barr scripted and starred in the top-rated ABC TV sitcom *Roseanne*, a groundbreaking deviation from comedy-as-usual that focused on the nonconformist working woman. The concept, a throwback to the rustic charm of poverty in the Ma and Pa Kettle movies and urban slums in Jackie Gleason's *The Honeymooners*, was the brainchild of production team Marcy Carsey and Tom Werner, designers of *The Cosby Show*. The style cross-bred Barr's individual and highly unpredictable stand-up routines with the domestic living room in Landford, Illinois, a containment that symbolized social and patriarchal forces constraining women. Adopting the persona of a disaffected and transgressive housewife, Roseanne Connor, Barr exulted, "I was fat and pushy and unapologetic about it all. Now that was revolutionary" (Loncaric, 2007). She exploited the stereotype of the obese underclass woman by lolling on furniture, slouching before the camera, and letting her words spew uncensored into slovenly excess that defied the cult of thinness.

For material, Barr mined the lives of her family and childhood friends and neighbors. The action coped intelligently with domestic violence, poverty, unemployment and labor unions, racism and sexism, substance abuse, gambling, and teen pregnancy. Viewers and critics blurred the line between the fictional Roseanne and her creator. Flourishing in 30 countries, the series ran for nine seasons and earned an Emmy, an American Comedy Award, a Nickelodeon Kids' Choice Award, a Peabody citation, six People's Choice Awards, a Lucy Award, and two Golden Globes for Roseanne and Emmys for costars John Goodman and Laurie Metcalf.

Toppling from the Top

Barr accumulated not only wealth but also opportunities usually denied to comediennes. The year she collaborated with actor Meryl Streep in the Gothic comedy *She-Devil* (1989), Barr appeared on more magazine covers than any other person. She extended her fame by publishing an autobiography, *Roseanne: My Life as a Woman* (1989), in which she characterized her appetites from infancy as "gargantuan" (Barr, 1989). She provided the infant voice-over for *Look Who's Talking Too* (1990) and for *Little Rosey* (1990), a cartoon based on her childhood. On July 25, 1990, Barr overstepped audience tolerance after singing the national anthem off key before a matchup of the Cincinnati Reds and San Diego Padres in San Diego, California. To satirize male jocks, she pawed her crotch and spat on the ground. Outraged fans defamed her for mocking the players and for desecrating "The Star-Spangled Banner." The next day, the media and President George H. W. Bush concurred that Barr was out of line.

On September 21, 1991, Barr's childhood insecurities reinvaded her new life. She ignited family uproar by declaring at a conference of recovering incest victims and to an interviewer for *People* that her father and mother molested and beat her. Her parents refuted the allegations with lie detector tests; her sister Geraldine charged Roseanne with lying to spark publicity. Barr recanted her story, which estranged family members for a decade. Supported by costars Goodman and Metcalf, Barr relied on coworkers to help her guide her 14-year-old, Jessica, through withdrawal from alcohol.

During a 5-year marriage to actor Tom Arnold, Barr collaborated with him on visits to military wives at California bases while their husbands served in Desert Storm. In 1991, when the couple reenacted their marriage vows, Barr took his surname. He converted to Judaism and became her executive producer. She ended the marriage with charges that Tom was violent and abusive. She sought the reversal of her tubal ligation and underwent in vitro fertilization to conceive another child, Buck, with her third mate, her driver and security guard Benjamin "Ben" Thomas. The couple resided in Brentwood Hills in a Tudor-style manse. The marriage collapsed after she charged him with alcoholic bingeing and plots to kidnap their son.

New Venues

Barr's creative urge found more outlets. At age 42, she paired admirably with Uma Thurman in the satiric film *Even Cowgirls Get the Blues* (1994). Barr appeared in the movie *Smoke* (1995) and published a second memoir, *My Lives* (1994), which toyed with the idea that she suffered from multiple personalities. In 1997, she ended an intense period of star-struck self-indulgence to acclimate to normal life. Semiseriously, she bemoaned, "What am I going to do? I can't boss people around any more—sad but true. There is no one to frigging fight with any more" (Rampton, 2007). She romped through a reprise of *The Wizard Of Oz* at Madison Square Garden as the Wicked Witch of the West. In March 1998, Barr ventured far enough into weight control to risk a gastric bypass, a stomach-stapling operation by which Dr. Mal Fobi reduced her stomach to a small pouch. A second procedure attached the pouch to her small intestine to bypass the part of her intestines that absorbed calories. The hospital stay ended after 3 days. Because she felt satisfied by smaller meals, her size dropped by more than half.

Barr's next venture was on daytime talk TV in *The Roseanne Show*, which survived until 2000. Appearing with her were daughters Brandi, Jennifer, and Jessica. In 2002, Barr shared stable romance with songwriter Johnny Argent. At age 51, she attempted simultaneous roles as cook on *Domestic Goddess* and star of a reality feature, the *Real Roseanne Show*. She withdrew from performing to recuperate from food poisoning and an appendectomy. Her next undertaking in television was a cyclical role in 2004 on ABC TV in *Desperate Housewives*.

In 2004, film satirist Michael Moore pulled Barr away from the camera and back to a live audience of conservatives in Salt Lake City. She enjoyed the old feeling of being in control: "It's a great art form that can bring down governments and religions. The jester/fool/critic is a powerful entity" (Loncaric, 2007). Her mockery of President George W. Bush began with thanks for his perpetuation of private assault rifle ownership. She smirked, "You never know when God is going to call on you to shoot an abortion doctor" (Rampton, 2007). Her whip-smart jibes earned a lifetime tribute from *Entertainment Weekly*, which named her one of television's 50 greatest icons.

Remaking Roseanne

Within months, Barr returned to her comic roots with a global tour of stand-up patter. The program, *Let the Healing Begin*, took her to a comedy fest at De Montfort Hall in Leicester, England. She described the scripting and delivery as a way of pondering the world and locating inconsistencies and ironies that are both ridiculous and poignant, such as the adult dress and makeup that turned Jon Benet Ramsey into a baby vamp. Barr introduced children's entertainment to her repertoire with a 40-minute DVD, *Rockin' with Roseanne: Calling All Kids* (2005), a fun sing-along recorded by her own production crew. On November 2, 2001, she depicted a nun on NBC TV in *My Name Is Earl*; 2 days later, HBO debuted a special DVD, *Roseanne Barr: Blonde 'N Bitchin'*. Constant screen exposure earned her a 1-hour phone-in radio talk show on KCAA in Los Angeles and the job of host on *The Search for the Funniest Mom in America*, which featured women who had suffered the same hardships and self-doubts as Roseanne. She rewarded herself by purchasing a macadamia farm in Hawaii.

Barr sometimes reeled from the self-delusions of fame. Her penchant for controversy resurged after she generalized about gays and lesbians. On the April 6, 2007, edition of her radio show, she charged the gay community with narcissism that excluded interest in other political and economic issues. She lambasted herself for making a divisive statement. A general overhaul—substantial weight loss, face-lift, breast and abdomen liposuction, chin implant, eyelid enhancement, a nose job to correct sleep apnea, and a lighter hair color—coincided with middle age, when she quelled some of the neurotic outrages of her past life. The breast reduction saved her from a life of backache and shoulder pain. She described the venture as an investment of $60,000 in a "whole new body" (Gilman, 1999, 219). She settled in El Segundo, California, to raise and homeschool Buck. With the zip of her old self, she bought an ad in the *Hollywood Reporter*, sneering, "This town is a back-stabbing, scum-sucking, small-minded town, but thanks for the money" (Rampton, 2007). Her awards include recognition in *Ms.* magazine's 20th anniversary special, a Children's Film Festival Humanitarian Award, listing as one of Comedy Central's 100 all-time best stand-up performers, and selection by *Ladies' Home Journal* as a fascinating individual.

Sources

Auslander, Philip. *From Acting to Performance: Essays in Modernism and Postmodernism*. New York: Routledge, 1997.

Barr, Roseanne. *Roseanne: My Life as a Woman*. New York: Harper & Row, 1989.

Butler, Jeremy G. *Television: Critical Methods and Applications*. New York: Routledge, 2006.

Dworkin, Susan. "Roseanne Barr: The Disgruntled Housewife as Stand-Up Comedian." *Ms.* (July–August 1987).

Gilman, Sander L. *Making the Body Beautiful: A Cultural History of Aesthetic Surgery*. Princeton, NJ: Princeton University Press, 1999.

Lavin, Suzanne. *Women and Comedy in Solo Performance: Phyllis Diller, Lily Tomlin, and Roseanne*. New York: Routledge, 2004.

Loncaric, Terry. "Back on the Stand-Up Circuit, Roseanne Barr's Still Dishing It Out." *Northwest Herald* (McHenry County, Ill.), September 28, 2007.

Rampton, James. "Roseanne: She's Big Again." *Independent*, December 10, 2007.

Tasker, Yvonne. *Working Girls: Gender and Sexuality in Popular Cinema*. New York: Routledge, 1998.

■ Bipolarity
Kaye Gibbons

Burdened by years of treatment for out-of-control emotions and depressions, Kaye Gibbons has flourished as a writer of redemptive feminist fiction. The third of three children reared on a tobacco farm on Bend of the River Road in Nash County, North Carolina, Bertha Kaye Batts Gibbons was born on May 5, 1960, and lived in a tin-roofed frame house lacking electricity and heat. In childhood, she treasured the antics of grandmother Martha and stored up the sufferings of her parents, farmer Charles "Charlie" Batts, a self-defeating alcoholic, and Alice "Shine" Batts, a semi-invalid from rheumatic fever, heart surgery, and a mood-shifting syndrome. Shine's fragile state required five weeks of treatment at Dorothea Dix Hospital in Raleigh with the antipsychotic drug Navane. Gibbons recalled, "I know what it's like to live with someone who's unhappy" (Jarvis, 2005). In self-defense, she read newspaper headlines, *Child Craft Encyclopedia*, and Bible stories before entering first grade at Coopers School. Recalling her escape through books, she later mourned, "I had nowhere else to go" (Brodeur, 1996).

Burdened by poverty, Gibbons coveted brick houses and families unscathed by mental illness and alcoholism, two motifs of her first novel. The suicide of her mother in March 1970 by an overdose of the pulse-suppressing drug digitalis foreshadowed the author's own sieges from the same disease, cyclical bipolarity, commonly called manic depression. Gibbons bore the survivor's onus of guilt for not being the perfect little girl. Without maternal guidance,

Kaye became the woman of the house, paying the bills and tending her father during his binges. Her fantasy world strayed from television episodes of *Green Acres* and *Get Smart* to Nancy Drew mysteries and visions of herself as a lab scientist searching for cures. At Christmas, in lieu of a visit by Santa Claus, she treated herself to a King James Bible, a fount of lyricism and wisdom lore that impacted her fiction.

Nested Once More

Until age 12, Gibbons ricocheted from one relative's home to another before entering a foster home near Wilson, North Carolina. On vacations from Spaulding Middle School at Spring Hope, North Carolina, she worked in tobacco fields and attended the Children's Bible Mission Camp at Falls of the Neuse River outside Raleigh. With a show of the resolve that marks her adulthood, she selected her own parent, Mary Lee, a tender rescuer who ended the era's insecurity. In spring 1973, Gibbons' older brother, 26-year-old David Batts, and his nurturing wife, Barbara Atkins Batts, of Englewood, took over the roles of surrogate parents. The author, hardened by lengthy stretches of hopelessness, recovered self-esteem through part-time employment at Bobby Mears' grocery store, Englewood Supermarket, Sunset Nursery, Cardinal Theater, and B. Dalton's. At age 17, she found the courage to enter the Miss North Carolina National Teenager Pageant but felt decidedly dowdy and out of place in her makeshift ball gown.

With a diploma from Rocky Mount Senior High School, serious reading of the Brontë sisters and John Steinbeck, and the encouragement of English teacher Elizabeth "Betty" Hardy, Gibbons was ready for literature and political science studies at North Carolina State University in Raleigh. She attended college with funding from the Veterans Administration and a governor's scholarship. Her intelligence and capacity for learning earned the regard of writer-professor Lee Smith. Supporting a plan to teach English and write scholarly articles, Gibbons tutored football players, shelved books in the library, and waited tables at MacGregor Downs Country Club. She entered the class of Cleanth Brooks, a passionate teacher of reading comprehension and analysis.

The First Hospitalization

The shadow of Shine Batts' bipolarity fell on Gibbons at age 20, when she began taking anticonvulsants to control restlessness and poor concentration during all-night bouts of reading. Heavy doses of psychotropic drugs wilted her writing voice and dulled the edge of her artistry. On May 12, 1984, she wed landscape architect Michael Gibbons, settled in a duplex apartment in west Raleigh, and gave birth to Mary, the first of three daughters. The completion of *Ellen Foster* (1987), a self-revelatory novella, boosted the author from unknown first-timer to author of a young adult classic. The work oppresses its protagonist with neglect, makeshift diet, near rape, and a Dickensian court system that robs her of a happy foster home with her art teacher by tossing her back to unfeeling relatives. At a poignant moment in the heroine's reflections, she states, "Every day I try to feel better about all that went on when I was little" (Gibbons, 1987, 121). Gibbons denied direct connections to the homeless, unloved protagonist but admitted that the vernacular first person style derived from the author's childhood in North Carolina's eastern tobacco land. For teaching her authentic voicing and for supporting her during edits and publication, she thanked

Southern literature scholar Lewis D. Rubin, Jr., the editor of Algonquin Press and a necessary father figure to Gibbons' literary coming of age.

Paradoxical bouts of ill health continued to dog Gibbons. Before the birth of Leslie Gibbons in 1987, the author suffered gestational diabetes and required 3 months of psychiatric therapy for bipolarity. She dissected debilitating mental states in an award-winning short story, "The Headache," a treasure of Southern gothic published in the June 1987 issue of the *St. Andrews Review*. While awards cropped up from the Ernest Hemingway Foundation, with the first North Carolina State University D. H. Hill Library author-in-residence honor and a Louis D. Rubin Writing Award from the University of North Carolina (UNC), Gibbons valued reader letters about hopeless, motherless lives similar to Ellen's. She made up for missing coursework to finish a B.A. degree in English literature from the UNC at Chapel Hill and came into two windfalls, $33,000 for the paperback rights to *Ellen Foster* and the sale of film rights to Paramount Pictures and Hallmark Hall of Fame. About the time that Gibbons gave birth to daughter Louise, substantial royalties expunged her obsession over childhood poverty.

Assertive Womenfolk

Gibbons disciplined her days with the writing of a second novel, *A Virtuous Woman* (1989), a compassionate reflection on the off-kilter romance of "Blinking" Jack and Ruby Woodrow Stokes, tenant farmers who occupy the rural microcosm of Milk Farm Road. The fallout of difficult composition while mothering a toddler and an infant was Gibbons' return to a psychiatric ward and the realization that her marriage had no future. From meetings of Adult Children of Alcoholics, she outgrew childish self-blame for her parents' slide into substance abuse and mental illness. The National Endowment for the Arts supplied a $20,000 grant for work on her third novel, *A Cure for Dreams* (1991), a celebration of strong Irish-American matrilineage, Bridget O'Donough O'Cadhain, Lottie O'Cadhain Davies, and Betty Davies Randolph. The mother-daughter duo of Lottie and Betty, a war bride, weathers the 1930s through talk-story, strategies of self-rescue, and the birth of Betty's daughter, Marjorie Polly Randolph, delivered by midwife and baby doctor Polly Deal. For authenticity, Gibbons amassed details from mill workers, farmers, ex-slaves, and female survivors who banked their stories with the Federal Writers' Project of the Great Depression. The emergence of feminist pride gave the author the courage to admit to attendees at an American Booksellers Association convention in Washington, D.C., that Kaye Gibbons was Ellen Foster.

Admiration for female autonomy and courage spurred Gibbons' later works, which she filled with realistic views of hard-pressed womanhood. For *Charms for the Easy Life* (1992), which earned a $1 million contract, she surveyed elements of her own character to flesh out a three-generation saga. The plot extols the cooperation of self-educated herbalist Charlie Kate Birch and her overly romantic widowed daughter, Sophia Snow Birch. The treasure of the all-woman household, Sophia's daughter Margaret, flourishes as a pragmatic intellectual and volunteer in military hospital wards at the height of World War II. Gibbons depicts the third generation as strong enough to survive international cataclysm and wise enough to choose a worthy mate.

While the book absorbed readers, a thirty-city book tour taxed the author's strength. On September 25, 1992, she married corporate and civil rights attorney Frank P. Ward, Jr., and added to the household two stepchildren, Frank, III, and Victoria. Nestled in affection and appreciation, she began a hurtful return to childhood suffering with her fifth novel, *Sights Unseen* (1995), a first-hand study of family chaos during the manic-depressive excesses of Maggie Barnes, a farm wife and mother. Amid the pathos of mercurial behaviors, the author inserted incongruities and comic relief through Maggie's delusions of preparing dinner for Robert Kennedy. As a literary foil, Gibbons created Pearl Wiggins, the cook-housekeeper whose surrogate parenthood eases the "undermothered" Hattie Barnes through her mother's psychotherapy and eight sessions of electroconvulsive therapy at Duke Hospital.

The author's psychiatrist eased the panic of reliving past calamities by comparing cyclical mood swings to diabetes, a physical ill controlled by medication. Gibbons reported on melancholic black holes and surges of elation that she knew from experience. She declared that tackling so personal a reflection made her "reaffirm" her "pledge to stay well," adding, "I try hard every day, even though it's much easier to give in to this illness" (Paddock, 1995). She predicted that the authenticity of her memories would enable her daughters to understand their mother's lapses into emotional spirals. Health care workers lauded the book as a first-person recall of children witnessing the episodes encountered by a parent ill with chronic manic depression.

Historical Fiction

Gibbons' emerging control over mental instability produced periods of hypomania, a transitional wellness that emerged between ravings and total withdrawal. Feelings of normality allowed her to venture into a girlhood love of history. She launched a 10-month research of Civil War domestic history as the basis for *On the Occasion of My Last Afternoon* (1998). Written from the perspective of a professional woman, surgical nurse Emma Garnet Lowell, the text covers the onset of revolt, waves of wounded demanding care and rehabilitation, the displacement of slaves from plantations, and the unabated sorrow of war widows. During a light-hearted moment in difficult preparation, she joined 16 local authors in writing a round-robin gothic mystery, *Pete & Shirley: The Great Tar Heel Novel* (1995). In February 1996, an insightful viewing of playwright Aaron Posner's 1994 adaptation of *Ellen Foster* placed Gibbons alongside her brother David for the bittersweet story they remembered from life. Returning to the toil of her civil war novel, she finished the manuscript, rested with the family at Wrightsville Beach, and then retreated to a hospital to recover from exhaustion from 40- to 60-hour writing sessions over a 3-month period.

Regard from readers, critics, and colleagues buoyed Gibbons' spirits. In Paris, the French minister of culture, Philippe Douste-Blazy, made her the youngest writer to receive the Chevalier de L'Ordre des Arts et des Lettres. Closer to home, an honorary Ph.D. in letters from N.C. State University followed the 35th annual North Carolina Award for Literature, the state's highest civilian honor for achievement in the arts, literature, public service, and science. Oprah Winfrey's selection of *Ellen Foster* delighted Gibbons by urging more people to read. The *Hallmark Hall of Fame* version of *Ellen Foster*, which aired on December 14, 1997, added to the versions of Gibbons' works available to the public. To relieve the miseries of unwanted children, she raised funds for the "Read to Me" program and established an ongoing charity to libraries in schools, homes for abused women and children, and orphanages. She championed the donation of new books as "spiritual possessions" for inmates: "Children in these situations too often get used things, and feel used themselves" (Brodeur, 1996).

Giving Back to the World

The defeat of bipolarity infused Gibbons with enthusiasm for benevolent works. She delivered the Rosamond Gifford Lecture, "My Life with Manic Depression So Far," a witty summation of deep mopes, verbal agitation, and unforeseen delusions over 2 decades that made her appreciate rare spans of sanity. Still anguished by mother hunger, she longed to glimpse Shine Batts as a woman free of mental swoops and dips. A hard-fought divorce from a second husband depleted Gibbons' finances and endangered her college fund for her three daughters. She adopted a mindset of challenge, chopped her budget to manageable size, and instituted double-shift writing sessions. The push to support a four-woman household preceded a serendipity, a new diagnosis of freedom from bipolarity.

In recent years, Gibbons' recovery capped a list of successes. In addition to her readings of audiocassette versions of her works, the public embraced the Showtime TV version of *Charms for the Easy Life*, which aired in August 2002. She dramatized more woman-to-woman networking in *Divining Women* (2004), a dramatization of in-house misogyny and spiritual battery by Troop Ross, a domestic villain. The historical fiction interlaces Maureen Ross' recovery from the stillbirth of Ella Eloise with the demands of World War I and the losses of the influenza epidemic of 1918, which include the two young sons of the family servants, Zollie and Mamie. Gibbons returned to her fictional persona with *The Life All Around Me by Ellen Foster* (2006), which revisits the author's alter ego as she enters college. Gibbons explained her need for a sequel: "If I only live twice and one of those times is through Ellen, I may have her avoid all the mistakes I've made" (Krentz, 2006). The height of the novel is the benevolent synergy generated by Ellen and Laura, a saintly foster mother on whom the author projects her adoration and whom she thanks on behalf of other unmoored children.

Savoring health and security after her daughters matured, Gibbons entered a phase of self-motivation and accomplishment. She established a home away from the South in Manhattan, where her flat overlooks the East River. She enjoyed idle strolls, charities aiding the homeless, rap recordings, and camp movies, which moderated the tensions of writing. By pursuing more fictional scenarios, she used novels to correct and cleanse past errors and to avenge herself on privation and cruelty.

Sources

Brodeur, Nicole. "So They'll Know They're Not Alone." *News & Observer* (Raleigh, NC), November 27, 1996.

Gibbons, Kaye. *Ellen Foster*. New York: Algonquin Press, 1987.

Jarvis, Craig. "The Life All Around Her: Kaye Gibbons Returns to the Character That Made Her in Order to Remake Herself." *News & Observer* (Raleigh, NC), December 25, 2005.

Krentz, Jeri. "Hard Journey Back to 'Ellen.'" *Charlotte Observer*, January 29, 2006.

Paddock, Polly. "Kaye Gibbons Recalls 'Sights Unseen' As a Tough Project." *The Charlotte Observer*, August 27, 1995.

Biracialism
Sandra Cisneros

Essayist and fiction writer Sandra Cisneros survived the traumas and diminution of the Anglo-Chicana experience to become a feminist pathfinder during the Latino literary renaissance. She was born into poverty in Chicago on December 20, 1954, to an Amerindian-Mexican, English-speaking mother, Elvira Cordero Anguinao, and Alfredo Cisneros del Moral, a Spanish-speaking Mexican construction worker and upholsterer. At home, the author developed a love of stories—classic literature from her mother and Famile Boron comic books, photonovelas (adult comic strips), and telenovelas (soap operas) from her father. Like a silent mouse perched in the corner, she absorbed the tradition of La Llorona, the weeping wraith, and memorized family anecdotes and genealogies reaching back several generations before her birth. Among the less amusing stories was an account of President Woodrow Wilson, who, in 1914, dispatched U.S. Marines to destabilize Mexican President José Huerta's regime. The story foreshadowed her own destabilization in a borderland where whites stripped browns of power and ignored the resultant labeling and ostracism. Her father, who started the business A. Cisneros & Sons, retaliated against the era's racism by naming the family dog "Wilson."

In girlhood, Cisneros was *la consentida* (daddy's little princess) at home. Pampered to expect the best from life, she longed for the white frame houses engulfed in green lawns like the ones on *Father Knows Best* and *Leave It to Beaver*. She was shy and culturally displaced in a neighborhood demarcated by skin color and language. Out of distaste for crowds, she chose to deal with relationships one person at a time. While growing up in a series of urban tenements and studying at Catholic schools, she tried to think of her surroundings as temporary. At the library, she repeatedly checked out a sentimental children's book by Beatrice Schenk de Regniers called *A Little House of Your Own* (1958). The gendered social order troubled her. Long before the author's maturity to womanhood, she realized that the silencing and tyrannizing of women was destructive to individualism. She resolved to avoid the ball and chain that awaited women who were compliant enough to place their necks on the doorsill.

The budding author became a keen observer and analyst of reality, from jack rocks and jump rope rhymes, cursed horoscopes, and taxi dancing to fly-by-night renters escaping decrepit housing and the social maneuvering at baptism celebrations and *quinceañeros*, the traditional coming-out parties for 15-year-old girls. She scrutinized the miseries of the barrio—illegitimacy, illegal immigration, patriarchal marriage, joblessness, domestic abuse, desertion, neighborhood violence, petty crime, and venereal disease. Not having a sister made her lonely; the family's nomadic moves prevented the formation of lasting friendships. Among privileged hothouse blossoms from white families, she envisioned herself as the outsider, the pseudocitizen devalued like a yellowed weed popping up between cracks in the sidewalk.

The Formative Years

When the family returned to their homeland, biculturalism subjected them to an abrupt shift from minority to majority. As described in *Caramelo* (The Shawl, 2003), which she dedicated to her father, each summer, Alfredo and the uncles drove the Cisneros household in a caravan of three cars through St. Louis, Tulsa, Dallas, and San Antonio. At the border at Laredo, the children experienced an ethnic welcome from Mexico's colors, flavors, smells, and delights and to the gendered atmosphere of swaggering macho males. In Hispanic surroundings, they sped on like a parade through Monterrey, Saltillo, Matehuala, San Luis Potosí, and Querétaro to a house on Destiny Street in Mexico City to visit her paternal grandmother. As Cisneros explained in "Ghosts and Voices: Writing from Obsession"

(1987), the absorption of family lore illuminated her musings over family secrets and embarrassing episodes: "I write about those ghosts inside that haunt me, that will not let me sleep, of that which even memory does not like to mention" (Cisneros, 1987, 73). Picking over the scrap pile of stored images and anecdotes, she later composed coming-of-age and female-centered vignettes and girl quest scenarios.

Following the death of a baby sister, Cisneros thrived as the only girl among six brothers but squirmed in the preset role of only daughter in a patriarchal home. For a respite from rowdy, girl-excluding boys, she retreated to the public library to read and write. Her imagination provided an on-the-spot escape from the unpromising ghetto. One of her favorite folk tales, "Six Swans: A Story about the Only Daughter among Six Sons" by Jacob and Wilhelm Grimm, guided her thinking on her family role. In 1966, the Cisneros settled in a small house in a Puerto Rican barrio, which she described in the semiautobiographical *The House on Mango Street* (1983), a suite of 44 continuing prose poems composed from the point of view of a seventh-grader, and 20 years later in *Caramelo*. Written in semiliterate Spanglish to reflect the awkward communication skills of a bicultural speaker, the texts found places on school and college reading lists and in thematic units on postmodernism, feminism, alienation, ethnicity, self-definition, patriarchal marriage, and female sexuality. Both earned kudos from young adult writer and friend Gary Soto, who found in Cisneros' prepubescent heroines the clear purpose, drive, and energy of survivors. Critic Julian Olivares, a teacher at the University of Houston, looked deeper into the narratives to admire the grit of marginalized women whose men flourished in the outer world. In contrast, Chicana women occupied circumscribed territory comprised of cooking, cleaning, laundering, nurturing children, and making do on crumbs of love and appreciation.

At Loyola University on scholarship, Cisneros began to see herself apart from the American white-bread stereotype. She produced her first fiction in 1974 in a creative writing class before she earned a B.A. degree in English. Her father assumed that study on a prestigious campus would increase her chances of meeting a better class of suitors. She disappointed him by remaining single. She read Chicano fiction and sketched human scenarios in a prose style less intense than that of Rudolfo Anaya or Juan Rulfo. Instead, in the mold of Emily Dickinson or Merce Rodereda, the author cultivated fleeting images that tease the mind with deeper, more disturbing possibilities. Cisneros laughingly dismissed her loose, miniaturist narrative as lazy poetry. In 1978, as the only Latina at the University of Iowa Writers Workshop, she discovered her unique writing voice in a session entitled "On Memory and Imagination." She completed an M.A. in creative writing and launched a career in pro-woman fiction. Influenced by the output of poets Richard Hugo, Donald Justice, Theodore Roethke, Mark Strand, and James Wright, she composed feminist verse and recorded two sessions of her poetry, a personalizing touch she continued with the audio taping of *Caramelo*.

Classrooms and Writing

Higher education awakened in Cisneros a long-suppressed Chicana persona endowed with unique experiences. While her brothers continued to live under parental control, she startled and dismayed her father by vacating the family home to live on her own. In the poem "His Story" in *My Wicked Wicked Ways* (1987), the father recites a roll call of the bad ends awaiting audacious women like Sandra: jailed, alone, widowed, cursed by voodoo, all punishments for disobeying the man of the house. In "Original Sin," anthologized in *Loose Woman* (1994), biculturalism again traps the female in a dilemma of conflicting expectations.

The poet pictures herself flying from San Antonio to Mexico City and presenting herself to relatives like the dutiful daughter her father claims she is.

Cisneros crafted her career from trial and error. While teaching dropouts at the Latino Youth Alternative High School in Chicago in 1978, she felt sapped by classroom routine, yet energized by an ethnic mix similar to her childhood milieu in Chicago. In varied jobs—poet-in-residence, arts administrator, secretary at Loyola University, creative writing tutor, and college recruiter and teacher in California, Michigan, New Mexico, and Texas—Cisneros freelanced poems and essays in *Contact II*, *Glamour*, *Imagine*, *Los Angeles Times*, *Ms.*, *New York Times*, *Nuestro*, *Poets & Writers*, *Progressive*, *Revista Chicano-Riqueña*, *San Antonio Express-News*, *Si*, and *Village Voice*. She broke ground for Hispanic authors with *The House on Mango Street*, a best-selling survey of insecurity and yearning in a preteen barrio dweller promoted by Houston's Arte Publico Press. The vivid story earned a Before Columbus American Book Award. She followed with the collection *Woman Hollering Creek and Other Stories* (1991), the first Latino work issued by a major American publishing house.

Mounting Success

The author's writings uplifted the nonwhite ghetto female from tyranny and denigration. In 1983, in *The House on Mango Street*, she probed the longings and insecurities of a preteen barrio girl named Esperanza Cordero, a name suggesting "hope of the heart." The girl's brief vision of prosperity captures the longings of the ghetto's have-nots: "I want a house on a hill like the ones with the gardens where Papa works" (Cisneros, 1983, 86). She adds that people so high above the disadvantaged forget "those of us who live too much on earth" (Ibid.). Returning her gaze to her real home, she regrets, "I am tired of looking at what we can't have" (Ibid.). In place of plans for advancement, Esperanza's mother murmurs her faith in winning the lottery, a cruel hoax on people who can ill afford to gamble. Esperanza prefers storytelling as an escape from apathy and squalor, but she must accept the fact that ghetto life has permanently impacted her being. The epiphany resonates from the author's inner voice to typify a love-hate relationship with the bicultural past.

Cisneros perpetuated her perspective on the sadness and trauma of her childhood by viewing events and challenges from a preteen perspective. After publication of *Bad Boys* (1980) and *My Wicked Wicked Ways* (1987), she moved rapidly into the inner circle of ethnic and feminist fiction writers. Success made her feel like a mapmaker, a plotter of directions in a literary world seriously lacking in Hispanic realities. In 1986, she told attendees at the Second Annual Hispanic Achievement Festival that she wrote candid glimpses of the underclass primarily to validate and strengthen downtrodden women like her own mother. She extended her fan base by producing *Hairs/Pelitos* (1999), a bilingual children's book honoring diversity in a single family. For their frank witness to the female microcosm, her stories won first and third prizes at the Segundo Concurso Nacional del Cuento Chicano (Second National Convention of Chicano Short Fiction).

As family members entrusted Cisneros with family stories, awards continued to reimburse her for verisimilitude and candor. She became a "walking Smithsonian" of reality tales. *Woman Hollering Creek*, which describes the renewal of the liberated female, earned the PEN Center West Award for Best Fiction of 1991, the Quality Paperback Book Club New Voices Award, and the Anisfield-Wolf Book Award. Subsequent citations came from the University of Arizona's Lannan Foundation and the State University of New York and a genius grant from the MacArthur Fellowship foundation. In 2003, United Press International named as book of the week *Caramelo*. The semihistorical family tree novel enlarges on the symbolic title, a weaving of contrasting strands into a sturdy, multipurpose wrap that women adapt as a baby carrier, blanket, and hammock. The narrative features the hero, Innocencio Reyes, and an alter ego, his mother Lala, the bossy, intrusive "awful grandmother" typical of a matriarchal society. Based on Alfredo Cisneros' life, the work was 9 years in the writing. In addition to referring to exotic dancer Josephine Baker and ventriloquist Señor Wences, the author included historical tidbits, like the refusal of Elvis Presley to kiss a Mexican woman and the ingenuity of Spanish conquistador Hernán Cortez in describing the terrain of Oaxaca, Mexico, by crumbling a piece of paper. Written during two trips to Europe for her publisher and time off during her father's illness and death from cancer, the composition of *Caramelo* set Cisneros in another place and time apart from family and friends but clarified for her fans a life-affirming trust in creativity.

Greeting Fans

Success engulfed Cisneros in touching flesh with the reading public. She gave interviews and book signings and received invitations to lecture; she toured Europe on the first of two National Endowment for the Arts grants, addressed a rally on International Women's Day, and read Chicana texts in France, Germany, Italy, Mexico, Sweden, and the United States. At her retro metal-roofed house in King William, the historic district of south of downtown San Antonio, Texas, where she settled in 1984, she was happy in a funky, laidback, savory atmosphere. To add to the Mexican flavor, she painted the exterior pink, two shades of purple, and turquoise, a combination that violated a house code enforcing period authenticity. She fought the enforcers for ignoring the tastes of the city's Mexican settlers. By the time that the purple faded to lavender, city protests died out.

Cisneros refused to be bulldozed or structured. She kept cats, dogs, and parrots and read the writings of essayist Colette, poets Emily Dickinson and Grace Paley, and novelists Marguerite Duras, Jean Rhys, and Virginia Woolf. Cisneros maintained a stray-writer-in-residence room for visiting artists, but she reserved an attic space for her reclusive office. She promoted the peace movement and, as a Buddhist-Guadalupana, venerated both the Buddha and Our Lady of Guadalupe. Of her bicultural heritage, she claimed to love American freedoms and to be nostalgic for the generosity, resilience, spirituality, and *cariño* (affection) of her Mexican heritage. She considered herself an amphibian and a bridge—an infiltrator and negotiator between warring cultures. To interviewers, she admitted that she felt guilty for not being able to rescue the Chicanos still trapped in the ghetto.

Sources

"Caramel-Coated Truths and Telenovela Lives: Sandra Cisneros Returns with an Ambitious Novel about the Latino Community." *World and I* 18 (3) (March 2003): 228.

Cisneros, Sandra. *Caramelo*. New York: Vintage Books, 2002.

———. "Ghosts and Voices: Writing from Obsession." *Americas Review* 15 (Spring 1987): 69–73.

———. *The House on Mango Street*. New York: Vintage Books, 1989.

———. *Loose Woman*. New York: Vintage Books, 1994.

———. *My Wicked Wicked Ways*. Berkeley, CA: Third Woman, 1987.

Mena, Jennifer. "A Story Woven from the Heart; Author Sandra Cisneros Gives a Female Voice to Her Complex Latino Family Tale." *Los Angeles Times*, September 13, 2002, E1.

Novarro, Mireya. "Telling a Tale of Immigrants Whose Stories Go Untold." *New York Times*, November 12, 2002, B1.

Shea, Renee H. "Truth, Lies, and Memory: A Profile of Sandra Cisneros." *Poets & Writers Magazine* 30 (5) (September–October 2002): 31–36.

■ Birth Defect
Jim Abbott

James Anthony "Jim" Abbott, a beginning starting pitcher for the Anaheim Angels, played professional baseball despite the absence of his right hand. Born disabled to teen parents Kathy and Mike Abbott, a car salesman and meat packer, in Southfield, Michigan, on September 19, 1967, he was the elder brother of Chad. The two grew up in East Village, a residential area of Flint, Michigan. Jim's underdeveloped right arm, shorter than the left by several inches, concluded in a small malformed finger. Subconsciously, he tucked in the stub to hide it from the curious. Kathy set an example of drive by finishing college through home courses and becoming a teacher and attorney. Mike advanced to manager of a dealership. To ease Jim's maturing, his parents taught themselves to tie shoelaces with one hand and tried to interest the boys in soccer. Chad settled on soccer, but Jim chose baseball. At age 4, he played catch with his father in the front yard of their apartment. A year later, he rejected a steel hook that therapists fitted to his right arm because kids called him "Mr. Hook" and feared his approach. Contributing to Jim's personal humiliations, a reporter asked if any other members of the Abbott family were disabled.

Out of a love for sports, Abbott concentrated on devising ways of throwing and catching baseballs and fantasized about pitching professionally like his sports hero Nolan Ryan. Abbott dismissed his birth anomaly as the absence of four fingers and concentrated on strengthening his legs. As he bounced a rubber ball off a brick wall, the compensatory "catch and switch" method, like tying his shoes, evolved from habit strength. The quick shift required him to thrust his glove against his chest while extracting the ball with his left for a quick throw. At the high point of his career, teammate Rich Monteleone crowed, "He was better than anybody else out there . . . . He was just so quick, it was just amazing how he could turn the glove over and be ready to field the ball" (Tan, 2006, 182).

Abbott used athletic ability as an in with suspicious peers. They treated him as different from the norm but respected his pitching prowess for the Little League team, for which he turned his first game into a no-hitter. In his preteens, he learned to ignore gibes from competitive teams that called him "Claw" and "Stumpy." Contributing to his efforts were his parents, teachers, and friends who wanted to see him succeed. While attending Flint Central High School, he played golf and racquetball, quarterbacked and punted for the Flint Central Indians, and boosted the basketball team as star forward. He proved a doubting coach wrong by manning first base, left field, and shortstop for the baseball team. He batted .427, averaged two strikeouts per inning, and won an American League championship for a baseball team in Ypsilanti. In the summer, he joined the Grossi Baseball Club and served as umpire.

College Sports Hero

At age 18, Abbott, then 6-foot-3 and weighing over 200 pounds, chose a baseball scholarship to college over a $50,000 signing bonus to play for the Toronto Blue Jays. During

3 years of majoring in communications and playing for the Wolverines at the University of Michigan, he racked up points for two Big Ten championships in his freshman and junior years. In 1987, his performance netted him the Most Courageous Athlete honor from the Philadelphia Sportswriters Association. In his second year, he hurled 31 scoreless innings in a row. He became the first pitcher to receive the Amateur Athletic Union's James E. Sullivan Award as the best amateur athlete in the United States. He also earned election to the Sporting News college All-America team and a Golden Spikes Award for the outstanding college baseball player in the United States.

Abbott turned athleticism into patriotism. As pitcher for Team U.S.A., on July 18, 1987, in front of 50,000 viewers, he became the first American pitcher in a quarter century to beat a Cuban team on its home turf. The win secured a silver medal at the Pan-American Games in Indianapolis, Indiana, and the U.S. Baseball Federation's Golden Spikes award for the nation's top amateur. With a 5-to-3 victory over Japan, he brought home a gold medal from the Summer Olympics in Seoul, Korea, after carrying the U.S. flag in the opening ceremony. The rise to fame earned him election as the Big Ten male athlete of the year. He returned home to notoriety and invitations to appear on ABC News *Person of the Week*, CNN News, ESPN, *The George Michael Sports Machine, Good Morning America, Larry King Live, Late Night with David Letterman, NBC Nightly News,* and *The Phil Donahue Show.* To interviewers, he refused that he thought of himself as defective or an amputee.

Abbott and the Majors

At age 21, Abbott quit college at the end of his junior year and became the rare athlete to move directly from amateur sports into a starting position for a professional major league baseball. After Bob Fontaine, lead scout for the Los Angeles Angels, extended the offer of a contract and a $207,000 signing bonus, skeptics doubted that Abbott could manage a competitive career because he couldn't conceal his pitching hand in his glove. Some cynics called the signing of a one-armed pitcher a publicity stunt intended to gain sympathy for the man and the team. Abbott acknowledged his uniqueness: "I know the way I played and the differences I had growing up were bound to attract attention . . . . It's something I don't take lightly" (Goldman and Ryan, 2006, 186). Farm team director Bill Bavasi recognized Abbott's drive: "He had gone through things most other kids never had to go through" (Goldman and Ryan, 2006, 186). Bavasi suggested introducing a special glove to smooth out a limited curveball, but coach Marcel Lachemann stuck to the "catch and switch" technique that Abbott had refined from childhood.

In spring camp, under the direction of manager Doug Rader, Abbott—dubbed "Abby" by the rest of the team—pitched and managed one-arm batting by wrapping left hand and abbreviated right digit around the wood. On April 8, 1989, he played his first professional game in Yuma, Arizona, to which reporters flocked. He sported wicked fastballs and sliders but lacked polish on his curveball. To the snipes of sportscasters, Rader retorted, "He's the least handicapped person I know" (Goldman and Ryan, 2006, 188). Other Angels laughed about the five or six bats that Abbott smashed per game. By his third public outing, Abbott led the team to win over the Baltimore Orioles. Four Japanese cameramen caught his motions on film. On August 31, 1989, at Fenway Park in Boston, his shutout against the Red Sox merited a standing ovation in the stands and dugout. A second stunner, a major league no-hitter in 1991 against the Red Sox in Anaheim, California, affirmed that Abbott was more than a sentimental favorite. As star rookie for the Angels, he was selected the Most Inspirational Player by the Baseball Writers Association of America and won the

Tony Conigliaro Award for winning more games his first year than any other major league beginner.

Uprooting from Anaheim came as a shock. Biographers describe a contract negotiation with his agent, Scott Boras, who demanded a 4-year salary of $19 million, a raise of $3 million. Instead of dickering, Angels owner Jackie Autrey and general manager Whitey Herzog refused to deal. In December 1992, the swap surprised the pitcher, who returned from vacation to hear the news from his mother-in-law. He despaired at being traded to the Yankees. The shift east occurred a year after he wed Dana Douty, an economics major and basketball standout at the University of California, Irvine. After their January 1991 wedding, the couple settled at Newport Beach, California. For their sake, he doubted he wanted to reestablish his family in New York.

A Miracle for the Yanks

The next year in Yankee Stadium, on September 4, 1993, Abbott bobbed back by pitching the team's first no-hitter in a decade. Unaware that greatness lay in his path, days before the event, he purchased from 7-year-old Jessica Morz, a one-handed vendor, a good luck Yankee troll, which he hung in his locker. He also wore lucky jeans, shirts, and shorts, which he marked with an X. In the final three innings, fans caromed between wild cheering and whispers to keep from jinxing the unfolding drama on the mound. The exhausting pennant-race game, which cost the Cleveland Indians a 4–0 loss, made Abbott feel like he occupied the hurricane's eye. By the last two innings, he felt so charged that he stopped gauging his efforts. Manager Buck Showalter was so riveted to the action that he feared leaving the scene long enough to go to the bathroom. The win came at a crucial point in division play, when New York evened the score against Toronto. Abbott recalled, "I didn't know how to react. I didn't know whether to be supremely confident or supremely thankful" (Tan, 2006, 182).

Although Abbott didn't think of himself as a role model, he was generous in thanking his hardy wife and crediting fans, particularly children. Backed by Tim Mead, director of publicity for the Angels, Abbott began making time for visiting handicapped children as well as for admiring retired players like Ernie Banks and Warren Spahn. Parents asked for meetings and autographs for disabled children. Kids lined the fence to chat with their idol and overwhelmed him with 300 letters per week. When fan mail piled up in shopping baskets, he returned from road trips to answer as many as possible, especially tragic stories about children who lost digits and limbs from fireworks, an explosive left in toothpaste in a shopping mall, and the jaws of a mountain lion. In November 1995, the birth of a son suffering from Down syndrome named Cade to player Rex and Jennifer Hudler inspired Abbott to encourage the parents to expect a miracle. His employer, George Steinbrenner, objected to Abbott's humanitarian work among New York children with disabilities, but the pitcher persisted in encouraging physically challenged youth. He greeted kids with limb differences and birth defects and kept up with their progress into their teens. His efforts won him a Freedom Forum's Free Spirit Award as well as cover stories in *Baseball America*, *Newsweek*, *PARADE* magazine, *People*, *Sports Illustrated*, *Time*, and *USA Today*.

End of an Era

At age 27, Abbott experienced a downturn in his prospects during a players strike that preceded the ebbing of his 94-mile-per-hour fastball. He continued pitching for the Chicago White Sox and, in 1996, again for the Angels. Although he scored a base hit to right field against the Los Angeles Dodgers in 1996, his record plunged, costing him self-confidence and fans. He dropped to the minor leagues. He agonized over having to clean out his locker in front of teammates and drove home alone over the Arizona desert. A former manager restored his spirit by trusting Abbott's resilience. The pitcher began rebuilding his throwing power. After worry about inherited disabilities, Dana and Jim Abbott produced a healthy daughter, Madeleine, on December 15, 1996.

Following a 2-year breather, in 1998, Abbott rejoined the White Sox and posted five wins in the first five games, beginning with the Hickory Crawdads in North Carolina, a Class A South Atlantic League. For strength training, he lifted weights that favored his torso and right arm and practiced with coach Lachemann several times a week. The comeback amazed his backers, who called him a "gamer." While pitching in 1999 for the Milwaukee Brewers, a National League team, he took his first professional turn at batting. On June 15 at County Stadium, he scored the first of two hits in the major leagues against the Chicago Cubs. Two weeks later, at Wrigley Field, he smacked another ball to center.

Subsequent slumps convinced Abbott that he was no longer major league material. He saw his fastball drop to around 85 miles per hour. After 254 career starts in ten seasons, at retirement on July 21, 1999, at age 31, he achieved a 4.25 earned run average, a strikeout score of 693 batters, and a career record of 87 wins and 108 losses. To sports journalists, he described his parting emotion as fulfilled and satisfied by the people he met and his experiences on the pitcher's mound.

Career Change-Up

From his home at Harbor Springs, Michigan, in 2000, Abbott and his wife began his career in platform lecturing. He chose upbeat themes about letting challenge define character and about approaching goals with passion. He created the signature acronym ADAPT from five traits—adjustability, determination, accountability, perseverance, and trust. His credo echoed grit: "The only thing that could stop me was myself" (Mack and Casstevens, 2001, 40).

Abbott extended his benevolence through technology. His Web site offered advice to parents rearing one-handed children and techniques for handicapped athletes and typists. To the California relief agency *Amigos de los Niños* (Friends of the Children), he donated $100,000. His honoraria include the Jesse Owens Award as Big Ten Male Athlete of the Year, a March of Dimes Athlete of the Year award, the Academy Awards of Sports, Courage Award, two Geoff Zahn Awards as Michigan's most valuable pitcher, induction into the Michigan Sports Hall of Fame, and a 1991 Victory Award presented at the Kennedy Center in Washington, D.C. At age 35, he opened game seven of the 2002 World Series by throwing the first pitch. In 2007, he was inducted into the College Baseball Hall of Fame.

Source

Berkow, Ira. "A Most Extraordinary Fella." *New York Times*, December 25, 1992, B-7.

Bernotas, Bob. *Nothing to Prove: The Jim Abbott Story*. New York: Kodansha America, 1995.

Goldman, Rob, and Nolan Ryan. *Once They Were Angels*. Champaign, IL: Sports, 2006.

Karpin, Howie, and Joe Torre. *Yankees Essential: Everything You Need to Know to Be a Real Fan*. New York: Triumph Books, 2007.

Mack, Gary, and David Casstevens. *Mind Gym: An Athlete's Guide to Inner Excellence*. New York: McGraw-Hill, 2001.

Marantz, Steve. "Time Is Throwing a Curve to Heroic Jim Abbott." *Sporting News* (March 31, 1997).

Stout, Glenn, and Richard A. Johnson. *Yankees Century: 100 Years of New York Yankees Baseball*. New York: Houghton Mifflin, 2002.

Tan, Cecilia. *The 50 Greatest Yankee Games*. Indianapolis, IN: Wiley, 2006.

■ Brain, Lung, and Testicular Cancer
Lance Armstrong

Cyclist Lance Armstrong exhibited courage and determination in his fight against cancer. Named Lance Edward Gunderson at birth on September 18, 1971, he bore the name of Dallas Cowboys player Lance Rentzel. His maternal grandfather, Edward Mooneyham, was so pleased at having a grandson that he gave up drinking and joined Alcoholics Anonymous. Growing up fatherless in the projects of Plano, Texas, Lance developed into a hard-charging athlete in his own right. His teenaged single mother, realtor Linda Gayle Mooneyham, divorced Eddie Charles Gunderson, an abusive mate who blamed her for the teen pregnancy. On her own, she supported her family with welfare checks and jobs at a grocery and fast-food restaurant and as an office temp. By night, she finished a high school diploma and moved to Richardson outside Dallas. The athlete later declared, "She instilled all her drive, motivation, and toughness in me" (Stewart, 2000, 5).

Three-year-old Lance took the surname of his stepfather, Terry Keith Armstrong. The father-son link foundered from Terry's eagerness to punish with a paddle for normal infractions like launching cannonball dives, squirting squirrels with the water hose, jumping rose bushes, climbing trees, playing in traffic, and kicking balls into trash cans. His anger at being betrayed by his birth father drove him to daredevilry, including games with flaming gas-soaked tennis balls. Clashes with Gunderson and with Mooneyham's three subsequent husbands turned Armstrong toward his mother for love and support. She arranged with bike shop owner Jim Hoyt to buy her son a used brown model with yellow wheels. The new set of wheels became afterschool fun as well as an escape from a tenuous home atmosphere.

A Budding Contender

From childhood, Armstrong recognized his gift for endurance and his need for speed. He summarized, "I do everything at a fast cadence: eat fast, sleep fast" (Armstrong and Jenkins, 2001, 1). A physical anomaly, the underproduction of lactic acid, spared his body the burning lungs and throbbing legs that most people experience. In elementary school, he played football and Little League baseball and swam at Los Rios Country Club. By fifth grade, he ran track with a lucky charm, a silver dollar dated the year he was born. In his early teens, he entered triathlons—biking, running, and swimming—and pedaled 40 miles a day round trip to the practice pool. His mother exulted and remarked, "What a great idea God had when He sat down at the drawing board and mapped out how He could make the most of two legs, two lungs, a brain, and His own breath" (Kelly and Rodgers, 2005, 6). She backed her son's success by driving him to triathlon events.

In 1986, Armstrong first identified as a goal the Tour de France, reputedly the world's most grueling sports challenge. Older contenders called him "Junior" and "the Kid" and taught him to focus his energy solely on winning. His mother provided cross training shorts, a fast-drying shirt, a toolbox for his equipment, and his first professional bike, a Mercier road racer. When they stopped at motels, she slept on the floor to allow him adequate rest on the only bed. One of his wins occurred after he ripped stitches from his head and foot after a car struck him. To accusations of brashness, he excused himself as normal: "I wasn't trying to be a jerk. I was just Texan" (Armstrong and Jenkins, 2001, 42).

Going Pro

In 1987, Armstrong became a professional road racer and spent his winnings for a used red Fiat. To outpace other contenders, he developed a strong, graceful showing up to 120 rpm in low gears. The pedaling style spared him fatigued leg muscles, exploited the strength of his enlarged heart, and enhanced his pacing over longer stretches of road. Key to his success was a mental imaging by which he imagined his way over the entire course. On the sidelines, he heard Linda cheering. She declared, "Somehow a little of your soul gets transferred into their system and gives them this little snap-crackle-pop of energy" (Kelly and Rodgers, 2005, 129). In one race in Philadelphia, he pedaled over the finish line with enough advantage to blow a kiss to his mother, his one-woman pit crew. In a crush of reporters, he took time to embrace her and weep for joy. By 1989, he scored a junior world championship in the Soviet Union for the junior national team of the United States Cycling Federation.

After moving to Austin, Texas, Armstrong chose retired cyclist Chris Carmichael as coach and Belgian athlete Johan Bruyneel as performance adviser. Additional advice from Italian athlete Michele Ferrari and Pete Aldred readied Armstrong for the ordeal. More boy than man, at the 1990 world championship in Utsunomiya, Japan, Armstrong defied coach Carmichael and rode out front in hot headwinds. At the Settimana Bergamasca in 1991, he entered an awkward situation—a 10-day course in northern Italy against former teammates. In a grim anti-American atmosphere, he learned some Italian and befriended a superb contender, Fabio Casartelli. Armstrong won for the U.S. team and set his sights on the Tour de France. At age 21, he signed with Subaru-Montgomery to race in the 1992 Olympic Games in Barcelona, Spain, where he finished in fourteenth place.

Armstrong became the youngest contender to win one stage of the Tour de France, 114 miles of course from Châlons-sur-Marne to Verdun. The 2,290-mile, 23-day race wiped him out on the twelfth stage in the Alps from his inexperience with uphill pedaling in a bitter climate. He later described the event as heartbreaking, exalting, and surprisingly scenic. Three years later, with his mother's assistance, he trained in Spain and on the French road course to compete in the 1995 Tour de France. His technological backing derived from experts at AMD, Bontrager, Giro, Oakley, Shimano, and Trek. For equipment, he promoted manufacturing synergy among sponsors and suppliers of his frames, handlebars, and tires. He followed with a signal victory—a win on October 2, 1996, at the U.S. National Road Race Championship with the largest margin in competition history.

Armstrong in Trouble

On October 2, 1996, Armstrong sought medical aid for chronic back pain, headaches, coughing up blood, and strep throat. Biopsy of a cancerous testicle and MRI scans of metastasis to his brain and lungs threatened his life expectancy and his ability to sire children. He admitted, "My illness was humbling and starkly revealing, and it forced me to survey my life with an unforgiving eye" (Armstrong and Jenkins, 2001, 4). Before treatment, he read up on cancer and gauged his chances the way an athlete surveys competition. His mother faxed initial test results to specialists in Indiana. On the last day before poisons sterilized him, he deposited sperm in a San Antonio cryopreservation bank to extend his options for a family. He worked out his diet with a nutritionist and devoted himself to a more purposeful life. One difficult regimen was the banning of caffeine from coffee, which he missed during tense hours at the Indiana University waiting room.

Armstrong chose aggressive action—brain and testicle operations. A treatment advocate, Steven Wolff, offered advice on anticancer protocols less likely to compromise his competitive career. At home, his mother charted his treatments and appointments and supervised his meals. At low points, she cried in private. On the way to surgery in Indianapolis, she carried his medical records and superintended a Ziploc bag of prescriptions and vitamins. The thought of cutting into his skull terrified him, forcing him to rely on family, friends Bart Knaggs and Kevin Livingston, girlfriend Lisa Shiels, attorney Bill Stapleton, and Jim "Och" Ochowicz, director of the Motorola cycling team. Armstrong's oncologist, Dr. Craig Nichols, gave him, at most, a 65 percent chance of a complete cure. The procedure sounded cold and cavalier: "We're just going to cut a little hole, pop it out, remove the lesions, put it back in, and cover it up" (Armstrong and Jenkins, 2004, 87). When his mother ran out of vacation time, she flew home to Plano, leaving Lance to cope alone.

For the athlete, cancer galloped so rapidly through his body that the oncologist moved directly to chemotherapy, which became a "living death" (Armstrong and Jenkins, 2004, 136). Five-hour sessions of an IV cocktail—bleomycin, cisplatin, etoposide—from Monday through Friday every 2 weeks sapped his energy from nausea, shrank his muscles, suppressed his immunity, and parched his skin. On flights home during his down time from chemo, the American Airlines crew commiserated with the athlete's thinning hair, eyebrows, and eyelashes. He lay in bed feeling disoriented, dozy, and out of sync with day and night. His gums bled; his mouth developed canker sores. When his appetite disappeared, Och brought apple fritters from the hospital cafeteria. More troubling to Armstrong was the lessening of concentration from depletion of his hemoglobin, which bears oxygen to the brain.

In the midst of illness and self-doubt, Armstrong faced a representative of Cofidis, a French team that cancelled a 2-year contract promising him $2.5 million. On the positive side, he made friends with fellow patients who shared the intimate thoughts and sensations common to cancer victims. One doomed girl named Kelly weakened rapidly from cancer. Armstrong tried to brighten her childhood with bike rides and rollerblading in the hospital hall. He gained strength from her courage. On his way out of the hospital, he refused a wheelchair and exited on foot. To cancer researchers, his recovery became known as the "Lance Armstrong Effect" (Chung, Isaacs, and Simon, 2007, v).

Back to Business

At first, the racer exercised without trying to halt muscle atrophy or boost fitness. On simple bike rides, he collapsed in neighbors' yards. By March 1996, he returned to bike training and channeled his fame and wealth into the Lance Armstrong Foundation. With compassion for other victims, he promoted emotional support and raised $13 million for research to prevent more pain and loss. His signature token, the Livestrong wristband, encircled the arms of others who either survived cancer or who loved victims who succumbed to the same scourge that weakened Armstrong. To impress on fans his resilience, at the 1999 Tour de France, he flaunted the *maillot jaune* (yellow jersey) of the time trial leader.

Revived by his physical regimen, Armstrong won seven Tour de France titles. On May 8, 1998, he wed Kristin "Kik" Richard, a devout Catholic and mother of son Luke and twin daughters Grace and Isabelle. The marriage ended in September 2003. During this period, he coauthored *The Lance Armstrong Performance Program: 7 Weeks to the Perfect Ride* (2000), the autobiography *It's Not about the Bike: My Journey Back to Life* (2001), and *The Noblest Invention: An Illustrated History of the Bicycle* (2003), a timeline of innovation from the first wood machine to the technologically advanced mountain bike. To establish his feisty spirit, he opened his memoir with a stunning image: "I want to die at a hundred years old with an American flag on my back and the star of Texas on my helmet, after screaming down an Alpine descent on a bicycle at 75 miles per hour" (Armstrong and Jenkins, 2001, 1).

Other threats to his recovery began in 1999 with demands for urine samples to assess his use of performance-enhancing pharmaceuticals. The results proved that trace amounts of corticosteroids from skin ointments dated to his treatment for saddle sores. Five years later, new charges of sports doping from journalists Pierre Ballester and David Walsh cited as evidence the claims of the cyclist's masseuse, Emma O'Reilly, that she trashed evidence of injectables and provided a cream to hide injection sites on his arm. Another eyewitness, Steve Swart, incriminated himself, Armstrong, and other athletes on the Motorola team for using steroids to bulk up leg muscles. In June 2004, Armstrong retaliated with lawsuits against editor Alan English and *The Sunday Times* (London) for libel. The newspaper renounced Swart's accusations and apologized in print. On July 24, 2005, after contending in the Tour de France, Armstrong retired from competitive sports with a world record of seven consecutive wins.

Another blow to Armstrong's record occurred on March 31, 2005, when a disgruntled former employee, valet Mike Anderson, claimed that the athlete stored containers of Androstenine in his apartment bathroom in Girona, Spain. Seven months later, the two settled out of court. More negative publicity haunted Armstrong on August 23, 2005, when the French journal *L'Équipe* linked the athlete to drugs in a urine sample submitted before the 1999 Tour de France. In June 2006, *Le Monde* cited Betsy and Frankie Andreu, who claimed that Armstrong resorted to drugs after brain surgery. Armstrong identified postsurgical treatment as Epogen, a standard drug prescribed by Dr. Nichols to build red blood cells destroyed by chemotherapy. Ensuing litigation generated conflicting claims, gossip, and unsubstantiated evidence that incriminated the claimants but cleared Armstrong's name and titles.

During public and court acrimony, Armstrong lived at his home in Austin, Texas, vacationed at a rural getaway, and ran the New York City marathon to raise $600,000 for his foundation. He began a 3-year relationship with composer and singer Sheryl Crow and discussed with President George W. Bush opportunities to run for governor of Texas. Armstrong abandoned thoughts of a political career that might infringe on his time with his three children. In 2004, he wrote the foreword to Dr. Anna L. Schwartz's handbook *Cancer Fitness: Exercise Programs for Cancer Patients and Survivors* and increased his activism with anticancer initiatives. On May 16, 2006, he drove the Chevrolet Corvette Z06 pace car before the Indianapolis 500. His honors include a Nickelodeon Kids Choice Favorite Athlete Award, membership in the Presidential Delegation to the 2002 Winter Olympiad, being named *Sports Illustrated* sportsman of the year, *VeloNews* cyclist of the year, *ABC's Wide World of Sports* athlete of the year, and Associated Press and ESPN athlete of the year four times, and the naming of an asteroid after him.

Sources

Armstrong, Lance, and Sally Jenkins. *Every Second Counts*. New York: Broadway, 2004.
———. *It's Not about the Bike: My Journey Back to Life*. London: Berkley Trade, 2001.
Chung, Leland W. K., William Brewster Isaacs, and Jonathan W. Simons. *Prostate Cancer: Biology, Genetics, and the New Therapeutics*. Totowa, NJ: Humana Press, 2007.
Kelly, Linda Armstrong, and Joni Rodgers. *No Mountain High Enough: Raising Lance, Raising Me*. New York: Broadway, 2005.
Stewart, Mark. *Sweet Victory: Lance Armstrong*. Minneapolis, MN: Millbrook Press, 2000.

■ Capture
Jessica Lynch

Army clerk Jessica Dawn "Jessie" Lynch stirred controversy after her rescue from enemy capture during the Iraq War. Born to a working-class family on April 26, 1983, in rural Palestine, West Virginia, she grew up amid modest means in fundamentalist Christian Wirt County. Her elder brother, Greg Lynch, Jr., gave up college when tuition proved too costly. At age 17, Jessica realized that the penury doomed her wish to teach kindergartners. She consulted a recruiter about a future in the army. After the 9/11 terrorist attacks on New York City and Washington, D.C., she began basic training on September 19, 2001, at Fort Jackson, South Carolina. At 5 feet 4 inches, she weighed 105 pounds. Advanced training as a unit supply specialist at Fort Lee, Virginia, prepared her for combat. Under command of Sergeant Shirley Atma, Lynch was based in Fort Bliss, Texas, with 12 mechanics, computer specialists, cooks, and supply clerks of the 507th Ordnance Maintenance Company.

The capture occurred during a plateau in the war effort when global support lagged. While serving as a private in the Quartermaster Corps, on March 23, 2003, Lynch joined a supply train of 15 vehicles packed with food and ammunition and headed north from Kuwait at dawn toward an antiaircraft battery. For an undetermined reason, her maintenance convoy strayed deep into the enemy-held urban territory. The drivers allegedly took wrong turns as a result of fatigue and inadequate communications. She sustained injury in the crash of a Humvee at an engagement outside Nasiriyah on a stretch along the Euphrates River called "ambush alley." Under tracer fire amid bursts of tank barage and bullets from all sides, a tractor-trailer mired in soft sand, leaving behind two vehicles not quipped to destroy the enemy. Propelled by a rocket-propelled grenade, the Humvee, driven by twenty-three-year-old Private First Class Lori Ann "White Bear Girl" Piestewa, smacked into the truck.

Lynch, the only one of five passengers to survive, fell into Fedayeen hands. Because her weapon jammed, she fell to her knees in prayer for safety before lapsing into unconsciousness. Piestewa, her Hopi tentmate from Tuba City, Arizona, took a bullet to the head while rescuing Lynch from the disabled vehicle. After Iraqi troops seized Lynch, Specialist Edgar Hernandez, Specialist Joseph Hudson, Specialist Shoshana Nyree Johnson, Private Patrick Miller, and their leader, Sergeant James Riley, the army listed them as missing in action.

Jessica as News Fodder

The Fedayeen kicked, tied, and blindfolded their prisoners. Iraqi media made sport of the capture on Al Jazeera television by airing tapes of Lynch and Piestewa filmed at Saddam Hospital, which the enemy regiment used as a military base. Included in the exhibit were American soldiers with bullet wounds in the head. The Fedayeen boasted that enemy fire killed eleven Americans, including Piestewa, who succumbed to a cranial wound upon arrival at a treatment center staffed by Dr. Harith Al-Houssona and Dr. Anmar Uday. With 3 pints of blood, 2 donated by the staff, the physicians treated Lynch for a bleeding head wound, a dislocated ankle, and a fractured arm, right foot, and thigh suffered in the collision.

Lynch remained unconscious for 24 hours before speaking her fear of capture. Nurse Khalida Shinah calmed the patient with orange juice and crackers and a promise of evacuation. The doctors declared themselves humanitarians for assigning her the hospital's only specialist bed and half the two-person nursing staff and for protecting Lynch from beating and torture. A week after the ambush, Al-Houssona tried to ferry Lynch out of danger by ambulance but aborted the delivery when the vehicle came under U.S. fire. Mitch Potter, a Middle East bureau chief for *The Toronto Star*, affirmed that Iraqi military abandoned the medical compound on March 31.

The Real Hero of the Lynch Story

Information reached Americans from a prominent Iraqi attorney, 33-year-old Mohammed Odeh al-Rehaief, the grandson of a sheikh and brother of a 17-year-old Fedayeen draftee. On a visit to his wife, Iman, a nurse in the hospital dialysis unit, al-Rehaief detected an air of heightened tension and asked about increased security measures in the medical compound. He tracked Lynch to her room and found her lying under a white blanket, her face bruised, her left forehead cut and swollen, a disk fractured in her back, and her left leg, right arm, and right foot broken in numerous places. A chart identified her in Arabic script as "Jessica Ameriqia" (al-Rehaief, 183). Lacking the English to reassure her, he pledged, "You are not dying anytime soon" (Ibid., 184).

After seeing a colonel back-handing Lynch, al-Rehaief walked to a marine checkpoint to inform authorities of the prisoner's peril. When soldiers learned her name, they cheered and applauded, "Lynch! Yes! *Yes!* [italics in original]" (Ibid., 196). He outlined an unmarked basement room and space for a helicopter to land on the hospital roof. A map highlighted in felt-tip markings noted his route in black, staircases in silver, patient rooms in yellow, and Fedayeen posts in red. Walking a 12-mile round trip, on April 1, the attorney infiltrated the hospital with a hidden camera to survey the situation and Lynch's exact location. He learned that surgeons anticipated an operation on her damaged knee, a procedure that the Fedayeen might have arranged at a larger facility in Baghdad. For his risky videotaped report to the Defense Intelligence Agency on staffing and security, on April 10, the United States granted refugee status to him, his wife, and their 5-year-old daughter, Abir. At Malden, West Virginia, sympathizers formed Friends of Mohammed, a political pressure group that lobbied for citizenship for the family. In safety from Iraqi retaliation, al-Rehaief published *Because Each Life Is Precious: Why an Iraqi Man Risked Everything for Pvt. Jessica Lynch* (2003). At a high point in the narrative, he admitted to endangering his father and uncles by collaborating with the Americans but concluded, "I felt no regret about helping Jessica; I had gone to her with a clear head, because it was the right thing to do" (Ibid., 204).

Gung Ho Rescue

The capture required intervention by Special Forces to retrieve Lynch from the Iraqis. A diversionary assault on Iraqis at 12:30 A.M. on April 2 preceded a combined raid by Air Force Pararescue Jumpers, Army Rangers, Delta Force, Green Berets, and Navy Seals. Al-Rehaief watched through field glasses. At CENTCOM, the military nexus with the media, Jim Wilkinson and other strategists worked through the night to coordinate intelligence. Planners perched at a cinder block table before loading jeeps, trucks, and choppers for the intervention. Using night vision cameras, the six male insurgents taped the 6-minute raid, the first prisoner of war retrieval since World War II.

In the aftermath of an Iraqi military withdrawal, the team encountered gunfire only on entry and departure from the city. After breaking through doors, they corralled the medical staff, handcuffed one patient to a bed frame, ransacked equipment, and recovered two bodies from the hospital morgue and nine more from shallow graves. Soldiers reached out to shift Lynch to a stretcher, causing her voice to quaver from back pain. The Special Forces, led by air force Major General Victor Renuart, returned from the building with the corpses and ferried Lynch from the second floor to safety by a Black Hawk helicopter. She managed a smile for the camera as attendants draped her with an American flag. General Vincent Brooks, a military spokesman in Doha, honored the raiders for following the tradition of leaving no soldier behind. Eight of the remains were identified and the soldiers honored posthumously with Purple Hearts.

Since that time, most points of the reported events have come under scrutiny. President George W. Bush broadcast the successful retrieval. The Pentagon immediately aired an edited version of the taped raid and transmitted reports on the survivor's physical condition. Under intravenous sedation, Lynch traveled by medical evacuation plane to Kuwait and north to Ramstein Air Base in Landstuhl, Germany. During prime time on April 2, a Pentagon video of the Special Forces operation described Lynch as a prisoner of war cruelly interrogated while under treatment for bullet and stab wounds. A head-and-shoulders shot of Lynch on the helicopter stretcher focused on her fragile blonde, fair-skinned good looks, and vulnerability. Concealment of the uncut tape enraged British journalist Simon Wren, who demanded the whole truth of the capture and rescue and an accounting of all casualties. Dr. Greg Argyros, deputy chief of the Department of Medicine at Walter Reed Army Medical Center, justified Lynch's poor memory as the result of trauma. Her prognosis indicated hopes for full recovery. To restore feeling to her lower limbs, on April 3, military surgeons relieved pressure on her spinal cord from a displaced vertebra. Two days later, she greeted her family with smiles. Her father was pleased that none of her injuries resulted from gunfire. He allowed Jessie to suppress the cause of her wounds.

The former captive received a Purple Heart, a Prisoner of War Medal, and a Bronze Star for meritorious service in combat. She delivered a poignant encomium exalting her friend Lori as a war hero. On April 12, Lynch flew to Washington, D.C., for care and rehabilitation at Walter Reed Army Medical Center to undergo specialized treatment and therapy that enabled her to walk again. Five days later, surgeons repaired a bone in her foot injured during her recapture. Her 3-month convalescence drew so many gifts and bouquets that the family requested cards rather than flowers and directed well-wishers to give money in Jessica's name to charities and relief efforts. By June, Lynch was courted by publisher Simon & Schuster and by media specialists from the *New York Times* and MTV, correspondent Jane Clayson of CBS News, anchor Katie Couric of NBC News, and ABC interviewer Diane Sawyer. On June 17, the *Washington Post* furthered the controversy over Pentagon hype by running an updated version of Lynch's capture and rescue. The second article retracted claims that Lynch, the American Joan of Arc, fought to the death, emptying her clip of bullets before succumbing to hostile fire and stabbing. On July 22, she returned home in full uniform by Black Hawk helicopter. West Virginians welcomed her back along with her brother and her fiancé, army Sergeant Ruben Contreras. On a medical discharge, she claimed a disability pension. Hunched over a walker, on August 27, 2003, she mustered out of the army.

An Exploited Casualty

While the media ignored 30-year-old Shoshana Johnson, an Afra-Latina and a single mother from El Paso, Texas, the first black female prisoner of war in the nation's history, and failed to acknowledge Lori Piestewa as the first woman and the first female Native American soldier killed in combat, Lynch remained in the public eye. For a variety of reasons, her name and faced resounded in country music lyrics and on refrigerator magnets, T-shirts, and highway signs. Feminists denounced the exploitation of Lynch, "a liberated woman, fighting in the war; still feminized, still helpless, still a victim, and still marginalized" (Sjoberg, 2006, 194). Critics declared the made-up superwoman menaced by stereotypical Iraqi hypermasculinity a reprise of the actual bravery of Shoshana Johnson, a black soldier who resisted the enemy and sustained wounds to both ankles. Authors Krista Hunt and Kim Rygiel charged that media manipulation was "designed to increase support for the invasion of Iraq and validate the continued presence of U.S. and U.K. forces" (Hunt and Rygiel, 81).

For the film *Saving Jessica Lynch*, NBC TV used Dallas, Texas, as a substitute for Iraqi terrain. The film aired on November 9, 2003; Canadian actor Laura Regan played the lead. The 40-minute ambush ran without commercial pause. The action depicted Lynch's endangerment and the aid of informant al-Rehaief in orchestrating the night raid to rescue Lynch. Two days after the film debut, *Hustler* magazine publisher Larry Flynt exploited the public's interest in Lynch by purchasing pictures of her topless at an army barracks. He wrapped himself in false patriotism by claiming to suppress the photos for the sake of an American hero. In fall 2005, on a military stipend, Lynch entered West Virginia University at Parkersburg. She wore a brace on her left foot to support damaged nerves. On January 19, 2007, she gave birth to daughter Dakota Ann, fathered by Wes Robinson, delivered by caesarian section, and named for deceased friend Lori Ann.

Lynch was dismayed by claims in the *Washington Post* that she took part in a firefight and shot attackers before her capture. She refused a Rambo-style heroism that she didn't deserve and demanded a recanting of the hype and Pentagon lies. With the aid of journalist Rick Bragg, Lynch received from Alfred A. Knopf a $1 million advance for writing *I Am A Soldier Too: The Jessica Lynch Story* (2003). Bragg narrated the audio version. The text fantasized she was sodomized by Iraqis, an assault unsubstantiated by medical examiners or by Lynch's recall. On April 24, 2007, during the inquiry into the death of army Ranger Pat Tillman, Lynch testified to the U.S. House Committee on Oversight and Government Reform that she couldn't fire her M16 rifle because it malfunctioned. Left unconscious when her vehicle crashed, she was aware of treatment in an Iraqi hospital. When she learned the extravagant tale of a heroic recapture, she charged the Pentagon and the media with fabricating a blood-and-thunder tale to romanticize the war effort. To redeem herself from being the dupe of Pentagon glorifiers, on July 23, 2007, she donated cash and stuffed animals to hospitalized children.

Sources

Bragg, Richard, and Jessica Lynch. *I Am a Soldier Too: The Jessica Lynch Story*. New York: Alfred A. Knopf, 2003.

Daniel, Sara. *Voyage to a Stricken Land: Four Years on the Ground Reporting in Iraq: A Woman's Inside Story*. New York: Arcade, 2006.

Hunt, Krista, and Kim Rygiel. *(En)gendering the War on Terror: War Stories and Camouflaged Politics.* London: Ashgate, 2006.

Knightley, Phillip. *The First Casualty: The War Correspondent as Hero and Myth-Maker from the Crimea to Iraq.* Baltimore, MD: Johns Hopkins University Press, 2004.

Rehaief, Mohammed Odeh al-. *Because Each Life Is Precious: Why an Iraqi Man Risked Everything for Pvt. Jessica Lynch.* New York: HarperCollins, 2003.

Sjoberg, Laura. *Gender, Justice, and the Wars in Iraq: A Feminist Reformulation of Just War Theory.* Lanham, MD: Lexington Books, 2006.

■ Career Dissatisfaction
Sean Covey

A force in the self-help and corporate and civic leadership market, Michael Sean Covey writes down-to-earth books, workbooks, peripheral materials, and speeches to guide people through the obstacles that once stumped him. Born in 1965 during his parents' mission for the Latter-Day Saints (LDS) in Belfast, Ireland, he is one of the nine children of Sandra Merrill and Stephen M. R. Covey, the grandparents of 44. Sean has resided in Boston and Dallas, but grew up primarily in a Mormon atmosphere in Provo, Utah. In the 1970s, his family set his thinking on a moral path by debating values and discussing the worth of competition, learning, and aims.

Covey followed his parents' example by volunteering for Mormon religious service far from home. On his own for the first time, he evolved a personal credo of the purpose-driven life. During an LDS mission in Cape Town, South Africa, during the fall of apartheid, from age 19 to 21, Covey devoted his talents to church projects. To make the most of his volunteerism, he disciplined himself and developed a scheduling philosophy of completing one task at a time. The 3-year mission refined his leadership skills. From a variety of demands on his time, he learned the worth of self-control, time management, and relaxation. In his off hours, he scrimmaged in local football games and learned from black teens to speak the predominant Dutch-African dialect called Afrikaans, a predominant language in black-white negotiations and business in Angola, Botswana, Namibia, South Africa, Swaziland, Zambia, and Zimbabwe.

Schooling in Business Administration

On return to the United States, before selecting a college, Sean Covey made a typically immature survey of varsity sports programs. He chose from those campuses that claimed the highest number of all-American quarterbacks, which was his sports ideal. He entered the English Department at Brigham Young University (BYU) and played quarterback for the university football team, the Cougars. At a tough game in 1988, he suffered a concussion but led his team to two subsequent bowl games. In 1989, for excellence in passing and scoring, he received the first of two Entertainment and Sports Programming Network (ESPN) Most Valuable Player awards. He graduated with honors.

A bachelor's degree was not enough for Sean Covey. Like his father, he entered Harvard Business School and earned a master's degree in business administration. In Salt Lake City, Utah, he and his wife, Rebecca Thatcher, of Madison, Idaho, established a home for their six children. To put his evolving outlook to good use, he wrote *Fourth Down and Life to Go: How to Turn Life's Setbacks into Triumphs* (1990), an introit to his creation of a win-win philosophy for youth. In 1991, the Deloitte & Touche management consulting firm hired him. He excelled in business projects at Trammell Cross Ventures and Walt Disney Productions but sought a more personal career based on his own experience. To add creative energy and perspective to his work, he took the position of vice president of product innovation at the family firm, Franklin Covey, a global time management and productivity enhancement corporation formed in 1987 at Parkway Boulevard in Salt Lake City.

Selling Success

In developing the focus and logic of success, Sean Covey mastered self-refinement in four spheres—mental, physical, social, and spiritual. He had a superior role model in his father, 57-year-old business mogul Stephen M. R. Covey, author of *The 7 Habits of Highly Effective People* (1989), a best-selling handbook promoting methods of life proficiency and character ethic. In the family-run company, Sean's brother, David Covey, administered the firm's activities and outreach in Asia and Australia; formerly on staff at BYU, their uncle, Dr. John M. R. Covey, directed the domestic and family division of Franklin Covey. John Covey also laid the groundwork for a major breakthrough in self-help philosophy, *The 7 Habits of Highly Effective Families* (1997), coauthored by Stephen Covey and his wife, Sandra Merrill Covey.

Based on his parents' belief system, in 1998, Sean Covey collaborated with agent Jan Miller, a trainer in employment evaluation and work assessment. They compiled *The 7 Habits of Highly Effective Teens*, a youth application of self-improvement to everyday problems of high school students. Covey adapted adult situations, concepts, and logic in models from his father's original text. During Sean's research into character formation and self-esteem, he questioned high school students in Joliet, Illinois, where he discovered that "[t]here was rich and poor, white and black, it was a real cross-cut of America" (Nash, 1998). From round table discussions, he took notes on the impact of low self-esteem, failure, and depression between junior high and college admission. His choice of life principles and morality centered on honesty, affection, and dedication to tasks that establish lifelong habits. Volunteers guided him in removing clichés, restructuring motivation, and avoiding teen stereotypes about such issues as anorexia, family blowups, boy-girl relationships, and gang formation. Copy editors winnowed out Covey's intrusive personal perspectives, which he expressed in examples from his life, especially playing football and working for large corporations. To convince readers of his sincerity and the book's validity for teens, he worked one-on-one with students at Joliet to hone his intention and to project sympathy, understanding, and optimism. Overall, he tried to communicate hope.

Hands-On Philosophy

Covey learned something from leaving the corporate world and involving himself with teenagers in day-to-day dilemmas. He respected and admired individuals who had come from dysfunctional homes and who had overcome such obstacles to their future as low grades, spiritual depletion, venereal disease, pregnancy, abusive relationships, loss of a sibling, substance abuse, and lapsed career plans. Against film, television, and newspaper slants reflecting cynicism about teen immorality, he found reason to anticipate goodness, momentum, and prosperity from their choices. He admired their decency, accomplishments, and streetwise resourcefulness. Dedicated to his mother, Covey's work flourished in paperback in English and Spanish and on audio tape and CD.

Covey set up his manual to appeal to readers, engage them in debate, and lead them to private contemplation. He identified the essentials: taking responsibility for oneself, organizing actions, thinking positively about oneself and other people, listening intently to speakers, collaborating with a group, and renewing the self to prevent exhaustion and distractions. In a jaunty reminder, he declared, "It's all about brain waves. Get some" (Covey, 1998). On the issue of selecting a life mission, he reminded the young reader that "a personal mission statement is like a tree with deep roots," a suggestion of permanence and of ongoing replenishment from ready sources (Ibid.). The text promised sincere readers to expect efficiency, contentment, freedom from addiction, pride and self-awareness, and an enjoyable, balanced life. In brief alerts, Covey warned about materialism and advocated trust, kindness, reduction of destructive habits, steady work, time allotment, and dedication to results. Ruling all progress, he counseled, was patience. He suggested as antidotes to arrogance, jealousy, and perilous habits a commitment to good health, honesty, and respect for human limitations, both in the reader and in others, teens and adults.

A Proactive Lifestyle

Covey explained in detail proactive habits—shrewd planning and allowance for failure, tolerance, and forgiveness. He commended these outlooks as "the most stable, immovable, unshakeable foundation you can build upon" (Ibid.). He relieved individuals of concern over such irremediable problems as past errors, the weather, discourteous teachers and authority figures, race prejudice, insubstantial upbringing, and difficult parents, including divorced, separated, remarried, and absent fathers and mothers. To matters beyond individual control, he recommended self-help through will power, ingenuity, conscience, and self-improvement by obliterating such bad habits as impulsive behaviors, shifting anger, shame, guilt, and blaming others. His life scheme called for mature thinking beyond the allure of the moment by keeping in sight satisfying goals and by steering toward a long-range personal destiny. His perspective on savvy aims charged readers with guarding themselves from wrong friends, violence, and escapism through sexual promiscuity, smoking, alcohol, and drugs. In place of negative stimuli, he chose good reading, worthy heroes, meditation and spirituality for long-term serenity, and fun based on talents and interests.

The Covey prospectus looked ahead to opportunities for friendship, exercise, and relaxation as cures for worry, risky behavior, and such phobias as the fear of heights, snakes and spiders, gaining or losing weight, performing before an audience, taking tests, riding elevators, or walking or sleeping in darkness. To clarify obstacles, he suggested listing sources or causes of pressures and fears as the first step toward conquering them. He posited that planning tasks, unpleasant duties, and responsibilities would allow the individual to intersperse them with pleasurable events and opportunities, particularly spontaneous humor and games played for fun and excellence rather than winning. As examples of self-destructive behaviors, he chose television, gossip, fads, grudges, exhibitionist driving, junk food, casual sex, and aimless telephone and online chats as time and energy wasters.

Solutions to Problems

Sean Covey's *The 7 Habits of Highly Effective Teens* does more than sermonize or scatter platitudes over daunting situations. To improve long-term relationships and decrease frustration and disillusion, he stresses realistic expectations about self and others. He recommends a commitment to human relations through loyalty, keeping promises, avoiding competition and superiority, and performing small good deeds, especially unexpected kindnesses. In a brief hint on owning up to hurts and omissions, he urges a first-strike mentality: "Apologies disarm people" (Ibid.). He lauds synergy for advancing and improving projects like a school club, chorus, or band. Covey's guide book names brainstorming and teamwork as solutions to misunderstandings caused by bias, closed mindedness, dominators and know-it-alls, longstanding feuds, generalizations about personal beauty and body types, and exclusion and cliques.

Certain aspects of Covey's step-by-step advice on attaining a rewarding life sounds almost motherly: stay physically fit; build stamina and vigor; eat a nutritious diet; pace yourself; and balance work with relaxation, clean living, solitude, and sleep to avoid lethargy and low moods. In anticipation of plateaus in commitment, he warns, "It takes faith to live by principles, especially when you see people close to you get ahead in life by lying, cheating, indulging, manipulating, and serving only themselves" (Ibid.). For a positive challenge, he suggests keeping up with current events, cultivating new friends, laughing at personal failings, learning demanding skills, keeping a journal, travel, volunteering, stimulating conversation, prayer, exposure to the arts, gardening, and spending time with nature and animals. In times of personal loss, such as serious financial setbacks, life-staggering losses, family trauma, or even world cataclysm, his text promotes habits that uplift and refuel the flagging spirit and that anticipate good feelings and positive returns. He also warns of inescapable seasons of imbalance, especially the transition from graduation to a job or the military.

Credit Due

The 7 Habits of Highly Effective Teens sold over three million copies and was translated into 16 languages. When Sean Covey's work became a bestseller, he returned to the source to give credit to the real winners, the teens at Joliet Central High School, many of whom improved their lives by following the book's precepts. Together, Covey and the student body greeted fans at Barnes & Noble in Joliet and autographed books. Readers stated that they identified with quotations, Garfield cartoons, analogies, stocktaking, and visual models, such as a description of the giant sequoia. Buoying self-image were Covey's biographical models from varied spheres of interest, including composer Ludwig von Beethoven, physicist Albert Einstein, singer Judy Garland, activist Jesse Jackson, athlete Michael Jordan, feminist Helen Keller, and Abraham Lincoln, who led warring citizens during a major threat to the United States. Covey built immediacy with stories of teens around the world, particularly anecdotes on urgent and life-threatening situations, such as acquaintance with a hashish user and the vulnerable targets of a serial rapist.

Parents and professional readers valued Covey's work for basing self-improvement on realism. They added *The 7 Habits of Highly Effective Teens* to school reading lists and coordinated parent workshops, counseling sessions, character development courses, and scouting and religious programs based on Covey's models of the proactive mindset. Covey began touring the country to address adults and youths, earning fees ranging from $10,000 to $12,000 per session. He varied his themes to suit the needs of each group—urban violence, relationships with family and friends, analyzing fads and peer pressure, defeating inferiority, and setting and achieving aims. At an appearance in November 2000, he blamed technology for complicating management problems and offered specifics for increasing contentment in a rushed, jangled world overloaded with cell phones, computers, e-mail, and instant communication.

Covey's subsequent self-help publications clarified and augmented his original ideas on the can-do spirit and urged a celebration of such human variables as age, culture, and physical abilities. To encourage self-expression through writing, he issued *The 7 Habits of Highly Effect Teens Journal* (1999); for a day-by-day guide to internalizing good habits, he published *Daily Reflections for Highly Effective Teens* (1999), an inspirational guide for future go-getters. As his successful philosophy drew more attention from teachers, parents, counselors, and scout and church leaders, he produced *The 7 Habits of Highly Effective Teens Personal Workbook* (2003), which advocates listing and taking stock of attitudes and actions at the reader's pace. Three years later, he returned to his original dilemma—making a sweeping change in his own life—by compiling *The 6 Most Important Decisions You'll Ever Make: A Guide for Teens* (2006). The handbook identifies opportunities and life choices, including higher education, the military, career, religion, marriage, and family.

Sources

Barnet, Andrea. "Self-Help Strategies." *Working Mother* (February 1999): 65.

"Class Aims to Teach Setting Priorities." *St. Louis Post-Dispatch*, July 10, 2006.

Covey, Sean. *The 7 Habits of Highly Effective Teens*. Minneapolis, MN: Sagebrush Education, 1998.

Covey, Stephen R. *The 7 Habits of Highly Effective Families*. New York: Golden Books, 1997.

Forman, Gayle. "Get It Together." *Seventeen* 59 (1) (January 2000): 96–97.

Nash, Pati. "For Author, Joliet Teens 'Highly Effective' High Schoolers Helped with Book on Character." *Chicago Tribune*, November 27, 1998.

Parish, Thomas S. "Tips on How to Turn Life's Setbacks into Triumphs." *Education* 115 (4) (Summer 1995): 537.

Rock, Brad. *Tales from the BYU Sidelines*. Champaign, IL: Sports Publishing, 2003.

Shellenbarger, Sue. "Wed., 1:30 P. M., Lunch: Emotional Discussion with Family Member." *Wall Street Journal*, March 27, 2002, B1.

Stepp, Laura Sessions. "Books Help Teens Strategize for Life." *Los Angeles Times*, September 12, 2000, 3.

■ Cerebral Aneurysm
Patricia Neal

A survivor of three consecutive brain malfunctions, actor Patricia Neal returned to her career with renewed enthusiasm and compassion. A Kentuckian from Packard, Patsy Louise Neal was born on January 20, 1926, to William Burdette "Coot" Neal, the traffic controller for a coal company, and Eura Mildred Petrey Neal, a housemother for Pi Kappa Phi fraternity house at the University of Tennessee. "Patsy Lou" spent her childhood in Knoxville with siblings Margaret Ann and William Petrey Neal. She observed the glamour of a white-robed evangelist at the Magnolia Avenue Methodist Church revival and developed a yen for acting and tap dancing. She began learning stage presence by delivering church monologues and public readings. In 1937, her supportive parents sent her to Emily Mahan Faust for 1-hour acting classes that covered diction, elocution, improvisation, pantomime, and stage technique.

Opportunities abounded for the lanky, poised young thespian. In fifth grade, she performed in Paul Bliss's two-act operetta *Twilight Alley*. In her mid-teens, she directed an English class presentation of William Shakespeare's *Romeo and Juliet*. On vacation from high school, she acted in summer stock with the Tennessee Valley Players and debuted at age 15 at the Barter Theatre in Abingdon, Virginia, in *Penny Wise*. Working at hands-on stage basics, she painted scenery, tagged and placed props, and stitched and ironed costumes. With training in drama and speech at Northwestern University in Chicago, she made the most of intelligence and an arresting beauty and stage presence. After 2 years, she and drama coach Alvina Krause found opportunities in summer theater in Eaglesmere, Pennsylvania.

A Rapid Rise to Stardom

Neal dropped out of college and gravitated toward a stage career on Broadway. She took a train to New York City, rented a flat on Morningside Drive, and supported herself at odd jobs. Under the name Patricia, in 1944, she landed a $150-a-week understudy role to Vivian Vance in John Van Druten's comedy *The Voice of the Turtle* (1943). In the midyears of the studio-controlled star system, she was a founding member of Lee Strasberg's Actors Studio. Instructed by George Shdanoff and Michael Chekhov, she mastered the trade of naturalistic drama method founded by Constantin Stanislavski. After a stunning debut at the Theatre Guild's summer production of *Devil Take the Whistler*, playwrights Lillian Hellman and Eugene O'Neill and musical theater mogul Richard Rodgers picked Neal as a promising actor. At age nineteen, Neal won the Drama Critics Award, the Ward Morehouse Partners in Care (PIC) award, and a Tony for the featured role of Regina Giddings in Hellman's classic play *Another Part of the Forest* (1946). The success won Neal a Hollywood contract with Warner Brothers, her picture on the cover of *Life* magazine, and features in *Charm*, *Harper's Bazaar*, *Junior Bazaar*, *Newsweek*, and *Redbook*. During this period, her voice shifted lower "through drinking and cigarettes and staying up late" (Shearer, 2006, 17). The alteration increased her sultry allure.

Three years later, guided by filmmaker Otto Preminger, Neal seized the attention of moviedom. She tackled cinema with Ronald Reagan in a boy-meets-girl role for *John Loves Mary* (1949). Cast with the era's heartthrobs, she appeared as a nurse with Reagan in the World War II British melodrama *The Hasty Heart* (1949), in the tobacco industry saga *Bright Leaf* (1950) with Gary Cooper, and in the spy thriller *Diplomatic Courier* (1952) with Tyrone Power. To play the provocative dominatrix Dominique Francon in the filming of Ayn Rand's *The Fountainhead* (1949), Neal gave up being "a taxicab girl" and mastered horseback riding (Shearer, 2006, 63).

Dangerous Choices

Neal began a 5-year affair with costar Gary Cooper, a married man and father who was 25 years older than Neal. Within months, Veronica "Rocky" Cooper dispatched a wire asserting her intent to keep Gary in their marriage. Their 22-year-old daughter Maria spit at Neal in public. He coerced his paramour to abort their unborn child and drove her to a Los Angeles residential area. Neal completed the appointment alone and paid the physician. The bleeding continued for 5 months. The decision grieved Neal, who was reared Roman Catholic: "For over thirty years, alone, in the night, I cried. For years and years I cried over that baby. . . . I regret it with all my heart" (Shearer, 2006, 108). Neal developed admiration for Swedish actor Ingrid Bergman, who bore public scandal after opting to bear her illegitimate son rather than abort him.

After Warner Brothers dropped Neal's contract, she lost a part in *Ivanhoe* (1952) to Elizabeth Taylor. Neal suffered a nervous collapse. She left California and returned to Broadway to star in a second run of *The Children's Hour* (1952), a groundbreaking feminist classic by Hellman on the theme of gossip about lesbianism. In a busy period of film roles, Neal finished the screen version of Ernest Hemingway's *The Breaking Point* (1950), the sci-fi thriller *The Day the Earth Stood Still* (1951), and *Operation Pacific* (1951), a submarine drama costarring leading men John Wayne and Ward Bond. She flourished in England in productions of *The Children's Hour* and Tennessee Williams's drama *Suddenly Last Summer* (1958).

Grim Realities

At age 27, Neal fell for Norwegian-Welsh short story author and screenwriter Roald Dahl, whom she met in 1951 at a fête hosted by Hellman. On July 2, 1953, they wed at New York City's Trinity Church. The actor developed versatility by starring in *A Roomful of Roses* (1955), as Marcia Jeffries opposite Andy Griffith in Elia Kazan's bleak political satire *A Face in the Crowd* (1957), as Helen Keller's mother Kate in the Broadway production of William Gibson's classic *The Miracle Worker* (1959), and as George Peppard's benefactor in *Breakfast at Tiffany's* (1961). The first of Neal's children, 7-year-old Olivia Twenty, succumbed to measles encephalitis in 1961. Over the next half decade, the actor produced four more children, Chantal Tessa Sophia, Theo Matthew Roald, Ophelia Magdalena, and Lucy Neal Dahl. The Dahls' only son suffered hydrocephaly and, at age 4 months, irreversible brain damage after a Manhattan taxi collided with his carriage.

At the height of success, Neal played meaty parts demanding a range of emotions. Opposite Paul Newman, she wore designer Edith Head's dowdy ranch costumes in *Hud* (1963), for which Neal enhanced the role of housekeeper Alma Brown with dignity and warmth. Her triumph of sense and sensuality won a British Academy of Film and Television Arts (BAFTA) award for best foreign actress, a New York Film Critics Circle Award, and an Oscar. In 1965, she played Lieutenant Maggie Haynes, a mature navy nurse, and lover of John Wayne's character, Captain Rock Torrey, in Otto Preminger's *In Harm's Way*, source of her second BAFTA award. The film cast her opposite male powerhouses Kirk Douglas, Brandon De Wilde, Dana Andrews, Burgess Meredith, and Henry Fonda. At age 39, she worked the first 3 days at MGM with Anne Bancroft and Eddie Albert under John Ford on *Seven Women*, a part that cast Neal as an atheist doctor amid a mission expedition to China.

On February 17, 1965, during the first trimester of Neal's last pregnancy, her career seemed doomed from the rupture of three aneurysms on the left side of her brain. In late afternoon, she collapsed in her bedroom at home from two bouts of cranial hemorrhage of the left carotid artery. After resuscitation and emergency transport to UCLA Hospital at 6:30 P.M., she suffered a third stroke on the X-ray table. The *Los Angeles Herald-Examiner* reported slim hope of Neal's recovery. *Variety* issued an erroneous banner head 5 days later declaring her dead in her prime. Fellow actor Mildred Dunnock intervened with the

Dahl children to explain their mother's grave condition. After neurosurgeon Charles Carton completed a 7-hour cranial operation to remove blood clots from Neal's left temporal zone, she lingered in a coma for 3 weeks.

The Way Back

On the 22nd day, Neal awoke to aphasia, word blockage, memory loss, and paralysis of the right side. With a struggle, she uttered one unintelligible word. She mourned, "Oh, what a mess I was. I wanted to give up. I was tired. I felt certain I was as good as I would ever be" (Kutscher, Downey, and Riedel, 1982, 15). Because of a monotone voice and lapses of comprehension and expression, she communicated poorly with best friend Anne Bancroft, who gave Neal time to shape thoughts into words. The patient described her quandary with a cage metaphor: "You're like a soul with no body, but the soul is drugged. Then the soul awakens into a body you cannot command. You are a prisoner in a private hell" (Prigatano and Schacter, 1991, 198). Neal feared she would never act again, but Dahl pushed her to stay alert and believe in her abilities. He lifted her eyelids, shouted her name, and smacked her on the cheek to summon signs of recognition. She was grateful that his slave driver methods forced her to want to survive.

Neal's recovery drew on years of language study and disciplined acting. She celebrated health: "Simple things like waking up in the morning and finding out I'm alive" (Shearer, 2006, 153). She submitted to speech therapy and to voice articulation and motion training under Dahl, who played the drill sergeant while demanding refinement of her primitive gurgly noises. On a complex schedule, Roald enlisted friends and neighbors in the regimen and drew on his wife's interests and strengths as material for exercises. The two began reading aloud the journalistic sentences of Ernest Hemingway. Neal worked her way up to Beatrix Potter's *Peter Rabbit*, which she read to her children. During the televised Academy Awards on April 5, 1965, actor Audrey Hepburn raised hopes with a general announcement, "We're all pulling for Pat Neal who couldn't be here tonight" (Newborn, 1998, 181). Neal thrived in singing sessions and composition, which resurrected more lost words from oblivion. Theo Neal contributed his own flash cards and guided his mother through quick recall trials.

Neal turned from self-absorption to concern for others. The success of therapy assured a normal birth on August 4 for daughter Lucy. In an outreach to other stroke victims, Neal and Dahl perfected a system by which volunteers could restore patient autonomy. The method aided patients in thirty British stroke clinics. By May 17, she was well enough to visit Jackie and John F. Kennedy at the White House. Neal challenged herself further to fly to London for a press conference and to exhibit wellness before a gathering of brain-damaged people at the Waldorf Astoria Hotel, where fans gave her a standing ovation. She reclaimed her role as housewife and mother and began sharing newfound wisdom about recovery with other stroke survivors. The public embraced her as a model of courage.

Great Performances

The actor's resilience in Hollywood won her a film offer for the part of Mrs. Robinson as the seducer of Dustin Hoffman in the comedic drama *The Graduate* (1967). She let the role pass to Anne Bancroft. A year later, Neal won an Oscar nomination for playing Nettie Cleary, the unfulfilled mother figure in *The Subject Was Roses* (1968), opposite

Martin Sheen as the son and Jack Albertson as her mate. At age 46, she created the Golden Globe-winning role of Olivia Walton, the belabored mother figure in the TV film *The Homecoming: A Christmas Story* (1971), which was the pilot episode for *The Waltons* television series. After her appearance in *Tail Gunner Joe* (1977), more Emmy nominations followed for a title role in *A Love Affair: The Eleanor and Lou Gehrig Story* (1979) and a TV remake of Erich Remarque's World War I combat classic *All Quiet on the Western Front* (1979), in which she played the mother of Paul Baumer. Four years later, she returned to maternal sufferers as the dying widow placing her children in foster homes NBC TV's *Little House on the Prairie* (1975). Three years later, she appeared in an episode of *The Bastard.*

In her home in the southern Appalachians, Neal challenged other victims of stroke. In 1978, Fort Sanders Regional Medical Center on Clinch Avenue in Knoxville honored her in the naming of the Patricia Neal Rehabilitation Center, a treatment clinic for paralytics and victims of spinal cord trauma and disease. The revered 73-bed hospital aided some 50,000 patients with restoration of function and education in self-care. Neal raised cash and spirits at a string of fundraisers. A filmed biography, *The Patricia Neal Story* (1981), captured her own experience with stroke and featured Glenda Jackson as the actor and Dirk Bogarde as Roald Dahl. The love match ended in 1983 after Neal rejected Dahl for his 9-year fling with her friend Felicity Crosland. Neal received the Women's International Center 1986 Living Legacy Award. She surveyed her experiences in love and on screen in *As I Am: An Autobiography* (1988).

Neal settled in New York City and summered in Martha's Vineyard, Massachusetts. She began lecturing, taping ads for Anacin pain remedy and Maxim coffee, and advocating education on speech impairments and physical handicaps. She performed at the Theatre Guild's Theatre at Sea and made appearances on television, including a 1990 episode with Angela Lansbury in *Murder She Wrote* and a remake of *Heidi* (1993), in which Neal played the grandmother. In 1999, she teamed with Glenn Close in the role of Cookie Orcutt in *Cookie's Fortune*. Honoring her years of professional excellence, the Last Frontier Theatre Conference in Valdez, Arkansas, offered the Patricia Neal Acting Award. She appeared at the Tribeca Film Festival in 2007. At age 81, she accepted a Lifetime Achievement Award at the SunDeis Film Festival in Waltham, Massachusetts.

Sources

Farrell, Barry. *Pat and Roald*. New York: Random House, 1969.

Greenberg, Gary, and Ethel Tobach. *Cognition, Language, and Consciousness: Integrative Levels*. New York: Lawrence Erlbaum, 1987.

Kutscher, Austin Harrison, John A. Downey, and Georgia Riedel. *Bereavement of Physical Disability: Recommitment to Life, Health, and Function*. Manchester, NH: Ayer, 1982.

Neal, Patricia. *As I Am: An Autobiography*. New York: Simon & Schuster, 1969.

Newborn, Barbara. "The Language Loss of Patricia Neal and Helen Wulf." In *After Stroke: Enhancing Quality of Life*, edited by Wallace Sife. Binghamton, NY: Haworth, 1998.

Powling, Chris. *Roald Dahl*. New York: Carolrhoda Books, 1998.

Prigatano, George P., and Daniel L. Schacter. *Awareness of Deficit after Brain Injury: Clinical and Theoretical Issues*. Oxford: Oxford University Press, 1991.

Shearer, Stephen Michael. *Patricia Neal: An Unquiet Life*. Lexington, KY: University Press of Kentucky, 2006.

■ Child Abuse
David James Pelzer

A survivor from age 4, confessional memoirist and inspirational writer David James "Dave" Pelzer turned childhood tragedy into material for a career in self-help lectures and books. The third of the five sons—Keith, Richard, Ross, and Scott—of Catherine Roerva Christen Pelzer and fireman Stephen Joseph Pelzer, Dave was born on December 29, 1960. He grew up on Crestline Avenue in the San Francisco Bay area in sight of the Golden Gate Bridge. While living in a middle-class neighborhood in Daly City, California, the boy weathered years of his parents' neglect, brutalizing, mental aberrations, and alcoholism. His mother, a Mormon reared in Salt Lake City, Utah, had been a secret boozer since age 13. Afternoons of marathon drinking and dancing altered his parents' behavior and precipitated neglect, physical abuse, and, eventually, separation and divorce.

Of her five children, Roerva targeted Dave for torment because he was the most compliant and malleable. The persecution begin in 1964, when she reported to a doctor that he had fallen from an upper bunk and broken his arm, a lie to cover up her brutalizing of a 4-year-old. Dave made no effort to refute her story. She quartered him on an army cot in an unheated garage and played life-threatening games with his trust and safety. Advancing from berating and scolding, she denied him meals, smashed his head into a mirror, forced him to vomit his food and to sit in cold bath water, and assigned wearying scrubbing jobs that dried his skin. After the birth of their baby brother Keith, Roerva flung a soiled diaper at Dave's face and made him eat feces. To win their mother's approval, the other boys contributed to Dave's misery. For his complicity, Richard referred to himself as Roerva's "Little Nazi" (Pelzer, 2005, 36).

Fear of Death

Dave began to focus less on obedience and more on survival. After receiving roller skates for Christmas, he realized that his mother intended to lock him out of the house and make him skate up and down the street. At a peak of fury, Roerva made him inhale and swallow ammonia and chlorine bleach, which scarred his esophagus. At a climactic point in child torture, she stabbed him in the upper abdomen with a kitchen knife, gashing and infecting the skin that he treated with dirty rags. To conceal her dehumanizing of Dave, she alienated herself from neighbors and friends. Her mother stopped visiting the children. Dave's father distanced himself from home. In complete control of her family, she gloated to Dave, "You are all mine now. Too bad your father's not here to protect you" (Pelzer, 1995, 152).

Lost in a fantasy of love and security, Dave constantly dreamed of food. He escaped the school playground and stole bread, chips, cookies, and graham crackers from a local grocer. He fed himself on scraps of Lucky Charms and milk from his brothers' cereal bowls, competed with the dog for leftovers, and begged from neighbors under the ruse that he forget his school lunch. His father did less to defend Dave from Roerva's cruelty and withdrew to bars on his days off. The family developed a code of silence: "If we don't acknowledge a problem, it simply does not exist" (Ibid., 91). In winter 1970, at age 9, Dave tried to escape to Johnson's Beach on the Russian River in Guerneville, where police found him at a pizzeria. Although he considered himself the butt of school jokes and the "reject of the fifth grade," he congratulated himself that he didn't "let her take away my will to somehow survive" (Ibid., 9, 4).

Rescue

At Thomas Edison Elementary School, the worsening condition of the troubled, unruly child alerted the staff nurse and Steven A. Ziegler, Dave's homeroom teacher. Dave wore ragged clothes, lied about bruises, and concealed raw skin from his mother's dousing his hands in cleaning solution. Ziegler later described Dave's home plight as the third-worst case of child abuse in California history. At lunch break, teachers wept over the child and plotted a rescue from his unbearable situation. One witness, teacher Atehan Konstan, declared that Dave was the most severely abused student she had seen in her 31-year career. On March 5, 1973, officers took 12-year-old Dave from the police station to San Mateo Medical Center, the county hospital. Nurses bathed him and noted ragged clothing and shoes, slash marks, scarring, chipped and missing teeth, and lumps and contusions on his head. He passed from the county juvenile department to a foster home.

Ostensibly safe from his mother's vengeance, Dave still dreamed that Roerva would find him and stab him with a knife. Pam Gold, an agent of the San Mateo County Child Protective Service, elicited details of his past and held him during fits of weeping. At a reunion with his mother and brothers Robert and Richard, Roerva fabricated charges against Dave for disobedience and harming other children. Out of earshot, she threatened to retrieve him and punish him more. At a custody hearing, she pretended to grieve for Dave. The boy begged to live with the judge, who made the child a permanent ward of the court, a guardianship lasting 6 years. The legal investment cost the state of California $100,000.

The cycle of violence took a new twist. At Dave's removal from home, his mother targeted her younger son, Richard B. Pelzer, who was unable to free himself like Dave. Richard later published two books on the Pelzer home: *A Brother's Journey: Surviving a Childhood of Abuse* (2005) and *A Teenager's Journey: Overcoming a Childhood of Abuse* (2006). He reported his own role in the perverted family scenario: "I was happy to watch my brother as he was beaten or forced to perform some disgusting punishment. It was exciting to watch. It is horrifying to remember" (Pelzer, 2005, 7). He later regretted contributing to Dave's sufferings.

Foster Care

In foster care, Dave vented frustration. He hoarded food in his only bag, which carried all his belongings. As his school skills deteriorated, he associated with delinquent boys who stole candy bars from a grocer. His family declined to contact him. Placed with Lilian and Rudy Catanze, Dave received new clothes and a house pet, a red-eared turtle. He cleaned his own room, helped out around the house, and played in the neighborhood. His privileges included seeing a James Bond movie and attending a Fourth of July picnic at Junipero Serra Park overlooking Mount Diablo. His mother returned his bike, which his brothers vandalized. He saved over 4 dollars to pay for repairs.

A diffident, skinny stutterer and high-risk student wearing glasses, Dave experienced adjustment problems. Larry Junior, another foster child of the Catanzes, needled and humiliated him. While receiving counseling, Dave disliked the psychologist, who called him the wrong name and viewed him impersonally. During their second session, Dave fainted from reliving the day that Roerva burned his arm at the gas stove. He ventured on his bike toward his family home. The next day, he grieved that his father failed to visit as he promised. To salve a damaged ego, Dave escaped to the Marsh home in the neighborhood and read magazine articles on military jets. After watching actor Clint Eastwood in *Dirty Harry*, Dave began mimicking his tough-guy one-liner before the mirror: "Do you feel lucky? Well, do ya . . . punk?" His imitation won the regard of street-hardened boys.

Upon entry into the sixth grade, Dave courted attention by stealing from Wal-Mart. Under threat to be sent to "The Hill," a home for wayward juveniles, he ran away to the Serramonte Six Theaters on Junipero Serra Boulevard to watch James Bond movies for 2 days and to dine at Denny's Restaurant at Serramonte Center. The Denny's manager reported Dave to Rudy Catanze. The next day, Pam Gold questioned Dave about disobedience. The boy longed to contact his parents. With a gang of boys, on January 10, 1974, Dave was involved in arson at a classroom module at Monte Cristo Elementary School. Authorities remanded him to San Mateo County Juvenile Hall on C-Wing, the quarters for hyperactive delinquents. Roerva plotted to place Dave in a mental institution to rid herself of him permanently. He exonerated himself at a trial by proving that he extinguished rather than started the school fire.

Into Manhood

In July 1974, Dave returned to the juvenile hall until he could locate a stable foster home. While living with Alice and Harold Turnbough, Dave attended Parkside Junior High and received psychiatric counseling. From jobs shining shoes at bars and working at a watch repair shop, at age 16, he graduated to busing tables and cooking at a fast-food restaurant and selling cars. Because of his heavy work schedule, he dropped out of high school and ended temporary placements in five foster families. Longing to be a movie stuntman, he earned a GED (General Educational Development) diploma and, at age 18, banged on the recruiter's office door until he gained enlistment in the U.S. Air Force. In summer 1979, he was stationed in the Florida swamps, where he worked as a cook and finished jump school. He advanced to Beale Air Force Base in Yuba County, California, and built confidence by bonding with flight crews who taught him teamwork and trust. On crews of the SR-71 Blackbird and the F-117 Stealth Fighter, he refueled planes in midair in Afghanistan and Iraq during operations Desert Shield, Desert Storm, and Just Cause. On leave time, he traveled the country. During his military career, his father died. Dave consoled himself that his military buddies took the place of his dysfunctional family.

In adulthood, Dave developed a strong relationship with his son Stephen but continued to battle low self-esteem. In 1990, he earned the J. C. Penney Golden Rule award as California Volunteer of the Year for advocating children's rights. When the Pentagon phased out the SR-71 Blackbird in May 1991, Dave retired from the Air Force at age 30. He launched a career in public speaking, seminars, and workshops on child neglect and abuse. His materials targeted both victims of abuse and the human service professionals who rescue them, particularly foster parents and youth volunteers, single parents, educators, social workers, and police officers. At Rancho Mirage, California, his wife and former editor, Marsha Donohoe Pelzer, managed their company, D-Esprit, and served as its vice president. In the formative years of his career, his mother died at age 63.

Dave's Mission

After winning the Ten Outstanding Young Americans Award in 1993, Dave wrote *A Child Called "It"* (1994), the first of a trilogy on his survival of early childhood mistreatment under an insane mother and indifferent father. He returned to his elementary school and distributed copies to his former teachers. The book received a Pulitzer Prize nomination as well as a visit from his rescuer, Steve Ziegler. Essential to the book's message, a statement of the survivor encouraged readers to look inward for strength: "I knew the black hole was out there, waiting to suck me in and forever control my destiny—but only if I let it" (Pelzer, 1995, 157). Unfortunately, he knew nothing of business. His book agent embezzled the profits, leaving the Pelzer family broke and struggling. Under the management of Nancy Lauterbach, president of Five Star Speakers and Trainers, he flourished as a witty, engaging monologist. He avoided sensationalizing his childhood experience and pledged himself to adaptation and motivation.

Writing set Dave on a new path of self-expression. He followed his first book with *The Lost Boy: A Foster Child's Search for the Love of a Family* (1997) and *A Man Named Dave: A Story of Triumph and Forgiveness* (2000). The trio maintained bestseller status on the *New York Times* and international lists for an unprecedented total of 448 weeks. In 2000, CBS TV began the filming of a biopic to air in May 2001. Dave followed with self-help handbooks: *Help Yourself: Celebrating the Rewards of Resilience and Gratitude* (2001), *The Privilege of Youth* (2004), *Life's Lessons* (2004), and *Help Yourself for Teens: Real-Life Advice for Real-Life Challenges* (2005), a guide through realistic adolescent dilemmas. At one point, he had three books on the bestseller list at one time. Subsequent awards and recognitions for his candid reflections include the Outstanding Young Person of the World citation in Kobe, Japan, the 2005 national Jefferson Award, and being the centennial flame carrier in the 1996 Olympic Torch Relay. Dave received honors from four U.S. presidents—Ronald Reagan, George Herbert Bush, Bill Clinton, and George W. Bush.

D-Esprit continued to boost spirits of tormented people. Dave tours the globe at the request of communities and institutions and, dubbing himself "Robin Williams with glasses," speaks over 270 days per year. In summer 1997, his outreach began its soar after he made the first of four appearances on *The Montel Williams Show*. In January 2002, he increased his name recognition after an interview on *The Oprah Winfrey Show*. More media appearances— *The Leeza Gibbons Show*, *The View*, *Larry King*, and *Sally Jessy Raphael*—extended his promotion of youth charities. The publication of anti-Dave tabloid stories in the international press—"Is He Making 'It' All Up?" in the *Daily Mail* (London) and "Dysfunction for Dollars" in the *New York Times*—failed to dampen his enthusiasm for his mission to be a Samaritan to lost and hurting children. His projects include arranging donations for school trips and assisting relief for victims of Hurricane Katrina. In June 2006, he visited troops in Iraq. He speaks directly to listeners of his radio program, *The Dave Pelzer Show*, which airs every Friday morning. Additional resources, like live call-in number, are available at his Web site, http://www.voiceamerica.com. His program honors individuals and groups who intervene on behalf of endangered or neglected children.

Sources

Baker, John F. "Lost No Longer." *Publishers Weekly* 246 (4) (January 25, 1999): 14.

Kellaway, Kate. "No Pain, No Gain." *Manchester Guardian*, February 15, 2004.

Maryles, Daisy. "A Triumphant Finale." *Publishers Weekly* 246 (43) (October 25, 1999): 19.

Neumark, Victoria. "Beaten But Not Defeated." *Times Educational Supplement*, February 6, 2004, 17.

Pelzer, Dave. *A Child Called "It."* Deerfield Beach, FL: Health Communications, 1995.

Pelzer, Richard B. *A Brother's Journey: Surviving a Childhood of Abuse.* New York: Time Warner Books, 2005.

Singh, Subhashni D. "A Child Called 'It.'" *Journal of Child & Family Studies* 7 (2) (June 1998): 257–260.

■ Civil War
John Bul Dau

A victim of Sudan's civil war, human rights warrior John Bul Dau inspired Americans with the survivalism of a refugee. Born in Duk Dayul in 1973, he lived in the oil-rich south of his country in Duk County south of Duk Faiwil, where health services lay a 75-mile walk from home. The sickest required twenty men to carry them the distance. He survived typhoid fever by a folk healing method—hot metal balls lined up on his shoulders. Some 30 miles from the nearest road, he and his siblings shared sleeping quarters in a cramped hut. Despite poverty in the outback, he developed into a hale 6-foot-8. Reflecting on his childhood, he recalled his Dinka village east of the White Nile surrounded by cattle and goats that pastured in lush savannahs.

In 1983, the situation shifted to terrorism, random murder, and genocide under the tyranny of Arab President Gaafar Muhammad Nimeiri, a proponent of strict Sharia law and the ouster of Christians and animists. Dau described the resultant civil war as a face-off between Nimeiri's Arab conquerors and a Dinka freedom fighter, Colonel John Garang de Mabior of Wagkulei village. The American-educated Christian leader and career soldier trained 3,000 men of the Sudanese People's Liberation Army (SPLA) in Ethiopia. In the lower quarter of Africa's largest nation, Garang led the SPLA in a war against colonialists in Darfur 700 miles to the west.

Religious Extremism

At a height of Arab-Sudanese fanaticism from the north, for 16 years, government forces and the Muslim militia attempted a forced conversion of all black Christian males to Islam. Those who refused the faith the Arabs condemned to genocide. Dau's father, a village headman of an agropastoral people, received anti-Islamic refugees and offered protection, supplies, and freshly slaughtered cattle in exchange for information. His parents learned that the Arab insurgents targeted Dinka boys to limit the growth of the all-male army. His 48-year-old mother, Anon Duot, began reducing meals to prepare her children for periods of hunger. She urged them to clasp hands to avoid being separated. The admonition proved unlikely as civil war uprooted 27,000 black youths from homes and cattle camps.

At age 13, Dau began his flight from home in 1987 and completed it fourteen years later in Syracuse, New York. During the night in August 1987, while sleeping in the men's quarters, he had an end-of-the-world epiphany. He awoke to the thumps of exploding mortars, his mother's screams, and the flight of villagers from bullets. On the run with his father and brothers, Dau fled to the bush and knelt in tall grass. Behind them, soldiers raped women, slaughtered or enslaved children and the elderly, rustled herds, and burned homes. The family assumed that Dau died in the onslaught. He and 55 other boys remained lost to villagers for 20 years. In 2002, he assured his mother over the phone that he was really a man now. She left a refugee camp in Uganda and reunited with Dau at Syracuse Airport with a salaam and a wail of discovery.

With the aid of Abraham, an adult neighbor, Dau eluded leopards, lions, and hyenas as well as hunger and thirst. The exodus continued at sunrise, when Dau ran naked, his knees scraped and feet bleeding, his skin stung by mosquitoes, and his stomach growling. Abraham and Dau joined a woman and her two daughters on the way east over sub-Saharan

Africa to Ethiopia. Their only rations were wild roots, grass stems, and stolen pumpkins. In a surprise militia foray, Arabs seized and flogged Abraham but left him alive. Dau, Abraham, and the women veered southeast to escape Arab patrols. They survived another week of walking. Another clutch of Arabs beat Abraham and Dau over the head, yanked out hair, and kidnapped the three females.

In Flight to Freedom

Dau seesawed over 1,000 miles between Ethiopia and southern Sudan for 7 years before reaching a settlement camp farther south in Kenya. By night, he escaped the cold by sleeping close to Abraham. Frog harrumphs led the two through high grass to pools of water, and Dau had to learn to submerge all but his nose to avoid encounters with Arabs. Weeks later in mid-October, the duo approached the Pibor Post basin of Sudan and joined two adults and 17 naked boys. The size of the company forced them to walk by dark and hover under trees in daylight. One of the adult males and a boy disappeared while scouting in leopard territory. While avoiding Dinka enemies in the pro-Arab Murle tribe, the walkers encountered hot, dry weather and shrinking food supplies. At the Kangen River, a tributary of the White Nile, they faced a cracked riverbed and the death of a second adult refugee, whom the Murle slew.

Abraham set the example of persistence and led his impressionable compatriots to a muddy pond, where they swallowed mud to moisten swollen tongues. They stepped over corpses on the trail, where vultures picked at remains. As the followers declined to only four boys, Dau turned ashen and emaciated from dehydration. When his eyes ceased to produce moisture, he prayed for succor. Two hunters offered him a sip from a gourd. Abraham made him drink urine to rehydrate his body. Dau revived his spirits with Christian songs and prayers for water. In the Kangen marsh, the five refugees toasted grasshoppers and roasted tortoises, a welcome source of protein.

Children Leading Children

Upon entry into western Ethiopia, Dau and the four others reached the anti-Arab Anyuak, a remote tribe that loaded the five refugees with corn for their journey. In late November, the group ended a 4-month walk at the Pinyudu camp on the border of Ethiopia and Sudan. In response to Dinka duty to the vulnerable, Dau fostered 200 boys as young as five and warded off famine, exhaustion, and stalkers from thousands of children. An overload of refugees reduced available rations to cereal twice a week and housing to the shade of a few trees in heat that reached 116 degrees Fahrenheit. Before the arrival of U.N. supplies of food, clothing, and medical aid, Dau coped with a cholera outbreak and the digging of graves with bare hands and sticks. More boys succumbed to chicken pox, measles, and whooping cough at the rate of two or three a day. The camp cemetery was so shallow that hyenas scavenged through loose dirt for the limbs of corpses.

Beneath physical stress, the children suffered hidden trauma, hysteria, and hallucinations. They feared death in the wild or permanent displacement from village, home, and family. As the population rose to 1,200 boys, Dau worked at camp organization. He distributed donated clothes, milk, and food and erected mud shelters with traditional conical thatched roofs. Latrines helped to curb sanitation problems. Venturesome boys raided farms and orchards for more food. The Anyuak retaliated by abducting the children and using them as bait for leopard traps.

By 1991, a local coup forced the boys out of Pinyudu and back to Sudan. To prepare, the refugees made backpacks from plastic and cloth sacking. The departure was a moving sight—27,000 barefoot boys tramping single file down the path toward home. At the Gilo River, crocodiles lurked on shore. While the expeditioners pondered their next move, Ethiopian rebels forced the boys into the water with gunfire. Dau survived a panicky swim that cost 9,000 lives to drowning, crocodiles, bullets, and torture. The remaining 18,000 plodded on toward home. For 9 months, survivors huddled in Pochala until the Arab-led government targeted the town twice a day with bombs. Dau led 1,200 boys toward Kenya. For 6 months, the children dodged ambush and airplanes while scavenging for water and food. Only 800 limped into Kakuma, a U.N. refugee receiving center in north Kenya.

Learning and Teaching

Dau was 17 before he learned to read by drawing letters and numbers in dirt with a stick. At the U.N. school, he quickly educated himself for the task ahead. For a decade, he taught refugees civics, English and reading, geography, history, and math. By age 27, he earned a high school diploma. His efforts caught the attention of a film crew, who immortalized the subsistence of homeless Sudanese boys in May 2001. He helped his mother, 18-year-old sister Akuot Leek, and 24-year-old fiancée, Martha Akech, to emigrate from East Africa but left behind most of his relatives and friends.

In 2001, the International Rescue Committee chose Dau among the 3,800 granted political asylum in North America. Sponsored by the Church World Service, he traveled 7,000 miles and reached Syracuse in company with 140 refugees appropriately named the "Lost Boys of Sudan." Three of his uncles and their families died in the war; his father and some of his brothers and sisters remained in Africa. Halfway round the world, he encountered his first electric lights on the runaway, which he thought resulted from a grass fire. For the first time, he flushed a toilet in the airport, slept in his own apartment on a mattress covered with linens, ate a doughnut, and saw a whole aisle of pet food at the supermarket. Because of rampant famine in Sudan, he was astounded that Americans devoted so much of their food money to domesticated animals.

Dau acclimated to the winter and layers of clothing but missed the communal lifestyle of Sudan. To his taste, American food seemed too sweet or too salty. His rewards—a peaceful land of plenty and medical care for his mother—outweighed the loss of his father, village, and Dinka food and culture. On the proceeds of a 60-hour a week job as a security guard at St. Joseph's Hospital and Health Center and part-time work cooking at a McDonald's and packing gaskets, he earned tuition for Onondaga Community College and Syracuse University, where he majored in civics, immigration law, and public affairs. Every 8 weeks, a film crew recorded Dau's life in Syracuse and interviewed him for up to 48 hours about such normal activities as grocery and window-shopping. They returned for Christmas Eve celebration and for community prayers after the 9/11 attacks on Washington, D.C., and New York City.

Dau developed into an articulate public platform speaker and related to privileged, well-educated audiences the privations of the Sudanese. In addition to his fee of $10,000 to $20,000, donors supported the Sudanese Lost Boys Foundation of New York, an organization Dau headed that offered scholarships, job counseling, and psychological healing. A second charity, the American Care for Sudan Foundation of New York, advised by "Lost Boy" Paul Ariik and sponsored by the Reverend Craig Lindsey and the First Presbyterian Church of Skaneateles, raised $230,000 to open and equip the Duk Lost Boys Clinic, a seven-room, 4,000-square foot medical facility at Duk Payuel. A central committee shipped the unassembled 36 by 96-foot steel building by air, accompanied by an engineer from Tech Serve International in Arkansas. Cement preceded the materials by flatbed out of Nairobi, Kenya, for final assembly in March in 120-degree heat. To raise the health standard for 195,000 Sudanese, the project specialized in treatment of bilharzias, chicken pox, diarrhea, guinea worm, h-worm, kala-azar, malaria, malnourishment, sleeping sickness, and trachoma. In the pediatric treatment room, staff scheduled immunizations as well as prenatal, maternity, and well-child services. He smiled approval and said, "I'm really looking forward to that. Our women have never given birth in a hospital before" (Tucker, 2007). His plans grew in 2007 to a network of six clinics some 50 miles apart.

Spokesman for the Sudanese

Dau became an American citizen. He returned to Africa in 2005 to propose to Martha Akech, a "Lost Girl" who emigrated to Seattle. For a dowry, he paid her family 80 cattle. The coupled married, settled at Green Street, and, in November 2006, produced daughter Agot. Still haunted by his ordeal, he used his example and advocacy to bring hope and peace to his homeland. Of the tenuous state of Sudanese peace, he said, "If the world lets us down, I don't know if I could bother myself to say there is an international community. I don't know if I would want to live on Earth" (Ordoña, 2007). To ensure the most for his money, he sent regular checks directly to Sudan. In February 2007, Dau's foundation dispatched seven American volunteers to break ground for the clinic project, which they opened in May 2007.

Contributing to Dau's fame was director Christopher Quinn's 85-minute documentary film *God Grew Tired of Us* (2006), winner of two Sundance Film Festival awards. The text, narrated by Nicole Kidman, produced by Brad Pitt, and promoted by Angelina Jolie, examined the lives of Dau and two fellow refugees, translator Panther Bior and inspirational leader Daniel Abul Pach, who emigrated to Pittsburgh. The next year, The National Geographic Society published Dau's memoir by the same title, coauthored by Michael S. Sweeney. The two media ventures limited the anonymity of a refugee who found himself alerting the world to a humanitarian disaster in East Africa. Dau's honors include a Good Society Award, Barney II Foundation Leadership Award, Distinguished Alumni of Onondaga Community College, Above and Beyond the Call citation for community service, 40 under 40 Award for Leadership, and a Martin Luther King Jr. Award.

Sources

Burleigh, Nina. "He Walked 1,100 Miles to Flee War." *People* (January 29, 2007): 107–108.

Dau, John, and Karen Kostyal. "John Dau: A Survivor's Story." *National Geographic* 211 (1) (January 2007).

Hecht, Joan. *The Journey of the Lost Boys: A Story of Courage, Faith and the Sheer Determination to Survive by a Group of Young Boys Called "The Lost Boys of Sudan."* Jacksonville, FL: Allswell, 2005.

Lee, Bonhia. "Documentary on John Dau, of Syracuse, Other Ex-Sudanese Refugees to Open Nationally." *Post-Standard* (Syracuse, NY), December 31, 2006.

Ordoña, Michael. "'God Grew Tired of Us' Tells the Stories of Young Sudanese Refugees Who Came to the U.S. after Escaping Brutality in Their Homeland." *Los Angeles Times*, January 5, 2007.

Seely, Hart. "Where They're Going, There Are No Roads." *Post-Standard* (Syracuse, NY), February 11, 2006.

Tucker, Neely. "He Escaped Sudan, but Not the Tug of a Heavy Heart." *Washington Post*, January 20, 2007.

Wilson, Craig. "'Lost Boy' Finds New Path Far from Home in Sudan." *USA Today*, January 23, 2007.

■ Congenital Glaucoma
José Feliciano

Singer and virtuoso guitarist José Feliciano overcame a life of darkness to become the first Latino to thrive in an English market. Second-born in the mountains of Lares, Puerto Rico, on September 10, 1945, Puerto José Montserrate Feliciano García was the son of farmers. He suffered congenital glaucoma, a form of optic neuropathy or nerve damage resulting from internal eye pressure, narrowed visual field, and destruction of the optic nerve. His neighbors proposed that he beg on the streets, but ethnic music proved the salvation of his dignity. In a household of eleven brothers, he displayed musical talent in toddlerhood, when his father introduced him to mariachi. His mother preferred radio sing-alongs.

Feliciano tapped a tin cracker box to his uncle's ten-stringed cuatro and gravitated to the concertina. The family emigrated to New York's Spanish Harlem and settled on 103rd Street. He later observed, "I knew, by their confidence, that America was the answer to their prayer for survival" (Downs, 2003, 81). He began entertaining classmates at age 8 at Public School 57 and took roles the next year in the Bronx at the Teatro Puerto Rico. On a guitar presented by his grandfather, he mastered fingerpicking and chording by listening to recorded blues and pop tunes along with Mozart classics. Mixed into his formative years were rock and roll by Sam Cooke and Ray Charles, jazz works by Wes Montgomery, the riffs of Joao Gilberto and Django Rheinhart, and the classical intricacies performed by Julian Bream and Andrés Segovia.

Developing a Career

Under mentor Harold Morris, a Segovia disciple, Feliciano trained on the 12-string guitar into his mid-teens and sang in four languages. During his father's unemployment from dock work in 1962, José abandoned his junior year in high school and, at age 18, left home permanently. He supported the family on proceeds from coffeehouse performances in Greenwich Village and at the Old Town School of Folk Music in Chicago and LaCave in Cleveland, Ohio, and with salaried gigs at the Retort Coffee House in Detroit, Michigan. A critic catching his folk, flamenco, R&B, and pop guitar act at Gerde's Folk City claimed Feliciano as a wizard and star in the making. During the folk boom, alongside singer Julio Iglesias, Feliciano gained radio airplay for soft ballads that suited Hispanic listeners, who tuned in over 30 hours per week. He made a significant showing at the 1964 Newport Jazz Festival at Newport Beach, Rhode Island. He held his own against stars Joan Baez, Bob Dylan, Judy Collins, and Peter, Paul, and Mary with "The Flight of the Bumblebee" and a flamenco resetting of "La Bamba." Two years later, he advanced to the Festival de Mar at Del Plata, south of Buenos Aires, Argentina.

Finding favor with RCA Victor agents, Feliciano cut his first single, the novelty tune "Everybody Do the Click" (1964), and the first of his 70 albums, *The Voice and Guitar of Jose Feliciano* (1964). He followed with *Bag Full of Soul* (1965), a collection of bolero torch songs in Spanish that he reworked with overtones of jazz and rock. The romantic album debuted two hit singles, "Poquita Fe" (Little Faith) and "Usted" (Thou), which made him a teen idol. About the time he married club manager Hilda Perez, he boosted his name recognition in Buenos Aires, where he entertained an audience of 100,000. En route to London, England, in 1967, Feliciano faced inflexible border rules against bringing his female guide dog into Great Britain. The incident soured him on English appearances for years. A more fearful incident in Toronto resulted in the poisoning of another lead dog. His blindness rattled the host of *The Ed Sullivan Show*, who feared for Feliciano's safety on stage. To prepare the audience, Sullivan burbled, "Now, ladies and gentlemen, on our stage, a gifted guitarist who is not only blind, but also Puerto Rican" (Mott, 2005, 213).

José the Star

After migrating to Los Angeles, Feliciano developed stardom throughout the Americas, especially in Mexico and the Caribbean. At the urging of producer Rick Jarrard, he popularized a bilingual adaptation of "Light My Fire," an original performed by the Doors in 1966. Sung to acoustic guitar, woodwind, and soulful vocal backup, Feliciano's version rose to first place on the 1968 pop chart and won his first gold album and first Grammy. The passionate, enticing lyrics set the tone of his early career. Recorded on the album *Feliciano!*, "Light My Fire" and remakes of tunes by John Lennon and Paul McCartney won audiences in Canada, Brazil, Australia, the United States, and England for his blend of rock and jazz set to Spanish-style strumming. Jarrard backed the song with "California Dreaming" (1968), a soft rock solo set to a freestyle obbligato. Feliciano's fans boosted "Hi-Heel Sneakers" (1968) and its flip side, "Hitchcock Railway," into his next greatest hit, the foundation of two Grammy Awards for the best new artist of 1969 and for the year's best popular song. At age 22, he stirred controversy with a Chicano soul-inflected rendition of the national anthem during the fifth World Series game at Detroit's Tiger Stadium on October 7, 1968, between the Tigers and the St. Louis Cardinals. Angry call-ins overwhelmed NBC's switchboard with aspersions on the singer and even his guide dog Trudy. Ironically, the performance rose to number 50 and stayed there for 5 weeks on *Billboard*'s pop chart, becoming the first recording of a stylized setting of "The Star-Spangled Banner." He appeared at the Schaefer Music Festival in Central Park and made inroads into the British market with "And the Sun Will Shine" (1969) and "Marley Purt Drive" (1969). He established himself as a crossover star with the album *Souled* (1969), which featured two more Feliciano standards, "Hey! Baby" and "My World Is Empty Without You."

Feliciano's style combined energetic riffs with peppy, often erotic delivery in both English and Spanish. He segued to feel-good music in 1970 with a Christmas classic, "Feliz Navidad" (Merry Christmas), a familiar holiday addition to seasonal albums featuring multiple artists. At age 26, he married Detroit fan Susan Omillion, mother of Melissa Anne, Jonathan "Jonnie" José, and Michael "Mikey" Julian. The couple made their home in a colonial era tavern in Fairfield County, Connecticut, where he performed on the talk show *Speaking of Music* over the Westport radio station WMMM. That same year,

Feliciano performed an Italian ballad, "Ché Sarà" (What Will Be, 1971), at an annual music festival in San Remo, Italy. The recorded version flourished in eastern Europe, the Balkans, and Asia. He remixed a Spanish adaptation, "Que Será," that sold well in the Americas. An English version, "Shake a Hand," pleased fans in Scandinavia. His appearances in movies and on stage, radio, and television included playing with the London Symphony, the U.S. Air Force Band, and the Los Angeles Philharmonic.

José in the Media

Feliciano's upbeat style has earned him a place preceding the White House Christmas Tree lighting with President Bill Clinton, at the Kennedy Center, on PBS television, in Motown and Las Vegas, and at Club Tropigala in Miami's Fontainebleau Hotel. The singer rated a television special on April 27, 1969, featuring Burt Bacharach, Glen Campbell, and Dionne Warwick. In August, he released "Rain," a rhythmic classic. Feliciano performed "Old Turkey Buzzard" as background for *Mackenna's Gold* (1969), a star-laden screen vehicle for Gregory Peck and Omar Sharif scored by Quincy Jones. On October 16, 2007, Feliciano performed a lengthened version of the song on *The Late Show with David Letterman*. The singer's last top 40 album, *Alive Alive-O!* (1970), reaped his third gold release.

Feliciano became a force in Spanglish culture. In a departure from album production, he recorded the theme song and wrote music for the detective series *McMillan & Wife* (1971–1977) and for episodes of *Kung Fu* (1972–1975). On television, he made a guest appearance as Pepe Fernando, the skirt-chasing cousin of Chico, title figure in the series *Chico and the Man* (1974–1978) starring Freddie Prinze, Jack Albertson, and Scatman Crothers. For director Gordon Parks' blaxploitation film *Aaron Loves Angela* (1975), Feliciano wrote the soundtrack and made a cameo appearance. He added his unique vocals, rhythms, and strumming to other albums—congas on Michael Nesmith's *Tantamount To Treason* (1971), "Ain't No Sunshine" on Bill Withers' *'Justments* (1974), electric guitar on "Free Man in Paris" for Joni Mitchell's *Court and Spark* (1974), acoustic guitar backup for 1950s hits on John Lennon's *Rock 'n' Roll* (1975), the duet "More Than the Stars" on Natalie Cole's *Everlasting* (1987), and the duet "Tengo Que Decirte Algo" with Gloria Estefan on *Alma Caribeña* (2000). In 1978, he cameoed in the film *Sgt. Pepper's Lonely Hearts Club Band* alongside the Bee Gees, Wolfman Jack, and Tina Turner.

A Spate of Awards

Feliciano's versatility won accolades from fans of English and Spanish rock and ballads. His cabinet of honoraria holds 45 gold and platinum records. *Guitar Player* magazine voted him top performer for five consecutive years for classic, jazz, and rock, and named him a top guitarist. *Playboy*'s reader's poll named him the best in jazz and rock. At a peak in the 1980s, he snagged four Grammys for Latin music—*Me Enamore* (1983), "Lelolai" (1986), "Ceilito Lindo" (1989), and "Por Que Te Tengo Que Olvidar" (1990). At age 42, he posed alongside his star at the Hollywood Walk of Fame and contributed wax sculptures of his hands to the Madame Tussauds Museum's "Wall of Fame" in London. His homeland awarded him another star in company with the stars of actors José Ferrer and Raul Julia. In 1987, Feliciano's popularity in Austria grew from the hit single "The Sound of Vienna." He performed it with the Vienna Symphony Orchestra and sang it to an audience of 50,000 at

Vienna's Danube Park. In 1989, he teamed with wife Susan to compose 12 songs for sci-fi author Ray Bradbury's play *The Wonderful Ice Cream Suit*, which debuted at the Pasadena Playhouse.

The singer won hearts with his inclusive canon and his dedication to cultural diversity. At age 50, he received a signal honor—the renaming of New York City public high school 155 to the José Feliciano Performing Arts School, an exemplary alternative arts center in East Harlem. Developing mainstream American appeal, he appeared in the film *Fargo* (1995) and sang an original ballad, "Let's Find Each Other Tonight," his only country hit. The next year, *Billboard* presented him a lifetime achievement award. He continued promoting Hispanic talent by singing "Behind the Mask," the theme song of the action series *Queen of Swords* (2001).

Feliciano returned to Puerto Rico in 2001 to join protests of American military bombardment of the island of Vieques. Joining in civil disobedience on May 1, 2001, he trespassed on the island along with singer Ricky Martin, militant clerics, athletes Chi Chi Rodriguez and Félix Trinidad, actors Edward James Olmos and Martin Sheen, Nobel Prize winner Rigoberta Menchú, Reverend Alfred Charles Sharpton, and politicians Rubén Berrios, Jesse Jackson, Robert Francis Kennedy, Jr., and Charles Rangel. Concealed in a swamp while a SWAT team combed the area and soldiers surveyed the protesters from Coast Guard cutters and helicopters, Feliciano risked arrest by U.S. marshals and Marine MPs. For this and other humanitarian and artistic contributions, in 2001, Sacred Heart University in Fairfield, Connecticut, presented him an honorary doctorate.

Greathearted Performer

Feliciano's urge to create kept him busy in his 50s on traditional and electric guitars and bass, banjo, mandolin, percussion, keyboard, and synthesizer. He equipped his studio with digital 32-track recorder and computer. He returned to bolero, his original medium, in the album *Señor Bolero* (1997). The title song reaped double platinum in the United States, Venezuela, and the Caribbean and gold in Argentina, Costa Rica, and Mexico. Los Premios Globos chose him as Artist of the Millennium and presented him the Alma Award. In December 2003, the Banco Popular de Puerto Rico saluted the island star with a television special, *Guitarra Mía*, a showcase of his works. The singer teamed with artist David Diaz in a children's picture book entitled *Feliz Navidad: Two Stories Celebrating Christmas* (2003). Two years later, he honored ties with Mexico by recording mariachi favorites to José Hernandez's orchestrations in the album *A Mexico . . . con Amor* (To Mexico . . . with Love, 2005). Universal Records released a Spanish album, *Jose Feliciano y amigos* (José Feliciano and Friends, 2006), a collection of singles in harmony with Latino stars Marc Anthony, Ramón Ayala, Cristian Castro, Raúl di Blasio, Gloria Estefan, Luis Fonsi, Ana Gabriel, Ricardo Montaner, Luciano Pereyra, Rudy Perez, Lupillo Rivera, and Alicia Villarrea. Feliciano composed original English songs for *Soundtrack of My Life* (2007). In honor of his "Feliz Navidad," ASCAP listed it among the 25 holiday greats of the 20th century.

Feliciano freely gives his time and prestige to his adopted land, including visits to the veteran's home in Tilton, New Hampshire, with his German shepherd, Buddy. He urged citizens to "band together in solidarity, for as a nation, there has never been an equal, and as a people, there will never be a dilemma we cannot overcome" (Downs, 2003, 81). To touch people with similar threats to eyesight, Feliciano addresses audiences on behalf of Citibank and Nissan of Japan on overcoming blindness. For Life Span, Inc., and the One

Touch Glucose Monitoring System, he targets Latino audiences with motivational speeches on diabetes, a common threat to vision, especially among Hispanics. For his concern for others, in September 2006, the Hispanic Heritage Foundation honored the singer at the Kennedy Center as a role model and leader in the fields of education, the arts, culture, and global good will.

Sources

Aparicio, Frances R. *Listening to Salsa: Gender, Latin Popular Music, and Puerto Rican Cultures*. Middletown, CT: Wesleyan University Press, 1998.

Downs, Hugh, ed. *My America: What My Country Means to Me by 150 Americans from All Walks of Life*. New York: Charles Scribner's Sons, 2003.

Gabbard, Krin. *Black Magic: White Hollywood and African American Culture*. Piscataway, NJ: Rutgers University Press, 2004.

Melendez, Miguel. *We Took the Streets: Fighting for Latino Rights with the Young Lords*. New York: St. Martin's Press, 2003.

Morales, Ed. *Living in Spanglish: The Search for Latino Identity in America*. New York: St. Martin's Press, 2003.

Mott, Robert L. *Radio Sound Effects: Who Did It and How in the Era of Live Broadcasting*. Jefferson, NC: McFarland, 2005.

■ Custody Battle
Elián González

Shortly before his 6th birthday, Elián Brotons González survived a shipwreck, the loss of his mother, and a custody battle that brought two nations into conflict. He is a native of Cárdenas in north central Cuba, born December 6, 1993, to Elizabet Brotons Rodriguez, a secretary and chief housekeeper at the Paradiso Punta Arenas Hotel, a high-rise resort in the city of Varadero east of Cárdenas. Her husband, Juan Miguel González Quintana, served the tourist hotel as a doorman and cashier. The couple had difficulty conceiving Elián and lost seven babies to miscarriage before his birth. They took the first letters of Elizabet and the last letters of Juan to create the boy's name. In 1996, Elizabet and Juan Miguel separated and later divorced but continued to live together. Elizabet saved $2,000 to pay for transporters to take her and Elián to Florida.

On November 20, 1999, Elián's 24-year-old mother picked him up at school around noon. Elizabet, Elián, and his Miami-born stepfather, Lazaro Rafael Munero García, departed the mangrove swamps outside the port town of Cárdenas in the province of Matanzas, Cuba, on an escape across the 90-mile Florida Strait to political asylum in the United States. Elián, who left without his father's knowledge, understood that the journey was a fishing trip and a visit to his uncle's. According to one report, he cried to be left behind.

The motor failed, requiring the émigrés to return, hide in the swamp during repairs, and make a second departure 2 days later. At midnight on November 22, the crew dumped the broken motor into the sea to lighten the load. Cuban patrol launches pursued the 17-foot homemade aluminum boat and tried to overturn it. The poorly soldered craft lacked seats, roof, and life preservers and towed three inner tubes for protection. Adult emigrés held up Elián to protest endangerment of a child. Of the 14 passengers, 11 perished when the motorboat lost power on November 26 and flipped on its side in rough waters. Among them were Munero, his parents and younger brother, and Elán's mother, who apparently drowned. Her body was not found among the seven corpses returned to coastal waters.

Surviving an Ordeal

Two survivors, 22-year-old Arianna Horta Alfonso and Nivaldo Fernandez Ferran, washed up at Key Biscayne and reported the boy missing. For 2 days, Elián recited a prayer and floated the rest of the way on the inner tube into which his stepfather wedged him. Before his mother sank, she left him a bottle of water. On November 25, 1999, Thanksgiving Day, 20 miles off Miami, a seaman, 44-year-old Donato Dalrymple and his cousin Sam Ciancio were fishing for mahimahi when they approached what they thought was a floating doll. They retrieved the refugee from the sea 3 miles off Fort Lauderdale and placed him in the custody of the U.S. Coast Guard. Elián's recall of the near-death experience was limited. He remembered going to sleep: "When I opened my eyes, I didn't see anyone" (De Valle, 2005). Nightmares of his mother's disappearance tormented him. Cuban exiles in Miami embraced the boy as a miracle child and respected his mother's wishes to rear him in freedom in the United States.

At the Joe DiMaggio Children's Hospital in Hollywood, Florida, Elián required overnight care for dehydration, sunburn, and the shock of separation from his mother. In Miami, Immigration and Naturalization Service (INS) agents remanded him to his 48-year-old great uncle Lázaro González, a Cuban refugee, and to Lázaro's 21-year-old daughter Marisleysis González, who became the boy's foster mother. She chose to conceal Elizabeth's death from Elián until he was stabilized. On November 28, 1999, 31-year-old Juan Miguel telephoned the family to demand Elián's return and to charge that his ex-wife took the boy without permission. Members of the anti-Castro Cuban exile faction in Little Havana, Miami's Cuban-American community, agitated for the boy's expatriation into the United States by issuing T-shirts, banners, billboards, and 4,000 posters of the boy under the heading "Another Child Victim of Fidel Castro." After reporters headquartered under a dozen canopies opposite the residence, activist Armando Gutierrez, a family friend, mediated between the González household and the press. Proponents of the boy's asylum declared him fearful of Cuban persecution. U.S. Senator Connie Mack of Florida proposed making the boy an American citizen. Meanwhile, the child enjoyed American amenities, front yard play with friends, gifts and television notoriety, and a trip to Disney World.

Exploited by Left and Right

Pro-Cuban factions took the face-off as an opportunity to remind Americans that Elián would live in a crime-free environment and receive universal medical care and free public schooling through university. On January 21, 2000, Elián's grandmothers, 51-year-old Mariela Quintana, Juan's mother, and Eleodra Raquel Rodriguez, Elizabet's mother, arrived from Havana to present for themselves and their husbands a request for the boy's release from U.S. relatives. Supporting their position were the *Chicago Tribune*, *The Christian Science Monitor*, Congressional Black Caucus, *The Miami Herald*, National Council of Churches, and the *Wall Street Journal*. On the opposing side stood the Cuban lobby led by U.S. Congressman Lincoln Diaz-Balart, who valued Elián as a bargaining tool in a series of press conferences, candlelight vigils, and protests of Fidel Castro. Elián met his grandmothers on neutral turf in the Miami Beach residence of a Dominican nun, Jeanne O'Laughlin, president of Barry University. Sister Jeanne sided with the Miami relatives because she detected Elián's fear of his grandmothers. During the 9-day visit, the grandmothers sought the intercession of congressmen and Attorney General Janet Reno. On January 26, the Congress rejected a bill to naturalize Elián and, under the philosophy that parents speak for minor children, supported the INS procedures that would reunite the child with his father. In the midst of constant media coverage and press speculation, the women flew home to Cuba.

Elián's status gained European recognition on January 28 after Spanish Foreign Minister Abel Matutes recommended that the father raise the boy in Cuba. Rumors muddled legal issues with charges that Cuban-Americans bribed Juan Miguel with a home and car if he would cede custody of his son and move north to Miami. The father communicated through letters to INS officials, to Cuban Foreign Minister Felipe Perez Roque, and to U.S. newspapers that he gave no ground on the issue of a father's right to his son. Supporting him, according to polls, were 66 percent of American citizens, who thought children should grow up in the care of their birth parents.

Deciding on Custody

On March 21, 4 months after Elián's arrival in Florida, U.S. District Judge K. Michael Moore overruled a petition for asylum in the United States. Eight days later, Miami Mayor Joseph Carollo and Dade County Mayor Alex Penelas backed the city manager, police chief, and 20 civic leaders, defied federal authorities by refusing assistance by police or social services in uprooting the child. On April 12, Reno met the relatives in Little Havana and ordered them to relinquish the child. Two days later, Elián confirmed to Juan Miguel on videotape that he wanted to remain with the Miami Gonzálezes. Attorneys for the father renounced the message as the result of child brainwashing. At age 11, Elián claimed to interviewers from *60 Minutes* in September 2005 that his Miami relatives coerced him into remaining in Florida by turning the child against Juan Miguel. Siding with the Cuban claimants, author Gabriel García Márquez charged Democratic leadership with keeping the child in Florida lest his return cost Democratic presidential candidate Al Gore popularity among Cuban-Americans, most of whom are conservative Republicans. The bicultural battle came to a lull on April 19 after the 11th Circuit Court of Appeals judge in Atlanta decreed that Elián stay with his Miami relatives until an asylum hearing in May.

The child custody quandary highlighted the resentment between Cuban leftists and successful Cuban-Americans in Florida. The debacle reached a height on April 13, the date that Attorney General Janet Reno set for the return of Elián to Juan Miguel. Because the Florida Gonzálezes refused the conditions, a gaggle of press, protesters, and police surrounded Elián's Miami residence. Among those attempting to normalize the situation were singer Gloria Estefan and actor Andy Garcia. Round-the-clock negotiations reached no accord. Reno agreed with a Florida family court judge that temporary custody should end and that Elián should be deported to Cuba. On April 20, she planned a foray on the Miami home despite the foster mother's threat to retain custody through violence. Supporters of the Florida family ringed the house; cars jammed the roadway to circumvent the approach of federal vehicles. Authorities arrested over 350 for disorderly conduct.

A Rambo-Style Rescue

At 5:15 A.M. on April 22, eight U.S. marshals and SWAT team members of the Border Patrol's BORTAC entered the home and used mace and pepper spray to subdue Elián's protectors. Donato Dalrymple grabbed the boy, who screamed at the raiders. Residents hurled bottles, rocks, and a stool at the agents while the boy's 46-year-old great aunt, Angela Maria Lázaro, her niece, the niece's son, and Dalrymple shielded Elián behind a locked door to the room the boy shared with his foster mother. Agents with an MP5 machine gun breached the door, damaged a bed, pushed adults to the floor, and threatened Elián and Dalrymple, who cowered in a closet. During the 3-minute raid, photographer Alan Diaz from the Associated Press caught the standoff with his camera. He discredited federal authorities for seizing a screaming child from the arms of his blood kin and passing him to a Spanish-speaking woman. Within days, U.S. Senator Jesse Helms denounced the coordinated foray as grotesque.

Some 100 protesters surged over the barricades, waved a Cuban flag while savaging an American flag, drew swastikas on U.S. posters, and assailed the emerging SWAT team with cries of "Assassins!" Authorities charged the INS with overreaching federal authority and with violating the Fourth Amendment guarantee of freedom from capricious search and seizure. Civil disobedience swelled as the number of demonstrators tripled. While blacks and Anglos championed federal intervention and Haitian-Americans protested antiblack favoritism, Hispanic workers boycotted area businesses. They overran a ten-block quadrant swinging baseball bats and set over 100 fires in dumpsters, tires, and trees. Police in riot gear suppressed violence with tear gas. In the aftermath, Dalrymple pressed suit against federal authorities for the use of excessive force in seizing a 6-year-old boy. In 2000, Delfin Gonzáles, Lázaro's brother, turned Elián's bedroom into a shrine, Unidios en Casa Elián (United in the House of Elián). The tourist attraction preserved the boy's race car bed, toys, and clothing while honoring Christianity, democracy, and patriotism. On September 17, a television documentary, *The Elián González Story* (2000), raised more questions on bias in media coverage of the boy's repatriation to Cuba.

In mid-morning, Juan Miguel, on temporary resident alien status, took custody of his son at Andrews Air Force Base and, in private, reunited Elián with his stepmother, Nelsy Carmeta González, 6-month-old half brother, cousin, kindergarten teacher, and pediatrician at a safe house at the Aspen Institute Wye River Conference Center in Bethesda, Maryland. While courts battled issues of custody and asylum, guards turned away New Hampshire Senator Bob Smith and a contingent of the Miami relatives. A week later, Elián received a visit from his teacher and school friends from Cárdenas. The Cuban-American newspaper *Granma* published a photo of Elián in uniform as a Young Pioneer, the Cuban Communist youth league. On May 6, 2000, Juan Miguel, his son, and attorney Greg Craig dined in Georgetown. Judge Edmondson of the 11th U.S. Circuit Court of Appeals decided Elián's future on June 1, 2000, by decreeing that the father alone could speak for his son. On June 28, 2000, after the U.S. Supreme Court refused to intervene, Elián González and his relatives boarded a plane to Cuba.

Back Home with Dad

In his homeland, the boy and his father gained hero status at island rallies and designated Cuban president Fidel Castro as a surrogate father. Elián settled with his father, who waited tables at an Italian restaurant near Cárdenas, attended meetings of the Cuban Communist Party, and, in 2003, won a seat in the national party assembly. Juan Miguel reported that his son feared the press, hated being alone, and retained memories of his unsettling 9-month juggernaut. Bodyguards sometimes patrolled the boy's daily route; the Cuban government withheld letters from the United States. A home video showed Elián content at the family's new home with his younger half brother and at a karate studio. In 2003, Albert A. Fox, Jr., president of the Alliance for Responsible Cuba Policy Foundation, reported on the normalization of the González household, "You only have to see father and son together to know that's where he belongs" (Fields-Meyer and Trischitta, 2004, 182). A mediator, Reverend Doctor Joan Brown Campbell of the National Council of Churches, monitored Elián's progress over eight visits. She verified his sense of humor, delight in Legos and in math and computers, and mourning for his mother, whose picture sat by his bed.

Elián presented a normal persona to interviewers but declared he still loved his Miami family. Annual press photos pictured Castro or his brother Raoul attending Elián's birthday parties. At Esteban Hernandez Junior High and later in high school, he earned good grades, participated in student government, and won a 25-meter swim meet. Meanwhile, his Miami relatives continued to mourn when they caught glimpses of the boy on television. Each December 6, Cubans celebrated the confrontation between Cuban and U.S. officials as the "Battle of Ideas." A local museum, the Museo a la Batalla de Ideas (Museum of the Battle of Ideas), featured an exhibit honoring Elián with a life-size bronze statue. The pose pictured the boy lifting a defiant fist.

Sources

De Valle, Elaine. "Elián González Recalls Tumultuous Time during Custody Fight." *Miami Herald*, October 2, 2005.

Fields-Meyer, Thomas, and Linda Trischitta. "Elián Five Years Later." *People* 62 (22) (November 29, 2004): 180–183.

Gay, Kathlyn. *Leaving Cuba: Operation Pedro*. New York: Twenty-First Century Books, 2000.

Horowitz, Irving Louis, and Jaime Suchlicki. *Cuban Communism*. Edison, NJ: Transaction, 2003.

Paterniti, Michael. "Fidel and the Magic Boy." *Esquire* 136 (3) (September 2001): 182–193.

■ Deafness
Lou Ferrigno

The Hulk of pop sci-fi, athlete Lou Ferrigno stands tall as a cult muscle man and as a role model to the deaf. Born Louis Jude Ferrigno on November 9, 1951, he grew up in the Bensonhurst section of his hometown, Brooklyn, New York. The environment was the inspiration for the Italian family in the film *Saturday Night Fever* (1977). In 1953, Lou lost over 80 percent of his hearing to an ear infection that received poor medical treatment. The son of Victoria Ferrigno and an Italian-American cop, Lieutenant Matthew "Matty" Ferrigno of the New York City Police Department, he suffered pain and deafness in both ears but wore only one hearing aid because his family could not afford two. He managed by favoring one ear for 6 months and switching his hearing aid to the other side for the rest of the year as a means of preventing further depletion of his auditory senses.

Ferrigno stored frustration and fury his whole life. Teased and bullied by kids as "Deaf Louie," "the Mute," and "Dumb Louie" and chided by his father for his disability and resultant speech defect, Ferrigno was a skinny preteen who declined to think of himself as disabled. He retreated into Action Comics featuring Superman and identified with two Marvel comic book protectors, Hulk and Spider Man. He reminisced, "I would pull my hearing aid out and completely tune out the rest of the world and fantasize that these super-heroes were me" ("Lou," March 2003). "Big Lou" built heft at age 12 with weightlifting and learned physique sculpting in childhood from his abusive father. He moved on to a neighborhood gym, the R & J Health Club, where he preferred dark private rooms to "go heavy" with quarter-ton weights. The workouts plumped up biceps and self-esteem. Nonetheless, his father forced him into a factory job making sheet metal. Lou salved the hurt of parental rejection by eating clams and shrimp at Sheepshead Bay and watching girls stroll by.

A Lucky Challenge

Hearing loss and the inability to pronounce clear sounds served Ferrigno as an impetus to success. He chafed at family favoritism toward his younger brother Andrew (Andy), the perfect son: "I wanted to prove [myself] so my father would love me.... But the relationship didn't improve at all" (Leamer, 2005, 105). Animosity turned the actor into a determined loner. In retrospect, he remarked on determination and setting goals: "The mind is everything. The mind is the most powerful tool" ("Lou," 1994). He later reflected that the handicap forced him to maximize his strengths in other talents by working out with Andy in the basement and, later, by playing professional football in Canada for the Toronto Argonauts.

In 1970, Ferrigno was goggle-eyed at his first glimpse of an Austrian contender, Arnold Schwarzenegger, who carried through the streets of New York City a Mr. Olympia trophy. Ferrigno got his own audience by just being himself. He confided to an interviewer for *Sports Psychology*, "I get attention no matter where I walk, regardless being an actor or celebrity, because big as I am people always look at me" ("Lou," 1994). In 1970, he came in last out of a field of 21 for the Mr. New Jersey Open Hercules, held in Trenton. After decades of fantasizing about movie heroes, he chose weight training for a hobby. Multiple strongman roles set Ferrigno's ambitions on acting. He chose as a model "Mr. World" body builder Steve Reeves, who played the mythic Hercules, Goliath, Romulus, Aeneas, and Pheidippides, the Greek runner of Marathon.

Early Achievements

With a diploma from Brooklyn Technical High School, Ferrigno developed his 6-foot 5-inch frame into a rippling 285 pounds. At ages 21 and 22, he set a standing *Guinness Book* record for the youngest winners and the only consecutive bearer of the Mr. Universe title, decided in Geneva, Switzerland, and Verona, Italy. With his earnings, for the first time, he was able to afford two hearing aids. The competitions served as an impetus for the cult documentary *Pumping Iron* (1977) and its sequel, *Raw Iron: The Making of Pumping Iron* (2002). Both peruse the motivation and entertainment facets of professional bodybuilding. In the background, the casting of Matty Ferrigno as Lou's coach masked the emotional battery that Lou suffered from his father for losing to Schwarzenegger.

Ferrigno dreamed of playing a unique role in the *Star Wars* series but found steady work in more mundane jobs. From 1974 to 1994, he posed for cover shots for *Bodybuilding Lifestyle*, *Flex*, *Iron Man*, *Muscle & Fitness*, *Muscle Mag International*, *Muscle Training Illustrated*, *Natural Bodybuilding*, and *Strength & Health* magazines. Under the supervision of a physician, he competed at the upper end in height in Mr. International and Olympia Masters. He won competitions for teen and adult Mr. America, Mr. Universe in the tall division, and a third place in the Mr. Olympia contest in the heavyweight class. At age 26, Ferrigno came in fourth for the first World's Strongest Man contest. Twice, he lost to Schwarzenegger and charged the failures to inadequate posing and flexing routines.

Family Man and Monster

In his late 20s, Ferrigno was briefly wed to Susan Groff. On May 3, 1980, he married his manager, psychotherapist Carla Green, mother of Shanna, Louis, Jr., and Brent. Ferrigno migrated from muscle contests to play the "mean and green" star of *The Incredible Hulk* (1978–1982), a popular television series that built a fan base among children and teens. He remarked on the screen test, "[T]hey liked the way I showed my emotions without speaking," a compliment to a lifetime of compensating for deafness and of concealing self-doubt and anger (Suss, 1993). At Vince Gironda's gym in North Hollywood, Ferrigno trained under Milton Katselas, Howard Fine, and Bill Bixby, Ferrigno's *Hulk* costar, who played the mute Hulk's alter ego, scientist David Banner. To transform Ferrigno into an irate green apparition, daily filming for 80 episodes required over 3 hours in body makeup, beginning at 5:00 A.M. Because he is impossible to replace with a body double, he performed his own stunts, which involved leaping over rocks in the sea, vaulting over a camera, and facing off against two advancing bulldozers. One off-kilter battle left an opposing stunt man with a torso gash requiring 35 stitches. Ferrigno's favorite episodes showcased retaliation against bullies who tormented the fictional Dr. Banner. The entire cast mourned the cancellation of the series at the end of the fifth season.

While coauthoring *Weight Training for Beginners: For Good Lifting Habits for a Lifetime* (1982) with Bill Reynolds and *The Incredible Lou Ferrigno* (1983) with Douglas Kent Hall, Ferrigno caromed across television series *Mister Rogers' Neighborhood* (1979), *The Fall Guy* (1981), *Matt Houston* (1982), and *Trauma Center* (1983). His menacing television personae included the Klondike Butcher in *Night Court* (1984) and the demigod and son of Zeus in the sagas *Hercules* (1983) and *The Adventures of Hercules* (1985), which dramatize the rescue of Princess Cassiopeia and the recovery of Zeus' lightning bolts. He reprised the part in the Italian screen myth *L'Avventure dell'incredibile Ercole* (1985), filmed among monuments dating to the Roman Empire. The action featured the tough guy battling two warriors at a time, breaking leg and iron chains, halting a moving chariot, and hurling a massive wooden drum.

Ferrigno maintained his flexibility and coordination while sculpting bulk and physique through daily ninety-minute workouts. The roaring, shape-shifting Hulk recurred in Remote Control Man in *Amazing Stories* (1985) and the teleplays *The Incredible Hulk: Death in the Family* (1977), *The Bride of the Incredible Hulk* (1979), *The Incredible Hulk Returns* (1988), *The Trial of the Incredible Hulk* (1989), and *The Death of the Incredible Hulk* (1990). In the same era, he studied blade fighting under the master who had trained Errol Flynn and Tyrone Power. The bodybuilder played Han in the Italian film *The Seven Magnificent Gladiators* (1983) and depicted Zerak in *Desert Warrior* (1988). In the starring role in *Sinbad of the Seven Seas* (1989), the actor wielded a 4-foot sword.

Global Superstar

Ferrigno is not limited to the small screen or U.S. production companies. His stage roles in *Arsenic and Old Lace*, *Requiem for a Heavyweight*, and *Of Mice and Men* earned critical regard in Canada, Chicago, and Texas. Along with his parts in 20 feature films are leads in the series *All's Fair* (1976). From parts as Smitty in *Hangfire* (1991), Detective Extralarge in the Italy TV series *Yo Yo* (1991), and as Zwei Supertypen in the German TV production *Miami: Der Kleine mit der großen Klappe* (1991), he experimented with a drag part in *The Naked Truth* (1992), set during a beauty pageant. A year later, he played Ranger John Jones in *Frogtown II* and Cain in… *And God Spoke*, a spoof of the Hollywood bible epics of the 1950s. In addition to the pilot role of Captain America, he starred as Billy Thomas in the action flicks *Cage* (1989) and *Cage II: The Arena of Death* (1994), in which army veterans become adversaries and grapple in a steel cage. Ferrigno later named *Cage* his favorite film.

After a decade and a half of retirement, at 41, Ferrigno reclaimed his childhood dream by beefing up for the 1992 Mr. Olympia title, judged in Helsinki, Finland. In 1994 in the Olympia Masters finals, he snagged a second place before retiring at age 43 and recapturing the feat in the film *Stand Tall*. Television became his vehicle for continued guest appearances, advertisements for a Canadian insurance firm and for Longhorn Steakhouse, and telephoning fans for Hollywood Is Calling, a company offering personalized birthday messages. The satire *The Godson* (1998) reprised Ferrigno in comedy about mafia stereotypes; another send-up, *Frank McKlusky, C.I.* (2002), paired Ferrigno with Dolly Parton. He accepted a contract role in *The King of Queens* (2000–2007), in which he and Carla played sedate suburban neighbors of the main characters. He returned to his early persona in a cameo as a security supervisor in Ang Lee's movie adaptation of *Hulk* (2003). In place of a human monster, Universal Studios replaced tedious makeup with a computer-generated figure twice Lou's height and weighing half a ton.

Varied Venues

Ferrigno's active life involves him in varied media creations and the marketing of a stamina drink called California Protein, fitness equipment, brochures on bulking up specific muscle groups, as well as posters, T-shirts, and training videos by Carla and Shanna

Ferrigno. He took pride in the success of Lou, Jr., a linebacker for the University of Southern California Trojans, and exulted in Shanna's stardom in E! reality TV series, *Filthy Rich: Cattle Drive* (2005). For a quarter century, Lou served as personal trainer to such celebrities as Michael Jackson, Chuck Norris, and Mickey Rourke. The bodybuilder compiled photos and text for *Lou Ferrigno's Guide to Personal Power, Bodybuilding and Fitness for Everyone* (1996), an inspirational handbook to would-be contenders and a glimpse into father-son antipathies in Lou's childhood. His role as Slave Master in the TV series *Black Scorpion* (2001) followed roles in *The Misery Brothers* (1995) and *Conan* (1998) and a part as a dogcatcher in the movie *Ping* (2000). He lost the part of Tigris of Gaul in the Roman epic drama *Gladiator* (2000) to Sven Ole Thorsen and took a lesser role in *From Heaven to Hell* (2002). Ferrigno cameoed in *Surge of Power* (2004), a camp flick based on the Hulk motif, and in the adventure comedy *Miss Cast Away and the Island Girls* (2004), a vehicle for Bob Denver and Pat Morita. Ferrigno provided a voice-over for the cartoon series *The Incredible Hulk* (2004) opposite actors Mark Hamill, Kathy Ireland, and Peter Strauss.

Nearing age 60, Ferrigno remains versatile in his creative outlets, including interviews for CNN, *Noonday*, and the BBC. He builds his fan base with motivational speeches, fundraising for the deaf, and the rereleases of his Hulk, Hercules, Sinbad, and iron-pumping images on DVD. For communications, he lip-reads and sometimes signs, a skill his family did not learn. His voice is the deaf-accented speech of someone who hears sounds but not words. Making the most of sound technology, he acquired a pair of Starkey digital hearing aids, the DaVinci PXP, which fit behind his ears and offer alternate programs for quiet and noisy settings. For watching DVDs, he uses a t-coil, which amplifies dialogue. For telephone conversations, his wireless Starkey Ear-Level Instrument projects calls directly into his ear devices.

Ferrigno still resides on 17th Street in Santa Monica, California, and continues to devote himself to good citizenship. After classroom and site training in first aid, CPR, weaponry, and high-speed driving, in summer 2005, he took oath as a reserve deputy of the Los Angeles County Sheriff's Department on February 13, 2006. His volunteer duties included recruitment of new officers and promotion of a youth league and a victims bureau aiding abused children. He chose a guest role on the ABC TV sitcom *My Wife and Kids* and promoted the Sit Up-Sit Down Home Gym and Sferoflex eyewear. Along with his self-published beefcake snapshots and DVDs, his autobiography, *My Incredible Life as the Hulk* (2003), provides photos and insight into his compensation for deafness by playing a Jekyll-and-Hyde fantasy caricature. Featuring his metamorphosis from calm, self-effacing adult to the wild-eyed shape-shifter and teeth-gritting green demon on the cover, the text applauds the actor's ability to transform reality to fantasy and to escape stress, emotional excess, and alcohol abuse by self-control and meditation. He summarized his philosophy in terms of self-image, "If you're out in the public, you want to give them the best attention you can. . . . To be a champion you must act like one, act like a champion. You must feel good about yourself" ("Lou," 1994).

Sources

"Ferrigno Achieved Superhero Dreams." *Herald* (Sharon, PA), October 7, 1999.

Ferrigno, Lou. *The Incredible Lou Ferrigno: His Story.* New York: Simon & Schuster, 1982.

Leamer, Laurence. *Fantastic: The Life of Arnold Schwarzenegger.* New York: St. Martin's Press, 2005.

"Lou Ferrigno: Interview." *Sports Psychology*, April 9, 1994.

"Lou Ferrigno." *Iron Age*, March 14, 2003.

"Lou Ferrigno—the Incredible Hulk—Discusses Hearing Loss and Hearing Aids." PR Newswire. Available at http://www.highbeam.com/doc/1G1-109651130.html (last accessed November 4, 2003).

Mills, David L. "Review: The Incredible Lou Ferrigno." *Library Journal* 107 (14) (August 1, 1982): 1476.

Suss, Elaine. *When Hearing Gets Hard.* New York: Bantam, 1993.

"Where Are They Now?" *Biography* (October 2003): 24.

■ Death of a Brother
Daniel Berrigan

A model of holy lawlessness, Daniel Joseph Berrigan follows the example of Philip Francis Berrigan (1923–2002), leader of a backlash against violence and social injustice against the poor. A literature teacher and proponent of the Catholic left, Philip preceded his elder brother's involvement in protesting the Vietnam War and the spread of nuclear weapons. Both were born to German-American parents of five brothers in Two Harbors, Minnesota— Daniel on May 9, 1921, and Philip on October 5, 1923. During World War II, Philip served as a sharpshooter and was a hero at the battle of Bulge. He entered the Josephite brotherhood in 1955 under the influence of Dorothy Day, founder of the Catholic Worker Movement, which operated soup kitchens, hospices, and drug and vocational counseling centers for some 1,200 transients. Setting an example of succoring the urban poor during the civil rights movement, he became a prominent protester at freedom rides, transportation boycotts, black voter registrations in the Deep South, and lunch counter sit-ins. Philip's civil disobedience netted him 11 years of active cell time for over 100 illegal acts on behalf of human rights.

A pacifist poet, playwright, and theology teacher at LeMoyne College, Daniel Berrigan entered the priesthood in 1952 and trained at the Jesuit seminary in Poughkeepsie, New York, and at the Gregorian Institute in Rome. While traveling through France, he absorbed the energy and direction of the worker-priest movement, a parallel to Philip's example in North America. Daniel was as yet uncommitted to demonstrations, but his moral poetry and essays appeared in *The Atlantic*, *Catholic Worker*, *Commonweal*, *Poetry*, and *Saturday Review*. After abandoning his self-effacing personal style, he emulated his activist brother, the first American priest to be arrested for civil disobedience. In tandem, the Berrigan brothers launched the "lamb's war" by voicing outrage at American materialism and apathy toward the underclass. In the late 1960s, Daniel joined Philip at a civil rights march against bigotry in Selma, Alabama, and collaborated with Trappist monk and theologian Thomas Merton in denouncing militarism in southeast Asia, a conflict similar to the genocide under Hitler's Third Reich.

Following Philip's Example

At age 42, Daniel used a clerical sabbatical as an opportunity to combat the installation of Cold War weaponry in Bulgaria and Czechoslovakia. In December 1966, he flaunted antiwar posters outside the homes of Secretary of State Dean Rusk and of Secretary of Defense Robert McNamara, whom Daniel had debated in 1965 and demeaned by calling him as bigoted as a Selma sheriff. On the following October 21 at a protest rally of 10,000 at the Pentagon in Arlington, Virginia, Daniel targeted American defense by mocking the cowardice of Attorney General Ramsey Clark, who peered down from an upstairs window. After Daniel's arrest for failure to disperse, he went on a hunger strike. For outraging the Catholic hierarchy in the archdiocese of New York, he earned a private scolding for breaching vows of humility and obedience and served a five-month penance in ten Latin American countries, ostensibly on a journalistic fact-finding mission. Supporters picketed the office of Francis Cardinal Spellman; the laity and priests published a demand for Daniel's recall in the *New York Times*.

In defiance of the U.S. State Department and the FBI, in late January during the 1968 Têt holiday, Daniel joined war hero Howard Zinn, a history teacher at Boston University, in a peace mission to enemy headquarters in Hanoi. By liberating three U.S. fliers—air force Captain Jon D. Black, navy Ensign David P. Matheny, and air force Major Norris M. Overly—from North Vietnamese prisons, the crusaders intended to acquire Matheny's memorized roster of 70 cellmates. In early February, the mission succeeded at freeing the men. Daniel chronicled the effort in *Night Flight to Hanoi* (1968), a primary literary document of the Vietnam War.

Activism at a Price

That spring, Daniel resided in the 98th Street Jesuit community in Manhattan and joined the staff of Cornell University. Philip urged him to adopt radical policies to stem denuding of Vietnamese jungles and the burning of peasant villages with napalm. On May 17, 1968, the Berrigans along with two women and five men formed the Catonsville Nine in a foray in the parking lot of a draft board in Catonsville, Maryland. With homemade napalm, a gelled form of gasoline, they heaped 378 files into two mesh wastebaskets and lit the papers. The conflagration drew the media, who publicized Daniel's charge that Christians and Jews condoned with their apathy American atrocities against southeast Asians.

Philip, who had a longer record of lawlessness, netted a 6-year sentence, twice that of his elder brother. Before entering cells, in spring 1970, the duo became "fugitives from injustice" by eluding federal officials. Daniel belittled FBI agents and U.S. marshals by ducking in and out of public protests, where he delivered harangues and rallied critics of the military. G-men nabbed Philip in Manhattan in April 1970 in a closet at St. Gregory the Great Roman Catholic Church and padded charges against him with warrants for plotting to sabotage government heating systems in Washington, D.C., and to capture National Security Adviser Henry Kissinger. After slipping past federal officers by joining a puppet troupe, Daniel remained at large until August, when agents seized him at the residence of attorney William Stringfellow on Block Island, Rhode Island, and transported him to a low-security lockup in Danbury, Connecticut. From his cell, he made use of idle time and spiritual influence by enlisting New York advertiser Mitch Snyder in interceding on behalf of urban street wanderers. In a busy chapter in his activism, Daniel honored his brother's spirited draft board raid in an Obie-winning free-verse play, *The Trial of the Catonsville Nine*, the source of a Hollywood film featuring Douglass Watson and Ed Flanders as Philip and Daniel Berrigan.

A Controversial Example

Daniel remained loyal to his brother's example of Christian advocacy for justice and against doomsday warfare. In France in 1972, Daniel held a peace conference with Buddhist dissident Thich Nhat Hanh, a Vietnamese exile. The next year, Philip and his wife, Elizabeth "Liz" McAlister Berrigan, a former nun, accepted excommunication for their marriage, which violated priestly celibacy. Daniel stepped up his involvement by issuing a public denunciation in the *New York Times* of prisoner maltreatment in Vietnam. In all, 78 pacifists signed the document, including radical folk singer Joan Baez.

Nearing age 60, on September 9, 1980, Daniel worked at an AIDS hospice in Manhattan. He supported Philip's organization of two women and four men into the Plowshares Eight, an antinuclear disarmament effort dubbed the "Silo Pruning Hooks." By breaching security at a test lab of the Mark 12A first-strike multiple warhead for Minuteman III missiles in Hangar 101 at the General Electric Nuclear Missile Re-entry Division in King of Prussia, Pennsylvania, they doused war files with a symbolic baptism in the activists' blood. The eight created additional havoc by hammering the nose cones and wings of two B-52 nuclear bombers waiting for shipment to Amarillo, Texas. Their sabotage complete, they prayed the Lord's Prayer and discussed Revelation 9:16, a prediction of world's end. Armed guards apprehended them and forced their faces into mud.

The Berrigans in Jail

During incarceration for felony trespass and destruction of property, the Berrigans and their six abettors lifted the spirits of cellmates and guards. While painting Christmas scenes, they sang carols and spirituals that drew others into the holiday mood. They remained behind bars until sentencing and parole in April 10, 1990, when a retired judge wearied of the ongoing legal farce. On gaining his freedom, Philip set the example of blatant pacifist lawlessness on March 31, 1991, by disarming the USS *Gettysburg*, a guided missile cruiser berthed at Bath, Maine. Meanwhile, shortly before the Persian Gulf War erupted on August 2, 1990, Daniel applauded a New York flag burning in Times Square and charged the government with fomenting violence to control oilfields. In 1992, Daniel veered to the antiabortion movement by courting arrest with lesbian activist Donna Marie Kearney during demonstrations at the Planned Parenthood headquarters in Rochester, New York.

At Seymour Johnson Air Force Base in Goldsboro, North Carolina, on December 7, 1993, Philip upped his public image by pouring blood in the air intakes of two F-14 nuclear-capable Strike Eagle fighter-bombers. The trespass escalated to battering equipment with ball-peen hammers, a crime that sent Philip to the Chowan County jail at Edenton for 4 months. An unrepentant radical, on February 12, 1997, he led the Plowshares to the USS *The Sullivans*, an Aegis destroyer, in Bath, Maine, for additional mayhem involving splashed blood and swinging hammers against nuclear missiles. By October 27, 1997, he faced 24 months in a cell at Petersburg, Virginia. Upon early release on November 20, 1998, he rallied 1,000 pacifists at the School of the Americas, a notorious spy and terrorist academy at Fort Benning, Georgia.

Philip continued setting the pace by directing the strike force against the arms race in over 80 pacifist, pro-life forays in Australia, Europe, and the United States. On December 20, 1999, the group marred and disarmed Gatling guns on A-10 Warthogs at the Warfield Air National Guard Base in Middle River, Maryland. For trespass and sabotage, Philip netted $2\frac{1}{2}$ years at Roxbury Correctional Institution in Hagerstown, Maryland. In the interim, Daniel counseled Philip's family, who feared that he would die in prison. Weakened by kidney and liver cancer, Philip died in Baltimore at age 79. At his funeral, Daniel delivered the homily.

Daniel Alone

In a reflection on his famous brother, "Father Dan" joked with an interviewer on the biblical blessing on holy extremists like Nelson Mandela, Martin Luther King, and Cesar Chávez. Daniel rejected a similar celebrity, but he declared himself committed to doing good works—harangues, leadership retreats, protests, interventions—without concern for the penalties. In June 2000, while recovering from spinal surgery at a Jesuit community in New York City, he lashed out at the jailing of freedom fighters by fools, bigots, and charlatans, all unaccountable for the powers they wield. In retrospect, he thought of Philip as a lifeline, a dependable source of rescue who defied the stereotype of the sententious, do-nothing cleric. Daniel revered his brother as a bearer of hope and perpetuated Philip's radical campaign against American soullessness, hypocrisy, arrogance, and imperialism. Daniel marveled at his idol's willingness to batter the national powers and to risk repeated imprisonments for the sake of justice. To publicize Philip's stalwart activism, Daniel included in his prison verse "My Brother's Battered Bible," which exalts Philip's piety and devotion to scripture.

An unreformed holy desperado, Daniel vilified the social and economic disorder that continued to erupt from the Reagan administration's meddling in the workings of Central American governments. In a jeremiad ringing with Old Testament gravity, Daniel predicted that the world would continue its moral decline. He described the 9/11 attack on the Pentagon and the World Trade Center as "Babylon remembered," a deserved comeuppance for wanton ruin in other lands. Instead of sharing the humanity of others on the forefront of terrorism, he remarked, the United States has set out to "obliterate an enemy we can't find" (Cipolla, 2006, 6). In 2002, he joined notable activists in a symposium, Vigil for Peaceful Tomorrows, and warned his disciples of "a very rough time, very twilight time" for world leadership (Sullivan and Boehrer, 2002, 56). He promoted the Plowshares action in Shannon, Ireland, in 2003, when protesters poured blood and clobbered a troop carrier as it was secretly refueled before advancing to Iraq.

Devotion to Nonviolence

Without Philip's bold strategizing, Daniel continued his cerebral approach to combating civil rights violations against the poor and publicizing U.S. breaches of nuclear arms agreements. Still a controversial figure shunned and alienated by Catholics for his outspoken pacifism, he surveyed the field of young Jesuits and encouraged their education in humanism. He applied ethical clout to protests of indiscriminate worldwide killing and of military budgets wasted on conflict in Grenada, Nicaragua, the Persian Gulf, and Kosovo and the advance of U.S. military in Afghanistan in 2001 and into Baghdad. He blamed the media for exalting the worst models of vapid celebrity, greed, chicanery, and vengeance. In 2002, he opposed the normalization of imprisoning more Americans and the simulated bombing of Iraq at the SS *Intrepid*, a ship turned into a war museum in New York. With his signature clarity, he mused, "There's a big room. You go in there in the dark and you're alone and you bomb Iraq. That's the way we're starting kids out" (Sullivan and Boehrer, 2002, 53). He organized resistance to federal funding of the *Intrepid*, which he impugned as a model of war idolatry.

Still feisty at age 83, Daniel regretted the burgeoning of "irresponsibility, naked power, high-level duplicity" by leaders intent on running the world (Kozlowski, 2004, 15). He charged President George W. Bush with justifying world slaughter as an element of empire building. In 2006, he repudiated the concept of a just war and challenged blind U.S. support for Israel as "all the wrong moves on the part of a superpower to guarantee its own demise" (Cipolla, 2006, 6). He supported the resistance of First Lieutenant Ehren K. Watada to deployment from Fort Lewis, Washington, to Iraq. On March 2, 2007, Daniel promoted a desert campaign at a nuclear test site in Indian Springs, Nevada, and called for the abolition of nuclear weapons. Days later, he celebrated Lent by encouraging peacemakers at a vigil at Lockheed outside Martin, Pennsylvania. Accolades from Pacem in Terris, Pax Christi, and the War Resisters League and the Thomas Merton Award and Vasyl Stus Award acknowledge his one-man lawbreaking for peace.

Sources

Cipolla, Benedicta. "Pacifism Is a Way of Living, Not a Tactic, Says Berrigan." *National Catholic Reporter* 42 (39) (September 8, 2006): 6.

Kozlowski, Carl. "Q&A Daniel Berrigan." *Progressive* 68 (3) (March 2004): 15.

Miller, Richard Brian. *Interpretations of Conflict*. Chicago: University of Chicago Press, 1991.

Polner, Murray, and Jim O'Grady. *Disarmed and Dangerous: The Radical Lives and Times of Daniel and Philip Berrigan*. Boulder, CO: Westview Press, 1997.

Sullivan, Dennis, and Fred Boehrer. "The Practice of Nonviolence in the Contemporary World." *Contemporary Justice Review* 5 (1) (2002): 53–61.

Welch, Michael R. *Flag Burning: Moral Panic and the Criminalization of Protest*. Edison, NJ: Aldine Transaction, 2000.

■ Death Threat
Salman Rushdie

A literary powerhouse on three continents, eclectic essayist, fabulist, and novelist Sir Ahmed Salman Rushdie survived a Muslim death threat. Born the oldest and only male of four children in Bombay, India, on June 19, 1947, he developed a scholarly outlook from his parents, teacher Negin Butt and Maulvi Anis Ahmed Rushdie, a Cambridge-educated attorney and businessman from Delhi. Reared at Solan in a two-story bungalow among Shia Muslims in the tradition of the Indian diaspora, he enjoyed a serene childhood in view of the Indian Ocean and studied drawing and sculpture. In a bilingual environment, he learned English but admired Urdu and Hindi storytelling for their natural tendency toward metaphor. Although his grandfather was an Urdu poet, his parents disapproved of writing as a career. He acquired a liberal attitude toward religion and admired the Sufis, energetic mystics who seek oneness with the divine through whirling and dance. For English reading, he preferred Charles Dickens, Laurence Sterne, and translations of Gogol. He completed a liberal education at the Cathedral and John Connon School, a mission school staffed by English and Scottish teachers.

At 14, Rushdie left India for the first time to enter Rugby School in Warwickshire, where he flourished at debate. White boys persecuted him. He recalled, "People would go into my room and tear up my essays or write slogans on the wall. I found it odd because I had never thought of myself as foreign before" (Rushdie, 2000, 32). He suffered depression and homesickness for Bombay, where he spent vacations. In 1964, his parents moved to Karachi, Pakistan, a city he found eerily repressive because of Islamic gender segregation. Under pressure from his father, on scholarship, he completed a history degree at King's College, Cambridge, Anis Rushdie's alma mater. Among older males, Rushdie's light complexion and British accent protected him from the racism he dodged at Rugby.

Rushdie learned early the power of fundamentalist fanaticism while he lived in Pakistan with his parents. For a time, he toyed with the notion of becoming an actor, a profession he admired from campus productions at Rugby and Cambridge. While producing material for a government television station, he wearied of religious control after censors removed the word "pork" from a text. The final break with the Islamic Pakistan resulted from censorship of an article he wrote for a magazine. He immigrated to England. For a decade, he wrote advertising copy part time for Ayer Barker and for Ogilvy & Mather. In his free time, in 1971, he composed a first novel that was never published. He jettisoned the sham of commercialism and initiated a writing career. Influencing his style were cross-cultural readings in Jorge Luis Borges, Italo Calvino, Lewis Carroll, Günter Grass, and James Joyce.

Writing Allegory

The author raised no critical stir with his sci-fi allegory *Grimus* (1975), which he set on an imaginary island. The next year, he wed Clarissa Luard, and they raised their son Zafar Rushdie at a comfortable London residence in Tufnell Park. The magical realism of his second opus, the comic epic *Midnight's Children* (1981), gripped reader attention for its allegorical depiction of India's escape from the British Raj on August 15, 1947. The postcolonial novel won a Booker McConnell Prize and listing among *Time* magazine's 100 best English-language novels. He influenced beginning Indian authors seeking a voice in the English language market yet found his own work speed of four pages per day halved by interviews and the claptrap of celebrity. In 1982, he deepened his criticism of bigotry, immigrant bashing, and nonwhite immigrant stereotyping in the essay "The New Empire within Britain," a bold charge against snooty Anglo-Saxons.

Rushdie next published *Shame* (1983), historical fiction surveying political leader and Pakistan president Zulfikar Ali Bhutto and General Muhammad Zia-ul-Haq, who unseated Bhutto in the July 5, 1997, coup. The novel won France's Prix du Meilleur Livre Étranger (Best Foreign Book) and short-listing for a second Booker Prize. He returned to Bombay to script the documentary *In Search of Midnight's Children* for British television. In response to an enlightening tour of Nicaragua under the sponsorship of the Sandinista regime, Rushdie composed *The Jaguar Smile: A Nicaraguan Journey* (1987). The ironic political travelogue exposed both in-country censorship and the CIA for supporting the rebel contras who destabilized the Nicaraguan government and economy. Following a divorce, on January 28, 1988, he wed novelist and photographer Marianne Wiggins of Lancaster, Pennsylvania.

Censorship and Terrorism

Rushdie attained global sympathy in September 1988 after publishing *The Satanic Verses: A Novel*, a controversial dreamscape novel accused of ridiculing the prophet Muhammad through the fictional character Mahound, the messenger of Mecca. The text developed an ambiguous apocryphal writing later expunged from the Koran for being devil inspired. According to Islamic Hadith (tradition), Muhammad, under the influence of Allah's messenger, the Archangel Gibreel or Gabriel, authored additional suras (scriptural verses) for the Koran about three female divines beings, Allat, Manah, and Uzzah. Muslim communities disseminated photocopies of offensive passages and bridled at the irreverence to the prophet and his wives. Religious extremists banned the book, bombed bookshops, and hosted public bonfires to destroy copies. On February 14, 1989, Rushdie and his wife learned from a

BBC news reporter that the Ayatollah Ruhollah Khomeini, Iran's spiritual tyrant and Shia scholar, wanted the novelist executed. Khomeini delivered over Radio Tehran a fatwa (religious decree) calling for the execution of Rushdie and his publishers, Viking Penguin, for blasphemy.

Global repercussion rippled out from the edict. At home, the couple locked doors and shuttered windows, but the author ventured out to a scheduled interview with a CBS TV morning show. On his return, he found 75 film crews clustered around his door. He camped out at his agent's office and then attended the funeral of fellow writer Bruce Chatwin, where reporters and photographers trailed him. A friend rescued Rushdie and his wife and whisked them away in a BBC limousine. For privacy, Marianne rented an apartment close to home. In a riposte to pious Muslims, Rushdie stated, "I see this as an innocent book, wrongly accused and much persecuted" (Rushdie, 2000, 130). Westernized Muslim intellectuals concurred with the author and petitioned Khomeini to rescind the fatwa.

Frenzy threatened public chaos. In London, cries of "Kill Rushdie" echoed from 30,000 Muslims processing outside Parliament. Rival author John Le Carré chided Rushdie for thinking that Islam should be as open-minded about critical satire as Christianity; Naguib Mahfouz labeled Rushdie an intellectual terrorist. Echoes of disapproval rose from British rabbi Sir Immanuel Jakobovits, former President Jimmy Carter, and Cardinal John O'Connor in New York. The press battered the novelist as an arrogant opportunist and renegade. Muslim countries experienced spontaneous rioting that killed six and injured a hundred. The Lebanese Organisation of the Mujahidin (divine soldiers) of Islam denounced Rushdie as an apostate. The $4 million bounty on the author's head lured headsmen to pursue him. Even translators of the work faced assassins—one assailant stabbed Hitoshi Igarashi to death; other stalkers injured translator Ettore Capriolo and publisher William Nygaard of Norway. Under protection of Scotland Yard's Special Branch, provided by Prime Minister Margaret Thatcher, Rushdie retreated from the public to shield his household. Fellow authors—Paul Theroux and Tom Stoppard—rallied to his cause. On March 7, 1989, the United Kingdom expressed outrage for the manhunt by breaking diplomatic ties with Iran.

Unsought World Renown

Under the fatwa, Rushdie lived on the run and restricted human communication to telephone calls. In exile, he gave up driving and cinema, one of his prized pleasures. Surrounded by watchmen with guns, he retreated to television and videos. He repined, "What I miss is ordinary life: walking down the street, browsing in a bookshop, going to a grocery store, going to a movie" (Rushdie, 2000, 127). Religious authorities reissued the edict annually on its anniversary. In seclusion, he combed the offending novel for overt insult to people of faith. His marriage foundered. He concealed his residence and met officials at undisclosed locations. When he appeared in public, bodyguards surrounded him. At a meeting in Toronto, the Canadian government dispatched their high echelon corps of the Royal Canadian Mounted Police. Scholars and bibliophiles attending his reading at the University of Toronto waved photo identification to pass through security.

The confrontation between the novelist and Islam dominated headlines. On August 3, 1989, the premature explosion of a book packed with RDX explosives demolished two floors of a Paddington hotel and killed Mustafa Mahmoud Mazeh, an operative of the Hezbollah paramilitary, without harming the author. Iranian fanatics declared Mazeh a martyr to Islamic ideals and enshrined him in central Tehran at the Behesht-e Zahra graveyard.

Publishers Weekly advised Viking Penguin to shelve plans to produce *The Satanic Verses* in paperback to circumvent more radical violence. The Media Coalition, proponents of free speech, viewed the halting of a paperback version as appeasement to enemies of civil liberty. Rushdie saw both sides of the issue—the unnecessary endangerment of the publisher and booksellers and the need for a paperback copy for use by students, teachers, historians, and researchers. In 1990, a filmmaker Jan Mohammad depicted Rushdie in the movie *International Gorillay* as an enemy of Muslim Pakistanis and a victim of Allah's holy lightning bolts. Rushdie, in the interest of normalizing international relations with Muslims, insisted that the British Board of Film Classification not ban the movie.

While in hiding away from his son Zafar, the author wrote for him the children's allegory *Haroun and the Sea of Stories* (1990), an encomium to storytelling as a builder of character. He met Islamic scholars on December 24, 1990, and achieved a consensus that *The Satanic Verses* exhibited no insidious motives. Days later, the scholars reneged their reconciliation and mouthed the official demonization of Rushdie. Surrounded by the New York City Police Department bomb squad, police dogs, and plainclothesmen, on December 11, 1991, he addressed the Columbia University School of Journalism about his life in a leaking hot air balloon, a bulletproof bubble in which he felt both exposed and concealed. He summarized his quandary with wit: "A man may become the bubble that encases him, and then one day— pop!—he's gone forever" (Rushdie, 1997, 770). He denounced the politically motivated death edict as a breach of international law. To relieve isolation, he made a show of giving up atheism and becoming a sincere Muslim "to show to the people who viewed . . . [him] as some kind of terrible enemy that . . . [he] wasn't one" (Gonzalez, 2004, 137). The devout had no faith in his sudden conversion. He gave up the pose because it cloaked his true persona and suppressed his creative output. A decade after the death warrant, on September 24, 1998, British ambassadors negotiated a new accord with Iran. A moderate authority, Mohammad Khatami, withdrew support for the fatwa. At this point in a decade of false alarms, Rushdie abandoned his hermitism.

After the "Verses"

As Rushdie's titles began updating college and university reading lists, his later writing deviated little from its original focus on international and intercultural relations. In *The Moor's Last Sigh* (1995), he examined religious, ethnic, and business plurality in Iberia through the eyes of Moraes Zogoiby, scion of Boabdil, Granada's last Moorish sultan. On August 28, 1997, Rushdie married Elizabeth West, mother of their son Milan Rushdie. He took time to have eye surgery for ptosis, a weakening of the tendons that made his eyelids droop. Four years later, the author completed a mystical novel, *The Ground Beneath Her Feet* (1999), a study of rock music that he began in longhand in 1991 in amorphous notes. The text opens with a metaphoric earthquake on Valentine's Day, 1989, and develops the rivalry of two men for Vina Apsara, a character drawn from an Indian myth.

A respite from Muslim hitmen made Rushdie feel like a cowboy stereotype. He reported to Anthony Wilson Smith of *Maclean's* magazine a sense of being: "[T]he aging gunslinger sipping bourbon in a saloon. Even if you mind your business, some kid will always come after you to take you down" (Smith, 1999). In 2005, he received the Hatch Crossword Fiction Award and short-listing for an International IMPAC Dublin Literary Award and a Whitbread Book Award for the fictional panorama *Shalimar the Clown*, a jihadist who kills the former U.S. ambassador to India. Following the Ayatollah Ali Khamenei's revival of the death decree, he commissioned the Islamic Revolutionary Guards to carry it out. Rushdie defied censorship in an essay anthology, *Free Expression Is No Offence* (2005), and stated publicly his denunciation of female veiling.

Rushdie defended artists beset worldwide by censors and oppressors. On May 12, 2006, he guest-hosted *The Charlie Rose Show*, on which he questioned Canadian movie mogul Deepa Mehta about her experience with religious fanatics criticizing her film *Water* (2005). In mid-August 2005, the *Times* (London) and the *Washington Times* printed his speech calling for a Muslim Reformation retrieving the faith from medievalism and intolerance. At a reading before the Harvard Humanist Chaplaincy in Cambridge, Massachusetts, in October 2006, he declared himself a humanist. His honors range from a Booker of Bookers citation, James Tait Black Memorial Prize, and English-Speaking Union Award to Knight Bachelorhood on June 16, 2007, during Queen Elizabeth II's birthday celebration. From outside the United Kingdom, he received the European Union's Aristeion Prize for Literature, fellowship of the Royal Society of Literature and Commandeur des Arts et des Lettres, a Premio Grinzane Cavour, presidency of the PEN American Center, Sweden's Kurt Tucholsky Prize, Switzerland's Prix Colette, Austria's State Prize for Literature, and Writer of the Year Award in Germany. British acknowledgement stirred protests in Iran, Malaysia, and Pakistan and renewed assassination threats from fanatic Islamists, notably, al-Qaida deputy Ayman al-Zawahiri. Rushdie continued his post as distinguished writer in residence at Emory University in Atlanta, Georgia, to which the author bestowed his archive.

Sources

Gonzalez, Madelena. *Fiction after the Fatwa: Salman Rushdie and the Charm of Catastrophe.* Amsterdam: Rodopi, 2004.

Luyat, Anne, and Francine Tolron. *Flight from Certainty: The Dilemma of Identity and Exile.* Amsterdam: Rodopi, 2001.

Reder, Michael R., ed. *Conversations with Salman Rushdie.* Jackson, MS: University Press of Mississippi, 2000.

Rushdie, Salman. "Author Salman Rushdie Cries Out from a Life 'Trapped inside a Metaphor.'" In *Lend Me Your Ears: Great Speeches in History*, ed. by William Safire. New York: W. W. Norton & Co., 1997.

Smith, Anthony Wilson. "Salman Rushdie." *Maclean's* 375 (2) (May 24, 1999).

■ Dyslexia
Henry Winkler

Actor Henry Franklin Winkler escaped the low self-esteem from learning disabilities to become a media star. His multilingual parents, German Jews Harry Irving and Ilse Anna Maria Winkler, escaped Nazi persecution in 1939 and immigrated to New York. Their parents died in the Holocaust. Henry was born without grandparents on October 30, 1945, in Manhattan, New York, where his parents headed an international lumber firm. He and older sister Beatrice came of age in 2 environments—urban New York City and a country home on Lake Mahopac near Carmel, New York. In retrospect, he recalled feeling like a dope because his educated parents did math in their head. He accused them of failing to listen to him and of ridiculing him as *"stummer hund"* (dumb hound) (Winkler, 2008). In kindergarten at Hilltop

Nursery School, he appeared in a play on hygiene as a tube of toothpaste. By age 7, he knew he could excel at acting. A year later, he marveled at Jimmy Stewart's control in the Alfred Hitchcock classic thriller *Rear Window*.

The diagnosis of dyslexia came too late to prevent severe blows to Winkler's confidence. Under fourth grade teacher Mrs. Adolf at P.S. 87, he struggled to understand academics and vowed to do a better job at fostering his own children. He knew that he had valid ideas, but his eyes refused to track a line of reading without skipping words. His math skills were so low that he couldn't count change or envision an isosceles triangle. Spelling was out of the question. He recalled the boyhood miseries of a drooping self-image: "For a long time it was around my ankles and I spent a lot of time pulling it up" (Winkler, 1989). While classmates scribbled marginalia in their books and applied to Princeton, he pictured a life of day labor in the family wood business. At a private college prep academy, McBurney School for Boys, the headmaster, who was also the drama coach, predicted that Winkler was not suited for theater. Advice from a psychiatrist worsened frustration. To focus more thoroughly on studies, Winkler bought blue and yellow highlighters from a stationery store and defeated the purpose by marking every word in his textbooks. The result was worse confusion and despair that he might have brain damage.

A Way Out of Ignominy

Taking cues from the real world, Winkler compensated by learning problem solving. By eighth grade, he nourished a dream of acting on stage after playing the title role of Herman Melville's novella *Billy Budd*. Graduating third from the bottom from McBurney, he moved on to Emerson College in Boston. The Winklers agreed he could participate in campus dramas if he enrolled in something more practical. He didn't pass required geometry until the fourth try. He dickered between a stage career and rescuing the vulnerable as a child psychologist. In 1970, on his father's advice, he earned an M.F.A. from the Yale School of Drama and performed with the Yale Repertory Theater and at the Manhattan Theatre Club, Cubiculo, and St. Clement's Church. Agent Tina Jacobson helped land his first 30 jobs in TV ads and as a guest on *The Mary Tyler Moore Show* and *The Bob Newhart Show*. At age 28, he moved to Hollywood and allotted himself 1 month to click with the film world. He made his cinema debut as a Brooklyn gang member opposite Sylvester Stallone as Butchey Weinstein in *The Lords of Flatbush* (1974). Winkler was so pleased with the reviews that he posted copies to his high school principal.

The hoodlum-in-boots part morphed into Winkler's signature persona as Arthur Herbert "Fonzie" Fonzarelli in the ABC TV series *Happy Days*, a spin-off of *Love, American Style*. The part earned Winkler two Golden Globes, three Emmy nominations, and a star on the Walk of Fame outside Pantages Theater on Hollywood Boulevard. A lovable high school dropout, motorcyclist, and Italian-American greaser, the Fonz didn't smoke, never chewed gum, but scored with bimbo girlfriends. His street tough attitude emerged from the New York Italians whom Winkler knew and feared in his teens. In the first episode, which aired on January 15, 1974 and opened with the familiar "Rock Around the Clock" theme song by Bill Haley and the Comets, the Fonz admired his TV persona in the mirror and modeled the hip voice on that of Sylvester Stallone.

The bike-loving clown, the owner of Bronco's Garage, at first parked his motorcycle at Arnold's Drive-In but had limited interaction with squeaky clean teens played by Ron Howard and Erin Moran and with three adults, Mr. and Mrs. Cunningham and Arnold, played by actor Pat Morita. Winkler injected into the tough guy facade the fiercely loyal friend who acted on his principles to protect more vulnerable teens. His character performed engagingly with cousin Charles "Chachi" Arcola, with girlfriend Pinky Tuscadero, and with Moran's character, Joanie Cunningham, whom he called "Shortcake." From a professional standpoint, Winkler glimpsed each episode as a one-act play and spruced his performance with intuition: "It's all about timing and trusting your instinct" (Ramuno, Winkler, and Belli, 2004, 10). His advice to others trying to shape so distinct a character was a matter of internalization: "Take what's there and make it you" (Ibid, 11).

The Fonz's Rise to Fame

Viewer demand rose to 50,000 fan letters per week and moved Fonzie to a pervasive presence, billed third in the credits. Actor Suzi Quatro, as Leather Tuscadero, composed and performed "Do the Fonzie" for one episode. In 1980, the Smithsonian Institution ex- hibited the Fonz's black leather jacket as an emblem of television sitcoms. On the set, no other actor dared try on the sacred token. Only the series mom, Marion "Mrs. C" Kelp Cun- ningham, played by Marion Ross, was allowed to call the Fonz "Arthur." In one episode, she pulled him into a tango. For a stunt, she kissed him on the mouth in front of a live audience. In 1983, the entire cast appeared in a parade before 100,000 in Milwakuee, Wisconsin.

The network considered renaming the series *Fonzie's Happy Days* but retained the title to keep Ron Howard from leaving the cast. Astute and articulate, Winkler played up gesture with sidelong looks, double takes, struts, and flicks of the eyebrows. He wrote Fonzie's lines from the gut and applied university training to the dialogue: "Comedy is very serious. If you act as if it's funny you blow the timing, you blow the elegance, you blow the comedy" (Kubey, 331). In scanty dialogue, he popularized the broad-faced "Aaaay!" and "Whoooa!," the term "nerd" for the uncool, and his smart-mouth parting shot, "Sit on it." With Howard and other cast, the Fonz joined in a group sing of "Blueberry Hill," a tribute to the 1950s' great Fats Domino. In 2005, the cast regrouped for a 30th anniversary reunion. Winkler learned from American prisoner of war Terry Anderson that hostages in Lebanon relaxed with security guards by watching reruns of *Happy Days*.

Fully engaged in a team effort, Winkler came to think of Paramount Studios as home, the cast and crew as a second family, and Ron Howard as a brother. Winkler made home movies of interaction on the set. With coaching from Howard on how to pitch, Winkler joined the Cunningham Hardware team for entertainment league softball at Dodger Sta- dium, Shea, and Wrigley Field, where fans yelled "Fonzie! Fonzie!" When the company toured Germany and Okinawa by a Black Hawk helicopter, he enjoyed USO baseball games with American soldiers. From 1974 to 1984, his leather jacket and thumbs-up exuber- ance impacted family entertainment history with a character that smashed the stereotype of streetwise belligerence. His face and finger-snapping pose cropped up on posters, lunch- boxes, and T-shirts. During his stardom as the Fonz, he rewarded himself with a BMW and, at age 33, escaped the emotional baggage that dragged him down from childhood. Erasing the stigma of his youth, one episode pictured Fonzie applying for a library card. The on-air salute to reading raised library enrollments nationwide to five times their nor- mal numbers; other episodes revealed that the Fonz earned a GED in night school, bought into Arnold's drive-in, and taught classes and counseled students as dean of boys at George S. Patton Vocational School. An ABC TV special, *Henry Winkler Meets William Shakespeare*

(1974) allowed the actor to turn Fonzie's appeal into a validation of English drama. In a *TV Guide* listing of the all-time greatest characters, the Fonz won fourth place.

A Professional Actor

Winkler patterned his career on the European system, under which actors are professionals rather than megastars. During the last 3 years of *Happy Days*, he opted for less salary and an investment in profits. While taping narrative for the documentary *Everybody Has a Song* (1976), Winkler found the name of his affliction: "It started to dawn on me. I'm not lazy. I'm not stupid. I'm dyslexic" (Winkler, 1989). He discovered that learning disabilities can be either genetic or generated by infection. He identified as the best teacher for an at-risk student the one who introduces the slow learner to internal strengths. He found movie roles in *Heroes* (1977), *The One and Only* (1978), *Ebenezer Scrooge in An American Christmas Carol* (1979), and *Night Shift* (1982), for which director Ron Howard drew quality performances from Winkler and Michael Keaton. On May 5, 1978, Winkler wed his publicist, child welfare advocate Stacey Weitzman, and settled in Los Angeles and made a family with her 6-year-old son Jed and their two birth children, Emily and Max. The actor began looking at the media from the aspect of parenting and presented quality programs to vulnerable children. One spin-off, *Fonz and the Happy Days Gang* (1980–1981), featuring the Fonz's dog Cupcake, offered animated fare on Saturday mornings.

To broaden his appeal, Winkler moved on from adolescent roles by turning down the part of Danny in the hit musical *Grease* (1978). At age 40, he ventured behind the camera to produce *Dead Man's Gun* (1997–1999), *Mr. Sunshine* (1986), *First Response* (1999), and the Disney drama *So Weird* (1998). He directed a winner, *MacGyver* (1985–1992) as well as *Memories of Me* (1988), starring Billy Crystal; *Cop and a Half* (1993), featuring Burt Reynolds; and *Sabrina, the Teenage Witch* (1996). He provided the voiceover for the biker Ramrod in a 1989 episode of *The Simpsons* and depicted Principal Himbry, doomed to die in the Wes Craven psycho flick *Scream* (1996). Subsequent parts eclipsed his typecasting as the Fonz with a variety of personas, including screen parts in *Ugly Naked People* (1999), *Dill Scallion* (1999), and as Barry Zuckerkorn on *Arrested Development* (2003).

In his 50s, Winkler built a résumé of solid performance. He worked with top stars— with John Ritter in *The Only Way Out* (1994), with Randy Quaid in *P.U.N.K.S.* (1999), and in *Ground Control* (1998) opposite Kiefer Sutherland, Sean Leonard, and Kelly McGillis. Winkler played Blockbuster Award-nominated coach Klein opposite Adam Sandler in the movie *The Waterboy* (1998) and teamed with Freddie Prinze, Jr., in *Down to You* (2000). Winkler's TV roles moved from the failed series *Monty* (1994) to successful stints on *The Practice* (1997), *Crossing Jordan* (2001), and *Out of Practice* (2005). At the Mark Taper Forum in Los Angeles, he appeared in Neal Simon's satiric comedy *The Dinner Party* (1999–2000). For a guest appearance on the series *Battery Park* (2000), he won an Emmy nomination. He played himself in *King of the Hill* (2004); for the PBS TV animated series *Clifford's Puppy Days* (2005), he provided a voice for Norville, which won an Emmy.

Help for Dyslexic Kids

Still sensitive about boyhood labeling as a loser, Winkler collaborated with Lin Oliver and Jesse Joshua Watson to write ten novels for the series *Hank Zipzer, the World's Greatest Underachiever*, a popular introduction to dyslexia in at-risk students. He kept individual titles upbeat, yet fraught with childhood's quandaries: *I Got a D in Salami*, *The Night I Flunked My Field Trip*, *Help! Somebody Get Me Out of Fourth Grade!*, *Barfing in the Back Seat: How I Survived My Family Road Trip*, *Who Ordered This Baby? Definitely Not Me!*, and *The Curtain Went Up, My Pants Fell Down*. Amid the humor of one volume, *The Day of the Iguana*, the text pictured a kid's version of underachievement as a brain that "flopped out of . . . [his] head and turned into mashed potatoes" (Winkler, 2003, 1). A later image pictured the hero, Hank, confronting electronic devices, which dazzled him with a cabinet "filled with lights. Red ones, green ones, white ones. Blinking ones, flashing ones, steady ones. Digital numbers changing constantly on dials" (Ibid., 36). The display echoed his boyhood attempt to sort out a mélange of coded signals. Hank, like his creator, chose altruism over failure by plotting a program guide to television for disabled readers.

Winkler extended his concern for the flustered by coauthoring *The Sitcom Handbook: A Guide to the Louder, Faster, Funnier World of TV Comedy* (2004). The text summarized conventions and form and defined terms like show runner, dry blocking, spec script, callback, and room tone. He didn't hesitate to criticize the medium that made him a multimillionaire for disrespecting young viewers and limited his own son to no more than one hour of viewing per day. In addition to empathizing with the disadvantaged learner, Winkler promoted the Epilepsy Foundation of America, National Committee for Arts for the Handicapped, Special Olympics, Toys for Tots, and United Cerebral Palsy Telethon, a cherished activism he held for 2 decades. He joined his wife in establishing the Children's Action Network, a source of immunization for 200,000 children, and became a spokesman for the Dyslexia Foundation.

Sources

Brant, Marley. *Happier Days: Paramount Television's Classic Sitcoms, 1974–1984*. New York: Billboard Books, 2006.

Fantle, David, and Tom Johnson. *Reel to Real*. Middleton, WI: Badger Books, 2004.

Kubey, Robert William. *Creating Television: Conversations with the People Behind 50 Years of American TV*. New York: Lawrence Erlbaum Associates, 2003.

Ramuno, Phil, Henry Winkler, and Mary Lou Belli. *The Sitcom Handbook: A Guide to the Louder, Faster, Funnier World of TV Comedy*. New York: Back Stage Books, 2004.

Winkler, Henry. "A Man's Reach Should Exceed His Grasp." *Perspectives* 17 (3) (January 1989).

Winkler, Henry, and Lin Oliver. *The Day of the Iguana*. New York: Grosset & Dunlap, 2003.

"Winkler Battled Through School." *Sioux City Journal* (Iowa), January 4, 2008.

Family Secrets
Joseph Bruchac

A skilled storykeeper, philosopher, and mythographer, Joseph "Joe" Bruchac III arrived late among his woodlands Indian roots. Born in Saratoga, New York, on October 16, 1942, of Abenaki, British, and Slovak heritage, he was the only son and eldest of three children. His parents—first-generation Czech taxidermist Joseph E. Bruchac II and Marion Flora Bowman Bruchac, the daughter of wealthy orchardists and cider mill owners—had him baptized Catholic with a three-generation name honoring a Christian saint. Without knowledge of his half-breed birth, Joe lived among Indians who passed as French-Canadians or Gypsies by concealing their customs and language. In the 1930s, those easily identified as indigenous people underwent forced sterilization through the Vermont Eugenics Program. A few passed for white because of strong Caucasian genes. Bruchac later wrote about how Indians survived "not only the stereotypes and the deeply held prejudice against Indians in the Northeast but physically surviving, not being killed as an Indian—an easy target" (Feltzer, 1997, 196).

Bruchac came of age among native basketmakers in Greenfield Center in the foothills of the Adirondack Mountains. He walked the woods with the first Joseph E. Bruchac, an eastern European immigrant and nature worshipper who professed an animistic faith. Lonely and undersized, from age 2, Joe imagined ghosts along the river but feared most of all his hardhanded father, a wife and child batterer who bore his own shame and anger for being a "brownhead" Slovak (Fetzer, 1997, 200). The boy pondered family secrets about his stillborn brother and about his grandmother Bowman's dead son. For amusement, he listened to *Straight Arrow* and *The Lone Ranger* on the radio, watched Hollywood cavalry murder bloodthirsty Indians at the movies, and fantasized about being a naturalist or a uniformed ranger in a national park. Bruchac felt abandoned by his father, who made a living during the Great Depression by working at a paper mill and by trapping muskrats and selling their pelts. Joe realized in adulthood that he was "the son that... [his] father had lost, the son who was within sight but never to be touched in a gentle way" (Bruchac, 1997, 133).

Life with the Bowmans

Bruchac parted permanently from his birth family at age 3, when his parents and little sister Mary Ann moved to an acreage called "The Farm." A quarter mile from his parents' home by the wayside of State Route 9N and Middle Grove Road, Bruchac lived at the gas station and general store run by his grandparents, attorney Marion Flora Dunham Bowman and Jesse Elmer Bowman, a semiliterate teamster, road builder, and merchant and the son of an Abenaki villager from Odanak, Canada. The New York home rested on the remains of Joe's great grandparents' residence, which burned to the foundations. A minority among hostile whites, Grandpa Jesse abandoned traditional ways to shield his family from bigotry.

Intuition helped Bruchac penetrate family secrets. His grandmother successfully battled for custody of Joe. She surrounded him with books and hinted in 1949 that he had a secret identity. He imagined he was Captain Marvel and dressed in a makeshift cape. On Sundays, he reluctantly shared car rides with his parents and Mary Ann. He realized in childhood, his grandmother "didn't talk about being Indian, they just did things Indian," like respect their dreams, honor nature, and rear children by nonabusive talk therapy (Bruchac, 1997, 24). As he described in his memoir, *Bowman's Store: A Journey to Myself* (1997), his grandfather reassured Joe of his uniqueness: "Yer a mongrel. Jes' like me. But that's all right. Mongrels is tough" (Feltzer, 1997, 201).

Acquiring an Identity

Without guessing his grandfather's native American origins, Bruchac evolved an awe of the Owner Creator, a non-Christian name for God. Called "Sonny" in boyhood, he learned from Grandpa Jesse to creep through the woods, to value animal fables and gentle humor, and to reason out moral dilemmas without vengeance. He roamed ancient Mohawk hunting grounds, gathered Indian corn, and visited a stone cairn called High Rock, the site of a healing spring called the Medicine Spring of the Great Spirit. His perceptions of Indians pictured greathearted people who lived without locks and keys in crime-free communities. More important to the development of humanism was his grandfather's demonstration that "the rights of children were implicit" (Felzer, 1997, 201). His great-aunt Katherine Bowman, wife of Jesse's brother Jack, wrote Joe about his Abenaki heritage. He said of the letter, "It is enough, for I want to claim no land, no allotments, only part of myself" (Bruchac, 1995, 244).

Bruchac came to think of himself as a Métis or middle man, a Lakota term indicating a bilingual translator in at least one Indian dialect. In exchange for fishing trips with Jesse, Bruchac stocked shelves, waited on customers, and washed car windshields. When business slowed in winter, he sat in a homemade pine chair by a potbellied stove among local lumberers and farmers to hear their songs and stories. Reflecting on childhood inklings, he remembered, "They were careful about how they mentioned Indians. One never knew who might be listening" (Bruchac, 1997, 10). A half century later, he honored his grandfather in the novel *Young Hunter and Rabbit Stick from Dawn Land* (1993), a pairing not unlike his childhood mentorship by the wise Abenaki elder.

Creative Stirrings

Bruchac stoked his imagination with Walt Disney nature movies, Tarzan novels, Albert Payson Terhune's dog stories, and the Hardy Boys adventure series. By age 7, he began writing poems, a skill that pleased teachers but provoked hostility from other boys. At school, he was an outcast relegated to the back row. To hide his nonwhite ancestry, he claimed to be French Canadian. Even though bullies from the Saratoga Springs School beat him up, he continued expanding his vocabulary by collecting tales filled with wonder and delight and elements of spiritual survival. In his teens, as "Jumping Joe" Bruchac, he wrestled and played football at Saratoga High School. While studying wildlife conservancy and vying at heavyweight wrestling at Cornell University, he demonstrated at antiwar pickets and civil rights protests. After veering into poetry, Joe finished college with a dual degree in English literature and zoology. Along the way, he mastered native hand drum, rattle, wooden flute, and the double wooden flute, which can sound up to three notes at a time. He began associating with other native boys to sample first person ethnicity and collected native stories that he later related to his sons, James Edward and Jesse Bowman Bruchac.

Ironically, Bruchac was living in West Africa when he embraced the oral tradition that threaded through Abenaki tradition and history. During a stint as a volunteer English teacher at the Keta Secondary School in Ghana in the 1960s, he met a soul mate. He befriended Nigerian folklorist and author Chinua Achebe, a survivor of colonial attempts to exterminate ethnic pride in the Igbo. The concurrence of the two authors on story significance validated Bruchac's belief in reciprocity of the learning circle, a cooperative experience that compels participants to listen, watch, recall, and share. To express action to his audience, he recreated the circle of life, an image of the cycles, sights, smells, feel, and sounds in nature. For greater clarity, Bruchac chose Swift Eagle, an Apache Pueblo elder and storykeeper, to advise on the use of the sweat lodge as a source of inner understanding. In company with Lakota medicine man Leonard Crow Dog, Bruchac experienced the spiritual cleansing that stripped away anger, bitterness, and jealousy. In subsequent steam bath ceremonies, he experienced the reverence of the seeker: "When I enter the sweat lodge, I do so on my knees, close to the Mother of us all, this Earth" (Bruchac, 1993, 8).

Joe the Celebrity

After marrying Carol Worthen, director of a nonprofit organization, on June 13, 1964, Bruchac completed his education with a master's degree in literature and creative writing from Syracuse University and a doctorate in comparative literature from Union Institute in Cincinnati, Ohio. For hobbies, he pursued gardening, music, and martial arts, three interests tied to his Abenaki legacy. During graduate school, he rode his Harley motorcycle to the Onondaga Reservation in central New York State to discuss parenting with the Iroquois Head Clan Mother, Alice Papineau, called Dewasentah, who believed in stories as a source of child discipline and guidance. For his reverence for pacifism, she dubbed him Gah Neh Goh He Yoh, an Onondaga name meaning "the Good Mind." At Comstock Prison in Comstock, New York, he taught extension courses in African lore and creative writing for the Great Meadows Institute, an outreach from Skidmore College to felons. As a venue for maximum security inmates, he founded the *Prison Project Newsletter*.

At age 33, on the advice of editor Elaine Gill at the Crossing Press in Freedom, California, Bruchac published his first mythography and one of his most anthologized poems, "Birdfoot's Grampa" (1975). His works, based on the Haudenosaunee or People of the Long House, formed around common themes of mutual respect and reverence for the Earth. In 1976, he made his first appearance at an elementary school, the start of an annual schedule of over a hundred sessions of drumming, chanting, and legends. Among his venues were the British Storytelling Festival, Smithsonian Institution Discovery Theater, National Storytelling Festival, Stone Soup, and annual National Council of Teachers of English convention.

Completing the Circle

The author spent his middle adult years filling the gaps caused by incomplete identification of self. With grandpa Jesse, Joe and Carol settled at Bowman's Store and turned an upstairs area into a home library and office. The couple founded the Greenfield Review Literary

Center, home of a regional and aboriginal publisher, Greenfield Review Press, for which he edited *Kite*, *Nickel Review*, *Prison Writing Review*, and *Studies in American Indian Literature*. Greenfield issued his historical fiction, folklore, drama, and picture books about earth tenders and "wampum keepers," a native term for storytellers. Only in late 1985, as his father neared death from coronary disease, did the author breach the secrecy and quell the mistrust that had separated them for 44 years.

Bruchac collaborated with writer and ecologist Michael J. Caduto for the three-volume "earth keeper" series and disseminated indigenous tales of the trickster Gluskabe on audiocassette. For material, Bruchac committed himself to years of research on a range of subjects—sacred sites, healing with native plants and sweat lodges, Sacajawea's guidance of the Lewis and Clark Expedition, Iroquois longhouse governance, the route of the Trail of Tears, the achievements of Squanto and of football great Jim Thorpe, the Vermont eugenics program, and native American patriotism during two world wars. For *Dawn Land* (1993) and its sequel, *Long River* (1995), he perused paleontology to imagine the life of an Abenaki warrior living about ten millennia ago. His short works appeared in *Aboriginal Voices*, *American Poetry Review*, *Cricket*, *National Geographic*, *Parabola*, *Paris Review*, *Smithsonian*, and *Tale Trader*; and his lectures, poetry clinics, and public appearances took him around the globe. With son Jim, he addressed groups at the Ndakinna Native American Interpretive Center, a consortium of native crafters and historians.

Returning the Gift

In 1992, Bruchac invested his energies in Returning the Gift, an Oklahoma-based culture sharing project and source of the Wordcraft Circle of Native Writers and Storytellers and the Native Writers' Circle of the Americas. He visited indigenous peoples, including the Cheyenne of Oklahoma, the Navajo of Canyon de Chelly, and the Lacadon Maya of Mexico. Through essay and interview, he fought the historical misrepresentations of Indians in such children's classic literature as *The Sign of the Beaver* and the *Little House* series. Joined by his sons and younger sister Margaret, he formed the Dawnland Singers, who recorded traditional Abenaki tunes on the album *Alnobak*, featuring percussion by the Awassos Signan drum ensemble. He earned an American Book Award from the Before Columbus Foundation for *Breaking Silence: An Anthology of Contemporary Asian American Poets* (1983), an International Reading Association Teachers' Choice citation for *Thirteen Moons on Turtle's Back: A Native American Year of Moons* (1992), and an American Folklore Society Aesop Accolade and Scientific American Young Readers Book Award for *The Story of the Milky Way* (1995). Contributing to his notoriety are a National Endowment for the Arts Writing Fellowship for Poetry, Cherokee Nation Prose Award, Hope S. Dean Award for Notable Achievement in Children's Literature, New York Public Library Knickerbocker Award, PEN Syndicated Fiction Award, Rockefeller Humanities fellowship, and 1998 Writer of the Year and Storyteller of the Year Awards from The Wordcraft Circle of Native Writers and Storytellers.

Bruchac's contributions to world literature extend to writing, interviewing, teaching, and compiling. In 2005, he delved into military heroics with an historical novel, *Code Talker: A Novel about the Navajo Marines of World War II*, which recaptured native contributions to the Pacific theater by creating an unbreakable code. After learning about the Navajo communicators in the 1970s, he incubated the story for 3 decades. Contributing to the authenticity were interviews with former U.S. Marines Carl Gorman, Jesse Samuel Smith, and

Keith Wilson. Throughout his career, Bruchac interviewed Indian authors like Navarre Scott Momaday, Gayle Ross, and Leslie Marmon Silko from the Native American Renaissance and pulled together examples of their works to impress on readers the dearth of perspective on America's first persons. Of American disparateness, he insisted, "We are a nation of nations [in] an era which is alive with exciting new poets" (Lincoln, 1985, 73). He identified Indian writings as healing songs relieving Earth's suffering. With his usual grace, he exulted, "A good anthology is always a reminder of how much more there is in store, like picking one berry at the edge of the woods and knowing from its taste that a whole summer full of berries is ahead" (Lincoln, 1985, 64).

Sources

Bruchac, Joseph. *Bowman's Store: A Journey to Myself*. New York: Lee & Low Books, 1997.
———. "Notes of a Translator's Son." In *Growing Up Native American*, by Patricia Riley & Ines Hernandez. New York: HarperCollins, 1995.
———. *Heroes and Heroines, Monsters and Magic: Native American Legends and Folktales*. Freedom, CA: Crossing Press, 1985.
———. *Hidden Roots*. New York: Scholastic, 2006.
———. *The Native American Sweat Lodge: History and Legends*. Freedom, CA: Crossing Press, 1993.
Fetzer, Philip L. *The Ethnic Moment: The Search for Equality in the American Experience*. Armonk, NY: M. E. Sharpe, 1997.
Lincoln, Kenneth. *Native American Renaissance*. Berkeley, CA: University of California Press, 1985.

■ FBI Most Wanted List
Angela Davis

An outspoken feminist intellectual and proponent of justice, Angela Yvonne Davis incurred stalking and surveillance by the Federal Bureau of Investigation. Born on January 26, 1944, in the racially mixed section of Birmingham, Alabama, she, younger sister Fania, and younger brothers Ben and Reginald grew up in a learned family. Their mother, activist Sally E. Davis, taught elementary school. Their father, history teacher B. Frank Davis, ran a gas station. Both parents supported the National Association for the Advancement of Colored People. They encouraged free reading at home and educated their children on methods of defying Jim Crow racism.

As Birmingham generated more diverse neighborhoods, the bombing of residences on "Dynamite Hill" in the 1950s introduced the Davis family to the extremes of exclusion and the hostility of nightriders. Angela witnessed segregation at Carrie A. Tuggle Elementary School and at Parker Annex Junior High. At age 15, she engineered a retreat from the prejudice at Birmingham High School. In 1959, the American Friends Service sent her at a small radical institution, Elizabeth Irwin High School in Greenwich Village, New York. During the experiment, which introduced Southern children to integrated Northern schools and communities, she boarded with whites in Brooklyn. Amid enthusiasm for communism from friends like lesbian intellectual Bettina Aptheker, Davis learned socialist principles and formed the Advance Club, a Marxist youth faction that picketed Woolworth's in support of sit-ins in the South. Contributing to Davis's formation of ideals were readings of the French existentialists Albert Camus and Jean-Paul Sartre.

Becoming an Activist

On scholarship, Davis joined two other black students in the integrating Brandeis University, where she majored in French literature. A favorite exploit involved her addressing a Southern shoe clerk in French and netting privileged treatment because he identified her as a West Indian exotic rather than an Alabaman from Birmingham. She extended her knowledge of ethnicity by befriending exchange students. During the Cuban Missile Crisis, she came under the influence of German philosopher Herbert Marcuse, a proponent of the student movement. With savings from odd jobs, she paid her way to Geneva, London, and Paris and attended the World Festival of Youth and Students in Helsinki, Finland. Among 18,000 teens from 137 countries, she rallied for pacifism and world harmony. The trip brought her to the attention of the Federal Bureau of Investigation (FBI), which sent agents to inquire about the procommunist gathering.

Davis's scholarship earned her a third year program at Hamilton College in Clinton, New York. While living in a French home, in 1963, she studied at Biarritz and in Paris at the Sorbonne. Stationed far from home, on September 16, she read in the *International Herald Tribune* of the deaths of four young friends murdered in Birmingham at the 16th Street Baptist Church, which three members of the Ku Klux Klan dynamited. She supported North Vietnam by attending a Têt New Year festival. After completing her degree with honors and membership in Phi Beta Kappa, on $300 per term, she moved in with a German family and entered the University of Frankfurt to major in philosophy. At a demonstration at the U.S. embassy, she denounced U.S. involvement in Vietnam. Travel to East Berlin convinced her of the wisdom of communist Germans in eradicating post–World War II fascism and liberating the working class from capitalist overlords.

A Radical Voice for Equality

Membership in the Sozialistischer Deutscher Studentenbund (SDS) precipitated Davis's radicalism, which she represented with a thick Afro hairstyle. She transferred to the University of California, San Diego, to attend lectures by Marcuse, who became her faculty adviser. He shaped her into a dedicated freedom fighter. At a socialist conference in London, she met Caribbean dissident "Michael X" de Freitas, a revolutionary from Notting Hill, and Stokely Carmichael, a Trinidadian-American civil rights activist. She and Carmichael concurred on the need to liberate black people from racism but disagreed on the role of socialism in establishing justice for nonwhite people. Still working out her feminist and Marxist ideals, she completed an M.A. and a doctorate in philosophy from Berlin's Humboldt University.

Employed at the University of California, Los Angeles, as an associate professor in the philosophy department, in 1967, Davis made no secret of her support of the Communist Party's Che Lumumba Club, the Student Nonviolent Coordinating Committee (SNCC), the Black Panther Party, Chicano organizations, and rebel Bobby Seale. Her organizing included the formation of the SNCC Youth Corps and the suppression of police brutality through the protests of the People's Tribunal Committee. She and her parents faced daily persecution while she fostered the first wave feminist militancy and sided with Fidel Castro in founding Cuban communism. To infiltrate and criminalize black nationalists, J. Edgar Hoover, director of the FBI during the conservative administration of Richard M. Nixon, ordered agents to monitor her contacts and activism. In September 1969, Governor Ronald Reagan had the Board of Regents fire Davis for overt leftist beliefs. On her appeal, in 1970, supporters demanded her right to teach at a state college and to expound communist polemics.

A Prison Revolt

In summer 1970, Davis joined the Black Panthers in challenging the prison sentences of the Soledad Prison Brothers—John Clutchette, Fleeta Drumgo, and George Jackson—who assassinated a prison guard in retaliation against the security officer who murdered three black dissidents. As head of the Soledad Brothers Defense Committee, Davis arranged rallies to inform citizens of court and prison injustices. She declared, "Three Black men who are unarmed, who are not attempting to escape, are killed, and this is called justifiable homicide" (Aptheker, 1999, 8). She plotted their flight from custody on August 7, when Jackson's 17-year-old brother Jonathan held Judge Harold J. Haley at automatic gunpoint while the three prisoners fled the Marin County Hall of Justice chamber in San Rafael. In the melee, a shotgun blast nearly decapitated Haley, and a bullet paralyzed District Attorney Gary Thomas. More gunfire from four San Quentin guards and the prosecutor killed George Jackson and three accomplices for conspiracy, riot, kidnap, and first-degree murder.

The recovery of the shotgun and a .380 pistol caused police to seize Davis, who bought them to protect herself from death threats. Although she was not present during the prison revolt, she left California under suspicion of conspiracy to commit a capital crime. On August 18, 1970, the FBI proclaimed her "armed and dangerous" and made her the third woman ever listed as a most wanted fugitive from justice (Aptheker, 1999, xi). President Nixon declared her a terrorist. Agents distributed head shots of Davis, rifled her apartment, and seized for questioning her sister, Fania Davis Jordan, and old friend Bettina Aptheker.

Because of Davis' African-American looks and thick, unprocessed Afro, police vilified her and any black woman who wore a natural hairstyle. During the 3 months she fled capture, officers and U.S. marshals grabbed and manhandled black females and flung them into jail on flimsy evidence. Black business owners and residents posted handbills offering shelter to Davis and other hunted females. People who had contact with her or who circulated pro-Angela petitions found themselves targets of FBI investigation, arbitrary job loss, traffic stops, jailing, and beating.

Organizing in Jail

After 2 months at large in New York City, on October 13, 1970, Davis and David Poindexter incurred an FBI dragnet. Special agents arrested her in a Howard Johnson motel and confined her to a dark cubicle, cell 4B, in the Women's Detention Center in Manhattan. President Nixon and Ronald Reagan applauded the FBI for diligence. Rodger McAfee, a California farmer, raised the $100,000 bail. During a 16-month incarceration, cell rules denied her books on any subject except her case. She organized inmates to support a bail project for the poor and wrote in longhand an apologia of radicalism, *If They Come in the Morning: Voices of Resistance* (1971). Rock idol John Lennon and the Rolling Stones composed ballads to her courage and in defiance of the establishment. Fania supported her sister on December 16, 1970, with a rally in Battle Creek, Michigan, before the Sojourner Truth statue.

Two months later, while supporters along Greenwich Avenue chanted, "Free Angela!" and distributed bumper stickers and buttons, Davis engaged lawyers to free her of all charges. The world press, singer Aretha Franklin, and authors Maya Angelou, James Baldwin, Toni Cade Bambara, Nikki Giovanni, and Sonia Sanchez pressured New York Governor Nelson Rockefeller to exonerate Davis. Agents extradited her to Hamilton Air Force Base in

San Jose, California, where she passed through ranks of soldiers guarding her route. Sheriff Matthew Carberry pledged "extreme precautions" during Davis' trial (Aptheker, 1999, 12). Before the judge in Marin County Superior Court on January 5, 1971, Davis declared herself "a target of a political frameup" that could send her to the gas chamber (Aptheker, 1999, 26).

After a change of venue to San Jose County, on June 4, 1972, one Chicano and 11 white jurors found Davis not guilty of conspiracy, kidnap, murder, and flight from federal agents. She reflected, "That period was pivotal for me in many respects. I came to understand much more concretely many of the realities of the Black struggle" (Felder, 248). She joined Carmichael and Black Panther leader Huey P. Newton in Cuba, where black islanders embraced her as a political refugee and elevated her to revolutionary stardom. At a press conference in Tucson, Arizona, on November 21, 1972, she called for viewers to join the struggle for justice and equality. In 1974, she penned a political memoir, *Angela Davis: An Autobiography*, stating her side of public misperceptions of the radical black agenda. She concluded that Cubans had achieved a better amalgamation of democracy with socialism than the American version of democracy and capitalist monopolies that exploit production and consumption. After 2 years on the faculty at Claremont College, she roamed Bulgaria, Czechoslovakia, East Germany, and Russia to promote a global consensus on racial, ethnic, gendered, and individual repression. At ages 36 and 40, she ran on the Communist Party ticket for the U.S. vice presidency.

Teacher and Freedom Fighter

For 35 years, David taught critical thinking skills and advised graduate students. At Florida A&M, Grinnell, Stanford, and San Francisco State Universities, she lectured on racial inequalities, particularly among Asians, blacks, Latinos, native Americans, poor whites, and women in jails and high-tech penitentiaries and on death row. Her feminist diatribe, *Women, Race, and Class* (1981), appeared on graduate level reading lists as a classic study of elitism, racism, and sexism. In 1983, she accepted an honorary Ph.D. from Lenin University for her contributions to the National Alliance against Racist and Political Repression.

Davis's writings chastised a wealthy nation in which the homeless, uneducated, and impoverished looked to opportunities in the military as their only option. She lobbied for uplift of the underclass and for more equitable ways of punishing criminals, especially in California, where the "landscape ... [had] been thoroughly prisonized [*sic*] over the last 20 years" (Davis, 2003, 12). Her treatise on prison abolition read, "How can we imagine a society in which punishment is not based on race and class" (Davis, 2003, 107). She called for a debate on the purpose and efficacy of incarceration of some two million Americans, who returned to the outside stripped of citizenship and dignity. Among her solutions to dehumanization were improved cell conditions, schooling and vocational training, paid employment for prisoners, and an end to violence and sexual assaults by guards and inmates.

Women's Champion

In 1995, Davis guided feminist studies and occupied the presidential chair of the history of consciousness, an interdisciplinary graduate humanities program conducted at the University of California, Santa Cruz. She was the faculty's first black female to obtain tenure. She decried the conservatism of the U.S. Supreme Court and the erosion of affirmative action. On behalf of all women, she denounced gangsta rap and Louis Farrakhan's Million Man March for promoting male dominance of females. In her mid-50s, she allied with fellow lesbians and black feminists and published *The Angela Y. Davis Reader* (1999) and *Blue Legacies & Black Feminism* (1999), an overview of black feminism based on the legacies of singers Billie Holiday, Gertrude "Ma" Rainey, and Bessie Smith. Central to Davis' activism were protests of the Gulf War and a denunciation of the prison-industrial complex for victimizing vulnerable women who turn to prostitution and drug trafficking to feed their children. She served on the advisory board of the Prison Activist Resource Center. Her book *Abolition Democracy: Beyond Empire, Prisons, and Torture* (2005) compelled readers to ponder inequities—"who goes to prison and who does not, who attends university and who does not, who has health insurance and who does not" (Davis, 2005, 30).

Davis' progressivism fostered radical and innovative strategies to solve human problems. She charged the American military with enhancing economic and military superiority at the expense of poor women and children, who remain "man's eternal servant . . . guardians of a devalued domestic life" (Felder, 2006, 250, 251). Of wasted tax dollars, she said, "Resources that ought to be available to address urgent health issues such as HIV/AIDS are being devoured by both the military and prison industrial complexes" (Siliman, 2002, 327). She described the post-9/11 government ploy as marketing the American flag "to adorn every imaginable aspect of daily life" less as a boost to patriotism than as a way of spreading fear of terrorism and obeisance to militaristic policies (Ibid.). In June 2006, before attendees at the American Library Association convention in New Orleans, she praised the Black Panthers for shaming the federal government into providing milk for school children. She advocated that individuals devote themselves to acts of conscience. Still idealistic in her mid-sixties, she proclaimed, "It is only for the sake of those without hope that hope is given to us" (Davis, 2005, vii).

Sources

Aptheker, Bettina. *The Morning Breaks: The Trial of Angela Davis*. Ithaca, NY: Cornell University Press, 1999.

Davis, Angela Yvonne. *Abolition Democracy: Beyond Empire, Prisons, and Torture*. New York: Seven Stories, 2005.

———. *Angela Davis: An Autobiography*. New York: Random House, 1974.

———. *Are Prisons Obsolete?* New York: Seven Stories, 2003.

Felder, Deborah G. *A Bookshelf of Our Own*. New York: Citadel Press, 2006.

Siliman, Jael Miriam, Anannya Bhattacharjee, and Angela Yvonne Davis. *Policing the National Body: Sex, Race, and Criminalization*. Cambridge, MA: South End, 2002.

■ Foreign Birth
Katherine Wolmendorf Paterson

Author of picture books and young adult novels, Katherine Clements Wolmendorf Paterson learned to function in contrasting worlds. Born on October 31, 1932, at Qing Jiang in eastern

China, she was the middle one of the five surviving children of Mary Goetchius Womeldorf and Southern Presbyterian missionary George Raymond, an amputee from World War I. Brought up with an Asian mindset, Paterson came of age in a Chinese neighborhood, where she learned traditional humility and patience as elements of friend making. Her father supported the family by preaching and heading Sutton 690, a boys' school. She and her siblings—Sonny, Lizzie, Helen, and Elizabeth—read aloud from *The Wind in the Willows*, *The Secret Garden*, the Winnie the Pooh series, and Beatrix Potter's fables. They studied scripture to define themselves as people of faith. Frequent moves among strange environments made her identify with the wandering Children of Israel, refugees living among the powerful and alien.

While learning Chinese, Paterson gained respect for Asian traditions and civilization. She published juvenilia at age 7 in the Shanghai American School newspaper. In July 1937 at the beginning of the Second Sino-Japanese War, when insurgents attacked the Marco Polo Bridge in Beijing, the Paterson family fled to Lynchburg, then Richmond, Virginia. The abrupt departure was the first of 15 moves over a 13-year span. Within a year, they resettled on the Pacific coast in the British sector of Shanghai, but George Paterson ventured back to Qing Jiang to continue itinerant preaching. She stayed in touch through letters. A subsequent evacuation of Westerners because of Japanese slaughter, arson, and looting forced the Wolmendorfs out in 1940 to North Carolina. For the remainder of World War II, while her older brother, George Raymond Womeldorf, Jr., served the navy as a fighter pilot, Katherine cultivated a rich fantasy life free of world turmoil. By age 10, she aspired to be either a missionary or a film star.

Stranger in a Strange Land

While learning to read and write English, Paterson felt like a Chinese refugee living in the American South and surviving on an unfamiliar diet. She reflected, "I remember the many schools I attended in those years mostly as places where I felt fear and humiliation. I was small, poor, and foreign" (Paterson, 1995, vii–viii). She acclimated to classmates in the Calvin H. I. Wiley School she attended in Winston-Salem, North Carolina. Her "missionary barrel" attire and crisp British accent set her apart from slow-talking Carolinians. Of her craft, she explained that her inner child felt rejected and jealous during adolescence and longed for satisfaction through revenge. Her payback took the form of written stories. During the family's many migrations, to compensate for missing Asia and for being an outsider, she retreated to the library, played all the roles in her mental dramas, and wrote plots and scenarios for her friends to act out.

While her family lived in Winchester, Virginia, in 1954, Paterson graduated summa cum laude with a degree in American and British literature from King College in Bristol, Tennessee. While working as a Christian education assistant, Paterson aided 11 pastors in rural Japan and taught sacred studies and English in rural Lovettsville, Virginia, and in Pennington, New Jersey. She worked for the next year at Lovettsville's only elementary school. She advised her students to read to learn how language works. Of her love of books, she later asserted the power of literature to change and reclaim the reader. In 1956, she received a master's degree in Bible and English from the Presbyterian School of Christian Education in Richmond, but the stolid Chinese communist regime prevented her return to teach in her birth country. Although she viewed the Japanese as an enemy, at age 24, she took a 6-year classroom post at a missionary enclave on the sparsely populated island of Shikoku in southern Japan. In 1957, she began 4 years of study at the prestigious Naganuma School of Japanese in Kobe.

From Loner to Mother

Paterson's ambitions shifted during her matriculation at Union Theological Seminary in New York. At the nondenominational graduate school, which readied men and women for the pulpit or mission field, she completed an M.A. in Christian education. On July 14, 1962, in Chatham, Virginia, she married a fellow student, Reverend John Barstow Paterson of Barre, Vermont. The couple lived in Takoma Park, Maryland, and Norfolk, Virginia. As she reared sons John Barstow and David Lord and adopted daughters Elizabeth Po Lin and Mary Katherine, she wrote at the dining room table in 10-minute stints. In 1964, she became a fulltime writer of church school curriculum for parochial school fifth- and sixth-graders and published *Who Am I?: Exploring What It Means to Be a Child of God* (1966). The next year, she began a Christmas tradition by supplying a story for her husband's holiday sermon.

After 9 years of attempts at fiction, the author advanced to picture books and young adult historical fiction, beginning with an Asian adventure tale, *The Sign of the Chrysanthemum* (1973). The story tells of Muna's orphaning and his search for a long lost father, a tattooed Heike samurai in feudal Japan. She followed with nonfiction, *Justice for All People* (1973) and *To Make Men Free* (1973), and another fiction, *Of Nightingale That Weep* (1974), a romance featuring Takiko, a girl who embraces the warrior's code of her deceased father. The stories took shape one chapter at a time in a creative writing workshop.

Midlife Misgivings

In her mid-40s, Paterson grappled with operable cancer, with her mother's illness and death, and with the vicissitudes of a burgeoning writing career. Correlating Chinese and Southern American events and cultures, she based her narratives on the activities of her children and their friends. She earned a National Book Award for *The Master Puppeteer* (1977), a favorite of young teens for its juxtaposition of juggling, magic, beggary, and famine in 18th-century Osaka, Japan. Rich with suspense and daring, the story lauds the character of Jiro, a puppet maker who connects puppeteer Yoshida and his theater with the bandit Saburo. The author returned to American settings for *The Great Gilly Hopkins* (1977), a perusal of preteen escape into fantasy by Galadriel Hopkins, a homeless child who racks up three foster placements in less than 3 years. A winner of the Christopher Award, the work filled a need in rootless children who vacillate between illusions of the perfect nuclear family and the chilling truth of growing up under the direction of social services.

For her controversial masterwork, *Bridge to Terabithia* (1977), a plot she designed by instinct, Paterson won a Newbery Medal and a second National Book Award. She created the novel's central friendship from the relationship of her son David with 8-year-old Lisa Hill, whom lightning struck and killed in Lovettsville. Although the fictional account of a child's mourning over a death by drowning made Paterson a top YA (young adult) author, the work achieved ninth place on the American Library Association list of the 100 most frequently censored books of 2000. At issue are its inclusion of sorcery and a hero who punctuates his thoughts with "Lord." Paterson takes to heart the courage of professionals: "Every time [the book] is challenged, some teacher or librarian is in trouble because of me" (Chattaway, 2007). In fall of that year, after the Patersons left Maryland for Norfolk, Virginia, the author labored over *Jacob Have I Loved* and chose to focus the drama of jealous twins on the fictional Rass Island in the Chesapeake Bay area in the years following World War II. The novel won the Kerlan Award, a University of Southern Mississippi de Grummond Collection Medallion, and nomination for an American Book Award.

Into Her Own

In 1978, King College conferred an honorary doctorate on the author, who attained name recognition among teachers, parents, and librarians. The next year, she won a best book commendation from *School Library Journal*. She began a series of holiday anthologies with *Angels and Other Strangers* (1979), a compendium rich in peace and tolerance. In 1981, Paterson returned to China to translate *The Crane Wife* (1981) and to research *Rebels of the Heavenly Kingdom* (1983), a tale of banditry and kidnap under Manchu overlords in imperial China during the 1850s. The text peruses the female perspective on footbinding, an archaic practice intended to increase the delicacy and sensuality of women. In 1985, *Come Sing, Jimmy Jo*, a story of West Virginia country-western musicians, received best book of the year citations from the *New York Times* and *School Library Journal*. The narrative tackles troubling domestic issues—an affair between a mother and uncle and a boy's discovery from a stranger of his real parentage.

Paterson directed her intellectual curiosity into multiple directions. She collected holiday stories in *Star of Night* (1980), published a child pleaser, *The Smallest Cow in the World* (1988), and, with her husband, coauthored nonfiction in *Consider the Lilies: Plants of the Bible* (1986) and *Images of God* (1998). Her enthusiasm for literacy resonated in the title of a speech, "Stick to Reality and a Dream: Celebrating America's Young Readers: A Lecture for the Year of the Young Reader," which she delivered on November 17, 1988, at the Library of Congress. She collected her platform addresses in *The Spying Heart: More Thoughts on Reading and Writing Books for Children* (1989). She combined spirituality and word skills in *The Puzzling Book* (1990), a pencil-and-paper challenge. In 1991, she depicted the exploitation of young females and immigrant women at New England fiber mills in *Lyddie*. The glimpse of women's history describes clanging looms, slipping shuttles, and ragged warp threads along with more mature concerns for worker health and sanitation and sexual harassment of vulnerable children who toil for as little as 50 cents a week. In 2006, Paterson's *Bread and Roses, Too* returned to real events from labor history during the 1912 textile strike in Lawrence, Massachusetts.

In 1997 at Jersey City State College, Paterson delivered an acceptance address for the Scott O'Dell Award to *Jip: His Story*, a plot pairing a Vermont orphan at a charity asylum with Put, a lunatic at the poorhouse farm. She stated her reverence for classics by Robert Louis Stevenson, Charles Dickens, and Mark Twain, to whom she returns for guidance. Acknowledging her own limitations, she described to her audience the mental refitting that shaped the youth Jip to a particular Northeastern environment in Hartford, Vermont. Her husband aided the narrative with fact-finding; Nancy Graff and Virginia Buckley provided external text edits and critiques. The author continued to reap respect for nonpreachy works like the fable *The King's Equal* (1992), a dozen modern Christmas stories in *A Midnight Clear* (1998), the female quest tale *Celia and the Sweet, Sweet Water* (1998), and Arthurian romance in *Parzival, The Quest of the Grail Knight* (1998). In 2001, she returned to authorial questions about character building in young readers with two essays, "Diagnosis, Please" in *Horn Book* and "The Spiritual Reading Life of Children" in *U.S. Catholic*.

A Model of Authorship

Paterson's versatility grew out of humanism. After receiving the Hans Christian Andersen Medal at an international congress of children's authors in New Delhi, India, in 1998, she composed an essay on the strivings of authors worldwide to set up publishing houses producing works for impressionable readers. She gravitated to animal lore in *The Field of the Dogs* (2001) and published a rewrite of *Anne of Green Gables* (2001), *The Adventures of Tom Sawyer* (2002), and *Pride and Prejudice* (2006). She adapted Beatrix Potter's "Tale of Jemima Puddle Duck" to the musical stage and issued the domestic novel *The Same Stuff as Stars* (2002), a salute to children who survive abandonment. In 2001, she collected lectures, essays, and four acceptance speeches from the late 1970s and early 1980s in *The Invisible Child: On Reading and Writing Books for Children* (2001).

Paterson bases her child advocacy on sympathy and faith and promotes readership among children to encourage healing and to allow youth to experience varied locales, conflicts, and loss at a safe distance. In her words, "Books give us emotional practice" (Chattaway, 2007). In a later interview, she described the plot of *Terabithia* as a death rehearsal. Currently, she resides and works at an antique farmhouse in Barre, Vermont, where her husband retired from the Presbyterian pastorate. Her hobbies range from tending seven grandchildren and drawing in pastels to singing, sailing, tennis, and playing the piano. Her canon merited sizeable critical acclaim—the Colorado Blue Spruce Award, Janusz Korcazk Medal, Le Grand Prix des Jeunes Lecteurs citation, Lewis Carroll Shelf Award, Michigan Young Reader's Award, and New York Public Library Award. In 2006, in Stockholm, Sweden, she received the Astrid Lindgren Memorial Award. The following year, David Paterson's screenplay of *Bridge to Terabithia* engaged filmgoers in its second movie version. She followed with biblical biography, *The Light of the World: The Life of Jesus for Children* (2008). Her collected works reside at the University of Minnesota.

Sources

Abramson, Ilene. "The Kids' Reading Room." *Los Angeles Times*, February 5, 2007, E.18.

Aspan, Maria. "A Tale of Fantasy Rendered Different, At Least in the Trailers." *New York Times*, February 19, 2007, C.4.

Bostrom, Kathleen Long. *Winning Authors: Profiles of the Newbery Medalists*. Westport, CT: Libraries Unlimited, 2003.

"'Bridge to Terabithia': David Paterson's Mother Wrote the Book for Him. Now He's Made the Movie." *Washington Post*, February 15, 2007, C-14.

Chattaway, Peter T. "An 'Unsafe' Bridge." *Christianity Today* 51 (2) (February 12, 2007).

Fisher, Bonnie. *Social Influences on the Writing of Marion Dane Bauer and Katherine Paterson*. Lampeter, Dyfed, UK: Edwin Mellen Press, 2001.

Hornaday, Ann. "'Bridge': Crossing into the Heart of Childhood." *Washington Post*, February 16, 2007, C.1.

Maglaty, Jeanne. "Helping Burgeoning Bookworms." *Washington Post*, March 12, 1998, M.1.

McGinty, Alice B. *Katherine Paterson*. New York: Rosen, 2005.

Paterson, Katherine. "Back from IBBY." *Horn Book* 75 (1) (January 1, 1999): 1.

———. "Scott O'Dell Award Acceptance Speech." *ALAN Review* 24 (3) (Spring 1997): 51–52.

———. *A Sense of Wonder: On Reading and Writing Books for Children*. New York: Plume, 1995.

Polette, Nancy. *Books Every Child Should Know*. Westport, CT: Libraries Unlimited, 2005.

"Premonition." *Washington Post*, March 16, 2007, T.39.

Silvey, Anita. *100 Best Books for Children*. Boston: Houghton Mifflin, 2004.

Smedman, M. Sarah. *Bridges for the Young: The Fiction of Katherine Paterson*. Lanham, MD: Scarecrow, 2003.

■ Foster Care
Ben Nighthorse Campbell

Politician Ben Nighthorse Campbell overcame a troubled childhood to become a compassionate, charismatic U.S. congressman. Born April 13, 1933, in Auburn, California, he is the grandson of an illegal alien and the son of nurse Mary Vierra, a Portuguese immigrant from the Azore Islands. She lived in a Hispanic community outside Sacramento from age 6. During treatment for tuberculosis, she met his father, World War I army veteran Albert Valdez Campbell of Pagosa Springs, Colorado, who entered the hospital's alcohol addiction ward. Albert joined the domestic staff of the Weimar Joint Sanatorium and invested in three rental cabins. A year after their marriage in 1929, the couple produced daughter Alberta. The parents suffered chronic separations from Mary's declining lungs and from Albert's unemployment, binge drinking, spousal abuse, and jailing for public drunkenness and nonsupport. Campbell later remarked on his periods of hunger and hardship during the Great Depression, "Those experiences are not conducive to what you might call a normal life of opportunities" (Campbell, 2007).

Campbell set as a lifetime goal avoiding the damage that alcohol does to individuals and families. During the children's youth, Albert Campbell concealed his Northern Cheyenne heritage, which included progenitor Ruben Black Horse, a warrior wounded at the Little Bighorn who rode with Dull Knife, Little Wolf, and Crazy Horse. To escape the contagion of their mother's illness, Ben and Alberta avoided maternal cuddling and required foster care and residence in Catholic orphanages, beginning in 1939 with entry into St. Patrick's Home in Sacramento. Strict discipline by nuns and priests did little to satisfy the need for parenting and affection. In one incident, a nun punished Campbell for unclean hands by locking him in a pigpen. He and his sister also suffered discrimination against half-breeds. He picked up jobs at fruit packers and worked in Newcastle at a fruit shed loading nails into a box assembly device. He grew apart from Alberta. At age 44, she killed herself with liquor and narcotics, leaving no note to explain her self-destruction.

At age 18, about the time that he learned his true ethnicity, Ben suffered problems with delinquency, skipping school to cut lumber, and poor classroom performance. He admitted that he was "probably the world's worst student" (Ibid., 30). When his mother returned to fulltime hospital care, at the end of football season, he dropped out of Placer High School to enlist in the U.S. Air Force. At Amarillo Air Force Base in Texas, for the first time in his life, he learned structure, obedience, and the management of a regular salary. He worked in traffic control for the military police in the Korean War, gaining the rank of airman second class. For combat roles from 1951 to 1953, he won the Air Medal and the Korean Service Medal. He reflected, "If it hadn't been for sports and the Air Force, I might have ended up in a different kind of institution than the U.S. Senate" (Ibid.).

After Korea

A civilian once more, Ben picked tomatoes and fruit in California for 15 cents per bushel. A truck driver took an interest in Ben and taught him to maneuver a big rig. With the friend's help, Ben applied for a commercial license, joined the teamster's union, and began driving professionally. With his earnings, he enrolled at San Jose State College in police science and improved his skill at judo by joining the judo team. The sport enabled him to work off hostilities that had previously gotten him in trouble with the law. Under the coaching of Yosh Uchida, Campbell became the youngest black belt in the country. In 1957, he earned a B.A. in fine arts and physical education and, after the annulment of his first marriage, wed Elaine Morgan.

Three years later, Ben settled in Tokyo to conduct a research project on Japanese culture at Meiji University in Chiyoda. During his residency in Japan, he studied metal lamination and jewelry fabrication under a Samurai sword maker. Ben continued competing in judo and achieved three U.S. national championships. In 1963, he participated in men's judo at the Pan American Games in São Paolo, Brazil, and won one of the three U.S. gold medals. The following year, he captained the U.S. judo squad at the 1964 Summer Olympics in Tokyo. In the second round of openweight competition, he thwarted his athletic career after tearing a ligament in his right knee and ceding the bronze medal to his opponent. During the closing ceremony, Campbell carried the American flag. He declared, "My knee hurt like hell, . . . but I was not about to let someone else have that flag" (Ibid., 67). Dedication to sports, however, cost him his wife, who felt neglected by his lengthy practices and competitions.

From graduate study and athletics, Campbell moved toward a period of serenity and prosperity. He bought a red Jaguar XKE and pursued women, but his needs were deeper than romance. To nourish empty places in his background, he isolated small details of his Cheyenne heritage and began researching his native genealogy. After the end of his second marriage, at age 33, he wed Linda Price, a rancher from Montrose, Colorado, and mother of their children, Colin Arrowtaker Campbell and Shanan Longfellow. She influenced him to stop wasting money and encouraged his trading the Jaguar for a VW bus. Campbell extended his involvement in judo by teaching and, in 1974, by authoring a beginner's handbook, *Championship Judo Training Drills*. For young male athletes, he maintained high standards of physical achievement and pride by teaching them discipline, strategy, and self-respect.

Talent and Self-Expression

Campbell trained and showed champion quarter horses at his ranch at Ignacio in southwestern Colorado, where his children became expert riders. While he served as deputy sheriff, he operated a food and clothing drive for the needy. At age 47, he enrolled in the Northern Cheyenne Nation and was inducted into the 44-member Council of Chiefs on the Lame Deer Reservation in Montana. To reconnect with his Indian forebears, he visited and brought gifts to Wolf Voice and to Alex and Mary Black Horse, who occupied a cabin in the Wolf Mountains. Campbell expressed his free native spirit by decking himself in a bandana and string tie, riding a Harley, and letting his ponytail float in the wind. For native rituals and powwows, he opted for braids. Among his services to American Indians was promotion of honors to Navajo code talkers, a famed cadre of U.S. Marines who befuddled Japanese spies during World War II.

Campbell earned 200 awards for original jewelry. He crafts armbands, bolos, bracelets, buckles, dome rings, earrings, pendants, and wedding bands adorned with coral, jade, lapis lazuli, malachite, mother of pearl, onyx, and turquoise. He works in gold, silver, and mixed metals and inlaid natural gemstones in authentic Anasazi and Navajo beadwork, ritual items, and rock art iconography found at the ancient sites at Canyon de Chelly, Chaco Canyon, and Mesa Verde. He also honors Rocky Mountain wildlife with symbolic jewelry featuring bear, bighorn rams, buffalo, cougar, deer, eagle, elk, horses, and peyote buttons. His business, operated by his wife in the Four Corners area, began to net more profit after he got a pilot's license to limit the time spent on marketing. Some of Ben's pieces are exhibited at the National Museum of the American Indian, which he sponsored as a division of the Smithsonian Institution to honor native peoples and cultures of the Western Hemisphere. On September 21, 2004, he was one of three speakers at the groundbreaking ceremony.

Elected to Office

In 1982, Campbell won election to a 1-year term in the Colorado General Assembly. After an abrupt decision to oppose a lawyer campaigning for the Colorado legislature, Campbell ran on the Democratic ticket and won. He intended to develop his own method of changing government to be more responsive to the citizenry. Service to the public gave him an opportunity to build community, fight crime, promote veterans' issues, improve education, and work toward lower tax rates and a balanced budget. His vigorous advocacy won from the *Denver Post* a designation as one of the ten best legislators of 1986. Famed for his Western libertarianism and native individualism, he flouted protocol, wore black jeans and cowboy boots, and parked his red, white, and blue motorcycle among the sedate town cars of stuffy politicians.

On January 3, 1987, Campbell entered the U.S. House of Representatives from Colorado's third district, replacing Michael Strang. For much of his incumbency, Campbell served the U.S. Congress as its only native American and its unofficial spokesman for Indians. In October 1987, he oversaw the removal from the House interior committee room of an offensive painting by Seth Eastman picturing an Indian scalping a white male, a pose that the Congress commissioned in 1868. Campbell led committees on agriculture and interior and insular affairs and produced gains for the Colorado wilderness, for aboriginal land and resources claims, and for the water rights of the Ute in the western part of the state. In 1987, he cosponsored the Indian Gaming Regulatory Act, which set national standards for gambling on native lands and reservations. He verbalized Indian anger that the Department of Energy proposed 17 out of 19 potential sites for nuclear waste disposal on ancestral Indian lands.

In 1991, Campbell championed preventive measures to halt fetal alcohol syndrome and spearheaded the demand for honoring some 10,000 Arapaho, Cheyenne, and Lakota warriors by renaming the Custer Battlefield Monument at Big Horn, Montana, Little Bighorn Battlefield National Monument. Campbell made a significant gesture of racial reconciliation on New Year's Day in 1992 during the Tournament of Roses "Voyages of Discovery" parade in Pasadena, California. Dressed in beaded buckskins and in eagle headdress and double trailers of 72 feathers, he rode his black and white paint, Black War Bonnet, at the head of the procession alongside Cristóbal Colón, a descendent of Christopher Columbus. Campbell also issued an ethnic treatise, *Reflections on the Columbus Quincentenary, 1492–1992*. He rode a second time in plains regalia down Pennsylvania Avenue in Washington, D.C., at the inaugural parade of President Bill Clinton.

Senator Ben

After Scott McInnis won the congressional seat for Congress, Campbell then moved on to a greater challenge. On January 3, 1993, Campbell succeeded Timothy E. Wirth in the U.S. Senate, becoming the first native American senator in six decades and the first Portuguese-American legislator in history. Two years later, he dumped the Democrats and joined the Republican Party but puzzled pundits by continuing to support the platform of President Bill Clinton, which included raising the minimum wage and protecting affirmative action and foreign aid funding for abortion. Campbell received appointment to the Helsinki Commission and the Senate Appropriations Committee and election to deputy majority whip. He ignored the prevalence of right-wingers and warmongers by designating no religion and by voting against Operation Desert Storm. Reelected in 1998 with 62 percent of the vote, he held the office for three terms. In 2001, he chaired the Committee on Indian Affairs, which passed bills that improved native health and welfare, education, self-government, energy development, arts and crafts, and sovereignty. Additional committee labors spread his influence over agriculture, forestry, nutrition, children's health insurance, and veterans' affairs.

Much of Campbell's effectiveness influenced land use and law enforcement. For the Committee on Energy and Natural Resources, he chaired the commissions on historic preservation and recreation and parks, forests, and public land management. He sponsored legislation to eradicate the tamarisk plant, an invasive weed clogging waterways in drought-prone areas. Upon his retirement in January 2005, he earned regard for sponsoring creation of the Animas-La Plata water project, Black Canyon of the Gunnison National Park, Great Sand Dunes National Park and Preserve, and Sand Creek Massacre National Historic Site. He promoted federal funds for bulletproof vests for the nation's 870,000 law enforcement officers and advocated the observation of National Peace Officers Memorial Day and the construction of the National Law Enforcement Museum. For honoring the courage and sacrifice of law officers, he earned the Distinguished Service Award from the National Law Enforcement Officers Memorial Fund.

Retirement and Family

At age 70, Campbell chose to end his political career. In an interview with *Time* magazine, he proudly said, "[I]f you look at every emerging country, the kind of government they try to emulate is ours" (Duffy and Waller, 2004, 32). He scheduled time to improve his health and to enjoy his wife, children, and three grandchildren—Lauren Campbell, Luke Longfellow, and Saylor Longfellow. Their time together comprises a precious heritage to a man who grew up in a splintered home. He joined a speakers' bureau to book lectures at colleges and universities and briefly pondered running in the 2006 Colorado gubernatorial race. In March 2006, he came under consideration for the office of the secretary of interior. The appointment would have made him the first Indian appointed to the United States Cabinet, overseeing the agency that oversees the Bureau of Indian Affairs and the National Park Service.

In retirement, Campbell visits Washington, D.C., every 3 weeks. He advises the Indian Law Practice Group of the capital firm Holland and Knight. As a former senator, he retains privileges to sit in on caucuses and visit the chamber before votes. He buttonholes members of the Congress to support native American issues, particularly the reauthorization of Indian health care, which the George Bush administration failed to support. In a political climate driven by hot-button issues like partial birth abortion, carry laws, and gay marriage, he continues to fight for native peoples, who have the lowest standard of living in the country and the highest averages of citizen joblessness and homelessness, inadequate education, fetal addiction syndrome, infectious disease, substance abuse, and suicide. Reflecting his love of lawmaking, he stated, "Sometimes in the wintertime, when the snow is on the ground here and [I] see this building in the moonlight, it's just hard to explain the feeling that I get" (Ibid., 34).

Sources

Campbell, Ben Nighthorse. "The American Dream." *Forbes*, March 22, 2007.

Duffy, Michael, and Douglas Waller. "What We'll Miss and What We Won't." *Time* 165 (22) (November 29, 2004): 32–34.

Reynolds, Jerry. "Catching Up with Ben Nighthorse Campbell." *Indian Country Today*, June 15, 2007.

Viola, Herman J. *Ben Nighthorse Campbell: An American Warrior*. New York: Crown, 1993.

■ GANGS
Luis J. Rodriguez

Memoirist, children's author, journalist, and poet Luis J. Rodriguez disclosed the terrors of gang membership, which he knows firsthand from growing up in Watts, a notorious ghetto in East Los Angeles, California. The great-grandson of a Raramuri Indian from southern Chihuahua and the son of Mexican immigrants, he is a native of El Paso, a Tex-Mex border city. He was born in 1954 and lived in Los Angeles after age 2. Nicknamed *Grillo* (grasshopper), he leaped from one culture to another because his mother, María Estela, chose to rear her two sons and two daughters in California rather than repatriate to Juárez, Mexico. Their income fell because her husband, Alfonso Rodriguez, lost his position as school principal. He wed his secretary, mother of their son, José René "Rano" Rodriguez, and served a prison sentence for embezzling from the school budget.

The Rodriguez family moved to the Watts ghetto in the San Gabriel Valley, where Luis hid from his parents the fact that José incurred a severe pummeling by white toughs at a South Gate grocery store. While Luis attended first grade at the 109th Street School, Alfonso taught temporarily at Taft High School and purchased a residence in Reseda. In 1957, Maria gave birth to Luis' sister, Gloria "Shorty" Rodriguez. Unemployed once more, Alfonso moved the family to the home of Seni, Luis's half sister, and their grandmother, Catita, until a family uproar forced the Rodriguezes to move once more. The Sheriff's Department tagged Luis for scaling a playground fence to play late evening basketball. During the trespass, Luis's friend Tino died in a tumble from the cafeteria roof. A riot in Watts earned international headlines from August 13 to 17, 1965, publicizing to the world the tenuous situation in East L.A. Luis recalled, "The fires that swept through my old neighborhood that summer swept through me, cutting deep lines, as it swept through America" (Rodriguez, 1993, 164). Its cleansing effect alerted Americans to a class and cultural divide that belied the ideals of the U.S. Constitution.

The Ghetto and Trouble

Moved to the crime-ridden neighborhood of South San Gabriel, Alfonso maintained biology labs at Pierce College. Luis, a student at Richard Garvey Middle School, became a *cholo* (street punk) and cofounded a gang, Thee Impersonations. Flirtations with Elena, Marina, and Socorro influence him to be tattooed with a cross. Although Alfonso and María Estela disapproved of Luis's gang membership and sporting with local girls, he joined four boys in establishing the Animal Tribe. The gang drank wine and vandalized an old house by writing on the walls. A territorial dispute with Sangra hoodlums resulted in an automatic weapon and shotgun assault that blinded Luis's friend Clavo in one eye. While the gang hung out at Huntington Beach, police seized members for possessing beer, marijuana, and mescaline. A judge sentenced one of the group, Black Dog, to juvenile hall.

In his early teens, Luis realized his plight. As he matured, he "felt disoriented, out of balance, tired of just acting and reacting" and admitted that "violence was eating . . . [him] alive"

(Ibid., 113). He worked at legitimate jobs delivering the *Progress Post Advocate* and polishing at a car wash. Another member of the Animal Tribe named Yuk Yuk organized shoplifting from malls, a record store, and supermarkets and robberies at gas stations and residences. While Jandro Mares masterminded gang car theft, junk man Shed Cowager turned the proceeds from bikes, electronics, and guns into cash. Yuk Yuk plotted armed robberies at truck stops and forced Luis to rob the concessionaire at an outdoor movie. Amid bursts of bullets, the gang fled. Terrified by the outcome, Luis ingested aerosol, liquor, and pills to kill himself. After a period of expulsion from home, María let him live in the garage.

The Animal Tribe

Upon enrollment at Mark Keppel High School, Luis entered classes for mentally disabled students and opted to become an outlaw and housebreaker. The Animal Tribe robbed whites at a football stadium, where Police targeted Chicanos and beat Carlitos. A riot halted the game. After expulsion from school, Luis's escape was snuffing aerosol vapors and romancing Payasa, a fellow drug abuser. More violence followed with the slaughter of John Fabela at a wild party at Nina's house, and Luis's cruel initiation to the Lomas gang by stabbing a bystander with a rusty screwdriver. At age 16, Luis sought a new direction by studying karate at the community center. More gunplay killed Little Man and Wilo; the Sangra girls shot at Luis's sister Gloria. Luis prowled other ghettos with Chicharrón while drinking, getting high, and stalking girls. María begged a former elementary school principal to rescue Luis, who lasted at Continuation High School for one week. Alfonso transferred him to Taft High School, where Luis studied typesetting in shop class and tuned auto engines.

Luis left high school during a teachers' strike and survived on his own before returning to the family garage. Into his late teens, while reading the writings of black revolutionaries Claude Brown, Eldridge Cleaver, Le Roi Jones, and Malcolm X and writing poems in the library, Luis reentered the hell of drugs, gang activity, and street crime. The sheriff arrested him in 1970 for nonpayment of a restaurant meal. Luis joined the Neighborhood Youth Corps and studied boxing. Meanwhile, two of the Animal Tribe, Daddio and Yuk Yuk, died in a car mishap after a botched robbery. Luis collapsed at a community center from a drug overdose. His felonies ranged from fighting, riot, and assault on a police officer to thievery, rape, and attempted murder.

A turning point in his life occurred on August 29, 1970. In company with 30,000 protesters, Luis was chanting, singing, and demonstrating at the Chicano Moratorium to protest the Vietnam War held at Belvedere and Laguna parks, when a deputy struck him with a nightstick. At the Los Angeles County Jail, Luis served more cell time than white and black protesters. At the Hall of Justice in downtown L.A., he and other juveniles were booked with adults. Luis shared a cell on murderers' row with two killers next to crazed cult murderer Charles Manson until Maria intervened. The overreaction of arresting officers resulted in looting, arson, hundreds of injuries, and three deaths, which included Ruben Salazar, a Chicano reporter for the *Los Angeles Times* whom police shot in the head with a tear gas casing. The cataclysm awakened in Rodriguez the need to restore justice and peace to society.

On Again, Off Again

On readmittance to Keppel High School, Luis became a school mascot and earned respect as a peacekeeper. He organized a school walkout to publicize the lack of Chicano history and culture in the curriculum. During a standoff against bikers, at 2:30 A.M., Luis obtained a rifle and scope. The San Gabriel police nabbed him for assault with intent to commit murder. Adults promoted dances, jobs, and athletic events to end the cycle of violence and grudges. Luis contributed to a mural project for the city of Rosemead, but the peaceful lull gave place to race wars, firing on a police helicopter, and the shooting of Indio, Santos, and Miguel Robles.

At a point in his life when 25 friends had died violently, Luis Rodriguez worked his way out of the ghetto. California State College offered him $250 and a trip to Berkeley as a prize for a literary contest. After graduating from high school, in 1972, he described himself as a combat veteran overwhelmed by posttraumatic stress syndrome. He enrolled at the college in broadcast journalism and Chicano studies. He launched a rescue effort for disaffected students at East Los Angeles high schools. Another shooting killed David Alcón and sent Tiburón and Chicharrón to prison. Luis's imprisonment for heroin use ended his mission. Friends persuaded a judge to lessen the sentence to a state prison term to a term in the county jail. Luis worked in a paper factory, lived briefly in Chicago, and resettled in California to work in construction and industrial jobs. In summer 1974, he married Camila Martínez and sired their son Ramiro. When mechanical jobs withered and the growth of electronics lessened employment opportunities for Los Angeles Hispanics, gang activity declined.

Luis in Adulthood

While driving a bus and working short term at carpentry, construction, foundry and refinery labor, trucking, and warehouse and janitorial jobs, Rodriguez composed poetry. In 1979, his wife gave birth to Andrea; the next year, Camila sued Luis for divorce. After completing night courses in creative writing, journalism, and speech at East Los Angeles College, in 1980, he entered a summer program in minority journalism at the University of California, Berkeley. He graduated valedictorian and joined a local newspaper to photograph and gather stories. At age 26, he landed a post at the *San Bernardino Sun*. In his free time, he ministered to homeless shelters, migrant labor camps, Lakota and Navajo reservations, men's conferences, juvenile halls, and prisons. Five years later, he began editing the *People's Tribune* in Chicago, where he lived for the next 15 years. His pro-youth speeches heartened audiences in Canada, Central America, Europe, Mexico, and Puerto Rico.

After he wed his second wife, Trini Cardenas, in 1988, they produced Rubén Joaquín. That winter, the couple worried over Ramiro, whose behavior grew more extreme from involvement in Chicago gangs. The next year, Luis ran a coffee shop and bookstore, Tía Chucha's Café & Centro Cultural, a nonprofit multiarts learning and cultural center. The center, sponsored by Chicago's Guild Complex, became one of the largest arts promoters in the Midwest and developed a satellite location in Lake View Terrace, California. Volunteers sponsored holistic learning through media workshops, readings and performances, computer literacy, healing and spiritual events, and family activities. Programming extended to art, dance, drama, film, graphics, literature, music, radio, technology, and television in Chicano, Mexican, and Central American communities of the northeast San Fernando Valley. An outgrowth of the center is Tía Chucha Press and a film production company called Rock a Mole. Rodriguez also edits a Chicano e-zine, Xispas.com.

Luis the Writer

Luis continued to vent his distress over urban violence in print by promoting decision making, appropriate rites of passage, and accountability in youth. His verse, lectures, and essays have appeared in the *American Poetry Review*, *Bello*, *Chicago Tribune*, *English Journal*, *Grand Street*, *LA Weekly*, *Los Angeles Times*, *Nation*, *New York Times*, *Philadelphia Inquirer*, *Prison Life*, *Progressive*, *Rock & Rap Confidential*, *Roots*, *Mercury News*, *Speakeasy*, *U.S. News & World Report*, *Utne Reader*, and *West* and in two stand-alone editions—*Poems across the Pavement* (1989) and *The Concrete River* (1991). The lawlessness he opposed worsened in 1991, when over 600 Los Angeles youth perished from drugs and gang violence. That summer, Luis sought psychiatric counseling for Ramiro. The following year, Luis photographed and recorded anecdotes revealing the boredom and false glorification of gangs for a book, *East Side Stories: Gang Life in East LA* (1998)

To teach his son the perils of gang membership, in 1993, Rodriguez wrote a cautionary tale, *Always Running: La Vida Loca: Gang Days in L.A.*, a vigorous, candid view of teen violence amid a crumbling social order. Dedicated to 25 deceased gang members, the popular memoir spawned a 30-city tour. A classic young adult work for Hispanic youth, for its raw depiction of senseless killings, it became one of the 100 most censored books in America. Nonetheless, the book won a Carl Sandburg Literary Arts Award for Nonfiction, Poetry Center Book Award, Joseph Miles Literary Award, Silver Book award from *ForeWord* magazine, and *Chicago Sun-Times* award along with two *Skipping Stones* nominations, a citation from Parent's Choice, and being named a *New York Times* notable book. In August 1995, he delivered the keynote speech at the Network of Educators on the Americas in Washington, D.C. A 30-minute PBS TV film, *Making Peace: Youth Struggling for Survival, Like father, Like Son* (1997), honors the author's work in 1994 mentoring wayward youth and healing fractured lives among 250 youth at the University of Illinois, Chicago. Ironically, that same year, Rodriguez's son Ramiro began a 28-year prison sentence at the maximum security Cook County Jail for three counts of attempted murder.

Luis and Trini Rodriguez and sons Ruben and Luis returned to L.A. in 2000. Still working toward gang transformation and reduction and toward Hispanic unity with blacks and Asians, Luis Rodriguez remains devoted to his message of justice, literacy, and peace, which he broadcasts over California Public Radio and issues in print and online and at school book fairs. He has appeared on *The Oprah Winfrey Show*, National Public Radio's *Morning Edition*, CNN's *Sonya Live!*, and BBC London to characterize gangs as "unstructured groupings, our children, who desire the same as any young person. Respect" (Ibid., 250). He warned that demoralized and discounted youth need a work ethic. Lacking employment, they sell sex or drugs as an alternative.

With Mexican illustrator Carlos Vazquez's drawings, Rodriguez composed a children's picture book, *América Is Her Name* (1998), a hopeful vision of school days in Chicago's Pilsen barrio. His more recent publications on urban life include the juvenile novel on gangs, *It Doesn't Have to Be This Way: A Barrio Story* (1999), *Hearts and Hands: Creating Community in Violent Times* (2001), the verse CD *My Name's Not Rodriguez* (2002), *The Republic of East L.A.: Stories* (2002), the novel *Music of the Mill* (2005), and *My Nature Is Hunger: New and Selected Poems, 1989–2004* (2005). Subsequent honors include an Unsung Heroes of Compassion Award from the Dalai Lama and an Illinois Author of the Year citation. In 2006, Rodriguez won a City of Los Angeles Individual Artist Fellowship from the city's Department of Cultural Affairs. Still fractious at age 53 while nursing a bad back, he urged dissidents to protest the Iraq War, a killing field for working-class soldiers.

Sources

Deitz, Roger. "Luis J. Rodriguez Award-Winning Chicano Writer and Poet." *Hispanic Outlook in Higher Education* 13 (12) (March 24, 2003): 7.

Dick, Bruce Allen. *A Poet's Truth*. Tucson, AZ: University of Arizona Press, 2003.

Fernandez, Maria Elena. "Poet of the Streets." *Los Angeles Times*, December 18, 2001, E1.

Rodriguez, Luis J. *Always Running: La Vida Loca: Gang Days in L.A.* New York: Touchstone, 1993.

Salas, Abel. "A Writer with a Rich Sense of Place." *Los Angeles Times*, May 5, 2002, 1.

Valadez, John, dir. *Beyond Brown*. Oakland, CA: Firelight Media, 2004. Video.

■ Gender Misidentification
Jamie Koufman

A handsome, prominent throat surgeon, Dr. James A. Koufman felt incomplete until he underwent surgery to alter his gender. Born to Beverly and Joseph Koufman in Boston, Massachusetts, on November 2, 1947, Jamie grew up a favored only child. His wealthy, privileged family hobnobbed with the Kennedys. In preschool days, he fantasized about being female, chose girlish tea parties, and strolled into the girls' restroom in kindergarten. In 1954, without understanding the significance of his secret life, he began cross-dressing in his mother's outfits, hose, and high heels. At the same time, he layered on a crusty protective coating that assured him that he was not a transsexual.

Puberty dismayed Koufman. In his teens, secondary sex characteristics reminded him that he would never have smooth cheeks or womanly breasts. He mourned, "It's all the wrong stuff, it's not the stuff you want" (Deaver, 4/17/2005). In high school in 1965, at the death of his father, an attorney with Peabody, Koufman, and Brewer, Jamie admitted that he would have to use guile to conceal his yearnings: "I'm not going to survive this way. I have to butch it up. And I did" (Deaver, 4/17/2005). He chose the macho model of football and dated a cheerleader. Inside, he longed to change places and wear the flirty skirt and shake pompoms before the fans.

Developing Brilliance

Koufman soured on law after watching the dissolution of his father's firm. Instead of law, he chose general surgery for a more satisfying, nurturing career. He spent a year at Boston University. In 1969, he completed a B.A. degree from Brandeis University in Waltham, Massachusetts. At Boston University School of Medicine from 1969 to 1973, he specialized in laryngology, the treatment of diseases and disorders of the throat and voice. In 1971, he completed research in public health and, 2 years later, began a 2-year residency at Tufts University, which involved head and neck surgery. He developed a reputation for innovative treatment and aggressive surgical perfectionism.

Koufman married but continued to seek relationships with men. In 1972 and 1974, the couple produced sons Joseph and H. Clifford. From chief resident in 1978, the surgeon advanced to the Bowman Gray School of Medicine in Winston-Salem, where he shared an otolaryngological residency research award for perfecting the injectable free fat graft. Among his projects was a study of silent gastroesophageal reflux, a painless regurgitation of acids that jeopardized the esophagus, lungs, vocal cords, and sinuses. He publicized the danger: "There's a whole population of people out there who are living with symptoms, some of which are trivial, some of which will never have a problem, and some of which are time bombs" (Wilson, 1992).

The surgeon taught diagnosis, physiology of the vocal cords, and throat surgery, progressing from assistant professor to full professor by 1994. For consulting purposes, he teamed with speech pathologists and specialists in endocrinology, gastroenterology, and neurology and offered diagnostic and therapeutic innovations to patients. He pioneered laryngeal framework phonosurgery and custom-carved plastic implants and refined surgical techniques with the versatile pulse dye carbon dioxide laser. The bladeless knife improved breathing by allowing the removal of papillomas (warts) from vocal cords without general anesthesia or a surgical team. The cost of the procedure dropped by 80 percent. He predicted far-reaching improvement to medicine through use of the Pentax Scope, a fiber-optic scope on a flexible tube that threaded from the throat into the chest: "This technology will probably have applications in laparoscopic surgery, colon and rectal surgery, urinary tract surgery" (Deaver, 2/1/2005).

A Global Reputation

At age 37, Koufman established the Center for Voice and Swallowing Disorders at Wake Forest University Baptist Medical Center. By 1994, he built a reputation for treatment of the effects of long-term acid reflux (regurgitated stomach acid) on the esophagus and larynx and on throat cancer. In February 1995 at the January meeting of the Southern Section of the American Laryngological, Rhinological, and Otological Society in Key West, Florida, he presented emerging theories of long-term maladies from heartburn, which worsens with middle age. In 1999, he was appointed adjunct clinical professor of otolaryngological surgery at George Washington School of Medicine and Health Services in Washington, D.C., and took a similar post in 2004 at Drexel University in Philadelphia, Pennsylvania, and in 2007 at the New York Eye and Ear Infirmary. He presented symposia on hyperalimentation through feeding tubes, cranial and throat cancer, thyroid tumors, tracheal intubation, throat constriction, nasal polyps, laser surgery of the throat, radiation treatment, and spastic dysphonia and other voice anomalies.

In a productive era, Koufman garnered awards, including a 1989 citation from the American Academy of Otolaryngology and, in 1990, recognition for a Triologic Society thesis on gastroesophageal reflux, a Broyles-Maloney Award of the American Broncho-Esophagological Association, a Rorer Award for his study of chronic hoarseness, and a 1991 Casselberry Award. He published textbooks in his field and articles in *Laryngoscope, Ear, Nose and Throat Journal, Patient Care, American Journal of Gastroenterology, Journal of the American Academy of Dermatology, North Carolina Medical Journal, American Journal of Radiology, Phonoscope, New England Journal of Medicine, Journal of the American College of Surgeons,* and *Visible Voice.* In 1995, he released studies he shared with voice coach Teresa Radomski at the American Academy of Otolaryngology, describing damage to the throats of bluegrass, choral, country-western, gospel, jazz, musical theater, operatic, and rock singers from tension in the vocal cords. In 2002, he extended his study to the types of acting and announcing voices that people prefer, including Katie Couric, Sam Donaldson, Mel Gibson, James Earl Jones, Meg Ryan, and Diane Sawyer.

Turmoil amid Success

Despite a procession of triumphs, Koufman was willing to risk ridicule and possible firing to realize his feminine potential. He knew from interviews the amount of pain suffered by transsexuals and the despair that thrust them over the edge of hope to suicide. In 1986, he ended his first marriage and united with Marsha Leonard, a graduate of Dan Mohr School of Real Estate, whom he described as a soul mate. At West End, they reared his sons and her two sons. To ease their conjugal dysfunction, he sought psychological therapy and counseling and identified himself as a homosexual. In 1997, Koufman gave up pretense, dressed in female outfits, and cruised gay bars. Relationships with males brought out his female affectations, which gay men disdained. Friends suggested that he was a transsexual. He studied resources and joined the Triad Gender Association before questioning specialists in transgender psychology. By age 53, he became one of 30,000 males whom the American Psychiatric Association identified as sexually misidentified. Rather than abandon his job and patients, he readied himself for gender reassignment. He explained, "I wanted to finish what I started" (Deaver, 4/17/2005).

In 2002, Koufman began taking estrogen, the introit to an irreversible gender swap. At a conference of the Triad Gender Association in December 2002, he learned of a theory that diethylstilbestrol, an estrogen that saved around 10 million women from miscarriage from 1948 to 1971, may have created transgenderism in the brain tissue of unborn baby boys. The information fit his family history, which included the miscarriages that afflicted his mother before his birth. That same year, he discovered results from a Dutch study revealed in the November 1995 issue of *Nature* which contributed another clue, that the hypothalamus of transsexuals looked like female tissue. Anecdotal data forced the surgeon to admit, "I lied to myself my whole life" about his biologic drive (Deaver, 2005). He summed up the dilemma with two choices—to be a Nobel Prize winner for medical research or to be a woman.

Farewell to the Masculine Self

By December 2002, Koufman had strategized the vast change that would retrieve him from posturing as a man. The next November, he underwent breast augmentation, which required a second plastic surgery in February 2004 at a cost of $5,000. The complete reassignment, including electrolysis to remove facial and body hair ($3,500), reshaping his cranial features ($40,000), shaving his trachea ($3,500), skin graft ($1,000), removal of his genitals, and labioplasty, a plastic surgery to make a vulva and vagina ($3,500), would cost him a total of $100,000. The announcement that he intended to cease being a man crushed his youngest son and shocked his wife, friends, and the staff at Wake Forest University Baptist Medical Center in Winston-Salem, North Carolina. In essence, his boys lost a father and gained an unknown female relative. After a quarter century of prestige as a specialist in reflux laryngitis, he found male posturing no longer tolerable to his internal female spirit. He intended to debut once more before the medical community with a different persona.

Rather than lurk about large cities seeking treatment, Koufman chose a series of procedures with the full knowledge of friends, family, and colleagues. The reassignment of gender resulted from an identity disorder that produced conflicting self-presentation. Directors Daniel McKinny and Laura Hart McKinny at School of Filmmaking at the North Carolina School of the Arts detailed Koufman's gender change in the graphic documentary, *In Broad Daylight* (2005). The surgeon began the project for personal reasons: "If I went from being this great person to a devil in six months, I would have some documentation" (Deaver, 4/18/2005). The filming also prevented lawsuits against Koufman.

At a San Francisco hotel during her annual summer sabbatical on June 6, 2003, the new Jamie A. Koufman savored surviving a 10-hour surgery that cost $15,500. The procedure broke and reconfigured her facial bones into a feminine shape marked by rounded jaws, slim nose, and smooth forehead. The day after surgery, she sat up in bed and examined her skull swathed in gauze and drain lines from her temples that removed accumulated fluid. On the second day, she enjoyed an epiphany, a spiritual serenity from completing a painful, emotionally dangerous sex change. The transformation required skills in shopping for clothes and shoes and choosing hairstyles and makeup suited to a surgical office. Within weeks, she bobbed her hair and learned to walk like a woman.

The Result of Change

The journey from male to female took 54 months, including 5 months of recuperation ending in June 2004 following genital surgery on June 8 in Trinidad, Colorado. A peek in the mirror at her form in stretch capri pants was reassuring. On the plane trip home, however, she suffered a hormonal meltdown at O'Hare Airport and wept. At home, she had to schedule a half hour to an hour of genital exercises for healing and more time than usual to dress for work. Drug treatment for a urinary tract infection weakened her tendons and precipitated a tear in her left Achilles tendon. Healing of her foot and ankle required weeks in a cast and maneuvering to walk on crutches. During the transition, she reflected on her former life as a man who was often brusque and dismissive of women.

In 2005, 57-year-old Koufman relished the success of the painful and expensive transition from male to female. She regretted not being a girl in his teens and denounced the marginalizing of females, particularly the mistreatment of middle-aged women by taxi drivers and restaurant managers. Her voice remained husky rather than feminine and demanded some retraining from a voice coach. To ameliorate the problem for others, Koufman began devising surgical techniques to feminize the voice. No longer conflicted or success driven, Jamie developed compassion that replaced a former brash, abrasive, and sometimes bullying personality. She had some difficulty with defiant clergy but lost only one patient from distribution of brochures explaining the James-to-Jamie alteration. She made friends and worked more harmoniously with staff like Janet Fox, manager of patient care in the otolaryngology operating room, who found Jamie completely altered in tone and behavior.

Less work-oriented in her new life, Jamie was happy to cook for friends, enjoy movies, and make an effort to connect more personally with patients. In March 2005, she took a part in Eve Ensler's feminist classic *The Vagina Monologues*, which she coproduced at the Arts Council Theatre in Winston-Salem. For fellow misgendered people, she became a professional advocate and cultural hero, except for the disgruntled few envious of her wealth and professional clout. She compiled information about her personal triumph on the Internet at http://www.inbroaddaylight.net. At one point, she traveled to Colorado to aid a transsexual through the removal of male genitals and fashioning of a female body.

Distribution of the film documentary and its presentation at the RiverRun International Film Festival eased pervasive fears of transsexuals by presenting the misery and frustration people suffer from living in the wrong body and acting out the part of the wrong gender.

Two articles in the *Winston-Salem Journal*—"Inner Woman Emerges" and "Practicing Being Herself"—elicited congratulations for Koufman's courage as well as Bible-based denunciations for altering a divinely created body. In August 2005, she answered questions of viewers at the series "OUT at the Movies," presented at the North Carolina School of the Arts. In 2007, she opened and directed the Voice Institute of New York in Manhattan. To broadcast her joy in being her true self, she equipped her car with a vanity plate reading "Trans Girl."

Sources

Deaver, Danielle. "Inner Woman Emerges: Renowned Doctor, Haunted by Mixed Feelings, Decides at 55 That It's Time to Change Genders; 'I Wanted to Be Good . . . to Have a Normal Life.'" *Winston-Salem Journal* (North Carolina), April 17, 2005.

———. "Lighting the Way: Procedures Here Is 1st to Use Hollow-Core Optical Fiber and CO_2 Laser in Surgery." *Winston-Salem Journal* (North Carolina), February 1, 2005.

———. "Practicing Being Herself: With Painful and Costly Sex Change Behind Her, Doctor Nourishes Her Softer Side As She Works to Find and Understand Her Role as a Woman." *Winston-Salem Journal* (North Carolina), April 18, 2005.

———. "Sounding Off: Poll Looks into Which Voices Please or Annoy." *Winston-Salem Journal* (North Carolina), January 31, 2002.

"Rock, Gospel Hurt Voice, Study Finds." *San Francisco Chronicle*, September 19, 1995.

"Study: Stomach Acid Linked Strongly to Throat Cancer." *Herald-Sun* (Durham, NC), February 27, 1995.

"Voice Disorders Treated." *News-Record* (Greensboro, NC), April 21, 1991.

Wilson, Bonnie. "Understanding Reflux: Doctor Has New Insight into Old Problem." *Fayetteville Observer* (North Carolina), March 30, 1992.

Wronski, Richard. "Even Gospel Music Seems to Be a Tension Getter." *Chicago Tribune*, September 19, 1995.

■ Genetic Defect
Lorenzo Odone

Lorenzo Michael Murphy Odone, a victim of an incurable neurodegenerative disease, survived years beyond the prognosis through his parents' intervention. Born to economist Augusto Odone of Gamalero, Italy, and Irish-American linguist and English teacher Michaela Teresa Murphy Odone on May 29, 1978, Lorenzo grew up normal outside Washington, D.C., in Fairfax, Virginia. He profited from having scholarly parents and two older stepsiblings, Cristina and Francesco Odone, who fostered his genius. By age 6, Lorenzo was fluent in English, French, and Italian. He loved reading Greek mythology and listening to classical symphonies, especially Bach's *Brandenburg Concertos* and Handel's *Water Music*.

When Augusto worked for the World Bank, the Odones moved from East Africa to the French-speaking Comoros Islands for 3 years. While he produced the nation's economic plan, Michaela edited his French and headed a clinic distributing pharmaceuticals donated by world charities. Lorenzo befriended Oumouri Hassane, who returned to the family after December 1983, when Lorenzo began to exhibit problems with balance and regressed to the level of a toddler. Because of his loss of coordination and mood swings, hyperactivity, and tantrums in elementary school, the Odones insisted on psychological and neurological tests. On Easter Sunday 1984, reports from the Washington Children's Hospital diagnosed the cause of change in Lorenzo as adrenoleukodystrophy (ALD), a sex-linked genetic adrenal anomaly preventing enzyme breakdown of fatty acids in cells.

ALD, which had been identified only a decade before, offered a prognosis of 1 to 10 years of rapid decline from unmetabolized acids in the nervous system. Victims with less severe forms of ALD lived normal life spans. Like multiple sclerosis, the disease affects brain chemistry by destroying myelin, the white lipid sheath that insulates nerve fibers. An X-linked or mother-to-son defect is present at birth in male and female infants. As nerve signals slow and halt altogether, ALD gradually afflicts the brains of 35 percent of males born with the defective gene. At ages 5 to 10, the neurological breakdown begins, causing dementia and memory lapses, spastic limbs, weakness, and seizures. Progressive buildup of toxic fats in the bloodstream disrupts behavior and depletes the intellect and motor control. ALD and other myelin degenerative diseases afflict 2 million people annually. Because ALD resembles multiple sclerosis, many of the 2 million are misdiagnosed.

Lorenzo's Decline

Frail, deaf, and bedfast, the patient required round-the-clock monitoring by his parents, Oumouri, and hired caregivers. His paralysis progressed to dangerous levels, causing swallowing and breathing problems that threatened pneumonia or asphyxiation. Despite his parents' removal of dangerous fatty acids from Lorenzo's diet by withholding peanut butter, pizza, spinach, and unpeeled fruit like apples, grapes, and peaches, experts predicted that the boy could not survive progressive brain atrophy more than 24 months. In May 1984, the Odones took Lorenzo to Boston for a therapy requiring huge doses of immune system suppressants over a grueling 21-day period. The treatment not only failed, but it also killed his hair follicles and weakened him from weight loss and nausea. In midsummer, the Odones attended a session of the ALD Foundation and discovered the gap of knowledge between researchers and laypeople. On November 10, 1984, at the First National ALD Symposium, scientists corroborated the effectiveness of oleic acid in patients.

In November 1984, Lorenzo could not walk. Michaela described the loss in dramatic terms: "He climbed on to a couch and would not get off, he could no longer walk. A few days later he stopped talking" (Odone, 2000). Within 2 months, he could not communicate or control his bowels and bladder. By the next April, he was neurologically isolated and survived on nasogastric tube feeding. The Odones took an aggressive stance. Augusto explained, "I wouldn't like it that people think our efforts were out of intellectual curiosity. This is a story of love" (Seaward, 2006, 334). They located other victims who were mute, blind, deaf, and paralyzed and investigated the decline of children who died of ALD.

Amateur Research

Horrified by the outlook for patients, the Odones became lay activists for boys like Lorenzo. They broke professional protocols in 1986 by convening experts to discuss glitches in research of methods to intervene in patient deterioration and restore damaged myelin. They badgered airlines to donate seats for experts flying long distances. Michaela located medical references to a 1979 issue of the *Polish Journal of Biology* that described an experiment in rats that used oleic acid to reduce dangerous long-chain acids in the bloodstream. In 1987, Augusto, at age 54, retired from finance to study medical records and clinical trials and to superintend a search for a cure. To support the family, he established a consulting firm, Augusto Odone Associates, Inc., in Washington, D.C. Although he lacked training in biochemistry, cell biology, genetics, and cerebral disorders, he camped out in medical libraries and began piecing together the cause of myelin breakdown from the buildup of long-chain fatty acids in the brain.

During daily therapy, Michaela taught her son to communicate through blinking and rolling his eyes, lifting his eyebrows, and wiggling his fingers. Lorenzo's parents defied the medical power structure, buttonholed researchers, combed animal experiments on lipids, and interviewed top pediatricians worldwide in search of glimmers of hope. In less than a year, Augusto Odone achieved a breakthrough, a treatment of oils that rid the blood stream of long-chain fatty acids. The couple began experimenting with a blend of plant oils from olives and rapeseed, a pale yellow concoction that contained two specific long-chain fatty acids that became a dietary basic for Lorenzo. Doctors and biochemists were at first skeptical that a layman had succeeded where professionals had failed. They warned that rapeseed oil could endanger the heart, but as their son rapidly declined, the Odones accepted the risk.

To obtain supplies, Michaela Odone telephoned a hundred firms before locating a retired English chemist who purified erucic acid at Croda Universal, an English industrial chemical firm. On November 21, 1984, he distilled a formula to the Odones' specifications. The treatment required restriction of fats from Lorenzo's diet and daily doses of corticosteroids and the distilled oil mixed with two monounsaturated dietary oils, glycerol trierucerin and glycerol triolein. The oil normalized the accumulation of long-chain fatty acids in Lorenzo's brain and stopped his neurological decline. Lorenzo's oil prevented the onset of nerve inflammation, but it required careful monitoring to prevent a fall in platelet counts and a threat of fatal hemorrhage from blood that failed to clot. The Odones safely tested the oil on the first human guinea pig, Michaela's sister, Deidra Rufino of Reston, Virginia, a carrier of ALD. Her levels of demyelinating fatty acids dropped to normal.

Lorenzo's Rescue

Michaela Odone systematized a daily care that satisfied Lorenzo's endocrinological, metabolic, and neurological needs. He began the oil regimen on September 27, 1986; by December, his blood levels of toxic fatty acids fell dramatically. Two months later, he could swallow normally. According to Dr. Hugo W. Moser, a professor of neurology and pediatrics at the Kennedy Krieger Institute of Johns Hopkins University in Baltimore and the global expert on ALD, the special oil reduced the myelin destroyers more effectively than drugs. The infusion was so promising in test cases involving 250 boys that Moser prescribed it for other ALD victims. By the summer 1987 ALD Family Conference, parents emulated the Odones and involved themselves in their sons' treatment regimens and diet. The Odones conferred with Alfie Stafford, the father of 7-year-old Barry Stafford, who became the first British patient to profit from the protocol that improved Lorenzo's condition. Barry's 2-year-old brother, Glenn, had the defective gene but no symptoms. Hugo Moser made Glenn the first symptom-free patient to take Lorenzo's oil. The treatment raised false hopes in the Staffords and other parents whose children died despite the oil regimen. In 1993, Dr. Patrick Aubourg of St. Vincent de Paul Hospital in Paris wrote for *New England Journal of Medicine* a negative report on the 24 subjects who had tested the oil blend. Those parents with the least understanding of medical research felt alienated from laboratory experts and blamed physicians for failing to work miracles.

In 1989, the Odones founded the Myelin Project, a global confederation of families and experts that raised funds for research on demyelinating diseases. Headquartered in Amarillo, Texas, in the Laura W. Bush Women's Research Center on the Texas Tech University Health Sciences Center campus, the project maintained ties with laboratories in Canada, Dubai, Germany, Italy, Switzerland, and the United Kingdom and with the European Leukodystrophy Association in France. The volunteer consortium promoted cooperation among clinics to rid research of duplicated efforts and dead ends and to focus on applicable treatment rather than double-blind research involving placebos given to control groups. Unlike other medical foundations, the Odones' endeavor placed parents in direct communication with medical authorities in the area of myelin repair at Yale University, the University of Wisconsin at Madison, the Istituto Superiore di Sanità and San Raffaele Scientific Institute in Italy, the Hôpital de la Salpêtrière and the Institut Pasteur in France, the University of Cambridge in the United Kingdom, and the Max-Planck-Gesellschaft in Germany, and the Queen's University at Kingston, Ontario. Among the most promising treatments were bone marrow or gene transplants with Schwann cells, which built myelin sheaths for peripheral nerves in patients with multiple sclerosis. By age 14, Lorenzo could swallow his meals and express his thoughts.

Lorenzo's Fame

Lorenzo's Oil (1992), a biopic filmed in Pittsburgh by Universal Studios, depicted the title curative as a miracle nutriment capable of alleviating crippling in thousands of young victims. Starring Zack O'Malley Greenburg as Lorenzo and Nick Nolte and Susan Sarandon as the boy's parents, the film portrayed his rapid decline and the Odones' desperation to find a cure before he was irreversibly brain damaged. At a meeting of parents, Augusto stated his outrage with a simple comparative: "Our children seem to be at the service of medical science. We thought medical science was the servant of suffering children" (Crellin, 2005, 78). Nolte dramatized the effects of a single enzyme in the oil treatment on screen by linking paper clips.

For empathetic mothering, Sarandon earned an Oscar nomination. Of her fierce and energetic portrayal, Augusto remarked, "There was a physical resemblance. She seemed to have the same 'tiger mother' instinct [as Michaela]" (Tucker, 2004, 51). The actor developed the part after witnessing Michaela's devotion to Lorenzo. She channeled the caregiver's drive, "becoming primal in her clarity in protecting and watching over Lorenzo.... She is so uncompromising and so pure" (Ibid., 52). Ethics, humanities, philosophy, and science teachers profited from a teaching kit that presented the film along with motivational tools and a study guide plus a slide program explaining how the oil relieves the body of toxic buildup. In 1996, the Odones provided singer Phil Collins with lyrics to the song "Lorenzo," which Collins recorded on the album *Dance into the Light*. After a decade of study, the BBC TV documentary *Medical Mysteries* revealed that the oil does little to revive victims' nervous systems and brain cells but does protect children like Glenn Stafford who are born with genetic susceptibility to ALD.

After attending and stimulating Lorenzo for 16 hours a day, Michaela died on June 10, 2000, of lung cancer. The loss left Augusto to fight their son's disease alone and to normalize activities for him. Augusto continued rehabilitating Lorenzo while looking for a cure and empowering the Myelin Project. He aimed for collaborators to discover a method of reducing or halting blockage of nerve impulse conduction and of remyelination of diseased cells to restore lost sensory motor function. He launched annual meetings and teleconferences to exchange leads, to foster ties among authorities, to facilitate the approval and funding of research, and to motivate experts to factor in the time element in the ebbing lives of Lorenzo and his fellow victims. Another goal was the screening of at-risk newborn males to target boys like Lorenzo before the onset of symptoms. Augusto's project produced genetically engineered mice with ALD symptoms and offered the National Institutes of Health a basis for new studies. By June 2002, the Myelin Project had raised $4 million to finance 29 research endeavors. Lorenzo's oil began appearing in medical protocols throughout North America, Europe, and Japan.

In September 2002, Dr. Moser deduced from a decade-long study of American and European boys that Lorenzo's oil treatment circumvented symptoms in 66 percent of the 105 subjects. A July 2005 issue of *Archives of Neurology* affirmed that Lorenzo's oil might protect at-risk boys from developing ALD. Augusto directed royalties to the Myelin Project and to a trust fund for Lorenzo. Augusto appeared on talk shows and, for setting biochemical research in motion and patenting Lorenzo's oil, earned multiple honorary doctorates for pioneering protocols to fight myelin destruction. He retired from the Myelin Project in April 2007, shortly before Lorenzo's 29th birthday. Cared for by nurses and by Oumouri Hassane, Lorenzo's friend from the Comoros Islands, the survivor continued to amaze physicians with his resilience and the absence of regression. He ate soft food and distinguished colors, shapes, and right from left. After regaining his sight and his neck mobility, Lorenzo enjoyed letters and e-mails from friends and sitting in a swimming pool. He spent his days listening to classical music or stories either read aloud or taped by Michaela. He died of pneumonia on May 30, 2008, the day after his thirtieth birthday.

Sources

Akoh, Casimir C., Oi Ming Lai, and American Oil Chemists' Society. *Healthful Lipids*. Urbana, IL: American Oil Chemists' Society, 2005.

Crellin, J. K. *Public Expectations and Physicians Responsibilites: Voices of Medical Humanities*. Abingdon, UK: Radcliffe, 2005.

Lorenzo's Oil: The Full Story. BBC News, July 21, 2004.

Masters, Colin, and Denis Crane. *The Peroxisome: A Vital Organelle*. New York: Cambridge University Press, 1995.

Odone, Augusto. "Obituary: Michaela Odone." *Independent* (London), June 21, 2000.

Saxon, Wolfgang. "Michaela Odone, 61, the 'Lorenzo's Oil' Mother." *New York Times*, June 13, 2000.

Seaward, Brian Luke. *Managing Stress: Principles and Strategies of Health and Wellbeing*. Boston: Jones & Bartlett, 2006.

Smith, Virginia A. "Lorenzo." *Philadelphia Inquirer*, August 11, 2005.

Snowbeck, Christopher. "The Mixed Legacy of 'Lorenzo's Oil.'" *Pittsburgh Post-Gazette*, May 8, 2001.

Tucker, Betty Jo. *Susan Sarandon: A True Maverick*. Tucson, AZ: Wheatmark, 2004.

Vedantam, Shankar. "A Real-Life Sequel to 'Lorenzo's Oil': After His Death, Scientist's Work May Bear Fruit." *Washington Post*, January 28, 2007, A.1.

■ Ghetto Upbringing
Colin Powell

A Jamaican-American, Colin Luther Powell advanced from ghetto child to the nation's 65th secretary of state. A Harlem native, he was born on April 5, 1937, to emigrants from

Jamaica—Luther Theophilus Powell from Top Hill, Kingston, and Maud Ariel "Arie" McKoy Powell, a seamstress from Westmoreland. Arie achieved higher status than her husband because she was reared in polite British Anglicanism and graduated from high school. Luther departed the West Indies in 1920 to find better work than his janitor's job. In a section of New York lacking black-owned businesses, he worked his way up from stock clerk to shipper and foreman. While growing up in a four-story brick tenement at 952 Kelly Street in Hunts Point, South Bronx, Colin lived in a marginally tolerant mixed neighborhood of blacks, Hispanics, Italians, Jews, and whites. He and his sister Marilyn, 5 years his senior, hobnobbed with other kids from Barbadian, Jamaican, and Trinidadian heritage. At age eight, he observed the inequalities awaiting veterans of World War II—substandard schools and colleges, limited job and salary opportunities, and toilets and water fountains marked "colored."

Unlike other latchkey kids, Powell received steady home supervision. While his parents worked in the garment district, he became the ward of his maternal grandmother, Gram Alice McKoy, a boardinghouse manager to Jamaican immigrants. Boyhood activities ranged from baseball games on an empty lot and maneuvering razor-tailed kites to cut loose a rival's kite from its string. He recalled in his memoir "'making the walk' from Kelly Street, up 163rd Street around Southern Boulevard to Westchester Avenue and back home" (Powell, 2003, 16). At the high point of bad boy behavior, he got ejected from church camp, joined a street gang, and received his father's rebuke for catching him in a poker game at the shoe shop. Powell described a constant face-off at home—his father's optimism and his mother's skepticism at each family crisis, an opposition characteristic of his adult job of national diplomat and peacekeeper. In the background, the neighborhood seethed with crime—"from gang fights to gang wars, from jackknives to switchblades, from zip guns to real guns from marijuana to heroin" (Ibid., 29). For Colin, the lure of marijuana, controlled substances, and illegal weapons made no inroads.

From School to Army

A lackluster math and science student, Powell failed to gain entrance to Stuyvesant High School, one of New York City's specialized academies that admit students by competitive examination only. Advancing from unloading baby buggies at Sickser's department store at Fox and Westchester streets, he took a menial summer job at a furniture factory screwing hinges onto cabinet doors. He graduated from Morris High School and set out to major in engineering at The City College of New York where the tuition was ten dollars. Unlike his social climber sister, a student at Buffalo State Teachers College, he fit in with "sons and daughters of the inner city, the poor, the immigrant" (Ibid., 36). Before completing a B.S. in geology, he joined the Reserve Officers' Training Corps and did target practice with the Pershing Rifles, the beginning of his love for the military. As a second lieutenant, he trained with the airborne rangers at the National War College in Fort Benning, Georgia. In 1962, he married audiologist Alma Vivian Johnson of Birmingham, Alabama, mother of their son, Michael Kevin Powell, current chair of the Federal Communications Commission.

Powell served his country as a soldier for 35 years. During the "nuke baiting" of the Cold War, his assignments began with the Third Armored Division in Gelnhausen 25 miles east of Frankfurt, West Germany. From 1958 to 1960, he learned to care for and defend his troops against potential communist attack. As hostilities heated up in southeast Asia, he, like many black Americans, supported the presidential candidacy of Lyndon B. Johnson. Later, Powell admitted his naïveté of the commander in chief's influence on the war: "I had no penetrating political insights into what was happening" (Ibid., 100). During two hitches as an adviser in the Vietnam War and leader of an ARVN unit, Powell experienced the daily threats to jungle patrols. He returned home with a Purple Heart and a Bronze Star. The medals marked a serious injury to his right foot from detonating a bamboo punji stick while he patrolled the Laos–Vietnamese border. Spreading infection from dung poisoning required his evacuation to a Hue hospital by helicopter. In recuperation, he returned to a nation that continued to refuse hotel and restaurant service to blacks. From supervising an airfield and intelligence collection during combat, he advanced to major in 1966 and to assistant chief of staff of operations of the 23rd Infantry and investigator of the My Lai Massacre. During his second posting to combat at the Duc Pho outpost in 1968, he received a medal for retrieving soldiers from a flaming helicopter that caused his second combat injury, a broken ankle. For valor, he won the Soldier's Medal and the Legion of Merit.

Plunge into Politics

Powell returned to college. He earned an M.B.A. in 1971 from George Washington University and received a White House fellowship and an assignment to the Office of Management and Budget during the Nixon administration. By the time that Powell posted to South Korea in the mid-1970s as a battalion commander, he bore the rank of lieutenant colonel and achieved the rank of brigadier general in 1979. Following postings to Fort Carson, Colorado, and Fort Leavenworth, Kansas, in the 1980s, he was named senior military assistant to Secretary of Defense Caspar Weinberger during the invasion of Grenada and the raid on Libya. During this period, Powell's son sustained a broken pelvis, torn bladder and urethra, and cracked vertebrae, injuries that required a year's recuperation at Walter Reed Army Medical Center in Washington, D.C. Under President Jimmy Carter, Powell assisted both the deputy secretary of defense and the secretary of energy. In 1986, Powell returned to field command of the Fifth Corps in Frankfurt, Germany. As national security adviser to Ronald Reagan, Powell managed presidential summits with Soviet President Mikhail Gorbachev. In 1989, Powell rose to four-star general and commander in chief of the U.S. Forces Command at Fort McPherson, Georgia. His supervisory extended over all army and National Guard troops in the United States and Puerto Rico.

Powell's stellar rise placed him over the Joint Chiefs of Staff from 1989 to 1993. A cautious moderate, he earned the nickname "reluctant warrior" for choosing negotiation and diplomacy over attack mode. Under his command, the United States invaded Panama, deposed General Manuel Noriega, and, in 1991, launched operations Desert Shield and Desert Storm to drive Iraq out of Kuwait at the onset of the Persian Gulf War. At the outbreak of the Iraq War, he feared that prolonged combat was too open-ended to reach a conclusion. He anticipated that the occupation of Iraq would stretch soldier power to capacity and leave Americans vulnerable at home. To the West Wing war cabinet, he was the only voice opposing military intervention against dictator Saddam Hussein and campaigning at the highest levels for economic sanctions and the fortification of Kuwait. Rather than go in shooting, he championed talks with Iran and Syria and warned Bush that war in the Middle East might escalate into a Vietnam-style quagmire. Powell called for an exit strategy as an integral part of U.S. military strategy. As an acknowledgement of his stature among moderates, in late 1993, Queen Elizabeth II appointed him an honorary Knight Commander of the Order of the Bath. He extended his reputation as a peacemaker in 1994 by joining Senator Sam Nunn and President Jimmy Carter in ousting a dictator from Haiti and returning the island to democracy.

Adviser to the Powerful

In retirement, Powell became a lecturer and reflected over an impressive career in his memoir, *My American Journey*. Both Democrats and Republicans courted him for his war record and popularity, but he rejected bipartisanship by calling for formation of a third party. In 1996, he opted not to oppose the presidential candidacy of Arkansas Governor Bill Clinton. Instead, in 1997, Powell established America's Promise Alliance, a collaboration advancing the well being of 15 million vulnerable children and youth. According to biographer Karen De Young, an associate editor of the *Washington Post*, in 2000, Powell realized that neither his head nor his heart urged him to run for office.

Unlike party faithfuls, Powell remained his own man. Cool and resolute, he supported women's right to choose, affirmative action, and handgun control. In reference to homosexual rights to military enlistment, he declared, "[G]ays and lesbians should be allowed to have maximum access to all aspects of society" (Pincus, 2007, A3). Nonetheless, Bush rewarded Powell's overall wisdom and loyalty by naming him secretary of state, a post that hawks wanted reserved for an ultraconservative. Although Powell distanced himself from presidential foreign policy deliberation, particularly from Secretary of Defense Donald Rumsfeld and White House adviser Karl Rove, Powell attended the Organization of American States General Assembly and promoted the Inter-American Democratic Charter. At a tenuous point in the secretary's relationship with the president, Bush locked Powell out of a staff meeting. When terrorism shook national confidence on September 11, 2001, Powell followed Bush's orders to convince citizens that war was both justified and necessary. He superintended relations with foreign heads of states to achieve a consensus on global terrorism and to raise money and troops. His reasoning was sound: "Where we have a principled position, what we will do is explain that principled position to our friends, try to see if we can find compromises, so we can join consensus" (Gordon and Shapiro, 2004, 51).

Powell viewed a deteriorating situation in Iraq as a sectarian civil war between violent Shi'ites and more peaceful Sunnis. He advised George W. Bush on foreign policy with a warning from Pottery Barn: "You break it, you pay for it." Powell warned Bush that invasion and occupation of Iraq was detrimental to Americans and the global community. Powell stated, "I took him through the consequences of going into an Arab country and becoming the occupiers" (Baxter, 2007). In 2003, Powell shifted stance on the invasion of Iraq to prevent stockpiling of weapons of mass destruction on condition that the U.S. press the issue at a U.N. assembly and that the global community agree on the removal of Saddam Hussein from office. On February 5, 2003, Powell reached the pinnacle of his career when he harangued the U.N. Security Council on the necessity of military action. As proof, he claimed that Iraqis admitted producing 4 tons of VX, a lethal nerve agent. He promised to present evidence that al Qaeda and Osama bin Laden plotted and executed the sabotage of the Pentagon and the World Trade Center. He mouthed a course of action promoted by the Bush administration, Vice President Richard Cheney in particular. Unknown to Powell, the Bush war cabinet concealed evidence that refuted Powell's U.N. declaration. In 2005, he stated regret at being manipulated as the administration's fall guy. As the scapegoat, Powell lost credibility with politicians, the press, European allies, and U.N. delegates. He recouped respect by declaring a need to reorganize the U.S. intelligence community to assure sharing of secret information.

A New Direction

On November 15, 2004, Powell was forced out of the Bush administration and replaced by Condoleezza Rice. Although citizens regretted his sacrifice to dirty politics, the break gave Powell more time with his grandsons, Bryan and Jeffrey Powell. In July 2005, Powell signed on with Kleiner Perkins Caufield & Byers as a venture capitalist. Within two months, he earned headlines for lambasting federal emergency services to the impoverished Louisiana and Mississippi victims of hurricane Katrina. He continued clashing with hawks and conservatives by challenging elements of the terrorism bill that reduced or endangered constitutional rights of citizens and violation of the Geneva Conventions. On an NBC TV broadcast of *Meet the Press*, he further disgruntled militarists by recommending immediate closure of the U.S. prison at Guantanamo Bay, Cuba, for its blot on American character. He denounced the use of torture against alleged terrorists as an obstacle to "the way the world perceives America" (Pincus, 2007, A3). Powell expressed his anger at learning about torture at the prison several years after the White House discovered infractions. He proposed that detainees return to the United States for immediate processing under federal law.

As a private citizen, Powell continued to win support for his humanitarianism and concern for world safety and security. He shunned right-wing extremists but did not remove his name for political candidacy. Instead, he stated, "I make myself available to talk about foreign policy matters with whoever wishes to chat with me" (Pincus, 2007, A3). In late September 2007, he assisted Time Warner Chairman Richard D. Parsons in the search for a new president for Howard University. He joined boxer Sugar Ray Leonard, evangelist Robert Schuller, and inspirational speaker Zig Ziglar for a fall 2007 session of Get Motivated! and addressed an audience at St. Xavier University in Chicago with his view on terrorist threats. Like a staunch professional soldier, he assured listeners, "We will rebuild, and we will mourn, and we will go after them . . . with all the forces at our disposal. There's one thing terrorists and terrorism cannot do—it cannot change who we are as a people" ("Terrorists," 2007, 22).

Sources

Baxter, Sarah. "Powell Tried to Talk Bush Out of War." *Times*, July 8, 2007.

De Young, Karen. *Soldier: The Life of Colin Powell*. New York: Alfred A. Knopf, 2006.

Dutty, Brian. "The Kid of No Promise." *U.S. News & World Report* 139 (16) (October 31, 2005).

Gellman, Barton, and Jo Becker. "The Unseen Path to Cruelty." *Washington Post*, June 25, 2007, 15.

Gordon, Phillip H., and Jeremy Shapiro. *Allies at War: America, Europe, and the Crisis over Iraq*. New York: McGraw-Hill, 2004.

Johnson, Chalmers. *The Sorrows of Empire: Militarism, Secrecy, and the End of the Republic*. New York: Henry Holt & Co., 2004.

Myers, Richard B., Richard H. Kohn, Mackubin Thomas Owens, Lawrence J. Korb, and Michael C. Desch. "Salute and Disobey?" *Foreign Affairs* 86 (5) (October 2007): 147–156.

Pincus, Walter. "Powell Calls for Closure of Military Prison at Guantanamo." *Washington Post*, June 11, 2007, A3.

Powell, Colin, and Joseph E. Persico. *My American Journey*. New York: Ballantine, 2003.

"Terrorists Can't Change Us, Powell Says Here." *Chicago Sun-Times*, September 20, 2007, 22.

■ Grief
Mitch Albom

Memoirist, sportscaster, and essayist Mitchell "Mitch" Albom won the nation's attention by describing his personal encounter with a sick man. The camaraderie introduced Albom to terminal illness, which he viewed as slow-motion death. A native of Passaic, New Jersey, he was born on May 23, 1958, to Ira and Rhoda Albom and grew up in Philadelphia with brother Peter, a would-be actor who is two years younger. From a legacy of anecdotes and family history that grandparents, aunts, and uncles told over the Thanksgiving table, Albom mastered storytelling. It became a means of inserting into their mutual genealogy his own experiences with world events. After he enrolled at Akiba Hebrew Academy, he resolved to become a journalist.

While completing a B.A. in sociology from Brandeis University, in spring 1976, Albom became friends with Dr. Morris "Coach" Schwartz, a Bronx-born expert on treatment of the mentally ill and a mediator in racial unrest at Brandeis. Morrie earned a reputation for compassion at Chestnut Lodge, a mental hospital outside Washington, D.C. To enhance humane care, he formed personal bonds with patients through one-on-one conversation. A Russian-Jewish agnostic, Morrie drew life lessons from Buddhism, Christianity, and Judaism and dedicated his career to instructing others on the perplexing issues of mortality.

In 1977, Morrie taught Albom in two sophomore- and junior-level courses in group process and urged him to learn how to be fully human. Morrie valued individualism and, over shared lunches of egg salad at the college cafeteria, encouraged Albom to pursue his dream of playing jazz piano. Albom witnessed Morrie's divergent thinking at a basketball game in 1979, where the professor informed fans to be satisfied with being number two. Out of altruism, Morrie also started Project Greenhouse to provide the needy with mental health care. More impressive was Morrie's gift of top grades to male students during the Vietnam War to keep them eligible for military draft deferments.

Making a Career

In his senior year in college, Albom wrote a yearlong honors thesis on "how football in America . . . [had] become ritualistic, almost a religion, an opiate for the masses" (Albom, 1997, 67). Morrie was so impressed that he suggested that Albom attend graduate school. Albom promised to stay in touch with his mentor. After earning an M.A. in business administration and journalism from Columbia University, in 1981, Albom joined the sports staff at the *Queens Tribune* in Flushing, New York, and dreamed of becoming a jazz pianist. He moved on to write for the *Fort Lauderdale News/Sun Sentinel*, the *Philadelphia Inquirer*, and *SPORT*.

Across the country, Albom developed name and face recognition. By 1985, he became a nationally syndicated newspaper columnist for the *Detroit Free Press*. Constantly on deadline, he became famous for creating the nation's first talk sports program, *The Mitch Albom Show on the Weekend*, for WJR-AM in Detroit. Albom's on-the-scene commentaries broadcast to 125 U.S. stations and Canada. The addition of electronic media to his workload began a soul-wrecking spiral of constant interviewing, writing, interviews, and public appearances. He interacted with the panel on ESPN's Sports Reporters, wrote a regular column for *Playgirl*, and published in *GEO*, *GQ*, *New York Times*, *WorldTraveler* (Northwest Airlines' in-flight magazine), *PARADE*, *Sports Illustrated*, *TV Guide*, and *USA Today*.

Apart from daily and nightly reportage on athletics, Albom sought stability. He bought a house in the Detroit suburb of Farmington Hills and, in 1995 after a 7-year courtship, married professional singer and guitarist Janine Sabino. He expanded his talent for lecturing, stand-up comedy, nightclub singing, and amateur boxing. Subconsciously, at age 37, he deluded himself that he controlled his life, which was dominated by cell phones, the electronic media, and interviews with rich, ego-sensitive athletes and media stars. His after-11 evenings with Janine were spent at Denny's restaurant, where they tried to stay awake to share the remains of their day. He confessed, "Over the years, I had taken labor as my companion and had moved everything else to the side" (Ibid., 32).

Rekindling Friendship

In July 1995, Albom paid a visit to his former college professor and scolded himself for failing to keep in touch. The two reconnected at a fearful passage for Morrie, who, at age 78, was diagnosed with a fatal and humbling illness, amyotrophic lateral sclerosis or Lou Gehrig's disease. The prognosis of creeping paralysis was 2 years, but Morrie knew that the time was possibly less. At the window in his home study, Morrie looked out on the final round of seasons and declared his intent to be a bridge to help other people face the final life passage to death. Albom later reflected on Morrie's concern for human suffering during the Bosnian war, "Maybe death is the great equalizer, the one big thing that can finally make strangers shed a tear for one another" (Ibid., 51).

The reunion of former student and teacher altered Albom's outlook during the final months of Morrie's life, which ended on November 4, 1995. Over 14 weeks of discussions, Albom visited Morrie at his home in West Newton, Massachusetts, and began structuring a new perception of a meaningful existence. Albom learned that Morrie had given up dancing the previous summer and taught one last session of social psychology before yielding to declining strength. He hired a valet and began swimming at the YMCA to bolster his muscles. By January 1995, Morrie required daily care and needed a wheelchair for mobility.

After TV anchor Ted Koppel interviewed Morrie on *Nightline* on February 25, 1995, Albom heard the broadcast and resolved to visit his wise old mentor. The visit coincided with a low point in Albom's life, after an assignment in April to write about the Wimbledon tennis tournament. In London, the author grew disillusioned about the purpose of publicizing self-important sports stars. On July 13, Albom found himself jobless and bored following an unforeseen union strike that idled the *Detroit Free Press*. He remarked, "I was stunned at how easily things went on without me" (Ibid., 45).

Gifts from Grief

On July 18, Albom began weekly visits with Morrie, who faced his own dilemma of becoming dependent on others for daily necessities and constant health treatments. Albom's gifts to Morrie were simpler—deli salads and bagels and spirited conversation. Morrie's gifts were life-sustaining lessons in coping: "Study me in my slow and patient demise. Watch what happens to me. Learn with me" (Ibid., 10). Reduced to living in a recliner, Morrie ruminated on sources of compassion and on the causes of self-pity and sadness, which he sensed in Albom's life.

On August 1, Albom introduced a tape recorder to capture Morrie's life story along with quotations from philosophers Martin Buber, Erik Erikson, and Erich Fromm. Through personal reflections, Morrie introduced such extraneous topics as the worldview of the Desana Indians of South America, who believed that birth and death are necessary to balance earth's energy supply. Morrie shed light on the trivialities of modern obsessions, citing as examples the narcissistic football hero O. J. Simpson's double murder trial, Princess Diana's rocky marriage to Prince Charles, and Atlanta media mogul Ted Turner's greed for his own television network. Morrie assured Albom that, whatever life's tensions and distractions, love is always triumphant. Morrie put the concept into existential terms: "Love is the only rational act" (Ibid., 52).

By August 29, 1995, Albom pressed on to the unspoken issue, Morrie's preparation for death. By September 5, Morrie ate only liquid or soft foods and depended on an oxygen tank, yet he convinced Albom that fear did not dominate the thoughts of the dying. As the disease further debilitated Morrie, Albom expressed unconditional love by lifting his fragile old friend from the chair and holding him on the toilet. On Albom's eighth visit, Morrie introduced a crucial topic, the danger of substituting materialism for love. He typified examples of caring for others in shared time, community, storytelling, and volunteering. The theme struck a sore spot in Albom's personal life and influenced him to try to call his estranged brother, Peter, a drug addict and victim of pancreatic cancer who enjoyed 5 years of remission in Spain. On October 3, Morrie spoke on the importance of a long-lasting husband–wife relationship. Albom saw that love in action when his wife Janine accompanied him on a visit and sang to Morrie the romantic ballad, "The Very Thought of You."

Another Separation

Good times rapidly came to an end. Albom realized that the renewed friendship was reaching the final separation and faced a burden of sadness and regret. The next week, he learned how to pound Morrie's back to loosen congestion to prevent pneumonia in his failing lungs. In a gesture of love, Albom massaged Morrie's ankles. By October 17, Morrie felt it was time to teach his former student to let go of grudges and to forgive himself and others. At a quirky moment in his thinking, Morrie vowed to return to earth as a gazelle, a sprightly image opposite to the old man's immobile state. Albom pledged to visit Morrie's grave to verbalize personal dilemmas.

By October 31, Albom witnessed a pivotal moment in Morrie's decline, when he declared himself ready to let go and embrace death. He asserted, "It'll get my body. It will not get my spirit" (Ibid., 163). Morphine reduced Morrie's interaction with Albom, who held his teacher's hand. Morrie praised Albom for his good soul. Albom wept when he kissed Morrie. Within the week, Morrie came under fulltime hospice care, lapsed into a coma, and slipped away peacefully one morning while his wife and sons surrounded him. With the help of his brother David, the family buried Morrie's ashes on a nearby hill under a shade tree that Morrie had preselected.

Redirecting Sorrow

The 14 intense chats with Morrie changed Albom. He reflected on lessons on mortality, terror, aging, greed, marriage, family, society, forgiveness, and meaning. Morrie reminded him to take responsibility for other people and to value everyday joys and the wisdom of advanced age. Albom recalled Morrie's instruction in how to be silent and alone with the inner self. At Morrie's urging, Albom located his younger brother Peter by phone and stated his love for him. The lessons in life influenced Albom to write *Tuesdays with Morrie: An Old Man, a Young Man, and Life's Greatest Lesson* (1997), which required a 9-month delving into sorrow by reviewing the taped interviews. For the writer, constant replays and conversations with Morrie's spirit produced a unique form of afterlife for the elderly humanist. The result was an antidote to Albom's grief—a 4-year bestseller that sold 5 million copies in Australia, Brazil, England, Japan, and the United States. It found its way into high school, college, yeshiva, and seminary reading lists in courses on nursing, philosophy, psychology, sociology, and theology. Out of honor to his professor, Albom donated the publisher's advance to pay Morrie's medical bills.

Albom ranged far from sports broadcasting to a new career as the author of eight stories, each a tribute to a unique human situation. He told anecdotes on *The Early Show* on CBS, *Dr. Phil*, *Good Morning America*, *Larry King Live*, NBC's *The Today Show*, *The Oprah Winfrey Show*, *The Rosie O'Donnell Show*, and *The Late Late Show with Tom Snyder*. On December 6, 1999, Winfrey's teleplay *Tuesdays with Morrie* debuted on ABC to an unprecedented audience of 25 million. The presentation won four Emmys for Hank Azaria as Mitch and Jack Lemmon's end-of-career role as Morrie. Lemmon claimed that it was his favorite part. In 1999, the National Hospice Organization named Albom their Man of the Year. He wrote two biographies and a popular stage comedy, *Duck Hunter Shoots Angel* (2003), a humorous look at spiritual reclamation. Five years after writing *Tuesdays with Morrie*, Mitch collaborated with Jeffrey Hatcher to adapt the text for the stage. It opened in Poughkeepsie, New York, in summer 2002 and flourished on a 25-city tour in the United States and Canada.

Becoming a better visitor to the sick and a better listener to survivors, Albom saw himself as Morrie's permanent teaching assistant. Rather than allow the bestseller to dominate his output, Albom reengineered his encounter with death and grief for a spin-off bestseller, *The Five People You Meet in Heaven* (2003), an afterdeath encounter with a failed amusement park repairman. The blockbuster novel evolved from Mitch's uncle Eddie, a cab driver and World War II veteran, and his memories of a near-death experience. Albom's screen version appeared on ABC TV on December 5, 2004, starring Jon Voight, Ellen Burstyn, and Jeff Daniels. Albom followed with *For One More Day* (2006), a tribute to motherhood and redemption through forgiveness. The work, which dramatized a son's reunion with his mother's ghost, sold well in Australia, Brazil, England, France, Germany, Japan, Korea, and New Zealand. Oprah Winfrey's Harpo Films produced a screen version for ABC TV scheduled for airing in December 2007.

Still writing at his home in Franklin, Michigan, Albom gave up his former workaholism. As Morrie suggested, the writer devoted himself to love, community, and creativity. He developed his relationship with Peter and with Peter's daughter Lilly. Albom and his wife support charities for needy children and the elderly, food banks, literacy and scholarships, hospitals, and the homeless and collect donations for Hospice, Forgotten Harvest, Meals on Wheels, and Habitat for Humanity. The couple founded two charities, Detroit: The Dream Fund and A Time to Help, a monthly roundup of volunteers.

Sources

Albom, Mitch. "Love Boat? It's More Like Food Boat." *Detroit Free Press*, August 8, 2004.

———. *Tuesdays with Morrie: An Old Man, a Young Man, and Life's Greatest Lesson.* New York: Broadway Books, 1997.

Bueher, Jack. "Mitch Albom Visits Fremont." *News Messenger*, May 3, 2004.

Carpenito-Moyet, Lynda Juall. "Facing Death." *Nursing Forum* (April–June 2002): 3–4.

De Botton, Alain. "Continuing Ed." *New York Times*, November 23, 1997, 20.

Geller, Conrad. "A Lesson in Living." *Writing* (April/May 2003): 11–13.

Grossman, Lev. "Words of Paradise." *Time* (October 13, 2003): 82.

Hutton, Carole Lee. "Mitch Albom's Book: Decision to Kill Review a Tough, But Right One." *Detroit Free Press*, October 5, 2003.

Lauer, Charles S. "Listen to This." *Modern Healthcare* (February 10, 2003): 34.

Omega, Julie L. "Thursdays with Morrie: The Use of Contemporary Literature in a Death and Dying Course." *Omega* 47 (3) (2003): 245–252.

Webber, Bruce. "A Life Examined As Death Inches Closer." *New York Times*, November 21, 2002, E1.

■ Heart Disease
Martin Sheen

A radical Catholic respected as a proponent of American civil disobedience, Martin "Marty" Sheen faced a crisis during his early success as a screen actor. At his birth on August 3, 1940, in Dayton, Ohio, he was named Ramón Gerardo Antonio Estévez for his father, Spanish emigrant Francisco Estévez, a machine inspector. Sheen suffered permanent motion impairment from crushed bones in his left arm and shoulder during forceps delivery. The seventh in a family of one sister and eight brothers, he lived temporarily in Bermuda and attended Mount Saint Agnes School outside Hamilton. In 1949, he masterminded a caddy strike at the elitist country club where he earned pocket money from stingy, self-important players. He developed sympathy with the underdog from his mother, Mary Anne Phelan Estévez of Tipperary, Ireland, who died when he was 11. He admired her honor to ancestors in the Irish Republic Army during three years of combat during the Anglo-Irish War of 1919.

Living in the South Park section of Dayton under the care of his grandmother, Sheen went to Chaminade Julienne Catholic High School. At age 18, he opted to quit his education. On borrowed cash, he moved to New York City to find acting parts at the avant-garde Living Theater and in film. He took a stage pseudonym honoring Archbishop Fulton John Sheen and pursued "angry young man" roles in the style of James Dean. To finance acting lessons, Sheen swept theater stages, delivered newspapers, and worked a soda fountain. In 1961, he married artist Janet Templeton, mother of their four actor children, Emilio Estévez, Ramón Luis Estévez, Renée Estévez, and Charlie Sheen. After 5 years of regular performing in *As the World Turns*, on May 25, 1964, Sheen made his name at the Royale Theatre as World War II veteran Timmy Cleary in Frank Gilroy's Pulitzer Prize-winning drama *The Subject Was Roses*. The film version, costarring Jack Albertson and Patricia Neal, earned Sheen a Golden Globe and a Tony nomination. His string of youthful triumphs continued with the role of a homosexual mate opposite Hal Holbrook in *That Certain Summer* (1972) and as a sociopathic killer opposite Sissy Spacek in *Badlands* (1973). During long shoots on location, Sheen insisted that his family accompany him.

The influence of heroes turned Sheen toward benevolence. He revered the Marianist brotherhood at the University of Dayton for dedication to piety, service, justice, and nonviolence. He studied the goodness of St. Francis of Assisi, the martyrdom of Gandhi, and pacifists in the Women's Strike for Peace and the ban the bomb movement. He absorbed the altruism of Mother Teresa among the poor in India and of settlement worker Dorothy Day, initiator of the Catholic Worker Movement. Sheen found male models in the passive resistance of Indian attorney Mohandas Gandhi and in the libertarianism of Dr. Martin Luther King, Jr., and Pope John XXIII. For contemporary exemplars of American freedom fighting, Sheen emulated labor leader Cesar Chavez and brother Jesuit priests Daniel Joseph Berrigan and Philip Francis Berrigan. With Chavez, in 1965, Sheen supported the unionization of farm laborers in Delano, California. In 1968, he joined a generation of peaceniks in exposing the genocide and waste of the Vietnam War. While comparing himself to the Berrigans, he says, "[I began] to reevaluate everything about myself and the world in which I lived. Eventually it forced me to look at social justice in an entirely different light" (Thomas,

2002, 311). The transformation redirected his outlook toward debased and disenfranchised people and to the sufferings of non-white and exploited stoop laborers.

Acting as Social Criticism

Sheen made career selections based on his character and liberal perspective, including antimilitary roles in *Catch-22* (1970), *The Andersonville Trial* (1970), and *Rage* (1972), an exposure of nerve gas danger to civilians. Subsequent roles acknowledged a rogue sheriff in *The California Kid* (1974), bioterrorism in *The Cassandra Crossing* (1976), and child endangerment in *The Little Girl Who Lives down the Lane* (1976). In the Emmy-winning title role of *The Execution of Private Slovik* (1974), the actor introduced a new generation to the execution of a deserter during World War II. During Francis Ford Coppola's filming of *Apocalypse Now* (1979), the anti–Vietnam War cinema version of Joseph Conrad's *Heart of Darkness*, Sheen played army Captain Benjamin L. Willard. From Christ-like mystic, he develops into a covert military assassin destroyed by close contact with evil. For the unscripted mirror scene in a Saigon hotel, Sheen was truly intoxicated, sobbing, striking out, and bleeding from a cut on his hand. He admitted, "I was swacked—couldn't hardly stand up . . . , [and I was] myself, the enemy" (Patterson, 2001). Reflecting over the arduous filming of contrasting passions, Peter Cowie notes in *The Apocalypse Now Book* (2001), "This scene tapped into demons that Marty was maybe not as aware of as he thought" (Cowie, 2001, 101).

Filmed in the Philippines, the demanding role of Benjamin Willard placed Sheen in jungly backcountry accessible only by boat, plane, and jeep. He recalled, "You had to fly there by private [DC3]. It was so remote, you couldn't get there any other way" (Patterson, 2001). The script required his performance in nearly every scene plus narrative voice-overs explaining the action. Stress increased after typhoons washed away sets and props; in the Do Long Bridge scene, Sheen performed for days in the rain. The movie placed such strain on his body and emotions that, at age 36, he suffered a breakdown, developed an erratic pulse rate, and collapsed from a heart attack. He crawled to a road to seek help. A priest conferred last rites, but Sheen survived with no coronary damage. Coppola misled the media that Sheen was hospitalized in Manila with heat exhaustion. Adding to the emotional strain, Sheen's grandmother died about the same time.

On the Mend

While Coppola and the cast and crew anguished over their downed lead player, Sheen sat in the sun in a wheelchair playing catch with his 11-year-old son Charlie. Of the actor's alcoholism, he admitted, "I was shattered. It was a long time coming back together" (Murphy 2002). The two reversed roles in 1998 when Sheen helped pull Charlie from an overdose of cocaine and vodka. While Sheen recuperated, the film crew shot views of body doubles and of the back of Joe Estévez, his younger brother, whose voice was close enough to Martin's for redubbing. Joe remained Sheen's voice double and stand-in through March and April 1977 until the star could recover during recuperation in Palm Springs, California. Sheen refused to view the harrowing film until weeks after it opened.

The near-death experience impacted Sheen's consciousness of mortality, causing him to give up alcohol, drugs, and cigarettes and to avoid overwork. For 4 years, he struggled with his faith: "Spirituality is what I was searching for. That was at the core of my recovery" (Murphy, 2002). He began reading Fyodor Dostoevsky's *The Brothers Karamazov* (1880), an epic saga of crime and retribution. While filming in Paris, in 1981, the actor located St. Joseph Church, an English-speaking Catholic congregation on Avenue Hoche, and requested his first confession in years. He described the cathartic experience as "the journey home" (Kupfer 2003). To steady himself, he reclaimed the Catholic beliefs of his childhood, celebrated mass daily, and carried a rosary in his pocket to discourage indulgence in cursing.

One of the steadiest workers in the entertainment field, Sheen continued to play parts that expressed his involvement in altruism and personal sacrifice. He chose a reporter's role in *Gandhi* (1982), a failed father in *Man, Woman and Child* (1983), and the title figure Artaban in *The Fourth Wise Man* (1985), which cast the actor as a Christ-like dawdler too concerned with human need to travel to Bethlehem with the Magi to visit the Christ Child. He continued depicting men of character—a mournful expatriate son in *Da* (1988), the title part in *JFK* (1991), General Robert E. Lee in *Gettysburg* (1993), a presidential adviser in *The American President* (1995), and narrator of the documentary *An Act of Conscience* (1997), which honors the perseverance of tax resisters who fight violence by refusing to finance the American military.

Making a Difference

From the 1980s to the present, Sheen incurred over 70 arrests while demonstrating for peace and justice. He opposed apartheid in South Africa and sought political asylum for refugees. He joined actor Ed Asner in regular assaults on the Los Angeles Federal Building to draw attention to American aid to the moral corruption and death squads in El Salvador. At Fort Benning, Georgia, he accused the military of covert promotion of peasant repression, kidnap, and mass murder by training Third World assassins at the army's School of the Americas (SOA). Along with Maryknoll priest Patrick Bergin, Sheen experienced his first arrest in 1986 by blocking an entrance to employees of the McGraw-Hill Building on 42nd Street in Manhattan. The action drew media attention to the nuclear Star Wars Initiative spawned under the administration of President Ronald Reagan. Sheen ventured into his own sphere of expertise by denouncing peddlers of child pornography and screen violence. For the poor and homeless, he built showers at Payatas outside Manila in the Philippines to reclaim the physical integrity and dignity of garbage pickers and championed greater rewards and safer working conditions for fruit and vegetable harvesters in the American Southwest.

Sheen declared to an interviewer the need to be accountable for acts of conscience. In 1986, the actor courted arrest in New York City by promoting the Sanctuary Movement, a rescue operation that Father Luis Olivares engineered in Los Angeles, California, on behalf of Central American political refugees. Sheen and Greenpeace chemist Pat Costner vilified the incinerators of Waste Management, Inc. (WMI), a Swiss-owned double kiln that polluted New York City residents with toxic particles. The actor and Costner also lambasted WMI for spewing airborne waste along the Ohio River and into homes in East Liverpool (Ohio), Pennsylvania, and West Virginia. In Washington, D.C., on October 13, 1991, Sheen joined Paul Connett, a toxicologist for Work on Waste U.S.A., in leading protesters in choruses of "Amazing Grace." The hymn, an anthem to moral transformation, overwhelmed an Environmental Protection Agency discussion and preceded the seizure of Connett and Sheen for trespass. The actor later explained the drive to protest wrong: "I do it because I can't seem to live with myself if I do not. I don't know any other way to be" (Kupfer, 2003).

Varied Causes

In middle age, Sheen diversified his defense of animal and human rights with overt demonstrations of compassion, including collecting donations for the poor and sleeping on sidewalks among the homeless. Additional acts of conscience allied him with radical protesters from Earth First! and People for the Ethical Treatment of Animals, with the press for affirmative action by the group called By Any Means Necessary, and with Consistent Life, an effort to halt abortion, euthanasia, execution, and combat. During the Persian Gulf War, he was touched by the synergy of Mother Teresa and Pope John Paul II in deploring hostilities in the Middle East. In 1993, Sheen joined Reverend Jesse Jackson in demanding benevolence toward illegal aliens, a category that once included Sheen's father, who slipped in through Cuba. While challenging the Canadian Sealer's Association on the Magdalen Islands southeast of Quebec, on May 16, 1995, he joined chemist Paul Watson of the Sea Shepherd Conservation Society in confronting 300 seal killers. Because of a free-for-all that threatened both conservationists along with journalist Stephen Douglass of the *London Daily Mirror*, Sheen insisted that U.S. authorities intervene to protect Americans. In 1996, he costarred as Peter Maurin with Moira Kelly as Dorothy Day in the biopic *Entertaining Angels: The Dorothy Day Story*. This stage of Sheen's career saw two craft-affirming awards, an Imagen Foundation Lifetime Achievement Award for portraying Latinos and a Catholics in Media Associates Lifetime Achievement Award. A left-handed compliment to his activism were two requests—from the Democrats and the Green Party—to run for president. He reminded politicians that his real job was that of a journeyman actor.

While developing a fan base from 1999 to 2006 for his role as liberal U.S. President Josiah "Jed" Bartlet in the TV series *The West Wing*, Sheen contracted for free time to join demonstrations, processions, and rallies. He reignited his pacifist mission on August 9, 1999, by leading prayers with Franciscan friars at the Los Alamos National Laboratory in New Mexico against nuclear proliferation. For his leadership, police booked him and 60 confederates for trespass. Fourteen months later, Sheen and nurse Lawrence "Butch" Turk of Greenpeace invaded Vandenberg Air Force Base outside Santa Barbara, California, to protest space warheads and global spying. On November 21, 2000, Sheen again attacked the SOA by shedding fake blood, a symbol of the sufferings and death worldwide caused by American-trained torturers and executioners. Military security arrested him and 2,000 activists.

American involvement in war spurred Sheen into his 60s. In 2003, he wrote a statement in the *Los Angeles Times* declaring the Iraq War foolish and immoral. On August 28, 2005, the actor denigrated the George W. Bush administration by honoring U.S. "peace mom" Cindy Lee Miller Sheehan at Camp Casey, her tent in Crawford, Texas. Hunkered down opposite the Texas white house of President George W. Bush and First Lady Laura Bush, Sheen and Sheehan expressed their outrage at the flimsy justification of the Iraq War, which killed Sheehan's son. Months later, Sheen repatriated to the National University of Ireland in Galway, his second home, to study English literature. During his sojourn, he denounced mushroom farmers for paying alien laborers one-third of the going rate. On April 1, 2007, he bobbed back into headlines at a peace rally 70 miles northwest of Las Vegas at the nuclear test grounds in Mercury, Nevada. In company with Franciscan priest Louis Vitale, retired Colonel Ann Wright, and Carrie Dunn, head of People Helping People, Sheen and 35 other peace walkers for the Nevada Desert Experience faced charges of trespass on government land.

Sources

Cowie, Peter. *The Apocalypse Now Book.* New York: Da Capo, 2001.

Kupfer, David. "Interview." *Progressive* 67 (July 2003): 38.

Murphy, Mary. "The Sheen Team." *TV Guide* 50 (9) (March 2, 2002): 16–21, 43.

Patterson, John. "Typhoons, Binges . . . Then a Heart Attack." *Guardian Unlimited*, November 2, 2001. Available at http://film.guardian.co.uk/interview/interviewpages/0,585052,00.html (last accessed April 3, 2008).

Thomas, Marlo. *The Right Words at the Right Time.* New York: Simon & Schuster, 2002.

■ Hillbilly Background
Barbara Kingsolver

A leader of ecofeminism, Barbara Kingsolver acquired a love of the land while growing up in the eastern Kentucky hills. Born in Annapolis, Maryland, on April 8, 1955, she learned to appreciate nature from her father, Wendell R. Kingsolver, a navy physician, and a hillbilly mother, Virginia Lee Henry "Ginny" Kingsolver, a student of bird lore. With her younger sister Ann, an anthropologist at the University of California, Santa Cruz, and older brother Rob, an entomologist at Kentucky Wesleyan College, Barbara grew up in a white clapboard house on East Main in the village of Carlisle amid the alfalfa, burley, and hayfields of Nicholas County. She later recalled the microcosm as "a wrinkle on the map that lies between farms and wildness" (Kingsolver, 2000, x). Amid the poverty of Appalachia, the trio cohabited with backwoods children and spent summers scouring the hill country around Horse Lick Creek for treasures—pawpaws, snakes, swallowtails, and sweet peas. She later wrote that her "best memories all contain birdsong and trees" and groves "rich in the pecky music of birds seeking forage" (Kingsolver, 2002, 11, 12).

In early girlhood, the author developed an enduring humanism based on her family's compassion for the underclass. She later drew on memories of survivors and nosy neighbors: "After I left, I understood what a rare thing it is to live among people who care that much about your business" (Donahue, 1993, F3). Like others reared in the Appalachians, she became adept at storytelling before graduating to reading children's classics by Louisa May Alcott, Christina Rossetti, Robert Louis Stevenson, and Laura Ingalls Wilder. Kingsolver internalized the strengths of poor Kentuckians who had no telephones, shopped in no bookstores, and weathered crop shortfalls and calamitous labor strikes. Modeling altruism for his intuitive daughter, her father, the community's lone doctor for 36 years, shielded his family from materialism and greed by treating the sick in a "place where doctors don't play golf and don't get rich" (Neill, 1993, 110). In lieu of cash, he traded treatment for vegetables, an agrarian barter system that Kingsolver later incorporated in her fiction.

A Promising Future

The Kingsolvers anticipated that their intuitive daughter would perpetuate the family devotion to human dignity and personal excellence. They read aloud to her and recommended the outdoors as a hands-on learning lab. In place of television viewing, they encouraged her to keep a journal and to select "books—big, good books—and one day go to college." She says, "Nobody else I knew had that sort of expectation" (Epstein, 1996, 33).

Offsetting the contentment of mountain life, the Cold War introduced global issues and impacted her with the terrors of the Cuban Missile Crisis. She recalls tales of lurking Russians, black paint obscuring the local water tower, and the filling of basement shelves with root crops and canned goods to last out a nuclear winter. She and other second graders "had 'duck and cover' drills, fully trusting that leaping into a ditch and throwing an Orlon sweater over . . . [their] heads would save . . . [them] from nuclear fallout" (Kingsolver, 1995, 213).

A propitious sojourn in the Congo at age 9 introduced Kingsolver to a different level of poverty while her parents worked for the public health service. Amid huts lacking utilities and children growing up unprotected by inoculation, she surveyed the great racial divide between black peasants and the missionary elite. At age 12, she followed her father's new posting to a convent hospital in St. Lucia, one of the Windward Islands. She encountered the poor black children of sugarcane cutters and millers, stories about Anansi the spider, and the goat sacrifices integral to west African Obeah. The Kingsolvers returned to Appalachia to reside once more among country folk, more of the world's have-nots, who subsisted in a milieu apart from the mine owners, bureaucrats, and storekeepers.

Teens and Causes

Kingsolver's political consciousness took shape during the war in southeast Asia, which aroused the teenager's hostility toward militarism and exploitation of the working poor. A devout pacifist by the time she entered Nicholas County High School, she furthered a more personal campaign during first wave feminism against gendered curricula. For hillbilly students, educational expectations ranged from unchallenging shop for boys and cooking and sewing for girls to two paltry introductions to math and science. At a time when intellectual curiosity outweighed interest in males, Kingsolver, an awkward adolescent, kept watch on the pairing and dating that preceded early marriage for country kids. She allied with the few ambitious souls, about whom she says, "[We] just swore that as soon as we could, we were going to kick the dust of this place from our heels and go away as far as we possibly could" (Barnette, 2000).

At age 16, Kingsolver discovered escapism by writing verse and devouring literature. The school librarian, Miss Truman Richey, guided the high school junior to Edgar Allan Poe, Margaret Mitchell, William Saroyan, and Leo Tolstoy. On reflecting over her midteen rescue, she exulted, "I'm of a fearsome mind to throw my arms around every living librarian who crosses my path, on behalf of the soul they never knew they saved" (Kingsolver, 1995, 46). Reading an array of classics from Flannery O'Connor's short stories to Henry David Thoreau's *Walden* (1854), Kingsolver grew wings of the mind: "I started to dream up intoxicating lives for myself that I could not have conceived without the books" (Rubinstein, 1999, 254).

From the University to the World

After a summer at the University of Kentucky in Lexington, Kingsolver remained close to home by absorbing the Southern scenarios and backwoods themes in the novels of William Faulkner, Carson McCullers, Reynolds Price, and Eudora Welty. While studying classical piano at DePauw University in Greencastle, Indiana, she developed an idealistic outlook on American imperialism, art, feminism, labor, reproductive rights, and violence. To stave off snickers at her hillbilly dialect, she nurtured an uptown persona free of Kentuckyisms.

Although urbane on the exterior, inside she recoiled at age 19 from date rape, a crime that haunted her thoughts with guilt and despair.

Before entering her junior year, Kingsolver chose the road less traveled by majoring in English and zoology. The margins of her lab notes became testing grounds for verse innovation. After earning admission to Phi Beta Kappa and a magna cum laude grade point average, from age 23 to 24, she worked in an X-ray lab and did domestic and clerical chores to pay for sojourns in communes in Athens and Paris and Beaurieux in France. To her surprise, a broader vision of the world solidified her determination to return to Carlisle to live "inside" the "amazing beast, poking at its belly from the inside" with "one little life and the small, pointed sword of . . . [her] pen" (McMahon, 2002).

From Mountains to Desert

Kingsolver created a plan of bicultural living in 1979 by moving from Kentucky to Tucson, Arizona. An unfamiliar form of outback, the Sonoran Desert satisfied her love of unique landscapes and biota. Along with doctoral study of ecology and animal behavior at the University of Arizona, she mastered composition with mentor Francine Prose. In-between years as a research assistant in the university physiology department and technical writer for the Arid Lands Institute preceded her decision to freelance essays for *Architectural Digest*, *Biomass Magazine*, *Economic Botany*, and *New York Times Magazine*. Her journalistic interests reached out to miner's wages, Amnesty International, the Cold War arms race, nuclear waste, and, during the Reagan administration, Central American human rights. Closest to her heart lay concern for the Earth and the "responsibility to our future, the political choices we make, how to begin paying back the debt to rivers and air and oceans and soil we've been borrowing on, cheating on, for decades" (Ross, 19192, 289).

At age 30, Kingsolver married Joseph "Joe" Hoffmann, a chemistry professor at the university. Their Tucson farm combined the isolation of the Kentucky farm and livestock of her childhood with the xeriscape and pantheism of a desert bosque. Before the birth of daughter Camille, the author joined the Sanctuary Movement, which fostered a modern underground railroad for political refugees fleeing Chile, El Salvador, and Guatemala. Combining images of motherhood with the stealth of rescuers, she published a bestseller, *The Bean Trees* (1986), featuring a Kentucky hillbilly heroine, Taylor Greer, living in Arizona, rearing an abandoned Indian baby, and speaking the familiar idiom of home. The characters—tire repair workers, single mother, an elderly blind babysitter, refugees, and 7-Eleven and salsa factory laborers—affirmed the author's egalitarian perspective and her respect for underappreciated Americans.

Fame

Kingsolver's first novel earned an American Library Association Notable Book, an Enoch Pratt Library Youth-to-Youth Books Award, and *New York Times* Notable Book. Her hometown celebrated their local star with a gala at the rail depot. Success in the outside world brought questions about her background. She marveled, "I was stunned to discover the world knows almost nothing about 'hillbillies,' and respects them even less. An undercurrent of defensiveness about this has guided my writing and my life, I think, as I've tried to seek out the voices of marginalized people" ("Barbara Kingsolver: Coming Home").

In 1989, the author extended her honor to female courage with investigative journalism into working-class issues. Her next work, *Holding the Line: Women in the Great Arizona Mine Strike of 1983*, chronicles collective bargaining with the Phelps Dodge Copper Corporation in Morenci, Arizona. Over a year and a half, Hispanic and native American workers incurred civil rights infractions for striking to thaw a wage freeze affecting 2,300 miners laboring 7-day weeks. Kingsolver recorded the bravery and solidarity of Berta Chavez and Flossie Navarro in the face of menacing deputies and national guardsmen, SWAT teams, company goons, and tear gas. Subjectively allied with the underdog, she explained, "I grew up in eastern Kentucky, so honestly union membership has always been profoundly associated with things like honor, integrity, responsibility towards community, and basically survival, security" (Kjos, 2000, 13). Kingsolver's empathy for female protesters won her a Citation of Accomplishment from the United Nations National Council of Women of the United States.

Combative Fiction

During America's illegal covert wars, Kingsolver's liberal leanings invested her writings with outrage against callous disregard for Central American peasants. She revisited elements from the last two books in *Animal Dreams* (1990), a diatribe against corporate polluters. A winner of the Edward Abbey Award for Ecofiction and Pen/USA West Fiction Award and named American Library Association Notable Book and Best Book for Young Adults, Arizona Library Association Book of the Year, and *New York Times* Notable Book, the novel preceded work on a masterpiece, *The Poisonwood Bible* (1998), an anticolonial allegory that she incubated for a decade. In distress over the Gulf War, she withdrew to the safe environs of Tenerife in the Canary Islands and filled poems with anger at planes raining death on Baghdad.

During wrangles over property rights throughout her divorce from Joe, Kingsolver sheltered once more in her Kentucky home. After a month of research in Benin, she completed *Pigs in Heaven* (1993) and met environmentalist and ornithologist Steven L. Hopp of southwestern Virginia, her second husband. They married in Kentucky "in the sight of pine-browed mountains, a forget-me-not sky, and nearly all the people . . . [they loved] most" (Kingsolver, 1995, 268). The couple chose to combine residency near the Tohono O'odham and Yaqui in Arizona with summers in a Kentucky log cabin, where Camille and baby sister Lily enjoyed the same childhood pleasures as their mother.

A Union of Habitats

Publication of *The Poisonwood Bible* introduced readers to the author's complex perspective on Southern privations and Third World economic calamities. Energized by empathy for vulnerable Congolese, the text delved into racist and misogynistic sins dating back to the Eisenhower administration. Awards poured in from the English-speaking world—American Booksellers Book of the Year, Book Sense Book of the Year Award, Britain's Orange Prize of £30,000, the National Book Prize of South Africa, Pulitzer Prize, and the Sierra Club's Edward Abbey Award for Ecofiction—along with a mention as one of Canada's North Forty-Nine Books Most Valuable Picks, *Los Angeles Times* Best Book, one of New York Public Library "25 Books to Remember," one of *New York Times* "Ten Best Books of 1998," an Oprah Book Club selection, and the Village Voice Best Book and nomination for the PEN/Faulkner award. To critics annoyed by her criticism of condescending attitudes toward the black world, she replied: "There is a nervousness in this country about art that addresses issues of social change and social justice. It's a very provincial and backward attitude that is pretty much absent in the rest of the world" (McMahon, 2000).

After Kingsolver published her pro-wilderness novel *Prodigal Summer* (2000), she won more accolades—Best American Science and Nature Writing honor and Kentucky Governor's Award in the Arts. For personal reasons, she narrated the audio version, which her husband adorned with authentic birdcalls. Still defensive of her Kentucky background, she commented, "I wanted to do it myself—I didn't trust a hired actor to get those accents right, and I can't abide a fakey, condescending hillbilly accent" ("Barbara Kingsolver: Coming Home"). With proceeds, she continued strengthening America's wild places through donations to the Huron River Watershed Council in Michigan, the San Diequito River Project in California, and the Washington State Environmental Learning Center. On December 20, 2000, Kingsolver received a National Humanities Medal from President Bill Clinton and First Lady Hillary Rodham Clinton. Months later, she accepted the National Award to a Kentuckian who has achieved national acclaim.

Sources

"Barbara Kingsolver: Coming Home to a Prodigal Summer." Available at http://www.ivillage.com/books/intervu/fict/articles (last accessed June 3, 2007).

Barnette, Martha. "Back to the Blue Ridge: A Kentucky Writer Rediscovers Her Roots." *Courier-Journal* (Louisville), June 24, 2000.

Donahue, Deirdre. "Interview." *USA Today*, July 15, 1993, F3.

Epstein, Robin. "Barbara Kingsolver." *Progressive* 60 (2) (February 1996): 33–37.

Kingsolver, Barbara. *High Tide in Tucson: Essays from Now or Never*. New York: HarperCollins, 1995.

———. *Last Stand: America's Virgin Lands*. Washington, DC: National Geographic Society, 2002.

———. *Prodigal Summer*. New York: HarperCollins, 2000.

Kjos, Tiffany. "Kingsolver Touts National Writers' Union." *Inside Tucson Business*, February 28, 2000, 13.

McMahon, Regan. "Barbara Kingsolver: An Army of One." *San Francisco Chronicle*, April 18, 2002.

Neill, Michael. "La Pasionaria." *People* 40 (15) (October 11, 1993): 109–110.

Ross, Jean W. "Interview." *Contemporary Authors*. Volume 134. Detroit: Gale Research, 1992.

Rubinstein, Roberta. "The Mark of Africa." *World & I* 14 (4) (April 1999): 254.

HIV
Magic Johnson

Magic Johnson turned a life sentence to the human immunodeficiency virus (HIV) into a reason to prevent infection of others. Born Earvin Effay Johnson, Jr., on August 14, 1959, in Lansing, Michigan, he is the sixth of the ten children of Earvin Effay Johnson, Sr., a laborer at a General Motors assembly plant, and Christine Johnson, a school custodian. Dubbed "June Bug" as a boy, he grew up in a Christian setting and began playing sports in early boyhood. He was a poor shot with a baseball but a natural at shooting hoops. On his walks down urban sidewalks, while flashing his signature smile, he marked the rhythm of his steps with the bounce of a ball. By age 14, when he worked as a janitor in a high-rise office, he reached 6 feet 5 inches. In his midteens, when his height climbed 4 more inches, he wowed fans at Lansing Everett High School with energetic turns and passes on the court.

An admirer, Fred S. Stabley, Jr., a journalist for the *Lansing State Journal*, chose "Magic" as the ideal name for Earvin for his clutch shoots, easy layups and rebounding, post-ups, and pinpoint no-look passing. His mother, a Seventh-Day Adventist, reviled the name as blasphemy. Magic hit a junior year slump and risked punishment for laziness. Because of the death of his buddy Reggie Chastaine that summer, Magic and his teammates pledged to snag a state championship and dedicate it to Reggie. The competition pressed the last of 28 games into overtime, when Lansing Everett snatched the title. Leading the hustle, Magic averaged 28.8 points, primarily by taking advantage of other players' mistakes and weaknesses.

Teen Marvel on the Courts

Inundated with offers from colleges and universities, Magic chose to stay in East Lansing, enroll at Michigan State University, and play basketball for the Spartans. He majored in media communications and set his goals on becoming a courtside commentator. His dependable fast break court performance the first year took the team to a Big Ten Conference championship and the finals of the National Collegiate Athletic Association (NCAA) tournament. He became the only freshman named to the All American college team. At age 20, his versatility as a 235-pound forward and point guard in the sophomore year redefined the guard position. His dual talents boosted the Spartans to the NCAA finals and won him acclaim as the Most Outstanding Player of the Final Four.

Because of his host of high school and university trophies, Magic chose basketball over education and entered the 1979 National Basketball Association (NBA) draft. As the primary selection of the Los Angeles Lakers on an annual salary of $600,000, he played for coach Jack McKinney and developed synergy with a top scorer, Kareem Abdul-Jabbar. The first season proved Magic an asset to the Lakers and to fans for his ebullient style, good manners, and sportsmanship. Sports analyst Elliot Kalb remarked that Kareem granted Magic the front-row spot as the team's spirit and spokesman. On private time, Magic developed a reputation for chasing female fans. When his team chalked up a 60-22 season, sports mavens named his court razzle-dazzle "Showtime." His position altered after Kareem injured his ankle and Magic took the pivot post. In a rush to fame, he ruled the court and snagged the NBA Finals Most Valuable Player award. With consecutive NCAA and NBA championships, he placed himself among the game's all-time stars.

Millionaire Player

At age 21, Magic played 37 games but missed 45 while nursing a torn cartilage in his knee following a clash with the Seattle Hawks' Tom Burleson. Magic's recovery was so spectacular that he received a precedent-setting offer from Lakers owner Jerry Buss— $25 million for 25 years of play. The contract made Magic one of the league's highest paid stars. A confrontation with coach Paul Westhead over pacing dampened Magic's enthusiasm for the team. After he requested a trade to another venue, Buss chose his star player over the coach and replaced Westhead with assistant coach Pat Riley. Magic acquired a reputation for petulance and arrogance. The contretemps threatened the Lakers' spirit and fan base. To redeem himself, Magic led the team once more to an NBA championship and won a second Most Valuable Player trophy and membership on the

All-NBA Second Team. With athletes Wilt Chamberlain and Oscar Robertson, Magic shared a season record of over 700 points, 700 rebounds, and 700 assists.

In 1984, Magic faced a formidable rival, Boston Celtics star Larry Bird, an Indiana State great, a former NBA rookie of the year, 1979 player of the year, and NBA title winner for the eastern division. In the NBA finals, Bird outshone Magic, whose publicity as ball-handling phenomenon began to slip. The two cemented a lifelong friendship during taping of an advertisement for Converse shoes. Their rivalry drew a new generation to NBA sports and increase television viewership.

The Lakers star turned loss into challenge and polished up his game for the 1984–1985 season. By 1986, he entered his best year and reached a pinnacle average of 23.9 points, 6.3 rebounds, and 12.2 assists and won the Most Valuable Player title. Fans of the Celtics and Lakers followed the heated Bird–Johnson rivalry to the 1987 NBA finals. At the end of the clock, Magic hooked a shot that ended the game at 107-106. The heart-stopping save earned Magic his third Finals Most Valuable Player trophy. In 1988, the year Magic married his college sweetheart, 31-year-old Earleatha "Cookie" Kelly, he maintained a 22.5 point average, but a pulled hamstring sidelined him. The Lakers lost to the Detroit Pistons. Kareem, Magic's idol, retired at age 42 at a farewell game. Magic spruced up his game in 1990, but the Lakers lost to the wizardry of Chicago Bulls shooting guard Michael Jordan, who switched hands in midair on scoring shots.

Foolish Behavior in Contemporary Culture

After a 12-season triumph, in 1991, listlessness in Magic cost him play. At a press conference on November 7, he stunned the sports world with a straightforward statement. With Cookie at his side, he identified an unspecified gastric disorder as HIV, which team physician Michael Mellman discovered after drawing serum during a physical for a life insurance policy. The athlete's ignorance of contagion muddled his perception of danger from acquired immunodeficiency syndrome (AIDS): "Like almost everyone else who has not paid attention to the growing AIDS epidemic in the U.S. and the rest of the world, I didn't know the difference between the virus and the disease" (Garber, Matlock, and Walkowitz, 1993, 265). Medical advisers feared that an 82-game season would compromise his immune system. Within an hour, male callers deluged AIDS hotlines along the East Coast with a 500 percent increase in requests for serum tests and advice on exposure to the AIDS virus. NBA investors quietly questioned other court stars to determine whether the disease could jeopardize the sport and its product endorsements. More important to younger players, college promoters surveyed the extent of hero worship that turned hoopsters into sexual adventurers.

Magic's shocking confession at the Great Western Forum sparked gossip in the tabloids and redirected medical coverage toward black and Latino communities and to threats to women and children. Nearly half of all media features on AIDS focused on Magic, with only 13 percent discussing infected tennis star Arthur Ashe. Analyst Cathy J. Cohen concluded that "declared heterosexual, drug-free, family-oriented . . . celebrity personas . . . propelled the media to label these two black Americans, in particular Johnson, one of the most important AIDS stories of the epidemic" (Cohen, 1999, 167). The media coverage coincided with AZT toxicity, a bout of daily nausea, malaise, and loss of appetite that downed Magic at the height of his physical greatness.

That evening on *Nightline*, AIDS activist Larry Kramer depicted the basketball phenomenon as a disease carrier marked for death. To refute crepe hangers and to establish his sexual orientation, Magic admitted to casual intimacies with over 200 women. Identifying freewheeling bachelorhood as his weakness, in a confessional aired in the November 18, 1991, issue of *Sports Illustrated*, he admitted, "After I arrived in L.A. in 1979, I did my best to accommodate as many women as I could—most of them through unprotected sex" (Garber, Matlock, and Walkowitz, 1993, 258). *The New York Times* printed an editorial charging Magic with egregious promiscuity. The *Los Angeles Times* added to the accusation editorial scoldings for indiscretion and reckless flamboyance, two outgrowths of American sports celebrity.

Giving Back to Fans

Forced into retirement, Magic took comfort that his pregnant wife and unborn son, Earvin III, escaped infection. The media correctly predicted that Magic would morph into the most effective poster child for awakening AIDS awareness in heterosexuals, both white and nonwhite. *USA Today* picked up on the story by printing a front-page feature encouraging people to beat the disease by getting tested for HIV in the earliest stages. Magic reassured fans with an appearance on *The Arsenio Hall Show* and with two articles, "Magic Johnson's Full-Court Press Against AIDS" and "Magic and Cookie Johnson Speak Out for First Time on Love, Marriage and AIDS," a husband-and-wife tell-all cover story for *Ebony* that indicated plenty of romance in the marriage.

Magic's notoriety emerged at a time when the majority of AIDS infections in the United States struck nonwhite citizens. The only HIV-positive players in the NBA, he returned to the court for the 1992 All-Star Game despite speculation that blood and saliva released on contact could infect other players. Although fellow player Karl Malone complained of risks, other teammates mobbed Magic and expressed respect for his prowess and sorrow at his illness. For his perseverance and devotion to the game, he received an All-Star Most Valuable Player trophy and appeared on the cover of the April 21 issue of the *Advocate*, a gay news journal.

At age 33, Magic presented a stoic face to fans with a cautionary work, *What You Can Do to Avoid Aids* (1992) and a candid autobiography, *Magic Johnson: My Life* (1992). He represented the United States at the 1992 Olympic Games in Barcelona, Spain, and helped add another gold medal to the total take. Forming the Dream Team were Larry Bird, Michael Jordan, and John Stockton, who bear-hugged Magic in a show of regard for an ailing player. Juan Antonio San Epifanio, Steffi Graf, and other Olympic competitors embraced Magic to impress on viewers that HIV need not turn the infected into pariahs. His knee problems benched him for most of the competition. He attempted a return to the Lakers that year, but halted his play after pre-season competition. *Sports Illustrated* paired Bird and Johnson on its December 14 cover as "Bird & Magic: Gone But Never Forgotten." A year after the Johnsons adopted daughter Elisa, a vote in 1996 placed Magic among the NBA's 50 all-time greatest players. By 2002, his jersey claimed glory at the Basketball Hall of Fame.

Magic turned from sports to activism. As a campaigner for sexual abstinence and safe intercourse, he spread the word that HIV is avoidable. His candor released from public misperceptions the facts about HIV, which strikes more people than just bisexual and gay men and needle-sharing junkies. To dubious teens at Cardozo High School in Washington, he declared that he frequently kissed Cookie. From President George H. W. Bush, Magic wrung an admission that the government did little to stem the AIDS epidemic. In response to Magic's letter of January 22, 1992, Bush looked into more funding for research, the Ryan White CARE Bill, and increased Medicaid coverage for HIV victims. After Magic served on the presidential AIDS Council, the lack of funds to slow the epidemic dismayed him. He resigned his role in Bush's investigation on September 25, 1992.

While serving NBC TV as a color sportscaster, Magic crusaded for more black AIDS workers and clinics. Simultaneous with his health initiatives, from an L.A. office on Wiltshire Boulevard, he championed more cinema houses in the Los Angeles ghettos, advocated investment in Harlem by opening a Starbucks coffeehouse, bought into TGI Friday's and Fatburger's chains, franchised Fitness Clubs and Loews movie theaters, built Las Vegas shopping malls, and traveled to Asia and Australia with an exhibition basketball team. In 1993, he coached the Lakers for 11 games and then bought 5 percent of the team. Another court comeback in 1995 ended after 32 games. In 1998, he hosted a talk show, *The Magic Hour*, on Fox TV before launching Magic Johnson Enterprises and Magic Johnson Theaters. Among his investments was the purchase of a minor league baseball team, the Dayton Dragons. His failed throw of a first-day pitch inspired him to try lofting a basketball. The hot toss to the catcher enthralled baseball fans.

A dormant virus and elevated T cell count have left Magic free of symptoms and energized him to do good. The Magic Johnson Foundation, created by Cookie and Magic, uplifts inner cities. The couple mobilized "I Stand with Magic," a 5-year, $60 million campaign in partnership with Abbott pharmaceutical laboratories. Cookie targeted black women, who were 20 times more likely to contract the virus than white females. Her platform derived from her admission to living with and loving an HIV-positive mate. Her husband pledged himself to a 16-city speaking tour drawing crowds of 200,000. At his urging, more people sought information and serum testing. His doctor commented, "I think if the president of the United States had contracted this disease, he could not have done any better" (Springer, 2001).

Sources

Cohen, Cathy J. *The Boundaries of Blackness: AIDS and the Breakdown of Black Politics*. Chicago: University of Chicago Press, 1999.

Garber, Marjorie B., Jann Matlock, and Rebecca L. Walkowitz. *Media Spectacles*. New York: Routledge, 1993.

Harper, Phillip Brian. *Are We Not Men?: Masculine Anxiety and the Problem of African-American Identity*. Oxford: Oxford University Press, 1996.

Johnson, Earvin "Magic." *Magic Johnson: My Life*. New York: Random House, 1992.

Shenton, Joan. *Positively False: Exposing the Myths around HIV and AIDS*. New York: Palgrave Macmillan, 1998.

Springer, Steve. "Magic's Announcement Ten Years Later a Real Survivor: Johnson Has Learned to Live with HIV and Thrived in Business Community." *Los Angeles Times*, November 7, 2001.

Sternberg, Steve. "Magic Johnson's Top Cheerleader Joins AIDS Fight." *USA Today*, November 29, 2007, 10D.

Weiner, Bernard. *Judgments of Responsibility: A Foundation for a Theory of Social Conduct*. New York: Guilford Press, 1995.

■ Holocaust
Elie Wiesel

Humanitarian and ethicist Eliezer "Elie" Wiesel survived Auschwitz, Birkenau, Buna, and Buchenwald with an indelible scar on his heart and soul. The only son of the four children of Sarah Feig Wiesel and theologian Shlomo ben Nissel Wiesel, he was born on September 30, 1928, in the Carpathian Mountains at Sighet, a Transylvanian town then part of Romania, where his father was a grocer. Elie bore the name of his paternal grandfather, Eliezer Nissel, who was killed during World War I. At school in Debrecen and Nagyvárad, Elie learned Torah Hebrew, the language of biblical patriarchs. At home, he mastered chess. By age 10, he was already writing Torah commentaries. Shlomo encouraged his son to learn astronomy, contemporary Hebrew, literature, and Freudian psychology. Sarah, the daughter of Reb Dovid "Dodye" Feig, an orthodox Jewish farmer and storyteller, directed her son toward scripture, religious commentary, and Hasidic mysticism. Thus, Elie developed from his mother and father the two sides of his personality, scholarship and faith.

In 1940, when Hungary annexed Sighet, 12-year-old Elie studied the Kabbalah with Moishe the beadle, the alcoholic caretaker of the shtetl synagogue. The worsening war alerted Moishe to rampant anti-Semitism and to capricious arrests and deportations by the Gestapo, who forced prisoners to dig their own graves before their deaths en masse by machine gun. Moishe terrified Elie by returning from a mass execution in Polish Galicia, where he escaped after lying limp in a heap of cadavers. The Wiesels and their neighbors dismissed Moishe as a madman. Although terrorism had already advanced as far as Budapest, Elie expressed his doubt that Adolf Hitler's Third Reich would commit genocide: "Was he going to wipe out a whole people" (Wiesel, 1986, 6). Shortly, Elie's grandmother Nissel was killed at Auschwitz.

In a compelling thanatography, *Night* (1960), Wiesel pictured the family's struggle against the Nazi "Final Solution" to rid Europe of its Jews. Because German defeat seemed certain, in spring 1944, Shlomo Wiesel refused to immigrate to a safer locale. Initially, German officers moved during the Purim celebration on March 19 and resided peaceably in the Jewish ghetto. The atmosphere darkened in Passover week, April 20, 1944, when synagogues closed and police incarcerated Jewish leaders. Anti-Semitic legislation countenanced the looting of religious treasures from synagogues and demanded the wearing of the yellow star in public, along with a 3-day house arrest for Jews, ousting of Jews from restaurants and railways, and confiscation of their valuables. At their home on Serpent Street, additional privations forced the Wiesels to block their windows and to board displaced relatives. Shlomo Wiesel ridiculed the yellow star and dismissed the mounting pressures as political posturing.

The Family Sundered

The Saturday before Pentecost, Shlomo learned that the Gestapo would empty Sighet's ghetto of Jews. Reportedly, deportees would work at brick factories. Hungarian police shoved residents about the streets, separating them from their bundles of food, clothing, and family treasures. At age 14, Elie joined his family at the railyard in boarding a cattle car, which carried 80 deportees to the extermination center at Birkenau, Poland. He described the refugees as "fallen, dragging their packs, dragging their lives, deserting their homes, the years of their childhood, cringing like beaten dogs" (Wiesel, 1986, 15). As they traveled through Kaschau, Czechoslovakia, deportees tied and gagged Madame Schächter, who shrieked at visions of flames. At midnight, the arrival at the gas crematoria confirmed her hysteria with plumes of smoke and gases that reeked of burnt flesh.

Among those who accompanied Elie to the death camp were his parents and 7-year-old sister, Tzipora, all victims of the Holocaust, to whom he dedicated his memoir. The last he saw of Sarah and Tzipora before they vanished forever, they were walking together among the doomed internees. In addition, Elie lost his maternal grandparents to Nazi extermination. Elie and Shlomo witnessed one of the cyclical horrors of the death camps, the selection process of Dr. Josef Mengele, an SS officer who separated healthy workers from rejects. Guards marched the doomed to the crematory. Father and son witnessed the unloading of truck filled with babies, whom the SS burned in a pit. A cynical deportee muttered, "You dumb bastards, don't you understand anything? You're going to be burned. Frizzled away. Turned into ashes" (Ibid., 28). Shlomo felt abandoned by humanity.

The Men Alone

Part of inmate dehumanization began with shaving of heads, delousing of naked bodies, and tattooing before inmates entered the mud-floored stone barracks at Block 17. Elie and Shlomo plodded through electric wires to another division, the work camp at Auschwitz. Three weeks later, they marched south of the Vistula River and through iron gates surrounding the electrical warehouse at Buna Werke. Before the liberation of camps in 1945, father and son, reduced to number A-7713, slogged along 400 miles west to Buchenwald, Germany. The camp held 28,000 men classed as criminals, deserters, foreign insurgents, gypsies, homosexuals, Jehovah's Witnesses, and Jews. Elie and other young men dreamed of immigrating to a Palestinian haven at Haifa. A dentist from Warsaw gouged out Elie's gold crown with a spoon. In another incident, a guard punished Elie with 25 lashes. After American bombers launched a 1-hour attack on Buna, the SS hanged a youth who stole soup during the alert. At Rosh Hashanah and Yom Kippur, Elie's faith in God plummeted.

While Elie dragged stone blocks, his father became weaker and more useless to the Germans. Fearing Dr. Mengele's next selection, Shlomo temporarily bequeathed his son a knife and spoon. In January 1945, without anesthesia, Elie survived a 1-hour surgery to drain infection from his right foot. He was still recuperating two days later when the advance of the Red Army forced the SS to evacuate inmates through snow to a subcamp at Gleiwitz. Elie and Shlomo watched over each other to prevent falling asleep and freezing to death. Shots pocked men around them as guards killed those who fell behind the march.

After three days without food and water, the inmates entered an open-top cattle wagon, one hundred in a car, for the 10-day journey. Along the way, prisoners fought to the death over scraps of bread. On arrival at Buchenwald, only a dozen men remained alive in the car. Depleted by starvation and exhaustion, on January 29, 1945, $2\frac{1}{2}$ months before rescue, Shlomo succumbed to dysentery. Elie castigated himself for feeling relieved of the burden of his father's care. Staff herded Elie in with 600 children to a separate block. The children gnawed grass and discarded potato peelings until April 10, when tanks of the U.S. Third Army forced their way through the gates.

Statelessness

After liberation, Wiesel entered the SS infirmary and weathered 2 weeks of food poisoning, which reduced his skeletal frame even further. He chose not to go home to Sighet, where Nazis had eradicated evidence of a community of 15,000 Jews. Instead, he joined orphans in awaiting placement under the aegis of Charles de Gaulle. After the Oeuvre au Secours aux Enfants (Children's Rescue Service) evacuation to Belgium, he and 400 other children sheltered at Écouis, a chateau in Normandy, France. He received a verbal offer of French citizenship, but he knew no French and remained stateless. In a welter of trauma, grief, and survivor's guilt, he reunited with Hilda, his oldest sibling, whom he discovered by accident in Paris. The two learned that Beatrice had returned to Sighet.

In 1946, Wiesel settled in Paris on a stipend of $16 per month. While secretly contemplating Kabbalah under the guidance of mystic Shushani, Wiesel entered the Sorbonne, where he studied literature, philosophy, and psychology and heard lectures by philosopher Martin Buber and existentialist Jean-Paul Sartre. Until the wee hours, Wiesel devoured the works of Fyodor Dostoyevsky, Franz Kafka, and Thomas Mann. The rejection of Wiesel's request for a visa to Palestine in 1948 quelled his urge to join Haganah to fight the Arabs for possession of Israel. From jobs as an orphanage choir director, tutor in Hebrew, and subtitler of movies, he gravitated to the French newspaper *Tsien in Kamf* (Zion in Struggle), which he translated from Hebrew to Yiddish for the armed Zionists of Irgun. He progressed to standard newspaper reportage in French and Yiddish for the Franco-Jewish magazine *L'Arche* and the Tel Aviv weekly *Yedioth Ahronoth* (Latest News).

A decade later, to speak for other survivors of the war, Wiesel published his first testimonial in Yiddish in Buenos Aires and introduced the term "holocaust" to world history as a descriptive of Jewish genocide. To gain an audience with Pierre Mendès-France, the Jewish president of France, Wiesel knocked at the door of Nobel Prize–winning fiction writer François Mauriac, a former member of the French Resistance and one of the president's advisers. Mauriac acknowledged Elie's sufferings in the straightforward recitation of Nazi atrocities. A devout Christian, Mauriac compared Elie to Lazarus arising from the dead. The author summarized the torment in Elie as "the death of God in the soul of a child who suddenly discovers absolute evil" (Wiesel, 1986, ix).

The author assisted Wiesel in publishing *Night*, originally written in Yiddish under the title *Un di Velt Hot Geshvign* (And the World Remained Silent). Translated into French as *La Nuit* (The Night), the memoir was slow to connect with a publisher. Most thought it too morbid. When the 800-page manuscript found a worthy reception in the United States at Hill & Wang, editors reduced text to 109 pages. It became a classic of Holocaust literature. The author, like Samuel Coleridge's ancient mariner, felt compelled to give further testimony to savagery. He followed with *L'Aube* (Dawn, 1961), and *Le Jour* (The Accident, 1962), both testimonials to German inhumanity.

Wiesel and the Postwar World

A peripatetic journalist skilled in languages and shrewd in the ways of politicians, Wiesel reported events in Argentina, Brazil, Canada, Morocco, India, and Spain and published a spy novel under the pseudonym Elisha Carmeli. He interviewed the leaders of the era—Hannah Arendt, Moshe Dayan, Anthony Eden, Dwight D. Eisenhower, Nikita Khrushchev, Golda Meir, and Georgy Zhukov. Wiesel witnessed the growth of Israel, an independent Jewish state that began receiving Holocaust survivors in the 1940s. In his

30s, he was on assignment to the U.N. headquarters on the Hudson River for an Israeli newspaper, the *Morgen Journal*, when a taxi struck him. The accident left him wheelchair-bound in a body cast for a year, when he started writing for *Der Forverts* (The Jewish Daily Forward), a Yiddish newspaper. In 1963, he ended decades of statelessness by seeking U.S. citizenship.

The world began viewing Wiesel as a brilliant reporter and an authority on genocide and its effects on targets. His classroom career advanced him from Distinguished Professor of Judaic Studies at City University of New York to Boston University, where he became the Andrew W. Mellon Professor in the Humanities in 1976. In 1982, he served a year as Henry Luce Visiting Scholar in Humanities and Social Thought at Yale. As chairman of the U.S. Holocaust Memorial Council, from 1978 to 1986, he dedicated himself to counseling other former inmates of death camps and family extermination and to researching, writing, and speaking on world peace and tolerance. His intervention in world suffering aided gypsies, Ethiopian and Soviet Jews, Cambodian and Vietnamese boat people, Biafran and South African blacks, Arab refugees, victims of tyranny in Argentina and Nicaragua, Kurds, Serbs and Bosnians, and victims of the Iraq War. On September 27, 1979, he submitted the chairman's report from the Holocaust Commission to President Jimmy Carter calling for the building of a Holocaust museum and for nonstop combat against injustice and oppression.

Defender of Goodness

Wiesel made a home near Central Park in New York City with his Austrian-born wife, Marion Erster Rose, and their son, Shlomo Elisha, who majored in computer science at Yale. Wiesel continued to crusade for human goodness. Overall, he received honorary degrees from Anna Maria College, Bar-Ilan, Boston University, Brandeis, Emory, Hebrew Union, Hofstra, Jewish Theological Seminary, Loyola, Manhattanville, Marquette, Notre Dame, Simmons, Spertus College of Judaica, St. Scholastica, Talmudic, University of Florida, University of Vermont, Wesleyan, Yale, and Yeshiva. His honors include the American Liberties Medallion, French Legion of Honor, Prix Livre Inter, Prix Medicis, Joseph Prize, Eleanor Roosevelt Memorial, Martin Luther King Jr. Award, Raul Wallenberg Medal, and, in 1985, a Congressional Medal of Freedom. The next year, he joined his sister Hilda at Oslo, Norway, to accept the 1986 Nobel Peace Prize. The judges lauded his efforts as a peacemaker and honored his atonement mission for humankind. Shortly after, Wiesel and his wife founded the Elie Wiesel Foundation for Humanity. Reprising his extraordinary life, he wrote two postwar autobiographies, *All Rivers Run to the Sea* (1995) and *And the Sea Is Never Full* (1999). At the request of First Lady Hillary Clinton, on April 12, 1999, he delivered a memorable speech, "The Perils of Indifference." The text blamed President Franklin Delano Roosevelt for failure to rescue Jews from their annihilators and elicited compassion from the world for prisoners, refugees, and ill-nourished children.

After retiring to Connecticut, Elie Wiesel returned to his hometown on July 29, 2002. The visit, filmed by NBC TV, coincided with the acknowledgement of his ghetto residence, restored as the Elie Wiesel Memorial House, where he accepted the nation's Star of Romania. Marion Wiesel, herself a survivor of the Holocaust, retranslated *Night*, which Oprah Winfrey added to her suggested reading list in May 2006. The next November, Elie Wiesel was knighted in London for educating the British about genocide. On February 1, 2007, Wiesel survived an assault in a San Francisco hotel by a denier of the Holocaust. Critics, out of respect, moderated commentary on his speeches and 40 publications. They challenged the author's subjectivity and his immersion in nightmarish reprises of Auschwitz, yet, overall, they exonerated the sad-eyed philosopher as a modern-day saint and near-martyr.

Sources

Chmiel, Mark. *Elie Wiesel and the Politics of Moral Leadership*. New York: Temple University Press, 2001.

Houghton, Sarah. *Elie Wiesel: A Holocaust Survivor Cries Out for Peace*. New York: Red Brick Learning, 2003.

Kolbert, Jack. *The Worlds of Elie Wiesel*. Selinsgrove, PA: Susquehanna University Press, 2001.

Leighton, Christopher M. "Oprah, Elie Wiesel, and My Fellow Christians." *Commentary* 121 (5) (May 2006): 59–62.

Wiesel, Elie. *Night*. New York: Bantam, 1986.

Winfrey, Oprah. "He Taught Us How to Answer Evil." *Time* (May 8, 2006): 198.

■ Hydrocephalus
Sherman Joseph Alexie

A wisecracking writer and filmmaker of the American Indian literary renaissance, Sherman Joseph Alexie, Jr., instructs white America on the disillusions faced by native "rez kids." He referred to his life as a quiet miracle. Born 45 miles northwest of Spokane, Washington, near the Idaho line on October 7, 1966, he is the middle child of five of a Spokane mother, social worker Lillian Agnes Cox, and Coeur d'Alene father, Sherman Joseph Alexie, Sr., a truck driver and logger. From birth, Alexie suffered convulsions from hydrocephalus, a neurological anomaly filling the cranium with an outflow of brain and spinal fluid. Hydrocephaly can also manifest itself in vertigo, double vision, vomiting, migraine, fever, and coma. At age 5 months, increased intracranial pressure and the risk of skull malformation and mental retardation required life-threatening surgery to drain excess liquid from his head. Doctors shunted fluids through a tube into his abdomen. The expertise and mystique of doctoring prompted him to want a medical degree. He later regretted the absence of professional native role models for young Indians.

Among 1,100 residents of the Spokane Indian Reservation, a 150,000-acre government installation at Wellpinit, the author grew up Roman Catholic and semifatherless in a laughter-loving household. During alcoholic binges, the elder Alexie left home. Sherman forgave his absent parent and admired him for his nontraditional narratives, which influenced the antiformalism of Alexie's verse and fiction. His mother clerked at the Wellpinit Trading Post and sold hand-stitched quilts to support the family of eight. The family lacked running water and indoor plumbing until 1973. During long periods of bed confinement, the boy profited from the loving care of his 63-year-old maternal grandmother, Etta Adams, a spiritual leader and traditional storyteller. His mother spoke fluent Spokane but chose not to pass native language to her children. He recalled living in his head, imagining himself in fictional tribes. He felt weird and deranged and wished that someone had visited the community to validate kids who escaped through narrative, songs, and visions.

By age 3, Alexie disproved predictions of retardation by displaying eidetic memory and by learning to read. In the neighborhood, other kids teased him about his seizures, uncontrolled bed-wetting, and odd shaped head, which members of his little league team dubbed "the globe." By age 5, he was hiding in the rocks to read superhero comic books and John Steinbeck's *The Grapes of Wrath*. Alexie's health regimen—daily phenobarbital, occupational therapy, physical rehabilitation, and speech correction—continued until age 7 along with frequent hospitalizations. For solace, he listened to country-western music and retreated into serious reading, including William Faulkner and Ernest Hemingway.

From Medicine to Literature

Isolated by his illness and his genius, Alexie managed to retain a quippy sense of humor and wry outlook on native American rage and self-hate. He confessed that he and his brother hitchhiked to Spokane to sneak into drive-ins by crawling under cars. Exerting his scout mentality, he entered an integrated public elementary school 20 miles south in Reardan, Washington, where he and the team mascot were the only Indians. Ambition thrust him into competitive situations as a debater and public speaker. He read every book in the school library. A jock adept at basketball, racquetball, softball, and volleyball, he rejected recruitment for a sports scholarship.

At Reardan High School, Alexie set himself apart as an academic whiz, a science geek, class president, leader of the Future Farmers of America, and a 6-foot-2 star player and captain of the basketball team. He set his sights on becoming a pediatrician. While attending Gonzaga University in Spokane on scholarship, he declared himself a double minority, Indian and liberal. He spoke of college as a period of finding his tribe and declared himself a member of the book-loving people. He later explained how belonging undergirded his success: "Good art doesn't come out of assimilation; it comes out of tribalism" (Franscell, 2000, 15). He performed brilliantly in three-dimensional calculus but developed his parents' addiction to alcoholic bingeing that required 3 years to whip. After premed school from 1987 to 1989, he transferred to Washington State University in Pullman to be with a girlfriend and finished his last four semesters in 1991. His college diploma was a first for his family, all of whom donated money to pay his tuition.

In a break from family weakness, Alexie shucked off alcoholism, which destroyed his parents' lives, and moved beyond the stereotypical "drunk Indian" view of dysfunctional reservation life. He lost hope of a medical career because of his tendency to faint in anatomy labs from the smell of cadavers. To an interviewer he smirked, "It's not really a good bedside manner to fall into your patients during surgery" (Saunders, 1998, N1). He chose American studies as a more suitable major. Through serendipity, he discovered verse by filling a slot on his schedule with a poetry workshop. Under the mentorship of writer and photographer Alexander Kuo, Alexie read the native American writings of Joy Hargo, Linda Hogan, Adrian Louis, Navarre Scott Momaday, Simon Ortiz, and Leslie Marmon Silko. He exulted, "It was a sledgehammer to the heart" (Ibid.). Their ethnic slant influenced his career in verse. At age 25, he won a Washington State Arts Commission Poetry Fellowship, followed a year later by a National Endowment for the Arts Poetry Fellowship.

Alexie in Print

Alexie's zany, mocking rebelliousness quickly found an audience. He completed two poetry collections—*The Business of Fancydancing* (1991) and *I Would Steal Horses* (1992), both of which parody media distortions of Indian culture. The first anthology won a *New York Times Book Review* Notable Book of 1992 citation and the author's picture on the paper's front page. In the latter collection, the poem "Little Big Man" reflects on a heritage of pain that "becomes so familiar we settle down and call it home" (Alexie, *I Would*, 3). The poem "Distances" received nomination for a Bram Stoker Award. He remarked to an interviewer that he dodged flak from disgruntled Indians. Nonetheless, his parents, two brothers, and two sisters were so proud of his achievement that they all attended his readings in Spokane.

The author next published a classic postmodern short fiction anthology *The Lone Ranger and Tonto Fistfight in Heaven* (1993), a moving portrait of Victor, a fictional alter ego. The vignettes ally grim sufferings—hunger, Christmas without gifts, illegal sterilization of Indian mothers, alcoholism and the DTs, drug abuse, divorce, absent fathers, and bums, among others—with an ethereal dream of a Ghost Dance to recover the Indians slain in the Indian Wars and to send white explorers back to Europe. Details typify native strengths from camaraderie, drumming, powwows, and conferring with wise elders. Alexie's hero enjoys native fry bread, storytelling, fancydancing, and stickball along with all-American pickup basketball, petty delinquency, and teen dreams. At first, critics dismissed Alexie's playful, disconnective style as disorderly and underdeveloped. Later evaluations acclaimed him for a mischievous humor, candor, and offbeat pacing in witnessing Indian despair from low self-esteem and social injustice. The collection won a Lila Wallace-Reader's Digest Writers' Award and a PEN/Hemingway Award for Best First Book of Fiction. The book, a frequent listing on high school and college reading lists, returned to print in 2005 with two additional stories. In retrospect of Alexie's dazzling prose, Comanche library progenitor Lotsee Patterson lauded the author as a breath of fresh air.

Alexie followed with a novel, *Reservation Blues* (1995), which reprises the storytelling career of a trickster, Thomas Builds-the-Fire, an affable reservation oddball and outcast. A mystic tale of the creative urge fostered by a spiritual overmother, the story depicts the rock music of the Coyote Springs band as a test of faith and will power. Alexie permeated the journey of the Indian musicians with traditional mythos, dreams, and historical catastrophes as well as with incongruities that question the status quo. The work won a 1996 Before Columbus Foundation's American Book Award, a Granta Best of Young American Novelists citation, and the Murray Morgan Prize. That same year, he published *Indian Killer* (1996), a shock novel featuring an Indian mass killer scalping and sprinkling with owl feathers white victims in Seattle. The story addresses opposites—the Indian wannabe and the native who lives the lie of white beliefs and culture. For material, Alexie read textbook studies of schizoid personalities that gave him nightmares.

Film and Personal Appearances

In Seattle, Sherman exploited a sassy, irreverent persona. He described the assimilated state of Indians as "the Brady Bunch School of Native American literature" (Franklin, 2003). He zinged his homeland for racism by calling the Dakotas, Idaho, Montana, Oregon, and Washington the heartland of Indian stereotypes. Nonetheless, he and his Hidatsa-Pottawatomi wife, psychologist Diane Tomhave, reared their two sons to be polite and respectful. To raise expectations for native artistry, the author developed a gift for storytelling, which he augmented with magical realism, gallows humor, paradox, ambiguity, and satire. He contributed nativist poems and short stories to *Another Chicago, Beloit Poetry Journal, Black Bear Review, Caliban, Esquire, Journal of Ethnic Studies, New York Quarterly, Raven Chronicles, Red Dirt, Salon, Slipstream*, and *Zyzzyva*. He also produced music and comic skits with Colville comic Jim Boyd, with whom he appeared in 1996 at a benefit for the Honor the Earth campaign. He used comedy as an antiseptic to cleanse deep spiritual wounds.

Alexie and Arapaho-Cheyenne artist Chris Eyre of Portland, Oregon, aired a mainstream "road trip with a buddy" film, *Smoke Signals*, at the 1998 Sundance Film Festival. A pop phenomenon, the film appealed to native audiences but generated in its perfectionist creator a dismissal of what he termed "pretentious mishmash" (Clodfelter, 2005). For its cult status, Alexie called it the "Rocky Horror Indian Picture Show" and "Gone with the Wind for Indians" (Ibid.). Based on the ambience of *Midnight Cowboy*, the plot featured Alexie's signature characters, Victor and Thomas Builds-the-Fire, in a Southwestern odyssey to collect Victor's father's ashes. The author joked about hearing grade-schoolers reciting the film dialogue and about seeing Indian trick-or-treaters dressed like the antihero Thomas. For its interplay of disparate images and the poignance of the absent father, the venture won multiple acknowledgements, an Audience Award, a Filmmakers Trophy, a Best First Screenplay from Film Independent, and the Christopher Award for promoting spiritual values. Alexie received a Florida Film Critics Circle Award, a San Diego World Film Festival Best Screenplay award, and an Outstanding Achievement in Writing award from First Americans in the Arts.

In this productive period, Alexie lived what he termed a vacation for first peoples. Affectionately known as the Richard Wright of the American Indian, he separated his worlds by opening an office that is a 5-minute drive from home. Afternoons playing basketball with his sons concluded with their bedtime, when the author returned to writing, sometimes until dawn. For his contribution to pop culture in a variety of genres, the *New Yorker* placed him among the top twenty authors of the 21st century; *People* magazine labeled him one of the nation's "25 Most Intriguing People." Critics claim he's a charismatic spokesman for Generation X. In the author's estimation, "It's my job to make people my age feel terrible about their lives" (Clodfelter, 2005).

Taking Bows

Alexie won the first of four World Heavyweight Poetry Bout competitions in Taos, New Mexico. He joined seven panelists and President Bill Clinton on July 9, 1998, in the Lehrer *NewsHour* Dialogue on Race. To a question about Indian poverty, Alexie described fourth world conditions on reservations. He debuted in comedy in 1999 at the Foolproof Northwest Comedy Festival in Seattle and the Vancouver International Comedy Festival. His comic skits appeared on *60 Minutes*, *NOW with Bill Moyers*, and *Politically Incorrect*. Alexie's notoriety brought new opportunities as a judge of the 1999 O. Henry Award and of the PEN/Amazon.com Short Story Award and a four-time member of the Independent Spirit Awards Nominating Committee. More critical responsibility in the 2001 Shelley Memorial Award and the Poets and Writers "Writers Exchange 2001" contest established his place among the American literati.

Alexie continues to find new horizons for his energies. In 2002, he directed the film version of *The Business of Fancydancing*. In February 2003, shortly before his father's death at age 64, the author showcased diversity in "Finding Our Families, Finding Ourselves," a project of the Museum of Tolerance in Los Angeles, California. Some months later, he earned a distinguished alumnus citation from Washington State University. He served as artist in residence at the University of Washington in 2004 and 2006, when he taught American ethnic studies. In 2007, he published his first young adult fiction, *The Absolutely*

True Diary of a Part-Time Indian, which returns to the Spokane reservation to survey growing up through the adventures of a 14-year-old cartoonist. Semiautobiographical scenarios reprise the obstacles that the author faced by choosing to attend an off-reservation school among racist white kids. A second innovative novel, *Flight* (2007), pictures a 15-year-old half-breed named Zits who time travels to a bank robbery and to Custer's Last Stand, the butt of Alexie's satire.

Sources

Alexie, Sherman. *I Would Steal Horses*. Niagara Falls, NY: Slipstream, 1993.

———. *The Lone Ranger and Tonto Fistfight in Heaven*. New York: Atlantic Monthly Press, 1993.

Clodfelter, Tim. "A Writer's Life: Sherman Alexie Reflects on Poetry, Pictures and Pretentiousness." *Winston-Salem Journal*, February 3, 2005.

Coulombe, Joseph L. "The Approximate Size of His Favorite Humor: Sherman Alexie's Comic Connections in *The Lone Ranger and Tonto Fistfight in Heaven*." *American Indian Quarterly* 26 (1) (Winter 2002): 94–115.

DeNuccio, Jerome. "Slow Dancing with Skeletons: Sherman Alexie's *The Lone Ranger and Tonto Fistfight in Heaven*." *CRITIQUE* 44 (1) (Fall 2002): 86–96.

Franklin, Joy. "We Shine Brightest When Laughter Overcomes Anger." *Asheville Citizen-Times* (North Carolina), August 24, 2003.

Franscell, Ron. "Tough Love from a Native American." *Chicago Sun-Times*, May 21, 2000, 15.

Gordon, Stephanie. "'The 7-11 of My Dreams': Pop Culture in Sherman Alexie's Short Fiction." *Studies in American Culture* 24 (2) (October 2001): 29–36.

Newton, John. "Sherman Alexie's Autoethnography." *Contemporary Literature* 42 (2) (Summer 2001): 413–428.

Saunders, Michael. "Alexie Sends 'Smoke Signals.'" *Boston Globe*, July 5, 1998, N1.

Winkler, Scott A. "Dreams Like Baseball Cards: Baseball, Bricoleur, and the Gap in Sherman Alexie's *The Lone Ranger and Tonto Fistfight in Heaven*." *Aethlon* 21 (2) (Spring 2004): 87–98.

Identity Crisis
Jamaica Kincaid

A woman from two worlds, author Jamaica Kincaid defined a new self to accommodate her shift from West Indian to American. Born Elaine Cynthia Potter Richardson on May 25, 1949, in St. John, Antigua, she claims African-Carib-Scots ancestry. Her mother, Annie Victoria Richardson Drew, maintained no relationship with Kincaid's birth father, Roderick Nathaniel Potter, an unschooled Afro-Scot cabbie. The family's wood frame house depended on kerosene lamps for light and a privy for sanitation. Kincaid learned in girlhood the daily chore of drawing water from a community standpipe. Although poor and socially devalued as an illegitimate girl child, Kincaid flourished amid warm family relationships with her maternal grandmother, a Dominican animist and devotee of obeah, and with Annie Drew's husband, carpenter David Drew, a loving stepfather.

Brilliant and sassy in girlhood, Kincaid learned to read at age 3. She absorbed island oral tradition from her mother, a well-read teller of tales and interpreter of dreams. The author's happy memories of perusing bookshops and the St. John Library on Redcliffe Street picture a contented bibliophile. She adored the sympathetic librarian, who understood book lust. To a budding writer, "[s]he was like food" (Ferguson, 1994, 174). Kincaid's readings consisted of scriptural study of Genesis and Revelation, William Shakespeare's sonnets and plays, Rudyard Kipling's colonial stories and fables, essays by Thomas Carlyle, Lewis Carroll's fantasies, and social novels by Charles Dickens and Thomas Hardy. For memory work, she preferred John Milton's epics and the romantic verse of John Keats and William Wordsworth. She found personal solace in feminist writings—fiction and nonfiction of Virginia Woolf and the novels of Charlotte and Emily Brontë and George Eliot. Kincaid advanced from a Moravian kindergarten to the Antiguan Girls School, an academy dedicated to the Eurocentric teaching methods and readings from the mother country. At the O level, Kincaid enrolled at the Princess Margaret School on scholarship, a testimony to her intellectual promise. In reflection on the absurdity of a British curriculum for second-class West Indian citizens, she sniped: "It was an attempt to make me into a certain kind of person, the kind of person they had no use for, anyway. An educated black person" (Bonetti, 1993, 329). Nonetheless, each January 1, she made a wish to become a writer.

Colonial Ambivalence

From the 1950s, Kincaid experienced a love-hate relationship with British colonialism and enslavement and with an island home reinundated by postcolonial exploitation in the form of tourism. She commented on the conqueror's advantage: "When you win, you can do anything. You can adopt another people's identity very easily" (Ferguson, 1994, 172). Within a milieu of poverty and deprivation, Brownie Scout leaders taught her table setting. Her mother insisted on European table manners at meals and at tea and on standard British English rather than Creole patois. Sessions with Miss Doreen introduced Kincaid to the prim stitchery expected of female islanders. Of the pressures from authorities figures, Kincaid repined, "I felt at the mercy of everybody" (Kaufman, 1997, 110). She chafed at textbook glorification of imperialism and the absence of West Indian slavery and European land grabs. Of her own attitude toward overlords, she joked, "If I'd been a slave, I would have been dead within ten seconds" (Kaufman, 1997, 109). To express her hatred of mastery, she defaced a sympathetic drawing of Christopher Columbus.

In her preteens, Kincaid experienced a wrench from happy girl to unloved prewoman. The birth of her oldest brother, Joseph Drew, in 1958, ended her oneness with Annie, whose favoritism for legitimate male children alienated and isolated Kincaid. When Annie rejected her only daughter, Kincaid analyzed a gendered dilemma: "When I became a woman, I seemed to repel her. I had to learn to fend for myself" (Snell, 1997, 28). Kincaid developed a truculent, unyielding self that defied home and island authority. The overlaying of a tyrannical mother with a domineering motherland resulted in Kincaid's balky classroom behaviors and her refusal to honor two British anthems, "God Save the King" and "Rule, Britannia." The situation worsened as the family's "Daddy Longlegs" grew to a buxom 6 feet tall. She fantasized emigrating from the islands in the style of Charlotte Brontë's feminist heroine Jane Eyre to make her own way in the world. She later reflected on a yearning for autonomy: "I was looking to close my door when I want to, open it when I want, come when I want" (Dilger, 21).

A Break from Home

West Indian gender prejudice needled Kincaid, who battered all forms of injustice directed at her. She later regretted, "If I had been a boy, there's no question that I would have been singled out" (Bonetti, 1993, 325). In 1961, the Drew family's worsening finances and the birth of a third son, Devon "Sugar" Drew, forced Kincaid to abandon school and dreams of a university education. She ducked home chores, shoplifted, stole from purses, and hoarded pilfered books under the house, her daily retreat. A blowup in 1964 erupted after Kincaid shirked diaper changing of Devon during babysitting. Annie retaliated by burning her 15-year-old's book stash.

In June 1965, Kincaid yielded to Annie Drew's insistence that she immigrate to Scarsdale, New York, as an au pair, a period she jokingly referred to as "just a few years off the banana boat" (Bonetti, 1993, 329). Into her early 20s, she tended the children of writer Michael Arlen at his toney Upper East Side residence. Depressed and alienated from home and family, she began a self-rescue, working from the outside in. After lopping her hair and bleaching her black curls blonde, she assembled outré outfits of jodhpurs and black motorcycle boots copied from ads in *Tan* magazine. A taste of liberty preceded her abandonment of a planned career in nursing and a refusal to communicate with her family or to send them money.

Self-Education

After setting in Harlem, Kincaid experimented with sexual promiscuity, marijuana, and street drugs. She survived a normal testing of limits: "My youth was exhausting, it was dangerous, and it is a miracle that I grew out of it unscathed" (Kincaid, 1995, 101). Ironically, in the late 1960s, her island home underwent its own coming-of-age angst of liberal mores, drugs, prostitution, and mafia gambling after the British gave Antigua more freedom. To reset her aims on learning, while earning a living singing, modeling, filing for a photo agency, and writing for *Art Direction*, she earned a high school diploma and enrolled at Westchester Community College in White Plains.

In 1969, Kincaid studied photography at the New York School for Social Research in Manhattan. Influencing her development of an expressionist style were the 5-minute French film *La Jeté* and the philosophical literary theoretician Alain Robbe-Grillet. After one year at Franconia College in New Hampshire in 1973, she dropped out, worked at an ad agency, and began directing her career in freelance reviewing and reporting for *Glamour*, *Harper's*, *Ingenue*, *Mademoiselle*, *Ms.*, *Paris Review*, *Rolling Stone*, and *Village Voice*. Driven by an urgency to write, she flourished at interviewing for *Ingenue* magazine. As a safety net against failure and island ridicule, she altered her name from the stiffly British birth identity to Jamaica Kincaid, a combination reflecting her Carib-Scots background.

Serendipity

In an elevator, Kincaid bumped into a connection with New York's elite entertainment and publishing empire. After her introduction to dramatist, editor, and nonfiction writer George W. Scott Trow, a cofounder of *National Lampoon*, she drew attention to her unique West Indian perspective in some 85 submissions to "Talk of the Town," a popular column in the *New Yorker*. The outlet for her talents came at an auspicious time when, she says, "I was just hungry. Hungry to say what was on my mind" (Trueheart, 1991, 1). Feeding that appetite, editor William Shawn assigned her a private office and nourished her eccentric reportage on the arts.

At age 29, Kincaid jolted readers with "Girl," a one-sentence mother-to-daughter directive laden with feminist perspectives. The next year, Shawn became her father-in-law after she married 31-year-old composer Allen Shawn, the father of their children, Annie and Harold. In their New York flat and later at their home in Bennington, Vermont, she indulged a domestic urge by growing potherbs, carpooling, and cooking American entrées. Her first bestseller, the autobiographical novella *Annie John* (1983), a young adult classic, earned $30,000 in prepublication royalties as well as an Anisfield-Wolf Book Award, a Lila Wallace-Reader's Digest Award, and second place for the Ritz Paris Hemingway Award. The rise in literary fame preceded employment for Kincaid and her husband at Bennington College.

Home Away from the Sea

Life in New England placed the tall, stately West Indian in a distinct racial and cultural minority. Nonetheless, she acclimated to the beauty of the White Mountains. In comparison to the tropical homeland she grew up in, she exulted in Vermont: "It changes. It's mountainous. It has seasons. I think I need that" (Kennedy, 1990). Central to her contentment were bulbs, plants, and herbs in her pine-shaded garden. On a visit to Antigua, she found it squalid, crumbling, and Americanized. She regretted that it was "owned by travel agents . . . not so big and so beautiful anymore" (Cudjoe, 1990, 225). Upon reflection on Antigua's shortcomings, she composed *A Small Place* (1988), an urgent diatribe resulting in the banning of her books in island shops and a restriction on her passport privileges.

At age 40, Kincaid experienced a wrench toward the past when her birth father visited her. Her first view of England as a tourist renewed her distaste for British menus,

Anglicanism, and mannerisms that conquerors forced on Antiguans. She charged, "England was a special jewel all right, and only special people got to wear it" (Kincaid, 1991, 13). She enlarged on the immigrant's severance of ties with home in a novella, *Lucy* (1990), a sequel to *Annie John*. Influenced by second wave American feminism, the text pictures ambivalence in a 19-year-old newcomer, who experiences unsettling attitudes toward female autonomy and sexuality and male fidelity.

In middle age, Kincaid felt at home with her adult self and with the accolades and honorary degrees that acknowledged her literary perspectives. She rebelled against shifts in the *New Yorker* toward celebrity worship and, in 1995, ended her long association. In a subsequent break with the past, Kincaid joined Bennington's Beth El Temple and involved herself in Judaic scholarship and oral tradition. Rabbi Howard Cohen discovered in her humanism an impetus toward universal issues: "She had a Jewish soul waiting to come out . . . She writes a lot about oppression and makes people uncomfortable, which is what the prophets did" (Kaufman, 1997, 110).

Peace with the Past

As a professional writer, Kincaid recycled the stiff curriculum of the British educational system into a springboard for words and images: "I'm hopelessly in love with language—with words, really—and what I can make it do" (Jones, 2002). She demonstrated tour de force style in the vignette collection, *At the Bottom of the River* (1992), an exotic montage of word pictures that relies on dreamscape and mythic scenarios. In it she incorporated the jablesse, an alluring female shapeshifter from West Indian mythology, who seduces men to their doom.

With *The Autobiography of My Mother* (1996), a critical favorite, Kincaid directed her island survey to Dominica, her mother's home. After the invalidism and death of Kincaid's youngest brother Devon, a bisexual Rastafarian who died of AIDS, the author extended honor and compassion to the sibling who shared her tendency to live in the head. In *My Brother: A Memoir*, winner of a Prix Fémina Étranger award and a nominee for a 1997 National Book Award and a PEN/Faulkner Award, she castigated Devon for remaining sexually active and spreading the disease, but she chose to rescue him from the ignominy of dying of a virus protracted through promiscuous sexual activity. To critics of the family tell-all, she rebuked, "Nobody should be shamed of [his death from AIDS]. Lies just lead to cruelty and pain" (Hayden, 1997). The eulogy broadened her audience to include more urban poor and Caribbean readers.

At Home in the Garden

Kincaid extended her links to the reading public with readings, lectures, and book-store appearances. She issued 85 columns in an anthology, *Talk Stories* (2001). Still linked to home, ten years after her biological father's death, she composed *Mr. Potter* (2002), a fictional embodiment of the sire who rejected her at conception. Her 21st-century writings for *Architectural Digest* moved from island memories to challenges of gardening, a seemingly apolitical realm that reflects the intrusions of European flora on North American landscapes. Unlike the yards she knew in Antigua that devoted space to dasheen and guava trees, she pictured North American horticulture as a visual representation of conquest and florid landscapes as hobbies of the wealthy and elite.

Nearing age 60, Kincaid enjoys a well-earned global audience and the publication of her works in standard high school and college texts. In *Among Flowers: A Walk in the Himalaya* (2005), she mused over the universal pairing of innocent lives among vanquishers, mercenaries, and tyrants. A teacher of creative writing and of African and Afro-American studies at Harvard, she continues to reflect in *Architectural Digest* on nature as an outlet for repressed feelings and yearnings.

Sources

Bonetti, Kay. "An Interview with Jamaica Kincaid." *Missouri Review* 15 (1993): 325–340.

Cudjoe, Selwyn R., ed. *Caribbean Women Writers: Essays from the First International Conference.* Wellesley, MA: Calaloux, 1990.

Dilger, Gerhard. "I Use a Cut and Slash Policy of Writing." *Wasafiri* 16: 21–25.

Ferguson, Moira. "A Lot of Memory: An Interview with Jamaica Kincaid." *Kenyon Review* 16 (1) (Summer 1994): 163–188.

Hayden, Chris. "Jamaica Kincaid Writes Out of Deep Desire." *St. Louis Post-Dispatch*, October 31, 1997.

Jones, Vanessa E. "A Personal Exploration: Jamaica Kincaid Invests Her Past in *Mr. Potter*." *Houston Chronicle*, July 6, 2002.

Kaufman, Joanne. "Jamaica Kincaid." *People* 48 (December 15, 1997): 109–110.

Kennedy, Louise. "A Writer Retraces Her Steps: Jamaica Kincaid Finds Herself in Her Words." *Boston Globe*, November 7, 1990.

Kincaid, Jamaica. "On Seeing England for the First Time." *Harper's* (August 1991): 13–17.

———. "Putting Myself Together." *New Yorker* (February 20, 1995): 20–27, 93, 94, 98, 100–101.

Snell, Marilyn. "Jamaica Kincaid Hates Happy Endings." *Mother Jones* 22 (5) (September–October 1997): 28–31.

Trueheart, Charles. "The Writer's Lessons from Literature and Life: Jamaica Kincaid Meets with Students at Dunbar High." *Washington Post*, November 2, 1991, 1.

■ Illegitimacy
Esmeralda Santiago

An emigrant from Puerto Rico, Latina feminist Esmeralda Santiago faced the combined torments of teen angst and coping with the rage of her mother, a *jamona* (unmarried woman), at an absent, dismissive mate. Born on May 17, 1948, in Santurce, a rural barrio in Tao Baja outside San Juan, the author bore the name of her paternal aunt, Titi Merín. Santiago preceded six more children—Delsa, Norma, Héctor, Alicia, Edna, and Raymond—all born illegitimately. Her mother, Ramona "Monín" Santiago, noticed early her eldest's powers of observation, which began in infancy. Called Negi, short for *negrita* (little dark one), she felt isolated after the family moved in 1951 to a dirt-floored stilted hut in rural Macún. Their poverty reduced them to an outdoor latrine concealed by palm fronds. Santiago began thinking of wives like Ramona as perpetual victims "whose voices cracked with pain, defeat, and simmering anger" (Santiago, 1993, 30).

The lack of wedded parents exposed the Santiago children to the erratic absences and inadequate support of their father, Pablo "Pablito" Santiago Diaz. A cheerful carpenter and food vendor, he charmed them by reciting verse in a resonant baritone. He frequently promised outings but then disappointed the children by breaking his word. She recalled that "[t]hey were locked in a litany choked with should have's, ought to's, and why didn't you's," and "[t]heir arguments accomplished nothing" (Santiago, 1993, 29). The constant domestic war made the whole family miserable. Worse for them were the embarrassing rumors about Provi, his *puta* (whore), and her daughter Margie, who moved from Santurce to New York City. Santiago based her view of gender and family on her illegitimacy: "Men, I was learning, . . . had no shame and indulged in behavior that never failed to surprise women but caused them much suffering" (Ibid., 29). At the height of in-house bitterness, Ramona hurled his wardrobe out the door before dousing it with water. When her anger abated over night, the next day, she laundered the clothes. In repeated episodes of fighting and accusations, Santiago hid her weeping inside, out of adult view. In adulthood, she supported programs to ease the hurt of domestic violence.

Good and Bad Times

Fatherlessness equated with constant need. After Santiago entered school, her mother moved the family to Santurce to live with grandmother Tata, who took the child to Mass and taught her to cross herself after praying the Lord's Prayer. Grandfather sold oranges from a cart at Calle San Cristóbal in Old San Juan. Among city kids, Santiago stood out as a *jíbara* (yokel). Following the birth of Alicia, Pablito lured Ramona back to Macún, where she conceived Edna. At the outback school, Monday through Saturday, Santiago received training in diet and cleanliness, free toothbrushes, and breakfasts of powdered eggs, sausages, canned juice, and bread with margarine from the Free Associated State. A nurse vaccinated students for polio. Social workers warned Ramona about internal parasites and offered her two bags of groceries. Santiago ate for the first time beets, canned peaches, cornflakes, fruit cocktail, grape jelly, peanut butter, pickles, and tuna. Pablito continued upgrading the fatherless home with carpentry and a cement floor to keep out insects.

After hurricane Santa Clara stripped the land of six mango trees and a grove of nine avocado trees on October 12, 1956, Pablito and uncle Cándido repaired the property. Ramona worked as thread cutter and seamstress at a lingerie factory in Toa Baja to pay for remodeling. In the absence of Gloria, the children's nanny, Delsa and Raymond rode a bicycle. When the chain mangled Raymond's leg, he required emergency care in Bayamón. Ramona's departure from the factory and the increased poverty severed her relationship with Pablito. The family moved to Doña Andrea's houseboat over a sewage lagoon in Santurce. At Pablito's apartment behind a bar, Ramona tended Raymond's injury while cooking for the landlord, cleaning houses, and doing laundry. To spare the child amputation, Ramona transported him to New York for 19 days. Her second journey north left the children with an unsuitable babysitter who fed them oatmeal at every meal.

Goodbye to the Caribbean

Santiago grew up blaming her father for any stress that worsened the family's primitive life. Ramona forbade her children from mentioning Provi or Margie. Futile attempts to form a nuclear family frustrated Pablito, who "disappeared into himself like a snail into a shell" (Ibid., 29). He shut himself away in a tool shed to drink, smoke, read prophecy, and contemplate Rosicrucianism. Santiago puzzled over moments of tenderness "that transcended the hurt and resentments, the name-calling and deceit" (Ibid.). After 14 years as a husbandless parent, Ramona demanded a legal union. The ultimatum caused a permanent breach. In August, she flew to New York with Edna, Negi, and Raymond. That fall, Pablito married Fela, a widow, and dispersed Alicia, Delsa, Héctor, and Norma among relatives. He ceased regular visits and stopped caring for their needs. In fury at his treachery, Santiago wrote to him that she would think of him as dead. The cycle of anger caused Pablito to accuse Ramona of poisoning the children's minds against him. Ramona completed the cycle by yelling at Negi. No one apologized, but Ramona insisted that the children honor Pablito as their father, even if he legitimized a new family and withdrew from Ramona's brood.

Ramona's introduction to America and feminism changed her from frumpy peasant wife to stylish matron. In the bilingual milieu of New York, at age 13, Santiago resided with her extended family in Brooklyn. She shopped with Ramona at *la marketa* in the Williamsburg section among blacks, Italians, and Jews. From their grandmother's two-room flat, the family progressed to a four-room apartment in the projects opposite Bushwick Avenue and facing Varet Street. On October 7, 1961, Ramona sent for the rest of her children. Santiago lived a fantasy that Pablito would materialize at the door to rescue Ramona "just as he had done countless times in Puerto Rico" (Santiago 2004, 5).

A Makeshift Father

At age 37, Ramona made a significant change in her children's lives. At her two-room apartment, free from her mother's meddling and disapproval, Ramona and her lover Francisco became the model parents that Santiago had lacked in childhood. In place of Pablito's duplicity and rancor, Francisco became Ramona's Prince Charming. Santiago recalled, "He was as close to a loving, warm-hearted, protective father as we could have wished" (Santiago, 2004, 12). The couple played cards in the evening at the dining room table; he treated the children to games of dominoes and gin rummy. He showered the family with candy, sodas, flowers, and happiness. In March 1963, Ramona and Francisco produced a son, Franky, within months of Francisco's death from cancer. The loss devastated her at a time when she struggled to be father and mother to her children. Santiago lauded Ramona's devotion: "We could count on her in a way we had never been able to count on Papi" (Santiago, 1993, 245).

Santiago maintained a distant relationship with Pablito. She sent holiday cards and copies of her school essays. Over 20 moves to more suitable housing, she rearranged her life to accommodate a maternal grandmother, mother, stepfather, and all six siblings. English sounded like a buzz to her Hispanic ears. She read from the public library to improve her English. She admired librarians for their generosity and regarded the institution as the nation's most democratic. She entered eighth grade and excelled in English, history, and social studies. To learn teen lingo, she read Archie comics, which taught her American slang. After a move to Ellery Street, she enrolled in ninth grade at P.S. 33 and determined to become an actor. She delivered a speech from Sidney Howard's play *The Silver Cord* (1926) and pantomimed trimming a Christmas tree with Bonnie, another auditioner for the prestigious Performing Arts High School.

Education and a Career

Santiago accepted the hassle of commuting daily to class while carrying books and dance clothes. More challenging, attending class with wealthy white students forced her to suppress embarrassment and shame over her family's growth to 11 children with the births of Charlie, Cibi, and Ciro. After graduating with honors in dance and drama, she pursued more education part time at a community college while acting in *Babu* and *A Box of Tears* for Children's Theater International Company, two Broadway musicals, and as a film extra in *Up the Down Staircase* (1967), an adaptation of Bel Kaufman's novel, starring Sandy Dennis and featuring Eileen Heckart and Jean Stapleton. Santiago supported herself as a telemarketer, mail sorter at Fisher Scientific, clerk for the Advertising Checking Bureau, model at a photography school, shoe seller, and office assistant at Lady Manhattan, a clothing manufacturer. On a tight budget, she continued studying speech, drama, and narration on full scholarship at Harvard University and graduated magna cum laude with a B.F.A. in film production at age 32. She earned an M.F.A. from Sarah Lawrence College, as well as honorary degrees from Pace and Trinity universities.

Santiago freelanced opinion pieces for the *Boston Globe*, *Christian Science Monitor*, *Los Angeles Times*, and *New York Times*. She also contributed to *Good Housekeeping*, *House & Garden*, *Latina*, *Metropolitan Home*, *New York Times Magazine*, *Ploughshares*, *Radcliffe Quarterly*, and *Vista*. She hosted television broadcasts of NPR's *All Things Considered* and *Morning Edition*. Her screen credits include two plays, *Beverly Hills Supper Club* (1980) and *Button, Button* (1982). For her contributions to cinema, she won a silver medal from the International Film and TV Festival and a gold medal from the Houston International Film Festival. No longer overwhelmed by bilingualism or intimidated by her déclassé origins, she addressed the International Reading Association, National Council of Teachers of English, and Smithsonian Institution. She initiated social programs for teens and for abused mothers and their children in a Quincy, Massachusetts, shelter.

Married to director Frank Cantor, the author settled in a Westchester County home with their children, Ila and Lucas. The couple collaborated on documentary and educational films at Cantomedia. Santiago wrote proposals, researched background, and composed narrations. With Joie Davidow, she edited *Las Christmas: Favorite Latino Authors Share Their Holiday Memories* and *Las Mamis: Favorite Latino Authors Remember Their Mothers*. As outlets for her generosity and love of America, Santiago promoted public libraries, chaired the Campaign for America's Libraries, and served on the education committee of the Jacob Burns Film Center.

Revealing Sources

Santiago expressed passion for the arts as a wellspring of the humanities. While addressing the demands of multiculturalism on Puerto Rican immigrants, she discussed issues of culture, gender, and history. In her autobiography, *When I Was Puerto Rican* (1994), she outlined candid views of the absent father and the effects of illegitimacy, welfare, alcoholism, and a single female parent on the children. She took the risk of family disapproval to ensure that no child felt so alone and uncommunicative as she had. Her relatives forgave her for spilling family secrets and for picturing Ramona as the backbone of the household and the in-and-out father Pablito as the villain.

Santiago continued championing young womanhood in the novel *America's Dream* (1997), the story of América Gonzalez, an abused maid on the island of Vieques who escapes an abusive relationship to work as a domestic in Westchester, New York. The story won acknowledgment from Literary Guild. For her second coming-of-age memoir, *Almost a Woman* (1999), the American Library Association presented her the Alex Award. The text revealed to readers the author's humiliation at having to translate for Ramona the intricacies of American welfare. In 2004, Connecticut readers chose the sequel as the One Book for Greater Hartford.

Santiago remained attuned to the degradation and strivings of other expatriate women in an androcentric, pro-white milieu. She followed in 2004 with another evocative memoir, *The Turkish Lover*, in which she honored Ramona, Pablito, and her siblings. Without castigating her father, she stated, "You have encouraged and supported this difficult work and have walked alongside me with grace and dignity.... That is the greatest gift anyone can receive" (Santiago, 2004, 340). The text depicts her maturity from ages 21 through 28 and her self-liberation from a dominator like Pablito. She ran away from home to live with screen director Ulvi Dogan of Istanbul, who was seventeen years her senior. A friend accused her of using Ulvi as a substitute father.

Past impressions of men strangled Santiago's heart. The stifling relationship reminded her that desperation undergirded the flight of her mother and siblings to opportunity in America. Contributing to her dismay was the sudden reappearance of Pablito, who reunited with her after an 8-year absence to discuss a threat to her virginity and to defend her honor. She longed to dash into his arms "collecting years' worth of hugs and father kisses" (Ibid., 67). Rattling around her head, the words, "Too late, too late, too late," summarized a past lacking in paternal concern (Ibid., 70). Nonetheless, on her first visit to Puerto Rico, she forgave his dissolute life and enjoyed an awkward visit with his wife Fela.

The filming of *Almost a Woman* validated the life of a notable expatriate. Santiago worried that a "Hollywoodized" version would lack authenticity. She labored at reducing the Spanish text with Puerto Rican inflections to an English screenplay. Integral to her task was recreating the feel of family camaraderie and trust in a woman-centered household. The choice of a Filipina-Spanish actor, Ana Maria Lagasca, to play the lead impressed Santiago for the girl's likeness to her. On September 14, 2002, the Exxon Mobil Masterpiece Theater broadcast the teleplay on PBS as part of a series featuring American classic authors James Agee, Willa Cather, Henry James, Eudora Welty, and Tennessee Williams. The film won a Premio Sol for Best Picture at the Houston Film Festival, an Imagen Award for Best Picture, and a George Peabody Award for Excellence in Broadcasting.

Sources

Brenner, Elsa. "A Bicultural Life on Paper and in Film." *New York Times*, August 8, 2004.

Constable, Pamela. "True Stories of Domestic Violence." *Washington Post*, May 23, 1996, J1.

Copeland, Libby Ingrid. "Cultural Go-Between: Author Esmeralda Santiago's Two Languages and Two Lives." *Washington Post*, November 12, 1998, C1.

Garcia, Elizabeth. "Degrees of Puertoricanness: A Gendered Look at Esmeralda Santiago's *When I Was Puerto Rican*." *Latino Studies* 2(4) (December 2004): 377.

Santiago, Esmeralda. *The Turkish Lover*. New York: Da Capo, 2004.

———. *When I Was Puerto Rican*. New York: Vintage Books, 1993.

■ Imprisonment
Martha Stewart

A one-woman industry, domestic designer Martha Stewart knows prison bars as well as autograph sessions. On August 4, 1941, in Jersey City, New Jersey, she was born Martha

Helen Kostyra, the second of six children to Polish-American teacher Harriet "Big Martha" Ruszowski Kolstyra and Edward "Eddie" Kolstyra, a pharmaceutical salesman from Buffalo, New York. He taught Martha how to sell herself as an antidote to poverty. Her parents and grandmother Franciska Albiniak Ruszowski demonstrated sewing, kitchen gardening, ethnic cookery, and canning and preserving. From age 13, while excelling in classwork and writing for *The Maroon and Gray*, the high school newspaper in Nutley, New Jersey, she turned fashion modeling for Bonwit Teller and *Glamour* magazine, catering, and party-planning into money makers. During her years on partial scholarship at Barnard College studying chemistry, European history, architecture, and art and composing a thesis on the Louvre Museum, she earned tuition by posing for TV ads for Breck hair spray, Lady Clairol hair care products, Lifebuoy hand soap, and Tareyton cigarettes.

In 1961, the designer wed Yale law student Andrew "Andy" Stewart, who met her when she catered a book release party for Abrams Publishing. She continued modeling until the birth of their daughter Alexis. At age 26, she joined the staff of Monness, Horstman, Williams, and Sidel, a brokerage house in New York City. In a shift to domestication at Westport, Connecticut, she plunged into remodeling Turkey Hill, a dilapidated farmhouse built in 1805, where she established an orchard growing apples, peaches, pears, and plums. In 1976, Stewart partnered with college pal Norma Collier in Uncatered Affair, a catering and take-out food service for business sessions, benefit dinners, and celebrity parties. The duo advertised through word of mouth as intelligent, tasteful kitchen divas.

On the side, Stewart managed the Market Basket outside a Ralph Lauren boutique at the Common Market, a gourmet foods and specialty supplies outlet, and freelanced articles and columns for the food section of the *New York Times*, *Family Circle*, and *House Beautiful*. At the urging of Alan Mirken, president of Crown Publishing, Stewart and fashion consultant Elizabeth Hawes cowrote *Entertaining* (1982), a photo cookbook featuring table settings and menus for informal gatherings and receptions. The popular work prefaced a line of bestselling coffee table volumes—*Martha Stewart's Quick Cook Menus* (1983), *Martha Stewart's Pies and Tarts* (1985), *Weddings* (1986), *The Wedding Planner* (1988), *Martha Stewart's Christmas: Entertaining, Decorating, and Giving* (1989), *Martha Stewart's Gardening, Month by Month* (1991), *Martha Stewart's New Old House* (1992), *Arranging Flowers* (1999), and *Martha Stewart's Hors d'Oeuvres Handbook* (1999). Martha's name became a synonym for upbeat consumerism and a rallying cry to second wave feminism.

Success Piled on Success

A multimedia dynamo in the late 20th through early 21st centuries, Stewart became famous for long hours, little sleep, and a fearless attitude toward obstacles. She progressed to lifestyle coordinator and spokeswoman for K-Mart, a conglomerate that merchandises Martha Stewart Everyday. She advised buyers on gift items, sheets and towels, tableware, paint, garden supplies, bedding plants, and laundry, nursery, and lawn care products. Steve Ryman, the company's divisional vice president, predicted more brilliance and market savvy from Stewart. She proved him right by editing *Martha Stewart Living* magazine and the quarterly journal *Martha Stewart Weddings* for Martha Stewart Living Omnimedia, Inc. She formed MarthaStewartFlowers.com and sold her goods through Martha by Mail. A media maven, she became a household name to fans of askMartha newspaper columns, free consumer Internet access, and the Westwood One syndicated radio show *Ask Martha*.

In 1990, the year of her divorce from Andy Stewart, the video series *Secrets of Entertaining* (1988) and *Martha Stewart's Living* magazine spread the author's home decoration concepts to Middle America. She launched a book tour to promote *Martha Stewart's New Old House* (1992) and earned accolades from *New York* magazine. In June 1995, she appeared on the cover of *Working Woman* and on holiday specials and interviews for *The Today Show*, *The Oprah Winfrey Show*, and *CBS This Morning*. By October 2000, Martha Stewart Living Enterprises supplied ideas and goods to Japanese homemakers through the Shop Channel. Using her Connecticut home and grounds as a backdrop, she published *Good Things for Organizing* (2001) and *Simple Home Solutions: Good Things with Martha Stewart Living* (2004) and taped relaxed, engaging television segments on practical upkeep, menus, and seasonal decoration. The series won an Emmy. In January 2001, she delivered a keynote address in Chicago at the International Housewares Show. *Ladies' Home Journal* named her one of America's most powerful women.

An Abrupt End to Stardom

An era of struggle tarnished the sheen of the Stewart name. In June 2003, only months after she obtained a seat on the board of the New York Stock Exchange, the Securities and Exchange Commission (SEC) released a 41-page indictment charging her with covering up for securities fraud from insider trading. A scandal arose from her profiteering the previous December 27 on sale of 4,000 shares in the ImClone Systems, a biotech conglomerate. On the day before the Food and Drug Administration rejected sale of Erbitux, an ImClone drug for colorectal cancer, the transaction earned her $51,000. On May 19, 2003, NBC TV exploited the brouhaha with the film *Martha, Inc.: The Story of Martha Stewart*, starring Cybill Shepherd.

Rather than yield to public persecution by the Department of Justice, Stewart risked her reputation and income to fight the charges in court. James B. Comey, the U.S. attorney for New York's Southern District, heightened the stakes by accusing her of manipulating her company's stock by pleading innocent of all wrongdoing. She purchased a full-page ad in *USA Today* denying culpability and vowing to exonerate herself of fraud. The fallout resulted in loss of advertisers, staff reduction from 650 to 470, cessation of a $900,000 annual salary, and dismay among fans. Her friend Marianna Pasternak refused to support her, but Stewart continued to mingle with public at Yankees baseball games, museums, and dinners.

Tried and Convicted

Stewart came to trial on January 20, 2004, before U.S. District Court Judge Miriam Goldman Cedarbaum. Five weeks later, the judge tossed out charges of securities fraud as unfounded. On March 5, 2004, a 12-member jury overturned a conspiracy charge but convicted Stewart and stockbroker Peter E. Bacanovic of four incidents of lying to FBI and SEC agents and of obstruction of justice. Both are felonies. The next evening, Larry King interviewed her on television and disclosed her ambivalence toward hard time. At the end of the politicized trial, on July 16, she faced a minimum sentence—a fine of $195,000 and of $58,062 in profits, a civil penalty of $137,019, 5 months in prison, and expulsion from the boards of the New York Stock Exchange, Revlon, and her own company until 2009.

Stewart turned public ridicule and incarceration to profit. While pressing an appeal, she sold her Greenwich Village flat and volunteered to begin her sentence. She requested assignment to Danbury Prison to put her near her 90-year-old mother, but the Bureau of Prisons denied Stewart's choice. In early morning on October 8, 2004, inmate 55170-054 entered "Camp Cupcake," the nickname of Alderson Federal Women's Prison Camp, a two-story brick facility on a 100-acre site along Ray Glen Road in Alderson, West Virginia. The crowded minimum security lockup features an open campus for unattended walks. The prison formerly held murderers Lynette "Squeaky" Fromme and Jean Harris, singer–drug addict Billie Holiday, presidential assassin Sara Jane Moore, and wartime radio commentators Tokyo Rose and Axis Sally. Despite its celebrity, Stewart learned that, contrary to public perception of soft cell time for the wealthy and privileged, 80 percent of its 1,000 to 1,200 inmates served time for drug-related felonies. She dressed in prison issue khaki work clothes and followed a rigid schedule under constant surveillance. Out of the whirl of public appearances, television, and publishing, she performed over 7 hours of day labor 5 days a week. For doing laundry, cleaning, waxing floors, and raking leaves, she earned from 12 to 40 cents per hour. On her own time, she exercised, wrote, lost weight, and planned a return to private life at her Manhattan apartment on Fifth Avenue and her homes—Bedford, a 153-acre residence in Katonah, New York; the DeWitt Talmage house on Lily Pont Lane in East Hampton, Long Island; the former Edsel Ford estate and three-story manse on Mount Desert Island, Maine; and her signature estate in Westport, Connecticut, north of Manhattan.

Making the Best of It

Because of reduction in female and male guard staff, Camp Cupcake earned a reputation for degradation, threats, sexual harassment, and up to 15 assaults and fights a year. Through an online journal beginning October 24, 2004, Stewart informed 2.5 million readers of daily events and thanked them for their support. For the sake of the poor and reviled fellow prisoners, she urged outsiders to show compassion to women who had survived depression, victimization, sexual abuse, and loss of their children. In an open section housing 125 females, she endured communal meals, food from vending machines, delousing, and strip searches. Her shower time was limited. She compared to sorority hazing crude name-calling—"scaredy cunt," "M. Diddy," and "fresh fish"—and spitting and feces-hurling incidents.

Stewart weathered the seamy side of prison life, in part from visits and hugs by her daughter Alexis, Rosie O'Donnell, and Oprah Winfrey. On October 20, Stewart earned a week of solitary confinement in a cement vault for combating physical pummeling and death threats. On return to her two-person cubicle, she befriended her black roommate by playing Scrabble. The woman armed Stewart with a "shiv," a sharp prison knife for self-protection. At Halloween, she proposed dressing up as an amusement for inmates. Stewart found outlets teaching night classes in yoga, crocheting, organizing picnics and a Christmas decorating contest, and creating microwave recipes featuring dandelions and wild greens foraged from the prison grounds. She also shared anti-Iraq War sentiments with activist nuns Carol Gilbert, Jackie Hudson, and Ardeth Platte, who served 33 months for pacifist civil disobedience on behalf of Plowshares by defacing three missiles at a Minuteman silo in Colorado.

Back to Business

Upon release on March 4, 2005, Stewart redeemed herself. Her company provided a flatbed truck for media coverage of her postmidnight departure. With daughter Alexis, the ex-con sped from Greenbrier Valley Airport by chartered plane home to Katonah, New York, where she lives alone. The first order of business was a reunion with five horses, her chow dog Paw Paw, and assorted canaries, cats, chickens, and donkeys. Meanwhile, projects resumed at her primary laboratory at Turkey Hill.

Stewart entered supervised probation and wore an electronic ankle monitor during five months of house arrest. It gave her access to her horse-drawn carriage, to lemons from trees in her greenhouse, and to sewing machines, vegetable beds, and beehives. Because of violation of confinement terms, she received 28 additional days of supervised parole. Until the end of the ordeal on August 31, 2005, she was allowed up to 48 hours of work per week. A trip to Annapolis Valley, Nova Scotia, required a temporary resident permit because the Immigration and Refugee Protection Act barred her entry to Canada. Critics of the Stewart style accused the beleaguered "kitchen commando" of arrogance and defiance of the law. Nonetheless, the town of Alderson flourished from tourism and from sales of T-shirts and mugs touting the slogans, "I Survived Alderson Prison" and "West Virginia Living, It's a Good Thing." The Dinner Bell chef added Martha Stewart Swedish meatballs to the menu. Local gardeners planted a Martha garden of 1,000 crocus bulbs. Her supporters contributed 1,000 daylilies to the effort.

Through aggressive self-marketing, Stewart revived her career as daytime television cook and publisher of the magazine *Martha Stewart Living*. Her stock rallied; Harvard Business School cited her career as a model of brand management. Martha Stewart Everyday promoted holiday ornaments and elegant home furnishings from her personal line produced by Bernhardt and marketed house paint through Sears. In September, she starred in a how-to series, *The Martha Stewart Show*, often bringing her champion cats and dogs on camera to promote animal care. On September 25, 2005, Cybill Shepherd again portrayed Martha in the 2-hour Showtime prison film *Martha: Behind Bars*, filmed for CBS TV at Humber College Lakeshore, Toronto. For insight into the character, Shepherd studied the author's prison notes and blog.

In late fall 2005, Stewart published *The Martha Rules: 10 Essentials for Achieving Success as You Start, Build, or Manage a Business* and *Martha Stewart's Baking Handbook*. She introduced a Sirius satellite radio network, a 24-hour-a-day vehicle for domestic and women's programs on child care, health issues, crafts, holidays, collecting, and whole living. A year later, she issued *The Martha Stewart Living Cookbook: The Original Classics* and a domestic handbook, *Martha Stewart's Homekeeping Handbook: The Essential Guide to Caring for Everything in Your Home*, and demonstrated cookery, crafts, and gardening on *The Today Show*. Her multimedia success earned six Emmy nominations for production and hosting. She added *Blueprint, Body+Soul*, and *Everyday Food: Great Food Fast* to the magazines of her publishing empire. In October 2005, she introduced moderately priced housing prefabricated in Cary, North Carolina. In fall 2007, she initiated Martha Stewart Vintage, a series of chardonnay, merlot, and cabernet sauvignon for Gallo Wines; endorsed fresh, refrigerated, and frozen foods for Costco; and boosted Macy's crystal, bath, bed, and kitchen goods with a swank line of 2,000 items. With Wendy Kromer, she published *Martha Stewart's Wedding Cakes* (2007), featuring a hundred model confections. On the private side, she declared, "Just knowing in your heart that you are a good person—an honest, good person—can get you through an awful lot of crap" (Allen, 2007). She snuggled into her lengthy relationship with Seattle software mogul Charles Simonyi. Of the many facets of her life, she credited change and transformation with rejuvenating her joy in creativity.

Sources

Allen, Jenny. "Martha Stewart Comes Clean." *Good Housekeeping* (October 2007).
Brown, Tina. "Martha Stewart and the Pros of Being a Con." *Washington Post*, March 3, 2005.
Crawford, Krysten. "Martha: The Exit Will Be Televised." *Money* (March 2, 2005). Available at http://money.cnn.com/2005/03/02/news/newsmakers/martha_exit/ (last accessed April 3, 2008).
Eichenwald, Kurt. "Prosecutors Have Reasons for Stalking Celebrities." *New York Times*, June 5, 2003.
Neligan, Myles. "Millionaires behind Bars." *BBC News*, October 7, 2004.

■ Integration
Melba Pattillo Beals

One of the nine black integrators of Southern schools, broadcast journalist Melba Pattillo Beals survives as a model of toughness and savvy. A native of Little Rock, Arkansas, she was born on December 7, 1941, during the Japanese bombardment of Pearl Harbor. She and her younger brother Conrad, currently a federal marshal, are the children of Lois Marie Peyton Pattillo, a junior high school English teacher, and Howell "Will" Pattillo, a worker on the Missouri Pacific Railroad. Within hours of Melba's birth, a forceps wound to the scalp threatened her life. A black janitor disclosed to the Pattillos that the white doctor left directions for bathing the baby's injury with Epsom salts, an instruction that the nurses ignored. Melba recovered, and by age 4 could read and write. The next Fourth of July at Fair Park, she experienced race prejudice for the first time. Her widowed grandmother, India Annette Ripley Peyton, a cook and domestic, reassured her with bible verses. Later, India fought sectional ignorance by organizing a boycott of a discriminatory grocer.

When the Pattillos parted, 7-year-old Melba acquired her maternal grandmother as adjunct parent with Lois. On May 17, 1954, Melba attended Dunbar Junior High School when the U.S. Supreme Court voted unanimously to outlaw segregation in public schools. Melba determined to better her education and to become a Rhodes scholar. She knew the virulence of racial bias from personal experience. She had eluded a white attacker who assaulted her on a vacant lot and tried to rape her. Still idealistic about human equality, Melba admired singer Nat King Cole and Reverend Martin Luther King, Jr., and chose as a role model Rosa Parks, the seamstress who, on December 1, 1955, demanded access to public transportation in Birmingham, Alabama.

Fighting Racism

A year later, Melba's mother set an example by graduating among the first blacks at the University of Arkansas. As Southern tempers simmered, the White Citizens Council plotted obstacles to racial mixing. Because Melba was safer at the all-black Horace Mann High School, Will Pattillo refused to let her integrate Little Rock's white bastion of education. On February 8, 1956, the National Association for the Advancement of Colored People (NAACP) filed a suit against the Little Rock school system. Strategists chose Melba Beals for her exemplary performance to challenge the all-white status of Little Rock's seven-story Central High School. The black group confronted Governor Orval Faubus, who promoted traditional Southern segregation. In mid-August 1957, Melba observed the first-class citizenship for blacks that Faubus denied black Southerners. During a vacation in Cincinnati, Ohio, with her great-uncle Clancey and cousin Cindy, she realized that much of the nation had freedom of access to businesses and schools.

On return to Little Rock, 15-year-old Melba angered her mother by planning to derail unconstitutional separation of the races. Melba's grandmother understood the crusade and urged her to carry equality's banner for black people. Melba joined 16 students whom the NAACP backed to integrate Central High. On September 2, 1957, Governor Faubus called out the Arkansas National Guard. As the opening of school loomed on September 4, threatening phone calls forced grandmother India to carry a shotgun and patrol the yard around the white frame house at 1121 Cross Street. In the turmoil, eight of the 17 volunteers opted to remain in black schools. That left Melba to accompany Minnijean Brown, Elizabeth Eckford, Ernest Green, Thelma Mothershed, Gloria Ray, Terrence Roberts, Jefferson Thomas, and Carlotta Walls, a clutch of teens known as the Little Rock Nine. Whites rallied against the mixing of races in public schools; black neighbors disapproved of a situation that threatened their children.

On the first morning, Elizabeth Eckford led eight followers before a slandering, mocking, spitting mob whom soldiers held at bay. Melba prayed the Lord's Prayer as she moved toward the school entrance. Behind the officers, whites gestured with fists, bricks, and baseball bats and screamed threats of lynching and shooting. In the heat of protest, some from the city police tossed down their badges to join the jeering mob. That evening, to avoid more confrontation, Grandma India kept Melba home from a wrestling match at Robinson Auditorium. In ensuing clashes, after a taunting white mob chased Melba and her mother to the car, Melba drove them home. Other black students fled unhurt. At a nadir of Melba's confidence, Grandma India reminded her that God had set a task for her.

Legal Obstacles

The school board's attempt to halt desegregation at Little Rock High school required the nine to appear before U.S. District Judge Ronald N. Davies. At a break in proceedings, the teens lunched with power players—activist Daisy Lee Gatson Bates, publisher of the *Arkansas State Press*, Wiley Branton, counsel for the NAACP, and Thurgood Marshall, the civil rights champion who argued *Brown v. the Board of Education* before the U.S. Supreme Court. On return to the hearing, the nine teens found Davies favoring integration. In the aftermath, reporters interviewed Melba. The flash of photographers' cameras and the clustering of newspapermen along the route to school prompted her to consider journalism for a college major. On Monday, September 23, Governor Faubus sided with racists by removing the National Guard. Margaret Jackson, an officer of the Mothers' League of Central High School, promised a demonstration by 1,000 local segregationists. To assure safety, Daisy Bates and Lois Pattillo drove Melba to a side entrance under police guard while four black reporters served as decoys at the front door.

Tensions eased after the boycott of die-hard segregations removed the more volatile students from school. When the nine black students received class schedules from girls' Vice Principal Elizabeth Huckaby, they found themselves separated into different rooms. Terrified of advancing alone, Thelma Mothershed fainted from stress on her weak heart. Melba entered room 339, where whites refused to sit near her. During a volleyball game in the second period physical education class, players aimed the ball at her head. Only the shorthand teacher, Mrs. Pickwick, quelled exclusion and denigration of Melba by welcoming the new student and conducting a no-nonsense class. Meanwhile, false rumors of violence and bloodshed circulated to parents and protesters outside.

To elude crowds thrusting limbs and weapons through campus barricades, Melba's student guide led her to the office. At 11:30, while Assistant Police Chief Gene Smith evacuated the nine black teens from the school, disgruntled racists attacked black reporters. Over the phone, Melba delivered a personal observation to a reporter from the *Arkansas Gazette*, which issued her words the next day. To stanch 3 weeks of rabble rousing, on Tuesday, September 24, President Dwight D. Eisenhower dispatched 52 planes carrying 1,200 paratroopers from the 101st Airborne Division from Fort Campbell, Kentucky, to escort Melba and her fellow black students to and from class. That night, a secret service agent reported to the Pattillo home. The next morning, while 50 soldiers surrounded Melba, helicopters flew overhead and jeeps equipped with turret guns drove around the site. Her bodyguard, a soldier named Danny, walked Melba to the English class but stopped at the door. Because protests worsened in the French class and study hall, a soldier named Sarge drove Melba to the Bates' home. Reporters from the *New York Post* asked Melba to write an eyewitness account of her first 2 days at Central High. The exercise initiated her love of fair reportage for the national news.

Singled Out

Late into September 1957, pressures worsened on numerous fronts. Incidents of hate crimes and noncompliance with the law proliferated. Gunshots jolted the barricades at the Pattillo residence. An office clerk dismissed Melba's reports of assaults because they weren't substantiated by an adult. In a school stairwell, Danny intercepted a stick of dynamite aimed at Melba's head and put out the fuse. At a pep rally, football players pinned Melba to a wall. On the weekend, Melba received roses from her boyfriend Vince, who respected her near martyrdom to civil rights. A minister prayed especially for the Little Rock Nine. On October 1, when the Arkansas National Guard took over security posts from the 101st Airborne, unseen assailants threw fiery paper wads at Melba in a girls' restroom cubicle. At a walkout of white students, protesters hanged and ignited a straw manikin at Park and 16th Streets. On Danny's return to duty, he rescued Melba and carried her to an optometrist to neutralize acid thrown in her eyes. His quick action saved her sight.

As more soldiers departed the Central High campus, on October 28, Lois Pattillo demanded from School Superintendent Virgil Blossom a security plan for the Little Rock Nine. By Thanksgiving, when Danny left Little Rock along with the rest of the 101st Airborne, Melba determined to think and act like a soldier. Black teens shunned her to save themselves from threats and harassment. Because white boys blocked Minnijean Brown's entry to the cafeteria, she spilled chili in their hair. After officials suspended her, a sorority honored her and the other eight students at a Christmas party. On return from the holidays, she received a suspension after white teens doused her with soup and she retaliated by calling them "white trash." The decision reduced the Little Rock Nine by one. When a racist student named Andy threatened to kill Melba, a friend named Link offered her the keys to his 1949 Chevy. After she arrived home, Grandma India hid the sedan by spreading sheets over it. To keep senior Ernie Green from graduating, segregationists stepped up threats in April.

Untenable Threats

The first week in May, racist pressures on the city department of education cost Lois Pattillo her job, a loss that also occurred in the lives of five sets of parents of the Little Rock integrators. Like her daughter, Lois fought for civil rights by informing the press and some American Methodist Episcopal bishops of the injustice. On May 27, Melba was thrilled when Ernie Green became the first black student to graduate from Central High. She felt defeat after Central High closed until September 1960 in an effort to influence other Southern school systems to resist forced integration. Her hope of graduating from Central was lost. Two days later, the *Chicago Defender* presented the remaining eight integrators the Robert S. Abbott Memorial Award. Because the Ku Klux Klan pledged $10,000 dead and $5,000 injured to any assassin willing to murder the students, the NAACP intervened to protect them. Officials dispatched Melba to Santa Rosa, California, where white volunteers from the NAACP met her plane. The staff housed her with Quaker activists Carol Adams McCabe and Sonoma State Professor George Elwood McCabe and their four children. Melba finished her senior year in an integrated high school as one of seven black students.

Melba Beals did not let her mission go unnoticed in American history. By age 17, she was composing reflective pieces in the media that credited God with protecting the Little Rock Nine. At San Francisco State University, she came under the mentorship of Lynn Ludlow, an editor of the *San Francisco Examiner*. On scholarship, she completed an M.A. from the Columbia University School of Journalism, where she met her future husband, Matthew John Beals, a white Irishman and father of their daughter Kellie Beals. Melba reported news for KRON TV and for KQED TV, a public station in San Francisco. She scheduled interviews and lectures, led seminars on diversity, wrote *Expose Yourself: Using the Power of Public Relations to Promote Your Business and Yourself*, and issued her memories of desegregation for *Essence*, the *San Francisco Examiner*, and *People*. In 1987, she was interviewed on a PBS TV documentary *Eyes on the Prize*, a testimonial to the civil rights movement. As evidence that integrating Central High was worthwhile, she named her brother Conrad, who became the first black captain of the Arkansas state troopers, and a cousin who was elected mayor of Little Rock.

Melba Beals cherishes her kinship with the Little Rock Nine. In 1994, she acknowledged the group's courage in *Warriors Don't Cry: A Searing Memoir of the Battle to Integrate Little Rock Central High School*, a first person recounting of integration in Little Rock she began writing in 1959. She wrote from a diary she kept during high school and from notes and magazine and newspaper clippings her mother saved. A portion of the text appeared in the *American Educator* in summer 1994. Guided by her agent Sandra Dykstra, Melba Beals presented the manuscript to a bidding war won by Simon & Schuster. The published memoir received a nomination as an American Library Association Notable Book for the 1995 Nonfiction Book of the Year, the American Booksellers' Association notable book award, and a Robert F. Kennedy Book Award.

Rewards

At a 40-year reunion in September 1997, Beals and the other eight students and their families met President Bill Clinton. In the East Room of the White House, he awarded the Little Rock Nine the Congressional Gold Medal and named Central High School a national historic site. She had already won a Spingarn Award from the NAACP and a Robert S. Abbot Award from the *Chicago Defender*. In 1997, Hillary Rodham Clinton honored Daisy Bates and the Little Rock Nine at a benefit fund-raiser for Little Rock Nine Foundation scholarships and for a Central High Museum and Visitor Center. Melba retired to Sausalito, California, to raise her daughter and adopted twins, Evan and Matthew Beals. Melba had an opportunity to step into her grandmother's role by encouraging Kellie Beals when, at age ten, she integrated a Lutheran school.

Melba's civil rights activism kept her busy. She toured the lecture circuit and published *White Is a State of Mind: A Memoir* (1999). In August 2005, the Little Rock Nine merited praise from a new generation that admired their statue outside the Little Rock Statehouse. The creation of Cathy and John Deering, it required 7 years of labor and completion at a foundry in Tesuque, New Mexico. The Deerings named the $360,000 bronze grouping "Testament." The U.S. Postal Service dedicated a 10-cent stamp to the nine.

Sources

Beals, Melba Pattillo. "Warriors Don't Cry." *American Educator* 18 (2) (Summer 1994): 43–47.
———. *Warriors Don't Cry*. New York: Washington Square Books, 1994.
"Ceremony Pays Tribute to Milestone in Civil Rights." *Los Angeles Times*, August 31, 2005, A13.
Riches, William T. *The Civil Rights Movement*. New York: Palgrave, 2004.

■ Japanese Internment
Jeanne Wakatsuki Houston

During her formative years, author Jeanne Toyo Wakatsuki Houston joined 120,000 Japanese-Americans in living out World War II in detainment camps. A native of Inglewood, California, she was born last of ten children on September 26, 1934, as a paternal Nisei (second generation) and maternal Sansei (third generation) Japanese-American. Her domineering father, Ko Wakatsuki, was a commercial fisher from Kage, Hiroshima; her mother, Riku Sugai Wakatsuki, a nurse, dietician, and fish cannery worker from Honolulu, Hawaii. Jeanne's paternal great grandfather was a magistrate of the Samurai class; her Japanese grandfather was a civil servant. With pride in notable ancestry, Jeanne pondered the role of the legendary "fire horse woman," an aggressive female of epic proportions. The Wakatsukis and granny Sugai lived at Ocean Park and Terminal Island in San Pedro Bay and helped "Skipper" Ko load and pilot his boats, the *Nereid* and the *Waka*, from Santa Monica pier. One of the family's happy memories involved late-night catching of grunion and the sizzling of fish for a midnight meal.

After the bombing of Pearl Harbor, Hawaii, on December 7, 1941, children like Jeanne puzzled over the rock throwing, shoving, and hate slogans and graffiti defaming "Slant-Eyes" and "Nips," epithets agitants used to equate people like Jeanne with Japanese insurgents. Under President Franklin Delano Roosevelt's Executive Order 9066, issued on February 19, 1942, curfews and roundups of Japanese-Americans—80 percent of them born in the United States—set the tone of suspicion and veiled accusation. Federal agents rifled homes, scoured documents, and arrested men like Ko who had access to offshore shipping for potential refueling of Japanese convoys. Among 3,000 Issei (native-born Japanese) locked in cells on the basis of rumor, Ko spent 9 months at a prison at Fort Lincoln in Bismarck, North Dakota, on suspicion of ferrying barrels of oil to offshore enemy submarines. He developed frostbite, alcoholism, and paranoia, which ended his close relationship with Jeanne, a "daddy's girl."

On February 25, the American-born Wakatsukis lost their home, farmland, boat, and belongings as well as civil rights. Beginning on March 24, the War Relocation Authority dispatched trainloads of evacuees to crude camps on surplus federal plots in Arizona, Arkansas, California, Colorado, Idaho, Utah, and Wyoming. Along the way, anti-Japanese signs asserted, "Japs Go Back Where You Came From" (Houston and Houston 1973, 109). The anti-Asian era exacerbated the author's fears and insecurities around rowdier, streetwise children and cold, distant classroom teachers. Easing the angst, Quaker volunteers from the American Friends Service helped the Wakatsukis make the best of their situation. Those who rebelled were remanded to the Tule Lake stockade.

A Desert Prison

In place of Ko, his second oldest son, 24-year-old Woodrow Mann "Woody" Wakatsuki, took charge of the household. In April 1942, formal charges uprooted the family from temporary residence at the ghetto of Boyle Heights to Owens Valley. At age 7, Jeanne, numbered and tagged for resettlement, boarded a Greyhound bus with her mother, siblings, and Granny Sugai at the strategic Long Beach Naval Station. In sight of Mount Whitney, they arrived in late afternoon for impounding at the Manzanar War Relocation Center, a gnarly landscape bled dry of water to satisfy the thirst of the Los Angeles County megalopolis. High in the eastern Sierra Nevada mountains, the internment camp—euphemistically known as a custodial "assembly center"—occupied 400 acres of a 6,000-acre military reserve. Surroundings on the Mojave Desert between Lone Pine, California, and the southern Nevada border tended toward boulders, arroyos, and sagebrush. The compound comprised guard towers, armed guards, and searchlight sweeps, all of which federal officials marked off-limits to photographers. At the center was a rock cairn holding an American flag.

Passenger trains and slatted trucks hauled adults and children of all social and economic levels to one ignoble sequestration. Evacuees shared pine plank and tarpaper shacks, concrete-floored latrines, and assembly halls hurriedly nailed together. One of 10,000 inmates, Jeanne lived the emotional turmoil of an American girl suspected of national disloyalty and incarcerated without a trial on the basis of her race. Until a move to Block 28, their home in Block 16 offered gritty, drafty shelter beset by rattlesnakes and sandstorms. Outside, a single standpipe and spigot provided water for the entire barracks.

With her mother and grandmother and siblings Lillian, May, Ray, and Kiyo, Jeanne shared one room of their two-room unit, which was lighted by a single overhead bulb. The other half of their quarters, walled off by blankets, housed her two married brothers, Bill and Woody, their wives Tomi and Chizu, and Woody's baby girl. The family awoke from their first prison sleep covered in silt resembling powdered sugar. They scrounged tin can lids and newspaper to cover holes and stuff crevices. Inoculations and spoiled food at the mess hall sickened Jeanne, as did the odor of sheet-metal sinks and overflowing toilets. Dining at long trestle tables disrupted Asian-style family conviviality and unity. Her mother declared, "Animals live like this" (Houston and Houston, 1973, 19). The guards issued army surplus pea coats, khaki pants, canvas leggings, caps, and earmuffs dating to World War I. In summer, Jeanne suffered a sunstroke. She described the misery as "an open insult to that other, private self, a slap in the face you were powerless to change" (Houston and Houston, 1973, 24).

Family Disintegration

Barbed wire, gated entrances, and machine gun mounts pointed inward defined the Wakatsukis' so-called protective milieu, which photographers Ansel Adams and Dorothea Lange captured in black and white. Riku cooked as a $19-a-month camp hospital dietician; Woody worked as a carpenter and clerked at the camp general store. Others wove camouflage netting for the military. The atmosphere worsened in September 1942, when Ko returned by Greyhound. Jeanne released pent-up tears at the sight of her father's emaciation, depression, and premature aging. To ease his emasculation and debasement at being called an *inu* (dog or collaborator), he hid in the barracks, strutted with a swagger stick, raged, and began moonshining rice wine in a home still. His binges produced marital outbursts, violence, and threats in an otherwise calm family. His 11-year-old son Kiyo attacked him with a fist to the nose.

Outside the quarters of the battling Wakatsukis, stints of rock gardening and conversation with neighbors eased the tension. In December 1942, a riot broke out among 2,000 pro-Japanese internees who wanted to renounce U.S. citizenship and repatriate to Japan. Military police shot and killed two dissident inmates. Jeanne huddled in bed at the sound of mess hall bells, which tolled until noon. In February 1943, at a climactic point in camp persecution, authorities forced inmates to sign loyalty oaths. While sorting out their loyalties, Jeanne and her family gathered at the oil stove in their living room to sing *Kimi Ga Yo*, the Japanese national anthem and credo of endurance.

Coping

Jeanne needed to escape the dreary surroundings and siege mentality as well as assaults on her modesty. She feared for her soldier brothers—Ray, who joined the Coast Guard, and Woody, whom the army drafted in November 1944 and shipped to Japan to suppress the postwar black market. While adults indulged in ideological debates, she chose hopscotch and picnics in sight of the Inyo Range. At Bair's Creek, she collected rocks, camped, and waded. At school, she flourished academically under a strict, but fair, Caucasian teacher from Kentucky.

Jeanne preferred American pastimes—glee club, ballet, the school play *Growing Pains*, talent shows, and baton—over *odori*, a native Japanese display of refined Geisha womanhood. She read Nancy Drew mysteries and the works of Hans Christian Andersen, Emily Bronte, and James Fenimore Cooper. Briefly, she studied Catholic catechism with Sister Bernadette, a Canadian-Japanese Maryknoll nun, and considered converting from Buddhism. The religious shift roused Ko to confront his daughter about turning over her autonomy to a controlling faith that offered no Japanese males for marriage. She fantasized that her baton was Ko, whom she would "throw ... high, again and again and again" (Houston and Houston, 1973, 84). By December 18, 1944, the family contretemps ended after the U.S. Supreme Court declared unconstitutional the incarceration of loyal citizens.

Home to California

Before the Wakatsukis decamped from Manzanar, an atomic bomb blast on Hiroshima on August 6, 1945, incinerated their relatives. In early October 1945, a month before the camp closed, Jeanne's brothers and sisters moved east to job opportunities in New Jersey. Like refugees, Jeanne and her parents settled 225 miles west in Long Beach at Cabrillo Homes, a rickety ghetto as unappealing as Manzanar. The family lost their Studebaker to repossession, the fishing trawlers to unnamed claimants, and their appliances and furnishings to a robbery at the warehouse where they were stored. Bigotry and ostracism flourished in newspaper headlines and among groups like the Home Front Commandos, No Japs Incorporated, and Pacific Coast Japanese Problem League. Nightriders threatened shootings, beatings, and arson. Jeanne described the blows to Ko's manhood as "another snip of the castrator's scissors" (Houston and Houston, 1973, 111).

While coping with her father's unemployment, her mother's overwork at the fish cannery, and racist bullies at school, Jeanne excelled in classwork. She edited the school newspaper, marched with uniformed majorettes, and applied for admission to the Girl Scouts, who rejected her. At Long Beach Polytechnic High School, she was desperate for acceptance. To salve the hurt, she cultivated an all-American girl pose by singing pop tunes, joining the girls athletic league, and appearing in parades as lead majorette and in a pageant as a sarong-clad carnival queen. At age 18, she lived in the Santa Clara Valley outside San Jose at a

100-acre strawberry farm that suited Ko's need to achieve and to rid himself of bitterness and gastric bleeding. In the war's aftermath, no allegation proved the Japanese-American guilty of espionage, sabotage, or collusion with the enemy.

After studying journalism and sociology from the University of San Jose, in 1957, Jeanne Houston became the first in the Wakatsuki family to hold a college degree. In 1959, the year of Ko's death, she worked as a juvenile probation officer and juvenile hall supervisor in San Mateo and, on Waikiki Beach, wed author and university professor James D. Houston. During a year on an ROTC post in England, she gave birth to their first child, Corinne "Cori" Houston. Jeanne completed postgraduate work at the Sorbonne and the University of Paris. In 1962, the couple settled at Cabrillo College in Aptos, California. Jeanne looked to Japanese minimalist writers Fumiko Enchi, Yasunari Kawabata, and Junichiro Tanizaki and feminist Maxine Hong Kingston for inspiration. She opened a ground floor office; Jim worked upstairs in the attic. The two collaborated at dinner over their manuscripts and lectures. For relaxation, they enjoyed yoga, swimming, cinema, and meditation.

Painful Memories

Houston, like other camp survivors, spent 3 decades suppressing her desert experience. In 1971, the year of her brother Woody's death, hysteria overwhelmed her as she struggled to answer the questions about internment from nephew Gary Nishikawa, who was born at Manzanar in spring 1943 to Jeanne's sister Eleanor and husband Shig. Houston feared she had triggered a nervous collapse. On a University of California faculty research grant, in April 1972, she, James, 11-year-old Cori, and 5-year-old twins Joshua and Gabrielle visited Manzanar to gather data for a bicultural wartime classic, *Farewell to Manzanar* (1973). At the same time that Jeanne's troubled past endeared her more to James, the three-stage tour of bleak ruins drenched her in guilt for having lived the part of enemy internee among 11,061 evacuees. At rock-ringed graves, she internalized grief for the inmates who died in camp. She felt sullied, like a rape victim. Based on tapes, research, a 1944 Manzanar High School yearbook, and interviews with camp survivors, the writing captured a coming-of-age story overlaid with family disintegration and national shame. She later viewed the text as a forgiveness of and tribute to Ko, the most damaged of the interned Wakatsukis.

The impressionistic memoir proved both cathartic and empowering. Cruz Bustamante, lieutenant governor of California, distributed copies, teacher's guides, and 10,000 video tapes to the state's libraries, junior highs, and high schools. It became the source of a teleplay written by the Houstons and by producer-director John Korty. On March 11, 1976, it premiered on MCA TV on *Thursday Night at the Movies* starring Yuki Shimoda as Ko and Nobu McCarthy in the dual role of Riku and Jeanne. Actors and former internees from Heart Mountain Minidoka, Topaz, and Tule Lake internment camps played roles that reduced them to tears. For its historical accuracy, the script and cinematography earned Emmy nominations. In December 2006, playwright Cynthia Gates Fujikawa adapted the screenplay for stage for debut at the Mark Taper Auditorium in the Los Angeles Public Library.

In articles for *California*, *Mother Jones*, *New England Review*, *San Francisco Chronicle*, *San Jose Mercury News*, and *West*, Houston extended her career through philosophic Buddhism, which rejected grudge-holding and vengeance. She and James projected the same humanism in two film projects, *Barrio* (1978) and *The Melting Pot* (1980). In 1984, the couple surveyed refugee camps in Indonesia, Korea, Malaysia, Okinawa, and the Philippines. She revisited war memories in *Beyond Manzanar and Other Views of Asian-American Womanhood* (1985). At age 61, she worked in Bellagio, Italy, as a writer in residence and, for 2 years, as a judge on the Kiriyama Book Prize panel. Her honors include a HUMANITAS Prize, Christopher Award, National Women's Political Caucus citation, Award of Excellence from the Japanese American National Museum, Hawaii International Film Festival special award, Japanese American of the Biennium, and a Warner Communication's Wonder Woman title. Residing in Santa Cruz, California, with Cori, Joshua, and Gabrielle, the two authors continue to support multiculturalism and tolerance by writing works that breach cultural borders. In 2001, *Publishers Weekly* honored *Farewell to Manzanar* in its 63rd printing as one of the all-time bestselling children's works.

Sources

Cooper, Michael L. *Remember Manzanar: Life in a Japanese Relocation Camp*. New York: Clarion Books, 2002.

Houston, James, and Jeanne Wakatsuki Houston. *Farewell to Manzanar*. New York: Houghton Mifflin, 1973.

Inada, Lawson Fusao, and the California Historical Society. *Only What We Could Carry: The Japanese American Internment Experience*. Berkeley, CA: Heyday Books, 2000.

Robinson, Gerald H. *Elusive Truth: Four Photographers at Manzanar*. Nevada City, CA: Carl Mautz, 2002.

Werner, Emmy E. *Through the Eyes of Innocents: Children Witness World War II*. New York: Westview Press, 2001.

■ Loss
Caroline Kennedy

The sole survivor of a family of six, Caroline Bouvier Kennedy is an American symbol of stoicism. The daughter of Jacqueline Lee "Jackie" Bouvier and John Fitzgerald "Jack" Kennedy, she was born of French-Irish descent in New York City on November 27, 1957, 14 months after the stillbirth of sister Arabella. During the last trimester before Caroline's birth, Jackie took extra care not to overexert herself by refraining from crowds and heat and relaxing at home. Caroline's maternal grandmother, Janet Jennings Auchincloss, was moved by Jack's delight in a baby girl, which turned him into a patriarch. Jackie chose her sister, Lee Radziwill, as Caroline's godmother.

The presidential election shaped Caroline's life. She spent toddlerhood in the Georgetown section of Washington, D.C., and cheered her father's campaign speeches from the Kennedy compound at Hyannis Port, Massachusetts. Her father declared his love for Caroline as approaching treason. Her infant brother, John, Jr., was born 2 months before the move on February 4, 1961, to the White House, where Caroline's room offered a rocking horse, canopied bed, and an original Grandma Moses painting. On his first morning after the election, Caroline awakened her father with a formal greeting, "Good morning, Mr. President" (Sommer, 2005, 62). She nurtured a series of pets, including two hamsters, a donkey, and a Welsh terrier named Charlie. The first babies in the White House in the 20th century, both children received an outpouring of gifts. Caroline earned notoriety as the focus of a pictorial fantasy, *The Caroline Kennedy First Lady Dress-Up Book* (1963), in which author-illustrator Charlotte Jetter pictured the little girl in historical costumes.

An Elite American Family

Caroline lived in an involved family that included secret service agents, pediatric nurse Luella Hennessey, and an English nanny, Maud Shaw, in a starched white uniform. Caroline's grandmother, Rose Fitzgerald Kennedy, demanded proper manners, posture, and deportment in young ones but showered her granddaughter with the hands-on love she had denied Jack and his siblings. Jack clapped his hands twice any time he broke away from national business to play with his daughter. He named his private Convair *Caroline*, taught his daughter to swim, and telephoned her any night they were separated. With other political wives, Jackie taught on alternate days at the White House nursery school in the solarium, an attempt at a democratic educational environment created by the children of friends and staff.

Training by example filled the growing-up years of the president's children. From her mother, Caroline learned refined manners, reverence for Impressionist art and European languages, and selection of fine clothing and decor. On August 7, 1963, Caroline's second brother, Patrick Bouvier, was born premature and died at a Boston hospital 2 days later of hyaline membrane disease, the result of undeveloped lungs. The president hurried to Squaw Island to comfort Caroline and "John-John." Adults explained to Caroline that the baby boy was in heaven with the angels. Her brother John retained his fascination with the sky, especially the arrival and departure of the presidential helicopter.

A Troubled Princess

The unofficial Dauphine of American royalty, Caroline won sympathies worldwide for her troubled childhood and introspection. On October 14, 1962, news reports of the Cuban Missile Crisis assured the public that the president would send Caroline and her brother to a locale safe from nuclear attack. In more peaceful times, she enjoyed storytelling with her father, who included characters named Caroline and John-John in tales of horse races and World War II naval exploits against the Japanese. She learned to read during play school and followed the 1960 presidential campaign in the newspapers, but she preferred being read to. Of the intimacy of a very public political family, she honored their sharing of books: "If our parents read to us as children, we remember the closeness of the moments together, the sound and power of voice and expression, the sense of wonder that a poem inspires" (Kennedy and Muth, 2005, 11).

Caroline delighted the White House press corps. Christopher Andersen, biographer of *Sweet Caroline: Last Child of Camelot* (2004), observed, "The public could not get enough of the irresistible, blue-eyed, blond-banged, crinoline-wearing Caroline," whom the reporters compared to actor Shirley Temple (Andersen, 2004, 65). Presidential photos pictured her dining in the High Chair Room, crawling with her father under his desk, dancing and smirking on the presidential seal carpet in the oval office, eating chocolates and jelly beans from his candy dish, and facing the wind from the stern of the family boat. She practiced ballet, attended the circus and theater, and rode her fat roan pony, Macaroni, at Camp David and on the lawn along 1600 Pennsylvania Avenue. At an end of patience with media exploitation, her mother forbade informal shots of her daughter playing unsupervised about the White House: "I want no more—I mean this" (Landai, 2000, 38). Jackie shielded her son and daughter from media star-making and public scandal, notably, Jack's affair with actor Marilyn Monroe. Jackie reputedly stayed married to the womanizing politician to spare her children the breakup she recalled in her own girlhood.

The President's Assassination

The public shooting and death of Caroline's father on November 22, 1963, in Dallas, Texas, uprooted her family. Grandmother Janet immediately took charge of Caroline and John. In the interim between the rifle shot and the president's death, Caroline murmured, "He's dead, isn't he? A man shot him, didn't he" (Andersen, 2004, 99). Two days later, an iconic photo of the children pictured them in matching coats and white gloves as their mother in black veil escorted them from the president's casket in the Capitol Rotunda, where Caroline knelt by her mother to pray for Jack's soul. A condolence note arrived with a flower from a Texas child: "I'm sorry Caroline and John-John. Forgive us. A nine-year-old Dallas girl" (Stein, 1993, 18). In public, Jackie and secret service agents protected Caroline and her brother from mourners who tried to embrace and kiss the fatherless children.

The children and Jackie shared 2 weeks of private mourning at their White House residence before moving to New York. Jackie urged her daughter to express sorrow by writing a love letter to daddy. Above the children's beds were pictures of their warm relationship with their father. At Caroline's confirmation, she chose the name Joan for Joan of Arc, the French warrior who died young, just like Jack Kennedy. Uncle Bobby Kennedy accepted the role of surrogate parent to his niece and nephew for birthdays, Father's Day, and school events involving fathers. For holidays, the children enjoyed free time with their cousins at Martha's Vineyard and riding horseback at the ten-room country farmhouse in Bernardsville, New Jersey. Jackie helped her daughter dress for competitions and practice dressage maneuvers. Caroline rode a dark brown hunter, Bit O'Irish. On Macaroni, she won a first prize at the Apple Barrel Pony Show.

For a year, Caroline observed her mother weeping in heavily guarded privacy at their apartment on 1040 Fifth Avenue across from Central Park in Manhattan. She wrote in a letter, "My mommy cries all the time" (Andersen, 2004, 89). Caroline suffered her own anguish, which broke her concentration and reduced her to pallor and verbal withdrawal. She developed hero worship for her trendsetting mother and followed her equestrian hobby by decorating her room with horse pictures and books on riding and harness. In one little girl's observation, she remarked, "I've seen a queen and my mommy looks better. Lots" (Andersen, 2004, 136). Three years later, Caroline christened the USS *John F. Kennedy*, a navy aircraft carrier that remained in service for 40 years. For her winsome ways, composer Neil Diamond wrote and sang "Sweet Caroline" (1969).

Writer and Public Figure

The president's daughter nestled in a family threesome. In her brother's description, "All our lives, there's just been the three of us: Mommy, Caroline and me" (Landai, 2000, 87). Caroline followed the example of the competitive Kennedys by studying at three private schools—Brearley, Convent of the Sacred Heart, her grandmother Kennedy's alma mater, and Concord Academy. Like her mother, she became fluent in French and coped with blended families, following her mother's 7-year marriage to Greek shipper Aristotle "Ari" Onassis. The union with an amoral Greek Orthodox Catholic distressed uncle Bobby Kennedy, but it offered the Kennedy children protection from the crazed factions who targeted Jack and his politically powerful brothers. For the first time, they escaped the rigors of Washington politics and explored exotic corners of the world.

The media poured out sympathy for Caroline. While training at Sotheby's auction house, at age 17, she escaped an Irish Republic Army bomb set under the right front wheel of a red Jaguar. Her mother insisted on immediate shadowing by officers of Scotland Yard. Acclimated to family arrangements, she completed her education in the fine arts at Radcliffe College and earned a law degree from Columbia University. Unlike her less scholarly brother, she adopted the family's demand for excellence. She passed her law exam on the first attempt but declined to practice. While her mother edited for Doubleday, Caroline served an internship in the U.S. Senate for her uncle, Edward "Teddy" Kennedy, and wrote for the *New York Daily News*. On staff at the Metropolitan Museum of Art, she managed the office of film and television. In private, she served the John F. Kennedy Library Foundation in Boston as president.

Caroline's love life drew press attention to the quality of three suitors—Nicholas Soames, athlete John Boswith, and Irish ale heir Jonathan Guinness. At age 23, she met an author and specialist in interactive exhibit design and layout, Edwin Arthur Schlossberg, a cultural historian of Ukrainian Orthodox Jewish ancestry and a fellow alumnus of Columbia. Six years later, the couple married at Our Lady of Victory Church in Centerville near Hyannisport, Massachusetts, where brother John served as best man. Like her own mother, Caroline focused on home and family. She gave birth to daughters Rose Kennedy and Tatiana Celia Kennedy Schlossberg and a son, John Bouvier Kennedy "Jack" Schlossberg. All were much loved by their "Grand Jackie," who took them out for ice cream cones or for playground fun on the swings at the 76th Street park. At home at Park Slope in West Brooklyn, the family enjoyed Prospect Park West and the historic churches and synagogues, gardens, museums, libraries, and conservatories that Jackie Kennedy introduced her children to in their early years.

Caroline and Family Losses

The sequence of Kennedy losses set a precedent for national tragedy. Much of the burden of death and sorrow belabored Caroline, beginning with her father's assassination when she was 6 and the shooting death of her uncle, Robert F. Kennedy, $4\frac{1}{2}$ years later. On May 19, 1994, Jackie Kennedy Onassis died of non-Hodgkin's lymphoma, leaving her estate to Caroline and John. Five years later on July 16, Caroline lost her brother and sister-in-law, Carolyn Bessette Kennedy, in a crash of his Piper Saratoga. The plane plunged from a hazy night sky into the Atlantic in sight of the family home on Martha's Vineyard, Massachusetts. The lone sister spoke a eulogy from William Shakespeare's play *The Tempest*: "We are such stuff as dreams are made on, and our little life is rounded with a sleep." She remained in charge of the investigation of a disaster apparently caused by pilot error and inexperience with night flying. After she explained the sudden death to her children, her son Jack wrote to great-uncle Teddy to ask him to replace John as his godfather.

Opting against the role of socialite, Caroline flourished at writing, editing, and public appearances. With author and former college friend Ellen Alderman, Caroline published *In Our Defense: The Bill of Rights in Action* (1990) and *The Right to Privacy* (1995) as well as two works on verse, a handbook on patriot activism, and a reprise of *Profiles in Courage*. In the introduction, she honored her father's political courage. She asserted that he "believed in the power of words to lead, to inspire, and to bring about change in the world" (Kennedy, 2002, 2). With her mother and brother, she established the Profile in Courage Award, named for her father's book and bestowed each year on May 29, Kennedy's birthday, to an elected official who displays grace under pressure. The award in 1998 honored Sinn Fein's Gerry Adams and John Hume for negotiating peace in Northern Ireland. In 2002, Caroline stood alongside her uncle Teddy to present the award to the elected officials, firefighters, medical teams, police officers, and soldiers who fought the 9/11 disaster in New York City the previous year.

Caroline maintains a full schedule of philanthropy chairing her father's foundation and the New York City Fund for Public Schools, acting as honorary president of the American Ballet Theatre, and directing the Commission on Presidential Debates and the legal defense fund for the National Association for the Advancement of Colored People. As the only living member of her nuclear family, she represented the Kennedy clan at the dedication of President Bill Clinton's library in Little Rock, Arkansas, and became a ceremonial presence at the funeral of Ronald Reagan, Gerald Ford, and Lady Bird Johnson. In 2007, Caroline collected personal memories and letters from her childhood in a holiday anthology, *A Family Christmas*, a gesture to the childhood that shaped her. She explained in 2004 in a new introduction to Jack Kennedy's Pulitzer Prize-winning book, "My father taught us all that we are never too old or too young for public service" (Kennedy, 2004, ix). She added, "It is up to us to redefine that commitment for our own time" (Ibid.).

Sources

Andersen, Christopher. *Sweet Caroline: Last Child of Camelot*. New York: Avon, 2004.

"Caroline Bouvier Kennedy to Wed Edwin Schlossberg." *New York Times*, March 2, 1986.

Kennedy, Caroline. *Profiles in Courage for Our Time*. New York: Hyperion, 2002.

———. "Introduction." In John Fitzgerald Kennedy, *Profiles in Courage*. New York: HarperCollins, 2004.

Kennedy, Caroline, ed., and Jon J. Muth, artist. *A Family of Poems: My Favorite Poetry for Children*. New York: Hyperion, 2005.

Landai, Elaine. *John F. Kennedy, Jr.* Brookfield, CT: Twenty-First Century Books, 2000.

Maier, Thomas. *The Kennedys: America's Emerald Kings*. New York: Basic Books, 2003.

Sommer, Shelley. *John F. Kennedy: His Life and Legacy*. New York: HarperCollins, 2005.

Stein, R. Conrad. *The Assassination of John F. Kennedy*. New York: Children's Press, 1993.

■ Low School Achievement
Ben Carson

Benjamin Solomon "Ben" Carson advanced from a slow learner to one of America's most gifted neurosurgeons. He was born on September 18, 1951, in an inner-city section of Detroit, Michigan, to Robert Carson, the minister of a small church, and Sonya Carson, a demanding mom with a third grade education and a background of foster homes. His ancestry linked him to the Lunda of Angola, Congo, and Zambia. His parents married when Robert was 28 and Sonya was 13; to find work, they moved from Chattanooga, Tennessee, to Detroit. His father, an employee at a Cadillac factory, seemed blessed with cash from unknown sources. He lacked Sonya's type A drive for security and stressed clothing, popularity, and materialism. She insisted on saving money and investing in a house. Ben grew up Christian in a Seventh-Day Adventist church on Burns Avenue and sought baptism at age 8. From regular bible study, he developed respect for Old Testament wisdom lore in Proverbs.

Carson's parents parted in 1959, after his mother learned that Robert Carson was a bigamist with five other children. He left with all the family's savings, provided little support for his sons, and forged checks bearing Sonya's name. For Ben, the absence of his cheery father left a loneliness that nothing relieved, even train hopping with his brother Curtis, who was 2 years older than Ben. Despite arthritis and heart disease, his mother determined to set an example of thrift and goal setting. She drove a failing car and, to save 40 cents bus fare per week day, supplied her sons with used bikes on which to ride to school. The trio moved in with their aunt Jean and uncle William and applied for food stamps for a few months until Sonya saved some money. The family environment improved, but, among superior white kids at Higgins Elementary School, Ben's performance was unpromising and his self-esteem low. Other kids ridiculed him as "dummy" for getting a zero on a math test. From her observations of successful clients, Sonya rejected any justification of failure: "You can always find a hook to hang excuses on, but they're only excuses.... Nobody else makes you fail" (Carson and Murphey, 2006, 49).

For the next 2 years, Sonya Carson rented a roach-infested flat in a Boston, Massachusetts, tenement on the railroad tracks and worked double and triple jobs as a domestic to send her sons to a religious school. To Ben's demand for a $75 Italian knit shirt, she turned over $100, her week's earnings for scrubbing floors and toilets, and left him to distribute it for groceries and bills. The effort to stretch little cash over support for three people sobered him. He was pleased to attend classes under Mr. Doakes, his first black male instructor. Because Ben's grades put him at the bottom of his class, she demanded achievement from him and Curtis. He recalled, "Our mother convinced Curtis and me that we could and would find success some day if we just followed the road of education to its natural end" (Carson and Lewis, 2000, 76). She turned off the television, limiting viewing to two preselected programs per week, and curtailed outdoor play while the boys completed school assignments. The first home lessons forced Ben to learn multiplication tables. Outside of class, she made them read eight books per month from the Detroit Public Library and to report on each in writing. With the help of friend librarians, he chose books on nature, animals, plants, and geology. He started a rock collection and ventured into the fine arts with strolls through a local museum. He improved his performance after the school provided him glasses.

No Longer the Dummy

At an upturn in his education, Carson surprised his classmates by identifying a sample of obsidian that his science teacher, Mr. Jaeck, exhibited to the class. The boy described the formation of obsidian from volcanic lava super-cooled in water. The breakthrough convinced him and his peers that he was not doomed to low school achievement. He enjoyed looking through Mr. Jaeck's microscope at protozoa and plant forms and nurtured a fantasy of becoming a doctor, a choice that pleased his mother. Within the term, he took first place in student grades. His subjects began to intrigue him. He and Curtis played on an integrated neighborhood football team. Because they were both fast, racists challenged them and demanded that the brothers stop competing with whites. On Curtis's advice, the brothers dropped out of the team and returned to reading and studying. Sonya rewarded them annually with a single extravagance, tickets to the Michigan State Fair.

In 1961, the family settled in Detroit, where Ben attended Hunter Junior High. Anger at poverty inflamed him in his early teens, when his peers ridiculed his ragged wardrobe. He attempted to stab his friend Bob in the gut with a camping knife. Fortunately for both boys, the victim's belt buckle deflected the blade and snapped it off at the hilt. Carson realized similar attacks would result in reform school, prison, or an early death. In a retreat to the bathroom, he read Proverbs 16:32 and vowed to restrain his temper. Daily, he returned to the passage to remind himself that he had to control anger, or it would control him. The habit of Bible reading and self-evaluation prepared him for tolerating stress and ridicule.

From High School to Yale

At inner-city Southwestern High School, Ben found summer work at the campus science laboratory. Like brother Curtis, he joined the Reserve Officers' Training Corps (ROTC). He progressed under the mentorship of an English teacher, Mrs. Miller, who guided him after school in correcting mistakes. She maintained her involvement in his education as he advanced through high school. He equated her involvement with Sonya's and tried not to disappoint either woman. The boy who had made zero in math in fifth grade enrolled in second-year algebra. He avoided the in-crowd, advanced in ROTC from second lieutenant to lieutenant colonel, and progressed in biology lab, for which teacher Frank McCotter assigned him to design and set up experiments. By the last term of twelfth grade, Carson topped an ROTC exam and was appointed city executive officer of Detroit's high schools.

Third in his class, Carson was an honor graduate from high school with an interest in social science. To ready himself for college, he read *Psychology Today* and fought off flashbacks to fifth grade, when friends called him "dummy." He grew arrogant from earning top grades and SAT scores in the low 90th percentile. The civil rights era blessed his efforts. Beginning in fall 1968, prestigious colleges clamored to recruit him and other promising black students. While watching *College Bowl* on television, he saw Yale swamp Harvard's team and opted to enroll at a winner. With his last $10 bill, he sent in an application. That summer, school counselor Alma Whittley helped him earn money for clothing, books, and transportation by requesting a job for him at the Ford Motor Company in Dearborn.

At Yale University on a 90 percent scholarship, Carson entered with a cocky opinion of his intelligence. In chats with other freshmen, he found that all his classmates were bright achievers. Contributing to his panic was a realization that he had wasted time in high school and relied on last minute cramming. The method failed him at Yale, where he struggled with chemistry. He determined to abandon the drive for peer approval and complete the course, a requirement for entry into premedical study. He completed a B.S. in premed and psychology in 1973. Out of a need to limit school tuition, he chose to remain in the state and attend the University of Michigan.

Becoming a Physician

At the University of Michigan Medical School at Ann Arbor, Carson found lectures boring. Because he made only so-so grades, he took charge of his education by studying textbooks from early morning until 11:00 at night. In his second year, he progressed by purchasing notes from fellow students. From James Anderson's instruction, Carson learned investigative radiology, an effective and efficient means of studying tissue; from George Udvarhelyi, Carson acquired respect for individual sufferings and patience in evaluating the victim's self-analysis. In his third year of medical training, when he began working in hospital wards, he felt confident of medical background and procedures. His mother's example rewarded him by compelling him to befriend aides and ward clerks. Unlike snobbish physicians, Carson exchanged observations and patient information with experienced ward personnel. From them, he gained valuable insight into patient health and hospital politics.

Carson made use of phenomenal eye-hand coordination by narrowing his focus on the human brain to neurosurgery. In his autobiography, *Gifted Hands: The Ben Carson Story* (1990), he described an epiphany: "Realizing that my hands were steady and that I could intuitively see the effect my hands had on the brain, I knew I had found my calling" (Carson and Murphey, 1990, 108). He earned honors for his work in medical school but chose not to stay at the university hospital because of a shift in hierarchy. After obtaining his M.D. in 1977, he married Yale-trained violinist, organist, and singer Lacena "Candy" Rustin, whom he met in 1975 at a freshman mixer at Grosse Pointe Country Club. The couple had formed mutual respect through campus walks, recruiting for minority students for Yale, and attendance at Mount Zion Seventh-Day Adventist Church. During Ben's residency, she clerked at an insurance company and worked as assistant to a chemistry teacher. They produced three sons, Murray Nedlands, Benjamin, Jr., and Rhoeyce, whom they reared in the Adventist faith.

For internship in fall 1976, Carson applied to Johns Hopkins Hospital in Baltimore, Maryland. Against competition from 125 applicants, he felt confident that his grades and scores on the national medical board exams would earn him one of two neurosurgery residencies. On the advice of a colleague, he based his oncological research on brain cancer in New Zealand rabbits. From 1982 to 1983, he served as senior neurosurgeon at the Sir Charles Gardiner Hospital, Queen Elizabeth II Medical Centre, a teaching institution in Western Australia. At the nation's only referral center for neurological cases, the constant demand refined his skills and gave him more experience than other surgeons gained in a career of medical practice.

Success at Johns Hopkins

By 1984, Carson became the youngest surgeon in the United States to be promoted to director of pediatric neurosurgery. He also codirected the craniofacial clinic and performed over 500 critical surgeries per year. He tended victims of brain injuries, brain stem and spinal cord tumors, dwarfism, neurological birth defects, skull malformation, and epilepsy. He performed the first intrauterine procedure to drain fluid from the brain of an unborn hydrocephalic twin and a hemispherectomy, the removal of half the brain in Maranda Francisco, an infant beset by seizures. One of his specialties involved treatment of trigeminal neuralgia with radio frequency and glycerol rhizotomy, a double assault on a pain so fierce that it drives patients to suicide.

Carson came to media attention in 1987, when he engineered the separation of the Binder children, Benjamin and Patrick, German twins joined at the back of the skull. Complicating the surgery was the sharing of brain tissue. He began training for the procedures when the boys were 2 months old and felt ready to begin 5 months later. In 22 hours of surgery, with the boys in suspended animation, he coordinated the work of seventy professionals and saved both patients. The two remained comatose for 10 days. Despite a Zeiss operating microscope, a 3-D visual imaging system, lasers, CAT scans and MRIs, angiograms, and ultrasound equipment, he could not save the children from mental handicaps.

Giving Back to Others

In 1997, Carson needed only a 50-member team at the Medical University of South Africa at Medunsa to separate Joseph and Luka Banda, 11-month-old Zambian boys joined at the top of the skull. Thirteen previous surgeries failed to release the boys because their separation required reconfiguration of a vascular network to each twin's brain. To ready for the surgery, Carson rehearsed the procedure for 6 months at a computerized, three-dimensional workbench that anticipated each anatomical maneuver. The boys survived the 22-hour session, which Carson attempted with only scalpels and a loupe, an eyepiece that magnified tissue. He took a year off to visit underachieving students to encourage them to aim high. A year after surviving an invasive prostate cancer, Carson plotted another rescue in July 2003 at Raffles Hospital in Singapore to separate Ladan and Laleh Bijani, 29-year-old Iranian lawyers from Shiraz. Following removal of a 12-inch bone strip with a high-speed drill, the women lost too much blood to survive the operation.

In reward for brilliant surgery to save children condemned to a diminished life, Carson received over 40 honorary Ph.D. degrees, the American Academy of Achievement Award, the Horatio Alger Award, and profiles in *Fortune,* the *New York Times, PARADE,* and *Reader's Digest.* He began advising the boards of America's Promise, Costco Wholesale Corporation, the Kellogg Company, and the governing body of Yale University. He maintained his dedication to God as an elder and health and temperance director of the Spencerville Seventh-Day Adventist Church. To realize individual intellectual potential, he delivered inspirational addresses to teens on delayed gratification and published bestselling self-help handbooks, *The Big Picture* (2000), *Think Big: Unleashing Your Potential for Excellence* (2006), and *Take the Risk: Learning to Identify, Choose and Live with Acceptable Risk* (2008). He coestablished the Carson Scholars Fund, a philanthropic endeavor rewarding youth for exemplary academic and humanitarian achievements. Over 2,800 scholarships have aided students in California, Delaware, Georgia, Indiana, Maryland, Michigan, Missouri, North Carolina, Pennsylvania, Washington, D.C., Washington State, and Wisconsin. In 2004, President George W. Bush named Carson to the President's Council on Bioethics. Two years later, PBS TV honored the surgeon on *African American Lives*. In Baltimore, Maryland, a stage biography, *Ben Carson, M.D.*, ran for 2 years.

Sources

Carson, Ben, and Cecil Murphey. *Gifted Hands: The Ben Carson Story*. Grand Rapids, MI: Zondervan, 1990.

———. *Think Big: Unleashing Your Potential for Excellence*. Grand Rapids, MI: Zondervan, 2006.

Carson, Ben, and Gregg Lewis. *The Big Picture*. Grand Rapids, MI: Zondervan, 2000.

———. *Take the Risk: Learning to Identify, Choose and Live with Acceptable Risk*. Grand Rapids, MI: Zondervan, 2008.

■ Lyme Disease
Amy Tan

A primary voice in first generation Asian-American fiction writing, Amy Tan faced an abrupt hiatus to her writing career from a mysterious nerve disorder. A native of Oakland, California, she was born An-mei Ruth "Amy" Tan on February 19, 1952, to Daisy Du Ching and Reverend John Yuehhan Tan, a Baptist evangelist and translator for the U.S. Information Service during World War II. Early on, Tan became trilingual in English, Mandarin, and Shanghainese. She revered life lessons from "the tapestry of who created us in our past, our parents, our grandparents, and beyond" (Kanner, 1995, 3). However, to become thoroughly Americanized, she did what other first generation children did—retreat from the culture that shaped her ancestry. Daisy Tan—an intrusive matriarch "just determined as hell" during house-wrecking, knife-wielding tantrums and emotional terrorism—upbraided her rebel daughter by combating Amy's in-house rebuff of the motherland (Somogyi and Stanton, 1991, 24). The conflict shaped Amy's personality and her will to survive.

The rattled household flitted along the California coast to temporary residences in Hayward, Oakland, Palo Alto, Santa Clara, and Sunnyvale before settling in Santa Rosa. Tan struggled with being the bicultural outsider and retreated for comfort to bedtime storybook readings by her low-key father and to "aunties," a maternal sanctuary among Chinese mah jong players. Because of Daisy's demands of perfection in her three children, from age 5, Amy developed depression and insecurities, wandering thoughts, and free-floating phobias while learning piano and earning only A's at Matanzas Elementary School. By night, she reshaped an Asian face by compressing her wide nose with a clothespin. Grimms' fairy tales, *Aesop's Fables*, scriptural stories, and the Laura Ingalls Wilder *Little House* series gave wings to Amy's fantasy and diverted her from suicidal urges. She later praised escapism through visits with her father to the Santa Rosa library: "Books were my salvation. Books saved me from being miserable" ("Interview," 1996). As an adult, she maintained her childhood love of literacy by defending intellectual liberty and free speech and repudiating book banning.

Whiz Kid

By age 8, Tan displayed the promise that later boosted her to a global bestselling author. She served her family as translator, go-between, and writer and interpreter of contracts and correspondence. For winning a competition with the essay "What the Library Means to Me," she received a transistor radio from the *Santa Rosa Press Democrat*, which published her effort. She advanced to reading novels by Harper Lee and J. D. Salinger and by delving into Richard von Krafft-Ebbing's *Psychopathia Sexualis*.

In her midteens, Tan suffered the loss of Peter, her 16-year-old brother, who died of a brain tumor after months of invalidism. The same disease killed John Tan 7 months later. The double loss left Amy under the care of a hostile widow. In anger at cosmic forces, Daisy abandoned religion and blamed a curse for their losses. Contributing to family confusion, Daisy admitted to a divorce in China at the end of World War II and to leaving behind three daughters before immigrating to the United States. In a major blowup over these disclosures, Amy rebelled against competition from previously unknown siblings. Her teen misbehavior exceeded the norm: "I was busy finding my own identity. I didn't want to be connected to all this family stuff in China" (Doten, 1991, 63).

More Moves

In 1968, Tan settled with her mother and brother John at a chalet in Montreux, Switzerland, and enrolled in language study at the Institut Monte Rosa. Daisy arbitrarily chose brain surgery and classical piano as careers for her daughter, who completed high school a year early and, at age 17, entered premed courses at Linfield, a Baptist college in McMinnville, Oregon. A steady beau, Italian-American law student Louis M. DeMattei, offered affection, stability, and a respite from late-teen angst. Tan transferred to San José City College and outraged Daisy once more by changing her major from medicine to English and linguistics. In 1973, Tan graduated from a third college, San José State University, and initiated advanced linguistics training at the University of California, Santa Cruz. She entered a Ph.D. program at the University of California, Berkeley.

At age 24-four, Tan wed DeMattei, a tax attorney, and established their home in urban San Francisco. Years of trauma left her weakened by depression and agoraphobia and determined to have no children who might share the brain anomalies that dogged her family. Following a move to Danville, California, as a speech therapist for Alameda County, she treated retarded children. After Daisy's first visit to China since World War II, she returned to California to end mother-daughter animosities through talk-story. Nourished by language, Tan took comfort in composition under the name May Brown, an un-Asian pseudonym. She began freelance writing in the newsletter *Emergency Room Reports* and, during 80-hour weeks, wrote speeches for Apple Computers, AT&T, IBM, and Pacific Bell.

From Business to Family

At age 35, Tan shucked off the meaninglessness of business writing and plunged into realistic voicing in the works of feminist authors Isabel Allende, Kaye Gibbons, Jamaica Kincaid, Maxine Hong Kingston, Alice Munro, Flannery O'Connor, and Eudora Welty. In imitation of Louise Erdrich's story cycle *Love Medicine*, Tan envisioned a reunion with her Chinese sisters in the episodic novel *The Joy Luck Club* (1989), a paean to mothering, sisterhood, and the truth. The work earned an American Library Association Best Book for Young Adults award, Bay Area Book Reviewers prize, and Commonwealth Club gold citation as well as nominations for the Los Angeles Times Best Book of the Year, a National Book Award, and a National Book Critics Circle's Best Novel. Its popularity held it on the *New York Times* bestseller list for 34 weeks and placed Tan at the forefront of an Asian-American literary renaissance. The screen version, coproduced by Tan and Oliver Stone for Disney Studios, was filmed in Richmond, Virginia, and Guilin, China. Tan enjoyed a screening of *The Joy Luck Club* with First Lady Hillary Rodham Clinton at the White House.

Renewed storytelling sessions with Daisy disclosed more secret family guilt and shame. Tan revamped the raw material into feminist scenarios of feudal marriage and the patriarchal silencing of Chinese women. A model storykeeper, she persevered against regrets and misgivings by writing about the disconnect between races and generations from miscommunication in Pidgin English. She valued collaboration with Daisy with a new-found appreciation for "a crazy quilt of love, pieced together, torn apart, repaired over and over again, and strong enough to protect us all" (Benedict, 1991, C10).

Fact into Fiction

Using the startling events from the combined Ching and Tan family history, the author produced *The Kitchen God's Wife* (1991), a roman á clef based on a period of marital rape, child loss, death threats, and imprisonment in Daisy's life. Tan turned the novel into a salute to *taonan*, a Chinese concept of overwhelming wartime starvation, pestilence, dislocation, confusion, and barbarism following the November 1937 Nanking Massacre. Introducing aspects of the Sino-Japanese War to Western readers, the autobiographical novel triumphed in the United States and Europe and in translation into over 20 languages. More important to the author, the publication built a new line of communication with Daisy. Still immersed in the calamities of Chinese womanhood, Tan fought hives, skeletal aches, and TMJ while writing *The Hundred Secret Senses*, a masterwork of dramatic irony that generated interviews on *Larry King Live* and *The Today Show* and a month's book tour across California, England, and Scotland.

In 1992, Tan treated herself to writing wisdom lore for young audiences with *The Moon Lady*, a tale of a child's loss during the moon festival. For illustrations, Tan allied with a friend, Gretchen Schields. The pair followed in 1994 with *The Chinese Siamese Cat*, another effort to introduce Asian culture to American readers. In spare time, Tan cochaired the National Kidney Foundation and fundraising for PEN writers' fund, the San Francisco library, Squaw Valley Community of Writers, the University of California, Berkeley, School of Journalism, and Yaddo artists' colony. For relaxation, she joined well-established authors— Ted Bartimus, Roy Blount, Dave Barry, Louise Erdrich, Robert Fulghum, Stephen King, Barbara Kingsolver, Al Kooper, and Ridley Pearson—in the Rock Bottom Remainders, Kathi Kamen Goldmark's band of professional writers, which performed rock classics at the 1992 convention of the American Booksellers Association. Their earnings supported First Amendment rights and library literacy programs.

Unease with Success

The restless search for security, which began in girlhood, pursued Tan into her 40s. She felt ill-prepared and inadequate and distrusted success and happiness. Following the demonstration of students and intellectuals against communism in Tiananmen Square in 1989, she began taking the antidepressant Zoloft to dispel fears of stalking and attack, a medical heritage from her mother and maternal grandmother. In the aftermath of a third novel, the gothic mystery *The Hundred Secret Senses* (1995), winner of the Bay Area Book Reviewer's Award, she worried less while composing about ghost-seers, missionaries, and banditry during the Taiping Rebellion. In a critique, Iain Finlayson raved, "The sheer buoyancy of Amy Tan's writing, her spirited genius for storytelling, the gutsy humor, the unsentimental expression of emotion, the sharp dialogue, and the sheer verve of the narrative as it bounces along from modern San Francisco to 19th-century provincial China, is entrancing" (Finlayson, 1996, 38).

After a tour of 33 cities, Tan returned home to a Thanksgiving Day surprise, erratic behavior in Daisy that preceded Alzheimer's disease. In addition, changing attitudes caused officials to halt Tan's visits to China. In a fourth novel, *The Bonesetter's Daughter* (2001), she offered a public farewell to Daisy, who died in a nursing home at age 83. The loss of a second parent increased Tan's jumpiness and exacerbated her vulnerability in hotel rooms during a 22-city book tour that included three Australian cities. She relaxed in Saratoga Springs, New York, at the Yaddo artist colony. On June 23, 2000, at the World Trade Center, she received an honorarium from the Museum of Chinese in the Americas for preserving the authenticity of Chinese-American perspectives and lifestyles.

Tick Bite Fever

In her late 40s, Tan ended a 4-month world book tour bereft of the buoyancy that Iain Finlayson once lauded. She entered a serious physical decline from a blood blister and rash, stiff neck, painful hips and knees, dizziness, tinnitus, and exhaustion. For no clear reason, she slept for days. She experienced prickling and numbness, attention and memory vagaries, dyslexia, hair loss, and unexplained nightmares. She jokingly named the surreal visual and olfactory illusions of nonexistent people in the room, the smell of a dead rat, and tremors the "Dolby Digital syndrome" (Behe, 2003). Diagnoses varied from travel stress and posttraumatic stress disorder to multiple sclerosis and Lou Gehrig's disease. A definitive test disclosed brain lesions on her front and parietal lobes resulting from neuroborreliosis or Lyme disease. She later discovered a long list of fellow victims—President George W. Bush, Governor George Pataki, golfer Gary Player, pitcher Tom Seaver, and authors Alice Walker and Rebecca Wells.

Tan dated the onset of Lyme disease to spirochetes inflicted by the bite of a deer tick in 1998, when she hiked and lolled in the grass in the Connecticut countryside beyond her Soho loft in New York City. In the midst of a fifth novel, she complained of "[dis]continuity, with segues and keeping pieces together," adding, "It feels like I have twelve pieces of fruit and vegetables being thrown in the air and trying to juggle them all. It's overwhelming"

(MacDonald, 2003). Worsening terror, the recall of her maternal grandmother's depression and suicide, her brother and father's deaths from brain tumors, and her mother's decline from Alzheimer's disease caused Tan to fear that her brain could no longer support the concentration and word skills that a writing career demands.

Helping Herself

After consulting her family doctor, an endocrinologist, a psychiatrist, a sleep disorder clinic, two neurologists, a cardiologist, and an orthopedist, Tan tracked the symptoms of late-stage chronic Lyme disease on the Internet and began a regimen of antiseizure medication and doxycycline. She improved steadily from personality changes, anxiety, and panic attacks and credited Dr. Raphael B. Stricker, a San Francisco hematologist and immunotherapist, who restored her brain to 85 percent of its normal function. To her credit, she accepted her fate as a learning experience: "I think that until you physically suffer and feel helpless and hopeless and wonder who is going to help you and how. I think that was the turning point" (Shafner, 2006). She lashed out at insurance providers and public health boards for refusing the expensive diagnostic testing to indigent victims.

Tan reassured readers and herself of improved health with the launching of a PBS series, *Sagwa: The Chinese Siamese Cat*, a daily half-hour program on Chinese folklore for Kids' Station. She also published *The Opposite of Fate: A Book of Musings* (2003), which devotes an epilogue to the misdiagnosis of Lyme disease, which experts call "the great imitator." She felt confident enough to show her Yorkshire terriers Bubba and Lili at the Westminster Kennel Club in 2002 and 2003 and to join protests of the U.S. invasion of Iraq. While researching *Saving Fish from Drowning* (2005), she ventured into Myanmar to witness human rights violations. On May 19, 2005, she joined other authors in forming Literati with Lyme and in offering firsthand accounts of the impact of Lyme disease on productive lives.

Sources

Behe, Regis. "Writer Amy Tan Relies on 'The Opposite of Fate' to Get By." *Pittsburgh Tribune-Review*, December 3, 2003.

Benedict, Kitty. "Mother to Daughter: Here Is the Truth of My Life." *Hartford Courant*, June 30, 1991, C10.

Doten, Patti. "Sharing Her Mother's Secrets." *Boston Globe*, June 21, 1991, 63.

Finlayson, Iain. "Chinese Whispers with Humour." *Chinatown News* 43 (9) (March 1, 1996): 38–39.

"Interview," June 28, 1996. Available at http://www.achievement.org/autodoc/page/tan0int-1 (last accessed on April 3, 2008)..

Kanner, Ellen. "From Amy Tan, a Superb Novel of Two Sisters, Two Worlds, and a Few Ghosts." *BookPage* (December 1995): 3.

MacDonald, Jay. "A Date with Fate." *BookPage* (November 2003). Available at http://www.bookpage.com/0311bp/amy_tan.html (last accessed April 3, 2008).

Shafner, Rhonda. "Amy Tan Goes on a Journey of Suffering: Her Work Explores How We Relate to the Agony That's Faced by Others." *Charlotte Observer*, January 15, 2006.

Somogyi, Barbara, and David Stanton. "Interview with Amy Tan." *Poets & Writers* 19 (5) (September–October 1991): 24–32.

■ McCarthyism
Pete Seeger

One of a generation of entertainers targeted by anticommunist fanaticism, Pete Seeger defied intimidation. A native of New York City born May 3, 1919, to composer and conductor Charles Seeger and violinist Constance de Clyver Edson, both teachers at Juilliard, Peter Seeger grew up in a musical haven. After his mother separated from Charles and settled in Nyack, she shelved an autoharp, marimba, penny whistle, portable organ, and concertina around the house for Pete and his brother, Alan and John, to explore on their own. As a youngster, Seeger attended a boarding school but returned home because the staff ignored his bout with scarlet fever. He considered becoming a sketch artist but shifted to other possibilities—a farmer or forest ranger, perhaps even an Indian, his ideal of cooperative living. He pitched a muslin tent in his grandparents' cow pasture, but, by age six, he was singing for audiences, just as his mother hoped. A year later, he took up the ukulele.

In 1927, Seeger came under the influence of his stepmother, composer Ruth Crawford Seeger, who produced four of Pete's siblings. His father, a colleague of composer Aaron Copland, conveyed humanistic ideals based on the belief that the arts belonged to everybody, not just the rich. Pete joined Charles and Ruth's son and daughter, Mike and Peggy Seeger, in a resilient career in American folk, gospel, and protest music, tavern and work songs and patriotic and holiday anthems. In the 1930s, Pete accompanied his father to square dances and songfests throughout the South, the people-friendly atmosphere that became Seeger's career milieu.

The Seeger Style

Seeger developed a precise falsetto above tenor in the low alto range. He specialized in unearthing neglected and obscure tunes from America's past. His compositions ran the gamut of human events—from childhood joys and personal triumphs to the hard traveling of pioneers, immigrants, farmers, seamen, factory hands, and miners. On his own, the troubadour fostered socialist sympathies and hitchhiked about the country to entertain church and PTA socials, picket lines, miners, chain gangs, migrant workers, and the down-and-out. His exuberant singing and clear lyrics encouraged groups to harmonize on the rounds and fun songs that once dominated American folk music.

At age 17, Seeger was attending the Mountain Folk Song and Dance Festival in Asheville, North Carolina, when he took an interest in the five-string banjo. The instrument dominated his 6-decade repertoire. He studied at the Avon Old Farms boarding school in Connecticut and on scholarship at Camp Rising Sun. During 2 years at Harvard's departments of journalism and sociology, he played with the tenor-banjo society and coedited the *Harvard Progressive*. In the last weeks of his sophomore year, he abandoned final exams to bike through New England, stopping to paint barns and fences. He captured croplands in watercolors to trade for meals in farm kitchens. While raising cash for the dairy farmers union, he performed with a puppet theater. Politically, he took the part of the unemployed against the New Deal politics of President Franklin Delano Roosevelt.

Moving Left

While clerking for folk collector Alan Lomax in Washington, D.C., in the Archive of American Folk Song at the Library of Congress, Seeger collaborated with Huddie William "Leadbelly" Ledbetter and Woody Guthrie, an itinerant Oklahoma balladeer, two giants of American proletarian and prison songs. In 1940, Seeger and Guthrie introduced radical tunes to the repertoire of their pick-up quartet, the Almanac Singers. The *Daily Worker*, the official communist newspaper, reported the group's circuit of Unitarian worship services, union rallies, and labor walkouts. Seeger collected pacifist compositions for the albums *Songs for John Doe* (1941), which featured his yodeling on his antimilitary satire "C for Conscription." The group followed with *Talking Union* (1941), their most popular effort.

In mid–World War II, Seeger married a 27-year-old Japanese-American dancer, Toshi-Aline Ohta, mother of Danny, Mika, and Tinya Seeger. The couple was living with Toshi's parents in Greenwich Village when Seeger received a draft notice. He trained in plane repair at Kiesler Field in Mississippi but spent his war months entertaining casualties on Saipan with songs like "Round and Round Hitler's Grave." In 1944, he performed "Peat Bog Soldiers" and "Valley of Jarama" as part of a suite of tunes honoring the Spanish Civil War. He mustered out in December 1945 and published folk and libertarian music for the distributor People's Songs. While living 60 miles north of New York City in Beacon, he settled on a cliffside lot in a former brickyard and chopped his own wood. In 1948, he, Guthrie, and Paul Robeson, a black actor and singer, involved themselves in the Progressive Party campaign for Henry Wallace for president.

Proletarian Music

At the beginning of the folk revival, Seeger joined Ronnie Gilbert, Lee Hays, and Fred Hellerman in coforming the Weavers. Their theme song, "This Land Is Your Land," recorded on *The Weavers at Home*, roused audiences to lock arms and sing along. At age 30, Seeger issued a hit record, "Goodnight Irene," one of Leadbelly's adaptations. Seeger promoted worker protest, integration, and pacifism through lyrics appealing to underclass issues, including "If I Had a Hammer," "Joe Hill," "Turn, Turn, Turn!," "Tzena, Tzena, Tzena," and "Where Have All the Flowers Gone." His top sellers for Decca Records included "Kisses Sweeter than Wine," "Rock Island Line," and "So Long, It's Been Good to Know You." He insisted on sending royalties to Solomon Linda, composer of the hit Zulu hunting song "Wimoweh," later reprised by Jimmy Dorsey and Yma Sumac. Seeger's compositions became vehicles for the Kingston Trio, Marlene Dietrich, Trini Lopez, the Byrds, and the trio Peter, Paul, and Mary. Seeger created the long neck banjo and compiled a handbook, *How to Play the Five-String Banjo* (1948).

Seeger's leftist principles aroused conservative and reactionary zealots. At a civil rights rally for Harlem held in the wilds of Peekskill, New York, he shared billing with Robeson, who favored communism for its egalitarianism. Ku Klux Klansmen intervened and ripped the stage apart. By 1950, Seeger's involvement in communism ended with the extremes of Josef Stalin's regime. Seeger joined Joan Baez in popularizing Guy Carawan's "We Shall Overcome" (1946), the theme song of civil rights activists. A sold-out reunion of the Weavers in 1955 at Carnegie Hall revived their fan base. Seeger rededicated himself to laborers by publishing *Union Songs* (1955).

Before HUAC

Seeger faced maligning by the House Un-American Activities Commmittee (HUAC), a force empaneled by the U.S. Congress in 1937 to root out communist cells and propagandists during a Red scare fomented by Senator Joseph McCarthy. To assure national security and stability, in 1947, chairman John Parnell Thomas, an attorney from New Jersey, and his aide, Congressman Richard Milhouse Nixon, an attorney from Yorba Linda, California, began grilling and libeling entertainers, homosexuals, immigrants, and Jews the stature of Lucille Ball, Bertolt Brecht, Charlie Chaplin, Walt Disney, Cary Grant, Dashiell Hammett, Lillian Hellman, Burl Ives, Ring Lardner, and Ronald Reagan. Because an informant named three of the Weavers as Reds, in 1952, the group disbanded.

On February 6, 1952, Harvey Matusow charged Ronnie Gilbert, Fred Hellerman, and Seeger before the committee as "pinkos." J. Edgar Hoover, director of surveillance, divulged Seeger's 5-year FBI file to Governor Frank Lausche of Ohio and to Frederick Woltman, a reporter for the *New York World-Telegram*. Woltman characterized Weavers members as the first American musicians suspected of treason, in part from singing the antiwar tune "Wasn't That a Time!" Because of the committee's curiosity about the lyrics, Seeger offered an a cappella performance. At the committee's rejection, he insisted, "I'm sorry you are not interested in the song. It is a good song" (Willens, 1993, 164). On May 1, 1952, Seeger launched a one-man guerrilla revolt in Manhattan by parading on Fifth Avenue with a sign reading, "The Censored Mike" (Dunaway, 1990, 156).

Red baiting worsened in the early 1950s, when Charles Seeger experienced the sudden revocation of his passport. On August 15, 1955, HUAC summoned Pete Seeger to testify concerning his membership in the American Communist Party and his writings for the *Daily Worker*. Mulling over his options, he said to his father, "I sometimes wonder if it wouldn't be more sensible just to give up and go to prison" (Dunaway, 1990, 166). Unlike 211 others who invoked Fifth Amendment rights against self-incrimination, the unrepentant singer refused under First Amendment rights to freedom of association. Coached by attorney Paul Ross, Seeger blistered HUAC members for challenging citizen associations and political and religious tenets. To questions about his performances in New Jersey and New York allegedly on behalf of the Communist Party, on the witness stand in 1956, he described his whole life as a contribution to national preservation. After a formal indictment on March 26, 1957, FBI agents stalked the singer. He came to trial in March 1961; on April 3, the court sentenced him to ten years in prison for noncooperation with a federal investigation. Along with playwright Arthur Miller, in 1956, Seeger faced a 1-year sentence for contempt of court until a court of appeals overturned the verdict on a technicality.

After HUAC

The insidious blacklisting in the anonymous publication *Red Channels: Communist Influence on Radio and Television* (1950) ruined 10,000 careers and crimped Seeger's popularity. DJs shunned his popular renditions of "Guantanamera," "Thoughts Are Free," and "We Shall Overcome" on radio; television producers banned so-called subversives from home screens. Even Decca Records and Local 802 of the American Federation of Musicians ousted Seeger.

His quartet faced bomb threats, stoning, impugning by the American Legion, anti-Seeger petitions, and spurious placards reading, "Red Pete" and "Khrushchev's Songbird." A committed organic gardener and recycler, he saved some of the stones to build the fireplace in his log cabin. His wife helped him distribute flyers to community clubs, camps, and schools so far apart that the couple kept on the move. Earning a pittance of his former income, in 1958, he played solo in community auditoriums and worked his way back into schools and collage sing-alongs.

Amid attacks on Seeger by the John Birch Society, the grassroots circuit revived Seeger's compassion for the underdog, the dissenter, and the working poor. During the Vietnam War, he became a force for the folk upsurge that emanated from Greenwich Village, New York, by performers he dubbed "Woody's children." Seeger expressed his love of libertarianism in *Broadside* magazine and *Sing Out! The Folk Song Magazine* and through Folkways Records. In 1963, he processed with dissenters in the March on Washington for Jobs and Freedom. After a family tour of Russia and India, in June 1964, he joined Dr. Martin Luther King, Jr., and the voter registration effort known as the Mississippi Summer Project.

Seeger returned to television in the mid-1960s with the television program *Rainbow Quest*, a venue for performers the caliber of Johnny Cash, June Carter, Judy Collins, and Doc Watson. To validate multiculturalism, Seeger featured Buffy Sainte-Marie and Mimi and Richard Fariña. Singing children's song, Seeger became a staple on *Sesame Street*. Still keen on vocal satire, in 1966, he mocked President Lyndon Johnson on the album *Dangerous Songs* with "Beans in My Ears," a verbal jest at "Mrs. Jay's little son Alby [LBJ]" for failing to listen to U.S. citizens. The next spring, Seeger angered producers of CBS TV for introducing on the *Smothers Brothers Comedy Hour* the allegorical lament "Waist Deep in the Big Muddy" (1967), a rebuke of Johnson for miring the nation in the Vietnam War.

In this same era, Seeger took seriously the decline of New York State waters from industrial and municipal pollutants. In 1966, he established the Hudson River Sloop Clearwater, a coterie of riverkeepers who built a floating swimming pool, patrolled the banks, and collected garbage. During the vessel's construction, he organized the Great Hudson River Revival, a two-day celebration at Croton Point Park to raise funds for the cleanup. Volunteers expanded the program to educate youth on the importance of waterways to the environment. On the sloop's maiden voyage in 1969, it traveled the river as far as the South Street Seaport Museum in New York City.

An American Treasure

Seeger's honors were late in arriving. At age 60, he accepted the Eugene V. Debs Award for his devotion to community and labor issues. In 1993, he received the Grammy Lifetime Achievement Award, followed the next year by a Kennedy Center Lifetime Achievement Honor and a National Medal of Arts from the National Endowment for the Arts. In 1996, he received an Arts Medal from Harvard and induction into the Rock and Roll Hall of Fame. In 1997, his recording of *Pete* won a Grammy Award for Best Traditional Folk Album of 1996. At age 80, the Cuban people bestowed the Felix Varela Medal for Excellence for his humanistic performances denouncing racism and defending the environment.

Seeger turned to narrative at the National Storytelling Festival in Jonesborough, Tennessee, where he recounted the legend of Abiyoyo. Before his 80th birthday, Seeger's admirers compiled a double CD, *Where Have All the Flowers Gone: The Songs of Pete Seeger* (1998). The vocals featured contributions from Bonnie Raitt, Bruce Springsteen, Roger

McGuinn, Judy Collins, and Odetta. Actively antiwar, Seeger issued "Bring Them Home" (2006), a denunciation of the Iraq War. At age 87, he sang at MerleFest 2006 in Wilkesboro, North Carolina, and issued a reflective collection, *Canciones de Las Brigadas Internacionales* (2006), which features eight songs about the Spanish Civil War. That April, Bruce Springsteen collected Seeger's greatest songs for an album, *We Shall Overcome: The Seeger Sessions* (2006). The next year, Pete joined others of the Seeger family singers at a performance at the Library of Congress in Washington, D.C. He published *The Deaf Musicians* (2007), a children's book that earned the Schneider Family Book Award. His song "Big Joe Blues" (2007) immortalized his disenchantment with communism under Stalin. One admirer shared with the press a morning vision of Pete in his late 80s standing by a roadside waving a scrawled sign on cardboard reading "Peace."

Sources

Dunaway, David King. *How Can I Keep from Singing: Pete Seeger*. New York: Da Capo, 1990.

Hornby, Nick. *Da Capo Best Music Writing 2001: The Year's Finest Writing on Rock, Pop, Jazz, Country & More*. New York: Da Capo, 2001.

Wilkinson, Alec. "The Protest Singer." *New Yorker* (April 17, 2006).

Willens, Doris. *Lonesome Traveler: The Life of Lee Hays*. Lincoln, NE: University of Nebraska Press, 1993.

■ Militarism
Pat Conroy

A provocative Irish-American author of memoir and semiautobiographical fiction, Donald Patrick "Pat" Conroy demands truth from memories of being a nomadic army brat. Born on October 26, 1945, in Atlanta, Georgia, he was the first of the five boys—Pat, Mike, Jim, Tim, and Tom—and two girls—Carol and Kathy—of Frances "Peg" Peek Conroy, a north Georgian social climber. Pat remembers her as a crafty beauty who couldn't cook but who concocted lies to cover her disastrous marriage. His father, hang-tough Colonel Donald N. Conroy, a Chicago-born bully, turned brutality into a career as a Marine fighter pilot. A member of the Black Sheep squadron, he fought in three wars, earned five distinguished flying crosses, and flew nuclear warheads. The belligerence slopped over on his home, a no-man's-land where he struck and degraded his wife and children. Two-year-old Pat observed from his high chair Don backhanding Peg, who threatened Don with a kitchen knife. Pat later jokingly identified his parents as Zeus and Hera, mythic deities at war for his psyche.

Pat grew up with a skewed vision of humanity. While his father spewed racism and irreverence, Pat learned refinement from his mother, who "raised her children to say *colored* [italics in original] and to bow their heads at the spoken name of Jesus" (Conroy, 1972, 5). From Peg, Pat gained a love of language, even when she instructed him to lie to deflect criticism of Don for bashing and bruising Pat. While Don flew jets during the Korean War, she stirred Pat's interest in the humanities by reading aloud *The Diary of Anne Frank* and *Gone with the Wind*. Peg described her style of mothering as raising the kind of children who would "hide Jews." Simultaneously, Pat's martinet father modeled for his children domestic abuse, racism, anti-Semitism, and sexism. When Pat signed up for a typing class, Don challenged, "Son, corporals type. Girls type. You'll be a fighter pilot. You won't need to type . . . . You're dismissed" (Breed, 2000). He forced Pat to play sports, a mutual interest that Pat manipulated into positive paternal attention.

Given to vicious mood swings and free-floating hostility, Don treated his son like a raw recruit by demanding discipline and unquestioning obedience. Pat matured unskilled at showing affection and spiritually needy. In adulthood, he joked about the family's "forced march of blood and tears": "The sound of gunfire on rifle ranges strikes an authentic chord of home in me even now" (Conroy, 1991, xvii, xix). At age ten, he learned to channel antimilitaristic angst through basketball by playing on a fifth grade team at St. James Elementary School in Orlando, Florida. He explained to an interviewer, "Athletics provided the single outlet for a repressed and preternaturally shy boy to express himself in public.... I lost myself in the beauty of sport and made my family proud while passing through the silent eye of the storm that was my childhood" (Weaver, 2002). While the military family moved to accommodate Donald's career, Pat, by age 15, had lived at 23 addresses and studied at 11 public schools in what he called "some of the more notable swamplands of the East Coast" (Conroy, 1972, 5). Frequent moves caused him to feel like a friendless outsider. He later blamed his funk on the dark macho posturing of his father.

Learning to Flourish

Because Conroy connected with fellow jocks, he learned to love school. In the year of the sit-ins at a segregated lunch counter at Woolworth's in Greensboro, North Carolina, junior English teacher Eugene Norris rid him of racial prejudice. At Christmas 1961, Norris sparked Pat's interest in Southern novels by giving him a copy of Thomas Wolfe's fictionalized autobiography *Look Homeward, Angel*. The novel set a pattern in Conroy's writing of salving past hurts through dramatic fiction. At his father's command, in 1960, Pat enrolled at the Citadel military academy, a state-supported college in Charleston, South Carolina. The camaraderie and militarism generated a love-hate response in Pat, who loathed the cruel plebe system. On his first phone call home, he described the atmosphere as worse than living with his father.

After surviving ridicule, forced marches, and gratuitous cigarette burns during his year as a knob, Pat played baseball and football and excelled as basketball captain, point guard, and most valuable player of the team. He described the value of sports to males as a perspective on glory and splendor, the place to escape self and troubles. Most important, he learned that he could complete a B.A. degree in English and write for a living. He respected the aim to become "a writer who wanted to create winged and roaring sentences, the kind that would set the language free and make people come to ... [his] house and sit on ... [his] knee and listen to the song ... [he] was born to sing" (Pate, 2002). While still an undergraduate, he paid $1,500 to self-publish his first nonfiction, *The Boo*, a reflection on an inspiring mentor, Bear Berrineau, the fictional incarnation of Lieutenant Colonel Thomas Nugent "Boo" Courvoisie, a professor of military science and commandant of cadets for 27 years.

At Home in Beaufort

Conroy chose Beaufort, South Carolina, as a hometown and searched for a residence on the Point, the historic end of town. Because of myopia and color blindness, he ruled out a military career and applied for the Peace Corps. In lieu of a placement in Africa, he became a teacher. In 1967, he devoted his first year to an English classroom at Beaufort

High School. In an era of racial unrest and civil disobedience against the military draft, he rebelled against the unjust southeast Asian war that caused the wounding and imprisonment of a schoolmate and the deaths of six other Citadel classmates. He later castigated himself for avoiding the draft and for protesting President Richard Nixon's Vietnam War campaign while his old friends died in combat. He mused, "I have come to a conclusion about my country that I knew then in my bones, but lacked the courage to act on: America is a good enough country to die for even when she is wrong" (Minzesheimer, 2005). Pat lobbied for the inclusion of black history to the curriculum. For his stance on racial equality, he lost a post as basketball coach.

At a party in May 1968, Pat met Barbara Bolling Jones, a Vietnam War widow whose husband had died the previous October. When Pat moved in with her in August 1968, she was a single parent to two daughters, Jessica and Melissa. Before Pat's marriage to Barbara on October 10, he began teaching impoverished black children grades five through eight at a one-room all-black school on Daufuskie Island. The kids called him "Mr. Patroy." For refusing to paddle students and for ignoring curriculum while teaching them practical skills and sex education, he was fired by an inflexible, intolerant school administration, which he ridiculed and resisted through passive aggression. He sued and lost his protest against a negative evaluation on his work record.

Pat in Conflict with Authority

In 1972, Pat exposed substandard schooling for island blacks in a nonfiction memoir, *The Water Is Wide*, his revenge against the educational establishment. Assigned to the fictional Yamacraw Island northeast of the Georgia–South Carolina line, the main character is a pragmatist who cultivates Gullah-speaking children isolated on a sea island lacking a bridge, paved roads, a doctor, and telephones. From him, they learn American values and icons as well as how to swim and to appreciate Beethoven's symphonies. The National Education Association presented Pat an Anisfield-Wolf humanitarian award. For *Conrack*, the screen version filmed by Martin Ritt for 20th Century Fox, Jon Voight played Pat's character. In 1987, composer Granville Wyche Burgess revived *The Water Is Wide* as a musical.

Conroy resettled Barbara, Jessica, Melissa, and baby Megan in Atlanta, where he wrote an autobiographical coming-of-age novel, *The Great Santini* (1976). The story broke the taboo of exploring the residue of child abuse on a damaged survivor. The book returned the author to the psychological terrorism of his father, fictionalized as Lieutenant Colonel "Bull" Meecham, an explosive sadist who made no differentiation between fathering and soldiering. The author exalted the composition as "the only way" he "could take to the skies in the dark-winged jets, move through those competitive ranks of aviators and become, at last," his "father's wingman" (Conroy, 1991, xxv). The Warner film version featured Robert Duvall as Pat's controlling father, Blythe Danner as the loyal military wife, and Michael O'Keefe as Ben, Pat's alter ego, a boy confused by loyalty to self and to his conflicted family. While reliving boyhood memories, Pat generated family antipathies. Members of the Conroy household picketed book signings and charged Pat with exploiting and profiteering from family secrets.

At a spiritual low point, Pat faced his own divorce from Barbara at the same time that his parents parted. Peg Conroy abandoned Don the day after his retirement parade and cited *The Great Santini* as evidence in a divorce hearing. Pat blamed the couple's breakup on his father's return to ordinary citizenship, which cost Peg the prestige she knew among Marine wives as the colonel's mate. Ironically, after leaving the Marines, Donald Conroy gentled his abusive personality and renewed his relationship with his eldest child. The author explained, "My father used my novel as a blueprint to reinvent himself and make a liar out of me . . . . He had the best second act in the history of fathering" (Minzesheimer, 2002). The two were close until Donald's death from colon cancer in spring 1998. At Beaufort's national cemetery, Pat buried his father under a headstone engraved "Great Santini."

Return to the Citadel

Pat dramatized the paranoia and sadism at the Citadel in a protest novel and cautionary tale, *The Lords of Discipline* (1980). The grim plot features a Catholic outsider named Will McLean. An egalitarian hero, he bucks the spying and intimidation of a Southern military academy where "the making of men was a kind of grotesque artistry" (Conroy, 1980, 6). Will challenges the tradition of physical and emotional brutality and its fostering of racism and elitism. The 1983 film version cast David Keith as Will, challenger of the Ten, a secret student society who haze students who lack the luster of an academy graduate. Alumni of the Citadel denounced Pat for two decades for vilifying their alma mater.

After marrying Alabama-born novelist Cassandra King and moving to Rome, Pat devoted his three years in Italy to composing *The Prince of Tides* (1986), a complex psychological novel about an adult settling issues left over from his dysfunctional family. The themes of codependence and pedophilia and the reunion of hero Tom Wingo with his suicidal sister Savannah so outraged the author's sister Carol that she cut all ties with him for years. On February 21, 1988, Pat defended Judith Fitzgerald, an English teacher at St. Andrews High School in Charleston, South Carolina, for teaching *The Prince of Tides* to a class of juniors. In a letter to the *Charleston News and Courier*, the author stated his purpose: "I see myself as bearing full witness to the times in which I live and explaining both the pain and beauty of my own life to myself" (White, 1992, 19). For his support of free speech and uncensored reading, the author won the South Carolina Library Association's Intellectual Freedom award.

Barbra Streisand filmed and starred in the 1991 screen version of *The Prince of Tides* opposite Nick Nolte, who garnered an Oscar nomination and a Golden Globe for best actor. Pat earned an Academy Award nomination for adapting the novel to the screen. After his youngest brother, Tom, committed suicide in 1994 and Peg Conroy died from leukemia, Pat set in Rome the novel *Beach Music* (1995), a poorly received work that he adapted for film. Reliving past hurts pushed the author over the edge and required psychiatric counseling to restabilize him. He refused psychotropic drugs that might undermine his art.

The Iconoclast Comes Home

Pat was still sorting out his revulsion toward militarism in 2000, when he was invited to deliver a commencement oration at the Citadel. The faculty, which had berated the author for supporting the female cadet Shannon Faulkner, conferred an honorary degree on him. He returned to the academy for another autobiographical novel, *My Losing Season: A Point Guard's Way of Knowledge* (2002), a perusal of his basketball experiences in 1966 and 1967 under coach Mel Thompson. The reflection on a humiliating 8-25 season allowed the author to examine subtle aspects of defeat. His reason for nostalgia was a personal need "to return to the boy" he "was": "I've called him the beaten boy, the ruined boy. But I needed to fall in love with that kid before I died" (Lanham, 2002). During the writing, former Bulldog teammates from the Citadel feared that the author would devastate them in print. Pleasantly surprised, the players bolstered the author after his wife sued for divorce, sending Pat into a suicidal free-fall from fear of losing his daughter. The author read the work aloud to his father shortly before Don's death.

While living on Fripp Island, South Carolina, Pat mellowed. He cultivated a long-term friendship with cartoonist Doug Marlette, a fellow army brat who probed emotional havoc in Pat's background. Pat compiled another memoir, *The Pat Conroy Cookbook: Recipes of My Life* (2004), which savors meals in Rome and the French Dordogne Valley alongside reveries of Southern barbecue, catfish, crab cakes, oysters, and peach cobbler. The anecdotal text and a hundred recipes savor Southern life through reflections on recipes, feasts, and friendships.

Sources

Breed, Allen G. "A Mid-Life, Pat Conroy Tries to Write His Own Happy Ending." *CNN Book News*, November 17, 2000. Available at http://archives.cnn.com/2000/books/news/11/17/pat.conroy.ap/ (last accessed April 3, 2008).

Conroy, Pat. "Introduction." In Mary Edwards Wertsch, *Military Brats: Legacies of Childhood inside the Fortress*. Bayside, NY: Altheia Productions, 1991.

———. *The Lords of Discipline*. Boston: Houghton Mifflin, 1980.

———. *The Water Is Wide*. New York: Bantam, 1972.

Lanham, Fritz. "Pat Conroy: 'My Losing Season.'" *Houston Chronicle*, October 11, 2002.

Minzesheimer, Bob. "Conroy Looks Back at His 'Losing Season.'" *USA Today*, October 15, 2002.

Pate, Nancy. "Winning Writer Scores with Basketball Memoir." *Orlando Sentinel*, October 20, 2002.

Weaver, Teresa. "A Memoir of Shattered Hoop Dreams." *Atlanta Journal-Constitution*, May 19, 2002.

White, Robert A. "'Pat Conroy's 'Gutter Language': Prince of Tides in a Lowcountry High School." *English Journal* 81 (4) (April 1992): 19–22.

■ Myasthenia Gravis
Wilma Mankiller

The first woman elected chief of the Cherokee Nation, Wilma Pearl Mankiller survived myasthenia gravis to advance health and education among the poor. Her great grandfather was among the 11,000 of the 17,000 Indian and black deportees to survive the Trail of Tears, a displacement from the southeastern states to Oklahoma Territory engineered in winter 1838–1839 by President Andrew Jackson. In 1907, her paternal grandfather, Yona (John) Mankiller, a World War I veteran, received a land allotment of 160 acres in the flinty Cookson Hills. For over a century, it served as the family homestead. His surname derived from tribal history when the hereditary title of "mankiller" denoted the security guard who protected each village from enemies. His granddaughter profited from being the scion of a tribal patriarch.

A native of Tahlequah, Oklahoma, the Cherokee capital, Wilma Mankiller was born on November 18, 1945, of Dutch, Irish, and Indian heritage to Charlie and Irene Sitton Mankiller. In Adair County, she grew up bilingual on the family farm at Mankiller Flats among spirited native debaters and poker and stickball players. She learned from storytellers who spoke of Mother Earth and the creation. Her great aunt Maggie Gourd Mankiller valued dreams for their glimpses of the future. For cash, her father and oldest brother, Louis Donald Mankiller, cut broomcorn in Campo, Colorado, planed railroad ties, and harvested beans, peanuts, and strawberries. With sister Linda, Wilma drew water from a spring a quarter mile from home. Her siblings went berrying, gathered watercress and wild onions, cleaned catfish and frogs, shot quail and squirrels for meat, and, lacking electricity, cooked on a wood stove fired with logs from local hickory, locust, and walnut groves. Her father nurtured self-sufficiency and encouraged reading among his six sons and five daughters by establishing a home library. By coal oil lamps, Wilma devoured books. During her education 3 miles from home at Rocky Mountain Elementary School, she gave no thought to going to college or becoming a tribal chief, an attainment reserved for males.

A Second Trail of Tears

Under the Bureau of Indian Affairs (BIA) Indian Relocation Program, Mankiller experienced a twentieth-century Trail of Tears based on the internment of Japanese-Americans during World War II. At age 11, she "came to know in some small way what it was like for . . . [he]r ancestors" (Mankiller and Wallis, 1993, 52). She witnessed the despair of her father, who abandoned his drought-ridden farm and traveled 2 days by rail from Stilwell to California. Lured by slick brochures of happy Indian households, he resettled the family in the industrial sector of San Francisco, which seemed like the surface of Mars. They lived for 2 weeks at the rundown Keys Hotel and then at the Hunter's Point project on Potrero Hill. Ethnic fragmentation sapped Cherokee political powers and reduced tribe members to low minority status. For its high black population, the ghetto was nicknamed "Harlem West."

At a low in her girlhood, Mankiller confronted middle school bigots who called her "nigger" and jeered at her dark skin and ominous name. Her self-esteem suffered. She reflected, "I learned to practice an ancient Cherokee value, being of good spirit" (Mattioni, 2005, 130–131). Kindly Latinos introduced her to the dial telephone and taught her to roller skate; from blacks, she learned the blues of B. B. King and Etta James. While her father struggled to support the family as a rope maker and stevedore, she left San Francisco to live for a year on the dairy farm of her maternal grandmother, Pearl Sitton, at Riverbank in central California 90 miles east of San Francisco. In 1960, Wilma grieved the death of her brother Bob, an apple picker who was trapped in a fire that destroyed a Washington State migrant shack. For courage, she emulated her father, who became a union organizer and Indian advocate.

Mankiller realized in her teens that the federal government underestimated the ability of the poor to solve their own social and economic problems. On return to the Bay Area, she studied law and treaty rights. She volunteered at the San Francisco Indian Center in the Mission District, where she felt accepted and needed. Attendance at seasonal stomp dances and powwows enlightened her on the difficulties engendered by the BIA in breaking up tribes and relocating Cherokee families to urban areas. She developed a love of Indian traditions and history along with political savvy about methods of coexisting with whites. After high school, she clerked in a finance office. In 1963, she married Hector Hugo Olaya de Bardi, a business and accounting major from Guayaquil, Ecuador. While he supported them with a night job at Pan American Airways, they had two daughters, Felicia and Gina.

An Indian Renaissance

At a pivotal point in Indian discontent, Mankiller, her father, and siblings James, Linda, Richard, and Vanessa Mankiller supported the American Indian Movement and Indians of All Tribes in a surprise revolt. On November 14, 1969, they overran and liberated the abandoned federal prison on Alcatraz Island in San Francisco Bay. The uprising sparked native pride in Wilma, who was too involved with child rearing to join the impromptu community forming on the sandstone bay island. Instead, she raised cash to supply the occupation force with food, equipment, and medicine. She developed activist sensibilities by fighting for civil rights, Indian self-affirmation, women's reproductive rights, and an end to the Vietnam War. Among the influences of her emerging activism were César Chavez, Dolores Huerta, and the striking Chicano farm laborers of Northern California.

For 7 years, Mankiller pursued a one-on-one form of tribal uplift by advancing kindergarten and adult education among the Pit River Tribe of Shasta, California, and by helping members regain traditional lands. In East Oakland, she coordinated musicals, led field trips to tribal gatherings, and hosted afterschool study sessions and youth projects. She studied sociology at Skyline Junior College in San Bruno and later at San Francisco State, an antidote to grief from her father's death from kidney failure in 1971 and the bankruptcy of the Cherokee Nation. During first wave feminism, when women discussed sexuality and male tyranny, her traditional husband refused her a car. In defiance, she bought a red Mazda with stick shift. In 1974, her liberation heightened tensions in her marriage, which ended after 11 years. She supported her family as a social worker for the town of Oakland.

A Search for Wholeness

When activism pointed her back to renewal among her Cherokee roots, in 1976, Wilma was broke and unemployed. She traded her Mazda for a buffalo robe. In a U-Haul, she returned to Tahlequah to camp at Cherokee Landing on Caney Creek, worked for the tribe, and introduced her girls to tent living, cooking over an open fire, swimming, and reading for pleasure. Although the family home had burned and the acreage flourished with weeds and scrub, her joy in her homeland and indigenous lifeways fostered hope: "By then I had an abiding belief that a distinct and vibrant Cherokee culture . . . existed in some historic Cherokee communities" (Mankiller et al., 2004, 74). To rekindle traditional collectivism, she worked at the Urban Indian Resource Center and read the self-help philosophy of Bangladeshi economist Muhammad Yunus, a warrior against Third World poverty. She exulted in volunteerism: "I wanted to be engaged in the world around me, to be involved in politics, civil rights, women's rights" (Mankiller et al., 2004, 48).

While completing graduate study at the University of Arkansas, Fayetteville, in 1979, Wilma suffered trauma in a head-on car crash on a blind curve. The impact killed her best friend, Sherry Morris, and smashed Wilma's face and ribs and slashed her neck. Out of devotion to her daughters, Wilma clung to life. For months, Linda Mankiller tended her sister until the removal of leg casts from a crushed right leg and a broken left leg and ankle. After seventeen surgeries on the right leg, Mankiller escaped amputation but not the guilt for Sherry's death. She rejected a life of leg braces by walking daily a quarter mile to the mailbox. When rehabilitation ended in 1980, Mankiller faced a diagnosis of myasthenia gravis, an autoimmune disease marked by neuromuscular weakness and exhaustion. Housebound over a lengthy period, she gained spiritual insight into tribal life and commitment. Of life-threatening illness, she remarked, "I never prayed for a long life. I prayed for a little space without treatments or major medical trauma" (Mankiller et al., 2004, 20). In 1981, the removal of her thymus gland restored her autonomy.

A Grassroots Organizer

Despite tribal sexism, Mankiller, a Democrat, rose in the ranks among predominantly Republican males. In January 1981, she established the Cherokee Community Development Department, increased tribal revenues, introduced solar technology in 25 new homes, and tackled the upgrading of the 16-mile water system. At the urging of Ross Swimmer, principal chief of the Cherokee Nation of Oklahoma, in August 1983, she won election to deputy tribal chief. She began writing grant proposals to advance female achievement and to assist 300 rural Cherokee families who lived in squalor and want in Bell, Oklahoma. Gradually, the standard of living rose as residents acquired jobs and homes. The success of the model town caught the attention of *CBS News Sunday Morning*, which aired film updates of the campaign. In Washington, D.C., she lobbied for improved health care, lower infant morality rates, maternal wellness and nutrition, and children's rights. Because of Swimmer's resignation on December 5, 1985, as head of the Bureau of Indian Affairs in Washington, D.C., she become the first female principal chief and the first woman in modern history to head a major Indian nation.

Mankiller naively assumed that a woman could thrive in a political setting. To her dismay, sexist opposition to a female chief resulted in slashed tires, telephone harassment, and death threats but no dialogue over issues. Males approached each council with complaints that electing a female chief violated religious principles and left the Cherokee defenseless before ridicule from other Indian nations. Mankiller sought help from a healer, who conducted a dawn ceremony to cleanse her thoughts of negativism. For clever comebacks, she called a folklorist on the *Ms.* Foundation for Women. Instead of witty remarks, the new chief adopted an impassive expression and refused to debate nonissues with fools. She arranged a catered reception and rally at a historic Tahlequah locale, but only five supporters attended it. On her first meeting at Stilwell with the Five Civilized Tribes—Cherokee, Chickasaw, Choctaw, Creek, and Seminole—men occupied all the chairs at the table. She ignored their discourtesy, fetched another chair, and continued discussing their mutual concerns, including the reunion of the Eastern Cherokee of North Carolina with the Western Cherokee of Oklahoma. After one rude male badgered her with obscure procedural regulations, she altered the sound system. When he continued interrupting, she silenced his microphone.

Fame

The media publicized the effectiveness of Mankiller's vigorous pro-people campaign and her spiritual force to the Cherokee. Her influence spread across 7,000 square miles. She governed a population of some 140,000 and superintended 1,200 employees and a budget of over $75 million. Her achievements built on Cherokee tenacity, a trait dependent on centuries of distinct heritage, interdependence, and coping. She boosted consensus building on necessary projects. Her platform of self-determination set goals to revitalize the tribe, end dependence on welfare, halt violence against women, and suppress teen substance abuse. She focused on raising high school graduation numbers, introducing native children to the Cherokee language and heritage, and launching small businesses. In 1986, she wed an open-minded full-blooded Cherokee, Charlie Lee Soap, the bilingual director of tribal development, but chose to retain her surname. His son Winterhawk increased the family to five. Together they launched a cultural renaissance based on five health clinics, a boarding academy, an $8 million vocational center, 24 Head Start centers, day care, and adult literacy. At the core of their values lay Mankiller's determination to slay the media stereotype of the lazy, drunken Indian.

In the midst of progress for the Cherokee, Mankiller faced kidney failure, a disease that first troubled her during her first pregnancy. Her brother Don donated a kidney that restored her to health. She established the Cherokee Nation Community Development Department, enrolled more natives in the Cherokee Nation, and upgraded Sequoyah High School. Two years later, she was named *Ms.* magazine's woman of the year. She won reelection, followed in 4 years by an even greater vote count of 82 percent for her third term. At her state of the nation address on September 1, 1990, she maintained an admiration for tribalism: "Despite everything that's happened to our people throughout history, we've managed to hang on to our culture, we've managed to hang on to our sense of being Cherokee" (Wright, 2005, 312). Employing fundamental animal fables and Indian history, she cowrote a memoir, *Mankiller: A Chief and Her People* (1993), a detailed recounting of her rise from naïveté to political acumen.

Mankiller's subsequent writings followed the indigenous reverence for holistic philosophy. She wrote of the earth's unity—"the gift of medicine from plants, the friendship of the wind, or ceremonies around the sacred fire" (Franck, Rose, and Connolly, 2001, 259). Without pomposity, she recounted meetings with Presidents Bill Clinton and Nelson Mandela and Gloria Steinem. A diagnosis of lymphoma in 1995 ended Mankiller's political career. Her honors include the Henry G. Bennett Distinguished Service Award from Oklahoma State University, an honorary Chubb Fellowship from Yale University, induction into the Women's Hall of Fame, and the Presidential Medal of Freedom. Of her remarkable stoicism after incurring myasthenia gravis, lymphoma, breast cancer, and double kidney implants, she stated, "How can I be anything but positive when I come from a tenacious, resilient people" (Mankiller et al., 2004, 172).

Sources

Franck, Frederick, Janis Roze, and Richard Connolly, eds. *What Does It Mean to Be Human?: Reverence for Life Reaffirmed by Responses from Around the World.* New York: St. Martin's Griffin, 2001.

Mankiller, Wilma, and Michael Wallis. *Mankiller: A Chief and Her People.* New York: St. Martin's Griffin, 1993.

Vine Deloria, Jr., and Gloria Steinem. *Every Day Is a Good Day: Reflections of Contemporary Indigenous Women.* Golden, CO: Fulcrum, 2004.

Mattioni, Gloria. *Reckless: The Outrageous Lives of Nine Kick-Ass Women.* New York: Seal Press, 2005.

Wright, Ronald. *Stolen Continents: 500 Years of Conquest and Resistance in the Americas.* Boston: Mariner, 2005.

Nazism
Johanna Reiss

An immigrant Dutch Jew, Johanna "Annie" De Leeuw Reiss wrote an eyewitness account of her survival of German dictator Adolf Hitler's subjugation of Holland. A native of Winterswijk on Holland's eastern tip, she was born on April 4, 1932, and came of age on the German border. The baby sister of 15-year-old Rachel, a talented artist, and 10-year-old Sini, she is the youngest daughter of an invalid, Sophie Spier De Leeuw, and stockman and cattle dealer Isaak "Ise" De Leeuw. He and the Gans family across the street formed a profitable partnership. On business excursions, Annie accompanied her father. On September 15, 1935, ease of travel for the De Leeuw family ended after the Nuremberg Laws revoked the rights and citizenship of Jews. By July 1937, Hitler's master plan began exterminating Jewish inmates at Buchenwald, a German death camp near Weimar, Thuringia. When Ise's brother, storekeeper Bram De Leeuw, immigrated to Pearl River, New York, Sophie was too ill with headaches to consider taking her family so far from home.

By spring 1938, Ise denounced Germany for scapegoating Jews for mounting unemployment and economic depression. He lambasted Hitler's forces during radio broadcasts, which followed the Nazi fortunes on November 9 during *Kristallnacht* (night of broken glass), when right-wing thugs destroyed 7,500 Jewish businesses and synagogues. Subsequent commentary pondered the Nazi invasion of Poland on September 1, 1939. Meanwhile, the De Leeuws coped with strictures on their freedoms. Rachel De Leeuw completed teacher education and began work at a nursery school.

The Seizure of Northwestern Europe

In spring 1940, the outlook for peace lessened as Germany overran Denmark, Norway, Belgium, Luxembourg, and France. On May 10, 1940, German pilots flew over Winterswijk, causing Dutch turncoats in the Dutch Nationaal Socialistische Beweging (NSB), a far-right, antiparliamentary, and National Socialist faction, to applaud the Nazi encroachment. By September, Ise and other Jews could no longer operate their businesses. The next month, Marie, the De Leeuws' maid, fled out of fear of Nazi retaliation against a Gentile working for a Jewish family. In November, after a year in the teaching profession, Rachel lost her classroom post.

The De Leeuws found themselves imprisoned in their homeland. In January 1941, Nazis terrified the Hebrew world by slaughtering 170 Bucharest Jews. Food and fuel rationing increased hardships; authorities loaded males into vans for transport by rail to Mauthausen, a prison in Austria. Annie entered Mr. Herschel's synagogue school. In October 1941, the De Leeuws moved to an unpainted house before it could be readied for occupancy. By the fourth grade, when the Nazi government prohibited Jews from public transportation and gathering places, including hotels, theaters, beaches, and parks, Annie withdrew from school. After the Nazi high command summoned the De Leeuw family in early October 1942, the five plotted to disappear over the Swiss border but found it closed.

While doctors treated Sophie for kidney disease and renal failure at a hospital, the four remaining family members could not gain visitors' passes. Johan predicted her death. The De Leeuws moved into Gentile residences. Annie recalled, "I was a child, and Jewish, and therefore undesirable" (Reiss, 1972, v). After Abbink refused to shelter Jews on his farm, Reverend Zwaal located a place for Ise with Hemmes, a retired bookkeeper living outside Rotterdam. Rachel remained behind to be near her mother and, in November 1942, became the last Jew to leave town. Sophie's death preceded Rachel's retreat to a parsonage in a hamlet on the outskirts of Winterswijk. Under the cover of night, Annie and Sini, a farm laborer, accepted the hospitality of a Gentile, Gerrit Jan Hannink, his wife, Johanna Derkje Overweel Hannink, and their daughter Dini, at Usselo, an agrarian crossroads offering little more than a church, school, bakeshop, and dry goods store. The migration was fraught with suspense. Sini peroxided her black hair and rode her bike to the Hanninks' farmstead. Annie cut her hair like a boy, dressed in a navy uniform, and posed as Jan de Wit for a bus ride to Enschede and a final pedal to Usselo.

Under Suspicion

The younger De Leeuw girls remained separate from Rachel and Ise from November 12, 1942, until 1943. The sisters learned from Miss Kleinhoonte of their mother's death and hasty burial. During calculated genocide of people unsuited to Hitler's master plan for a super race, German task forces combed the area for Jewish holdouts. On January 1, 1943, the investigations and interviews forced the De Leeuw sisters to the farmstead of Gerritdina "Dientje" and Johan Herman Oosterveld and his seventy-year-old mother, Mina Oosterveld, whom the girls called Opoe (granny). The family were respected citizens who had owned farmland for over a half century. For 36 months, Johanna and Sini slept in one room with the couple and cowered in a small, unheated niche while Nazis officers turned the lower floor into their local headquarters. By day, while Johan Oosterveld worked at the bleach plant in Boekelo, Sini helped Opoe repair socks. At night, the family huddled by the radio to listen to *Radio Oranje* to hear world news about the merger of Canada, France, England, Russia, and the United States against Germany and its allies, Italy and Japan. On February 2, the listeners celebrated the Russian defeat of the Germans at Stalingrad.

For extra security, Johann built a hiding place for the De Leeuws behind a closet shelf. Dientje borrowed a copy of Dostoevsky's *War and Peace* for the girls to read on boring afternoons. At Opoe's 71st birthday, she shared cake with the visitors. While storm troopers conducted a house-to-house hunt for a Jew who stole ration coupons in Enschede, Annie recited the alphabet backwards to control her panic. Because of heightened surveillance, outside exercise dwindled to walks to the dairy barn. On Dientje's bicycle, Annie visited Mimi among ten Jews in hiding. Brief treats included a game of Monopoly and, for Annie's 11th birthday, a copy of *Secrets of Nature*.

The End of Nazism

From an underground newspaper, Annie read about the death camps and corpse ovens in Austria, Germany, and Poland. Johan Oosterveld foresaw that Hitler's overthrow would require an Allied invasion of Europe. On July 9, 1943, the family heard on the radio that American and British forces were making a 2-day landing at Sicily. A week later, Italian Fascists jailed dictator Benito Mussolini, thus separating the Axis powers of Germany and Italy.

In fall 1943, Miss Kleinhoonte, while delivering textbooks to Annie, reported that Rachel was safe in hiding at the home of Reverend Slomp. Annie and Sini visited their older sister and shared a postcard from Sophie's brother, Uncle Phil, and from Grandmother De Leeuw. The handwritten message revealed the pair's transport by freight car to Poland, ostensibly for extermination and incineration in gas ovens that the girls read about in smuggled Resistance newspapers.

Increasingly the Oostervelds worried over dwindling finances, anticipation of a confrontation between local Nazis and the Allies, and the beginning of the De Leeuw sisters' third year in hiding. Johan loaded the girls into a wheelbarrow for an outing in the wheat field, where they were burned from basking too long in the sun. When Hitler's troops passed through Belgium into Holland, they conducted more searches and purloined goods and livestock. Because soldiers seized Annie's friend Mimi and nine other Jews, Johan executed the group's betrayer. Annie never learned Mimi's fate. Danger worsened after the Nazis began senseless torture and execution of hostages by the roadside.

Rescue at Last

On D-day, June 6, 1944, news of the Allied landing at Normandy, France, lifted hopes of rescue. By August 25, Paris was free of Nazi troops. On September 17, 1944, British paratroopers made drops for 9 days into Arnhem while the Allies freed parts of Holland. Hunger and the lack of fuel increased begging and homelessness. More Nazis headquartered their staff at the Oosterveld home. Johan walled off the remaining rooms and had the De Leeuw girls lighten their hair color and stay in bed to silence movements. A week later, the Germans decamped.

Heightened fears caused Dientje to press for new hiding places for the sisters. They migrated to the Hanninks' underground shelter. Ten days later, Johan returned for them. Hannink acquired forged papers identifying Annie's sister as Sini ten Broeke, a domestic from Arnhem. The Allies launched an offensive in Belgium. On February 22, 1945, Johan reported that the Canadian army was pressing into Holland. By early spring, the United States and Russia forced their way through German lines. On March 31, Annie hid in the air-raid shelter as planes bombed the bakery and parsonage to bits.

The arrival of Canadian soldiers on April 1 ended the standoff with a march through town toward Boekelo. The Oostervelds, Annie, and Sini emerged freely in public, where Sini climbed onto a Canadian tank. Annie swayed on stiff legs from 2 years and 7 months in the upstairs room. Neighbors proclaimed Johan a hero for keeping the girls safe. Before allowing the sisters to return home, he traveled to Winterswijk to determine the town's safety and to look for structural damage to their residence. By V-E day, May 7, 1945, the younger De Leeuw daughters reclaimed their home and spacious bedrooms, a contrast to their hiding place with the Oostervelds. The girls posted a notice in the square seeking the whereabouts of their father and older sister. Ise and Rachel resurfaced in town and reunited the family at a home where weeds had overtaken the garden. Bombs had reduced churches and inns to rubble. People lacked tires for their cars and bicycles and began recycling items that the Allied soldiers threw away. Annie recoiled from changes in her life—her sister Sini dating Canadian soldiers and relegating Annie's care to their father and older sister, Rachel becoming a Christian and nailing plaques of Bible verses on her bedroom wall, and Ise getting remarried. At times, Annie pretended to be living once more with Opoe, Johan, and Dientje.

Becoming an American

With a degree in elementary education, Johanna De Leeuw taught school before immigrating to the United States at age 23. After working as a governess and cheese cutter, she wed an American, James "Jim" Reiss, and gave birth to Julie H. and Kathy Reiss. While editing for a publishing house, she began writing to please her 7- and 9-year-old daughters, who were innocent of the turmoil that devastated their mother's childhood. At her husband's urging, in August 1969, she and the girls traveled to Holland to visit Dientje, Johan, and Opoe Oosterveld. Jim Reiss returned home early and committed suicide, leaving no note to explain his actions. The Reiss girls flourished—Julie as an art expert and Kathy as a school psychologist. Their children gave Annie a new kind of happiness as a grandmother.

In her role as witness to Nazism, Johanna De Leeuw Reiss produced classic historical works on the sufferings of families and children during the Holocaust. Reflections on World War II filled Reiss's young adult memoir, *The Upstairs Room* (1972), which begins with Hitler's rise to power and ends with peace in Europe and the De Leeuws back together again. Still eager to share more of her experience, she issued its sequel, *The Journey Back* (1976), and *That Fateful Night* (1988), the story of a flood. Her motivation was the residue of regret that tormented survivors and the difficulties of clothing and feeding families, treating the sick and traumatized, and reuniting with alienated neighbors and relatives. She recalled seeing people clustered around lists in the marketplace as they searched for the names of missing family members who never returned from camps at Auschwitz, Bergen-Belsen, Dachau, and Mauthausen. Some watched movies of the death camps and covered their eyes so as not to see the starvation, torture, and murder. Her personal struggles involved seeing her sisters leave home and acclimating to a snobbish stepmother who constantly found fault with Annie. Her re-creations reflected human fragility and the emotional trauma that required decades and generations to heal.

At Skidmore College in Saratoga Springs, New York, Reiss conducted symposia for the International Women's Writing Guild and tutored for the Fortune Society, a community outreach that informed the public on sources of crime, court justice, and prisons. While making library and classroom lectures and slide presentations, she earned $1,500 a day for book signings and speeches, which engaged audiences in Germany and Taiwan. While residing in New York City near her grown daughters, she counseled jail inmates and chaired the Prison Writing Program for Poets, Essayists, and Novelists. She made frequent visits to surviving family in Holland and, upon Johan Oosterveld's death in 1988, had "Onze Held" (Our Hero) carved on his tombstone.

Critics identified Reiss as a respected spokesperson for a generation of Jewish infants and youth whom Gentiles closeted from the Nazis during the late 1930s and early 1940s. Her reflective works earned the praise of Holocaust spokesman Dr. Elie Wiesel, a world peacemaker and humanities professor at Boston University. One critic for the *New York Times* compared *The Upstairs Room* to the *Diary of Anne Frank* (1952), Holland's most famous journal of childhood menace by Nazi invaders. Reiss's popular works dramatized wartime stress without bitterness or vengefulness. Her first memoir received notoriety as an American Library Association Notable Children's Book, a Jane Addams Peace Association Honor Book, the Jewish Book Council Charles and Bertie G. Schwartz Juvenile Book, and a Newbery Honor Book. She became the first American to earn the Buxtehuder Bulle, a German award for children's fiction, for the promotion of peace. Random House created a color filmstrip adaptation of the book. In 1998, Recorded Books produced an audiocassette version read by

Christina Moore. In 2008, Reiss issued a new installment, *A Hidden Life: A Memoir of August 1969*.

Sources

"Expletive Deleted." *School Library Journal* 21 (1) (September 1974): 48–49.

Fay, Mavoureen. "The Book Zone." *Scholastic Scope* 48 (3) (October 4, 1999): 5.

Gillespie, John T., and Corinne J. Naden. *The Newbery Companion*. Greenwood Village, CO: Libraries Unlimited, 2001.

Hearne, Betsy. *Choosing Books for Children: A Commonsense Guide*. Champaign, IL: University of Illinois Press, 1999.

Land-Weber, Ellen. *To Save a Life: Stories of Holocaust Rescue*. Champaign, IL: University of Illinois Press, 2000.

Reiss, Johanna. *The Upstairs Room*. New York: HarperTrophy, 1972.

Silvey, Anita, ed. *Children's Books and Their Creators*. New York: Houghton Mifflin, 1995.

Van Gorp, Hendrik. *Genres As Repositories of Cultural Memory*. Atlanta, GA: Rodopi, 2000.

■ Paraplegia
Ron Kovic

Antiwar activist Ronald L. "Ron" Kovic forced Americans to view his paraplegia as the true legacy of the Vietnam War. Born to Yugoslavian immigrants on July 4, 1946, in Ladysmith, Wisconsin, he came of age in Massapequa, New York, where his father clerked at an A&P grocery store. Ron's strong-willed mother reared their six children to follow conservative Catholic tenets. Both his parents, former members of the navy, and his uncles, all World War II veterans, recounted to the family the aims of America's "good war." Kovic, the eldest, grew up misinformed about the threat of communism and the glories of war. Secretly, he hoped that military heroism would spare him a boring job like his father's. He read Sergeant Rock comic books, played war with his pals, collected plastic green soldiers with bazookas and flamethrowers, and hero-worshipped actors Audie Murphy in *To Hell and Back* and John Wayne in *The Sands of Iwo Jima*. With macho zeal, in high school, Kovic wrestled, pole vaulted, and ran track and considered auditioning for a major league baseball team. He rooted for Mickey Mantle and the New York Yankees and wept during performances of the "Marines Hymn."

In September 1964, shortly after his 18th birthday, Kovic came under the spell of military recruiters at the high school. Mesmerized by their promise that "the Marine Corps built men—body, mind, and spirit," he signed up (Kovik, 2005, 74). After a silent drive with his father to the Long Island Rail Road station, Kovic took the oath at Whitehall Street and begin his first 2-year tour of duty. While completing a second voluntary tour in Vietnam in 1968, he earned a bronze star and a purple heart but shamed himself during a chaotic night battle by downing a young corporal from Georgia with unintentional friendly fire through the neck. The nighttime foray and destruction of a village resulted in the deaths of innocent women, children, infants and aged peasants. He identified with the soldiers involved in the My Lai Massacre and tried to punish himself for military atrocities.

Imprisoned on Wheels

Near the end of Sergeant Kovic's second voluntary tour, sniper fire ripped apart his right heel and ankle while he led an infantry platoon near the A Shau River Valley, a hotly contested part of the Ho Chi Minh Trail, south of the demilitarized zone. He continued to fight until a North Vietnamese army bullet tore through his flak jacket and into the right shoulder and lung during a firefight on January 20, 1968. He struggled to breathe as a tall black rescuer carried him through the fray to a foxhole. Medical evacuation personnel inserted IVs, loaded him aboard an Amtrac landing vehicle, and whisked him across the river to safety in a helicopter. At a hospital in Da Nang, a priest offered last rites and warned that the worst awaited him in recovery. Realizing he could never walk again or father children, Kovic felt betrayed by Hollywood's romanticized screen wars. He charged his injury to God's retaliation for past sins against the Vietnamese and reflected, "The score is evened up" (Kovic, 2005, 35).

The T4-6 spinal cord injury paralyzed Kovic's nervous system permanently from mid-chest down and condemned him to life in a wheelchair. In an intensive care ward among amputees and brain-damaged soldiers, he battled to survive and stay sane. On his return to the States, Governor Nelson Rockefeller issued a medal and citation from the state of New York for him; on February 14, Kovic's parents received praise from Lieutenant General Lewis William Walt for rearing a brave American. Out of combat, Kovic avoided photos and news footage of the war and dodged the vituperations of Americans angered by the southeast Asian conflict. Nightmares and flashbacks assaulted him with heart palpitations and anxiety attacks. Ironically, in late 1968, the year that the Congress passed the Architectural Barriers Act, his rehabilitation at a vermin-ridden neurological ward at St. Albans Naval Hospital in Queens worsened his sense of isolation. He and other paralyzed veterans spread crumbs on the floor to distract rats from chewing the men's toes.

From Warrior to Radical

To escape institutional routine, Kovac rifled shelves at the library on the hospital's first floor. As radicalism seized his imagination, he concealed his interest in revolutionary physician Che Guevara's diary. He chose philosopher Henry David Thoreau's essay *Civil Disobedience*, Alex Haley's *The Autobiography of Malcolm X*, comedian Dick Gregory's *Nigger: An Autobiography*, and Joseph Conrad's *Heart of Darkness*, the basis for the movie *Apocalypse Now*. Kovic grew bolder in selecting Vladimir Lenin's *State and Revolution*, *The Prison Poems of Ho Chi Minh*, and George Jackson's *Prison Letters*. Kovic was reading Senator Robert F. Kennedy's treatise *To Seek a Newer World* when the author was assassinated in Los Angeles at the Ambassador Hotel.

Feeling out of the action, Kovic sensed America's polarization by sit-ins at Columbia University, rebellious music at Woodstock, and the alternative radio station WBAI. On return home, Kovic lay on the living room sofa and recounted war memories to his mother. A former classmate who shirked the draft offered Kovic a job flipping hamburgers. On July 4, 1968, the city of Massapequa honored him with an ironic title—the grand marshal of the annual Independence Day parade. In 1969, Kovic broke a leg and ended his studies at Hofstra University. He extended his mobility by buying a hand-controlled car.

Champion of Democracy

Restless in captivity, Kovic was unprepared for rootlessness and emasculation. He channeled self-pity into liquor, hookers, apostasy, expatriation to Mexico, and dissent. Recruited by wheelchair-bound soldier Robert O. "Bobby" Muller, Kovic joined the Vietnam Veterans Against the War (VVAW) in the belief that the "war had not ended," remarking, "It was time for me to join forces with other vets" (Kovic, 2005). In 1969, at age 23, Kovic launched a crusade against violence at Levittown Memorial High School on Long Island. His youth and invalidism impressed teens and informed them about the perils of a gung-ho attitude based on clichés rather than reality. Modeling his campaign on the philosophy of Dr. Martin Luther King, Jr., Kovic asserted that silence was betrayal.

Kovic pushed his wheelchair at antiwar rallies, peace processions, and demonstrations. He addressed more high school groups and students of Hofstra University and pacifist Howard Zinn's classes at Brandeis University in Boston. Mixed in with patriotic pride and democratic zeal, he perceived survivor's guilt and a need for forgiveness. He incurred charges of betrayal, tapped phones, stalking by FBI infiltrators, police brutality, 12 arrests, and nights in jail, but he refused to think of himself as a victim. To arresting officers who wished he had died in Vietnam, Kovic twice identified his occupation as a "Vietnam veteran against the war" (Kovic, 2005)

While living at Redondo Beach, California, in 1970, Kovic relaxed with piano, painting, wheelchair basketball, and gardening but retained his eloquent disdain for war. He sold and auctioned some 1,000 paintings in Chicago, Los Angeles, and San Francisco to raise money for disabled veterans and the homeless, many of whom were former soldiers. He gained perspective on rhetoric from pacifist actor Donald Sutherland, who read from the war classic *Johnny Got His Gun*, by scenarist Dalton Trumbo. The film version of Trumbo's book and the National Guard's shooting of four students in a campus crowd on May 4, 1970, at Kent State University pressed Kovic into action.

On August 21, 1972, Kovic joined a convoy to Miami Beach, Florida, in company with 1,300 members of VVAW. In silence, they followed hand signals on a march in formation through a throng of some 10,000 picketers and protesters to the Fontainebleau Hotel. Kovic, Bob Muller, and Bill Wyman interrupted Richard M. Nixon's acceptance speech at the Republican National Convention with chants of "Stop the War" and "Stop the bombing." Kovic stated ardent personal convictions: "You have lied to us too long, you have burned too many babies. You may have taken our bodies, but you haven't taken our minds" (Lembcke, 1998, 101). A voice from the audience cheered, "Welcome home, Ronnie" (Boggs, 2003, 324).

After G. Gordon Liddy's crew dispatched secret service agents to escort Kovic and his buddies from the hall, news anchor Roger Mudd interviewed Kovic on CBS TV. The demonstration continued 3 days later when the VVAW left their camp at the municipal airport and processed in Gainesville for the arraignment of eight members of the Last Patrol. The men carried so much shrapnel in their wounds that metal detectors protested their entry into the courthouse. At Nixon's reelection headquarters in Los Angeles, a hostile crowd dumped Kovic from his chair and ripped his medals from his shirt.

At age 28, Kovic and a coterie of disabled, wheelchair-bound Vietnam Veterans held a 17-day hunger strike in Los Angeles at the office of U.S. Senator Alan Cranston. They sought a media airing of substandard conditions and medical care in veterans' hospitals. The men demanded respect for wounded soldiers and a congressional investigation of veterans' affairs. Following a conference with Donald E. Johnson, director of the Veterans Administration, the VVAW ended their demonstration. Within months, Johnson resigned; in 2006, the government renovated the Bronx hospital that caused Kovic's outrage.

A Nation's Conscience

Over 6 weeks in fall 1975, with the help of screenwriter Waldo Salt, Kovic composed a memoir, *Born on the Fourth of July* (1976), at his home in Santa Monica, California. Fearing that he would not survive to tell his story, without break, he pounded out his despair on a typewriter, filling the pages front and back with memories of a clash that kill 58,000 Americans and more than 2 million Vietnamese. He dedicated his life story to his country and its citizens. On July 15, 1976, in an address to the Democratic National Convention at Madison Square Garden, Kovic supported amnesty for draft evaders and spiritual redemption for the whole nation. He expanded his protests to nuclear power plants and CIA support of a corrupt regime in El Salvador.

When Kovic's book was published, the *New York Times* admired its candor and intimate testimony; the *Los Angeles Times* identified the author with American tragedy. Bruce Springsteen honored his experience with a ballad, "Shut Out the Light" (1998), and with the 1978 live performance of "Darkness on the Edge of Town" at Winterland in San Francisco. After meeting Kovic in Phoenix, Springsteen bought copies of his albums from Tower Records and left them at the door of Kovic's hotel room. A note read, "If this album can affect you half as much as your book affected me, then I will have done my job" (Kirkpatrick, 2006, 62). An anti-Vietnam War film romance, *Coming Home* (1978), starring Jane Fonda, Jon Voight, and Bruce Dern, drew on Kovic's trauma during posttrauma recovery and rehabilitation. Rather than run for office, Kovic chose direct confrontation of the American war culture with appearances at the 1988 Democratic Convention and on *Larry King Live*.

The cinema version of Kovic's autobiography, starring Tom Cruise, won a citation from the *New York Times* as one of the 1,000 all-time top movies. The shooting took place in the Philippines and in Dallas, Texas. To prepare, Cruise emulated Kovic's experiences maneuvering a wheelchair, dug a foxhole, and visited a boot camp and paralytics in veterans hospitals. When filming came to an end in early 1989, Kovic passed his bronze star to Cruise for recreating combat terrors. Disabled people and veterans lauded the film for its honesty. Kovic won applause at the Berlin Film Festival and a Golden Globe for the screenplay, and the film won eight Oscar nominations, including one for Cruise and one for the adaptation, coauthored by Oliver Stone, himself a Vietnam vet. Documentarian Loretta Smith echoed Stone's themes in *A Good American: The Ron Kovic Story* (1989). In July 2000, on the 10th anniversary of the Americans with Disabilities Act, he exhorted the Coalition for a Santa Monica Disabilities Commission to refuse a return to past apathy. The pace of his harangues sapped his strength but gave his zeal no rest.

Age and Idealism

In 2002, while Kovic received a medical checkup, he learned that potential cutbacks might force Iraq War casualties into the same miasma that had threatened his will to live. He expanded his hatred of combat to defiance of the George W. Bush administration and denunciation of the recklessness that prolonged aggression. On October 6, 2002, he led marchers on a foray against the Army Reserve Center in Santa Monica, California. Through a bullhorn, he rallied University of Californa at Los Angeles students to honor democracy and challenged the National Guard to embrace peace. On October 26, he took his protest to San Francisco to urge nonviolent revolt against American imperialism.

News anchor Wolf Blitzer of CNN TV questioned Kovic's patriotism and his intent to promote a citizens' march in San Francisco, Los Angeles, London, Paris, and the nation's capital on January 18, 2003. A month later, Kovic rejoiced that over 30 million citizens in over 100 nations banded for a global protest. He rolled through rain to invigorate a crowd with his memories of men and women forever diminished by war. In November 2003, he protested at Trafalgar Square and joined British pacifists at London's city hall to raise public consciousness of human costs of the Middle Eastern conflict. Still vehement in March 2005, he penned a new introduction to *Born on the Fourth of July* with a reminder to readers that "Life is so precious" (Kovic, 2005, 25). At age 60, he described his sleep as wracked by physical suffering. In March 2007, he required further treatment at the Ernst Bors Spinal Cord Injury ward of the Veterans Administration Hospital in Long Beach, California.

Sources

Anderegg, Michael A. *Inventing Vietnam: The War in Film and Television*. Philadelphia: Temple University Press, 1991.

Boggs, Carl. *Masters of War: Militarism and Blowback in the Era of American Empire*. New York: Routledge, 2003.

De Leon, David. *Leaders from the 1960s: A Biographical Sourcebook of American Activism*. Westport, CT: Greenwood, 1994.

Hunt, Andrew E. *The Turning: A History of Vietnam Veterans Against the War*. Albany, NY: New York University Press, 1999.

Kirkpatrick, Rob. *The Words and Music of Bruce Springsteen*. Westport, CT: Greenwood, 2006.

Kovic, Ron. *Born on the Fourth of July*. Second edition. New York: Akashic Books, 2005.

Lembcke, Jerry. *The Spitting Image: Myth, Memory and the Legacy of Vietnam*. Albany, NY: New York University Press, 1998.

■ Parkinson's Disease
Michael J. Fox

During a battle with Parkinson's disease, actor Michael J. "Mike" Fox directed his notoriety toward research and treatment. A native of Edmonton, Alberta, he was named Michael Andrew Fox at birth on June 9, 1961. The jobs of his parents, actor Phyllis Piper Fox and Royal Canadian Army Signal Corps cryptographer William "Bill" Fox, required frequent moves to new posts for their army brat children—Mike, Karen, Steven, Jackie, and Kelli. Mike spent toddlerhood in Permanent Married Quarters at Chilliwack Army Base near the Fraser River in British Columbia, where he tested boundaries by edging out of his mother's sight.

Fox was ambivalent about his future. He fantasized about a career with the National Hockey League and netted his share of chipped teeth and facial stitches crashing into larger skaters. He gravitated toward garage band guitar, cartooning and sketching, and creative writing, which had absorbed him from age 5. In 1971, Bill retired to Burnaby outside Vancouver, where the family had roots. Over a marathon of reunions, barbecues, and homecomings, family members became Mike's closest friends.

The Future on Stage

Fox embraced theater under Ross Jones, a junior high teacher who introduced him to drama. Fox's parents attended his performances in plays and rock concerts, but Bill demanded a pragmatic approach toward investing self and equipment in unremunerative work. At age 11, Mike suffered a setback after the death of Nana Jenny Piper, a maternal grandmother who understood and protected him. He called her adoration "a posthumous gift, an emotional trust fund" (Fox, 2002, 51). His mother mediated the contretemps with Bill in summer 1976 by landing Mike a job as office help at a cold storage plant on the docks. While attending Burnaby South Secondary School, he debuted on television as the character Jamie in 13 episodes of the Canadian Broadcasting Company sitcom *Leo and Me* (1976). For 3 years, he acted in local theatricals and found bit parts with American casts on location in Canada.

On April 18, 1979, Fox left Canada with Bill and drove to Los Angeles to seek a movie career. Producer Ronald Shedlo introduced Fox in the teleplay *Letters from Frank*

(1979), in which he played Jamie Miller, Jr. While registering with the Screen Actors Guild, Mike had to lengthen his name to distinguish himself from another performer. Honoring actor Michael J. Pollard, Mike chose Michael J. Fox. He curried exposure as a guest on *Lou Grant* (1979), *Family* (1980), *Trapper John, M.D.* (1981), *Love Boat* (1983), and *Night Court* (1984). He played Scot Larson in the Walt Disney feature *Midnight Madness* (1980), Willy Joe Hall in the TV series *Palmerstown, U.S.A.* (1980–1981), and Arthur Summers in *Class of 1984* (1982). In addition, he shot ads for McDonald's restaurants and Tilex bathroom cleaner. Overwork forced him to depend on alcohol for weekend respites. He shared down time with his girlfriend Diane, whom he had known from age 12.

Early Fame and Excess

Fox won a Golden Globe and three Emmys for playing Alex P. Keaton, a pompous Republican teen in the TV series *Family Ties* (1982–1989). The persona earned him a Golden Globe and three Emmys and enough cash to buy a Nissan 300 ZX and a home in Laurel Canyon. Simultaneously, he played the part of Jay-Jay Manners in the sitcom *High School U.S.A.* (1983) and as Dennis Baxter in the TV vehicle *Poison Ivy* (1985) while driving the 1,200-mile trip to Vancouver during vacations to visit his folks. In 1997, *TV Guide* immortalized one episode of *Family Ties*, "A—My Name Is Alex," as one of the best in the history of television for its depiction of emotional disburdening during a counseling session. Two years later, the magazine staff named the Alex character one of the medium's 50 best creations.

Fox scored as the foam rubber-padded, yak-haired star of *Teen Wolf* (1985) and amassed fans for the part of the skirt-chasing time tripper Marty McFly in Steven Spielberg's *Back to the Future*, which introduced time travel in a remodeled DeLorean. The smash hit trilogy began in 1985, was reprised in 1989, and concluded in 1990. Fox saw the footage for the first time in a London theater, where he boosted public interest. He found himself rich, adored in print, and mobbed in public. He guested on Johnny Carson's *The Tonight Show*; his name filled headlines in *Bop*, *Gentleman's Quarterly*, *National Enquirer*, *People*, *Playgirl*, *Rolling Stone*, *Star*, *TV Guide*, and *Us*. He confessed, "Gnawing at you always is the deep-seated belief that you're a fake, a phony" (Fox, 2002, 16). He invested in Las Vegas real estate with fighter Sugar Ray Leonard and flew on Leonard's jet. Fox described casual Hollywood friendships as the "I'm famous, you're famous club" (Ibid., 112). On one journey home in early January 1990, he shared with sister Jackie the grief of Bill's death from heart disease and kidney arrest. Other trips took him to hospitals for Make-a-Wish, Starlight, and charities supporting kids with cancer, cystic fibrosis, diabetes, and leukemia. He admired young patients who faced with dignity pain and limited life spans.

After filming *The Light of Day* (1987), Fox managed the dual role of Brantley Foster and Carlton Whitfield in *The Secret of My Success* (1988). He overindulged in local beer while collaborating with Sean Penn on location in Phuket, Thailand, for Brian De Palma's Vietnam War film, *Casualties of War* (1988). New York-born actor Tracy Pollan, whom Fox met while shooting *Bright Lights, Big City* (1988), visited him on the set. On July 16, 1988, at West Mountain Inn in Arlington, Vermont, the couple married. He credited Tracy with the success of *Family Ties*, on which she played the sophisticated love interest. While portraying Dr. Ben Stone during filming of *Doc Hollywood* (1991) in Gainesville, Florida, he drank heavily with pal Woody Harrelson. The two sparred in mock bar brawls that sometimes injured Fox.

Signs of Disaster

One night after Fox's bodyguard Dennis hustled him back to the University Hotel's presidential suite from a bout of pub crawling, Fox writhed with a hangover. He began noticing twitches in his little finger, a symptom of neurological malfunction that spread over his left hand and up the arm. At the top of his game, Fox admitted, "I woke up to find the message in my left hand. . . . My hand held nothing at all. The trembling was the message" (Fox, 2002, 1). The candid admission became the opening line of his bestselling autobiography, *Lucky Me: A Memoir* (2002). Lying to himself about fatigue and injury during a stunt, he feared the onset of delirium tremens and flexed his hands to stop the spasms. He avoided the truth by reducing beer intake, jogging along the shore, and retreating into family contentment. At their home at Martha's Vineyard, Massachusetts, on Menemsha Pond, he grappled with horseshoe crabs while son Sam bird-watched for osprey and learned to bike on Lobsterville Road. As though grasping the status quo, Fox cherished "the warm paternal satisfaction" he'd felt pointing out to Sam the various wonders of a Vineyard morning (Fox, 2002, 25).

At age 30, the actor realized the limitations on his career from a diagnosis of Parkinson's disease (PD), marked by garbled speech, swallowing problems, and unilateral palsy, exaggerated gestures, numbness, and rigid limbs. He tended to converge his left thumb with four fingers into a tent. A diagnostician in Manhattan described the anomaly as the early onset of a progressive and incurable degeneration of bodily control. There was no set timetable for advancing debility. Fox dreaded returning home to share the prognosis with Tracy. In December 1993, he sought professional counseling in New Haven, Connecticut.

Persistence

Fox continued performing in *For Love or Money* (1993), playing the title role in *Life With Mikey* (1993), collaborating with director Woody Allen in *Don't Drink the Water* (1994), and filming the satire *Mars Attacks!* (1996). His first adult role as political adviser Lewis Rothschild in *The American President* (1995) presaged similar characterizations in the hit TV series *The West Wing*. He ended his cinema career with *The Frighteners* (1996). In 1996, he performed a second time as a savvy politico, Deputy Mayor Mike Flaherty, in the New York City government spoof *Spin City* (1996–2002). The part earned him three Golden Globes, an Emmy and three Emmy nominations, two Screen Actors Guild citations, a People's Choice Award, and a Man of the Year Award from *Gentleman's Quarterly*.

The demands of a weekly series proved too demanding for Fox's decline from PD. After 7 years of treatment by Boston neurologist Allan Ropper, author of *Principles of Neurology*, Fox hoped for at least a decade of semicontrol of motor system disorders. He chose to beat the tabloids to the news. To reporter Todd Gold of *People* magazine, Fox went public about his advancing impairment. According to author Morton Kondracke, the shocking news "changed the landscape both politically and psychologically" (Kondracke, 227). Treatment required the cautious intake of the drug L-dopa and brain surgery—a thalamotomy—under the knife of neurosurgeon Bruce Cook in North Andover, Massachusetts, in March 1998. To prepare, Cook videotaped Fox without medication and on Sinemet to determine the need for intervention on the less dominant right side of the brain to remove a small lesion from the substantia nigra. Cook typified the seizures as quite severe and explained that disabling the nerve endings in the thalamus responsible for spasms was an effective method of restoring quality of life.

The operation required immobilizing Fox's shaved head with an aluminum frame for study of neuron messages under magnetic resonance imaging, then bolting the apparatus to the operating table. He entered the procedure under liquid Valium and remained conscious to answer questions about the location of the defective cells, which Cook obliterated with an electrode. The next month, while Fox recuperated in Anguilla, he discovered that the tremor had migrated from his left hand to the right. Realizing that he had half cured the spasms, he felt sad for himself and his family, but he clung to the belief that "a cure for Parkinson's disease is very close" (Kondracke, 2001, xvii).

From Actor to Activist

A 4-year sting playing Mike Flaherty and co-producing *Spin City* (1996–2000) reaped three more Golden Globes, two Screen Actors Guild Awards, a second Emmy, and, in 2000, a star on Canada's Allée des Célébrités (Walk of Fame) on King Street in Toronto. At the Republican National Convention in Philadelphia in August 2000, Fox posed at a reception alongside another PD victim, retired boxer Muhammad Ali. To demonstrate the crippling effects of PD, in February 2001, Fox went off Sinemet previous to testifying before the Senate Appropriations Subcommittee on behalf of the Parkinson's Action Network. He pressed the urgency of research: "For two years, you have had a parade of witnesses—scientists, ethicists, theologians of every school, and some celebrities—discussing every nuance of stem cell research. . . . I can't help but say, respectfully, 'Enough!'" (Solo and Pressberg, 2006, 68).

At age 39, Fox abandoned full-time acting. He soldiered on with a guest appearance as the twitchy Dr. Kevin Casey on *Scrubs* (2004) and as Daniel Post, a victim of terminal lung cancer in five episodes of *Boston Legal* (2006). The part won him an Emmy nomination. While rearing his four children—Sam Michael, twins Aquinnah Kathleen and Schuyler Frances, and Esmé Annabelle—he enhanced his reputation for professional excellence, taste, and taping voice-overs for the title character of E. B. White's classic children's story *Stuart Little* (1999) and its 2002 and 2006 sequels and for Chance in the production of Sheila Burnside's novel *Homeward Bound: The Incredible Journey* (1993) and *Homeward Bound II: Lost in San Francisco* (1996). He provided subsequent spoken parts as Milo James Thatch in *Atlantis: The Lost Empire* (2001) and as Marcel Maggot in *The Magic 7* (2006). Still vibrant in public, in 2006, Fox cheered the Detroit Tigers at all five World Series games.

The actor devoted himself to medical advocacy. In 2000, he established the Michael J. Fox Foundation for Parkinson's Research in New York City to raise and distribute funds. Over a decade of concentrated effort and the investment of $1.2 million, he pledged to locate promising clinicians and to explore holistic and multidisciplinary embryonic stem cell projects for insights into multiple catastrophic diseases. He intended to shorten the time between experimental cures and relief of individual patient sufferings. Still confident before the camera, he spoke on *Dateline NBC*, *Inside the Actors Studio*, *Biography*, *E! True Hollywood Story*, *Larry King Live*, three episodes of *Late Night with Conan O'Brien*, and four episodes of *Late Show with David Letterman*. On *Good Morning America* on July 18, 2006, he lobbied for expanded National Institutes of Health funding by enactment of the Stem Cell Research Enhancement Act, which President George W. Bush vetoed. *The New York Times* published an editorial contrasting Bush's adamance with the vision of Al Gore. To ensure the election of more visionaries who validated groundbreaking solutions to Parkinson's disease, Fox endorsed Tammy Duckworth for the Illinois legislature, Jim Doyle for governor of Wisconsin, Chet Culver for governor of Iowa, Virginian James Webb, Sherrod Brown of

Ohio, Missourian Claire McCaskill, Ben Cardin of Maryland, and Senator Bob Menendez of New Jersey for the U.S. legislature. The mockery of talk show maven Rush Limbaugh toward Fox's tremors raised an anti-Rush clamor. Fox graciously refused to rise to the bait. To news anchor Katie Couric, he asserted the right of victims to political support for advanced medical cures. Echoing his hope were actors Mary Tyler Moore and Christopher Reeve and former First Lady Nancy Reagan. In a plea to conservative forces, Fox demanded to know "why it is more pro-life to throw away stem cells than to put them to work saving lives" (Fox, 2002, 218).

Sources

Ebadi, Manuchair S., and Ronald F. Pfeiffer. *Parkinson's Disease*. New York: CRC Press, 2005.
Fox, Michael J. "A Crucial Election for Medical Research." In *The Future Is Now: American Confronts the New Genetics*, ed. by William Kristol and Eric Cohen. Lanham, MD: Rowan & Littlefield, 2002.
———. *Lucky Man: A Memoir*. New York: Hyperion, 2002.
Kondracke, Morton. *Saving Milly: Love, Politics, and Parkinson's Disease*. New York: Perseus, 2001.
Solo, Pam, and Gail Pressberg. *The Promise and Politics of Stem Cell Research*. Westport, CT: Greenwood, 2006.

■ Police Brutality
Dolores Huerta

A spirited feminist and labor activist, Dolores Fernández Huerta survived crippling from battering by police to continue plotting union strategy for day laborers. A scion of 17th-century New Mexicans and native of Dawson, New Mexico, she was born on April 10, 1930, and brought up Catholic. Her maternal grandfather, Herculano Chávez, and uncle, Marcial Chávez, were trapped in a mining accident. Herculano was permanently disabled; Marcial died. Her father, Juan Fernández, a miner and labor activist, traveled the migrant route from the Southwest to Wyoming. After her parents split up in 1933, Juan remained behind while his ex-wife, Alicia Fernández Chávez, a cannery worker and restaurant waiter and cook, reared her daughter and sons, John and Marshall, first in Las Vegas, then in the San Joaquin Valley at Stockton, California.

The birth of Dolores's two sisters deepened the family's need during the Depression years. Herculano tended his five grandchildren while Alicia and her second husband, James Richards, invested in a lunch counter, restaurant, and two hotels. Alicia exhibited concern for laborers by offering free housing to migrant harvesters. In 1938, Juan made a separate impact on Dolores by winning election to the New Mexico legislature. The Huerta family occupied rooms in one of the properties, the Richards Hotel, which a Japanese couple vacated in 1942 when the U.S. government lodged them in a concentration camp. Alicia's children learned inn keeping, cleaning, and laundry, but they enjoyed evenings off at their mother's insistence to attend plays and symphonies.

In summers, Dolores worked in fields and packing sheds. As Dolores progressed from Lafayette Elementary School to Jackson Junior High, Alicia supported her appearances as a majorette in local parades and encouraged Dolores to enter Girl Scouts. Because she envisioned herself as a flamenco dancer rather than a hotel drudge like her mother, Alicia paid for dance, piano, and violin lessons for Dolores. The girls in her troop came from black,

Caucasian, Chinese, Filipino, Hispanic, Japanese, and Jewish families. Throughout World War II, Dolores followed the model of community outreach by raising money for the USO.

Racism in California

Despite her family's greatheartedness and service orientation, Huerta experienced bias against Latinos. On August 15, 1945, a mob battered her brother Marshall and reduced his new suit to ribbons during Stockton's "Victory over Japan" Day celebration. Huerta won second place in a scouting essay competition but couldn't take the winner's trip to the Hopi Indian Reservation in Gallup, New Mexico, because a prejudiced dean of girls at her school refused permission. In 1947, when Dolores completed Stockton High School, she left embittered by another anti-Latino gesture. After earning top marks in English, she received a C for the course because the teacher suspected Dolores of turning in work written by others. The underlying message asserted that Latinas were incapable of excellence.

Huerta developed speaking skills from childhood and honed them for the classroom while earning a teaching degree. She married classmate Ralph Head in 1948 and bore daughters Celeste and Lori while studying at Stockton Junior College and the College of the Pacific. In her second marriage, she adopted the surname of her husband, activist Ventura Huerta. The first of her clan to earn a degree, Huerta taught English in elementary school. The profession offered her new perspectives on indigent workers, whose children arrived to class barefoot and undernourished. The daily sufferings of the underclass compelled her to become a union organizer for stoop laborers. At age 25, she cofounded a local division of the Community Service Organization (CSO), a Chicano civil rights effort, and lobbied in Sacramento on behalf of California's farm pickers and packers. Alicia promoted the effort by volunteering her own experience with uplifting the poor.

A Female Powerhouse

Huerta began making news as the driving force of the Agricultural Workers Association, which she established in 1960. Before the feminist and civil rights movements, she expressed herself forcefully in public and familiarized herself with power wielders in Sacramento and Washington, D.C. She demanded clean drinking water, toilets, rest periods, and the right of peaceful assembly for workers. A year later, her first triumph legitimized the demand for pensions, public assistance, surplus commodities, and disability insurance for undocumented workers. A second push toward empowering Hispanics required driver's license exams, federal pamphlets, voter information, and ballots to be offered in Spanish. In 1962, she fought the exploitive Bracero Program, a trans-Rio Grande partnership contracting workers like press gangs. A year later, she engineered the extension of Aid for Dependent Families to part-time and out of work laborers.

Influencing Huerta during her 30s were two mentors, Fred Ross, founder of the CSO, and labor hero César Estrada Chávez, a Southwestern icon of nonviolent mediation. Ross recruited Chávez and Huerta and taught them to plan protests and to engage in collective bargaining and civil disobedience to end segregation and brutality by landowners and police, who routinely beat up Mexicans. The trio built a community consensus on the need for public services for nonwhite Californians. They mobilized a voter registration drive of 150,000 Mexican-Americans to elect Ed Roybal, a Los Angeles City councilman and the first Latino to succeed by ballot in over a century. Over a 30-year period, Huerta and Chávez collaborated to establish the Farm Workers Credit Union, the Juan De La Cruz Farm Workers Pension Fund, the Robert Kennedy Medical Plan, the Spanish language Radio Campesina throughout the Southwest and Washington State, and the National Farm Workers Service Center, a source of 4,300 affordable residences. Reporting their advances was an in-house newspaper, *El Malcriado*.

Toward One Big Union

Chávez and Huerta resigned from the CSO to work toward the National Farm Workers Association (NFWA), a union of 1,700 families. A divorced mother, Huerta lived on $20 a month and drove her family in a failing jalopy to Delano, California, to become what she modestly termed a "trouble-shooter in the union" (Huerta, 1981, 215). She noted the hardships of single parenthood: "Any help I get from my two exes has to go for grub for my seven little hungry mouths" (Chávez, 2005, 246). She joined Chávez and Philip Vera Cruz, Filipino-American labor leader and International Workers of the World member, in 18-hour days campaigning for worker solidarity in fields, orchards, labor camps, and produce-loading docks throughout the San Joaquin Valley. Huerta's schedule juggled strategizing and platform speeches around door-to-door canvassing and house meetings in Acampo, Linden, Lodi, Manteca, Victor, and Woodbridge. Her crusade for raises for dollar-a-day laborers incurred vandalism, verbal abuse from growers, and death threats. The effort preceded a world first for migrant labor, the inauguration of the United Farm Workers Union (UFW).

On September 8, 1965, when Filipino vineyard workers walked off their Delano jobs, Huerta began shaping a crucial stage of American labor history. Eight days later, 5,000 members of the NFWA joined the strike. For the next 5 years, she and Chávez led a table grape boycott in defiance of a court injunction. In the background, Huerta got automobile insurance for union members and access to the Kern County hospital for Mexicans and persuaded the Department of Motor Vehicles to reinstate drivers. In late March 1966, 250 workers, armed with banners proclaiming "*Huelga*" (strike) and "*Viva La Causa*" (long live our cause), marched toward Sacramento 340 miles away. The procession ended on Easter, April 10, when disgruntled workers thrust "*la causa*" in the faces of state legislators. The aim of concerted action was a four-prong workplace upgrading to raise wages, end management abuses, secure health insurance, and shield workers from pesticides. Within months, Huerta mediated differences to secure a binding settlement with the Schenley Wine Company, the first contract negotiated by a Latina and mixed-race farm laborers. During deliberations, she stood firm against racist and sexist insinuations.

Over the next 3 years of the grape strike, Huerta aided the merger of the AWA and the NFWA into the United Farm Workers Organizing Committee (UFWOC). To land more contracts from agribusiness favoring the working class, she formed ranch committees, staffed hiring halls, trained unionists in leading demonstrations and work slow-downs and field strikes, and settled one hundred grievances. In addition, she fostered women's self-determination and cocreated Teatro Campesino, a cultural outlet for Hispanic performers. While Governor Ronald Reagan munched grapes publicly to thwart union efforts, she moved to New York City to coordinate an industrywide consumer boycott that dropped consumption by nearly one-quarter. Her accomplishments buttressed the underclass with safety protocols and medical and pension plans for *los viejitos* (the elderly). The benefits rescued agrarian workers from medieval conditions that kept them poor, ignorant, and vulnerable to disease and job mishaps. Simultaneously, Huerta alerted the media to an emerging issue, the endangerment of laborers, consumers, and air, soil, and water from such toxic chemicals as DDT and Parathyon. The death threats burgeoned after the John Birch Society began pressing for white Americans to deport Chicanos. Her poise and visibility during the 1968 California Democratic Presidential Primary and the boycotts of 10,000 in Bud Antle lettuce fields and the Gallo vineyards earned the regard of Senator Robert F. Kennedy of New York. In celebration, Joan Baez sang a tribute to workers at Fiesta Campesina.

In 1970, the efforts of Chávez and Huerta produced a breakthrough with the Freedman Ranches, the first contract between harvesters and megafarm owners. She exulted, "It never, ever, ever, ever crossed my mind that it couldn't happen" (Chávez, 2005, 248). However, the battle heightened from a conservative backlash against the UFW's "dragon lady" (Ibid.). When the first settlement expired in 1973, the imbroglio between pickers and growers went to court after teamster Jimmy Hoffa signed a "sweetheart deal" with farm owners. A revered egalitarian, Dorothy Day, founder of the Catholic Workers Movement, supported Huerta's direction of 3,000 picketers and lobbyists. In a heated atmosphere, police struck and shot dissidents, killing two and jailing thousands, including Chávez. In February 1975, Huerta responded by expanding work stoppages and consumer boycotts of the Gallo wines produced on seven family estates at Healdsburg in Sonoma County, California. In 1975, the California legislature passed the Agricultural Labor Relations Act, a precedent in labor law allowing farm workers to unionize and negotiate for fair wages and clean, safe working conditions.

Reprisals

Down and dirty dealings set the tone of the early 1980s. On September 21, 1983, Rene Lopez, an employee of Sikkema Dairy in Fresno, California, was assassinated for his vote in union election. The conspiracy outraged union adherents and boosted unity. Because growers conspired with Republican Governor George Deukmejian in 1984 to suppress worker civil rights, laborers faced job loss, blacklisting, and fear of retaliation. In 1985 Huerta denounced the federal guest worker system and demanded amnesty for 1,400,000 illegal migrants on the grounds of their faithful citizenship and contributions to the U.S. economy through labor and taxes. The drive resulted in the Immigration Act of 1985.

The mid- to late 1980s put Chávez and Huerta in more danger. In 1986, the UFW launched another grape boycott. On September 14, 1988, during demonstrations against Vice President George H. W. Bush, Huerta bore the UFW banner and distributed news updates on the grape boycott while Bush attended a dinner party at the Sir Francis Drake Hotel to raise funds for his presidential campaign. In Union Square outside the hotel, a tactical squad of the San Francisco police bludgeoned the 5-foot tall leader in the head, damaged her spleen, and broke six ribs. Video footage captured the assault while Huerta cowered and raised her arms against official nightsticks. Her son Emilio reported, "She was speared and stabbed to where her spleen was shattered" ("Family," 1988). Huerta's sidelining for emergency surgery at San Francisco General Hospital launched a worker outcry against police for beating a nonviolent protester and for hushing up the assault. Unionists vilified Mayor Art Agnos and Police Chief Frank Jordan for exonerating her attacker 3 days later.

Unbowed by Adversity

While Huerta recuperated, she won a lawsuit against the police for $825,000 on grounds of lethal crowd-control methods by SWAT teams. Meanwhile, Chávez began a 5-week fast in sympathy with workers poisoned by toxic dust and spray. With Reverend Jesse Jackson, performers Whoopi Goldberg and Carly Simon, and actors Edward James Olmos and Martin Sheen, Huerta protested cyclical pesticide use that threatened women breastfeeding their babies while they cultivated and picked beans, lettuce, onions, and strawberries. On return to action, she took a stand against police terrorism: "By doing whatever causes your anxiety, you overcome the fear and strengthen your emotional, spiritual, activist muscles" (Chávez, 2005, 240).

After Huerta married Richard Chávez and bore son Ricky and daughters Camilla, Juanita, and María Elena, her family shared the privations of migrants. Following Cesar Chávez's death in 1993, Huerta remained at the task of organizing farm workers and earned election to the National Women's Hall of Fame. She taught grassroots organizing at the University of Southern California and promoted gender equity through the Feminist Majority Foundation. A proud moment was the graduation of her oldest son from medical school as a result of affirmative action policies. As chair of the Dolores Huerta Foundation, she traveled the continent to raise horizons for women, nonwhites, and immigrants. Her selflessness earned an Outstanding Labor Leader Award from the California Senate, an American Civil Liberties Union Roger Baldwin Medal of Liberty award, a Consumers' Union Trumpeter's Award, an Ellis Island Medal of Freedom Award, and a Eugene V. Debs Foundation Outstanding American Award. She accepted six honorary doctorates from universities in California, Illinois, and New York. With a $100,000 grant from the Puffin Foundation/Nation Institute Award for Creative Citizenship, she opened the Dolores Huerta Foundation's Organizing Institute, an underclass leadership training center. *Ms.* magazine named her "Woman of the Year 1998"; *Ladies Home Journal* placed her among the "100 Most Important Women of the 20th Century."

Sources

Blee, Kathleen M. *No Middle Ground: Women and Radical Protest*. New York: New York University Press, 1998.

Chávez, Alicia. "Dolores Huerta and the United Farm Workers." In *Latina Legacies: Identity, Biography, and Community*, ed. by Vicki Ruiz and Virginia Sanchez Korrol. Oxford: Oxford University Press, 2005.

"Family Decries the Beating of a Union Leader." *New York Times*, September 16, 1988.

Huerta, Dolores. "Un Soldado del Movimiento." In *With These Hands: Women Working on the Land*, ed. by Joan M. Jensen. New York: Feminist Press, 1981.

Polio
Dianne O'Dell

A model of survivalism, Dianne O'Dell was the oldest polio victim to inhabit an iron lung. Born February 13, 1947, in Jackson between Memphis and Nashville, Tennessee, she fell victim to bulbospinal poliomyelitis at age 3. The upsurge in polio worldwide after World War II burgeoned in parts of the United States, in England and Wales, and into New Zealand, the South Pacific, and the Nicobar Islands of India. The elusive infection, spread by enterovirus in body wastes contaminating food or water, comprises 19 percent of paralytic cases. It begins with lung and throat infection, fever, nausea, and flu-like malaise and aches. Unlike spinal polio and bulbar polio, the complex viral contagion inflames the central nervous system in the spinal cord and destroys motor neurons above the cerebellum in the bulbar section of the brain. The result is atrophied muscles, paralysis of tongue and throat, stiff neck and immobile jaws, seizures, coronary complications, suffocation from a nonfunctioning diaphragm and swallowing muscles, and weakness. Victims tend to die from pneumonia from the inability to cough. More commonly in infants, patients succumb to encephalitis, an infection of brain tissue.

For Dianne O'Dell, polio struck in June 1950, a year before Jonas Salk, backed by the National Foundation for Infantile Paralysis, invented a polio vaccine. In a period that saw 20,000 new cases in the United States, the disease produced a pandemic farther south in San Angelo, Texas, where 420 patients required treatment and rehabilitation. Dianne woke in the night suffering from sore throat, head pain, fever, and throbbing legs. When her fever continued to rise, the initial diagnosis of strep throat proved wrong. Her 32-year-old mother, Geneva O'Dell, suspected the worst: "Children were being paralyzed and dying all over. It was a scary time" (Alligood, 2007). The next day, a spinal tap identified the poliovirus. Paralysis of her lungs and diaphragm required her removal to an isolation ward and encasement in a vacuum produced by a body-sheathing respirator. The pressurized chamber pumped air in and out of her immobile torso.

Attending Dianne was pediatrician Walton Harrison, Jr., a child advocate and civil rights champion who integrated the Jackson Children's Clinic in 1952. Of her lethal infection, he stated, "I didn't think she would last through puberty because her lung capacity was so limited" (Poovey, 2002). To the family, Harrison predicted that their 3-year-old could not long survive. He urged Dianne's father, Freeman O'Dell, an employee of the telephone company, not to touch his daughter lest he carry the infection back to his family. The directive prefaced a father–daughter relationship deprived of close contact with her torso and extremities. Her memories of normality dwindled to a walk to a ballgame, riding on a train, and playing in the mud.

Home Health Care

Sixteen months into Dianne's treatment and rehabilitation, Freeman O'Dell and his wife opted to return their daughter home in her "yellow submarine" iron lung. With the help of visiting nurses, Dianne avoided bed sores and always had someone nearby to bathe her, spoon in snacks, brush her hair, and scratch her nose. Geneva made a special effort to create holidays, girly sleepovers, and vacations at home with Dianne and her two younger sisters, Donna and Mary. Of past Halloweens, Dianne recalled, "I was a package of Lifesavers one year. I was a yellow submarine one year, and once I was a spaceship" (Baird, 1991, 16). Dianne accepted the possibility of dying young. She later gave thanks for quality home care: "I think God just looked at me and said, 'She is going to have a rough time. I better pick good parents'" (Poovey, 2002).

In constant pain from tissue atrophy, twisted spine, inflammation, and easily dislocated joints, Dianne reclined on her back in the metal cocoon, a 7-foot, 750-pound Emerson iron lung designed by Philip Drinker and Louis Agassiz Shaw. They invented the device in 1928 at Harvard for life sustenance of underground miners poisoned by lethal gas. The manager of a Pittsburgh ventilator factory acknowledged that only about 75 to 100 iron lungs still breathe for patients, some only part-time. Around thirty polio victims still require the mechanical stimulus to lung function. Ventilated by negative and positive pressure, a noninvasive bellows-like therapy that mimics human breathing, Dianne was able to speak on the machine's exhale function in a high-pitched tone. For auxiliary electricity in case of power outage, Freeman installed a backup generator in a separate building and sat up nights with Dianne when problems arose in the iron lung's function.

A Long-Term Prisoner

Sealed in for life, Dianne communicated with the outside world through a mirror angled from her face. In addition to doctors, nurses, and family, she welcomed visitors from her church and neighborhood. To the curious, she summarized her condition: "Even though I am paralyzed, I still have complete feeling in my body. Only the muscles are paralyzed, not the nerves. It is ironic that with polio the mind continues to grow and develop, even as the body weakens" ("Nation's," 2007). Leon Alligood, a reporter for the *Chicago Sun-Times*, described her environment as "a gentle sound, a constant whishing and whooshing that in her imagination could be small waves breaking for the ocean's shore" (Alligood, 2007). He added, "This is the soundtrack of O'Dell's existence, an affirmation that she will live to take her next breath and the next breath and the breath after that" (Ibid.).

Missing from Dianne's life were the tactile stimuli—fuzzy pets, holding her sisters' children, writing letters in longhand, wearing silk scarves and high-heeled shoes, and, most of all, being hugged by her own husband and children, a dream denied by her physical state. For entertainment, she learned to manipulate a telephone, television set, and tape player by sip and blow switches to access art, drama, comedy, and music. For brief periods, she departed the ventilator for up to 3 or 4 hours at a time and breathed on her own while attending church in a wheelchair and making patterns in her sandpile with her foot. By the 1970s, increasing weakness prevented even these few escapes from medical and technological intervention. She commented that a normal day in her metal housing involved watching a movie, helping kids with homework, and counseling the handicapped.

A Whole Person

Dianne developed her talents through compromise. She championed her parents as her mentors: "My family never told me I couldn't do things. As a child I wanted to learn to write, but [had] no use of my arms. My family helped me learn to write by using my toes" ("Nation's," 2007). Under the direction of volunteer teachers to the homebound, she continued her education via a home-to-class intercom system and earned a diploma from Jackson High School in 1965. Three years later, on a $5,000 scholarship, prize money from an essay contest, she attended Freed-Hardeman College, a liberal arts school in Henderson, Tennessee, sponsored by the Church of Christ. While Dianne boarded with a professor, students sometimes gathered in her room for lectures. Chronic migraine headaches limited classroom attendance, where her cousin took notes. Although Dianne's college education ended abruptly, in 1987, the college faculty awarded her a special degree in psychology, her major field. She began tutoring small children, who admired her iron lung as "magic."

Dianne achieved the dream of many would-be writers by publishing a children's picture fable. Using a voice-activated computer, which she received in the 1980s, she was able to dictate words such as "cat," which she encoded verbally as "charlie alpha tango." The first model made voice recognition bloopers. In 1998, with funds from bake sales and garage sales, she purchased updated word processing and voice input software that suited her reedy sounds. She began designing greeting cards and wrote an inspirational fantasy, *Blinky, Less Light* (2001), the story of Blinky, an undersized star who wanted to grant wishes. Of the story of Jonathan, a blind boy, and his lead dog, Lady, the author explained the principle of compensation: "Who else could see a star that can't be seen but a child who can't see. He sees it with his heart" (Baird, 1991, 16). The book required dictation and collaboration with illustrator Toni Wall, a bookstore manager in Clinton, Tennessee, and publication by Gospel Advocate in Nashville. The effort was worth it to young fans who wrote in thanking O'Dell and Wall for helping them accept compromises to wellness. Dianne planned a sequel and began compiling an autobiography to express to children that physical handicaps need not limit their everyday activities and aspirations. She asserted the importance of her accomplishments as role models to youth: "It's amazing what you can accomplish if you see someone do the same thing" (Poovey, 2002).

Dianne's Future

According to Frank McMeen, president of West Tennessee Health Care Foundation, Dianne O'Dell survived in an iron lung longer than any other patient. He and Dr. Robert Christopher, a polio specialist at the University of Tennessee, marveled at the quality of life she sustained through volunteer and family care givers, who visited her country home in south Madison County, 15 miles away from the nearest hospital. Her needs, however, burdened her aging parents and required more support from the foundation. On December 4, 2001, when the O'Dells reached their 90s, Dianne celebrated a Christmas Gala arranged by her mother Geneva and friend Libby Murphy. Of obstacles to her travels, Dianne declared, "I'm going if it kills me" (Poovey, 2002).

The patient and her respirator arrived by ambulance at the Jackson Fairgrounds Park in Jackson, Tennessee. Guests rose to applaud Dianne and her American flag, which topped the iron lung. The 1,100 attendees included actor David Keith and singer Gary Morris. Former Vice President Al Gore chatted with Dianne at the reception, where she posed above a purple satin pillow in a sequined gown created by a hometown designer. Gore kissed Dianne on the forehead below her twinkly gilt tiara. She mused, "People may ask, 'Why would my parents take on this responsibility?' and the answer is their faith. With God's help they knew they would find a way to take care of my needs" ("Nation's," 2007). Because her parents were nearing the end of their lives as parents and caregivers, supporters raised $110,000 to relieve worries about Dianne's maintenance in the future.

A Star in Her Own Right

The significance of Dianne O'Dell to friends and supporters derives from an infectious optimism. She dismissed a lifetime tethered to an iron monster as her normal environment: "You get used to it. What you don't want to do is let it control you" (Alligood, 2007). She declared herself the recipient of a good life blessed with friends and family, particularly her four nephews, who turned her iron lung into a jungle gym. She laughed at her role in their imaginary dramas: "I played Star Wars with them until it was coming out my ears. I got to be Princess Leia and my lines were, 'Help me. Help me. Darth Vader has me'" (Ibid.). Libby Murphy summarized, "Dianne has a way of bringing you into her life and you are better for it" (Poovey, 2002). In 2004, actors Jane Seymour and James Keach and their daughter Kate and twins, Johnny and Kris, sponsored "A Christmas Homecoming," a Holiday Tea and Cocktail Buffet Reception at Oakmont Place Jackson, followed by a concert at Freed-Hardeman University. Fundraising produced a corporate donation of $30,000 as well as gifts from service clubs and the Campbell Street Church of Christ. The actors offered a challenge gift of $10,000. They grew so involved in Dianne that they considered making a biopic about her parents' half-century of dedication and sacrifice.

In mid-November 2007, Dianne's friends threw a 60th birthday party and fundraiser at Jackson's New Southern Hotel. A visitor applied the honoree's makeup. Donors and guests presented her cash, CDs and DVDs of her favorite artists, and autographed photos of celebrities. It was the first time in 6 years that she had left home. The $50 tickets raised cash for the Dianne O'dell Fund at the West Tennessee Health Care Foundation to pay her annual medical debt of from $60,000 to $80,000. Former U.S. Senator Max Cleland, a triple amputee as a result of a grenade explosion during the Vietnam War, contributed a phone call; e-mail buddies tapped into some 600 Web sites that support Dianne's cause. Of her continued stamina despite a bout of kidney stones, she exulted, "It's just the way God wanted it" (Alligood, 2007).

More than 800 guests attended "An Evening in the Imperial Palace," a celebration featuring original scarf designs, an autographed copy of the book *Jane Seymour: Making Yourself at Home*, and oil and watercolor art by actor Jane Seymour, a promoter of support for Dianne along with Seymour's husband, who filmed a biopic of Johnny Cash near the O'Dell residence. Seymour stressed that she met Dianne in 2002 and learned that she received no federal funds because the paralysis falls outside Medicare parameters. Both actors admired Dianne for her spirit. Both Seymour and Keach described her as "an amazing woman" with an open heart for inspiring so many people worldwide to overcome adversity (Reed, 2007). In retrospect, Dianne contemplated her uniqueness: "I often wonder what kind of person I would be had I not been handicapped. I have a lot of friends who call with their problems and say I cheer them up a little bit. I like being that kind of person, but I might not have been" (Baird, 1991, 16). She died on May 28, 2008, at age 61 of asphyxiation after a power outage shut down her life support system.

Sources

Alligood, Leon. "Five Decades in an Iron Lung: 'I Try to Do Anything I Think I Can Do.'" *Chicago Sun-Times*, February 21, 2007.

Baird, Woody. "Spirit Thrives after Forty-one Years in Iron Lung." *Los Angeles Times*, October 13, 1991, 16.

Hillman, Jacque. "Seymour, Other Celebrities Coming to Fundraiser for Iron Lung Survivor." *Jackson Sun* (Tennessee), November 17, 2004.

———. "Sunshine and Rainbows Came to Dianne O'Dell's House on Friday." *Jackson Sun*, July 18, 2004.

"Nation's Longest Living Polio Survivor in Iron Lung Celebrates Milestone." *Business Wire*, February 13, 2007. Available at http://www.highbeam.com/doc/1G1-159246472.html (last accessed April 3, 2008).

O'Dell, Dianne. *Blinky, Less Light*. Nashville, TN: Gospel Advocate, 2001.

Poovey, Bill. "Fifty-One Years in Iron Lung Doesn't Hold Woman Back." *Athens Banner-Herald* (Georgia), February 20, 2002.

Reed, Tony, Jr. "Glittering Gala Raises Funds for Charities." *Jackson Sun*, November 16, 2007.

■ Political Asylum
Khaled Hosseini

A prominent two-career fiction writer, Dr. Khaled Hosseini turned political asylum into an opportunity to instruct readers on the Afghani experience. Born the first of five children of Kizilbash or Shi'ite Muslim descent on March 4, 1965, in northern Kabul, he is the son of Nasser Hosseini, an Afghan ambassador who grew up in Herat in western Afghanistan. Hosseini's Persian mother, Maimoona, one of a generation of women who flourished after the lifting of purdah in 1959, taught Farsi and history at a girls' high school. While growing up as an Iranian-speaking Tajik in a comfortable villa at Wazir Akbar Khan in the affluent northern ward of Kabul, Hosseini revered his father in adherence to a tribal style that lauded father–son relations. Hosseini enjoyed a stable era in Afghan history, but he witnessed the discrimination against the Hazara, a Mongol-Caucasian ethnic group clustered in central Afghanistan. The author learned storytelling from radio broadcasts and sessions of family and clan memories of his grandmother and father. While Kabul thrived with artistic vibrancy and intellectualism, he read classic verse, Lewis Carroll's *Alice in Wonderland*, Ian Fleming spy thrillers, and Mickey Spillane mysteries in Persian. He became a closet short fiction author and determined to write in adulthood.

From age 5 to age 8, Hosseini lived in Tehran, Iran, where his father was posted to the Afghan Foreign Ministry. At the Cinema Park Theatre, Hosseini and his younger brother viewed Hindi cinema and Hosseini's favorite, *Lawrence of Arabia*. They took in American action and crime movies featuring James Caan, Clint Eastwood, Robert Mitchum, and John Wayne. The brothers played in an abandoned cemetery and went to mosque each Friday with their dad. With cousins, Hosseini pursued soccer in summer, picnicked at Paghman, and flew warrior kites competitively each winter during the 3-month hiatus from school. In 1973, he taught a family servant, 30-year-old Hussein Khan, to read and write so he could correspond with family. The grateful servant named Hosseini "Professor Khaled." The author began outlining his first plot from a single incident—for a month, the Hosseini family's cook sodomized Moussa, an impoverished Hazara boy living with his mother across the street.

The Collapse of Security

On his father's diplomatic mission as second secretary to the Afghan embassy, Hosseini lived in Paris from October 1976 to fall 1980, after a coup ended the rule of King Zahir Shah while the monarch was visiting Italy. During the instability in the Afghan government following a Soviet invasion in April 1978 and the infighting of warlords, the family learned of imprisonments and executions, including the shooting deaths of friends and relatives and the loss of 70,000 Kabul citizens. Hosseini's father adopted extreme security measures. To protect his family from car bombing, he left them at the garage while he retrieved his car from a parking space across the street. After meeting Afghan boys who referred to each other as "comrade," Hosseini felt like a character in a Cold War spy movie.

In September 1980, the Hosseinis resolved not to return home and, like 8 million others, opted to emigrate. They little suspected that Afghanistan would founder under 25 years of internal conflict that destroyed farmland and irrigation systems. Among other expatriate professionals, the Hosseinis sought political asylum in the United States. Lacking their father's former elitist position and salary, the Hosseinis arrived in San Jose, California, with a few changes of clothes and lived in poverty. To Nasser's humiliation, Boy Scouts delivered boxes of used toys and clothing, canned goods, and a Christmas tree to the house. The elder Hosseini rejected food stamps and took minimum wage jobs to support seven people. Among them were stints at a Sunday flea market on Berryessa Road, where he sold used items from yard sales among fellow Afghan merchants, some of them relatives.

In a low-level course at Independence High School, Hosseini added English to his command of Farsi and French. His assimilation occurred about the time that the Taliban crushed Afghani spirits through 7 years of random slaughter, house arrest and silencing of women, and destruction of the Bamiyan Buddhas and antiquities in the Kabul Museum. Taliban officials outlawed movies, music, and other forms of pop culture, including, in 1996, the kite-flying contests that Hosseini loved in boyhood. In his homeland, musicians, writers, artists, and film directors saw their works burned. Meanwhile, he earned a B.S. in biology from Santa Clara University and advanced to an M.D. from the University of California, San Diego, School of Medicine. At age 31, he began practicing internal medicine at Cedars-Sinai Medical Center in Los Angeles, a profession that broadened his respect for human nature. Maimoona bussed tables in restaurants and worked as a beautician. His father became a driving instructor until diabetes and coronary disease weakened him. After rejecting further financial aid from San Jose's social services bureau, he became an eligibility officer supervising the allotment of welfare to fellow Afghani.

An Internist and Writer

In 1997, following a traditional courtship, Hosseini wed a 24-year-old Afghan-American, Roya Hosseini, an investment attorney for Intel Capital, and bought a townhouse in Sunnyvale, California. He sired son Haris and daughter Farah, to whom he dedicated *The Kite Runner*. At home, Hosseini spoke Farsi and followed Afghan tastes in food and music. In 1999, in the Mountain View section of the Bay Area, he opened a medical office with Kaiser Permanente. He became patriarch of an Afghan clan and took pride in exhibiting compassion in patient care and fictional characters. In his free time from office demands, he played racquetball, wrote short and long fiction, and savored the verse of the Sufi mystic Rumi, Hafez's *Divan*, Omar Khayyam's *The Rubaiyat*, Arundhati Roy's *The God of Small Things*, John Steinbeck's *The Grapes of Wrath*, and the fiction of John Irving, Stephen King, Wally Lamb, George Orwell, and Mary Shelley. When the United States enacted Operation Enduring Freedom on October 7, 2001, following the 9/11 al-Qaida attacks on the Pentagon and World Trade Center, Hosseini pitied native fears of lawlessness, violent extremes, and economic and social chaos when the Americans and NATO withdrew to fight Saddam Hussein in Iraq. He delighted to learn that Afghan boys were again flying kites.

After Hosseini ventured from composing gothic horror and thrillers, he had difficulty selling more contemporary scenarios to *Esquire*, *Harper's*, and the *New Yorker*. In March 2001, his wife and father-in-law suggested that Hosseini expand the unpublished short story "The Kite Runner" into a novel, a project that reached into June 2002. With a $500,000 advance from Penguin Books, in midsummer 2002, he began laboring each day from 5:00 to 8:00 A.M. and, for support, attended the Tamim Ansary Tuesday night writer's workshop in San Francisco. The text covered a time span ranging from the collapse of the Afghan king to the end of the Taliban. Celina "Cindy" Spiegel, the editor/copublisher, urged Hosseini to reshape one-third of the text by shifting Amir's American wife to the Afghan Soraya Taheri.

A Bestselling Author

Khaled Hosseini's popular morality story *The Kite Runner*, a tale of father-son redemption, describes the cowardice of Amir, a teenage Afghan and his protracted penance and self-forgiveness in manhood. Over 25 years of political upheaval in Kabul, the narrative depicts the protagonist's longing for redemption and his willingness to a rescue his nephew Sohrab from the Taliban as a debt owed to the boy Amir betrayed. The quest begins with a trek to a squalid orphanage and a challenge against the adversary Assef, a pedophile and an official of the Taliban. Amir sheds his shame for treachery by facing Assef, who arms himself with brass knuckles for a one-on-one scuffle. The outcome of Amir's pilgrimage to Kabul is a revival of self-respect and Islamic piety. By accepting the faults of his father and by fostering Hassan's orphaned son Sohrab, Amir cleanses himself of self-hatred and sleeplessness and builds with his wife Soraya a fulfilling marriage.

The first Afghan novel written in English, *The Kite Runner* became a 2005 bestseller. Hosseini's gripping semiautobiographical motif of family secrets and atonement surprised the American fiction market, but it produced outrage among countrymen when he read a segment to the Society of Afghan Professionals in Fremont. In one scene, the author reprised the suffocation of his cousin, a former kite-flying buddy, who died of fumes in a fuel truck that evacuated him from Afghanistan into Pakistan. The book appeared in English and translation in Canada, Denmark, England, Finland, France, Germany, Greece, Holland, Israel, Italy, Japan, Spain, and Sweden and in audio form read by the author. In March 2002, he halted work for a 2-week trip to Afghanistan, which he longed to see once more. After a 27-year absence, he visited his old residence, neighborhood, and school and the historic fortress walls at Bala Hissar near the royal palace of Darulaman, which artillery reduced to pillars. Among humbled Afghans, Hosseini flashed back to scenes of Ma and Tom Joad in *The Grapes of Wrath*.

Home Again

All was not well in Kabul. Whole neighborhoods had vanished into rubble. Amid dust, debris, and the reek of diesel fuel, he found that the Russians had lopped groves of trees to disclose snipers. He discovered that Afghani women's sufferings were fertile ground for a novel. He abandoned hopes that he had overstated Afghanistan's trauma: "What I'd written was so terrible, part of me was kind of hoping that it wasn't quite that bad. The reality was that it was actually worse" (Grossman, 2007). Amid the ongoing medieval "tong wars" in the east and south, nationalism foundered, and the drug economy threatened to transform the country into another Colombia.

In months, Hosseini's addition to American immigrant literature sold 5 million copies and alerted readers to a part of Asia at the center of Christian–Muslim misunderstanding. Readers applauded the thrilling escape element and duck-and-run scenes and sympathized with newcomers' struggles to Americanize themselves. At the crux of the action, Hosseini probed racism, the inflexible caste system that subjects the Hazara underclass to subjugation by the elite Pashtun Sunni. The guiding tone and motivation is Amir's self-castigation for abandoning a friend to the savagery of street thugs. The motifs overwhelm Amir's mind and spirit, robbing him of contentment in California. In a gesture to fellow exiles, Hosseini exonerates Amir by circumventing another child tragedy to Amir's nephew Sohrab.

During a ten-city promotional tour, Hosseini made 100 appearances and, on July 27, was interviewed on National Public Radio. In May 2003, the publisher released a paperback version of *The Kite Runner* and an eight-cassette audio edition read by the author. Contributing to Hosseini's success as a first-time author was the selection of the Connecticut Library Consortium for the One Book, One Region program. In 2003, DreamWorks and Wonderland Films began outlining a screenplay. The author visited the filming while *The Kite Runner* was shot in Kashgar in outback of western China for release in November 2007.

Hosseini credits independent booksellers with a verbal campaign hyping *The Kite Runner*. In 2004, Borders Books presented him an Original Voices Award. The book won Booklist's Alex Award, which listed the novel among the top ten adult books for teens. The novel merited a best book citation from *Entertainment Weekly* and the *San Francisco Chronicle* and the American Place Theatre's Literature to Life Award. In November 2004, author Prue Leith selected *The Kite Runner* as a New Statesman critics' choice of the year. Community reads, literary clubs, and classroom assignments of Hosseini's novel extended his influence on American readership. In 2006, Hosseini became the goodwill ambassador to the United Nations Relief Agency, which presented him an award for humanitarianism. Among his first travels was a visit to Darfur refugees from Sudan living in a dust bowl in Bahai, Chad. He began making public appearances to encourage support for global feeding stations and to plead for world sympathy for the dispossessed. The hands-on altruism relieved survivor's guilt: "I've this sense of being spared somehow and granted this incredible luck. It would be wasteful not to do something" ("Despair," 2007).

A Perspective on Afghan Women

Hosseini's life shifted after a sabbatical from medicine. He traveled more and met contemporary authors while committing himself to researching and writing a second novel. In 2007, he issued more complex wartime fiction in *A Thousand Splendid Suns*, a female-centered novel about the orphan Laila and Mariam, her adoptive mother. He drew characters from women whom he met and viewed on Kabul's streets in March 2003. For accuracy, he tried on a burqa, the black robe and veil concealing the bodies of oppressed Islamic women. He experienced shock from seeing the number of amputees crippled by explosives and of widows and their children who begged passersby for spare change. Like the character Amir, the author felt like a tourist in his native land. While identifying with Afghanistan's miseries, he regretted that he had left home before the oppressive Taliban and that his fellow countrymen had suffered while he lived unharmed in San Jose.

Hosseini chose the title of his female saga from a line written by Saib-e-Tabrizi, a 17th-century Persian poet. The work, like its predecessor, features Kabul as a character in torment and creates empathy for its citizens. He justified the negative angle: "I guess it's my Western sensibility, now that I've lived here for so long, that I feel like these are things we should talk about" (Grossman, 2007). The author reported distress at female honor killings and stonings for adulterers, genital mutilation, illiteracy, disempowerment, and limited health care. The book reached the market in paperback and as an audiobook and received a movie option from Columbia Pictures. In the aftermath of researching and writing, Hosseini longed to return to Kabul, but, for the sake of his wife, daughter, and son, he chose to remain in safe territory until Afghan conditions stabilized.

Sources

"Borders Announces 2003 Original Voices Award Winners; *The Kite Runner* by Khaled Hosseini Takes Top Fiction Prize." *Business Wire* (February 25, 2004): 5520.
"Despair in Kabul." *Telegraph Magazine*, May 19, 2007.
Grossman, Lev. "The Kite Runner Author Returns Home." *Time* (May 17, 2007).
Hosseini, Khaled. "Following Amir—A Trip to Afghanistan in Which Life Imitates Art." *San Francisco Chronicle*, August 10, 2003.
———. "Khaled Hosseini." *Lancet* 362 (September 20, 2003): 1003.
Zvirin, Stephanie. "The Alex Awards, 2004." *Booklist* 100 (15) (April 1, 2004): 1360.

■ Preeclampsia
Jane Seymour

A veteran of 50 movies and television shows and hundreds of interviews, British actor Jane Seymour risked her life to satisfy the maternal urge. Born Joyce Penelope Wilhelmina Frankenberg outside London in Hillingdon, Middlesex, on February 15, 1951, she grew up with two younger sisters, Sally and Anne. Seymour developed from girlhood into a graceful, poised, yet cheery beauty set apart by long reddish-brown hair, which adapts to myriad styles. She learned the value of an upbeat outlook from her father, German-Polish Jewish obstetrician John Benjamin Frankenberg. A student of ballet from age 3, she danced briefly with the Kirov before suffering a knee injury in 1964 at the London Festival Ballet that ended her stage career. In this period, she attended the Arts Educational Trust with designer Cheri Ingle, the actor's current makeup and hair specialist.

At age 17, Seymour displayed a characteristic pragmatism and versatility. She reshaped her ambition from dance to stage and gave herself the stage name of Henry VIII's beloved third wife, who died of postpartum complications in 1537 after giving birth to the future Edward VI. The following year, Seymour made a screen debut in *Oh! What a Lovely War* (1969), a star-heavy musical in which she performed as a chorus girl to World War I ditties. At this crucial time in her career, she came under the mentorship of director Richard Attenborough and received encouragement from actors Anne Bancroft and Maggie Smith. Seymour's next film, *The Only Way* (1970), depicted her as a Jewish refugee escaping the Nazis. She also performed in the 6-hour BBC radio series *Far from the Madding Crowd*, drawn from an 1874 Thomas Hardy novel. In repertory theatre, she tackled the starring roles of Lady Macbeth, Ophelia in Shakespeare's *Hamlet*, and the rebellious Nora Helmer in Heinrich Ibsen's landmark feminist drama *A Doll's House* (1879).

After playing Winston Churchill's lover, Pamela Plowden, in *Young Winston* (1972) and a 2-year run in the BBC television series *The Onedin Line* (1971–1980), the actor immortalized herself as a sex queen by dramatizing Solitaire, a Haitian-French lovely opposite Roger Moore's 007 in *Live and Let Die* (1973), an Ian Fleming classic. She took her work so seriously that the cast named her "Baby Bernhardt." Subsequent castings ranged from a dewy maiden in *Frankenstein: The True Story* (1973) and Bathsheba in *The Story of David* (1976) to Princess Farah in *Sinbad and the Eye of the Tiger* (1977), Serina in *Battlestar Galactica* (1978), and frontier orphan Genny Luckett in the three-part series *The Awakening Land* (1978). Although a public success, in private, her life with film director Michael Attenborough in 1971 foundered after 2 years; a subsequent union to businessman and old friend Geoffrey "Jeep" Planer in 1977 lasted half that long. After she began developing an

American accent, in 1977, she won a first Emmy nomination for the 6-hour television series *Captains and Kings*, the saga of an American dynasty. Her star appeal rose in the States and Canada with a television role as an investigative reporter in the exposé *The Dallas Cowboys Cheerleaders* (1979).

From Actor to Film Diva

At age 29, Seymour turned a nostalgic romance, *Somewhere in Time* (1980), into a cult favorite for her on-screen chemistry with Christopher Reeve. Her fan base rose from a single persona, Elise McKenna, an early 20th-century actress returned to youth at the Grand Hotel. Period costumes, elegant hairstyles, and John Barry's score featuring Sergei Rachmaninoff's *Rhapsody on a Theme of Paganini* earned Saturn Awards for costume, music, and fantasy. At age 30, Seymour departed from sweetness to play a devious femme fatale role, Cathy Ames, in a television miniseries adaptation of John Steinbeck's *East of Eden* (1981), which earned her a second Emmy nomination and a Golden Globe Award for best actress in a series. The emergence of aggression may have cost her depiction as Meggie Cleary in *The Thorn Birds* (1983), a vulnerable persona assigned to Rachel Ward.

Historical and costume drama suited Seymour's talents and taste. On Broadway, she introduced to Amadeus the role of Constanza Weber, the adoring wife of Mozart; on the screen, she played a spurned wife in *Crossings* (1986) and shared stardom with Michael Caine in the horror film *Jack the Ripper* (1988). In the television movie *The Woman He Loved* (1988), a fashion extravaganza, playing the egotistical Wallis Warfield Simpson, the American divorcée who became the consort of England's Edward VIII, required that Seymour age to the end of Simpson's widowhood. The actor paid tribute to her Dutch mother, Mieke van Trigt Frankenberg, a nurse who survived Japanese torment in an Indonesian concentration camp during World War II, by portraying Natalie Jastrow Henry, a victim of Nazi terrorism in the screen adaptation of Herman Wouk's epic war novel *War and Remembrance* (1988). Her variant roles extended to more demanding biography with the passionate, but temperamental, opera star Maria Callas, the long-term mistress of Aristotle Onassis in *Onassis: The Richest Man in the World* (1988), which won Seymour an Emmy. She played Queen Marie Antoinette in *La Révolution Française* (1989), which featured Seymour's children Katherine "Kate" Jane and Sean Michael Flynn as the French dauphine and dauphin.

Turning Point

In her mid-40s, Seymour faced a series of emotional challenges. She weathered her father's death from cancer and the flight of her alcoholic husband and business manager David Flynn to a series of affairs. His departure brought to light his mismanagement of $9 million of her cinematic income as the TV miniseries queen. In 1992, she found herself strapped for cash as the single parent of two children. Overnight, her agent advertised her availability and booked her for her most successful television production, *Dr. Quinn, Medicine Woman* (1993–2001). To relieve panic, she began painting on the set while playing the multifaceted emigration of Dr. Michaela Quinn, a Boston-bred physician challenging gender prejudices on the Colorado frontier. The part required horseback riding, driving a farm wagon, and rock climbing in company with her leading man, Joe Lando, in the guise of enigmatic mountain man Byron Sully. She drew on childhood experiences accompanying her father on medical rounds for scenes of patient diagnosis and treatment and of bone setting, childbirth, surgery, and epidemic control. For the sizeable wardrobe, she acquired vintage jewelry and antique English lace. The starring role won her a second Golden Globe in 1996 and spawned two televised spin-offs, *Dr. Quinn: The Movie* (1999) and *Dr. Quinn: The Heart Within* (2001).

Marriage to actor-director James Keach on May 15, 1993, stepmotherhood to his son Kalen Keach and to Jennifer "Jenny" Flynn, and the longing for more children inspired the actor to attempt in vitro fertilization. After painful injections for infertility and two miscarriages, one suffered during the Rose Parade on live television, she conceived fraternal triplets. During the high-risk pregnancy, one of the embryos was too immature to survive. Early on, her pregnancy ruffled emotions, absorbed her energies, and necessitated frequent naps. In the last 5 months, she lost weight as the babies consumed nutrients, stretching her waistline to 90 inches. Using a stunt double to ride horseback, play baseball, and climb in and out of a farm wagon, she worked into the 8th month and gave birth 2 weeks early.

Daring Motherhood

In the delivery room on November 30, 1995, Seymour slipped close to death from preeclampsia, a mysterious and unforeseen gestational hypertension marked by a dangerous spiking of proteinuria or protein in the urine. The syndome jeopardizes the endothelium or lining of the blood vessels in the kidneys and liver of parturient women bearing multiple fetuses. Toxicity develops through connection to the placenta. Seymour's symptoms appeared in high blood pressure readings, seizures, toxemia, and edema in the face and extremities. She practiced Lamaze breathing techniques and followed the advice of her father by opting for an epidural. Her obstetrician, Dr. Sheryl Ross, delivered the babies—5-pound Kris and 4.5-pound John—by caesarean section and concealed the medical near-calamity from the actor for 3 days while the babies recovered in the intensive care unit. Seymour honored colleagues Johnny Cash and Christopher Reeve by naming the boys John Stacy and Kristopher Steven. She breastfed the newborns in tandem and supplemented nursing with soy milk. Within a month, she overcame fears for her health and returned to filming *Dr. Quinn*.

For postpartum wellness, Seymour grew her own organic citrus fruits, berries, herbs, and vegetables at her Malibu home, avoided caffeine and alcohol, and strengthened her taxed body with golf, skiing, tennis, swimming, fly fishing, and horseback riding. In the gym, she relied on isometrics, pilates, weight lifting, and light yoga to sustain flexibility and strength and meditation for serenity. For upper respiratory disease, she developed strategies of complementary medicine that involved alternative cures and homeopathy. Continuing the popular frontier television series, she worked 16- to 18-hour days and compiled a guide to twinning, *Two at a Time: Having Twins, the Journey Through Pregnancy and Birth* (2001). Her career expanded in varied directions. Before the demise of the *Dr. Quinn* role, she renovated her Renaissance estate, St. Catherine's Court. Located some 4 miles outside Bath, it features a late Tudor stone manor house, vineyards, and 15 acres of gardens, where her father's ashes are buried. She starred in *Touching Wild Horses*, painted prints and greeting cards professionally in oils and watercolors, and launched Putting It All Together, a line of junior clothes and home decor for Saks Fifth Avenue, Inc., and her Seymour Signature Collection, a fashion line retailed through Blair's Crossing Pointe Web site and catalog. Her designs appear on stationary, children's togs, housewares, hotel accoutrements, fabrics, and handbags.

New Directions

Seymour channeled her energy into new directions that showcased her joy in wifehood and mothering and her advocacy for at-risk families. She published *Jane Seymour's Guide to Romantic Living* (1986), *Remarkable Changes: Turning Life's Challenges into Opportunities* (2003), *Making Yourself at Home* (2007), and three children's books—*Yum*, *Splat*, and *Boing*—for a series entitled *This One and That One* (1993–1996), coauthored by James Keach. In 1991, she joined the choir of stars including Kevin Costner, Ali MacGraw, Helen Reddy, Kenny Rogers, and Meryl Streep to sing "Voices that Care," an American Red Cross choral boost to American military personnel during Operation Desert Storm. She remarked, "I realize that I've been given many gifts, not least of which is my ability to communicate on behalf of people who don't have a voice" ("Impact," 2005). Seymour worked under her husband's direction in the family thrillers *Sunstroke* (1992) and *Blackout* (2001), in a survey of sexual harassment in *The Absolute Truth* (1997), and on the biopic *A Passion for Justice: The Hazel Brannon Smith Story* (1994), which reprises the courage of America's first female Pulitzer Prize-winning editor in Jackson, Mississippi, before integration. Guest appearances involved Seymour in *Murphy Brown* (1997) and *Dharma and Greg* (1998); she costarred with husband James as Anna and Jack Robinson in *The New Swiss Family Robinson* (1998). On December 31, 1999, at Buckingham Palace, she received from Queen Elizabeth II the Order of the British Empire.

Parenting is a pervasive motif in Seymour's filmography. Her recent work with James Keach reveals an easy synergy. She commented, "As a team, we have moved on from just acting to producing to directing and being involved in all aspects of the film business. We are trying our best to make the kind of movies that we believe in" (Hernandez, 2004). She paired with James Brolin in a mothering role for the television film *Marriage of Convenience* (1998) and played the reclusive Fiona in *Touching Wild Horses* (2001) and a heart transplant recipient in *Heart of a Stranger* (2002). Still confident of her physical beauty, she performed a nude wedding night scene opposite Keith Carradine in the antebellum Showtime TV biopic *Enslavement: Fanny Kemble* (2000), based on the life of a British actor and wife of Pierce Butler, a Georgian enslaver, who involves herself in the Underground Railroad; she appeared topless in the comedy *The Wedding Crashers* (2005), a zany role that revealed a quirky sense of fun. On April 20, 1999, declared "Jane Seymour Day" in Hollywood, she disclosed her star on the Walk of Fame.

Woman with a Heart

Seymour devotes herself to humanism. She explained that real beauty is internal. The people she admires possess spirit, understanding, and an overall down-to-earth quality. She campaigns for the American Paralysis Association, City Hearts, and Make-A-Wish. For the American Red Cross, she traveled Kenya promoting measles eradication; for UNICEF, she served as official spokeswoman on a tour of El Salvador. She earned a Woman of the World award for her benevolence as international ambassador for Childhelp USA and, in 2004, a Lifetime Achievement of the Arts Award from Chapman University. On February 11, 2005, she claimed naturalized American citizenship. Her interest in women's heart health underlay an appearance in Washington, D.C., on April 27, 2007, alongside her paintings of women wearing red to raise awareness of the danger of coronary disease to female longevity.

In fall 2007, at age 56, 2 years after she had spinal fusion to relieve a herniated disc, she paired with dancer Tony Dovolani and competed successfully on *Dancing with the Stars*. Most memorable to fans were her stunning extensions and footwork in the foxtrot and Viennese waltz. The appearance stretched over seven weeks against much younger women despite the death of her mother Mieke from a stroke and a wildfire that threatened the Keaches' Malibu property. At a reflective moment in her career she summed up a life philosophy: "I'm most happy playing women who make a difference. I feel that way about my own life: What matters is what you do to help and give back to the world—not money or fame" ("Top Ten," 1999).

Sources

Hernandez, Greg. "Power Couple." *Orange Coast* (November 2004).
"Impact Awards 2005 Honorees." *AARP* (January–February 2005).
"Jane Seymour and Family Turn Back Time to See in the New Year in Style." *HELLO!* (January 17, 2000).
"Jane Seymour: 'Why I'm No Neighbour from Hell.'" *Telegraph*, September 27, 2007.
"Medicine Woman: Jane Seymour's Favorite Family Remedies." *Healing Herbs* (December 2, 1997).
Seymour, Jane, and Pamela Patrick Novotny. *Two at a Time: Having Twins: The Journey Through Pregnancy and Birth*. New York: Pocket Books, 2001.

■ Public Ridicule
Jane Fonda

Actor Jane Fonda risked destroying a popular and critically acclaimed film career by expressing radical concerns for nonviolence and world peace. Born in New York City on December 21, 1937, to Frances Ford Seymour and screen giant Henry Jaynes Fonda, she was named Lady Jayne Seymour Fonda. At age 13, she nearly lost her 10-year-old brother Peter, who accidentally shot himself. On April 14, 1950, their mother, a mental patient at the Craig House sanitarium in Stockbridge, Massachusetts, killed herself by slitting her throat with a razor. Eight months later, Henry Fonda married socialite and actress Susan Blanchard, a fun-loving stepmother and mother of Jane and Peter's stepsister, Amy Blanchard. At a fearful time in their lives, Susan, dubbed "Mom Two," treated the emotionally needy Fonda children to a full summer at the beach.

In her teens, Fonda gravitated toward display of her talents and developing sexuality. While modeling, she appeared as a cover girl on *Esquire*, *Glamour*, *Ladies' Home Journal*, and *McCall's* and twice on the cover of *Vogue*. She teamed with her father in pro bono stage work at the Omaha Community Theatre for a performance of Clifford Odets' play *The Country Girl* (1953). Graduating after 6 years from the Emma Willard School in Troy, New York, and after 2 years from Vassar in Poughkeepsie, she studied language and painting in Paris. She entered the mentorship of drama teacher Lee Strasberg, joined the Actors Studio, and debuted as Toni Newton on the Broadway stage in *There Was a Little Girl* (1960), which earned her a Tony nomination. Fonda's rise to screen stardom began at age 23, when she appeared opposite Anthony Perkins as cheerleader June Ryder in the boy crazy romantic comedy *Tall Story* (1960). Subsequent roles accentuated her sexual appeal, from nurse Isabel Haverstick in *Period of Adjustment* (1962), Tennessee Williams's post–Korean

War domestic tangle, to Kitty Twist, a prostitute paired with Laurence Harvey in *Walk on the Wild Side* (1962). The second role won Fonda a Golden Globe for promising new talent.

Jane and Ridicule

In 1963, Jane Fonda experienced her first run-in with public humiliation after the Harvard Lampoon voted her the year's worst actress for the part of Eileen Tyler, a willing virgin in *Sunday in New York*. At age 28, Fonda surged to popularity in the title role of the gun-totin' schoolteacher in the comedy Western *Cat Ballou* (1965), her first blockbuster. After two romantic leads in *Any Wednesday* (1966) and *Barefoot in the Park* (1967), at age 31, she achieved name and face recognition in *Barbarella* (1968), a futuristic comic book spoof that pictured her naked in zero gravity. She balanced extremes of erotica with realism by depicting Gloria Beatty in Sydney Pollack's tragic film *They Shoot Horses, Don't They* (1969), the part that won her an Academy Award nomination. Along with Candice Bergen, Marlon Brando, and Anthony Quinn, on November 14, 1969, Fonda allied with 10,000 proponents of the American Indian Movement (AIM) in the liberation and 19-month standoff at Alcatraz Island in San Francisco Bay. That same year, vilification by the National Security Agency posed Fonda in company with protesters Joan Baez, Dr. Martin Luther King, Jr., Benjamin Spock, and Malcolm X under the category, "domestic subversive."

Before winning her first Oscar and second Golden Globe in 1971 for playing the prostitute Bree Daniels in *Klute*, Fonda intensified her image as a left-winger and an anarchist. On March 8, 1970, at Fort Lawton, Washington, in collusion with native American dissidents Leonard Peltier, Bob Satiacum, and Bernie Whitebear, she supported northwestern tribes in demanding the return of traditional tribal lands. Recovering from "graylisting" for civil disobedience, she launched her own production firm, IPC Films. After creating Workout Inc. and opening an aerobics studio, she eased back into fame with 23 aerobics exercise tapes, 13 audio tapes on fitness, five workout manuals, body sculpting, and yoga, a discipline she took up after an injury to her foot ended ballet practice. Simultaneously, she backed the Black Panthers, Huey Newton and radical fugitive Angela Davis, civil rights, feminism, RITAs (Resisters Inside the Army), and immediate withdrawal of American troops from southeast Asia. Her pacifism echoed the sentiments of media stars Lauren Bacall, Harry Belafonte, Bette Davis, Gene Hackman, and Jon Voight.

Jane on the Road

Fonda joined political activist Fred Gardner, dramatist Barbara Garson, comedian Dick Gregory, and actor Donald Sutherland in an antiwar road show called "Free the Army." The guerrilla vaudeville became the source of the film *F.T.A.* (1972), a documentary of soldier malcontent that parodies the U.S. army enlistment slogan "Fun, Travel and Adventure." In April 1970, the bus tour rolled along the California coast to bistros and military sites, where the players performed gags, droll music, folk music, and satires warning untried GIs about the bloody quagmire in Vietnam. At Fort Mead, Maryland, reporters covered Fonda's arrest by MPs. Because she circulated pacifist propaganda at Fort Bragg, North Carolina, the next month, the Criminal Investigation Division banished her from the base. She moved into Rowan Street Park in Fayetteville to harangue 2,000 fans on the fruitless Vietnam War. On Labor Day, 1970, she crusaded for peace at a protest march from Morristown, New

Jersey, to Valley Forge State Park that involved 200 veterans and military nurses. Addressing some 1,500 pacifists, politicians Joe Kennedy and John Kerry and U.S. Senators George McGovern and Edmund Muskie assured attendees of serious controversy in Washington over the lengthy war. In a climate of protest, Fonda raised some $10,000 for antiwar veterans by soliciting support from college students.

The tide of public protest encouraged Fonda to champion the underdog. In February 1971, in Valley Forge, Pennsylvania, she crusaded for nonviolence at a Vietnam Veterans Against the War rally. Some weeks later, she canvassed Las Vegas with freedom fighters Ralph David Abernathy, César Chávez, and Benjamin Spock on behalf of fatherless black families on welfare, the targets of racist state legislation. On March 14, 1971, Fonda performed a strident antimilitary parody at the Haymarket Square coffeehouse near the base entrance, an effrontery that made headlines the next day in the Los Angeles Times. The pacifist documentary *F.T.A.* (1972) interspersed stage slapstick with Fonda's interviews with disgruntled infantrymen. During a campus uprising at the University of California, Los Angeles, that spring, she praised students for demonizing ROTC recruiting on state campuses and for enticing enlistees with lies and half-truths.

In 1973, Fonda's dedication to liberalism involved her husband Tom Hayden in the mockery of President Richard Nixon in Paris, London, and his California mansion at San Clemente. The launching of the Indochina Peace Campaign spurred the Haydens' crusade to awaken Middle America to alternatives to international conflict. Central to their distaste for Nixon was his proposal of nuclear attacks on North Vietnam as early as 1969. She described herself as "shaking with fury: Here was Nixon, elected by promising he would end the war, expanding it into another country" (Fonda, 2006, 241). Because of her criticism of the new U.S. president, two motel managers in Albuquerque, New Mexico, refused to rent her rooms.

In July 1972, Fonda pressed her radical agenda to a new height by accepting an invitation to visit the enemy in Hanoi. Traveling with still and 8-millimeter cameras via Aeroflot from Moscow to Vientiane, Laos, she arrived in North Vietnam with Communist agitator Herbert Aptheker and historian Stoughton Lynd for a 2-week tour. Along the road to Nam Dinh, she observed bombed-out schools, hospitals, pagodas, factories, and homes. After a survey of the Nam Sach District, on August 22, she addressed the nation over Radio Hanoi, which the Reuters news agency reported verbatim.

Fonda was outspoken on the subject of Richard Nixon and his intent to turn North Vietnam into an American colony. She sided with farmers against the deliberate bombing of rice field terracing the Red River Delta by A-7s and Phantom jets and against a push of hostilities into Cambodia. In Hanoi, she stirred pity for eight prisoners of war, to whom she delivered a packet of mail. She experienced concussion from a burst of ground fire against U.S. jets and more flak from veteran John McCain, who refuted her claims that the North Vietnamese did not subject prisoners to brainwashing, starvation, and torture. She rallied pacifism over radio broadcasts, accused the Nixon administration of lying about escalation of the conflict, and sealed her public image by smiling in a helmet while mounting an inactive antiaircraft battery in sight of reporters' cameras.

Fonda's Popular Decline

Dubbed "Hanoi Jane," a sister to "Axis Sally," "Hanoi Hannah," and "Tokyo Rose," Fonda returned to a right-wing backlash against Jane the antisoldier. Still beloved by students, whom the press nicknamed "Fonda Reds," she found herself vilified as a Benedict Arnold. Detractors hanged her in effigy from a tree in Waterbury's Library Park; picketers charged her with Communism and waved anti-Jane signs outside her hotel room. In her own estimation, she says, "I was framed and turned into a lightning rod for people's anger, frustration, misinformation, and confusion about the war" (Fonda, 2006, 324). Although right-wing Hollywood actors Charlton Heston and John Wayne shunned her, she lobbied prowar legislators in Washington, D.C., for 6 weeks. She later reported, "Despite the saber rattling, the Justice Department found I had violated no statutes, including those covering sedition" (Fonda, 2006, 322). As of August 14, 1972, Attorney General Richard Kleindienst pressed no prosecution.

Fonda's resilience did not desert her. In February 1973, she concealed under a purple serape her pregnancy with son Troy Garity while she rallied at Claremont, California, with Vietnam veteran Ron Kovic, hero of *Born on the Fourth of July*. She boosted her popularity with filmgoers by starring in three political films, *Julia* (1977), *Coming Home* (1978), and *The China Syndrome* (1979), in which she portrayed television reporter Kimberly Wells investigating a nuclear nightmare about the attempted cover-up of a meltdown at a California power plant. For playing dramatist Lillian Hellman opposite Vanessa Redgrave in *Julia*, Fonda earned a fourth Golden Globe and another Academy Award nomination; the part of Sally Hyde, a volunteer at a veteran's hospital opposite Jon Voight as a wounded soldier in *Coming Home*, snagged Fonda's second Oscar and a third Golden Globe for best actress. She moved into new territory by fostering gay rights at the Elephant Walk, a San Francisco headquarters of protest against the partial exoneration of Dan White, who assassinated Mayor George Moscone and homosexual city supervisor Harvey Milk.

Extremes of Controversy

Sponsors sided with conservatives. After journalist Barbara Walters conversed with Fonda for an ABC TV interview, General Electric canceled sponsorship. Fonda maintained her zeal for pacifism by partnering with folksinger Joni Mitchell and consumer rights protester Ralph Nader to raise public consciousness of nuclear threat. In reaction to the Three Mile Island nuclear incident, on May 6, 1979, the trio addressed 75,000 who mobbed Washington, D.C. She disclosed in her autobiography signs at major airports declaring, "Jane Fonda Leaks More than Nuclear Power Plants," and demanding, "Feed Fonda to the Whales." Her film career remained upbeat with the workaday comedy *Nine to Five* (1980), in which she plays divorcée Judy Bernly, and as supporting actress to her father in *On Golden Pond* (1981). In 1984, she completed *The Dollmaker*, an Emmy-winning performance honoring Gertie Nevels, a hillbilly woman who turns the art of whittling into a redemptive act for herself and her blue-collar neighbors. The next year, Fonda teamed with Anne Bancroft for *Agnes of God* (1985), in which Fonda played a forthright psychologist, Dr. Martha Livingston.

Approaching age 50, Fonda persisted in public forums against classroom gender stereotyping, loss of reproductive rights, Taliban misogyny in Afghanistan, teen pregnancy, female genital mutilation of Kenyan girls, and other forms of violence against women. In September 1985, Fonda, Sally Field, and Sissy Spacek backed aid to farm families. Months later, Fonda boarded a bus tour, the California Clean Water Caravan, to win voters to Proposition 65, which promoted safe drinking water and public lands free of toxic pollutants. During a broadcast of *20/20* in 1988, she apologized to former prisoners of war for making hurtful, misguided statements on behalf of the enemy.

Work and Altruism

Fonda returned to the screen with actors Gregory Peck and Jimmy Smits in *Old Gringo* (1989), based on a Carlos Fuentes novel about the disappearance of Ambrose Bierce during the Mexican Revolution. Following her intent to promote worthy issues, in 1990, she starred in *Stanley and Iris* as Iris King, a bakery worker and tutor to an illiterate inventor, played by Robert De Niro. At age 55, she established the Jane Fonda Center for Adolescent Reproductive Health at the medical school of Emory University in Atlanta, Georgia. Two years later, she headed a delegation of women pressing the Mexican government to investigate the murders of hundreds of Juaréz women. The Film Society of Lincoln Center hosted a gala on May 7, 2001, honoring Fonda's lifetime achievements. In 2006, she and Vanessa Vadim, her 33-year-old daughter by first husband Roger Vadim, supported America's "peace mom," protester Cindy Sheehan, at Camp Casey, a pup tent pitched across from President George W. Bush's ranch in Crawford, Texas, and named in honor of Cindy's son, a casualty of the Iraq War.

Fonda expressed her unwavering support of peace with continued public protest and with a 624-page memoir, *My Life So Far* (2006), which fostered détente with her critics. She used her notoriety at a gathering at the University of Notre Dame to decry the feminization of poverty in America. While Americans rebelled against waste of money on war in the Middle East, in January 27, 2007, Fonda appeared opposite a flag-draped coffin topped by army boots. In league with activists Eve Ensler, Danny Glover, Sean Penn, Tim Robbins, Susan Sarandon, and U.S. Congresswomen Maxine Waters and Lynn Woolsey, Fonda drew a crowd at the Navy Memorial in Washington, D.C. Fonda rebuked President Bush for hubris and war mongering. She declared his administration mean-spirited and vengeful and warned that silence was not an option.

Sources

Fonda, Jane. *My Life So Far.* New York: Random House, 2006.

Hershberger, Mary, ed. *Jane Fonda's Words of Politics and Passion.* New York: New Press, 2006.

Holzer, Henry Mark, and Erika Holzer. *Aid and Comfort: Jane Fonda in North Vietnam.* Jefferson, NC: McFarland, 2006.

■ Racist Parent
Toni Morrison

A revered author and teacher, Chloe Anthony Wofford "Toni" Morrison is an American icon who emerged from a racist household. Born the second of four on Elyria Avenue in Lorain, west of Cleveland, Ohio, on February 18, 1931, she, her older sister, Lois, and two younger brothers came of age on the boundary between the industrial North and the plantation South. They are the great-grandchildren of a land-owning Afro-Indian woman and the granddaughter of an illiterate sharecropper and carpenter, John Solomon Willis, and Ardelia Willis, who struggled against racism in Greenville and Birmingham, Alabama. From age 5, John remembered the promise of the Emancipation Proclamation, which President Abraham Lincoln enacted on January 1, 1863.

After whites stole John Willis' inheritance of 88 acres, in 1910, the Willises moved north to better themselves and to protect their 12 children from the predations of the Ku Klux Klan. Ardelia Willis bore with her stories of magic, spirits, and ghost and a dream book filled with phantasms recovered from her night thoughts. John, a self-educated reader and violinist, transported north agrarian work and folk songs and peasant rhythms. To improve educational opportunities, the couple reared seven children first in the coal country of Kentucky, where Ardelia took in laundry, and next in Lorain, at the western rim of Ohio's industrial heartland. In this same era, Morrison's paternal grandparents fled Klan violence and Southern agrarian poverty.

The Wofford Household

Morrison's deeply diametric parents—George Wofford and Ella Ramah Willis Wofford—viewed racial issues over a divide. After departing Georgia at age 16 to leave Jim Crow behind, George lost his parents while still a youth. Employed at three jobs for over 17 years, he worked high-paying welding posts at a Northern shipyard and steel mills. Into each seam, he inscribed his name in molten metal as a statement of pride in craft, a quality he passed to his daughter Toni. On the side, he washed cars and labored on construction sites while remaining uninvolved in the lives of whites and European immigrants in surrounding neighborhoods. He never overcame antipathy toward whites, whom he considered a deceptive, lying race morally inferior to blacks. He once lost his temper and tossed a white male down stairs. Wofford ordered his children to think of themselves as other than the white opinion of blackness, which tended toward insult and abasement. In the role of family storykeeper, he advanced his bias toward the ruling class through oral narrative. From these sessions, Toni absorbed contempt and hatred that she later tried to spare her own two sons.

Unlike her embittered mate, Ramah Wofford, a high school graduate, set the example of the compassionate parent who encouraged learning and tolerance in her household. She sang jazz and arias, filled the children's minds with music and Bible lore, and joined a book club. She held high standards of the uncompromising mother figure and surrounded her daughters with tough, progressive women who expressed female dreams and aspirations while they cooked; their no-nonsense idealism demanded excellence from girl children. The model influenced Toni's life as a writer and as mentor to aspiring novelists. From her hours of listening and absorbing postures and gestures grew the female portraits that invigorate her works.

A Bookish Bent

In a mixed section of Cleveland on Lake Erie's southwestern rim, Morrison went to school with blacks, Greeks, Italians, Mexicans, and whites. She and her siblings got along well with others, even after a landlord set fire to their apartment when Morrison was 2 years old. From strong bonds with community women, Morrison valued stories and verses about the Underground Railroad and other episodes from the post-Reconstruction South. In the style of her idol, ballerina Maria Tallchief, Toni displayed brilliance in childhood and learned to read before entering elementary school. In fifth grade she encountered racism in an illiterate immigrant whom she taught to read. After recognizing Toni's race, the boy dismissed her as a nigger. At the depths of the Great Depression, Ramah Wofford refused to be diminished by dependence on welfare. Upon receipt of vermin-ridden meal, she reported the inedible rations in a letter to President Franklin Delano Roosevelt. While working after school at the Lorain Public Library to fatten the family budget, from age 13, Toni read Jane Austen, Fyodor Dostoevsky, Gustave Flaubert, and Leo Tolstoy and excelled at English. She graduated valedictorian from Lorain High and became the first in her family to merit a college diploma.

To attend Howard University in Washington, D.C., in 1949, Morrison relied in part on her parents' contributions, which stretched to cover the tuition of older daughter Lois. While studying in a cosmopolitan atmosphere, Toni shed the name Chloe, which bore "Aunt Jemima" overtones from Harriet Beecher Stowe's melodramatic slave novel *Uncle Tom's Cabin* (1852). Toni studied classics and English, French, and Russian literature and toured the South with a university theater group, the Howard University Players. In a production of William Shakespeare's *Richard III*, she played a queen. She profited from contact with two important influences, poet Sterling Brown and critic Alain Locke. In 1955, she completed a master's degree in English at Cornell with a focus on the suicide motif in the canons of William Faulkner and Virginia Woolf. For 10 years, Morrison taught English at Texas Southern and Howard universities.

Mother and Breadwinner

Morrison married a Jamaican, Howard-educated architect Harold Morrison, in 1957 and bore two sons, architect Harold Ford and artist-musician Slade Kevin. During her second pregnancy, she admitted the collapse of her marriage and moved back home to Lorain. In her professional career, she became more demanding as breadwinner for a family of three. She befriended poet LeRoi Jones and activist Andrew Young and impacted the careers of two students, Claude Brown, author of *Manchild in the Promised Land*, and Stokely Carmichael, cofounder of the Student Nonviolent Coordinating Committee.

In the early 1960s, Morrison stole time for her creative urge by joining a monthly author's consortium and maintaining an independent interior life. The discipline of writing and reading aloud for other writers initiated her regimen of plotting characterization in her head before jotting words and phrases in pencil on yellow legal pads. While her sons slept, she completed a story she had begun in high school, which became the kernel of her first novel,

The Bluest Eye (1970), which went through seven rewrites. The story of an unloved, sexually abused black child, the text draws on the generation of female children who looked to Shirley Temple as the epitome of beauty and grace. In 1965, Morrison worked as a textbook editor for the I. W. Singer division of Random House in Syracuse. As senior trade book editor for company headquarters in New York City, she developed works by black authors Muhammad Ali, Toni Cade Bambara, Wesley Brown, Gayl Jones, Angela Davis, and Andrew Young.

A Midlife Rise to Fame

While serving as Albert Schweitzer Professor of Humanities at State University of New York at Albany, in 1969, Morrison lived in a four-story residence renovated from a boathouse at Grandview on the Hudson River outside Nyack, New York. Four years later, she published *Sula* (1973), which *Redbook* excerpted. She followed in 1974 by editing Middleton Harris' *The Black Book*, an album of slave biographies, advertising, photos, recipes, patent records, and news clippings, one of which evolved into Morrison's *Beloved* (1987). After teaching at Bard College and Yale University, Morrison devoted herself to writing. Following her father's death on September 9, 1975, she wrote *Song of Solomon* (1977), a saga novel based on her family history and mythos. It garnered the National Book Award and Ohioana Book Award and a 1978 segment of the PBS television series *Writers in America*. She flexed her imagination into broader terrain with *Tar Baby* (1981), dedicated to her mother, Ramah, grandmother Ardelia, sister, Lois Brooks, and aunts Carolina Smith and Millie MacTeer. In this fertile period, President Jimmy Carter appointed Morrison to the National Council on the Arts.

Morrison labored over *Beloved*, her masterwork. For the background and motivation, she drew on research from slave quarters in Brazil, enslavers from Spain, Kentucky plantations, and the function of the Underground Railroad in Ohio River towns. The plot restructures the historical account of child-murderer Margaret Garner, who, unlike the protagonist Sethe, was reenslaved by her owner. Dedicated to 60 million black victims, the novel extols a savage maternal love and redemption. Morrison impacted readers with a rare feminine view of bondage as cyclical rape and dehumanizing motherhood. The failure of *Beloved* to receive a National Book Award roused 48 black authors and critics to fury, which they blazoned in the *New York Times Book Review*.

Subsequent works—essays for the *New York Times* as well as *Jazz* (1992), *Playing in the Dark: Whiteness and the Literary Imagination* (1992), *Paradise* (1998), and *Remember: The Journey to School Integration* (2004)—have settled Toni Morrison more firmly in the canons of feminist, African-American, and world literatures. The first black female author to earn world renown, Morrison was also the premiere black woman to publish a Book of the Month Club focal selection. Her awards include commendation from the American Academy and Institute of Arts and Letters and City College of New York Langston Hughes Festival and the Anisfield Wolf Book Award, and three consecutive Public Library's Books for the Teen Age nominations for her works. On March 30, 1981, Morrison appeared on the cover of *Newsweek* and delivered the keynote address to the American Writers' Congress. In an original drama, *Dreaming Emmett* (1985), she reprised the agitation of 1955 over the assassination of Emmett Till, a black 14-year-old whom white racists murdered in Money, Mississippi, for whistling at a white female. Unlike her disgruntled father, Morrison brought to the narrative a dispassionate interest. The play stirred the audience at the debut at Albany's Marketplace Theater on January 4, 1986, and earned the New York State Governor's Arts Council Award.

A Star Author

Into the decade, Morrison earned a Pulitzer Prize for *Beloved*, which flourished for 18 weeks as a bestseller and received nominations for the Ritz-Hemingway, National Book, and National Book Critics Circle awards. Honors continued to flow in her direction—the Melcher Book Award, Robert Kennedy Book Award, Peggy V. Helmerich Distinguished Author Award, Barnard Medal of Distinction, City of New York Mayor's Award of Honor for Art and Culture, Elmer Holmes Bobst Award in Arts and Letters, Modern Language Association Commonwealth Award, and 14 honorary degrees, including doctorates from Spelman, Oberlin, Dartmouth, Bryn Mawr, Columbia, and Yale. She served as the Tanner Lecturer at the University of Michigan and the Robert Goheen Professor in creative writing, women's studies, and African studies at Princeton. The latter appointment made history as the first chair of an Ivy League university to pass to a black female. Until her retirement at age 75, her contributions to classroom development of creative writing involved the pairing of promising pupils with skilled authors.

At her peak in the 1990s, Morrison rose to literary "divahood." Her essay for *Time* magazine on America's melting pot summarized her perspective on national history satirizing Americans as "Star spangled. Race Strangled" (Morrison, 1993). She ventured into postmodernism for *Jazz* (1992), a mélange of love and violence, and for *Love: A Novel* (2005), a symphonic blend of power and passion. Although she encountered withering reviews, she forced herself to read negative and wrong-headed commentary to help her understand white perceptions of African-American fiction. She paired with son Slade Morrison in publishing children's picture books—*The Big Box* (2002), *The Book of Mean People* (2002), and *The Lion or the Mouse?* (2003)—and with Richard Danielpour and Andre Previn as lyricist for their musical compositions. She won the Chianti Ruffino Antico Fattore International Literary Prize and became the eighth female and first black woman to receive a Nobel Prize, which carried a purse of $825,000.

The first American to receive the accolade since John Steinbeck in 1962, Morrison awed the selection committee, who acknowledged her debt to Faulkner and the African-American canon. They remarked, "She delves into the language itself, a language she wants to liberate from the fetters of race. And she addresses us with the luster of poetry" (Grimes, 1993). The committee summarized the lasting impression as humanistic, compassionate, and profoundly humorous. Colleague Henry Louis Gates, Jr., exulted that the selection marked a momentous occasion for blacks and for all Americans. With typical humility, Morrison rejoiced that her mother was still alive to share the prestige. Accompanied by son Harold to Stockholm, Sweden, the author thanked the public for their love and support and promised a sequel to *Beloved*. In her Nobel address, she challenged the young writer: "We will not blame you if your reach exceeds your grasp, if love so ignites your words that they go down in flames and nothing is left but their scald" (Larson, 2007).

In January 1995, Morrison dedicated the Toni Morrison Reading room of the Lorain Public Library. She became the Jefferson Lecturer, the federal government's highest honor for intellectual achievement. Director Jonathan Demme's 1998 screen version of *Beloved*, produced by Harpo Productions, starred Oprah Winfrey and Danny Glover with Thandie Newton in the title role as a drooling, demanding child-woman. The film reaped positive critical acclaim for its verisimilitude to slave escapes into southern Ohio. In 2001, *Ladies Home Journal* placed Morrison among the "30 Most Powerful Women in America." Four years later, Oxford University conferred on her an honorary doctor of letters; she also served a month in residence as guest curator of the Louvre Museum in Paris. *The New York Times* lauded *Beloved* as the outstanding American novel of a quarter century.

Sources

Gillespie, Carmen. *Critical Companion to Toni Morrison: A Literary Reference to Her Life and Work*. New York: Facts on File, 2008.

Grimes, William. "Toni Morrison Is '93 Winner of Nobel Prize in Literature." *New York Times*, October 8, 1993.

Jennings, La Vinia Delois. *Toni Morrison and the Idea of Africa*. Cambridge: Cambridge University Press, 2008.

Larson, Susan. "Awaiting Toni Morrison." *Times-Picayune*, April 11, 2007.

Morrison, Toni. "On the Backs of Blacks." *Time*, December 2, 1993.

Tally, Justine. *The Cambridge Companion to Toni Morrison*. Cambridge: Cambridge University Press, 2007.

Wall, Cheryl A. *Worrying the Line: Black Women Writers, Lineage and Literary Tradition*. Chapel Hill: University of North Carolina Press, 2006.

Yardley, Jonathan. "Toni Morrison: An Introduction." *Washington Post*, March 6, 2006, C1.

■ Rape
Oprah Winfrey

A single-name star, Oprah Gail Winfrey survived childhood rape to become America's listening ear. Her ethnicity dates to prehistoric Liberia and to native American stock. At the beginning of the Civil War, her great grandparents, Constantine and Violet A. Winfrey, were enslaved in Mississippi. A native of Kosciusko in Attala County, Mississippi, she was born on January 29, 1954, to an 18-year-old unwed domestic, Vernita Lee, and Vernon Winfrey, a soldier at Fort Rucker, Alabama, who later mined coal and owned a grocery store and barbershop. After her maternal grandmother, Hattie Mae Presley Lee, and a midwife delivered Oprah, her maternal aunt Ida Lee named her for the biblical character of Orpah in the book of Ruth. The name appeared misspelled on her birth certificate as "Oprah."

Because Winfrey's parents escaped welfare by migrating to jobs in the North, she grew up on Hattie Mae and Earless Lee's 2-acre farm, which lacked running water and indoor toilets. She learned to boil laundry and make lye soap and warded off solitude by telling stories to the chickens and pigs and to a corncob doll. Religion and reading colored Winfrey's upbringing at the Kosciusko Baptist Church, where she excelled at memorizing and reciting scripture. By age 3, she could read; 2 years later, she learned to write. At neighborhood churches, she recited poet James Weldon Johnson's *The Creation*. In kindergarten, she wrote a note to the teacher about her boredom and received an immediate advance to the first grade. In adulthood, she claimed Grandmother Hattie Mae as the source of her reason and strength. Life changed forever after her grandmother's illness in 1960.

Life in Two Worlds

Reared in a Milwaukee, Wisconsin, boardinghouse from age 6, Winfrey shared her mother's attention with baby sister Patricia and, later, with son Jeffrey. During temporary residence with her father and his wife Zelma in Nashville, Tennessee, Winfrey attended East Wharton Elementary School and clerked in Vernon's Grocery store. Her father demanded strict obedience; her stepmother taught her multiplication and vocabulary. On return to Milwaukee, Winfrey revered Mrs. Duncan, a teacher who inspired excellence in children.

The fourth grader considered becoming a teacher or a missionary to have the same influence over young lives. During a mission drive, she collected donations for the Costa Rican poor.

At her Uncle Trent Winfrey's house in Tennessee, young Oprah survived rape in summer 1963. The 19-year-old cousin who destroyed her virginity bought her silence with ice cream and a visit to the zoo. Cyclical molestation ensued by Trent and other relatives and by some of the men who came and went from Vernita's life. She was unaware that she could demand an end to their fondling and coupling. Instead, she accused herself of moral weakness. Until 1975, she suppressed her "big, looming, dark secret" and blamed her parents for failing to protect her from predators (Garson, 2003, 22). She introduced "Sexual Abuse in Families" on November 20, 1986, with a confession: "I was raped by a relative. . . . I'm telling you about myself because when it happened, I couldn't tell anyone, because I thought it was all my fault" (Nelson, 2005, 4).

A Promising Talent

In 1967, on scholarship, Winfrey entered Nicolet High School in Glendale, Wisconsin, a toney neighborhood where she embroidered her life history with lies to suit upper middle-class schoolmates. Because of long commutes from the ghetto, she received little adult supervision. She dressed in revealing costumes and consorted with street kids. To escape fights with Vernita, Winfrey ran away and lived in a hotel before negotiating her return home through a minister. Vernita ruled out sending her to a juvenile home and dispatched her pregnant daughter to Vernon and Velma for discipline. At age 14, Winfrey bore a son prematurely who died within weeks.

Winfrey returned to normal girlhood, church, and schoolwork. She won prizes for oratory and stagecraft and the title Miss Fire Prevention and got a job in radio news at WVOL. She dated Anthony Otey but, on Valentine's Day of her senior year, gave him up for her career. During her relationship with Randolph Cook, she took drugs. At Tennessee State University, where she majored in speech and drama, she fell in love with William "Bubba" Taylor and won the 1971 Miss Black Tennessee title. As coanchor of an evening news show on WLAC TV, she stood out as the youngest newscaster and first black female to rise to media prominence.

Winfrey managed to ally self-empowerment with sensuality and fellowship, the signature triad of her on-camera persona. Lured to Baltimore, at age 23, she gave up Taylor to coanchor evening news over WJZ TV and to host *Dialing for Dollars*. Her male companion, journalist Lloyd Kramer, gave her emotional support while she learned to deal for herself with tough station management. In 1978, she joined Richard Sher in presenting a talk show, *People Are Talking*. When Kramer moved to a New York post in 1981, Winfrey involved herself with an anonymous married man who reduced her to submission. Feeling trapped in a dead-end relationship, she put on weight and pondered suicide. In later reflections, she realized the destructive power of controlling males who reduce their lovers to handmaidens.

From Radio to Television to Cinema

At age 29, Winfrey advanced her gift for informal group therapy on a morning show, *A.M. Chicago*, over WLS TV. The give-and-take format, renamed *The Oprah Winfrey Show*, topped tabloid talk show host Phil Donahue's ratings within the month and made her a millionaire. She explained her appeal by claiming kinship with needy people: "We all want the same things" (Krohn, 2002, 58). At the urging of another beau, movie critic Roger Ebert, on September 8, 1986, Winfrey went national and hosted the 1987 Annual Daytime Emmy Awards, which presented her a total of forty honors. Critics warmed to her wit and greateheartedness and to her ability to empathize with the perplexed and downtrodden. Editors at the *Wall Street Journal* named her style of public therapy "Oprahfication." Her compassion for gays, lesbians, bisexuals, transsexuals, and transgendered people ushered them further into the mainstream. Her television income rose to $264 million a year. At a high point in success and popularity, she began a long-term relationship with educator and public relations consultant Stedman Graham and his daughter, Wendy.

Oprah outpaced male talk show themes by delving into women's heart diseases, breast cancer, meditation, imprisoned husbands, and substance abuse. She attacked the antiwoman lyrics of rappers and denounced the sale of handguns. One program on pacifism reaped extensive hate mail. The 1988 People's Choice Awards named Winfrey the favorite talk show host. In November 1988, *Ms.* magazine credited her with breaking barriers for plus-size women and for treasuring the inner worth of all women. Her personal involvement with the AIDS crisis derived from her dependence on Billy Rizzo, a staff member who died of the virus in 1989. Interviewees clamoring to appear with her included singer Michael Jackson and pop psychologist Phil McGraw. In 2002, Harpo Productions, her base company, established McGraw in his own venue, *Dr. Phil*.

Winfrey's energetic grasp of the media included the filming of Alice Walker's redemption novel *The Color Purple* (1985). Producer Quincy Jones hired Oprah to play Sofia, a shamed wife and survivor of prison. The part won Golden Globe and Oscar nominations and prefaced her next film jobs as Mrs. Thomas in an adaptation of Richard Wright's *Native Son* (1986), as Mattie Michael in *The Women of Brewster Place* (1989), as LaJoe Rivers in *There Are No Children Here* (1993), and, 4 years later, as producer and star of *Before Women Had Wings* (1997). In 1990, she opened Harpo Studios, featuring her logo, a capital O. At the company's peak, she entered *Forbes* magazine's list of the 400 wealthiest people in the United States. Harpo Studios produced for television *The Wedding* (1998), *David and Lisa* (1998), and *Tuesdays with Morrie* (1999), all films with character-building themes. Winfrey took a more demanding role as the former slave Sethe opposite actor Danny Glover as her lover Paul D in the screen version of Toni Morrison's novel *Beloved* (1998). The ghost tale reenacted the true crime story of Margaret Garner, a runaway from Kentucky to Ohio who slit her toddler daughter's throat rather than see her returned to sexual bondage.

An Influential Voice

Winfrey's media savvy gave her a platform from which to expose the sexual opportunism that threatened her girlhood. On September 4, 1992, she divulged the child molestation in her past as an introit to the television documentary *Scared Silent: Ending and Exposing Child Abuse*. The text featured six true accounts of intergenerational child molestation. Aired simultaneously on CBS, NBC, and PBS, it was the first theme-oriented program to receive major primetime coverage. To protect other vulnerable children, she related her story on *Good Morning America*, *This Morning*, and *The Today Show*. In response, the National Child Abuse Hotline handled 112,000 calls at the rate of 22,400 a day, many from frightened children.

The glamorous star turned prestige and fame to worthy use. She lent her support to President Bill Clinton's National Child Protection Act, a database of convicted child predators, and, over PBS TV, funded *One Child, One Dream: The Horatio Alger Awards* to acknowledge people who overcame difficulties. Joining her in the selection of recipients were author Maya Angelou, U.S. Senator Robert J. Dole, boxer George Foreman, Reverend Billy Graham, and General Colin Powell. In 1996, Winfrey's clout among viewers spawned a lawsuit from Texas cattlemen after she swore off hamburgers to avoid mad cow disease. Two months later, a jury in Amarillo, Texas, acquitted her of libeling an entire food industry. In 1998, she established Oxygen Media, a women's cable television network that featured her unscripted *Oprah After the Show* half hour. Her publications include coauthored self-help handbooks—*Homecoming When the Soldiers Returned from Vietnam* (1989), *Make the Connection: Ten Steps to a Better Body—and a Better Life* (1996), *A Journal of Daily Renewal: The Companion to Make the Connection* (1996), *Journey to Beloved* (1998), *The Uncommon Wisdom of Oprah Winfrey: A Portrait in Her Own Words* (2000), and *Live Your Best Life: A Treasury of Wisdom, Wit, Advice, Interviews, and Inspiration from O, the Oprah Magazine* (2005). Audiocassettes like *Oprah: An Autobiography* (1994) and *Oprah Winfrey Speaks* (1998) personalized her philosophy.

In 2000, Winfrey's woman-to-woman touch inspired two magazines, the monthly *O, The Oprah Magazine*, edited by her best friend Gayle King, and a 2004 spin-off, the quarterly *O at Home*. On December 23, 2004, the star joined actor Tom Cruise in hosting the Nobel Peace Prize Concert; the following year, she produced *The Color Purple* as a Broadway musical and aired a screen adaptation of Zora Neale Hurston's feminist classic *Their Eyes Were Watching God* (2005), featuring Halle Berry as journeywoman Janie Crawford. In the animated *Charlotte's Web* (2006), Winfrey provided the voice of Gussie the goose; a similar project in 2007 featured her as Judge Bumbleden in *Bee Movie*.

Good Deeds

Winfrey holds prominence as one of the media's most generous philanthropists. In 1996, her book club promoted literacy by selecting new works like *The Bluest Eye*, *She's Come Undone*, and *The Poisonwood Bible*, and classics like *Night*, *East of Eden*, *The Good Earth*, and *Anna Karenina*. She based her selections on humanistic themes and insight into difficult choices. With Stedman Graham, Winfrey offered a graduate course, "The Dynamics of Leadership," to a hundred students at Northwestern University. Through her Web site, Oprah.com, she coordinated interactive viewer and reader response, charity drives organized by Angel Network, and alerts through "Oprah's Child Predator Watch List." Her concern for children compensated for her own childlessness and concern for the welfare of the young and vulnerable.

At a Christmas gift program near Johannesburg, South Africa, Winfrey's team distributed school uniforms, dolls, soccer balls, books and school supplies, and food to 50,000 orphans and children displaced from home by poverty and AIDS. Bishop Desmond Tutu expressed thanks; President Nelson Mandela praised her investment in the future of Africa, which she identified as "our human family that is suffering across the ocean" (Nelson, 2005, 8). Her outreach raised funds for home construction in Alabama, Louisiana, Mississippi, and Texas following hurricanes Katrina and Rita. She extended her range in 2006 with a new radio channel, Oprah & Friends, over XM Satellite Radio. In 2007, she opened a leadership academy for 152 girls in South Africa and set up a temporary residence for herself among students who consider her a second mother. In May 2007, when she fought exhaustion and weight gain from hypothyroidism, she returned to South Africa to convalesce among the students.

The star, a prominent billionaire with fans as far away as Saudi Arabia and Beijing, China, made her home in Montecito near Santa Barbara, California, on a 42-acre site she named the Promised Land. For her busy life, she added homes in the Streeterville section of Chicago and in Lavallette, New Jersey, and getaway spots in Miami, Maui, and Telluride, Colorado, and a farm in Indiana. Her awards include a Peabody citation for individual achievement, being named *Newsweek*'s most important individual in the media, a Bob Hope Humanitarian Award, the *TV Guide* performer of the year, a gold medal from the International Radio & Television Society, induction into the National Association for the Advancement of Colored People Hall of Fame, being listed as one of *Time* magazine's 100 most influential people, a National Academy of Television Arts and Sciences Lifetime Achievement Award, and recognition as the world's first black female billionaire. In 2007, black historian and critic Henry Louis Gates, Jr., honored Winfrey with *Finding Oprah's Roots: Finding Your Own*, a guide to genealogy that urged tolerance and forgiveness as the routes to illuminating a personal past. Of her own rescue, she remarked, "You discover that you are not so bad after all. It's an amazing thing" (Krohn, 2002, 54).

Sources

Garson, Helen S. *Oprah Winfrey: A Biography*. Westport, CT: Greenwood, 2003.
Gates, Henry Louis, Jr. *Finding Oprah's Roots: Finding Your Own*. New York: Crown, 2007.
Krohn, Katherine E. *Oprah Winfrey*. Minneapolis, MN: Twenty-First Century Books, 2002.
Lowe, Janet. *Oprah Winfrey Speaks: Insights from the World's Most Influential Voice*. Indianapolis, IN: Wiley, 2001.
Nelson, Marcia Z. *The Gospel According to Oprah*. Louisville, KY: Westminster John Knox Press, 2005.
Rowe, Patricia. "Child Abuse Telecast Floods National Hotline—'Scared Silent: Exposing and Ending Child Abuse' Hosted by Oprah Winfrey." *Children Today* 21(2) (March–April 1992).

■ Religious Fanaticism
Betty Mahmoody

Betty Lover Mahmoody, a speaker and author on child abduction, denounced Islamic patriarchy for condoning child abduction. Born in Detroit, Michigan, in 1945, at age 18, she married an unaffectionate mate. She graduated from Alma College and worked in Elsie, Michigan at ITT Hancock as office manager. She was divorced and responsible for sons Joe and John. In addition to work, she volunteered annually for the Muscular Dystrophy Association canvass. In 1974, she met Sayyed Bozorg "Moody" Mahmoody, a 3-year resident osteopath from Shustar, Iran, 8 years her senior, and his nephew Reza, a student at Wayne State University. At the time, while she studied industrial management at Lansing Community College in Owosso, Sayyed treated her for migraines that blindsided her with vertigo, nausea, and weakness. Tests at Carson City Hospital showed no brain tumor. Eventually, the symptoms disappeared.

For 3 years, while Sayyed trained in anesthesiology at Detroit Osteopathic Hospital and moonlighted at the Fourteenth Street Clinic, he courted Betty with handmade cards, bouquets, jewelry, and perfume. The orphaned son of two physicians, he declared himself done with Iran and with an extended family that didn't understand him. Their weekends at his apartment satisfied her need for a gentle lover. She perceived in Sayyed brilliance, affection, and devotion to family alongside a callousness and cultural confusion. She also recognized his possessiveness in his insistence on holding her hand or shoulders in a roomful of people.

Marriage to Sayyed

When Sayyed received a job at Corpus Christi Osteopathic Hospital in 1977, the couple married and enjoyed travels in Canada and Mexico. They produced daughter Mahtob in 1980. Sayyed balked at sharing a checking account with his wife but gave in to American customs of joint finance. He enjoyed conversation and sought genteel comforts and healthful, hygienic home conditions. He lavished Betty and Mahtob with two cars, expensive furnishings, and a vacation home in Corpus Christi, Texas. Betty learned to cook rice Iranian style with basil, mint, leeks, and beans and to steam vegetables with spices, onions, and lamb chunks. At age 4, the child anticipated entering a Montessori kindergarten in late summer 1984. Sayyed looked forward to building the family's dream house.

The family planned a vacation to Tehran for August 3 to visit for two weeks with Sayyed's sister, Sara Mahmoody Ghodsi, the family matriarch, whom he had missed in 2 decades away from Iran. Betty arranged for her ex-husband to keep her sons during the vacation but concealed her destination from her parents. Sayyed provided a single Iranian passport for himself, his wife, and their daughter. Before the departure, he grew sullen and resentful and spent $4,000 on credit cards for gifts for his Iranian family. The vacation followed Sayyed's loss of his post at a Detroit hospital, which he initially concealed from his wife. Betty, at age 39, felt uneasy about 47-year-old Sayyed's depression, but she commiserated with his suffering a low point in his career far from home and family. He took an oath on the Koran that the family would return to Michigan but later recanted the oath as the only way to convince Betty to leave her homeland. Consultation with attorneys eased her fears of the trip, but panic returned as the British Airways jet approached Iran.

Marital Duties

At Sayyed's demand, Betty honored Iran's veiling laws by entering the plane's tiny restroom to put on a matronly suit, heavy black panty hose, and dark green head covering. At Teheran airport, she feared arrest for unintentionally revealing her hair and facial skin. To her surprise, over 100 relatives descended on the family. She recoiled from the dray labor of women in chadors and pitied how they struggled to cover their faces with a scarf while dragging luggage with their free hands. She later remarked, "The more devout Iranian women allowed only a single eye to poke through.... I marveled at the power their society and their religion held over them" (Mahmoody, 1993, 5). In the city, she feared a siege mentality. Among police and soldiers, she observed indiscriminate car searches for American tapes of rock music or for anti-Islamic literature. Most frightening were the ayatollah's secret police, which humiliated and punished women for unseemly behavior or public dress.

Betty discovered two extremes among her in-laws. Half were sophisticated and English-speaking; the other half were peasant drones obsessed with the Shi'ite sect. Her sister-in-law, Sara, and her husband, Baba Hajji, kept a filthy, vermin-ridden house and fomented trouble between the visitors and his family. When Betty fell ill with assorted complaints, Sayyed treated her. Relatives, speaking only Farsi, made no effort to conceal traditional hostility toward Americans and Christianity. The streets flooded with refugees; television news blared

Irani success in its war over Iraq and concealed from viewers any Irani casualties. At meals of oily entrées, the Iranis fawned over Sayyed while Betty and Mahtob sank into isolation and fought their distaste for greasy food. Mother and daughter retreated to the bedroom to relax on the mattress and hope the two weeks would pass quickly.

Under the pressure of Shi'ite religious fanatics, in mid-August, Sayyed rededicated himself to the fundamentalist faith and developed bizarre attitudes and behaviors. For the next 18 months, Mahmoody chafed at brutality, isolation from Mahtob, and virtual imprisonment that destroyed Mahtob's happy childhood and her filial trust in Sayyed. He stripped his wife and daughter of civil rights and forced Betty to wear her chador in Baba Hajji's house. Goodbye kisses were forbidden as inappropriate in front of young children. Sayyed placed his wife and daughter under house arrest in squalid rooms before resettling them under careful guard at his brother Mammal and sister-in-law Nasserine's apartment. In front of Mahtob, Sayyed predicted that Betty would remain in Iran until she died.

Maid and Inmate

In an atmosphere of screened windows covered by iron bars, Betty became a live-in domestic while Nasserine attended the university, studied scripture, and prayed. Among the culinary chores was the reduction of a lump of sugar into cubes through which to suck tea. At the market, she shopped with Mahtob and Nasserine's 1-year-old son, Amir, and selected fresh bread, fruit, meat, and vegetables. Sayyed spent heavily in Iran and networked with the medical community to locate job opportunities. Meanwhile, the family owed money for rent, utilities, and payments to the Internal Revenue Service, which Sayyed swore never to pay again. To recoup their losses, he instructed Betty to have her parents liquidate their assets and send the money to Iran. After 7 months of idleness, Sayyed rejoiced at an anesthesiologist's position that he landed by under-the-table dealings.

At home, Betty drew Sayyed into medical discussions, the best way to involve him with friends and outsiders. The ruse worked in the park, where Sayyed engaged a clinic office manager in shoptalk while Betty conferred with friend Judy. Betty concluded that "[Iranis] are used to living in a clandestine manner, probably under the shah as well as the ayatollah. Plots and counterplots abound" in offices and families (Mahmoody, 1993, 173). After Betty alerted her mother with a telephone call home, he restricted Betty from telephone use and confiscated her credit cards, cash, and American birth certificate and passports. She relied on her friend Ellen Rafaie, but discovered that Ellen confessed Betty's plot for escape to her fanatic husband, Hormoz. Betty feared that Sayyed would agree with Hormoz's conjugal terrorism and murder her for attempting to take Mahtob home to Detroit.

Desperation

While international efforts through the State Department and the American Embassy in Frankfurt dragged on, Betty filled out forms for new passports. She listened to advice from two American women, Suzanne and Trish, both married to Iranians, and from Hamid, a sympathetic merchant in a menswear shop. Like a prisoner of war, Betty endured interrogation, thrashings, and death threats and concealed a paring knife and table knife to use as tools to remove screws and pry hinges off doors for an escape. She agonized at Sayyed's cruel suspicions of Mahtob. Two days before the child's 5th birthday, Sayyed held her down while a physician sewed up a cut that Sayyed inflicted on Mahtob's upper lip with the back of his hand. Betty held her child's hand and fought off queasiness at the barbaric medical system. After teachers returned Mahtob from class for crying, he blamed his wife for every failure of the child to acclimate to Iran. Betty realized their vulnerability in a society where the Ayatollah Rumollah Khomeini's regime and his antiwoman laws elevated men to supremacy over women and children. Sayyed demanded a choice—remain in Iran and obey him or return to Detroit without Mahtob. She realized she had lost her, adding, "Darkness encompassed me now and I wrestled with my faith" (Mahmoody, 1993, 209).

When Betty protested at the U.S. Interest Section of the Swiss embassy, she learned that national law made her a citizen of Iran because she wed an Iranian male. Increasing her anxiety was the illness of her father, Harold Lover of Bannister, Michigan, who was taking chemotherapy. Sayyed exacerbated her fears by insisting that they sell their American property and belongings and invest the cash in Iran. On a marketing trip, she encountered an agent from an underground network that aided non-Muslim women to escape. To gain time for planning, she pretended to embrace devout Shi'ite customs and to study for conversion to Islam. Sayyed believed her act and moved the family to his brother's house. Mahtob enrolled at Madrasay Zainab, a government-operated religious school for girls; Betty took a scripture class from Englishwomen who demanded reading in unison and chanting unison prayers. While learning the Koran, Betty met another hostage wife who mailed a letter for Betty to her mother asking that her brother Jim and wife Robin help arrange a return to the United States. The act cost the wife a severe beating.

Betty's first attempts to escape failed because they were too obvious. In 1986, she shifted to another ruse to free herself and her 6-year-old daughter—a 500-mile flight northwest into Turkey, for which guides charged as much as $30,000. Despite ongoing civil war in the area, Betty insisted she could make the trip with her child. For the journey, Betty wrapped her head in fabric like Kurdish women wore. From the city, a courier named Amahl drove them to Tabriz. The trek over desert and mountains took them to safety on horseback, by car and pickup, and, finally, on foot through Kurdish holdouts. In the dark, they sped over serpentine curves to a farm and hid in an unheated cement barn. The crackling of ice under horse hooves threatened to summon avalanches from treacherous slopes. Along the way, Mahtob's cooperation amazed her mother that so young a child would risk death to escape her father.

The trip to Van in east Turkey required relays by teams of smugglers. At one point, Betty and Mahtob hid in a Red Cross ambulance. In the final dash over terrain too steep for horses, Mahmoody collapsed from carrying Mahtob. Their guides dragged her the rest of the way to the U.S. embassy. Still under threat from Sayyed and Shi'ite authorities, after a week of travel, she and Mahtob flew from Ankara to Oswego, Michigan, and adopted aliases. Betty was thrilled to find her father still alive. She borrowed cash to repay Amahl.

Betty as Social Reformer

In recovery, Mahmoody chose to expose fanatic Islamic males for abducting her and Mahtob. She founded One World: For Children, a pro-woman outreach to the children of bicultural marriages, which set up programs to alert other women and children of the danger of international parental kidnappings. Her bestselling eyewitness account, *Not Without My Daughter: A True Story* (1987), cowritten by William Hoffer, described Muslim misogyny. It flourished in book clubs and sociology and religion classes, as a Literary Guild/Doubleday Book Club selection and Reader's Digest Condensed Book, and among readers in France, Germany, and Sweden. Muslims protested the American stereotype that all male Muslims abuse their wives and daughters. She continued her story in a sequel, *For Love of a Child* (1992).

Mahmoody developed a reputation for insider knowledge about Iran. During custody trials between Iranian fathers and American mothers in Florida and Minnesota, Mahmoody served as expert witness. She also testified before the Michigan state legislature on international custody differences. The U.S. State Department hired her as a consultant on matters involving women's rights and male dominance under Islam. Her experience influenced passage of the 1993 International Parental Kidnapping Act protecting wives and children from kidnap. Publicity earned her invitations to speak on radio and television talk shows—*Donahue*, *Larry King Live*, *Oprah Winfrey*, *Sally Jesse Raphael*, and *20/20* with Barbara Walters. Betty often appeared with Mahtob, now a graduate of Michigan State University with a degree in psychology, who bore emotional damage from the hostage situation.

Betty Mahmoody's courage made her a feminist hero. She received a woman of the year citation from Germany, an Outstanding Woman of the Year citation from Oakland University, and a Pulitzer Prize nomination for her first book. Universal International turned *Not Without My Daughter* into a docudrama in 1991, featuring Sally Field as the courageous mother and Alfred Molina as Sayyed. Actor Sheila Rosenthal won a Best Actress Young Artist Award for depicting Mahtob. The movie, shot in Neve Ilan, Israel, and in Atlanta, Georgia, concluded with Betty's reverence for the American flag, which fluttered over an international haven. A Hindi film version of the story, *Shakti* (2002), resets the family's move as Canada to India and alters Shi'ism to militant Hinduism. In 2002, director Alexis Kouros filmed *Without My Daughter*, a documentary refuting Betty's claims and relating events of the visit to Iran from Sayyed's perspective.

Sources

Haddad, Yvonne Yazbeck, Jane I. Smith, and Kathleen M. Moore. *Muslim Women in America: The Challenge of Islamic Identity Today*. New York: Oxford University Press, 2006.

Hinz, Joan. "Captive in Body, but Not in Spirit: Woman Relied on God's Grace to Make Escape from Iran." *Western Catholic Reporter*, April 5, 1999.

Kamalipour, Yanya R. *The U.S. Media and the Middle East: Image and Perception*. Westport, CT: Greenwood, 1995.

Mahmoody, Betty. *Not Without My Daughter: A True Story*. New York: St. Martin's Press, 1993.

Steindorf, Sara. "Betty and Mahtob Mahmoody." *Christian Science Monitor*, June 6, 2000, 23.

■ Residue of Slavery
Ernest Gaines

A beloved Southern author and spokesman for "his people," Ernest James Gaines earned renown for smashing black literary stereotypes that date to the slave trade. The eldest child of Adrienne Jefferson Gaines and Manuel Gaines, a black Delta sharecropper, the writer claims Anglo-African-Native American lineage. Born in Oscar, Louisiana, on January 15, 1933, on River Lake Plantation near New Roads, Pointe Coupee Parish, he matured in Cherie Quarters, a compound of employees' shacks built by slaves. His Grandmother Jefferson cooked at the big house while Grandfather Gaines groomed the yard. The author, whom family called "Ernie," lived among elitist, violent Cajuns who once owned his ancestors, sugar plantation workers dating back five generations to the 1830s. From infancy, he lived among whites who had no interest in the black culture that thrived in the Delta for 300 years. He was baptized in the False River where local people washed laundry and fished for bream, catfish, and sac-au-lait. Like a slave, from age 8, he earned 50 cents a day chopping cane, pulling corn, digging onions and potatoes, picking blackberries, and harvesting cotton. On special occasions, he traveled by car beyond the quarter with an aunt who peddled cosmetics.

After Adrienne Gaines separated from her husband and moved to a plantation job in New Orleans, Gaines and his three sisters and eight brothers became the wards of their disabled great-aunt, Augusteen Jefferson, a Creole speaker and exemplar of physical and moral strength. Lacking a wheelchair, Aunt Teen set the example of survivalism by crawling to finish housekeeping chores, to gather pecans, and to weed and harvest a vegetable garden. She patched their clothes on a treadle sewing machine and cooked over a wood stove that the children stoked with kindling. Her stoicism set Gaines's philosophy: "Any person who's worth a goddamn must really struggle" (Gaines, 1995, 58).

The Gaines children absorbed an oral culture, a blend of black, Cajun, Creole, and standard English perpetuated by a preliterate people. For her children's edification, while peanuts and sweet potatoes roasted in the ashes, Aunt Teen asked guests to sit on the porch or by the fireplace. In good company, they sipped coffee and home brew and retold folk tales, jokes, and ghost stories. They gathered for folk ceremonies—sugar cane grinding, corn shucking, quilting, weddings, birthings, funerals, and wakes and discussed life issues and memories. From informal storytelling sessions on dirt banks and in swamps and cane fields, Gaines mastered the immediacy of first person Southern narrative. He reminisced, "For me there's no more beautiful sound anywhere—unless, of course—you take exceptional pride in 'proper' French or 'proper' English" (Callahan, 2001, 214).

Education activated Gaines's potential for mimicry and transmission of the past. From late October to early April, he studied at a one-room black school in nearby Mount Zion Baptist Church under an itinerant teacher commuting from Baton Rouge or New Roads, the town he recreated in his novels as Bayonne. People of the quarter admired and promoted his scholarship. In grade six, he entered St. Augustine School, a parochial school in New Roads. After mastering a legible longhand, he volunteered as neighborhood scribe and newspaper reader and penned letters for the illiterate. For classmates, he produced, directed, and acted in an original drama.

Discovering Literature

Because of educational inequalities for blacks, Gaines's Louisiana schooling ended in his midteens. Traveling by Trailways bus to New Orleans and 2 days by segregated train with a stash of fried chicken and tea cakes, at age 15, he moved to Vallejo, California. He lived with his mother and Catholic stepfather, Raphael Norbert Colar, a merchant marine, and seven stepsiblings. Decades later, he honored his mother and stepfather by creating St. Adrienne Parish and St. Raphael Parish, fictional microcosms of blacks and Creoles similar to the blacks and whites who populate William Faulkner's Yoknapatawpha County. The family occupied a government project among blacks, Chicanos, Chinese, Filipinos, Indians, Japanese, and whites. At his stepfather's direction, Gaines abandoned street loafing and tried boxing at the YMCA, where poor performance proved his unworthiness in the sport.

In lieu of money for expensive movie houses, Gaines frequented free libraries that were open to all races. Looking for works reflecting the lower South he knew from birth, he searched the shelves but found no settings equal to his home. The closest he came to Louisiana were the Nebraska plains described by Willa Cather and John Steinbeck's beloved Salinas, California. To fill a need, Gaines determined to write his own experiences. At age 16, while tending a little brother, he tapped out a first novel, *The Little Stream*, by rented typewriter on half sheets and bound the pages into a book. The text, which emulated European authors, vivified peasant life. A New York publisher rejected the pages; Gaines tossed the package in the backyard incinerator. A decade later, he reprised the text, published as *Catherine Carmier* (1964), which he set in the early 1960s.

Gaines studied at Vallejo High School and Vallejo Junior Collge and was drafted into the army in 1953 shortly after the death of his Aunt Teen. During training at Fort Ord, California, and Camp Chaffee, Arkansas, and a year in Guam, he won two short story competitions for a total of $25. A second hitch was tempting, but he chose schooling over security. On $110 a month from the GI bill, in 1957, he earned a degree in literature and writing from San Francisco State University (SFSU). Coursework introduced him to the autobiography of James Joyce, the polyphony of Sherwood Anderson, the Russian psychological fiction of Fyodor Dostoevsky and Ivan Turgenev, and peasant lore by Émile Zola, Auguste Flaubert, and Guy de Maupassant. Gaines attended Stanford University on a creative writing fellowship in company with authors Wendell Berry, Ken Kesey, and Tillie Olsen and mentors Malcolm Cowley, Richard Scowcroft, and Wallace Stegner.

A Slow Process

At a part-time job at an insurance agency, Gaines slipped into the bathroom to write fiction on paper towels. His focus was a universal struggle—the grace under pressure that American blacks mastered over 3 centuries of exploitation and mistreatment. He asserted, "I do respect men under pressure . . . that they go through hell but come through some kind of way" (Gaines, 1995, 19). After reading his story "The Turtles" (1956), which he published in *Transfer*, the campus literary magazine at SFSU, literary agent Dorothea Oppenheimer encouraged the 23-year-old aspiring writer to launch a professional career. He published in *Callaloo*, *CEA Critic*, *Negro Digest*, *New Mexico Quarterly*, *Sewanee Review*, *Southern Review*, *Stanford Short Stories*, and *Texas Quarterly* and completed two more novels, a Romeo and Juliet plot in *Of Love and Dust* (1967) and *Bloodline* (1968), a salute to black manhood in a setting still dominated by slave-era narrow-mindedness. He noticed that his novels crept back in time, first to the World War II era, then to the 1930s.

While working at his literary career at a flat at the corner of Divisadero Street and Golden Gate Avenue in San Francisco, Gaines supported himself with a series of odd jobs—dishwasher, shoe shiner, cab driver, printers' devil, postal deliverer, and mail room clerk. He surrounded himself with black and white photos that he took of his Louisiana home before the destruction of houses, stores, and open spaces along the river. Of visual stimuli from the South, he rhapsodized on place: "I have to touch, I have to be, you melt into things and you let them melt into you . . . the trees, the rivers, the bayous, the language, the sounds" (Gaines, 1995, 69). His grandmother filled his kitchen with the fragrances of gumbo, jambalaya, and shrimp creole. During the upheavals of the Vietnam War and civil rights movement, he stuck to writing and left protesting to others.

For 2½ years, Gaines remained strapped for living expenses until he published a bestselling novel, *The Autobiography of Miss Jane Pittman* (1971), the story of a woman who battles Southern bigotry by sipping from a fountain. Unlike his first three novels, it was a saga covering the range of Delta history from slavery to integration. The style drew on Works Projects Administration interviews with former slaves and exhibited the influence of Southern regional dialect in William Faulkner's *The Sound and the Fury*. For accuracy, Gaines listened to spirituals and sermons, the rural blues of Lightnin' Hopkins and B. B. King, and the musings of black elders. To background recordings of Mussorgsky's *Pictures at an Exhibition*, Gaines related the saga through the voice of a believable fictional character. In a 1978 issue of *Callaloo*, he published "Miss Jane and I," a reflection on his classic novel and its roots in his Louisiana homeland.

A Classic Author of the Black Experience

An engaging, introspective loner, Gaines no longer has to hide to write. In 1976, he tackled the alienated father and son motif for *In My Father's House* (1978), a novel about which he said, "[It had] been kicking my ass around for ten years" (Gaines, 1995, 100). He achieved critical respect in American and Southern literature and black studies courses, where his works appeared on reading lists. Shortly before taking a teaching post at the University of Southwestern Louisiana in Lafayette in 1981, Gaines was strapped financially and facing knee surgery. The administration allowed him to move to campus housing. He continued teaching and lecturing, wrote fiction daily, and served as writer in residence at Denison and Stanford Universities. In addition to giving readings, at age 50, he scheduled his first visit in eighteen years to his rural lowland birthplace. He settled permanently in Lafayette in 1984 and traveled to speaking engagements at the University of Mississippi and at the Sorbonne in Paris. He married for the first time at age 60 to Dianne Saulney Gaines, a Miami assistant district attorney, and continued teaching in the fall quarter as professor emeritus of English at the University of Louisiana at Lafayette. At age 70, he retired to a house on the False River. To accommodate arthritic joints, he depends on a cane.

Gaines's uniqueness lies in his ease with Southern rural folk and their complex social layering, the strength of *Mozart and Leadbelly: Stories and Essays* (2005). Set in the 1940s, the text bears the sense impressions of Gaines' childhood and his admiration of iconoclasts who defy long-standing racist tradition. *Time* credited the author with storytelling flair and with circumspection in reenacting the explosive issues of lynching, racial bias, injustice, and gradual biculturalism. Rather than follow trends toward a ghetto milieu, Gaines dipped into early black American history of agrarian communities for realistic characters, idiom, and patois. His characterization avoided the stark contrast of racists and victims to find a mix of qualities in his entire cast.

Gaines and Fame

A respectable list of honors accrued to Gaines—a Rockefeller grant, Guggenheim fellowship, Black Academy of Arts and Letters award, Southern Book Award, Langston Hughes Award, Wallace Stegner fellowship, Joseph Henry Jackson Award, National Endowment of the Arts stipend, National Humanities Medal, two citations from the Commonwealth Club of California, Louisiana Library Association award, and a San Francisco Arts Commission award. Denison University, Brown University, Bard College, Whittier College, Tulane, Loyola, Sewanee, Savannah College, and Louisiana State University conferred honorary degrees on him. From the John D. and Catherine T. MacArthur Foundation, in 1993, he received a cash prize of $355,000; the same year, he won a Dos Passos Prize and acclaim as the Louisiana Humanist of the Year. At age 67, he acquired a French Order of Arts and

Letters, the National Governors' Arts Award, an American Academy and Institute of Arts and Letters citation, and the title of Louisiana Writer of the Year. In 2002, he accepted the Anisfield-Wolf Book Award for lifetime achievement. Five years later, the Baton Rouge Area Foundation set up an annual $10,000 award to a black writer who perpetuates the Gaines legacy.

Three of Gaines' novels and one short work have adapted well to television. *The Autobiography of Miss Jane Pittman*, which CBS TV aired on January 3, 1974, featured Cicely Tyson in the starring role as a 110-year-old former slave. The film, which won nine Emmy awards and was named outstanding special of the year, created such verisimilitude that viewers thought Jane was a historic figure. Critics lauded the quality of Joseph Sargent's direction and the performances of Cicely Tyron, Lisa Arrindell Anderson, and Irma P. Hall. A short work, "The Sky Is Gray" aired in 1980 on WHMM TV as part of *The Humanities American Short Story* series. Directed by Stan Lathan and starring Olivia Cole, James Bond, Margaret Avery, and Cleavon Little, it is available on video. The screen version of *A Gathering of Old Men* (1983), also filmed for CBS TV on May 10, 1987, starred Lou Gossett, Jr., and Richard Widmark. A documentary—*Ernest J. Gaines: Louisiana Stories*—appeared on WHMM TV in 1992. On May 26, 1999, HBO showcased *A Lesson Before Dying* (1993), a prison novel of an actual murder trial that won a National Book Critics Circle Award, Pulitzer Prize nomination, and selection for Oprah's Book Club. The screen version featured Don Cheadle as convict Grant Wiggins and Mekhi Phifer as Jefferson. The novel, adapted by playwright Romulus Linney appeared on stage at the Alabama Shakespeare Festival in January 2000 and, in September 2000, off Broadway.

Sources

Auger, Philip. *Native Sons in "No Man's Land": Rewriting Manhood in the Novels of Baldwin, Walker, Wideman, and Gaines*. New York: Garland, 2000.

Brown, Dale W. "A Lesson for Living." *Sojourners* 31(5) (September–October 2002): 30–33.

Callahan, John F. *In the African-American Grain: Call-and-Response in Twentieth-Century Black Fiction*. Chicago: University of Illinois Press, 2001.

Doyle, Mary Ellen. *Voices from the Quarters: The Fiction of Ernest J. Gaines*. Lafayette, LA: Louisiana State University Press, 2002.

Gaines, Ernest J. *Conversations with Ernest Gaines*. Jackson, MS: University Press of Mississippi, 1995.

Gertjegerdes-Myricks, Petra. "Lest We Forget: Ernest Gaines's *The Autobiography of Miss Jane Pittman*." *Columbus Times*, January 18, 2000, 1.

"Remember When: Cherie Quarters Housed Family and Many Friends of Author Ernest Gaines." *Advocate* (Baton Rouge), June 20, 1999.

Sachs, Mark. "They Changed the Face of TV." *Los Angeles Times*, February 1, 2002, F 31.

Simon, Scott. "Interview: Ernest J. Gaines." NPR's *Weekend Edition*, February 5, 2005.

Weeks, Jerome. "Author Ernest J. Gaines Mines His Rich Southern Past." *Dallas Morning News*, February 28, 2001.

■ Rheumatoid Arthritis
Kathleen Turner

A passionate, funny screen and stage actor, Mary Kathleen Turner could not conceal the effects of rheumatoid arthritis. A native of Springfield, Missouri, she was born the third of four children on June 19, 1954, to Patsy "Pat" Magee, an employee of the United Nations, and Allen Richard Turner, a teacher and U.S. Foreign Service officer who survived interning by the Japanese during World War II. The family exhibited a strong Methodist tradition from her great grandfather, a missionary to China. While her family lived at embassies in Toronto, Canada; London, England; and Washington, D.C., she developed poise and the ability to adapt to new situations. Her father evacuated the family from Havana during the Cuban Revolution in 1958 and closed the American embassy. In Caracas, Venezuela, her favorite posting, she acquired a Spanish accent.

Turner prepared well for her career. She developed agility from swimming in the creek, running across fields, gardening, stacking hay bales into forts, and playing games demanding strength and coordination. While attending the American School in London, she trained in gymnastics and studied at the Central School of Speech and Drama. At the theater, she admired the skills of British stars Angela Lansbury, Christopher Plummer, and Diana Rigg and decided on acting for a career. Because her father disapproved of the profession, while his wife attended Kathleen's stage performances in Canada, he sat outside in the car. At age 17, she was a leggy beauty eager for success. In 1971, she ran away to Stratford-on-Avon and returned to turmoil an hour after her father's sudden death from a heart attack. The next year, she settled with her mother, brother, and sister on her grandparents' farm in Springfield and studied voice at Southwest Missouri State University. In 1974, she landed a bit part in Pat Conroy's biopic *Conrack*. To escape a culturally sterile environment, she transferred to the University of Maryland to complete a B.F.A. in drama. She left home for New York in 1977, worked as a waitress and hotel receptionist, found an agent, and auditioned for advertising and acting jobs.

From Soaps to Star

At age 24, Turner failed at her first job, as Nola Dancy Aldrich in the NBC TV serial *The Doctors*. The next year, she moved on to the Soho Repertory Theatre in New York to appear in *Mr. T* and to Broadway in 1978 in *Gemini*. With the help of agent and paramour David Guc, her screen debut in 1981 in *Body Heat* made her an instant star for the role of sexual predator Matty Walker. Teaming with William Hurt and Richard Crenna in the noir thriller, she played a sultry, disgruntled wife seeking murder for hire. Critics compared her overt vampishness to that of Lauren Bacall, Bette Davis, Ava Gardner, Barbara Stanwyck, and Lana Turner. For the erotic role, *Empire* magazine selected Turner as one of the 100 sexiest stars in cinema history.

To broaden her options, Turner worked at versatility. She depicted the patient, Dolores Benedict, opposite Steve Martin as brain surgeon Michael Hfuhruhurr in Carl Reiner's mad scientist comedy, *The Man with Two Brains* (1983). The synergy of Turner with Michael Douglas and Danny DeVito in box office hit *Romancing the Stone* (1984) increased her celebrity and earned her a Golden Globe for the part of romance novelist Joan Wilder. She followed in *The Breed Apart* (1984) and in the sexually complex role of fashion designer Joanna Crane and prostitute China Blue in *Crimes of Passion* (1984), a psychological study of female duality. Turner snagged a second contract to play Joan Wilder in *The Jewel of the Nile* (1985), a reprise of energetic adventure requiring the book writer to flee pirates. Because of the weak script, she tried to duck her contract obligations to a sequel, but the studio launched a $25 million lawsuit to force her to comply.

A Burst of Success

At a reform ceremony performed in Manhattan by Rabbi Seligman, in 1984, Turner wed Jewish realty developer Jay Weiss and settled on 65th Street near Lincoln Center. Three years later, the couple moved to Suffolk County, Long Island. As a volunteer, she read Greek mythology and William Shakespeare's plays in schools and worked with battered women at The Retreat. Despite a hectic film career, she bore daughter Rachel Ann and enrolled her in Jewish training. Turner's second Golden Globe resulted from casting with Jack Nicholson and Anjelica Huston in the Mafia crime comedy *Prizzi's Honor* (1985), in which Turner plays femme fatale tax consultant and hired gun Irene Walker. For Francis Ford Coppola's *Peggy Sue Got Married* (1986), a nostalgic satire of the 1950s opposite Nicolas Cage, she won an Oscar nomination in the title role of Peggy Sue Bodell, a high school sweetheart who outgrows romantic dreams. Her spate of leading men numbered some of Hollywood's most appealing. For *Julia and Julia* (1987), she caromed between Gabriel Byrne and Sting. She appeared with Burt Reynolds, Christopher Reeve, and Ned Beatty in the weak comedy *Switching Channels* (1988) and a second time with William Hurt in the screen version of Anne Tyler's redemptive novel *The Accidental Tourist* (1988).

Turner withdrew from the camera to take the lead in the Long Wharf Theater's 1987 production of *Camille* and to narrate *Dear America: Letters Home from Vietnam* (1987). She provided her signature gravelly alto voice for cartoon temptress Jessica Rabbit opposite comedian Charles Fleischer's title role in *Who Framed Roger Rabbit* (1988), a blend of human and animated characterization. The cynical anthropomorphism spawned three sequels, *Tummy Trouble* (1989), *Roller Coaster Rabbit* (1990), and *Trail Mix-Up* (1993). In a third teaming with Douglas and DeVito, she produced a lethally passionate role by doing some of her own stunts for *The War of the Roses* (1989), the comic tale of the marriage breakup of Barbara and Oliver Rose. Her onscreen daring resulted in a broken nose as the title figure in the detective movie *V. I. Warshawski* (1991), based on the feminist crime novel by Sara Paretsky. For *Serial Mom* (1994), she played a psychotic housewife opposite Sam Waterson and Ricki Lake.

The Body's War on Itself

At age 38, Turner suffered threats to her lifestyle from the painful onset of rheumatoid arthritis (RA). The disease, an autoimmune syndrome exacerbated by stress, began in her feet. It swelled the soft tissue of her neck, hands, and legs, reducing mobility and sapping her strength. She summarized, "It's lifestyle threatening...your sex life, your parenting, your work. Everything is affected by this disease" (Baron-Faust and Buyon, 2004, 50). She envisioned life in a wheelchair. During her months of low fever and limited stamina, she suffered flu-like ague, lost movement in her elbow and toes, and couldn't depend on a typically athletic body. She despaired that her daughter witnessed arthritic hands too weak to squeeze a bottle of body moisturizer. Damage threatened her elbow, knee, and shoulder. She sought help from a podiatrist, an orthopedic surgeon, and a spine specialist. On a shoot in Canada, she spent her lunch hour at a hospital having fluid extracted from joints. More vexing than physical agonies was a fear that daughter Rachel Ann would inherit the disease.

The final diagnosis was a year in coming and required the intervention of her general practitioner, who confirmed RA with a single blood test. She remarked, "My rheumatoid factor was sky-high; he didn't know how I was walking at all" (Baron-Faust and Buyon,

12004, 18). Wobbly on her feet and puffy from methotrexate and prednisone, she developed a reputation for indulgence in drink. She explained, "I didn't tell anyone what the problem really was because I was afraid I wouldn't get work" ("Trimmer," 1996). As she suspected, casting agents stopped calling. A Boston rheumatologist, David E. Trentham, disputed daily use of pain medication and exploratory surgery. Instead, he recommended low doses of antibiotics, avoidance of stair climbing, and daily pool therapy to loosen the joints. Turner gave up high heels, had boots specially made, and tried to ward off the cold of New York winters, which stiffened her joints. She avoided chemicals and salt by choosing fresh foods over canned or frozen. Because of the risk to overall well-being, she abandoned plans to conceive another child and harangued the Women's National Economic Alliance on the lag in women's health care and treatment for chronic illness.

Health and Career Strategies

Turner fought the advance of acute RA. She scheduled 30 minutes of daily yoga, walking in slippers lined with gel pads, diet control, and relief with acupuncture and massage. She worked out with a trainer 90 minutes four times a week with weight lifting, stretching, and cardiovascular stimulation via an elliptical runner, nonimpact aerobic exercise, and pilates. Instead of painkillers, which precipitated anger, fear, and depression, she chose warm paraffin baths for hands and feet. Her husband made a show of courtesies that masked assisting her out of chairs and vehicles. She took more narrative roles—*Hollywood Remembers: Myrna Loy* (1991), *Three Dances by Martha Graham* (1992), *We All Have Tales: Rumplestiltskin* (1992), *The Star* (1995), *American Cinema* (1995), *Love in the Ancient World* (1997), *Castles of the Sea* (1997), *Ancient Mysteries* (1998), *The Science of Sex* (1998), *Dashiell Hammett: Detective, Writer* (1999), and *National Geographic Kids: Creepy Creatures* (2000)—worked on BBC radio, directed *Leslie's Folly* (1994), produced audiocassettes of popular novels, and co-presented at Drama Desk, Oscar, and Tony award ceremonies. At the funeral of Israeli Prime Minister Yitzhak Rabin in November 1995, she recited Walt Whitman's "O Captain, My Captain," a Civil War era eulogy to Abraham Lincoln. In 1996, she managed a vacation to Israel, an evidence of her growing sensitivity to Judaism.

At an ebb in Jay Weiss' earning power, physical limitations ended Turner's stardom and precipitated contracts for unglamorous character parts—*A Day at a Time* (1992), *Undercover Blues* (1993), *House of Cards* (1993), *Moonlight and Valentino* (1995), *A Simple Wish* (1997), *The Real Blonde* (1997), *Baby Geniuses* (1999), *Prince of Central Park* (2000), and the animated thrilled *Monster House* (2006)—and for *The Conspiracy of Silence* (1995), a PBS TV documentary on spousal abuse. The CBS TV pilot for *Style and Substance* in 1997 fell through. A more successful venture, Sofia Coppola's *The Virgin Suicides* (1999), paired Turner and James Woods as the parents of the five Lisbon sisters, all of whom commit suicide. In the actor's late 30s, improved therapy with the disease-modifying antirheumatic drugs Enbrel, Celebrex, and Minocycline forced her RA into remission. Television roles on *Biography*, *Entertainment Tonight*, *Friends*, *Law & Order*, *Nip/Tuck*, *The Rosie O'Donnell Show*, and *Sunday AM* and in voiceovers for *The Simpsons* and a Lay's potato chip ad broadened her fan base and revived her career in the States, Australia, and Great Britain. She tried in vitro fertilization, but the drugs promoting conception almost jolted her into active RA. To assist other women facing difficult choices, she appeared on CNN and described the results of her treatment with drugs marketed by Amgen Inc. and Wyeth Pharmaceuticals.

The Actor Up Close

Turner branched out to stage in the 1990s with Broadway roles—in the title part of Maggie the Cat in Tennessee Williams's Pulitzer Prize-winning domestic drama *Cat on a Hot Tin Roof*, which earned her a Tony nomination, and, in 1995, as Yvonne in *Indiscretions*, an adaptation of Jean Cocteau's *Les Parents Terribles*. In 2000, she appeared in London at the Gielgud Theatre in a lucrative adaptation of *The Graduate*, in which she stripped to play the seductive Mrs. Robinson. For a weekly R and R from eight performances a week, she played poker with the cast and crew on Wednesday nights. In 320 performances on Broadway, she missed only four—two each for a torn hamstring and bronchitis. The play continued to draw playgoers in 2002 when it opened off Broadway at the Plymouth Theater. Additional dramatic challenges—as Titania, queen of the fairies, in William Shakespeare's comic romance *A Midsummer Night's Dream* in Washington, D.C., and as Nina in Anton Chekhov's drama *The Seagull* in Winnipeg—preceded a U.S. tour in *Tallulah!*, a one-woman comedy exploring actor Tallulah Bankhead, which debuted at the Chichester Festival. At a weak point in her control of drinking, in November, Turner blacked out. Fearful of turning alcohol into a regular analgesic, she signed herself into Marworth, a substance abuse treatment center in Waverly, Pennsylvania.

In 2004, Savannah College of Art and Design at the Savannah Film Festival presented Turner a lifetime achievement award. After a knee replacement in 2005, she competed against actors Stockard Channing, Christine Lahti, Jessica Lange, and Bette Midler to play Martha, the alcoholic professor's wife in Edward Albee's *Who's Afraid of Virginia Woolf?*, a poignant role popularized on stage by Uta Hagen and on film by Elizabeth Taylor. The performance netted Turner's second Tony nomination and a contract to reprise the play in London at the Apollo Theatre and on tour in 2007. In her free time, she supported Amnesty International, Childhelp USA, City Meals on Wheels, and People for the American Way. As a proponent of women's health, she chaired Planned Parenthood of America; as an advocate for RA victims, she promoted early diagnosis by a rheumatologist, immediate treatment to halt joint damage, and self-education on lifestyle options at www.arthritis.org. Her honors include *Glamour's* woman of the year and listing among *Vanity Fair's* Top 200 Legends, Leaders, and Trailblazers. For canvassing for donations and raising public awareness of RA, she received the Dr. John I. Sandson Lifetime Achievement Award from the Massachusetts Arthritis Foundation. In 2008, she completed an intimate memoir, *Send Yourself Roses: Thoughts on My Life, Love, and Leading Roles*, which won the praises of actor Michael Douglas and feminist leader Gloria Steinem. The core philosophy of Turner's autobiography captured her vibrancy, self-confidence, and determination to beat a crippling disease.

Sources

Baron-Faust, Rita, and Jill P. Buyon. *The Autoimmune Connection: Essential Information for Women on Diagnosis, Treatment, and Getting On with Your Life*. New York: McGraw Hill Professional, 2004.
Green, Jesse. "Kathleen Turner Meets Her Monster." *New York Times*, March 20, 2005.
Lindstrom, Pia. "Real-Life Role Helping Battered Women." *New York Times*, January 12, 1997.
"Trimmer Turner Back on Track." *Los Angeles Daily News*, June 20, 1996.
Turner, Kathleen, and Gloria Feldt. *Send Yourself Roses: Thoughts on My Life, Love, and Leading Roles*. New York: Springboard Press, 2008.

■ Sexism
Shannon Faulkner

In a classic Pyrrhic victory, Shannon Richey Faulkner risked ridicule and possible terrorism to integrate a bastion of male militarism. A native of Powdersville outside Greenville, South Carolina, she was born in 1975 to fence builder Edward "Ed" Faulkner and Sandy Richey Faulkner, a teacher at Powdersville High School. A solid 150 pounds and 5 feet 8 inches in height, she marched with the school band and built muscle by mall walking. For her own reasons, she chose a military education at the Citadel in Charleston. She stated, "I want the whole Citadel experience, and I can get it only at the Citadel" (Jarvis, 2003, 61). Along with the rest of the 2,000 cadets in the student body, she intended to sport the gray uniform, play in the band, and share living space with other band members. She was aware that the college was a tough Moorish fortress known over a 152-year history for rigorous parading, sexism, fanatic conformity, exclusivity, and intimidating the weak. The school allowed no deviation from strict hierarchy, regardless of a plebe's social status or his father's military rank. Faulkner's individuality posed a direct conflict of interest to a tradition founded on male solidarity.

A throwback to the Old South, the Citadel, originally named the Military College of South Carolina, took shape on feudal models of male bonding. Derived from the home guard, it protected Charleston's genteel white majority from a possible slave uprising. Simultaneously, the institution fostered masculine aggression and a contempt for underlings, which denigrated all females, including faculty members and mess hall wait staff. Because the school is a private institution, it hedged past a 1975 law allowing women entrance to U.S. service academies. Apologists declared that channeling male hostilities into socially acceptable outlets produced top-quality soldiers. In 1993, the Citadel corps, with tacit approval of staff and alumni, became a subculture of malice intent on protecting a male bastion from infiltration by coeds. President Claudius Elmer "Bud" Watts III declared that the school's integrity was on the line and vowed to fight coeducation to the end. Beneath euphemisms of brotherhood, duty, honor, and country lurked racism, sexism, obscenity, and a gleeful sadism. Campus misogyny, like the "womanhate" of rap music and pernicious urban gangs, promoted respect for inflicting and tolerating pain and soul-bruising indignities. Obedience to the warrior class became an introit to ideal manhood, soldiery, and obsessive nationalism.

A Bold Teenager

Based on her high school record and character, on January 1993, Faulkner gained admission as a freshman. Her acceptance letter read, "Dear Mr. Faulkner" (Salomone, 2003, 145). The tone altered the following month after the military board realized her gender. One published complaint described her as a "toxic kind of virus" who would infect and weaken the all-male tradition of turning boys into men (Faludi, 2002, 66). The college readied for battle by bolstering graduation requirements with a fitness test—"45 pushups and 55 sit-ups in two-minute sets, and a two-mile run in 16 minutes" (Ibid., 64). An assault on Shannon's home began with disabling the emergency exhaust valve on the water heater, tampering with a gas tank, demolishing a mailbox, tossing firecrackers and bottle rockets on the lawn, and coursing through flowerbeds. An interloper to the telephone voice mail recorded coarse antifemale rap lyrics. At 6 A.M., Ed Faulkner arose to whitewash the terms "bitch," "dyke," "lesbo," and "whore" painted on the clapboard walls and porch columns. The county sheriff's department did little to stem ongoing persecution.

On the counsel of attorney Valorie Kay Vojdik, Faulkner filed a discrimination suit in U.S. District Court in Charleston on grounds of equal protection under the Fourteenth Amendment from single-sex education at a state-funded institution. To the American Civil Liberties Union, the case suited parameters of the Women's Rights Project, cofounded in 1972 by Ruth Bader Ginsburg, an unstinting warrior against sex discrimination. Advocates and education experts flew in from various parts of the country to testify in *Shannon Faulkner and the United States of America v. James Jones et al., for The Citadel*. Second wave feminists vowed to remain close to the case to assure Faulkner's safety. Within days, a sign appeared in Charleston demanding, "Die Shannon." In 1994, Faulkner expressed doubts about ongoing litigation, but her legal team encouraged her to press on. Lead counsel, National Organization of Women (NOW) President Suzanne Coe, made the case a test of the government's sincerity to end sexism in education.

Partway There

After Judge C. Weston Houck cleared the way to admission, in January 1994, Faulkner became an official member of the student body. *Glamour* named her one of the women of the year alongside athlete Martina Navratilova, advocate Tipper Gore, singer Vanessa Williams, and feminist author Naomi Wolf. For 2 years, guarded by federal marshals, Faulkner earned a 3.0 average as a day student and ate and parked her car off campus. She made friends with classmates but remained in civilian dress and outside the corps. Judge Houck demanded that the college assign Faulkner to the barracks instead of making a special case of her by placing her in the infirmary. His ruling permitted the unremitting discipline exacted from all cadets. Attorney Dawes Cooke, speaking for school officials, chose to exempt her from the shaved haircut required of "knobs," the campus term for freshmen. The board attempted another dodge by inventing the South Carolina Institute of Leadership for Women, a parallel curriculum taught 190 miles away at Converse College in Spartanburg similar to the Virginia Military Institute for Leadership, a women's training program at Mary Baldwin College in Staunton, Virginia.

Liz Clark, the NOW Coordinator for South Carolina, rejected a modest girl's school as unequal to a real military education. Clark substantiated her rejection by citing the state's allotment of $3.4 million, over one-third of the cost of a program designed to extenuate androcentric education at the Citadel. Another flaw in the perpetuation of macho military elitism was the "glass ceiling" that inhibited female alumni networking and career advancement. Faulkner chimed in with her own observation that, as a state citizen, she paid taxes for half the student body, all out-of-staters, to attend classes in a school that refused Faulkner the same opportunity.

In Conflict with Tradition

Under a federal court order from Judge Houck, in April 1995, the Citadel dropped its alternate proposal and admitted its first female cadet. In June, a medical form listing her weight prompted school officials to try another ploy to reject her by claiming that she was 21 pounds above the height standard. U.S. Supreme Court Chief Justice William Rehnquist rejected further appeal. Justice Antonin Scalia concurred on the issue that public single-gender education is a violation of gender rights. Meanwhile, the Citadel's legal team appealed its plan to establish a separate women's program, to which Faulkner could be arbitrarily transferred.

On August 12 in her junior year, 20-year-old Faulkner arrived already physically and spiritually pummeled, her weight hovering at 195 pounds. She moved into a private room on the third floor of Law Barracks that worsened her alienation. The male preserve's strategy to set her apart and leave her head unshaved precipitated failure. For a total of $25,000, the school provided her a locked door, window blinds, a private bathroom, and a surveillance camera sweeping the approach to her quarters. Three days later at 7:30 A.M., she became the first female cadet to enter training at the Citadel. Protest banners, some lofted by Sallie Baldwin and a clique of hostile women, declared, "Women Don't Belong Here," and urged, "Save the Males" (White, 1997, 55). Bumper stickers and T-shirts chortled at Faulkner's weight: "1,951 Bulldogs and One Bitch," "Bovine," and "Save the Males. Shave the Whale." Some 50 Faulkner fans raised their own posters: "The Citadel Mentality Is Not Now a Reality" and "The Males are Saved." Because of death threats and vandalism of her family's home, her attorneys, parents, and four federal marshals encircled her, much as soldiers shadowed the first black students to enter all-white Little Rock High School.

Shannon the Cadet

With an air of normality, Faulkner refused comment to reporters. She entered a militant campus marked by student M-14 rifles, a submarine hatch, a Sherman tank, a Phantom jet called *Annette*, and cannons affectionately dubbed Betsy and Lizzie. A senior, cadet Alex Pettett, commander of India Company, received the newcomer to the campus. Other students carried her belongings to her quarters. To shield the school from lawsuits, Colonel Joseph W. Trez, the commandant of cadets, directed cadets to refer to Faulkner as "plebe" rather than "knob" or "dumb head." He warned them against pawing through her belongings. He limited the number of cadets who could interact with Faulkner and required campuswide training in sensitivity and gender fairness.

Faulkner began college life by carrying sheet music and flute case to a band audition. During "hell week," she began intense physical training to turn her into "the Citadel man" (Faludi, 2002, 70). She expected standard knob debasement, from obligatory silence in the presence of upperclassmen and walking in the gutter to dunking in toilet water, kneeing of genitals, and battery with rifle butts. All knobs would have to tuck chins to chest before meals, address upperclassmen's comments and rebukes with "Sir, yes sir!," "Sir, no sir!," or "Sir, no excuse sir!" (Ibid., 64). After the initial 4 hours of military indoctrination, Faulkner retreated to the infirmary with four male knobs, all reporting heat-related ailments. For 4 days, she required intravenous rehydration and hospital tests. On the 5th day, she withdrew by reason of exhaustion from a 30-month legal battle and emotional and psychological abuse from the press and cadets. She filed suit against the college.

In retreat from a stressfully insular environment, Shannon Faulkner was not alone. Some 30 others decamped trembling and weeping after hours of pointless verbal abuse by sophomore officers bent on humiliating and breaking the untried. Feminist essayist Susan Faludi explained in a feature for the August 23, 1995, issue of *New Yorker* that, "in a time when extreme insecurity and confusion about maculinity's standing run rampant, the Corps of Cadets once again seeks to obscure a domestic male paradise with an intensifying of virile showmanship and violence" (Ibid., 80).

Faulkner declined a campus car and police escort out an easier route. Ed Faulkner escorted his daughter from the barracks into a phalanx of reporters surrounding his jeep. Before her tormenters, she thanked her supporters and admitted the harrowing ostracism that followed 3 years of court battles. She wept but regretted having to leave the place she crusaded to make her alma mater. Her resignation released exuberance among male cadets, who cavorted about the campus amid rebel yells. As the jeep passed the stone gate, cadets formed an impromptu chorus line and did a cancan to their own version of "Ding, dong, the witch is dead." She told interviewer Oprah Winfrey that her attorneys chose breaking the all-male barrier as their goal. Faulkner feared that crusaders had exploited her to the detriment of her health.

Leaving the Fight to Others

The celebration was short-lived. Attorney Valorie Vojdik substituted 17-year-old Nancy Mellette of Irmo, South Carolina, as complainant in the lawsuit against the Citadel. Faulkner's breach of sexist barriers left space for the entrance of two more female cadets. Both quit the school because of extreme provocation based on gender. On June 26, 1996, after a 7-year battle led by the Justice Department, the U.S. Supreme Court struck down the male-only admission policy at the Virginia Military Institute, the nation's other state-funded, all-male military college, on grounds that it imitated the "separate but equal" philosophy of racial separation. Commandant of Cadets, Brigadier General James Emory Mace, joined the staff to superintend a shift to coeducation.

Federal authorities challenged the appeals court for validating misconceptions that women are more timid, less aggressive, and inept at boot camp training. The Citadel immediately altered its masculine image by recruiting females and by employing egalitarian Anne Sinkler Whaley "Angie" LeClercq to the faculty as director of the Daniel Library. By July 1996, the Citadel Board of Visitors instituted new policies of equitable staff promotions and women in leadership roles. The school pledged to inaugurate coed barracks and dress code, fairness in sports, privacy for all cadets, and an inclusive teaching philosophy. The next morning, coeds Petra Lovetinska, Nancy Mace, Jeanie Menavlos, and Kim Messer entered a bristly, antiwoman corps. Two stayed in despite heckling, brutality, and sexual terrorism involving strip-searching women. In a state where hazing is illegal, cadets doused female plebes with nail polish solvent and ignited it. The college disciplined the perpetrators but chose not to press criminal charges. In 1999, Mace's daughter Nancy became the Citadel's first female graduate strictly on her own merit. By May 2005, a decade after Faulkner's foray, 118 women cadets comprised 6 percent of the corps.

Proclaimed a feminist foremother, Shannon Faulkner found her niche as a high school teacher at Woodmont High School in Piedmont, South Carolina. She later explained her youthful determination: "I was a young girl who did it all right, and I thought I should go to the best college in South Carolina I could find" (Chesler, Rothblum, and Cole, 1995, 200). The National Organization of Women recognized her historic accomplishments with a Woman of Courage Award. One admirer, retired army Major Lillian Pfluke, retrieved Faulkner from ignominy by acknowledging her pioneer's spirit: "None of us do it alone, we all walk in the footsteps of those women who went before us" (Skaine, 1999, 84).

Sources

Chesler, Phyllis, Esther D. Rothblum, and Ellen Cole. *Feminist Foremothers in Women's Studies, Psychology, and Mental Health*. Binghamton, NY: Haworth Press, 1995.

Faludi, Susan. "The Naked Citadel." In *Sexuality and Gender*, ed. by Christine L. Williams and Arlene Stein. Boston: Blackwell, 2002.

Jarvis, F. Washington. *With Love and Prayers: A Headmaster Speaks to the Next Generation*. Boston: David R. Godine, 2003.

Manegold, Catherine S. *In Glory's Shadow: The Citadel, Shannon Faulkner, and a Changing America*. New York: Vintage, 2001.

Salomone, Rosemary C. *Same, Different, Equal: Rethinking Single-Sex Schooling*. New Haven, CT: Yale University Press, 2003.

Skaine, Rosemarie. *Women at War: Gender Issues of Americans in Combat*. Jefferson, NC: McFarland, 1999.

White, Christie C. *Wives and Warriors: Woman and the Military in the United States and Canada*. Westport, CT: Greenwood, 1997.

■ Sexual Harassment
Anita Hill

Anita Faye Hill put a face to the emerging issue of workplace sexual harassment of female employees. Born the youngest of the 13 children of farmer Albert Hill and Erma Elliott Hill of Arkansas on July 30, 1956, at Lone Tree in Okmulgee County, Oklahoma, she lived in a four-room frame dwelling opposite Lone Tree Mountain. She grew up in farm country amid families who cherished hard work, honesty, and candor. Her parents, the first in Anita's clan to own land, grew cotton and peanuts, both labor-intensive crops. She aided the womanly tasks of putting up fruit and vegetables in glass jars and making jams and jellies. In a setting cluttered with abandoned autos, a combine, a tractor, and farm equipment, her mother brightened a half-acre of land with jonquils and marigolds. After her parents' disabling car accident that broke Erma Hill's collarbone and shattered Albert Hill's right arm and punctured his lungs, Anita recalled the family's stoicism: "Farmwork had to be done regardless of sickness or death" (Hill, 1998, 43).

The Hills attended Lone Tree Missionary Baptist Church, a congregation begun by her paternal grandparents, taxi driver Allen Hill and Ollie Nelson Hill. Anita attended a two-room elementary school in Eram with sister JoAnn and brother Ray. On free afternoons, Anita played basketball on a clay court and shared a bicycle with JoAnn. She reached age 12 before seeing her first movie in a theater, *Bonnie and Clyde*. When her father's health failed and Ray left home, Anita, JoAnn, and their mother assumed the task of feeding the cattle and pigs. In a community where few blacks studied longer than 8 years, her parents insisted that their children earn high school diplomas and enter college or the military. From members of the Baptist congregation, she gained female role models who influenced her social and spiritual maturity.

From a Rural School to Yale

Hill gained little awareness of black history from courses in junior high and from the newly integrated high school at Morris. At age 21, she completed courses in law, social policy, and women's studies at an "aggie" college, Oklahoma State University in Stillwater. Three years later, among privileged, well-traveled classmates, she finished a degree from Yale Law School in a milieu far from her childhood home. After passing the Washington, D.C., bar exam, she joined the firm of Wald, Harkrader & Ross. Within months, she served as legal adviser to the assistant secretary of the Department of Education's Office for Civil Rights. In 1982, she made a momentous career shift by taking a post as special assistant to the same boss, 34-year-old attorney Clarence Thomas of Pin Point, Georgia, who chaired the Equal Employment Opportunity Commission (EEOC) until 1990.

Because of his coarse behavior and unseemly stares and remarks in the office, in 1983, after only a year in the position, Hill quit the job. In her view, Thomas' misbehavior was controlling rather than seductive: "Sexual harassment is the assumption that certain workplace conditions can produce a level of intimidation even though the harasser does not assault the target or threaten retaliation for not acceding to sexual requests" (Hill, 1998, 148). At first, she tried to believe that Thomas would stop badgering and embarrassing her if she ignored him. She confided to colleagues Thomas' appalling sexist tactics but omitted the worst details. With a letter of recommendation from Thomas, she quickly moved on to teach at the O. W. Coburn School of Law in Oral Roberts University in Tulsa to be near her family. When the evangelical Christian law school was sold to Pat Robertson and Christian Broadcasting Network University, in 1986, she joined the law staff at the University of Oklahoma, Norman. She found the campus more collegial, less racist, and more productive than Oral Roberts University.

Feminist Heroine

President George H. W. Bush's nomination of Thomas to the U.S. Supreme Court forced Hill to oppose the black attorney's appointment to the Senate Judiciary Committee. On July 1, 1991, she acted both as a citizen and legal professional to inform the public of Thomas' aberrant attitudes and behaviors toward females. Florence Kennedy, negotiator and spokeswoman for the National Organization of Women, had already condemned Thomas as an obstructer of women's rights and reproductive rights. Three other organizations—the Congressional Black Caucus, the National Association for the Advancement of Colored People, and the Urban League—opposed him for his disdain for affirmative action. Under grilling by the liberal media, Thomas sidestepped questions about his opinion of women's abortion rights under the Supreme Court decision concerning *Roe v. Wade*.

After watching Thomas' opening remarks on a hotel room television, on October 11, 1991, as Anita Hill testified on camera at a Senate hearing chaired by Senator Joseph R. Biden, Jr., of Delaware, she maintained poise and objectivity. Sixteen years later, she asserted, "From day one, for many women and men, the hearing was a test of whether elected public officials understood not just my experience but the experiences of working women throughout the country" (Hill, November 2007). Daytime viewers abandoned soap operas and the World Series to hear explicit sexual details enunciated by Senator Orrin Hatch of Utah.

The disgruntled employee reported violations of Title VII of the Civil Rights Act of 1964—gender discrimination and propositions, vulgar gestures, a melodramatic debacle over pubic hair on Thomas' can of Coke, and sexually provocative remarks he made in a government office about "Long Dong Silver," fellatio, and cunnilingus. Before 15 white male senators, Hill characterized sex as a perquisite of a male authority figure like Thomas.

She believed Thomas guilty of indifference to lewd behavior, namely, the intimidation of female underlings with offensive male–female badinage. Contributing to the drama of her revelations was the potential for Thomas to replace retiring Justice Thurgood Marshall, the first black American to serve on the highest court in the land.

In the presence of her 80-year-old mother and four sisters, Carlene, Elreatha, JoAnn, and Joyce, Anita Hill offered calm, straightforward recall of Thomas' boasts of sexual prowess and of his obsession with pornographic films of bestiality and group rape. She answered insinuating questions about her own dress and about any behavior that might have lured Thomas into sexual pursuit. In the tense give and take, U.S. Congresswoman Louise Slaughter of New York remarked on Hill's speaking out before a room full of white men: "I became so filled with emotion. . . . I was so nervous for her" (Foerstel and Foerstel, 1996, 93). Senator Barbara Mikulski of Maryland summarized the hearing as "one of the most grueling, humiliating experiences that anyone has ever endured before the U.S. Senate" (Foerstel and Foerstel, 1996, 1935). Angela Wright and Sukari Hardnett, two black clerks at EEOC at the time of Anita Hill's employment, testified that they experienced similar goading, comments on female body parts, and requests for dates from Thomas. With backing from colleague Rose Jourdain, Wright substantiated damning claims against Thomas. Senator Howell Heflin of Alabama compared the alleged harassment to date rape. Law student John W. Carr, Judge Susan Hoerchner, law professor Joel Paul, and office assistant Ellen Wells recalled how Thomas's coarse remarks rattled Hill. She wrote to Carr about the incidents. Hoerchner described her former employer as a "complete scoundrel" and voiced "dismay that inexcusable behavior had seemingly been rewarded" by elevation to the U.S. Supreme Court (Hill, 1998, 95).

Thomas rebutted the damaging testimony with claims that Hill espoused a radical feminism and that her demure demeanor in the courtroom concealed a less admirable character. He charged that the televised character assassination was a circus and a "high-tech lynching for uppity blacks." Senator Hatch, in the role of "fact finder," contributed more ammunition for Thomas by attacking Hill's credibility and by implying witness fabrication of the charges, despite her successful polygraph test (Ragan, Bystrom, Kaid, and Becks, 1996, 12). He insisted that Bush's nominee deserved to know what the confidential FBI report contained. Senator Alan Simpson of Wyoming trusted that the cross-examination would impugn Hill rather than Thomas. Despite Hill's denunciation and positive lie detector test results, both senators Hatch and Arlen Specter of Pennsylvania questioned the reliability and validity of polygraph evidence. In private, Republicans feared that abasing Anita Hill would prompt women voters to back female candidates. Still, the U.S. Senate, which was only 2 percent female at the time, confirmed Thomas' appointment by two votes, the smallest margin in 200 years of Supreme Court confirmation hearings.

Spokeswoman for Decency

The repeated TV clips kept Hill's claims before the public. Although she failed to halt Thomas' advancement, through guest appearances on *Face the Nation*, *60 Minutes*, and *Today*, she furthered public debate of sexual harassment against female employees who feared for their jobs if they reported lascivious employers. Some victims thanked Hill privately and out of media hearing for backing silent females. Feminists sported badges and T-shirts proclaiming, "I Believe Anita Hill." They lionized the attorney for speaking an unvoiced complaint of most women, who endured public and work place groping and aspersions at some time in their adult lives. Some had no choice but to endure crude man talk and racy jokes to guarantee a paycheck and health insurance for their families.

Novelist Toni Morrison and other learned authors of *Race-ing Justice, En-Gendering Power: Essays on Anita Hill, Clarence Thomas, and the Construction of Social Reality* (1992) questioned what Hill achieved for herself by daring to testify. As a result of her bold defense of decency in the work place, vindictive voices lambasted and maligned her. In the months succeeding the Senate hearing, the FBI investigated her telephone records and grilled family members. More stressful were brickbats from the black community, retaliation from university students and colleagues, and a demand from Oklahomans that she leave the state university faculty. At home, she recoiled from the phone: "People felt free to leave the most cruel and revolting messages imaginable," including threats of rape, sodomy, and murder (Hill, 1998, 129). Further revelations affirm that colleague David Brock, author of an attack article in the March 1992 issue of *American Spectator* and in a polemic, *The Real Anita Hill: The Untold Story* (1993), smeared his friend to deter another witness, Kaye Savage, from corroborating claims of Thomas' sleazy behavior. In Hill's essay in *Race, Gender, and Power in America: The Legacy of the Hill–Thomas Hearings* (1995), she posited that a woman lacking a patron or a husband had less chance of establishing credibility in a national forum. She warned, "Though the events of October 1991 are long past, the headlines being continuing reminders of the the [sic] issues raised during the hearings. These issues are far from resolved" (Hill, 1995, back cover). She declared a national need for awareness of gender and racial inequalities in the public sphere.

After Clarence

Within 5 years of the public bashing of U.S. vice presidential candidate Geraldine Ferraro in 1984, the navy Tailhook scandal of September 1991, and the Hill–Thomas controversy in October 1991, the number of EEOC sexual harassment claims rose from 6,127 to 15,342. During the rise in women's outrage at exploitation of women at school, in public, and on the job, court awards to victims quadrupled to $27.8 million. Anita Hill later noted that most 21st-century corporate whistle blowers and government witnesses to harassment are female.

Hill pursued her career in civil rights law with public addresses and guest columns, classroom work at the Institute for the Study of Social Change at the University of California, Berkeley, and a visiting professorship at the Newhouse Center for the Humanities at Wellesley College. For *Nova Law Review* and *Michigan Journal of Race & Law*, she produced scholarly articles on international law, civil rights, feminism, race, and perversions of power. In 1997, she taught at the Heller School for Social Policy and Management at Brandeis University in Waltham, Massachusetts. She repeated her allegations in an autobiography, *Speaking Truth to Power* (1998). Surprisingly lacking in animosity toward the Clarence Thomas hearings, the text describes Hill's intent to improve opportunities for youth.

Thomas' rancorous reflections, *My Grandfather's Son: A Memoir* (2007), revisited the original debate with ad hominem accusations that Hill was emotionally unstable and only a so-so worker. To an interviewer on *60 Minutes*, Virginia Lamp Thomas demanded that Hill apologize to her husband. In a review of his writings for the *New York Times* on October 2, 2007, Hill charged her former employer with lies and gendered disparities and rejected Virginia Thomas' call for an apology. In an essay for the *Boston Globe*, Hill acknowledged ongoing support: "Last month, when Thomas published his memoir, nearly 600 e-mails came within two days time. I have about 25,000 letters, cards, handwritten notes on bits of paper passed through crowds" (Hill, November 2007). She concluded, "If sent back in time, I would testify again" (Ibid.). She appeared on *Good Morning America* to assure listeners that the 1991 testimony was accurate. Of the intervening 16 years, she remarked, "Fortunately, we have made progress since 1991. Today, when employees complain of abuse in the workplace, investigators and judges are more likely to examine all the evidence and less likely to simply accept as true the word of those in power" (Hill, October 2007). Her awards include honorary doctorates from Dillard University and Simmons College. At age 49, she received a fellowship from the Fletcher Foundation, which promotes civil rights education.

Sources

Foerstel, Karen, and Herbert N. Foerstel, eds. *Climbing the Hill: Gender Conflict in Congress*. New York: Praeger, 1996.

Foskett, Ken. *Judging Thomas: The Life and Times of Clarence Thomas*. New York: HarperCollins, 2005.

Hill, Anita F. "Our Bittersweet 16." *Boston Globe*, November 19, 2007.

———. "The Smear This Time." *New York Times*, October 2, 2007.

———. *Speaking Truth to Power*. New York: Anchor, 1998.

Hill, Anita F., and Emma Coleman Jordan, eds. *Race, Gender, and Power in America: The Legacy of the Hill–Thomas Hearings*. Oxford: Oxford University Press, 1995.

Morrison, Toni. "Introduction." In *Race-ing Justice, En-Gendering Power: Essays on Anita Hill, Clarence Thomas, and the Construction of Social Reality*, ed. by Toni Morrison. New York: Pantheon, 1992.

Ragan, Sandra, Dianne G. Bystrom, Lynda Lee Kaid, and Christina Beck, eds. *The Lynching of Language: Gender Politics, and Power in the Hill–Thomas Hearings*. Chicago: University of Illinois Press, 1996.

Saguy, Abigail C. *What Is Sexual Harassment?: From Capitol Hill to the Sorbonne*. Berkeley, CA: University of California Press, 2003.

■ Speech Defect
Walter Dean Myers

One of America's foremost authors of young adult literature, Walter Dean Myers developed a determination and persistence in childhood that inform his biographies, verse, and complex fictional casts. His canon of 85 books totals the most pages published by any black American author. The model for his persona preceded the Civil War, when his great grandmother Dolly Dennis served the Dandridges, her white masters at the Bower, a plantation in Leetown, Virginia. Born Walter Milton Myers in 1939 in Martinsburg, West Virginia, the author and his seven siblings grew up 10 miles from the Bower and attended the Free Will Baptist Church. In 1940, the death of their mother, Mary Myers, in childbirth, robbed Myers of a maternal figure in his life. Family poverty caused his father to farm the boy out to Florence Brown Dean, a button factory laborer, and her husband, stevedore Herbert Julius Dean, who fostered Walter at their flat in central Harlem, New York.

Curious and lively, Myers absorbed the thrum of America's black haven—stalls at La Marqueta, the spiritual uplift of the Abyssinian Baptist Church, the singing of Josephine Baker, and the grace of Langston Hughes' poems. A lifelong interest in sports began with local boxer Sugar Ray Robinson and included baseball at Ebbets Field in Brooklyn and games of stickball, stoopball, and ring-a-levio with a blend of Jewish, Irish, and West Indian children living in brick tenements near Morningside Drive. In his 60s, Myers reflected, "There was a time when there was no gulf between my mind and my body. On the basketball court I wanted to bring my strong body against other strong bodies" (Myers, "Private," March 16, 2005). At home, Herbert's storytelling added monster and ghost tales to radio thrillers. Florence told German folk stories; "Pap" William Dean, a former wagoner, contributed Old Testament lore. By age 5, Walter read comic books, issues of *True Romance*, and headline news. To maintain a macho reputation, he devoured books in secret while wondering if a love of the written word set him apart from other boys.

Losing Confidence

Enrollment at P.S. 125 Ralph J. Bunche School on LaSalle Street reframed Myers' outlook on himself and his future. Although he enjoyed an oral reading of Laura Ingalls Wilder's *Little House in the Big Woods* (1932), school tortured him. Students marginalized him for his phonetic speech disorder and imitated his efforts to pronounce ch, r, sh, u, and w. In self-defense, he suppressed personal communication. He noted, "I had an inner life I couldn't share" (Myers, 2005, 14). By age 8, his grades dropped in everything but physical education. Mockery of "Mushmouth Myers" destroyed his concentration. He compensated for his articulation disorder with mischief and fighting that netted scoldings in the principal's office and whippings at home. In grade five, his teacher stereotyped him as a "bad boy," a denigration that shaped his self-image.

In 1947, as the nation recovered from World War II, Myers began his own recovery through the androcentric adventure books his teacher suggested. From perusing the boys' shelf of his day, he came to admire Robin Hood, the Three Musketeers, Huck Finn, and Louisa May Alcott's *Little Men*. A wise teacher, Mrs. Conway, freed Myers from the agony of reading aloud from textbooks by having him recite original poems. Liberation from lockstep classroom methods prompted his love of the public library, which provided a sanctuary from teasing and ridicule and a source of verbal outlets through reading and writing. He exulted, "It's not like going out there and playing basketball where everyone's watching you; it's private" (Graham, 2002). Completing the boyhood transformation, former Marine Irwin Lasher convinced the stammerer of his own potential. From weekly speech therapy, Myers advanced to flag bearer of the honor guard and mentor to disadvantaged pupils.

From Reader to Writer to Loser

In his teens, Myers experienced the emotional turmoil and racism that revived vulnerability. Once more, school saved him by offering classes for gifted students and the opportunity to complete seventh and eighth grades in two semesters. Writing seemed a promising career after he won an essay contest sponsored by *Life* magazine. A dedicated teacher during Myers' freshman year introduced him to British verse and encouraged memorization from Samuel Taylor Coleridge's symbolic voyage poem "The Rime of the Ancient Mariner" (1798), one of Myers' favorite narratives. At Stuyvesant High School, he composed short fiction and began to see himself as a professional writer. By analyzing characters in the fiction of Balzac, Camus, Mann, and Zola, Myers developed an affinity for the everyman who flourishes despite human flaws.

Challenging himself to read and analyze demanding literature, Myers tackled competitions in verse and essay, which he tapped out on a used Royal typewriter. Because he lacked the cash to apply to colleges and scholarship committees, he lost hope and dawdled in his junior year. Devaluing his positive self-image, at age 15, he quit school. He developed a punk persona, flashed a stiletto, and moped about the park. A run-in in a subway with a plainclothesman preceded a defining moment. To Myers' surprise, a guidance counselor probed his attitude toward being black. At a nadir in his life, he fled his Harlem buddies to escape a likely plunge into crime.

The Struggle

At age 17, Myers chose the army as his introit to manhood. From Fort Dix, New Jersey, he graduated to radio repair and a plum spot on a military basketball team. He gained insight from observing arctic seals and polar bears at a missile base on Baffin Island. On return home to Morristown, New Jersey, he clashed with Herbert, who disdained story writing as "real work." Myers moved to Manhattan, roomed at the Cort Hotel, and sorted mail for the Peerless Brokerage. While reading Gide, Joyce, Nietzsche, O'Neill, Orwell, and Sartre, Myers submitted manuscripts under a series of pen names. Seeing his writing in print in *Black Creation, Black Family Digest, Black Scholar, Black World, Essence, Liberator,* and *Negro Digest* boosted his morale.

After marrying Joyce Smith in 1959, Myers worked for the post office, played bongos in a band, and buddied around with drug users. While rearing his children, Karen Elaine and Michael Dean, in Queens, the author learned composition under Hungarian-Jewish author Lajos Egri and supervised hiring for the New York State Department of Labor. Myers studied languages at City College of the City University of New York while receiving speech therapy. He continued freelancing sports and blood-and-thunder in *Argosy, Bluebook, Cavalier, Delta Review, Espionage, Male, National Enquirer,* and *Star,* earning, at most, $20 per piece.

Writing for Black Kids

At the dawning of YA fiction for nonwhite readers, the Council on Interracial Books for Children awarded Myers $500 for an elementary reader, *Where Does the Day Go?*, a story of black parents and their children. A precursor of Myers' development of humanistic themes, the work echoed the lessons of his childhood in self-respect and ambition. The uptick in his fortune paralleled serious setbacks, the death of his brother, Sonny Myers, during the 1968 Tet offensive in Vietnam and a divorce from Joyce, who took Elaine and Michael out of the author's life. Adversity tempered Myers' idealism. He infused with racial realism a gritty prison story, "How Long Is Forever?," for the 1969 issue of *Negro Digest.* Eager for direction, he enrolled at Columbia University under writer-in-residence John Oliver Killens, founder of the Harlem Writers Guild, who found Myers a position on the acquisitions staff of publisher Bobbs-Merrill.

Myers advanced to senior trade book editor. Under the name Walter Dean Myers, in honor of his foster parents, he began picturing the success of black youth in white-dominated fields. For *The Dancers* (1972), he won a Child Study Association of America's Children's Books of the Year citation, the first of a stream of accolades for his depiction of praise-starved nonwhite achievers. At age 35, he kayoed Eurocentric folklore with a hip fairy tale, *The Dragon Takes a Wife* (1974), a dialectal paean to a close-knit black family invigorated by the American work ethic.

Myers pressed into new venues with fiction, allegory, and essays published in *Alfred Hitchcock's Mystery Magazine*, *McCall's*, and *Sunday News Magazine*, and in an anthology, *We Be Word Sorcerers: Twenty-five Stories by Black Americans* (1973). After marrying Constance Brendell and siring son Christopher, Myers began to travel Europe and to write urban scenarios that empowered disadvantaged youth. He justified his choice of Harlem as a focus: "I loved those streets.... It was where I was raised. These were the people I knew" (Sutton, 1994, 26). The author's comic novel *Fast Sam, Cool Clyde, and Stuff* (1975) netted a Woodward Park School Annual Book Award and an American Library Association (ALA) Notable Book citation. In 1976, he eulogized in *Black Scholar* author-photographer Gordon Parks, one of a series of black heroes whom Myers' writings introduced to readers.

A Voice for Black Youth

Settled at a row house in Jersey City, Myers branched out to biography, coming-of-age, fantasy, ethnic history, mystery, photography collections, verse, realism, and science fiction, which he submitted to *Black Creation*, *Black World*, *Boy's Life*, *Ebony Jr.!*, *Espionage*, *Essence*, *Parents*, and *Scholastic*. Acclaim poured in for *It Ain't All for Nothin'* (1978), winner of an ALA Notable Book citation and an ALA Best Book for Young Adults award for its depiction of moral floundering and dilemmas befuddling teens. In the same vein, *The Young Landlords* (1979), a fun story about community reclamation, earned a second ALA Best Book for Young Adults award, a second ALA Notable Book Citation, the Coretta Scott King Award, and a film option from Topol Productions. For *Interracial Books for Children Bulletin*, Myers felt compelled to issue "The Black Experience in Children's Books: One Step Forward, Two Steps Back," a demand for fair representation of all races and cultures as American.

Myers moved sure-footedly into young adult classics by picturing the maturing of the black athlete in *Hoops: A Novel* (1981), receiver of his third ALA Best Book for Young Adults citation and a finalist for an Edgar Allan Poe Award. He followed with a realistic survey of fostering a juvenile delinquent, *Won't Know Till I Get There* (1982), which snagged the Parents Choice Award for its psychological insight and compassion for dead-end teens. Through kid-simple dialogue, he validated language as a conduit to self-understanding: "Writing helps [people] bring things together, to see where they fit in life" (Myers, 1982, 1). After coursework in criminal justice and photography, in 1983, Myers launched a study at the Green Haven prison in Rahway, New Jersey, of progressive criminality. After completing a B.A. in communications from Empire State College, he published two solid teen pleasers, *Motown and Didi: A Love Story* (1984), receiver of Myers' second Coretta Scott King Award, and *The Outside Shot* (1987), winner of a Parents' Choice Award. Travels in Asia preceded publication of a masterwork, *Fallen Angels* (1988), a classic survey of the ghetto youth who filled military allotments during the Vietnam War. Myers dramatized urban temptations in the multiaward-winning *Scorpions* (1988) and challenged attendees at the National Council of Teachers of English with the speech "The Young Adult Novel: Writing for Aliens."

Continued Challenges

In the last 15 years, Myers has perpetuated his escape from stutterer to role model for teens. After winning the 1994 Margaret A. Edwards lifetime achievement award, the author remarked to an interviewer, "I'm trying to give a voice to the imperfect model in order to reach imperfect kids" (Pierleoni, 2005). In the introduction to *Now Is Your Time!*

The African-American Struggle for Freedom (1991), he delighted in "the joy and the light and the music and the genius and the muscle and the glory of these . . . [he writes] about" (Myers, 1991, x). His canon includes candid images of working-class blacks—from the historical *Malcolm X: By Any Means Necessary* (1992) and *The Great Migration: An American Story* (1993) to black genealogy in the saga *The Glory Field* (1994) and *Slam!* (1996), a vibrant narrative on values clarification. A venture into crime metafiction, *Monster: A Novel* (1999), peers into the twisted psyche of an accused felon who projects himself as a character on video. The defendant's terror of his own quasilegal behavior contests the white stereotype of soulless black delinquents.

As an antidote to apathy, Myers demands of himself and of his fans their "best and truest voice" (Myers, "YA Grows Up," 2001). In 2001, he revisited hurtful territory in *Bad Boy: A Memoir*, a reprise of his childhood torments. During a period of feverish literary experimentation, he produced an urban wisdom tale, *The Dream Bearer* (2003), an elegiac study of drug addiction in *The Beast* (2003), and a lyrical salute to his home turf in *Here in Harlem: Poems in Many Voices* (2004). In fealty to realism, he reset the Columbine massacre in *Shooter* (2004), a fair, but jolting, examination of the failure of parents to dissuade disaffected teens from guns as an avenue to peer acceptance. Ironically, he predicted the need for a book on kids and firearms 2 years before, when he remarked, "Life is far too complex for a simple shootout to solve our problems" (Myers, 2001, 62). Overall, Myers' books celebrate nonsexual boy–girl pairings, intergenerational learning experiences, and hopeful family dynamics. In 2007, his true-to-life recreations of confused, rudderless youth in troubled times earned from fellow author Robert Lipsyte an insider's praise of Myers as the moral compass of young adult literature.

Sources

Gallo, Donald R. "A Man of Many Ideas: Walter Dean Myers." *Writing* 26 (5) (February–March 2004): 10–11.

Graham, Adam. "Author's Just a Kid at Heart." *Detroit News*, May 6, 2002.

Lipsyte, Robert. "Novels with the Power to Change Young Lives." *New York Times*, April 28, 2003, E1.

Myers, Walter Dean. "And Then I Read. . . ." *Voices from the Middle* 8 (4) (May 2001): 58–62.

———. *Bad Boy: A Memoir*. New York: HarperCollins, 2001.

———. *Now Is Your Time! The African-American Struggle for Freedom*. New York: HarperCollins, 1991.

———. "Private Interview." E-mail to Mary Ellen Snodgrass, March 16, 2005.

———. "Walter Dean Myers." *Read* 54 (13) (February 25, 2005): 14–15.

———. *Won't Know Till I Get There*. New York: Viking, 1982.

Myers, Walter Dean, Laurie Halse Anderson, Meg Cabot, Chris Crutcher, Sarah Dessen, and Garth Nix. "YA Grows Up." Available at http://www.authorsontheweb.com/features/0108-ya/0108-ya.asp (last accessed April 3, 2008).

Pierleoni, Allen O. "Wrongs and the Writer." *Sacramento Bee*, March 29, 2005.

Sutton, Roger. "Threads in Our Cultural Fabric." *School Library Journal* 40 (6) (June 1994): 24–28.

■ Spousal Abuse
Francine Moran Hughes

Francine Moran Hughes survived marital torment and became a feminist icon of endurance. Born in Stockbridge County, Michigan, in August 1947, to Hazel and Walter Moran, she had seven siblings, two of whom died in infancy. She bore the name of a French singer whose radio music intrigued Francine's mother. The patriarchal home scene in Jackson, Michigan, set the course of Francine's life—her father drank and assaulted her mother, who meekly submitted to him and kept the attacks secret from her children. Francine took the standard route of escape from domestic discontent by dating a carousing dropout, James "Mickey" Hughes, 2 years her elder, whom she met at a school dance. At his direction, she quit Jackson High School in tenth grade. They had an argument over her use of his car. His flare-up terrified her, but she submitted to premarital sex and accepted his marriage proposal. He groused that she refused him additional intimacies until the wedding.

After their union on November 4, 1963, at Dansville Methodist Church, Francine discovered Mickey's alcoholism and his dark, controlling nature. To keep the peace in their coercive relationship, she attempted to placate him, a pattern common to the battered wife syndrome. On their honeymoon, Mickey flew into a jealous tantrum and struck Francine for allegedly glancing at another man. Mickey criticized her blouse as too sexy when she tucked it into ski pants and ripped her outfit apart. Humiliations and merciless backhanding surprised and shocked her. She tolerated the anxiety and pain out of ignorance of her rights. At first, Mickey repented, promised to control his anger, and reconciled with Francine with romance and sex. She examined her faults and lost self-respect for being a "bad wife."

Battered Wife and Mother

The couple settled in cramped quarters with Mickey's parents, Flossie and Berlin Hughes, and his siblings, Dexter, Donovan, Wimpy, and Vicky, at Dansville near East Lansing, Michigan. During marital blow-ups, Francine found herself locked out of the house when she ran away from Mickey's yelling and pummeling. In wintry weather, she sat in the car until he relented. She recalled, "I was a beaten-down, scared animal. There was no help" (Darling, 1980). Flossie did nothing to end Francine's devaluation but admitted her son's progressive derangement. Berlin shielded Mickey from the stigma of committal to a mental asylum and left home for two weeks to distance himself from the two intrusive females' solution of psychological treatment.

During pregnancy, to protect unborn life, Francine fled her confrontational husband and stayed with her parents. In 1964, she gave birth to Christy; 2 years later, Jimmy was born. Dana arrived in 1969, followed in 1970 by Nicole. Intermittently, Mickey and his brother Dexter sought jobs in Kansas and Missouri. Mickey's chronic sadism worsened to unexplained absences, womanizing, constant drunkenness, and job loss. He stopped looking for work, hunkered in his recliner by the television with a bottle, and took out his spite on his family. He slapped Francine and beat her with his fists. He splintered chairs, smashed cabinet doors, ripped telephone cords from the wall, struck the children, and choked Francine to near unconsciousness. He declared, "I'm gonna keep it up . . . until you're sorry you were born" (McNulty, 1980, 130). Francine, like a hamster on a wheel, ricocheted from housecleaning, laundry, cooking, and child care to Mickey's frequent demands for sex. After his injury in a car wreck in 1971, she bathed, fed, and cared for him until he recovered. The damage to his heart and diaphragm left him disabled. He retreated to the Wooden Nickel Bar. In intimate moments, he robbed her of affection and tenderness and turned their couplings into marital rape. She hated herself for complying. Gradually, his overpowering eroded her self-identity.

Variant Opinions

Francine received wise counsel from professionals. The physician who examined the contusions to her face and torso, split lips, and bloody noses urged her to rescue herself and her children from escalating assaults. She accepted a prescription tranquilizer but not the advice. She sought psychological counseling and proposed taking assertiveness training. The outside interference in his marriage embarrassed and infuriated Mickey. At his worst, he beat his mother for interfering and snatched up his children's kitten and snapped its neck. While Lady, the family collie lab, went into labor, he locked her outdoors and left her and the pups to freeze. Francine's mother advised her to avoid violence and to tolerate a bad marriage that Francine willingly entered.

Untrained outsiders blamed the wife for the husband's brutality, which extended to threats of slitting her throat with a knife and to garroting that left her near suffocation. The Hughes family charged her with fighting back, once by hurling a glass ashtray into the back of his head. Flossie and Berlin offered a lame retreat to the church, a paltry salve to Mickey's instability. To Francine, the daily tussle was addictive. She engaged in cat-and-mouse plots to avoid Mickey's cunning ambushes for imaginary faults. Lacking the support of her neighbors, the sheriff's department, social services agents, parents, and in-laws, she withdrew emotionally and gave up hope of escaping.

Isolation

When their money ran out, Francine stirred jelly in water to feed her toddlers and made popcorn for her meals. She repressed rage at a man who refused to support them, confined them to their rooms, and threatened her life. Bouts of cruelty and rage escalated, forcing her to escape to her parents' residence or to telephone police, who took no action against cyclical abuse. The Hughes' battles appeared regularly on police records. They witnessed his attempt to run over her with his car and heard his death threats. Part of her reluctance to demand police protection was the time lag between jailing and the trial. When Mickey posted bond, he would return home itching for vengeance. Because she chose not to press charges, he spent little time in jail. At times, Jimmy intervened and shrieked that he wished his father dead. Her reliance on the boy and on one sympathetic police officer, George Walkup, illustrated her need to grasp any scrap of solace.

Francine stayed in the marriage to the breaking point. In 1975, while she attended Lansing Business College, Mickey seemed perpetually disgruntled. She filed for divorce. When she sought a court decree, he sat with the children and refused to leave. The face-off worsened after a welfare agent intervened. He had no answers to Mickey's trespassing and struck the Hughes family from the welfare rolls because Francine allowed a male to live on the premises. When Francine heated TV dinners, Mickey called her a slut and hurled the children's meals to the floor. After she mopped up the food, he dumped it again, yanked her by the hair, forced her to kneel, and dragged her through the mess. He upended their dinner table, burned her textbooks and notes in a waste barrel, and forbade her from attending the business courses that would enhance her autonomy. Symbolically, the domestic eruption closed off Francine's escape through education and self-empowerment. In front of the police, he threatened to kill her and a protective officer and vowed to step up his battery to make her life more wretched.

The Burning Bed

On March 9, 1977, Francine killed Mickey after he passed out drunk on their bed. Preceding the murder, Christy Hughes telephoned police to halt the domestic tyranny and to remove Mickey from his ex-wife's residence. When investigating officers chose not to arrest Mickey, Francine packed her belongings with her children's help. Mickey forced her into intercourse and sank into sleep. At the moment of decision, she sank into an eerie calm and dressed her children in their winter coats. As though disembodied from her paralyzed self, she searched the basement for a gas can, removed the lid, and approached the bed. As an inner voice pressed her forward, she looked away from Mickey to the floor and began saturating the area with gas. She retreated to the doorframe and lit a match. The reality struck with the burst of flames. The fumes and explosion jolted her conscience. She experienced an uprush of thrill, elation, and terror followed by hysteria. Adrenaline coursed through her, forcing her to flee for her life, leaving Mickey to burn to death. She shuttled the children to the car and drove to the Ingham County Sheriff's Office to confess to arson and murder.

In police custody, Francine chose not to plead self-defense or justifiable homicide. A Detroit judge refused bail on the strength of her methodical murder of a sleeping man. He mused, "After all, what kind of woman would burn her husband?" (Jones, 2003, 58). She stayed behind bars until psychological tests freed her. The trial, held in Lansing, Michigan, drew throngs. The police raised barricades against protesters and the curious. Assistant prosecutor Lee Atkinson of Ingham County charged her with premeditated murder. Francine gained support from Michigan feminists, who considered the trial a political event. Beginning on October 24, 1977, her court-appointed defender, attorney Aryon Greydanus, built his case on Francine's thirteen years of terror from bullying, brutality, and threats on her life. She testified to Mickey's calculated evil toward his youngest child: "[He] had warned that if he found the cat on the porch he'd wring its neck. When he caught her with it the second time he took it out of her arms and just broke its neck in his two hands" (McNulty, 1980, 165). Flossie lied on the stand and covered up her son's derangement. On November 1, 1977, the jury found Hughes innocent by reason of insanity. The exoneration set a precedent nationwide for battered women who fight back.

The Aftermath

Freeing herself of murder charges did not end Hughes' hurts or guilt. Her in-laws wanted her dead or in prison for life. Schoolmates jeered at her children. Christy, at age 16, declared she would never marry. Jimmy, then 14 years old, required counseling to free himself of rage at his odious father. The smaller children seemed less troubled by the killing and trial. Hughes faced straightforward questions from 6-year-old Nicole, who demanded an explanation for the killing. The conversation reduced mother and daughter to tears. The media debated the case; skeptics alleged that other women might use her acquittal to justify spousal murder. Female inmates took hope from Hughes' example and demanded clemency for their acts of self-defense against bruisers and child beaters. Within 3 months of the verdict, feminist legal scholars Elizabeth Schneider and Nancy Stearns from the Center for Constitutional Law made use of Francine's battered woman syndrome defense in the Women's Self-Defense Law Project. She conducted her own questions and answers and wondered if she could have escaped Mickey without killing him.

Hughes settled her family with her mother. She stripped herself of emotion, smoked more heavily, and retreated into a filial dependency on the older woman. She found happiness in normal motherhood and in a home freed of terrorism, but she suffered panic attacks at the approach of the mail carrier and in stores. Her eyes took on a glassy quality. She refused to speak Mickey's name and reduced the burning to "it" and his personhood to "him." She marveled at the oppressed women who looked up to her as a symbol of liberation. To a woman who dismissed herself as "just a housewife," their hero worship seemed out of place (Darling, 1980).

Hughes dated Robert Wilson, a strong, sensitive man who encouraged her to express her thoughts and feelings. When they wed, she enjoyed dining, dancing, and summer excursions for fishing and swimming. Realizing how much she had lacked under Mickey's control, she began to shed her complacency: "Now I put in my two cents' worth whenever I please. I'm learning how to say what I feel when I feel it" (Darling, 1980). She fought stereotypes of the submissive wife and defended women's rights to self. Poet John R. Reed studied the grounds for murdering a madman in an ode, "House Burning." In a folk song, "The Ballad of Francine Hughes," composers Lyn Hardy and Donna Herbert elevated Francine from debased housewife to feminist hero.

Feminist Outrage

In 1980, children's book author Faith McNulty, a journalist and reviewer for the *New Yorker*, summarized Francine's self-liberation in a feminist revenge classic, *The Burning Bed: The True Story of Francine Hughes, a Beaten Wife Who Rebels*. The title, replete with anger, passion, and retaliation, caught the attention of book reviewers as well as civil authorities, psychologists, and social workers who dealt with wife beaters and child abusers. Fueling controversy over the story were McNulty's dramatic state-of-mind depictions: "Get in the car and go. Drive all night. Drive all tomorrow. Don't think about what happens after that! Don't think of anything except going! Go! And never turn back" (McNulty, 1980, 193).

In October 1984, when NBC TV producer Robert Greenwald aired Rose Leiman Goldemberg's screen version of McNulty's *The Burning Bed*, a public reexamination of the murder and trial further politicized Hughes' actions. Actor Farrah Fawcett stayed in a women's shelter for a month to prepare for the role. She surprised viewers by playing a haggard, robotic victim who wills herself to burn her husband and house to end a nightmarish marriage. She paired with Paul Le Mat, who justified the killing with his depiction of obsession and violent temper. Actor Richard Masur dramatized the attorney's case for exoneration. The made-for-TV film set a record at 75 million viewers and earned Fawcett Emmy and Golden Globe nominations. Second wave feminists used the true story as the basis for demands for protection of women and their families from conjugal violence, threats, marital rape, and incest. Hughes' example set the parameters of such drives as Take Back the Night and Fight Back!

Sources

Darling, Lynn. "Ring of Fire." *Washington Post*, November 5, 1980.

Fields, Suzanne. "The Raging Flames of a Battered Wife." *Washington Post*, November 27, 1980.

Fineman, Martha, and Martha T. McCluskey. *Feminism, Media, and the Law.* New York: Oxford University Press, 1997.

Jones, Jennifer. *Medea's Daughters: Forming and Performing the Woman Who Kills.* Columbus, OH: Ohio State University Press, 2003.

Lootens, Tricia. "Women Who Kill: The Burning Bed." *Off Our Backs* 11 (11) (December 31, 1983): 16.

McNulty, Faith. *The Burning Bed.* New York: Harcourt Brace Jovanovich, 1980.

Zoglin, Richard. "The Burning Bed." *Time* 124 (October 8, 1984): 85.

■ Stalking
Jodie Foster

On a career uptick, actor and singer Jodie Foster experienced personal terrorism from a crazed stalker. A child star from Los Angeles, California, she was born Alicia Christian Foster on November 19, 1962, to film publicist Evelyn Ella Almond "Brandy" Foster. Her father, air force Colonel Lucius Fisher Foster III, an inconstant realtor, abandoned his pregnant wife and their three children Lucinda, Constance, and Lucius, Jr. His family chose the postdivorce baby's name; Brandy called her Jodie. The child displayed genius at 8 months, when she began to talk. By age 3, she could read. Rearing her brood at Newport Beach on a slim budget, Brandy promoted art in the trio with visits to museums and to European art films. Jodie was captivated by the latter.

Because courts chopped the $600 per month child support in half, Foster and her siblings went to work. She began her career at age 2 as a model and, a year later, with commercials for Kellogg's Corn Flakes and a bare-bottomed ad for "Little Miss Coppertone" suntan lotion. She advanced to sassy, tomboyish gamins on television on *The Doris Day Show*, *The Partridge Family*, *Sesame Street*, *The Courtship of Eddie's Father*, *Bonanza*, and *Gunsmoke*. In third grade, she began outshining brother Buddy, a child star on *Mayberry R.F.D.*, by debuting in the Civil War era teleplay *Menace on the Mountain* (1970). Her income—$1,000 a week—became the mainstay of the family of five.

Foster became fluent in French at an emersion prep school, the Lycée Français de Los Angeles, where she delivered the class valedictory in French. While studying, she juggled the demands of a screen career that frequently cast her as a world-weary innocent made wise beyond her years by parental divorce, orphaning, abandonment, or bad company. Managed by stage mother Brandy, Jodie disengaged her real self from troubled characters in the films *Napoleon and Samantha* (1972) and *Kansas City Bomber* (1972). For *Alice Doesn't Live Here Anymore* (1974), a cult favorite, Foster played Audrey, a street-hardened alcoholic. Her mother balanced the demands of grittier parts with the more normal characterizations in the Disney films *One Little Indian* (1973), *Freaky Friday* (1976), and *Candleshoe* (1977). On television at age 11, Jodie appeared in *Kung Fu* and *The Addams Family* and as Becky Thatcher, the female interest in the young adult classic *Tom Sawyer*.

From Child to Adult Star

At age 14, Foster entered a new phase of notoriety as a "new woman" actor. She experienced her first adult critique from Dino de Laurentis, who derided her rounded figure. She began playing tennis and limiting meals to cottage cheese until she slimmed her 5-foot 1-inch frame down to 89 pounds. Male and female groupies fantasized claiming her as a sex partner; security guards collared a celebrity stalker on a movie set. Her mother worried about

Jodie's safety, yet capitalized on her sexuality by scheduling an audition for a mature part in *Raging Bull* and by arranging for alluring photos to add to Jodie's portfolio. The publicity set Foster on a course of morally complex films.

Foster hosted *Saturday Night Live* and costarred as Addie Loggins in the television series *Paper Moon* (1976) and with Martin Sheen as a neighborhood pedophile in *The Little Girl Who Lives Down the Lane* (1976), for which Jodie's more mature sister Connie served as her body double. Foster's singing and appearance as the 1920s flapper Tallulah opposite Scott Baio in the gangster film *Bugsy Malone* (1976) won British Academy of Film and Television Arts awards for supporting actress and best newcomer. Of the mature kiss in her part, she reflected on the act as a display of professional self-confidence: "I certainly don't look back on it as having a tremendous amount of sexuality" (Abramowitz, 2000). In France at age 15, she dubbed her movies in French and recorded pop tunes for the soundtrack of the film *Moi, Fleur Bleue* ("I, Blue Flower," 1977), in which she played the title character.

Foster's encounter with a deadlier intimate stalker began with the Oscar-nominated part as Iris Steensman, a drug-addicted child hustler in Martin Scorsese's *Taxi Driver* (1976), which the *New York Times* listed among the 1,000 greatest films. Under surveillance by a social worker from the Los Angeles Welfare Board, she teamed with Robert De Niro as a would-be savior and Harvey Keitel as her pimp, both of whom hesitated to enact the sexual exploitation of a child. During the preliminaries to filming, Scorsese and screenwriter Paul Schrader learned of a psychological study that identified Foster's backside-baring Coppertone ad as a turn-on for sexual deviants. Foster, at age 14½, drew on years of on-camera experience to perform graphic scenes—a seduction dance with her pimp and unzipping the fly of the taxi driver. For the latter action, Scorsese superimposed the hand of twenty-year-old Connie Foster.

The movie was Jodie's first attempt to shape a character. She realized the power of actors to express raw emotion: "This acting thing is not just a hobby, that it's actually a real thing you could do" (Abramowitz, 2000). Because of mixed reaction to the film's seaminess, attendees at the Cannes in May 1976 hooted during presentation of the Palme D'Or. At the Oscar ceremonies, Scorsese required an FBI escort because of a death threat for forcing Foster to perform so mature a role.

Forever Changed by Hinckley

Taxi Driver, a cult favorite, seized the imagination of 25-year-old John Warnock Hinckley, Jr., a Nazi-obsessed drifter and voyeur who viewed the movie fifteen times. A diagnosed narcissist, for three years, he dreamed of rescuing Foster from degradation, marrying her, and serving as the U.S. president. He wrote to *Time* magazine of his fixation on the unattainable love object: "The most important thing in my life is Jodie Foster's love and admiration. If I can't have them, neither can anyone else" (Nicol, 2006, 35). He visualized himself as Romeo to her Juliet and Napoleon to her Josephine. Hinckley purchased .22- and .38-caliber pistols and emulated De Niro's character, Travis Bickle, in seeking media attention by plotting to assassinate the U.S. president. He began merging with the screen figure by costuming himself in boots and army fatigues, sipping peach brandy, and writing his parents about squiring Lynn Collins, an imaginary girlfriend based on the movie character Betsy. He puzzled over his need to both adore and destroy Foster in what he described as an act of love.

Emboldened by erotic illusions and a loaded revolver, Hinckley relieved his social isolation by playing out psychopathic scenarios of redemption through violence. In early fall 1980, he stalked 17-year-old Foster on campus during her first year at Yale in New Haven, Connecticut, where she hoped to establish herself as a scholar independent of Brandy. In September, he taped his phone calls to Foster and then changed his modus operandi by shadowing President Jimmy Carter. Refocused on the actor, Hinckley plotted kidnap and rape and fantasized hijacking a plane and taking Foster to the White House. He watched her lodgings; he wrote love poems and letters and pushed them under her dorm room door. The notes claimed that Hinckley would shoot President Ronald Reagan to gain Foster's favor.

The perverse 7-month crush came to national attention on March 30, 1981. In a psychotic state generated by unconsummated passion, Hinckley declared that he fired six shots at President Reagan outside the Washington Hilton Hotel as a way to get her attention. The spray of bullets wounded police officer Thomas Delahunty and Secret Service agent Tim McCarthy, paralyzed press secretary James Brady, and pierced Reagan's lung. Foster made futile attempts to separate her identity from the assassin. Before the press, she wept while refusing to denounce her realistic acting in *Taxi Driver*. The media invaded her privacy and reported her daily activities. At Hinckley's trial in 1982, she denied having any relationship with the shooter. In a rage, he hurled a pen at the witness and threatened to "get" her.

The actor's college years incurred additional stalking from Edward Richardson. The university security force frisked playgoers who attended a campus production of Marsha Norman's prison drama *Getting Out*, in which Foster played a hooker who murders a cab driver. One of the fans who paid the scalper's price of $50 for a ticket was copycat assassin Richardson, an armed stalker who took a front row seat to make eye contact with Foster. He sent her a death threat and lied about hiding a bomb in her dormitory. The Secret Service seized him in New York City at the Port Authority Bus Terminal. A punk band exploited the contretemps by naming itself Jody [sic] Foster's Army.

Life after Hinckley

The hype depressed Foster, who feared the public. She rented an off-campus apartment and hired an armed security force to shadow her night and day. In December 1982, she addressed the issue of pursuit and harassment in *Esquire* with the article "Why Me?" She graduated magna cum laude with a degree in English literature, but her public notoriety eclipsed her professional career. After she gained 20 pounds, she played B parts and took movie roles in France to be near her mother. Contributing to her discontent was a poster designed by gay militants to divulge her lesbianism. In 1998, her estranged brother Buddy confirmed the message in his unauthorized biography, *Foster Child*.

Foster chose to shake off the image of the victim of an erotomaniac, a delusional person who imagines an intimate tie or relationship with a celebrity or prestigious person. Her triumphs in film continued with *The Accused* (1988), the feminist cautionary story based on a real multiple assault committed in New Bedford, Massachusetts. She played Sarah Tobias, a working-class victim of gang rape and public vilification aided by an understanding prosecuting attorney, played by Kelly McGillis. The stunning success earned $100 million and won the star her first Oscar and Golden Globe. At the Academy Awards, she named her mother as the source of her confidence. Foster validated her depiction of Sarah for its revelations about male-on-female brutality: "Cruelty might be human, and it might be cultural, but it's not acceptable, which is what this movie is all about" (Abramowitz, 2000).

Returning to Normal

The actor distanced herself from Hinckley by refusing an interview on NBC TV's *The Today Show* (1991) that included questions about stalking. She posed for numerous magazine covers and played FBI neophyte Clarice Starling opposite Anthony Hopkins's Hannibal Lecter in *The Silence of the Lambs* (1991). The authenticity of her battle against a monstrous serial killer won her second Academy Award for the balance of controlled terror and self-empowerment through logic and ingenuity. The same year, she directed and starred as Dede Tate in *Little Man Tate* (1991), an examination of the child genius. After establishing the production company Egg Pictures, she directed Holly Hunter and Robert Downey, Jr., in the quirky comedy *Home for the Holidays* (1995). In the film *Nell* (1994), set in the Appalachian backcountry, she produced and starred as feral assault victim Nell Kellty opposite Liam Neeson and Natasha Richardson. Foster's varied characters include Laurel Sommersby, a civil war widow in *Sommersby* (1994), and phony Southern belle Annabelle Brandford, the love interest of James Garner and Mel Gibson in *Maverick* (1994). Opposite Matthew Mc-Conaughey, as a research scientist in the screen version of Carl Sagan's novel *Contact* (1997), her character, radio astronomer Dr. Ellie Arroway, unraveled a mathematical signal from space and time traveled to a distant locale. The box office smash earned her $9.5 million and, the next year, the honor of having an asteroid named 17744 Jodiefoster.

In the years following Hinckley's incarceration, Foster craved privacy in the midst of celebrity. When she gave birth to son Charles Bernard Foster on July 20, 1998, she withdrew to a safe house far from media attention. In 1999, she allowed Charlie Rose to question her about the stalking experience on *60 Minutes II*. She won acclaim for the part of Welsh teacher Anna Leonowens at the nineteenth-century court of Siamese monarch Phra Maha Mongut in a remake of *Anna and the King* (1999). The media revived public fascination with Hinckley's stalking in 2000, when he wrote to killer Ted Bundy, hid 57 photos of Foster under his mattress, and requested a nude sketch of her. Against court orders, he smuggled a book about Foster into his quarters at St. Elizabeth's Hospital, a mental institution where he was incarcerated on the insane ward on June 21, 1982.

A devoted single mother like Brandy, Foster closed her production company to devote more time to her family, but she continued to act. During her pregnancy with second son Kit Bernard Foster, she played Meg Altman, a victim of in-home terror, in *Panic Room* (2002). Her cinema role as Elodie Gordes in the foreign language venture *Un Long Dimanche de Fiançailles* (2004), set during the battle of the Somme, preceded the psychological thriller as Kyle Pratt, a frenzied engineer and single parent in *Flightplan* (2005), a global success. She followed with appearances in Spike Lee's thriller *Inside Man* (2006), costarring Denzel Washington and Clive Owen, and as Erica in *The Brave One* (2007). In December 2007, at a breakfast for Hollywood Reporter's Women in Entertainment, Foster acknowledged her 15-year relationship with film producer Cydney Bernard. Her honors include listing among VH1's top child actors, honorary doctorates from her alma mater and from Smith College and the University of Pennsylvania, listing among *People* magazine's 100 greatest film stars and *Empire*'s hundred sexiest stars, and recognition as the only two-time Oscar-winning woman under 30.

Sources

Abramowitz, Rachel. "What It Means To Be Jodie Foster." *Us Weekly*, May 8, 2000. Available at http://www.geocities.com/jodiefosterph/us050800.html (last accessed April 3, 2008).

Andersen, Kurt. "A Drifter Who Stalked Success." *Time*, April 13, 1981.

Brakel, Samuel J., and Alexander D. Brooks. *Law and Psychiatry in Criminal Justice*. Buffalo, NY: William S. Hein, 2001.

Doan, Laura L. *The Lesbian Postmodern*. New York: Columbia University Press, 1994.

Foster, Jodie. "Why Me?" *Esquire* (December 1982): 101–108.

Meloy, J. Reid. *The Psychology of Stalking: Clinical and Forensic Perspectives*. Burlington, MA: Academic Press, 1998.

Nicol, Brian. *Stalking*. London: Reaktion Books, 2006.

Taylor, Stuart, Jr. "Witness Says Hinckley Trailed Actress with Gun." *New York Times*, May 26, 1982.

Wilson, Anna. *Persuasive Fictions: Feminist Narrative and Critical Myth*. Cranbury, NJ: Bucknell University Press, 2001.

■ Suicide of a Spouse
Louise Erdrich

Revered Ojibway (also Anishinaabe or Chippewa) writer and storyteller, Karen Louise Erdrich survived the loss of her mate and writing partner Michael Dorris. A native of Little Falls, Minnesota, where her paternal grandparents operated a butcher shop, she was born on June 7, 1954, and grew up in a Roman Catholic environment. The eldest of the seven children of German-American father Ralph Louis Erdrich and French-Ojibway mother Rita Joanne Gourneau Erdrich, she was reared in the Red River Valley by her grandmother Mary Cecelia Lefavor and grandfather Aunnish e-Naubay Patrick Gourneau, a bead crafter and dancer at powwows, at Wahpeton in southeastern North Dakota on the Minnesota border. At the Turtle Mountain Chippewa Reservation on the Canadian border, where her parents taught school, her grandfather served as tribal chairman and related accounts of scraping by during the Great Depression as a Wobbly, a member of the International Workers of the World.

Erdrich and her sisters Heidi and Lise attended public schools and developed literary gifts in girlhood from the cyclical storytelling sessions that defined family get-togethers. From family conversations and storytelling sessions, Erdrich developed a knack for sound, image, and cadence. In 1985 to interviewer Laura Coltelli, Erdrich divulged that her father read his daughters William Shakespeare's plays and recited the poems of Robert Frost and George Gordon, Lord Byron. He suggested that, like other family tellers of cyclic tales, the children compose original narratives. After her mother stapled the stories into construction paper covers and her father paid a nickel for each entry, Erdrich felt like an accomplished author.

Louise and Michael

Erdrich expanded her writing in high school by keeping a journal and by reading and imitating classic verse. She emulated folksinger Joan Baez by dressing in hippie outfits comprised of items from her father's army uniforms. She also cheered for the wrestling team. At her mother's urging, in 1972, she enrolled in creative writing, English, and native

American studies at the first coeducational class at Dartmouth College in Hanover, New Hampshire. The start of school took her far from home for the first time. To her delight, she met Modoc anthropologist and author Michael Anthony Dorris, director of Dartmouth's native American studies program, who stressed that she should maintain her ties to first peoples.

Through dense verse, Erdrich told stories metaphysically and sensuously, but she looked to longer, more complex genres to provide more opportunity for development. An English department member, A. B. Paulsen, recognized Erdrich's gift for verse. Her early pieces, published in *Harper's*, *Massachusetts Review*, *Ms.*, *New Yorker*, *Paris Review*, and *Prairie Schooner*, won citations from the Academy of American Poets in her junior year. In 1977, she assisted in production at Lincoln, Nebraska, of a PBS TV documentary on her ancestry, the plains Indians of the Dakotas and Canada. Before beginning study for an M.A. on fellowship at Johns Hopkins University in 1979, she supported herself with part-time jobs as a field hand harvesting beets and cucumbers, waitress at Kentucky Fried Chicken, lifeguard, poetry teacher at hospitals and prisons, and construction flag signaler and weigher of trucks for the interstate highway system. For the State Arts Council of North Dakota, she taught poetry and writing to youth.

A Literary Team

In her 30s during the second phase of the native American literary Renaissance, Erdrich initiated a career writing circular narratives and poems set on the Great Plains. She wove contemporary Indian lore that stressed the post-Columbian clash between Roman Catholicism and native animism. For professional idols, she chose feminists Kay Boyle, Toni Morrison, Flannery O'Connor, Grace Paley, and Amy Tan and native American writers Sherman Alexie, Linda Hogan, Susan Power, and Jim Welch. While editing the Boston Indian Council newspaper, the *Circle*, she encountered Dorris again. Interaction with urban dwellers helped rid her of anguish at being culturally mixed by introducing other forms of multiethnicity. Friendships and observations also contributed ideas for characters and motivation.

When Erdrich began composing the verse collection *Jacklight* (1984), she collaborated with Dorris long distance as he conducted fieldwork in New Zealand and lectured at Auckland University. Erdrich flourished at the MacDowell Colony in Peterborough, New Hampshire, and as writer in residence at Dartmouth. Dorris declared her his literary soul mate. They married on October 10, 1981, the year she published a second verse collection, *Imagination*. Their children participated in the ceremony. On the second floor of their Minnesota home, he kept a separate office from hers and served as her agent.

Erdrich became stepmother to Dorris' three adopted children—Reynold Abel, a developmentally challenged Lakota from South Dakota, Jeffrey Sava, and Madeline "Birdie" Hannah, all likely victims of fetal alcohol syndrome. The couple produced three daughters—Persia Andromeda, Pallas Antigone, and Aza Marion. To make time for herself among preschoolers, Erdrich set up trays of pencils and crayons to entertain the girls. When they entered school, she limited herself to writing during school hours. As she shaped images from her journal into text, she consulted with Dorris on pacing, voice, and structure. The couple wrote romances under the "ungendered" pseudonym Milou North, which joined the first syllables of their given names. After marking titillating sections with paper clips, she sent raw manuscripts for her father's commentary.

Literary Success

Success encouraged Erdrich to extend short stories to longer fiction. In 1982, she won the Nelson Algren Prize and a purse of $5,000 for the story "The World's Greatest Fisherman," which she wrote in her kitchen and expanded into the opening chapter of a first novel. She preferred visually meaty images that served as magnets to gather bits of recall, experience, or dialogue. For her the title of her best work, *Love Medicine* (1984), the first of a tetralogy of blended fiction, she referred to traditional Chippewa love potions known to her matrilineal relatives. The novel won her and Dorris a National Book Critics Circle Award for the postmodern layering of personal narratives over a half-century of reservation life, like a song that sets interrelated verses to a recurrent melody and refrain. The novel earned a citation from the Before Columbus Foundation, a Sue Kaufman Prize for Best First Fiction, a Virginia Scully Award for Best Book Dealing with western Indians, and the admiration of novelists Toni Morrison and Philip Roth. Chickasaw poet and scholar Linda Hogan praised Erdrich's objectivity in refusing to romanticize everyday lives and choices. In Erdrich's next venture, *The Beet Queen* (1986), she branched out from reservation communities to Argus, North Dakota, in the era preceding World War II to present more refined stories based on her father's side of the family. She explained to a book editor from the *Chicago Tribune* her dedication to cultural diversity and issues of mixed blood people.

The virtuoso styling annoyed contemporary novelist Leslie Marmon Silko, who accused Erdrich of drifting away from Indian motifs to dabble in artsy self-indulgence. Erdrich liberated herself by brushing aside attempts to fit her under the heading of feminist or Indian or experimental fiction writer. The short story "Fleur," issued in the August 1986 *Esquire*, captured an O. Henry Award. In further collaborations with her husband, *A Yellow Raft in Blue Water* (1987) appeared solely under Dorris' authoring. The couple published a historical romance, *The Crown of Columbus* (1991), under both their names. In 1988, Erdrich featured oral narrative and ethnic mythology in the novel *Tracks*, an inventive story that the author bore as a burden over a decade of writing. The story describes shapeshifter Fleur Pillager, a feminist survivor, shaman, and storykeeper. Of character androgyny and self-empowerment, Erdrich exulted in the spunk of second wave feminism: "[Fleur] messed with evil, laughed at the old women's advice and dressed like a man. She got herself into some half-forgotten medicine, studied ways we shouldn't talk about" (Erdrich, 1988, 12). With *The Bingo Palace* (1994), Erdrich perused the violation of native traditions with the building of gambling casinos and the crime and materialism nurtured by the capitalistic mentality.

Analyzing Family Pain

In 1989, Dorris wrote a family memoir, *The Broken Cord: A Family's Ongoing Struggle with Fetal Alcohol Syndrome*, with details of their 21-year-old son Reynold Abel's mental and physical difficulties with his medical legacy. Erdrich recorded in journal entries an ongoing battle with Abel's school expulsions, violent behavior, inappropriate sexual contact, arrests, sadism, and suicide attempts. Two years later, Abel died in a pedestrian car accident. Dorris sank into despair. The family situation worsened in 1994, when son Jeffrey Sava went to jail in Denver for torturing his girlfriend. He tried to extort $15,000 by charging his parents with child abuse. The parents moved their young daughters to Montana and countered with a felony theft suit.

Erdrich approached her next work from a womanly perspective. She captured the layered emotions of the parturient woman in a memoir, *The Blue Jay's Dance: A Birth Year* (1996), and won a World Fiction Award for *The Antelope Wife: A Novel* (1996). She wrote her first children's work, *Grandmother's Pigeon* (1996), a mystical voyager tale about an elder's ride to Greenland on a porpoise and the messages she receives from passenger pigeons. Replete with witty ironies, *Tales of Burning Love* (1997) pictured the renaissance of contractor Jack Mauser, who learned that pleasuring his mate could cure his impotence.

Unsuccessful litigation and Dorris' depression, insomnia, exhaustion, and longing for literary prestige pushed Michael and Louise apart. She rented a residence blocks from the family home but acquiesced to the girls' demand to return by posing each morning as contented mother until they boarded the bus to school. She regretted the breakup of the era's great literary romance and the couple's abortive attempts to reunite, yet, she produced an enigmatic response for reporters: "There's no one reason, and there's 25,000 reasons" (Streitfeld, 1997, F.1). Further complicating the situation were unsubstantiated claims that Dorris beat and molested one or more of his biological daughters, ages 13, 11, and 8, who filed charges in Hennepin County, Minnesota. The girls moved in with their mother after intervention in his substance abuse failed. He lost faith in the justice system that had sided with the defendant in his lawsuit.

Dorris and Erdrich separated without settling issues of child custody and ownership of property, royalties, and literary rights. On December 4, 1996, friends intervened in his alcoholic binges and convinced him to stay 27 days at Hazelden treatment center in Center City, Minnesota. After interviews conducted by St. Paul therapist Sandra Hewitt, his children left him permanently. He considered his life over and, on March 29 at a New Hampshire farm cottage, made an unsuccessful attempt on his life with a mix of applesauce, sleeping pills, and vodka. On April 10, 1997, the night before a district attorney would charge him with criminal sexual abuse of two adopted children, Madeline and Sava, Dorris checked in at the Brick Tower Motor Inn in Concord, New Hampshire, on a day pass from Hazelden. Using vodka, prescription sleeping pills, and tapioca, he asphyxiated himself by fastening a plastic bag over his head. He wrote an apology note to the motel maid for leaving a mess in the room. Judge Delores Orey sealed the records and placed all parties under a gag order. The unfinished business left Dorris' exemplary reputation clouded by charges in *New York* magazine and *Vanity Fair* of child rape of two of his biological daughters.

Life after Michael

Erdrich was not surprised that Dorris chose death over the entanglements of their family life. She viewed his public persona as "the third floor of a building with a very deep basement" (Lyman, 1997, A.14). She told the press that "[h]e descended inch by inch, fighting all the way" and requested "some self-respect and dignity" (Ibid.). She looked inward to a strong persona she named Nurse Louise and visited her children's classes to suppress speculation on their father's suicide. She and her daughters moved to Minneapolis to be closer to her parents. In a tense atmosphere, 21-year-old Madeline charged her mother with complicity and negligence and contested her father's will, which excluded his estranged wife and adopted children from a share of his $2.4 million estate. Erdrich predicted that her five children would drop their animosities toward their father and each other. Letters from fans overwhelmed her with support and kindness. On February 3, 1992, a screen adaptation of Dorris' *The Broken Cord* aired on ABC TV.

Erdrich supported herself and her youngest three children with royalties from writing and with a bookshop, Birchbark Books, which she ran with her sister. Because the store faced an elementary school, the author established a laissez-faire attitude toward young book browsers. For relaxation, she began taking piano lessons and learning to speak Ojibwa. She visited Manitoulin Island, Ontario, to study native porcupine quilling and beading. Like William Faulkner's saga of Yoknapatawpha County, Erdrich's fiction pictured tiers of family in the lives of repeat characters. Her saga *The Last Report on the Miracles at Little No Horse* (2001) featured a cross-dresser, Agnes DeWitt, who posed among rural North Dakota tribes as Father Damien Modeste, a savior of the lost. Erdrich drew on family heritage for the gothic novel *The Master Butchers Singing Club* (2003). Her lifetime achievements include an Associate Poet Laureate of North Dakota title, Pushcart Prize for poetry, Western Literacy Association Award, Los Angeles Times Award for fiction, National Magazine Award, and a Scott O'Dell Award for young adult historical fiction for *The Game of Silence* (2006). In April 2007 she rejected an honorary doctorate from the University of North Dakota to scorn the Fighting Sioux mascot, a diminution of Indians.

Sources

"Author Found Way to Cope with Suicide." *Seattle Post-Intelligencer*, September 25, 1997.

Erdrich, Louise. *Tracks*. New York: Harper & Row, 1988.

Lyman, Rick. "Writer's Death Brings Plea for Respect, Not Sensation." *New York Times*, April 18, 1997, A.14.

Rawson, Josie. "A Broken Life." *City Pages* (Minneapolis), April 21, 1997.

Stone, Brad. "In the Best of Families: Two Months after the Death of Troubled Writer Michael Dorris, His Story Takes an Ugly New Turn." *Newsweek*, June 16, 1997.

Stookey, Lorena L. *Louise Erdrich: A Critical Companion*. Westport, CT: Greenwood, 1999.

Streitfeld, David. "Sad Story." *Washington Post*, July 13, 1997, F.1.

Weisser, Susan Ostrov, and Jennifer Fleischner. *Feminist Nightmares: Women at Odds: Feminism and the Problems of Sisterhood*. New York: New York University Press, 1995.

■ Survivor Guilt
Jon Krakauer

Investigative journalist and environmentalist Jon Krakauer reported to readers on his climb to Mount Everest on a doom-laden exhibition. A second-generation American from Brookline, Massachusetts, he was born of Polish-Russian Jewish ancestry on April 12, 1954, the middle of the five children of Carol and Lewis J. Krakauer, a transplanted author-physician and sports medicine specialist from Brooklyn, New York. Jon came of age in the rugged outback of the Willamette Valley near Corvallis, Oregon. At age 4, he scrambled the lower reaches of Mount Hood, Oregon. Despite a tenuous relationship with his fiercely competitive father, at age 8, the author began mounting heights under Lewis' direction and topped the 10,358-foot peak of South Sister, the tallest of the three volcanic spires of the Cascade Range. Lewis was disappointed in his rebellious son, who refused to go to Harvard. Drug addiction from postpolio syndrome drove Lewis to madness.

In his youth, Krakauer fell in love with the mystique of heights. He later observed, "I'd always known that climbing mountains was a high-risk pursuit. I accepted that danger was an essential component of the game" (Krakauer, 1997). He fostered hero worship for his Oregon neighbor, Willi Unsoeld, who, on May 22, 1963, conquered Everest's west ridge with adventurer Tom Hornbein as part of a National Geographic expedition. Before graduating from Corvallis High School in 1972, Krakauer played competitive tennis. While majoring in environmental science at Hampshire College in Amherst, Massachusetts, he learned about the sport of climbing from explorer David Roberts, author of *The Mountain of My Fear* (1968). Krakauer produced an 80-page senior thesis on the pioneering of an unclimbed rock route up the 8,985-foot Kichatna Spire, Alaska.

Mountaineering

Laboring at carpentry and commercial salmon fishing in Boulder, Colorado, Krakauer became an Alaskaphile and challenged his skills with more summitry. While courting outdoorswoman and climber Linda Mariam Moore, he promised to abandon his hobby scaling but failed to keep his word to quit extreme sports. His list of conquered slopes included Arrigetch Peaks in the state's Brooks Range, which a party of seven challenged in 1974. The adventures inspired his amateur sport journalism for the American Alpine Club and a student venture in avalanche weather into Colorado's Gore Range. The next year, he and college pal Nate Zinsser followed with an ascent of unstable, rain-soaked ice on the Moose's Tooth, a treacherous cathedral spire in the Alaska Range that the author described and photographed. Two years later in May, he managed a solo ascent of the granite couloirs of the Stikine Ice Cap and of Devil's Thumb, a 6,700-foot rocky tor across the bay from Petersburg, Alaska, on the border of British Columbia. After crossing the Stikine Ice Cap, he awaited an airdrop of supplies. On his climb of the northwest face, he encountered rock under ice and had to descend the same way he came. For 3 days, he contemplated the climb: "You constantly feel the abyss pulling at your back. To resist takes a tremendous conscious effort; you don't dare let your guard down for an instant" (Krakauer, 1996, 142). After a failed assault on the vertical facet amid a blizzard, he started up the south face. His trek succeeded after 20 days.

Krakauer reported the 3-week adventure for *Mountain* magazine and in his first anthology *Eiger Dreams: Ventures Among Men and Mountains* (1990), his first book. The collection of 12 stories covered roughing it on Mount McKinley and his 1984 attack on the Eiger in Switzerland, an undertaking that jeopardized his marriage and introduced the subject of "accrued guilt" (Krakauer, 1990, 178). His preface acknowledged the draw of climbing to his imagination. He smoothed over the ruffled home front with a tender dedication to his wife, best pal, and editor, "Linda, with thoughts of Green Mountain Falls, the Wind Rivers, and Roanoke Street" (Ibid.). He admitted fearing that "the connubial arrangement was going to end," but he "managed to stay married and keep climbing" (Ibid.). A testimony to his skill at analyzing the egos of athletes emerged on the first page: "The trickiest moves on any climb are the mental ones, the psychological gymnastics that keep terror in check, and the Eiger's grim aura is intimidating enough to rattle anyone's poise" (Ibid., 1). Under the influence of writer David Roberts, at age 29, Krakauer quit woodworking and commercial fishing to freelance fulltime for *American Alpine Journal*, *Architectural Digest*, *Climbing*, *Men's Journal*, *Mountain*, *National Geographic*, the *New York Times*, *Playboy*, *Rolling Stone*, *Smithsonian*, and the *Washington Post*. One journal, *Outside*, financed his most harrowing expedition.

Climber Turned Author

In 1990, Krakauer issued his photographic journalism for Iceland: *Land of the Sagas* (1990), cowritten by David Roberts. The text covered the epic landscape of gravelly coastline, lava flows, glaciers, spring-fed lakes, and snow-glazed peaks. Two years later, Krakauer topped an Andean classic, Cerro Torre in Patagonia, Argentina, a tower of sheer granite. In the November 1993 issue of *Smithsonian*, he reflected on motorcycling in "A Hog Is Still a Hog, but the 'Wild Ones' Are Tamer."

In the January 1993 issue of *Outside*, Krakauer wrote "Death of an Innocent: How Christopher McCandless Lost His Way in the Wilds," the story of a transcendental hermit. In July 1992, hunters found McCandless' remains after 2 weeks of exposure at Denali National Park. He appeared to have poisoned himself on wild potatoes, which contained the alkaloid swainsonine. He starved to death in an abandoned bus. On January 4, 1993, *Outside* magazine featured McCandless on the cover. Ten months after the adventurer's bizarre demise, Krakauer flew over the Stampede Trail with McCandless' father and stepmother. With two companions, the author traversed the area that McCandless traveled and located items abandoned on the trail. Krakauer compared the tragic death to the failure of Sir John Franklin, who led an expedition into Canada in 1819. Starvation drove him to cannibalism. Métis rescued the survivors. In 1845, Franklin made a third trip to the Arctic and disappeared. Krakauer concluded that McCandless was just unlucky. Largely self-trained, Krakauer reprised his article with a classic of sports biography, *Into the Wild*, a *New York Times* bestseller that won the 1996 Entertainment Weekly Book of the Year award. One criticism charged him with amateur psychological analysis of a man he had never met.

Krakauer on Everest

The consummate adventure, a 29,028-foot climb up Mount Everest placed Krakauer in the troposphere, the atmosphere's lowest limit. He accounted for the allure: "Everest has always been a magnet for kooks, publicity seekers, hopeless romantics, and others with a shaky hold on reality" (Messner, 1999, 73). Following a year's training, he traveled with New Zealand guide Rob Hall's 1996 expedition, which cost American, New Zealand, Norwegian, South African, and Taiwanese adventurers $65,000 each. *Outside* magazine underwrote Krakauer's participation to study commercialization of sport climbing and its effect on camaraderie and teamwork. The climb began with his helicopter approach from Kathmandu to Lukla in northeastern Nepal for the April 6 scaling of rubble on the Khumbu Icefall, a 12-mile ice tongue on Everest's south flank. In harsh cold, a week later, while yak trains supplied the base camp, Krakauer and tentmate Doug Hansen, a postal worker, settled in at Camp One for serious strategizing. Krakauer developed climber's symptoms—coughing, insomnia, and suppressed appetite. Hansen suffered headaches from the ultraviolet radiation that scorched his eyes.

Three days later, Krakauer began shedding some of his boyish idealization of risk taking in an unpredictable competition that threatens mental acuity. His faculties felt muddled as though by a hangover. He slogged up the Western Cwm past two corpses to the second level for acclimatizing before reaching base camp on April 26. Hansen developed frostbite and a frozen larynx; Krakauer suffered solar radiation. The climbers quarreled over the task of stretching rope up Lhotse Face. The expedition initiated Krakauer's admiration for the Sherpa, native athletes from Phakding Village who carried loads ahead and guided a stream of traffic from would-be summiteers up the Nepalese access to the world's highest peak.

Topping Everest

From Camp Three on May 6, Hall's group sortied toward the final ascent, a death zone above 25,000 feet into thin air that caused high altitude brain, cardiac, and respiratory anomalies. Two days later, a boulder struck Sandy Harris in the chest; the next day, Chen Yu-Nan tumbled from a precipice to his death in a crevasse. In rough going, the crew rescued Tenzing Sherpa, Rob's assistant, from an ice bridge. A rogue gale throttled Camp Four, forcing Krakauer to start the final leg near midnight. For 24 hours, he tackled the South Col. He observed, "So little oxygen was reaching my brain that my mental capacity was that of a slow child" (Krakauer, 1997, 4).

Filled with apprehension after nearly 2 hours at the top of the world, on the afternoon of May 10, Krakauer descended toward Camp Four over a 7,000-foot abyss and along the Hillary Step, a treacherous notch requiring technical expertise. The risky descent killed Rob Hall, dimmed Beck Weathers' eyesight from scratched corneas and low barometric pressure, and separated three climbers from the group. Following the disappearance of Andy Harris, Doug Hansen, Yasuko Namba, and Beck Weathers and the crushing of a Sherpa guide by falling stones, the rigorous scale threatened Krakauer with exhaustion. For each step, he labored to draw four breaths. Rappeling 200 feet down an ice wall, he survived a whiteout, loss of oxygen, and temperatures below -100 degrees Fahrenheit before collapsing in his domed tent.

Krakauer blamed himself for sleeping rather than returning to help less able climbers descend through the dark in driving snow. After 5 days in the high country, he wept for the deaths of 12 out of 16 expeditioners and the stunting of lives from out-of-control grandstanding. He admitted that the events on Everest were "gnawing... [his] guts out": "I was a party to the death of good people, which is something that is apt to remain on my conscience for a very long time" (Krakauer, 1997, xvii, xviii). From the worst season of climbing on Mount Everest in 75 years, he boarded a helicopter to Syangboche and returned to Kathmandu. Beck Weathers survived but lost the fingers and thumb of his left hand and his right arm and nose to frostbite. After arriving home to Seattle airport on May 19, Krakauer carried the news of Hansen's death to his parents. In mid-June, Ngawang Topche's death from HAPE (high-altitude pulmonary edema) increased Krakauer's flashbacks to "intense competition and undiluted machismo" and his burden of survivor guilt (Ibid., 23).

From Everest into Print

To purge regret for profiting from the tragic venture, Krakauer sought catharsis. He defended his role in interviews and answered bitter, retaliatory letters from victims' relatives. Scott Fischer's sister Lisa charged, "[T]he book records] YOUR OWN ego frantically struggling to make sense out of what happened" (Ibid., 370). Krakauer compiled a 17,000-word redemptive piece for the September 1996 issue of *Outside*. After he earned a nomination for the National Magazine Award for the original article, *Into Thin Air* bobbed into prominence in other forms—public readings, large print, illustrated edition, e-book, CD, and, notably, "Summit Journal 1996: Jon Krakauer on Everest," aired on May 23, 1997, on *Outside Online*. Still traumatized by the eight deaths that paralleled his ascent, over 3 months, he composed *Into Thin Air: A Personal Account of the Mount Everest Disaster* (1997), a complex exposé of sport climbing and the commercialization of mountaineering. The judgmental bestseller that sold 2,600,000 copies stirred acclaim for climbers' courage and blame for their arrogance. The text acknowledged a lethal combination—nature's quirks and the party's wrongheadedness.

Brooding and self-castigating for not rescuing more of the team, Krakauer swore off Everest and gave up lecturing, even after an invitation to address the American Himalayan Foundation. With royalties topping $50 million, he began supporting charities for the indigenous Sherpa of the Himalayas and established the Everest '96 Memorial Fund at the Boulder Community Foundation. For National Geographic, he returned to climbing in Antarctica. In 1997, ABC TV aired TriStar's 90-minute adaptation of *Into Thin Air*, starring Peter Horton. The same year, Krakauer narrated a six-cassette, unabridged audio book and contributed to *High: Stories of Survival from Everest and K2* (1999), a compilation of mountaineering narratives.

Into the 21st century, Krakauer pleased his fan base with more adventure writing. He edited three historical works, *The Last Place on Earth: Scott and Amundsen's Race to the South Pole* (1999), *Starlight and Storm: The Conquest for the Great North Faces of the Alps* (1999), and *Francis Parkman, La Salle, and the Discovery of the Great West* (1999). After summiting First Flatiron outside Boulder, Colorado, in May 2000 and coauthoring *High Exposure: An Enduring Passion for Everest and Unforgiving Places* (2000), he returned to editing with *The Brendan Voyage* (2000), *Chauncey Loomis, Weird and Tragic Shores* (2000), and *The Shameless Diary of an Explorer* (2001). Less loved was Krakauer's agnostic's view of Mormonism in *Under the Banner of Heaven: A Story of Violent Faith* (2003), another literary venture into extremes. He compared the disturbingly glib motivation of a double execution of a Mormon mother and her infant daughter to the insane fundamentalism of Islamic terrorists. He continues to reverence the land and to promote rambles into nature's solitude and grandeur.

Sources

Beckwith, Christian, ed. *American Alpine Journal*. Seattle, WA: Mountaineers Books, 1999.

Bromet, Jane, "Summit Journal 1996: Jon Krakauer Turns His Eye—and Lungs—toward Everest." Outside Online (April 15, 1996). Available at http://outside.away.com/peaks/features/krakauer.html (last accessed on April 3, 2008).

Colford, Paul D. "One Man's Final Frontier Is Another's Gripping Bestseller." *Los Angeles Times*, April 8, 1996, 3.

Crouch, Gregory. *Rock & Ice Goldline: Stories of Climbing Adventure & Tradition*. Seattle, WA: Mountaineers Books, 2001.

Ermelino, Louisa. "Into the Wild." *People* 45 (6) (February 12, 1996): 35.

Krakauer, Jon. *Eiger Dreams: Ventures Among Men and Mountains*. New York: Anchor Books, 1990.

———. *Into the Wild*. New York: Anchor Books, 1996.

———. *Into Thin Air*. New York: Anchor Books, 1997.

Lichtenstein, Grace. "Against All Odds." *Washington Post*, September 26, 2004.

Messner, Reinhold, ed. *All Fourteen Eight-Thousanders*. Seattle, WA: Mountaineers Books, 1999.

"Plumbing the Depths of Faith." *New York Times*, August 17, 2003.

Roberts, David. *On the Ridge Between Life and Death: A Climbing Life Reexamined*. New York: Simon & Schuster, 2006.

Williams, Wilda. "Into the Wild." *Library Journal* 120 (19) (November 15, 1995): 96.

◼ Third World Poverty
Muhammad Yunus

An immigrant from Bengal, one of the world's poorest regions, economist Muhammad Yunus looked back on the poverty of his native land with fresh ideas. A native of the seaport of Bathua, he was born to a Muslim family on June 28, 1940, on Boxirhat Road in Hathazari, Chittagong, British India, now called Bangladesh. His home combined his father's jewelry workshop with a five-room residence on the second floor. During World War II, Yunus and his friend Salam acted out combat with imitation machine guns. Of his 13 younger siblings, five died in infancy.

Because his father, goldsmith Hazi Dula Mia Shoudagar, had only an eighth grade education, he wanted his sons—Muhammad, Ibrahim, Salani, Ayub, Azam, Jahangir, and Moinu—amply trained for business. Muhammad contributed by tutoring his younger brothers. Despite inherited mental illness and only a fourth grade education, his mother, Sufia Khatun, set an example of benevolence to the needy. At age 7, Yunus lived in Chittagong and attended Lamar Bazar Primary School. Although he escaped lessons in a humble village school, the local burden of hunger and homelessness followed him. As he matured, he learned that 118 million Bangladeshi lived on 55,000 square miles and earned only $210 per person annually.

Making a Difference

Yunus dedicated his brilliant career to ending the long history of world poverty. In his words, "I wanted to see if as a person, as a human being, I could be of some use to some people, outside of the university campus where the villages are" ("Interview," 2007). On scholarship, he enrolled at Chittagong Collegiate School in East Pakistan and participated in Boy Scouts. In his early teens, he attended jamborees in Canada, India, Japan, the Philippines, and West Pakistan. In his first years at Chittagong College, he flourished at campus drama productions. At age 17, he entered Dhaka University and completed an M.A. by age 21. From research assistant at the Bureau of Economics, he progressed to lecturer in economics in Chittagong College while operating a factory that packaged books, calendars, and greeting cards. On a Fulbright scholarship, at age 25, he completed a doctorate in economics and banking from Vanderbilt University in Nashville, Tennessee. For 3 years, he taught at Middle Tennessee State University in Murfreesboro. During this period, he joined other hyphenated Americans in protesting the Vietnam War.

During the Bangladesh Liberation War in 1971, Yunus organized the Bangladesh Information Center and promoted support with other Bangladeshi-Americans. Working out of his Nashville home, he formed a citizens' committee, gained inside information from fellow countrymen in Washington, D.C., and issued the *Bangladesh Newsletter*. After the revolution, when devastation demoralized the Bangladeshi, the new government named Yunus a member of the planning commission. He wearied of bureaucratic answers to age-old problems and returned to Chittagong University to head the economics department. He married a

Russian wife, Vera Forostenko, a student of Russian literature living in Trenton, New Jersey. In 1975, his research into cooperative economics resulted in a Nabajug Tebhaga Khamar (new era three-share farm), source of the Gram Sarkar (village government) program. In 1977, the couple immigrated to New Jersey with their infant daughter Monica, but parted because Vera refused to live in Bangladesh. In April 1980, Yunus married a native, Professor Afrozi Begum Yunus, a researcher in nuclear physics at Manchester University in England who later taught at Jahangirnagar University in Savar, Dhaka.

The Village Banking Project

During the famine in Bangladesh late in 1974, shortly after the nation gained independence from Pakistan, Yunus and local students from his economics class surveyed the difficulties of small business. He confessed, "I couldn't cope with this daily tragedy. It made me realize that, whatever I had learned, whatever I was teaching, was all make-believe: it had no meaning for people's lives" (Collopy, 2000, 75). Basing his theory on the paradigm created by Dr. Akhtar Hameed Khan, founder of Pakistan Academy for Rural Development (now Bangladesh Academy for Rural Development), Yunus and his assistants tackled the low profits earned by 42 female bamboo stool crafters. The low yield was the fault of misogynistic bankers and of loan sharks charging exorbitant rates of interest on amounts as small as 15 cents. The cost of financing materials undercut profits to pennies.

Yunus equated exploitation of workers as another form of slave labor and combated the sufferings of women with microfranchising. To raise village entrepreneurs to a more comfortable level of subsistence, he focused on women as the source of family well-being. He experimented with microcredit—interest-free loans equivalent to pocket change extended to villagers in Jobra. The cash served simple needs: to "pay for medical treatments, purchase school supplies, recapitalize businesses affected by natural disasters, and finance modest but dignified family burials" (Yunus, 2003, 57).

When the campus bank refused credit to the poor, Yunus became their guarantor for the first outlay of $27. The positive reaction astounded him: "The next few days, I thought if you can make so many people so happy with such a small amount of money, why shouldn't you do more of it?" ("Interview," 2007). In an androcentric country, social and economic change for women also earned Yunus and his staff the enmity of Communist radicals and from Islamic Imams. In Tangail, conservative clergy denied the women orthodox Muslim burial for violating Koranic commands against usury and profiteering. Men beat women for disloyalty and spread rumors that the bank was a front for Christian proselytizers, pimps, murderers, smugglers, or a Middle Eastern slave ring.

The Grameen Bank and Foundation

A loan from Janata Bank set Yunus' model in motion in December 1976. He used welfare lists as a source of people who needed help. To apply for unsecured loans, patrons drawn from the "un-lendable" organized a solidarity group, five acquaintances who attested to each borrower's integrity and to support the project to its conclusion. Decisions fell on bank committees, most of which were comprised of landless peasants or smallholders with under an acre each. The results vindicated the founder's original trust in Asian females: "As women become empowered, they look at themselves, and at what they can do. They are making economic progress and alongside that, making decisions about their personal lives" (Kennedy,Cuomo, and Richardson, 2000, 23).

Yunus' initial model diversified into the Gonoshasthaya Grameen Texile Mills, Grameen CyberNet Limited, Grameen Fund, Grameen Knitwear Limited, Grameen Krishi (Village Agriculture Foundation), Grameen Motsho (Village Fisheries Foundation), Grameen Software Limited, and Grameen Trust. Individual outlays went toward modest dreams—buying seed for a crop, milling grain, purchasing a milk cow, or stocking a henyard or fish farm. The bank and its donors promoted home gardens by distributing 3 million saplings and 6 million packets of corn, soybeans, and sunflower seeds to diversify traditional plantings of rice, sugarcane, and wheat. Preferential treatment fell on those areas suffering drought or natural disasters. Most of the profits returned directly to homes and families for improved water supply and sanitation through irrigation pumps and deep-drilled tube wells.

Nine years after the class project took wings, on October 1, 1983, Yunus established Grameen Bank (village bank), a peasant financial structure offering microloans to dreamers of a better life. Within 2 decades, Yunus headed a professional force of 25,000 at 2,381 branch banks serving 75,950 remote villages. His visionary network uplifted over 7.3 million people, 97 percent of whom were women. Within 3 years, patrons saw a 50 percent boost to their annual income and a rise in agricultural proficiency and equitable distribution of foodstuffs. Many borrowers aspired to found their own businesses; all sought dignity and self-worth through industry, education, and affordable housing for 640,000 families. The Grameen default rate was less than 1 percent. As 58 percent of borrowers pulled themselves above the poverty line, borrowers' children sprouted up to average height and weight. The bank began to turn a profit and expanded to insurance, pension fund, and savings departments. For empowering the bottom social and economic class, comprised mostly of women and children, in 1994 in Des Moines, Iowa, Yunus accepted the World Food Prize.

Capitalism among the Poor

The Grameen project spread worldwide, ridding the people from small hamlets of the suffering and oppression that Yunus remembered from childhood. By adding information and communication technology to the project, he founded Grameen Phone, a mobile phone company that aimed to put a major utility under control of the poor. The plan began with Yunus' first "telephone lady," Laily Begum from Patira Village. With seed money, some 300,000 other village women stocked mobile phones and contracted communications services to 10 million subscribers. By March 1997, 260,000 rural people in over 50,000 villages owned cell phones. The Grameen project also masterminded village eye camps and an eye care hospital to perform 10,000 cataract removals annually. For spindly, sickly children, the banking foundation built a yogurt factory supplying fortified yogurt for the malnourished.

Yunus described his innovative solution to homeland poverty in *Banker to the Poor: The Autobiography of Muhammad Yunus, Founder of the Grameen Bank* (2001), a rewrite of an earlier memoir published in 1999 and a forerunner of a third volume in 2003. That year, he developed a more daring attack on hunger and despair by providing financial aid to wandering mendicants—"the barefoot beggars with babies, women asleep on the sidewalk, children with deformed limbs and emaciated bodies" (Yunus, 2003, 86). The program loaned around $12 per client and enabled 85,000 itinerant people to sell household goods, snacks, and toys house to house. Within 3 years, 6 percent of the beggars had left the streets and settled into stable lives. By 2005, the Grameen Bank made over $500 million in loans.

Early in 2006 Yunus collaborated with Mahfuz Anam, Debapriya Bhattcharya, Dr. Kamal Hossain, Judge Muhammad Habibur Rahman, Matiur Rahman, and Professor Rehman Sobhan in launching a people's political party. To ensure integrity, the group proposed straightforward national campaigning by dependable candidates. On February 11, 2007, Yunus issued a letter in the Bangladeshi newspaper *Daily Star* requesting citizen input in a move toward clean government provided by Nagorik Shakti (Citizens' Power). On May 3, he abandoned idealistic plans to enter politics and opted to stay in financial altruism, the work he knew best.

The Nobel Prize

Upon receipt of the Nobel Prize for Peace shared with his banking foundation, in 2006, Yunus exulted as the first businessman and the first of his nation to win the honor. In a telephone interview on October 13, he declared poverty an artificial creation of faulty global economic systems. He stated modestly, "As a Bangladeshi, I'm proud that we have given something to the world. Our work has now been recognized by the whole world" ("Nobel," 2006). He planned to invest some of the $1.4 million award in the manufacture of a cheap, nutritious food for the poor "from below."

Yunus traveled to Oslo and, on December 20, delivered an acceptance speech. To an audience of bank patrons and executives, former students, and relatives, he thanked the many village clients of his bank who profited from his pragmatism and from his trust in social businesses, his term for village cooperatives. In his view of the global honor, it acknowledged lowly people and their efforts to better themselves. He used the platform to inform the world that peace depends on hope, altruism, and self-sufficiency. He linked an adequate living to stability, democracy, and civil rights and to education, a goal of 100 percent of his female clients. Within 3 decades of operation, the Grameen project offered 30,000 annual scholarships to promising youth and 7,000 student loans per year for advanced training in education, engineering, law, and medicine. Yunus described these achievers as a new generation who may never know the misery of homelessness, ignorance, famine, or beggary. As of mid-2007, Grameen Bank extended $6.38 billion to 7.4 million borrowers.

An Exemplar of Altruism

On July 18, 2007, Yunus joined a consortium in Johannesburg, South Africa, comprised of U.N. President Kofi Annan, Indian economist and feminist Ela R. Bhatt, Algerian peacekeeper Lakhdar Brahimi, Norwegian public health advocate Gro Brundtland, Brazilian sociologist Fernando Henrique Cardoso, former U.S. President Jimmy Carter, Myanmar freedom fighter Aung Sun Suu Kyi, Mozambican women's advocate Graça Machel, South African President Nelson Mandela, Irish freedom fighter Mary Robinson, South African Archbishop Desmond Tutu, and Chinese statesman Li Xhaoxing. Called the Global Elders, the group proposed to promote wise altruism worldwide through creative leadership. In addition to the global award, Yunus' cabinet of honors housed 26 honorary doctorates and 50 awards, including the Ramon Magsaysay Award, the Sydney Peace Prize, and a commemorative stamp from his native land. His signal achievement was the financing of 3.6 million bank patrons in 25 nations.

Still invigorated to merge business with benevolence, Yunus looked ahead to greater ventures. He explained, "Poverty isn't a space science, or about an intricate design of a complicated machine. It is a topic about people" (Arena, 2004, 136). His book *Creating a World Without Poverty: How Social Business Can Transform Our Lives* (2007) envisioned partnerships with generous investors and business schools willing to tackle troubling issues of global marketing, health care, infrastructure projects, and renewable energy for the poor. At the far end of his goals, he foresaw the collapse of world poverty through the long-term security, creativity, and contributions of the underclass. He began advising the World Bank's Advisory Council for Sustainable Economic Development and UNESCO's International Advisory Panel. His model took root in 250 institutions in a hundred countries in Malaysia, South America, and rural North America, transforming many of the world's bottom 2 percent with small investments in their aims and initiative.

Sources

Arena, Christine. *Cause for Success: Companies That Put Profit Second and Come in First.* Novato, CA: New World Library, 2004.

Collopy Michael. *Architects of Peace: Visions of Hope in Words and Images.* Novato, CA: New World Library, 2000.

"Interview with Muhammad Yunus." *CNN News*, November 20, 2007.

Kennedy, Kerry, Eddie Adams, Kerry Kennedy Cuomo, and Nan Richardson. *Speak Truth to Power: Human Rights Defenders Who Are Changing Our World.* New York: Umbrage, 2000.

"Nobel for Anti-Poverty Pioneers." *BBC News*, October 13, 2006.

Yunus, Muhammad. *Banker to the Poor: Micro-Lending and the Battle Against World Poverty.* New York: Public Affairs, 2003.

———. *Creating a World Without Poverty: How Social Business Can Transform Our Lives.* New York: Public Affairs, 2007.

■ Tyranny
Julia Álvarez

Bicultural children's author, poet, and fiction writer Julia Álvarez witnessed tyranny in her childhood home in the Dominican Republic and used the events as background for a Latin American dictator novel. She was born one of five daughters in New York City, on March 27, 1950, and spent her first decade in Santo Domingo. Her family was headed by a grandfather who was a U.N. cultural attaché and extended to relatives as well as a staff of duennas and servants. She lived in an age-segregated compound where "we, the younger members of *la familia*, would be off at our own table" (Álvarez, "Foreword," 2004, xiii). To conceal family secrets, the adults conspired in English. She reflected in her memoir, *Something to Declare* (1998), on the traditional gender roles expected by fathers and enforced by Catholicism. She later remarked on "how important it is to be able to tell our stories to those who have power over us" (Álvarez, 1998, 269).

At an impressionable age, the author chose as a champion the rebel Scheherazade, the lifesaver in *The Arabian Nights*. Education in folklore at home coordinated with boarding school, but her aunts rejected the child's original storytelling as lies. She disliked textbooks but loved reciting verse to visitors. Her favorite poems were the works of Rubén Darío, José Martí, Pablo Neruda, and Salomé Ureña. Her mother chose cautionary tales that warned the girls of Generalissimo Rafael Leonidas, a ruthless lecher. Of narrative during national upheaval, Álvarez later learned a vital truth, "that stories could save you" (Álvarez, 1998, 138).

Under Trujillo's repressive regime, Álvarez was aware of the terrorism of peasants, particularly 20,000 Haitian laborers, whom hit squads executed in 1937. In August 1960, her father, a physician and hospital manager, conspired with a cabal known as MR1J4 to unseat Trujillo and overthrow a police state that had garroted islanders for 3 decades. The family fled discovery by the Servicio de Inteligencia Militar (SIM), the regime's secret police. While eluding possible jailing and execution, the adults protected Julia from the most fearful episodes under "El Jefe" (the Chief) that spawned the Dominican diaspora. It brought 17,000 refugees to the United States that year, followed in the next 20 years by 230,000 more. She later wrote about the virtual house arrest, "the whisperings of terrified adults, the cries of uncles being rounded up, the sirens of the death squads racing by" (Shreve, 2003, x). By December 1960, when her father began a fellowship in coronary surgery in the United States, his co-plotters were dead. She could only dream of opening prison cells, relocating the "disappeared," tearing down island shanties, and offering vegetables to beggars. She lost touch with more than her West Indian residence: "I lost almost everything: a homeland, a language, family connections, a way of understanding, a warmth" (Sirias, 2).

English as a Second Language

In exile, the author began assimilation in American English, a language she connected with the colonization of the Spanish Caribbean. Classmates rejected her as a spic and threw stones at her. Because her mind refused to abandon her Dominican culture, at Abbot Academy she retreated into books, fantasy, and writing. While composing essays on her native land for class, she dreamed of making the world safe. The effort reduced her isolation and alienation from home. Because she studied each word and weighed the significance of each idiom, she developed professional skills. At first, Walt Whitman and Emily Dickinson's verse captivated her. In high school, she took up French and lost her ability to craft her mother tongue into art. She admitted, "I can't ride its wild horses" (Álvarez, 1998, 172). By age 15, she and her sisters began summering in the Dominican Republic, where the author recorded stories as a "portable homeland." Far from American technology, she wrote in longhand by a gas lamp. She later summarized her method: "I use structures to survive and triumph! To say what's important to me as a woman and as a Latina" (Brown, Finch, and Kumin, 204). In the poem "33," she declared herself more real on paper than in person.

Beginning in 1967, Álvarez studied at Connecticut College and earned a degree in literature from Middlebury College, from which she graduated summa cum laude and Phi Beta Kappa. In 1975, she completed an M.F.A. in creative writing from Syracuse University. At the Bread Loaf School of English, she studied American and British literature and turned her knack for words into a promising career. She published two narratives, "Father" (1977) and "The Rainfall" (1977), in *Barataria Review* and spent 5 years learning technique in creative writing workshops. She became a co-reader with Sandra Cisneros and studied the writings of Ana Castillo and Denise Chavez. Álvarez identified the foursome as *Las Girlfriends*, a clutch of Latinas united by the staff of *Vanity Fair*. At her father's insistence, she enrolled at Harvard and won a fellowship, but the drive for a Ph.D. belonged to the father, not the daughter.

Fostering Writers

On staff at California State University, Fresno, College of the Sequoias, Phillips Andover Academy, George Washington University, Middlebury College, and the universities of Illinois at Urbana and Vermont, the author advised Latino students and taught classes in composition, autobiography, and women's, immigrant, and Hispanic literatures. Simultaneously with classroom work, she compiled her first verse anthology, *Homecoming* (1984). During a visit to Santo Domingo to address the Caribbean Studies Association, an elderly islander berated Álvarez for not writing in Spanish. In school systems around Franklin, Kentucky, and in Fayetteville, North Carolina, and Wilmington, Delaware, she served as poet in residence migrating by a VW from post to post. Her itinerant job required giving recitations and writing workshops at public schools, colleges, libraries, and community venues. Her first financial boosts were grants—a 1986 General Electric Foundation Award for Young Writers and a 1987 National Endowment for the Arts. She published in the *Burlington Free Press* and small literary journals—*Academic Questions, Bellevue Literary Review, Callaloo, Calyx, Caribbean Writer, Kenyon Review, Latinos in the U.S., Massachusetts Review, Plainsong, Witness,* and *Womanspirit*—won some writing competitions, and compiled examples of her work in *Yo Soy/I Am* (1997). In 1998, she gave up the classroom for full-time writing.

With a push from agent Susan Bergholz, Álvarez burst onto the pop fiction scene with a first novel, *How the García Girls Lost Their Accent* (1991), winner of an ALA Notable Book citation and a PEN Oakland/Josephine Miles Award. The motifs of women of color in works by Zora Neale Hurston, Maxine Hong Kingston, Toni Morrison, and Alice Walker encouraged her to turn island experience into mainstream American literature. The candor of her memories cost her a breakup with her mother, Julia T. Álvarez, a traditionalist who preferred women to be silent. The caution derived from the 1950s, when Trujillo's cohorts caused people to disappear for speaking dangerous truths.

Feminism as a Fight for Freedom

While writing and teaching, Álvarez advanced feminist themes in two works of historical fiction—*En el tiempo de las mariposa* (*In the Time of the Butterflies*, 1994), an autobiographical reflection of her decade in the Dominican Republic, and *In the Name of Salomé* (2000), a study of educator Salomé Ureña de Henriquez, a women's rights advocate in the late 1800s. For *In the Time of the Butterflies*, a reflection of the survivors of Trujillo's depredations, she researched the tyrannous milieu in 1986 through encounters with Noris and Minou, children like herself who observed the dictatorship through the daring of their parents. Six years later, Álvarez encountered life insurance agent Dedé Mirabal, a storykeeper like the author who exorcised the horrendous Trujillo era by preserving in narrative a model of female defiance.

Álvarez set about developing a framework motif and a polyphonic style contrasting the perspectives of four island patriots—Dedé and her courageous sisters, attorney Minerva "Mate" Mirabal de Tavárez, María Teresa Mirabal de Guzman, and Patria Mercedes Mirabal de González, the most domesticated, who learned of island corruption while studying at a La Vega convent school, Inmaculada Concepción. The author's mother urged silence on the murderous Trujillo regime. Álvarez reasoned, "If I shut up, would I still be fanning the embers of the dictatorship with its continuing power of censorship and control over the imagination of many Dominicans?" (Álvarez, 1998, 111). Exposing the chauvinism of androcentric Latino society and its patriarchal accomplice, the Catholic Church, the story describes the courage of three women against a blatant skirt chaser and mass murderer. A subplot counters Trujillo's exploitation of preteen virgins of good family with the philandering of Enrique Mirabal, who sires an illegitimate daughter. The author implies that Trujillo seized power by advancing an island patriarchy built on male privilege and subjugation of women of all classes. In later works, she posed the male peacock in ludicrous scenes intended to deflate and abase men for their foolish machismo. Of women's makeshift methods of fighting back, she remarked on her own innovative style: "You use what you have, you learn to work the structure to create what you need" (Brown, Finch, and Kumin, 204).

Global Acclaim

Critics extolled Álvarez, the first Dominican-American published in the United States, as a feminist author on a par with novelist Isabel Allende, author of *The House of the Spirits* (1982). Álvarez's dramatization of the Mirabal sisters' defiance increased their notoriety worldwide. Because Trujillo's goon squad ambushed, tortured, and executed three of the sisters by the roadside outside La Cumbre on November 25, 1960, islanders elevated the "butterflies" to the status of freedom fighters and martyrs. The United Nations named their death date, November 25, the International Day against Violence against Women. On October 7, 2001, an adaptation of *In the Time of the Butterflies* aired on Showtime TV, featuring Salma Hayek and Edward James Olmos as Minerva and Trujillo. Critics lauded the novelist for her overlay of daily rural life and superstitions on the island with the menace of Trujillo, the persecutions of his henchmen, and the guile of radical underground spies and liberators.

The mother–daughter strengths of Álvarez's early works took more palpable shape in *In the Name of Salome* (2000), a memoir of Camila Henríquez Ureña and her mother, Salome Ureña, a national treasure whose patriotic verse heartened Dominicans in the late 1800s. To extend her muse to all, she began the island's first girl's school. In Álvarez's words, "She was going to build a nation, girl by girl" (Álvarez, "I came," 2004, 211). For research into Salome's letters, notebooks, and manuscripts, in October 1997, the author and her husband risked an illicit trip to the National Archives of Cuba in Santiago. Historian Ricardo Repilado supplied details and gave Álvarez a copy of Salome's poems issued in 1880. The author veered into a different direction that year with her first children's work, *The Secret Footprints* (2000), a tender myth about the *ciguapas*, timid creatures who venture out only at night. She and her husband compiled entrées for *The New Family Cookbook: Recipes for Nourishing Yourself and Those You Love* (2000). Another venture, *How Tía Lola Came to Stay* (2001), introduced Álvarez to preteen readers.

Álvarez currently teaches, supports and judges essay and poetry contests, and serves as a resource for the Boston Artists Foundation and an editor of *The Wadsworth Anthology of Poetry* (2006). Early on, she decided to remain childless. After two divorces, in 1989, she married Nebraska-born ophthalmologist Bill Eichner, a father of two girls from a pervious marriage. He farmed their land and orchards at Middlebury in the Champlain Valley of Vermont. She ran Alta Gracia, a 60-acre mountain plantation and literacy center on Pico Duarte outside Jarabacoa, where she grew organic arabica coffee. On visits, she lived among illiterate peasants in the high country without electricity or phones. After a 3-year effort in a local cooperative, she marketed their first harvest as Café Alta Gracia. She used the premises to operate DREAM, a school for adult peasants featured in *A Cafecito Story/El Cuento del Cafecito* (2001), a bilingual story that she coauthored with her husband and artist Belkis Ramirez. Of the fair trade standards of old-style farming, her text lauds "a built-in commitment to equity, dignity, respect, and mutual aid" (Álvarez, *Cafecito*, 2004).

The author's honors include the 2002 Américas Award, listing of her works as *Miami Herald* best book, an American Library Association (ALA) Notable Book, ALA Best Book for Young Adults, *Parent's Guide to Children's Media* outstanding book, Child Magazine Best Children's Book, and New York Library classic for the 21st century, Fray Antón de Montesinos Award, Sor Juana Award, Hispanic Heritage Award, Nebraska Book Award for Fiction, Woman of the Year by *Latina* magazine, Jessica Nobel-Maxwell Poetry Prize for 1995, a Reader's Choice Award, and degrees from Union College in Schenectady and City University of New York. From 1995 to 1996, the New York Public Library honored her skills by incorporating her verse in a literary overview, "The Hand of the Poet: Original Manuscripts by Hundred Masters, from John Donne to Julia Álvarez." Upon receipt of the ALA Pura Belpré Award, the author noted, "We have a tradition in Latin America of *el testimonio*, the testimony, bearing witness. The first step in the awakening of a people's fight for freedom is bearing witness" (Treviño, 2002, 30). Of her own witness, she explained that she offered young readers "the enormous cost of becoming a free person" (Ibid.).

Sources

Álvarez, Julia. *The Cafecito Story*. New York: Chelsea Green, 2004.

———. "Foreword." In Michelle Herrera Mulligan and Robyn Moreno, *Border-Line Personalities: A New Generation of Latinas Dish on Sex, Sass, and Cultural Shifting*. New York: HarperCollins, 2004.

———. "I Came to Help: Resistance Writ Small." In *Women Writing Resistance: Essays on Latin America and the Caribbean*, ed. Jennifer Browdy de Hernandez. Cambridge, MA: South End Press, 2004.

———. *Something to Declare*. Chapel Hill, NC: Algonquin, 1998.

Brown, Deborah, Annie Finch, and Maxine Kumin. *Lofty Dogmas: Poets on Poetics*. Fayetteville, AR: University of Arkansas Press, 2005.

Kafka, Phillipa. *"Saddling la Gringa": Gatekeeping in Literature by Contemporary Latina Writers*. Westport, CT: Greenwood, 2000.

Newton, Pauline T. *Transcultural Women of Late Twentieth-Century U.S. American Literature*. London: Ashgate, 2005.

Shreve, Susan Richards. *Dream Me Home Safely: Writers on Growing Up in America*. Boston: Houghton Mifflin, 2003.

Sirias, Silvio. *Julia Alvarez: A Critical Companion*. Westport, CT: Greenwood, 2001.

Treviño, Rose Zertuche. *The Pura Belpré Awards: Celebrating Latino Authors and Illustrators, 1981–2002*. Chicago: ALA Editions, 2002.

■ Urban Violence
Piri Thomas

A Puerto Rican-Cuban civil rights activist and memoirist, Piri Thomas turned his childhood experiences in Spanish Harlem into a weapon against random city sadism. Born the eldest of seven on September 30, 1928, Juan Pedro Tomás Montañez and his surviving siblings, José, Paulie, Ricardo, Miriam, and James, grew up in a fervid environment. Their black father, Catholic orphan Juan Tomás "Johnny" de la Cruz, a laborer for the Works Project Administration and would-be baseball player from Santiago, Cuba, wed a Seventh-Day Adventist mother, Dolores "Lola" Montañez Tomás, a seamstress in sweatshops in her native Bayamón in Cerro Gordo, Puerto Rico. She called her eldest son by an American name, John Peter Thomas, and nicknamed him "Piri" (spirit). The name helped to salve the inner misgivings derived from being a black Hispanic mestizo, a racial hybridity that thrust him on the borderlands of ethnic identity and predisposed him to a violent lifestyle.

Lola told Piri island folk tales and taught about the powers of darkness and of light. Through Hispanic oral tradition, she groomed him for the ministry. He participated in church activities, including a part as Tiny Tim in a stage version of Charles Dickens's *A Christmas Carol*. From a Pentecostal maternal aunt Angelita, Piri learned to chant verse. Called Pete by his hard-handed father, the author felt the mixed-race tension of not being Caucasian enough and not being black enough to fit in with other children. Among his adversaries were his multiracial Latinos siblings. Thomas suspected that dark skin made him less lovable to his father and a victim of Piri's younger brother José.

Native to New York City's Spanish Harlem, Thomas grew up in an El Barrio tenement as an identifiable and undersized Negrito (short black person), a target of bullies. He spoke Caribbean Spanish from birth and memorized scripture in Spanish. He played ball with street urchins, revered the movies as his day care center, and joined a Jewish Boy Scout troop. With his mother, he shopped at the multiethnic La Marketa; he sat beside his father during political orations by Vito Marcantonio, a freedom fighter for Puerto Ricans. During the Great Depression, Thomas suspended a blanket hammock on the fire escape for quiet reading. While his parents stored spare change in a jar in the closet to keep their kids in school, he struggled to understand classroom English. Because Spanish was forbidden in class, he damned English as the language of colonial oppressors. Although he failed English, one teacher, Mrs. Wright, championed his promise. At the Aguilar branch of the New York Public Library on 110th Street, he discovered the works of Ernest Hemingway and Jack London. He checked out the limit of two books and concealed twice that many in his jacket. By age 13, he was composing his own fiction.

Racism and Survival

After the death of baby Ricardo from a botched tonsillectomy, the family moved from 111th Street to 114th Street. Italian racists made life difficult for Piri, one of few Puerto Ricans on the block. Because Rocky threw asphalt into Piri's eyes, Johnny hailed a cab and sped Piri to Harlem Hospital and promised roller skates if Piri recovered. His parents squabbled after Johnny lost his job. The next day, to acquire money for groceries, Piri interpreted for Lola at the Home Relief Office. In winter 1941, Johnny dug ditches for the Works Project Administration to earn rent for their unheated Harlem apartment. As a result of the Japanese attack on Pearl Harbor, Hawaii, on December 7, Johnny got a job in an airplane factory. The family resettled on 104th Street in Spanish Harlem, where Piri entered Patrick Henry School and co-formed a gang, the TNTs, who battled the Jolly Rogers. Among male prostitutes, Piri drank rum and Five Star Pete, smoked marijuana, and experienced fellatio. To earn cash, he polished shoes on Lexington Avenue and, with buddies Crip and Louie, operated a lemonade stand with Kool-Ade, lemons, sugar, and a pitcher swiped from the A&P.

Thomas knew street violence even in the suburbs. After his father won a *bolia* (numbers) payout, in 1944, the Thomases moved east to Babylon, a coastal town on South Oyster Bay, Long Island. His brothers and sisters could pass, but Piri was the coffee bean in a deluge of milk. At a gym dance, a girl named Marcia caught his attention, who then rejected him as a nigger. At age 16, he dropped out of school. To protect himself from Irish and Italian white supremacists, he controlled his fears and prowled Babylon by night with gangs. From fellow disaffected teens, he acquired belonging, backup, and prestige. He returned to Harlem for fighting, dating, and pot smoking and survived on rooftops, backyards, and stairways. Alienation made him feel orphaned. The family fell apart after Johnny took a mistress named Ruthie while Lola battled terminal illness. Thomas worked in the kitchen at Pilgrim State Hospital in Brentwood and dated Betty, a white girl.

Life on the Dark Side

At age 15, Thomas fought with his father, who tossed him out of the house shortly after Lola's death at age 36. He grieved that she spent her final days in the charity ward at Metropolitan Hospital. Neither Hispanic nor black, Thomas found difficulty landing a sales job and spent 3 months homeless and hungry. He began selling marijuana to pay for his heroin addiction and signed on with the National Maritime Union. Aboard the tanker SS *James Clifford*, he and friend Brew worked in the ship's mess on the cruise to Mobile, New Orleans, and Galveston. Thomas gained insight into the difficulties of blacks living in the racist South after a run-in with an armed bus driver who forced him into the back of the bus with other blacks. On a return voyage to Norfolk, he traveled to the West Indies as a coal fireman. Subsequent journeys took him to England, France, Italy, and South America.

In the Greek merchant marines aboard the Panamanian freighter SS *Doris*, Thomas began keeping a diary during the late 1940s. Gang activities escalated to assault, heroin dealing, and theft. While working days at a restaurant, he sired a son, Pedro Luis Thomas, by Dulcien, Thomas' Puerto Rican mistress. The author mustered out of the army in 1951. He and his gang robbed a nightclub in Greenwich Village. During an exchange of gunfire, he suffered a serious lung wound, collapsed in a taxi, and rode to St. Vincent's Hospital in an ambulance. After recovering from a near-death experience, he transferred to Bellevue prison ward and on to the Tombs on 125 White Street, where he occupied a cell on murderers' row.

From Cell to God

Following 4 tense months of litigation over his crimes of first degree assault for shooting an undercover police officer and of attempted armed robbery, Thomas began a sentence of 5 to 15 years at hard labor as inmate #18193 in Sing Sing Prison in Ossining, New York. After gaining a transfer to Great Meadows State Prison in Washington County, New York, he languished apart from Jenny, his first love, and rejected courtship by prison homosexuals. His family withheld visits for 3 years. He chose solitude over inmate camaraderie and, in C513, a 6-by-8-by-9 prison cell, plunged into world religions under mentorship of Claude, the prison chaplain, whom Thomas called the White Haired Saint. Claude prevented guards from destroying Thomas' lengthy prison manuscript. In the years to come, the author came to value his time in prison as a painful blessing.

Thomas joined the black Muslims, learned to love his imperfect self, and adopted the Islamic name Hussein Afmit ben Hassen. While working in the jobbing shop and learning brick masonry, he studied to earn a G.E.D. During solitary time, he read Edgar Allan Poe's verse and gothic stories, the adventure tales of Robert Louis Stevenson, Westerns by Zane Gray, John Oliver Killens' *Youngblood*, John Howard Griffin's *Black Like Me*, the Bible and the Koran, and the philosophy of Karl Marx and Friedrich Nietzsche. For spiritual nourishment, he fantasized about Lola's love and encouragement for her Negrito. At the end of 4 years behind bars, in 1955, he applied for clemency but was rejected.

Success at Last

Upon his parole on November 28, 1957, after 6 years in jail, Thomas was home for Christmas. He found part-time employment at Macy's department store and as a handyman and janitor at a dress and shirt company in New York's garment district. He joined the Harlem Writers' Guild and, at 116th Street and Madison Avenue, continued his loner lifestyle. Like the unnamed protagonist of Ralph Ellison's *Invisible Man*, Thomas wrote in the basement of his aunt Angelita's church, Iglesia Rehoboth Pentecostal on 118th Street, where he cleansed himself of alcohol and drugs. In 1959, he married Daniela "Nelin" Calo, mother of San-Dee and Ricardo Thomas. In this domesticated phase, he wrote "Home Sweet Harlem," the nucleus of his memoir, *Down These Mean Streets*, a title suggested by mystery-detective author Raymond Chandler. After his children wrinkled his manuscript, it was accidentally burned in an incinerator at his Brooklyn flat. Thomas earned a grant from the Rabinowitz Foundation and completed a second version of his life story virtually from memory. He dedicated the work to Daniela and to the world's children.

Thomas' memoir made him the first U.S. Puerto Rican writer to gain renown. The text set the tone and direction for a generation of cathartic Puerto Rican slum and prison literature. *The New York Times* listed the book as one of the ten best written about New York City. Critic Daniel Stern lauded the autobiography for piercing to the heart of a submerged ethnic population. Channeling rage into narrative sapped his strength. For a subsequent title, *A Matter of Dignity*, he opted for a gentler, more humorous tone. In 1968, photographer and director Gordon Parks completed *The World of Piri Thomas*, a film for National Educational Television. Thomas co-authored *Puerto Rico: A Profile* (1970) and produced commentary on Harlem gang structure in *Savior, Savior, Hold My Hand* (1972) and prison terrors and indignities in *Seven Long Times* (1974) and *Stories from El Barrio* (1974). His works fit a number of college and university book lists, particularly the psychology of imprisonment, the social underpinnings of bigotry, street literature, and urban youth alienation.

In 1976, Thomas' hard-hitting autobiography *Down These Mean Streets* incurred threat of censorship during a 7-year court battle at the Island Trees Union Free School

District in Levittown, Long Island. Additional objections to street language arose in Salinas, California; Teaneck, New Jersey; Darien, Connecticut; and nearer home in Queens, New York. Undeterred, he continued giving recitations at patriotic gatherings and published "The Right to Write and to Read" (1976) for the *New York Times* and "Puerto Rico: 500 Years of Oppression" (1997) in *In Motion Magazine*. In 2003, PBS aired the program "Every Child Is Born a Poet: The Life and Work of Piri Thomas."

Counseling the Down and Out

On an initial visit to Puerto Rico at age 32, Thomas discovered a pro-Hispanic mind-set that devalued indigenous Taino and Afro-Caribbean islanders. He enrolled in advanced psychology at the University of Puerto Rico. He tried to identify with islanders but, because of his poor Spanish, he felt like an outsider. Because of his former addiction to heroin, he worked for Youth Development Incorporated at the Hospital of Psychiatry in Río Piedras as a physician's assistant. He counseled drug addicts and hosted a Sunday radio talk show, *The Voice of a New Race*. With the aid of New York Governor Nelson A. Rockefeller and U.S. Senators Jacob K. Javits and Robert F. Kennedy, Thomas acquired amnesty and had his prison record expunged. The act of clemency restored the author to full citizenship.

In 1983, Thomas moved his second wife, attorney-activist Betty Gross Thomas, a specialist in international law, and their children to San Francisco. In 1985, the couple traveled Cuba and Nicaragua. A year later, after 7 years of marriage, Betty died of cancer. As a member of the Nuyorican (New Yorker of Puerto Rican descent) Movement, Piri worked in drama, film, and street music: *Sounds of the Streets* (1994), *No Mo' Barrio Blues* (1996), and *Every Child Is Born a Poet: The Life and Work of Piri Thomas* (2004). His oral verse performances crossed the boundaries of gospel, Latino and Caribbean music, rhythm and blues, and salsa. In the thirtieth anniversary edition of *Down These Mean Streets*, in January 1997, Thomas relived the rejection and rage that undergirded the original text. In a new era of urban violence, he regretted the crack wars, drive-by shootings, homelessness, injustice, racism, and violence that afflict the poor. During hospitalization for herniated disks in his spine, he required surgery for kidney cancer.

At home in El Cerrito, California, with current wife Jennifer Suzanne Dod Thomas, the author continues lecturing at-risk youth, gang members, and hard-core prisoners. He publishes articles on travels in Cuba, Mexico, Nicaragua, Puerto Rico, and Germany and writes essays about endangered urban youth. Made famous globally for humanism, Thomas battles with Puerto Ricans for the recovery of the island of Vieques from the U.S. military. His lectures have taken him to Brown, Columbia, Cornell, Erlangen-Nuremberg, Fordham, Howard, Rutgers, and Yale Universities to remind listeners of the lasting hurt caused by inhumanity toward nonwhite children. Against would-be book banners, he crusades for uplifting literature that combats urban violence.

Sources

Coeyman, Marjorie. "The Shifting 'Canon' of Multicultural Lit." *Christian Science Monitor*, June 18, 2002, 14.

Gonzalez, David. "After Loneliness of Prison, Poet of the Streets Finds an Embracing Audience." *New York Times*, June 22, 1996.

Greenberg, Dorothee von Huene. "Piri Thomas: An Interview." *MELUS* 26 (30) (Fall 2001): 71–99.

McGill, Lisa D. "A Conversation with Piri Thomas." *Bilingual Review* 25 (2) (May–August 2000): 179–184.

Pearl, Nancy. "Companion Reads for Your Next Book Club." *Library Journal* 128(1) (January 1, 2003): 192.

Platt, Anthony M. "The Abyss." *Los Angeles Times*, July 4, 1999, 6.

Sanchez, Marta E. "La Malinche at the Intersection: Race and Gender in *Down These Mean Streets*." *PMLA* 113 (1) (January 1998): 117–128.

Stavans, Ilan. "Race and Mercy: A Conversation with Piri Thomas." *Massachusetts Review* 37 (3) (Autumn 1996): 344–354.

Thomas, Piri. "The Right to Write and to Read." *New York Times*, September 14, 1976.

■ Usurpation
Leslie Marmon Silko

Mixed-race mythmaker and radical fiction writer Leslie Marmon Silko contributes a dual perspective to the Native American Renaissance, a rebirth of native culture. Born of German, Hispanic, Laguna, and Pueblo forebears on March 5, 1948, she is a native of the Pueblo Indian Reservation in Albuquerque, New Mexico. The family residence in the old Santa Fe depot, the ancestral home of the Marmons for four generations, reflected the Americanization of first peoples through intermarriage. After the Civil War, Silko's great grandfather, trader Robert Marmon, surveyed pueblo boundaries for the U.S. government. His brother, Walter Gunn Marmon, set up a government school in 1871 at Acoma and married Mary Sarracino, the daughter of a shaman-chief. The growth of Marmons replaced tribal hierarchy with a blended culture. After World War I, the Laguna need for continuity alienated mixed-race members as interlopers.

Central to Silko's memories of gendering were the self-sufficient women who repaired washing machines and plastered walls alongside males. Her family lived apart from Laguna society near the San José River bordering the enclave, where she attended an Indian school. From a Norwegian teacher, at age 10, Silko learned to love Norse deity stories. From her parents, Virginia Marmon and photographer and tribal council treasurer Lee Howard Marmon, she and her younger sisters, Gigi and Wendy, acquired the egalitarian Laguna tradition, through which each reservation child received nurturing and training from each adult. By age 7, she rode horseback over the mesas and hunted deer with her father. From observations of nature, she acquired a humility and reverence for Earth powers.

Key to Silko's outlook was the Laguna belief that each human life has value, a pre-Christian tenet stretching over some 18,000 years of Pueblo Indian history. Her father, who ran the post office and Laguna Trading Post with the help of his father, Henry C. "Hank" Marmon, instilled awe for black and white photos of noble tribe members, whom Lee pictured as dignified preservers of the native past. His most famous portrait, "White Man's Moccasins," prefigures Silko's perspective on the merger of cultures with a glimpse of a Laguna elder dressed in native garments and high-top sneakers. The image captures in a single pose the author's dedication to native pride in nationhood and to the sovereignty of indigenous people.

Female Talk-Story

From Keres speakers—Great grandmother Marie Anaya Marmon, called Grandma A'mooh; Grandma Lillie Stagner Marmon, a Model A Ford mechanic; Great-aunt Alice Charity Marmon Eckerman; and Great-aunt Susan "Susie" Reyes, a teacher and native historian—Silko gained reverence for strong matriarchy, which salves the native hurt and grief from being a suppressed and landless people. Integral to home training were facets of spontaneous oral tradition—beast fable, chants, anecdotal humor, songs, talk-story, and trickster lore. Through repetition, nuance, and rebuttal, the participatory style of storytelling accorded worth to each comment and point of view. Silko described the narrative way of communication as "a whole way of seeing yourself, the people around you, your life, the place of your life in the bigger context, not just in terms of nature and location, but in terms of what has gone on before" (Graulich, 2003, 49–50). She enjoyed the 4-day winter solstice, when tellers reiterated stories about the origination of the Pueblo and their migration from their birth home. Family storytellers taught values through the goddess lore of benevolent Corn Woman, of life-restoring Thought Woman, and of the creator, Spider Woman. In Silko's recollection, all historical, scientific, technological, and theological information took the form of stories, which tapped the organic yearning of humankind to merge with earth, water, sky, and living things.

Silko's milieu broadened in her early teens, when she attended a Catholic high school 50 miles from the reservation. She earned a B.A. in English from the University of Mexico and studied native American law before choosing teaching as her life's work. In her junior year, she identified transcendental philosopher Margaret Fuller and feminist diarist Alice James as heroes. Silko's venture into the white world took on a messianic significance. Reflecting on Indian loss and anger over half a millennium of white insurgency, she envisioned herself as an intermediary for her people. After a brief marriage to Richard C. Chapman and the birth of son Robert William, she taught English and creative writing at Navajo Community College in Tsaile, Arizona. Simultaneous with her classroom work, she published stories and verse in anthologies and textbooks, including *The Norton Anthology of Literature by Women*. Her first success, "Tony's Story" (1969), appeared in *Thunderbird*, followed by "The Man to Send Rain Clouds" (1969) in the *New Mexico Quarterly* and "Lullaby" (1971) in the *Chicago Review*. The National Endowment for the Arts paid for her 2-year sabbatical in Bethel near Ketchikan, Alaska. Her first major anthology, *Laguna Woman* (1974), won a *Chicago Review* award. The same year, she issued *Laguna Women: Poems*.

A Mission to Complete

Mentored by poet James Wright, at age 29, Silko began fulfilling her mission with her first novel, *Ceremony* (1977), which she wrote while teaching in Alaska on a Rosewater Foundation grant and boarding among the Inuit of Ketchikan Creek. In the style of Arthurian Grail lore, the post–World War II study of Tayo, a veteran of the Pacific theater, describes redemption of a wounded soul from alcohol and rootlessness through myth, nature, and ritual. Led by the shaman Betonie, revived and adapted ceremonies reflect new threats and accommodate the needs and sufferings of men like Tayo, who incur flashbacks from war and tribal alienation. To account for deception in human life, Silko incorporated the Ck'o'yo con artist and gambler Pa'caya'nyi, who lures native people from their devotion to the corn mother. Loss of ties to the land causes an imbalance that leads to drought and famine. Critical evaluations were so positive that her novel quickly rose to classic status and found favor with high school, college, and university teachers of American literature, anthropology, religion, and women's studies. For the folkloric impact of *Ceremony*, critic Alan Velie named the author a native literary master in company with Navarre Scott Momaday, Gerald Vizenor, and James Welch.

Silko's early notoriety preceded an outpouring of brilliance. For the short film *Running on the Edge of the Rainbow* (1978), she played a native storykeeper, a part reflecting her family's respect for wisewomen. Her essay "An Old Fashioned Indian Attack in Two Parts," anthologized in *The Remembered Earth* (1978), vilified native fiction that profits from a retelling of native legend. She ventured into mythography with *Storyteller* (1980), which blends narrative with genealogy, melody, oral tales, and personal essay. The collection earned the John and Catherine MacArthur Foundation Prize Fellowship of $176,000, the Native Writers Circle of the Americas lifetime achievement award, and her selection as a Living Cultural Treasure by the New Mexico Humanities Council. A classic feminist sexual adventure, "Yellow Woman," featured a bold female uncowed by the predations of a seducer, Buffalo Man. Within the year, she authored *Western Stories* and the screenplay *Arrowboy and the Witches*.

Writing as Teaching

In 1981, the author was divorced from her second husband, attorney John Silko, father of her second son, Cazimir. Her career took on an urgency in the publication of *After a Summer Rain in the Upper Sonoran* (1984), letters in *The Delicacy and Strength of Lace* (1986), and two short works, "Landscape, History, and the Pueblo Imagination" (1986) in *Antaeus* and "The Fourth World" (1989) in *Artforum*. Of the impact of her artistry on the scholarly community, she chortled, "I don't want to write something that the MLA [Modern Language Association] will want. I want something that will horrify the people at the MLA" (Graulich, 2003, 47–48). In "Here's an Odd Artifact for the Fairy-Tale Shelf" (1986), a book review of Anishinabe author Louise Erdrich's *The Beet Queen*, Silko came down on the side of her Laguna-Pueblo ancestry. She lambasted Erdrich for self-indulgence at the expense of native American themes and motifs.

In 1986, during an intense period of composition, Silko allowed an aboriginal spirit to guide her work. The impetus was the election of a racist felon, Evan Mecham, to state governor. Silko halted her writing to spray graffiti on the wall of her office in downtown Tucson. A vision of a snake compelled her to work 6 months on the painting of a giant blue snake on the side of the rented building. To express menace, she drew skulls in the serpent's stomach. She completed the visual warning with a message in Spanish accusing a rich man of curtailing the people's freedom. The mural drew the attention of homeless women and children living in cars, the victims of 1980s conservative politics, until a new landlord whitewashed the work 6 years later. Silko exulted in the peeling whitewash, which failed to conceal the power of her reptilian symbol.

Fiction and Prophecy

In the compilation of Indian conflicts in a Eurocentric world, Silko produced a contemporary anticapitalist novel, *Almanac of the Dead* (1991), which bears the influence of her reading of 18 volumes compiled by Viennese neurologist Sigmund Freud. The urgent nonlinear collation lauds a borderless world—a decentralization effected via community action. Through a publication she jokingly termed cultural terrorism, she attempted to alleviate native American ignorance of their own history, particularly the imprisonment of the poor who take refuge in drugs. To expose the frailties of the Christian-capitalist society, she incorporated a Marxist perspective on worker exploitation and predicted a revolt of the powerless. For spirituality, she chose myth and epic genres akin to the Mayan scripture in the *Popol Vuh* to expose the soul killing caused by illegal drugs and global aggression. A complex and troubling diatribe, *Almanac* accounts for the residue of anger in native Americans some 5 centuries after the establishment of an illegitimate government on stolen land. To her delight, the Maya Zapatistas, invigorated by *Almanac*, launched a rebellion in Chiapas on January 1, 1994. She admired the spirit of aboriginal people still resisting usurpation.

Silko established herself as a major feminist author with the creation of Kochinnenako, a liberated heroine of *Yellow Woman* (1993), and as a native American maven by authoring *Sacred Water: Narratives and Pictures* (1993) and *Rain* (1996). She continued publishing short reflections on reservation upbringing with "A Laguna Portfolio" (1993) in *Studies in American Indian Literature*, "An Essay on Rocks" (1995) in *Aperture*, and "Interior and Exterior Landscapes: The Pueblo Migration Stories" (1995). Her essay collection, *Yellow Woman and a Beauty of the Spirit: Essays on Native American Life Today* (1996), touches on the oral themes of Aztec, Inca, Maya, Mixtec, and Pueblo, particularly ecology and a reverence for the inexorable powers of nature. She reprised her signature nature lore in *Love Poem and Slim Man Canyon* (1999) and *Gardens in the Dunes* (1999). The latter, based on stories her grandpa Hank related, is a historical novel replete with female bondage, male-on-female violence, and the healing release of gardening for Sister Salt and Indigo, remnants of the languishing Sand Lizard tribe. During visits to European capitals, Silko admired the resilience of paganism and remarked, "As hard as Christianity tried to wipe it out, and tried to break that connection between the Europeans and the earth, and the plants and the animals—even though they've been broken from it longer than the indigenous people of the Americas or Africa—that connection won't break completely" (Arnold, 1998, 6). Because of growing regard for Silko's environmental concerns, in March 2005, she received the annual American Indian Festival of Words Author Award.

Silko settled on a ranch in the Sonora Desert outside Tucson, where she takes photos, writes, and teaches English at the University of Arizona. During the heyday of Indian protest, she chose not to support the American Indian Movement, pan-tribal protest of reservation and urban Indian squalor and of widespread police brutality against minorities. Because of her belief in the power of the arts, she supports Flood Plain Press, a source of handmade books run by her son Robert on North Stone Avenue. For her intuitive revelations of peasant survivalism, she is numbered among tribal internationalists, individual artists who ally with global defenders. She promotes aboriginal traditions to defeat injustice and oppression by validating sacred life phenomena and rhythms like the Mayan almanac that realign and heal fragmented regional cultures. She collaborated with her father and with poets Joy Harjo and Simon Ortiz for the book *The Pueblo Imagination* (2004), a collection of photographic images similar in thrust to her storytelling about deinstitutionalized experience. Of native story cycles, she maintains with a fierce passion, "These things will only die if we neglect to tell the stories. So I am still telling the stories" (Silko, 2000, 31).

Sources

Allen, Paula Gunn. "Special Problems in Teaching Leslie Marmon Silko's Ceremony." *American Indian Quarterly* (Fall 1990): 379–86.

Arnold, Ellen. "Listening to the Spirits: An Interview with Leslie Marmon Silko." *Studies in American Indian Literature* 10 (3) (Fall 1998): 1–33.

Barnett, Louise, and James Thorson, eds. *Leslie Marmon Silko: A Collection of Critical Essays.* Albuquerque, NM: University of New Mexico Press, 1999.

Bellinelli, Matteo. *Leslie Marmon Silko.* Princeton, NJ: Films for the Humanities, 1995. Video.

Coltelli, Laura. *Winged Words: American Indian Writers Speak.* Lincoln, NE: University of Nebraska Press, 1990.

Donovan, Kathleen M. *Feminist Readings of Native American Literature: Coming to Voice.* Tucson, AZ: University of Arizona Press, 1998.

Goldstein, Coleman. "Silko's Ceremony." *Explicator* 61 (4) (Summer 2003): 245–248.

Graulich, Melody, ed. *Yellow Woman.* New Brunswick, NJ: Rutgers University Press, 2003.

Pratt, Mary Louise. "Arts of the Contact Zone." In *Ways of Reading: An Anthology for Writers,* ed. by David Bartholomae and Anthony Petrosky. Boston: St. Martin's Press, 1993.

Romero, Channette. "Envisioning a 'Network of Tribal Coalitions': Leslie Marmon Silko's Almanac of the Dead." *American Indian Quarterly* 26 (4) (Fall 2002): 623–640.

Silko, Leslie Marmon. *Leslie Silko.* Trumansburg, NY: Crossing Press, 1974.

———. "An Old-Time Indian Attack Conducted in Two Parts." In *The Remembered Earth,* ed. by Geary Hobson. Albuquerque, NM: University of New Mexico Press, 1979.

Silko, Leslie Marmon, and Ellen L. Arnold. *Conversations with Leslie Marmon Silko.* Jackson, MS: University Press of Mississippi, 2000.

Velie, Alan R. *Four American Literary Masters.* Norman, OK: University of Oklahoma Press, 1982.

Velikova, Roumiana. "Leslie Marmon Silko: Reading, Writing, and Storytelling." *MELUS* 27 (3) (Fall 2002): 57–75.

Wilson, Norma C. "Ceremony: From Alienation to Reciprocity." In *Teaching American Ethnic Literatures,* ed. by John R. Maitano and David R. Peck, 69–82. Albuquerque, NM: University of New Mexico Press, 1996.

Wartime Displacement
Yoko Kawashima Watkins

One of a generation of children to survive World War II, peace activist Yoko Kawashima Watkins published her memories of refugee survival. A native of Aomori in northern Honshu, Japan, and third in a family of three, she was born in 1933 and grew up in Harbin, Manchuria, in northeastern China. For 12 years, her intellectual father, Yoshio Kawashima, served in the Japanese diplomatic corps as head of the colonial ruling class coordinating growth of the Manchurian railway. After his reassignment to Manchuria, his family settled at Nanam in northeastern Korea, some 50 miles south of the Tumen River and the border separating Siberia from Manchuria. Visits to Yoshio's wife and children required a 100-mile train ride. To create a feel of home, he secured slips of yellow bamboo from Aomori.

The author was reared bilingual in Japanese and Korean and came to think of Korea as home. At dinner, her parents drew out their children with folktales and with compliments and questions about their schooling. In the bamboo grove, she walked with her father holding hands and discussing the strength of the imagination. She studied tea service, flower arranging, verse writing, and calligraphy by printing of 103 Japanese characters. At a temple, in 1938, she and her siblings, Ko and Hideyo, learned to clean and weed, to sit still, and to serve gracefully. Five years later, at age 18, Hideyo deliberately failed a military exam to avoid service in the Yokaren, the student force of the Japanese Imperial Army, and began packing machine guns in crates at a munitions plant 20 miles away. His absence left the women alone and unguarded.

At school, Yoko developed hostility toward her teacher for refuting an original beast fable depicting talking birds, which Yoko based on the pair of canaries that Yoshio gave her. Daydreamy and disobedient, she faced a failing report card that she feared showing her mother. Her father advised an impersonal approach of concentrating on the blackboard rather than the teacher's animosity. He soothed, "Little One, go at your own pace. Eventually you will succeed" (Hackett, 2002, 118). To end the standoff over birds, he mailed her first story, "Canary Birds," to a newspaper for publication. Her success enabled her to return to school to face friends and teachers.

Escaping the War

In July 1945, within weeks of the atomic bombing of Hiroshima and Nagasaki and of the Japanese surrender to the United States, Korean and Soviet Communists invaded Nanam. They provoked a war with Japan that cost the lives of both the sets of Yoko's grandparents. To promote patriotism, school children wore national Korean dress. Yoko aided the war effort by collecting empty cans and culling dented bullets from boxes of usable ammunition. At a Red Cross hospital, she dressed in traditional kimono and obi and entertained wounded soldiers with a refined odori dance. At home, Yoshio and Hideyo dug a backyard bomb shelter. After 2 weeks of nightly air raid alerts, the loving father and daughter relationship ended abruptly on the night of July 29, when Yoshio parted from his family. A recovering veteran warned Yoko's mother of a Russian landing. A military marauder rifled the house and kicked Yoko into unconsciousness for biting his hand. The veteran arranged for Yoko's mother to board a hospital evacuation train with Yoko and her 16-year-old sister, Ko, to safer territory in the south. Notes for Yoshio and Hideyo hidden under a rice bowl on the sewing machine explained the escape, a 2-day ride through Wonsan to Seoul that Yoko assumed was only a temporary displacement.

The family squeezed in among wounded soldiers and civilian patients. At 3:00 A.M. some 45 miles from Seoul, when bombers struck the train's two engines, Yoko, Ko, and their mother began a night walk through rough country. The mother encouraged the girls to endure whatever befell them. Three soldiers in Korean Communist uniforms threatened rape; a bomb blast killed them. Shrapnel burned the right side of Yoko's chest and temporarily deafened her. To ward off more opportunists, her mother armed herself with a ceremonial sword, shaved their heads, and dressed them in the men's uniforms. Ko fed them on moldy bread and orange and apple peelings retrieved from garbage. At a Red Cross tent hospital in Seoul, Yoko required 2 weeks of treatment for severe wound infection before the family could board a flatcar to Pusan on Korea's southern tip. By freighter, the trio and other war escapees made the 3-day crossing to Fukuoka, Japan. From a refugee center, they took a train to Kyoto, the only town that American bombers had left unscathed.

Life without Parents

At her mother's insistence, Yoko entered the Sagano Girls' School, where more privileged female students ridiculed her scraggly hair and ragged clothes and jeered at her work collecting trash. After her mother suddenly expired from sorrow and loss at the Kyoto train station, Yoko and Ko found shelter in a tiny room at the warehouse of a geta (shoe) factory. They made an altar to house their mother's cremated remains but concealed from authorities that they lived without parental supervision. The government provided futons and comforters for war survivors. While Ko attended Seian University, she scrounged fish and rice from hotel trashcans, polished shoes, and sewed children's clothes and beanbags to sell outside a Buddhist temple. Under privation, Yoko, the family's "Little One," matured and gave up pettish complaints of hunger, cold and ruined shoes. She learned to break ice at a stream, beat clothing clean over a rock with a bamboo stick, and heat water over a fire at their makeshift hibachi (grill). For a New Year's celebration, she boiled rice and heated water for green tea in an aluminum mess kit, their main cook pot. From the lining of their mother's wrapper, she and Ko recovered $300 in cash and reserved it for emergencies.

A period of inflation increased financial hardships. At school, Mr. Naido, the custodian, befriended Yoko and collected scissors, brushes, paper, glue, a compass, and other classroom gear to save her expenses. She reciprocated by scrounging cans and bottles for him to sell. In mid-March 1946, the author rescued herself and her sister from cold and malnutrition by writing "Understanding," which won 10,000 yen—about $300—in an essay contest at the *Asahi* morning newspaper. The prize included a formal dinner of more food than Yoko had seen in months. The cash kept them solvent for several months; the newspaper notoriety reunited them with Corporal Matsumura, a former soldier whom Yoko had entertained the previous year at the military hospital in Nanam. With his gift packages and paid employment for Ko at his silk factory, the girls' lives improved. Matsumura also issued radio requests for information about the girls' brother and father. In 1947, Hideyo returned from Korea, and, in fall 1951, their father repatriated to Japan from a Siberian prison camp. Ko worked in a department store sewing kimonos while Hideyo found odd jobs at the Kyoto city hall.

Postwar Bloom

Her education completed, Yoko entered an experimental English language school at Kyoto University. While employed as a typist and translator at Misawa, a U.S. Air Force base in Aomori, Japan, at age 20, she wed Donald Watkins, an American pilot and father of their four children and two Taiwanese adoptees. In 1955, the family moved to Minnesota and lived in Wisconsin and Oregon before establishing a home on Cape Cod in Brewster, Massachusetts. In 1976, Watkins again reunited with Hideyo, whom she had not seen since 1956. She questioned him about his route out of Korea during the war and about the Korean family who rescued him. To enlighten a privileged 15-year-old American girl who complained without reason, the author began reliving the pain of loss and deprivation. The death of Hideyo, who taught in Kyoto, thrust the author into a depression she called "the most darkest [sic], darkest pit" (Hackett, 2002, 123). She lacked the money for psychological counseling and chose for catharsis writing a biography of her brother, which she published in Japan. Another bout of despair over war in Bosnia jolted her thoughts to the war 51 years before and her own sufferings as a refugee. Anger inspired her to write a ten-page story, "Cherry Tree Sons," the source of a picture book. She explained her obsessions with the past: "The war happening. . . . You just cannot forget it. It is there all the time" (Ibid., 126).

While Watkins continued caring for her invalid sister, Ko, at the peak of the Asian-American literary Renaissance, she launched a career as a children's author. She presented herself as a mother addressing children to balance their lives and attitudes toward a troubled time in world history. In interviews, she described the difficulties of an English-as-a-second-language writer as frustrating, particularly translation of idiomatic Japanese expressions. At the height of torment, she halted composition long enough to vacuum the house. To release negative energy, she performed the traditional tea ceremony, a source of serenity. She explained, "If you are shaking, or if you are frustrated, or if your mind is a whirlwind, then you spill the waters, you spill the tea powder" (Ibid., 113).

Collecting Fragments of the Past

She initiated a 10-year writing project compiling childhood traumas in *So Far from the Bamboo Grove* (1986), a wartime memoir that took over a decade to complete. To spare Hideyo's saviors, she made up an escape route for him and fictionalized the family's location. For a test of the unedited manuscript, she chose a stranger to critique it and then continued reading and rewriting until the finished text satisfied her. The work struck a chord of family and racial pride, historical information, peace, and tolerance. In 2001, she issued an audiocassette that preserved her childhood perspective, a literary device similar to that of Laura Ingalls Wilder in the *Little House* series. A subsequent work compiled the Ainu and Japanese fables and folktales "The Fox Wife, "The Grandmother Who Became an Island," "Monkey and Crab," and "Why Is Seawater Salty?" in *Tales from the Bamboo Grove* (1992), an anthology of stories her parents chose for character building. Watkins' narratives found favor with teachers, librarians, homeschoolers, parents, feminists, and pacifists for its view of immigrant memories of survivalism in a period of unstable loyalties.

For the historical novel *My Brother, My Sister, and I* (1994), Watkins returned to memories of her early teens and living with her 21-year-old brother Hideyo and 17-year-old sister Ko. The reflection on Japanese loss of World War II pictured Yoko and her brother and sister subsisting on daikons and tangerine peel tea. During a warehouse fire that concealed the murdered remains of the Masudas, their landlord and his wife, Ko fell while attempting to salvage her mother's ashes. The injury to Ko's knee left her permanently disabled. Yoko depicted nine months of barely getting by. Brother and sister lived at Ko's hospital room while Hideyo paid for medical care by working two jobs. The author turned the story into a murder mystery and sleuthing adventure and concluded with the parentless Kawashima children living near starvation at a shack under a bridge. The return of Yoshio Kawashima ended the need to sell Ko's clothing to survive.

Ambassador of Peace

To introduce youngsters to the terrors of war, Watkins began lecturing in classrooms and library reading clubs with what she termed a cry from the heart. She explained, "I stress unto them that the heart comes first, love comes first, understanding comes first before anything else" (McLendon, 2007). Her appearances helped stanch Korean censorship of her regional ethnic fiction, which Koreans vilified as pro-Japanese and historically inaccurate for omitting Japan's wartime atrocities to colonials. Koreans accused the translator and publisher of *So Far from the Bamboo Grove* of disloyalty; Korean bookshops banned the book that locals belittled as "Yoko's Story" for its graphic images of soldiers raping girls (Hamamoto, 2007).

Critics claimed that Watkins wrote a sanitized version of World War II and of the career of Yoko's father, whom they labeled a war criminal for serving Unit 731, a Japanese biological warfare lab that experimented on living Koreans. She researched spotty documents to clear up a mix-up in identities. According to postwar records, a Japanese officer, Major General Kiyoshi Kawashima, faced a war tribunal at Khabarovsk, Russia, in December 1949 and began serving from 2 to 25 years in Siberia. After his release in 1956, he repatriated to Japan. The details and dates clash with Yoshio Kawashima's governmental job and his reunion with his children in 1951.

Watkins' honors include a Best Book for Young Adults award from the American Library Association, Boston Public Library Literary Lights for Children citation, Judy Lopez Memorial Award for the best American book for 9- through 12-year-olds from the Women's National Book Association, and best book honors from *Publishers Weekly*, *New York Times*, and *Parenting* magazine. *The Bulletin of the Center for Children's Books* proclaimed the author's memoirs "one of the most forceful forms of history" (Watkins, 1994, cover). Nonetheless, to stem complaints from Korean-Americans, public school librarians in Hawaii, Massachusetts, and Rhode Island pulled copies of *So Far from the Bamboo Grove* from library shelves. After apologizing at a press conference in Boston for creating controversy, on February 16, 2007, Watkins received the backing of John D'Auria, principal of Wellesley Middle School in Sherborn, Massachusetts. Having heard her antiwar lectures, he asserted, "There's no author that has . . . made more of a positive change in children than this woman" (Kocian, 2007). In May 2007, she visited Korea to promote peaceful coexistence between Asian nations.

Sources

Hackett, Jill. *I Gotta Crow: Women, Voice, and Writing.* New York: Watson-Guptill, 2002.

Hamamoto, Ben. "Book by Japanese American Author at Center of Controversy." *Nichi Bei Times,* February 22, 2007.

Kocian, Lisa. "Author Defends Memoir on Korea, Apologizes for Furor." *Boston Globe,* February 16, 2007.

McLendon, Gary. "Memoir Author Teachers City Students Lesson of Peace." *Democrat and Chronicle* (Rochester, NY), October 4, 2007.

Olson, Renee, and Randy Meyer. "Awards." *School Library Journal* 41 (7) (July 1995): 14–15.

Watkins, Yoko Kawashima. *My Brother, My Sister, and I.* New York: Simon & Schuster, 1994.

———. *So Far from the Bamboo Grove.* Bel Air, CA: Lothrop, Lee & Shepherd, 1986.

■ Whistle-blowing
Paula Coughlin

Navy Lieutenant Paula Anne Coughlin jeopardized a flying career to report gross public misogyny and nonconsensual fondling by male naval officers. Born to aviator Paul Gerard Coughlin and executive secretary Rena Thyne Coughlin in Virginia Beach, Virginia, in 1961, she grew to a petite 5 feet 4 inches and 125 pounds and served the area as its first female lifeguard. After ROTC training at Old Dominion University, in 1986, she mastered the piloting of Ch-53E helicopters, a ferrier of artillery, vehicles, and combat troops. As a career soldier, she resolved to compete with men by being the best officer she was capable of. She joined the female lobby to allow women to fly combat missions. By 1991, at the time of Iraq's invasion of Kuwait and the launching of Operation Desert Storm, she advanced to the post of flag aide as executive assistant to Rear Admiral John W. "Jack" Snyder, commander at Patuxent River Naval Air Test Center on Maryland's Chesapeake Bay.

One of the official duties took Coughlin to the Las Vegas Hilton on September 6–8, 1991, when 4,000 pilots gathered for the annual Tailhook Association convention. The notorious drunken bash had, for 18 years, reunited active, reserve, and retired officers from the ranks of Marine and naval aviators. Squadrons booked hospitality suites offering booze, leg-shaving booths, pornographic films and slides, and nude exotic dancers. Partying reached such extremes that managers at earlier venues in Mexico refused to book the convention. The worst, the nineteenth annual gathering, cost the association $23,000 in damage to the hotel and no end of trouble from felonious assault on women. Tailhook President Captain Frederick Ludwig summarized the debauchery as the "Mother of All Hooks" (McMichael, 1997, 49).

Coughlin at Tailhook '91

The second night of carousing began with a formal dinner at the Hilton. Coughlin retired to the Paddlewheel Hotel & Casino to change from her dress whites into a black tank top, denim skirt, and black cowboy boots. Accompanied by Lieutenant Scott Wilson, she returned up the Las Vegas strip to the Hilton in search of a friend, Lieutenant Michael "Trusty" Steed. Around 11:30 P.M., she entered alone a third floor corridor from the pool area amid raucous partying noises from both sides of the hall. A master of ceremonies directed women into harm's way and carried some victims, including Julia Rodgers, who tried to escape. At Coughlin's approach, the sweaty pack exulted "admiral's aide" and charged at her. She later exploded, "It was an outrage—that's what it comes down to—it was a crime" (Turner, 2000, 510).

Although Coughlin warned "woman on deck," eight of some hundred fellow officers from the Marines and navy formed a double line and intentionally jostled and grabbed her buttocks. Caroming from one groper to another, she experienced pinching, shoving, and yanks on her clothing while she forced a way out of the gauntlet. A Marine instructor pilot in an orange T-shirt, whom she later identified from a composite drawing as Captain Gregory J. Bonam, hoisted her from the floor. Amid shrieks of "bitch" and "whore," one man reached down her tank top and bra to grasp her breasts. Coughlin dropped out of reach, seized the man's wrists, and bit his left forearm and the webbing between his right thumb and index finger. In the tussle, another assaulter reached up her skirt to seize the crotch of her underwear. She began to fear gang rape. The drunken entourage laughed at her cries for help.

While another female struggled with the same molesters, Coughlin sought shelter in VA-128, an administrative suite. In shock, she contemplated a situation that escalated to assaults on 83 women, including six officers' wives. The next night, Admiral Snyder yelled at her during her telephoned recounting of the hotel corridor mauling and suggested she alter her account. Trauma forced her into bouts of weeping and serial food binges. In a letter dated September 29, she informed Vice Admiral Richard M. Dunleavy of the Tailhook debauchery. In June 1992, she wearied of the military's dawdling and broke her story to Gregory L. Vistica, a reporter for the *San Diego Union-Tribune*. Anchor Peter Jennings of ABC TV's *World News Tonight* and interviewers from the *Washington Post* reported Coughlin's eyewitness account and dug for more victims and details of the annual revelry. In response, a dozen female casualties echoed her demands for accountability. When naval intelligence questioned 36-year-old Lieutenant Commander Roxanne Baxter, she corroborated Coughlin's allegations. Others, including Anne Merritt, daughter of an army sergeant major, declined to press charges but demanded an apology.

A Flawed Investigation

Seven months after the fact, on May 1, 1992, the Department of Defense Office of the Inspector General, Navy Inspector General, and Naval Investigative Service made preliminary inquiries. The Hilton Corporation chairman, William Barron Hilton, asked the Las Vegas staff for special treatment of the Tailhook party. The management urged employees to watch for underage visitors. To accommodate pranksters and heavy smokers, hotel maintenance staff altered the fire alarm system to bypass the third floor. Security guard Milton Lawrence reported sexual liaisons between consenting adults but no in-house violence. Security officer Janeth Albrecht changed the tone of Lawrence's testimony by declaring that the management urged her and other female staffers not to venture onto the Hilton's rowdy third floor.

Investigators compiled 2,000 pages on the Tailhook '91 incident. Until February 1994, they grilled witnesses, victims, and assailants in 140 instances of public sexual misconduct, including a leg shaving and belly shot drinking incident involving Ensign Elizabeth J. "Beth" Warnick. In all, agents interviewed 1,500 convention attendees and 700 other witnesses to substantiate or refute claims of bodily assault by 12 female civilians and 14 female officers. To get at the truth of Coughlin's allegations, authorities granted 51 naval officers immunity. Contributing to military shame was the inaction of two attendees—Henry Lawrence Garrett III, secretary of the navy, and Admiral Frank Benton Kelso III, the navy's chief of naval operations. In the aftermath at the Norfolk, Virginia, naval air station, the military judiciary focused less on criminal assault and more on charges of career navy officers' lewdness at an annual drunken orgy.

The Tailhook Legacy

The save-face attitude concealed a history of assault and rape over the legendary history of Tailhook gatherings. Out of self-preservation from reprisals, one victim, Lieutenant Kara Hultgreen, a bomber pilot, refused to file charges after she punched out Jim Ibbottson, a randy visiting officer from the Royal Australian Air Force. Nonetheless, Secretary of the Navy Garrett, who resigned 2 days after Coughlin went public, admitted to attending the Las Vegas gathering and to chatting with the exuberant company on the patio while hookers and strippers stirred up business. In the courtroom of Captain William T. Vest, Jr., a navy judge, over 100 pilots faced charges of sexual misconduct. One witness reported three pilots chasing a terrified woman onto a hotel balcony until a hotel bartender demanded that the maulers desist. During Coughlin's parents' testimony, her mother cited the most troubling aspect of the spree was her daughter's assault by fellow officers.

Participants in female harassment attempted to laugh off the Tailhook debacle as harmless flirting, streaking, genital exposure, and mooning. While conferring with Coughlin, Lieutenant Commander Hank Sonday smirked, "You need to remember that in the grand scheme of things, you're not dead, you weren't raped, you have no missing body parts" (McMichael, 1997, 61). He warned that she had pushed "about every political button . . . [she] could push in the navy" (Ibid.). Some military apologists charged Coughlin with unseemly behavior, a blame-the-victim ploy that redirected inquiry toward the female. One officer testified that the allegations of impropriety were fabrications intended to discredit Coughlin for outing males for a traditional grab fest targeting women, some of whom fellow officers set up for strong-arming. Defensive billboards sprang up asserting, "Not in Our Navy." Headquartered at Quantico, Virginia, the investigation humiliated navy brass. Of the 43 men accused, only 28 officers incurred censure for conduct unbecoming an officer, failure to intercede on behalf of a fellow officer, and indecent exposure. Six were proved to have falsified and/or obstructed official testimony. None was found guilty of attempted rape, battery, or assault on a female.

Woe to the Navy

The navy's leadership credibility lapsed amid heightening curiosity from the press into the worst military scandal in U.S. history. Sean O'Keefe, acting navy secretary, stormed into the controversy on September 25, 1991. On October 30, the navy dissolved its relationship with the Tailhook Association, which cancelled the 1992 convention. President George H. W. Bush stated his "complete intolerance of such [military] behavior" and personally demanded the resignation of Secretary of the Navy Garrett (Breuer, 1997, 165). Coughlin accepted transfer to a quiet job at the Pentagon.

In November 1991, Admiral Kelso suspended Snyder, a former president of the Tailhook Association, from his Patuxent River command. U.S. Senator Barbara Levy Boxer of

California proposed demoting Kelso to rear admiral and reducing his pension from that of full admiral. Congresswoman Patricia Schroeder of Colorado, a senior member of the House Armed Services Committee, led a procession to the Senate demanding Kelso's demotion. She prodded the male-dominant Congress with a blunt accusation: "The Joint Chiefs simply are not getting it" (Breuer, 1997, 164). Her colleagues objected to scapegoating Kelso on grounds that he had believed Coughlin and had instituted stiffer penalties for sexual misconduct. The Senate vote, 54 to 43, left him a four-star rather than a two-star admiral. Among the careers of other senior officers lopped off by scandal were those of Admiral Snyder and Admiral Dunleavy. Snyder retired early. Dunleavy and two associates, Rear Admiral Riley Mixson, the navy's air warfare chief, and Rear Admiral Wilson F. "Bud" Flag, a hero of the Vietnam War, received official censure on October 15, 1993, for arranging the convention. An official remonstrance cost Dunleavy one star and $100,000 in retirement compensation.

Battling for Self

In summer 1992, Coughlin took her story to the White House. In the presence of First Lady Barbara Bush, Coughlin reported the group assault to President Bush. He wept at the obscene details and remarked that he had a daughter Coughlin's age. In retrospect, Coughlin summarized her experience with patronizing superiors, blackballing, and institutional sexism as a reality far below the public's ideal of navy standards. Her work evaluations fell from exemplary to mediocre. Contributing to bitterness and disillusion was the whistle-blower's isolation, exacerbated by a congressional hearing into gender disparities and female abuse in the U.S. military. Deserted by other victims of Tailhook '91, she found superior officers deaf to her complaints of injustice from the traditional hierarchy. Male peers derided her, hoisted a newly named sour cocktail, the Paula Coughlin, at the Miramar Bar, and claimed she teased men with flips of her miniskirt. Defended by Dennis Schoville, she joined eleven others in civil lawsuits. She testified in court that "[t]he rumors about . . . [her] were so rampant and so disgusting" that she addressed 600 peers on the subject of sexual harassment to define her maltreatment as criminal (Noble, 1994). Defense attorney Eugene Wait tried to establish that Coughlin was impulsive, immature, and deliberately provocative to men. He further defamed her as a suicidal officer who kept flying helicopters in spite of emotional instability.

On October 24, 1994, Judge Philip M. Pro awarded Coughlin $5.2 million in punitive damages and $1.7 million in compensatory damages from the Hilton Hotel chain for inadequate security at the Las Vegas Hilton. Additional settlements appeased victims Anne Merritt and Ensign Kim Ponikowski. Coughlin's payoff broadened the rift with navy cohorts, who tended to dismiss her as a grandstander and golddigger. Peppered with gossip and hate mail, she transferred to the office of Jeremy Michael Boorda, chief of naval operations. In the end of a lame weighing of charges and a diminution of the women involved, she lost weight; her health declined. On February 7, 1994, amid visions of suicide, she resigned from the navy, effective May 31. Her official statement declared, "[T]he covert and overt attacks on me that follows [Tailhook] have stripped me of my ability to serve" (Breuer, 1997, 188).

The Tailhook Association settled with Coughlin for $400,000. Four days later, the navy ceased prosecuting men accused of drunken indecencies at Tailhook '91. Aspiring to anonymity, she wanted to shut her door and redecorate her house. In the private sector, she found no work flying helicopters. Dogged and derided, she and husband Joe moved to Florida to raise their son and daughter in privacy. Coughlin opened a yoga studio and disseminated the peace denied to her in her first career.

Feminists and libertarians lionized Coughlin for forcing the U.S. military to admit to ongoing devaluation and maltreatment of women. Looking back over her ordeal, Coughlin asserted to the press, "I think justice was served. . . . This [court judgment] sends a message that you can't tolerate abusing women" (McMichael, 1997, 303). In 1993, former *Newsweek* staffer Linda Bird Francke, in an article for *Glamour*, proclaimed Coughlin "The Woman Who Changed the U.S. Navy"; *Virginia Press Women* named her "Newsmaker of the Year." As a major sop to an outraged public, in March 1994, at the urging of Congresswoman Schroeder, the navy began advancing women's careers. President Bill Clinton opened 250,000 previously male-only positions to females in the military. Under the command of Admiral Jay L. Johnson, the hierarchy assigned its first female crew to the *Nimitz*-class supercarrier USS *Dwight D. Eisenhower*, the first of 32 combat ships retrofitted to accommodate a total of 7,300 war-ready female crew and officers. Another 5,000 women found berths on support ships.

Sources

Breuer, William B. *War and American Women: Heroism, Deeds, and Controversy*. Westport, CT: Greenwood, 1997.

McMichael, William H. *The Mother of All Hooks: The Story of the U.S. Navy's Tailhook Scandal*. Edison, NJ: Transaction Books, 1997.

Mitchell, Brian. *Women in the Military: Flirting with Disaster*. Washington, DC: Regnery, 1998.

Noble, Kenneth B. "Woman Tells of Retaliation for Complaint on Tailhook." *New York Times*, October 5, 1994.

Skaine, Rosemarie. *Power and Gender: Issues in Sexual Dominance and Harassment*. Jefferson, NC: McFarland, 1996.

Turner, Marlene E. *Groups at Work: Theory and Research*. New York: Lawrence Erlbaum Associates, 2000.

■ Widowhood
Lisa Halaby

An American girl crowned Queen Noor of Jordan, Lisa Najeeb Halaby lost her global presence after her husband's death. A blend of Scandinavian, British, and Syrian heritage, she was born on August 23, 1951, in Washington, D.C. The eldest of three, she, her brother Christian, and sister Alexa enjoyed a privileged upbringing as granddaughters of oil importer Najeeb Elias "Ned" Halaby of Dallas, Texas, and as the children of Swedish-American Doris Carlquist and Syrian-American Najeeb Elias Halaby II, a pioneering navy test pilot and the head of Pan American World Airways. The home environment generated by a perfectionist husband and submissive wife turned Halaby into an introverted and socially inept loner. She was more relaxed at her grandmother's home riding a pony. At age 6, while living in Santa Monica, California, she learned from her mother the family's Arab and European roots. The link to distinct ethnicities broadened her horizons and instilled pride. During the opening of the Los Angeles International Airport, she attended the ceremony with her father, who headed the Federal Aviation Administration.

Over many changes in residence, Halaby attended kindergarten in Manhattan and studied at the National Cathedral School and Concord Academy in Concord, Massachusetts. She recalled, "I would find myself on the outside looking in—watching, studying, learning—having to familiarize myself with unfamiliar people and communities" (Noor, 2003, 14). She rode her own horse and debuted with daughters of the elite. During her enrollment at the Chapin School in Manhattan, she volunteered to tutor non-English-speaking pupils in Harlem public schools. In the glow of John F. Kennedy's Camelot years, she absorbed the methods of his war on poverty, watched newscasts of civil rights struggles, and fantasized about joining the Peace Corps. At age 14, she recovered from the threats of a deranged stalker. That summer, she toured Greece and learned how to bargain Mediterranean style.

Lisa the Scholar

Halaby profited from the advances of first wave feminism. Among the first women at Princeton University, she joined the coed cheering squad and mastered spoken French, Greek, and Arabic. On sabbatical in Colorado, she waited tables at a pizza parlor, did domestic work, and assisted the staff at the Aspen Institute while studying the achievements of architect Buckminster Fuller. She majored in architecture and urban planning in 1974 by combining the disciplines of anthropology, art, engineering, history, physics, psychology, religion, and sociology. Key to her success was the acceptance of criticism of her ideas and projects, a flexibility that came in handy after her elevation to queendom. Her first professional consultancies took her to Australia, Iran, the United States, and Jordan. While working in Tehran, she began to comprehend the vast gulf between Western and Middle Eastern culture and religion.

While working at the Amman Intercontinental Airport's dual terminal, 26-year-old Halaby weathered the divorce of her mismatched parents and considered seeking an M.A. in journalism from Columbia University. She studied the political situation throughout the Middle East and discovered that American media favored Israel as the lone non-Islamic nation facing down waves of evil Arabs. During her residence at a small apartment in al-Ma'wa, she admired local families for an intimacy lacking in the Halaby household. She learned to cook her favorite Jordanian entrées—*fava* beans, *bamieh* (okra), and *fasoulieh*, green beans in tomato sauce. She entered a 2-month courtship by King Hussein bin Talal, who met her through her father's aviation company at the unveiling of Jordan's first Boeing 747. She developed hero worship for the king, an idealistic pan-Arabist who had held the throne since August 11, 1952, amid enemy attacks and intrigue. Her father warned that a royal flirtation could jeopardize her safety in Amman. To ready herself for a pragmatic decision, she read books on Arab history and on Islam and delighted in discovering that seventh-century Islam liberated women to study, open businesses, and marry the husbands of their choice.

A Royal Love Match

On motorcycle rides, unchaperoned night tours of Amman, and a flight in an Alouette helicopter over the Dead Sea, the king seemed irresistible in his wooing. At his gold stone palace, he engaged Halaby in lengthy evening discussions, screened videos by John Wayne and Peter Sellers, and even sang rock lyrics for her. Despite the 16-year difference in their ages, his mania for flying jets and helicopters, his interest in Arabian horses, cats, and

architecture, his educational attainments, and his peaceful nature and pro-Palestinian loyalties matched hers. Of her suitor, she admitted to admiration for his decency and moral
convictions. Of his country, she later rhapsodized on the beauty of the Wadi Rum desert
under shifts of light: "I was overwhelmed by an extraordinary sensation of belonging, an
almost mystical sense of peace" (Noor, 2003, 2). On April 25, 1978, he proposed in a domestic setting at the Hashimya Palace—their mutual readying of his children for a nap. The
youngest, Princess Haya and Prince Ali, won Halaby's heart in their grief for their mother,
Alia Baha el-Din Toukan, who died in 1997 in a helicopter crash in Amman. On May 13,
the king completed a formal request for Lisa with a phone call asking the permission of her
father.

After a simple bicultural wedding on June 15, 1978, Hussein proclaimed Lisa his life
partner and queen. The royal couple honeymooned in London and at a small seaside house
at Aqaba. Halaby adopted the Arabic name "Noor al-Hussein" (Light of Hussein) and converted to Islam. Unlike Arab women, she chose to speak for herself at the altar rather than
allow a male relative to seal the marital contract. The union thrust Halaby into a Middle Eastern milieu as fourth wife to a Hashemite king, queen to 4 million Jordanians, and stepmother
to his eight children. In the first weeks, gossip threatened to swamp her confidence with its
vicious intent. To her credit, she made friends with her mother-in-law, Queen Zein al Sharaf,
and scored praise from the king's nieces and nephews, who loved their new aunt's spunk
and spontaneity. The palace offered little privacy, no guidance on protocol, and constant
intrusions by courtiers, security guards, and military officials. To the surprise of disapprov-
ing Jordanians and Americans, she refused to be a queen on a pedestal. She declared, "I
followed my own instincts and tried to be polite and respectful, but I had to also be myself;
otherwise I would have gone mad" (Noor, 2003, 133). Among her scandalous interventions
were the dousing of lights at night to save energy and the control of Hussein's diet to reduce
his cholesterol and triglyceride counts.

Learning to Rule

Halaby acclimated to her new homeland through activism on behalf of its subjects.
While the king involved himself in foreign affairs, the queen built consensus on a tangle
of interrelated issues affecting human welfare. She made personal contact with Bedouins in
their native language and received their written petitions for schooling, housing, transportation, or medical care for their children. To ease Hussein into the hearts of Westerners, she
taught him to drop ornate Arabic oratory in favor of off-the-cuff speaking. Late in 1981, the
couple collaborated on a speech at the Center for Contemporary Arab Studies at Georgetown University in Washington, D.C. The bold political agenda shocked the 500 attendees
and the press for its deviation from traditional queenly interests in children and culture.

Halaby's royal duties left time for skiing in the Austrian alps, sailing, horseback riding,
gardening, and photography as well as recording impressions of American, Arab, Israeli,
and Palestinian politicians in her journal. A state visit with President Sandro Pertini of Italy
dismayed Jordan's diwan or imperial council for the host's flattery of King Hussein's wife.
Less reassuring were clashes with President George W. Bush over the Gulf War and the
arrival of Palestinian Liberation Organization leader Yasir Arafat, who manipulated Hussein's
sympathies with farmers who had lost their smallholdings to Israeli insurgents. In Tokyo, she
received a guided tour of the Imperial Palace, where the elderly Emperor Hirohito discussed
the finer points of Japanese architecture and art. From an insider's perspective, she lost

respect for the U.S. military for using the ongoing clash with North Korea as an excuse for rejecting the Ottawa land mine ban treaty.

After a miscarriage in London in the fourth month of gestation, Noor bore four children—Prince Hamzah, Prince Hashim, Princess Iman, and Princess Raiyah. Of the offspring, Raiyah shared the ash-blond beauty of her mother. Hussein's love of Hamzah assured Noor that her husband treasured his ninth child as though it were his first. She reared Hamzah to be heir presumptive in line with Abdullah II, Hussein's first-born son by Muna al-Hussein and a descendant of the prophet Muhammad. Hamzah traveled at age two months for his parents' state visit to the White House and later to France, Russia, and Germany's Gymnich Castle. For overseas flights, the king took the controls of the Royal Squadron Boeing 727 with Noor seated behind him. To spare his family intrusive media, he registered them at hotels as "Mr. and Mrs. Brown & family."

From Queen to Widow

In 1980, the queen launched the Noor Al Hussein Foundation, which integrates community economic growth with such social concerns as the impoverished, refugees, and displaced persons. She pushed for uniform building codes and proposed a consortium to conserve Jordan's architectural legacy and to integrate new public works in harmony with ancient palaces, walls, and mosques. Her drive for pluralism and international accord heartened Hussein during the Gulf War and the 1994 agreement with Israeli Prime Minister Yitzhak Rabin. On issues involving freedom of speech and the press, she made few inroads. In 1998, she promoted the Ottawa mine ban treaty at the United Nations, which limits the use of land mines and establishes ongoing aid for survivors.

Halaby's outlook altered in the twentieth year of her marriage after her husband was diagnosed with non-Hodgkin's lymphoma, a cancer of the lymphatic system. For his last 6 months, under her care, he sought treatment at the Mayo Clinic in Rochester, Minnesota, where she celebrated his 63rd birthday in November 14, 1998. During stopovers in the United States, the couple occupied their house on the Potomac River. After his surgery in Amman, she remained by his bed for 10 days, prayed for him, and helped him drift back into a work schedule. On January 24, 1999, during a brief remission from symptoms, he named Abdullah his successor and Hamzah the second in line to the throne. After the return of fever and the failure of a bone marrow transplant on January 25, she attended the king until his death on February 6, 1999. At a state reception at the Zahran Palace, she greeting mourners and shared their sorrow. At her residence, the Bab al Salam Palace outside Amman, she grieved in private in Arab style. Tradition forbade attendance by a Muslim convert at the king's funeral, which concluded with his remains borne by a cortege through Amman to Raghadan Palace and burial in the royal cemetery. Her subjects extended their love to the widowed queen but asserted that she could never remarry.

The Afterglow

Halaby's articulate writings encouraged East-West understanding, beginning with *Old Houses of Jordan* (1999), a field guide to traditional building styles. She compiled *Hussein of Jordan* (2000) and commemorated her husband for his ability to clear his mind of worry and fear. She stated to Dominick Dunne, an interviewer from *Vanity Fair*, "He always felt his responsibility was to project only the most positive, constructive, caring, loving, comforting spirit to everyone he encountered, no matter what he was feeling inside" (Bennetts, 1999). Her bestselling memoir, *Leap of Faith: Memoirs of an Unexpected Life* (2003), described her extraordinary career as a Middle Eastern monarch and her state travels over the Western Hemisphere, the Middle East, the Balkans, Africa, and Asia. Of Noor's commitment to her new homeland, she commiserated with Jordanians: "Politically, economically, this society has been under enormous pressure through its history" (Goodwin, 2003, 267). To ease the sufferings of Middle Eastern females, she organized the Women and Development Project, promoted civil rights for Afghani women, and presided over the General Federation of Jordanian Women.

On November 28, 2004, Jordanian politics overturned Halaby's expectations by denying Hamzah a place in the royal hierarchy and clearing the way for Abdullah's son Hussein to be named heir apparent. She abandoned her intent to live in Jordan and to groom her son for rule. Instead, she joined the U.N. advisory board. While promoting international stability, justice, and benevolence, she began residing in Washington, D.C. Of roadside ordnance, a focus of her activism for the International Campaign to Ban Land Mines, she condemned the maiming and disfiguring caused by abandoned antipersonnel devices. She stated, "When war ends, the guns and mortars are stilled, but no one turns off the mines" (Noor, 2000, 161). In addition to demining former battlefields, her full schedule of speeches and activism covered human issues—female health and empowerment, civil rights, Arab relations with the Christian world, literacy and vocational training, wildlife protection, sustainable global development, and disarmament and banning of child soldiery. During a visit with President Nelson Mandela of South Africa, she promoted SOS Children's Villages, a global organization offering orphans long-term homes and parenting. As chair of the King Hussein Foundation, she awarded the annual King Hussein Leadership Prize for leadership. Her honors include the Temple of Understanding's Juliet Hollister Award for service to interfaith understanding and nomination for *Time* magazine's person of the year 2007.

Sources

Bennetts, Leslie. "Jordan's Royal Widow: Queen Noor after the Death of King Hussein." *Vanity Fair* (June 1999).

Goodwin, Jan. *Price of Honor: Muslim Women Lift the Veil of Silence on the Islamic World.* New York: Penguin, 2003.

Mandela, Nelson, and Bill Clinton. *Nelson Mandela: In His Own Words.* New York: Little, Brown and Company, 2004.

Pelton, Robert Young. *The World's Most Dangerous Places.* New York: Tembo, 2003.

Queen Noor. "Foreword." In *Landmines and Human Security: International Politics and War's Hidden Legacy*, ed. by Richard Anthony Matthew, Bryan McDonald, and Ken Rutherford. Albany, NY: SUNY Press. 2004.

———. "Her Majesty Queen Noor al Hussein." In *Architects of Peace: Vision of Hope in Words and Images*, ed. by Michael Collopy and Jason Gardner, with a foreword by Walter Cronkite. Novarro, CA: New World Library, 2000.

———. *Leap of Faith: Memoirs of an Unexpected Life.* New York: Miramax Books, 2003.

■ Glossary

adrenoleukodystrophy (ALD): a sex-linked genetic adrenal disorder in digesting fatty acids in cells that gradually afflicts the brain, causes dementia and seizures, disrupts behavior, and depletes the intellect and motor control in young male victims.

agoraphobia: a chronic anxiety disorder characterized by panic attacks outside the victim's safe zone, which is usually home. Symptoms include faintness, hyperventilation, irregular heartbeat, numbness, and an extreme fight-or-flight response to a person, setting, or events.

AIDS: acquired immunodeficiency syndrome results from HIV in humans and worsens to tumors, the collapse of the immune system, and invasion by such opportunistic infections as esophagitis, pneumonia, toxoplasmosis, and tuberculosis. *See also* **HIV**

alkaloid poisoning: toxicity from such amines as amphetamines, cocaine, codeine, methamphetamine, morphine, and solanine.

amyotrophic lateral sclerosis: a progressive degeneration of the motor neurons that control voluntary muscles that move the limbs and joints. Patients become mute and eventually die of strangulation or suffocation.

anorexia: an eating disorder emerging from an obsession over thinness. Victims may diet, exercise excessively, fast, purge, and vomit to rid themselves of fear of obesity.

aphasia: an impairment of language understanding and speech following trauma to the brain from disease, tumor, or cranial injury.

bariatric surgery: a form of obesity intervention that requires reducing stomach size with permanent staples. The patient feels satisfied by smaller meals and quickly loses weight.

Bell's palsy: an acute nerve inflammation of unknown origin that allows the muscles to droop on one side of the face.

bipolarity: a mental and emotional syndrome marked by cyclical mood swings from mania to melancholia, relieved in between extremes by hypomania, a more balanced feeling of wellness and normality.

bone marrow transplant: the implanting of functioning bone marrow into the body of a victim of cancer, immune deficiency, or hereditary heart, kidney, liver, or lung disease to restore red and white blood cells and platelets.

bulbospinal poliomyelitis: a viral infection spread by enterovirus in body wastes, contaminating food or water. It begins with lung and throat infection, fever, nausea, and flu-like malaise and aches. Infection inflames the central nervous system in the spinal cord and destroys motor neurons above the cerebellum in the bulbar section of the brain. The result is atrophied muscles, acute paralysis of tongue and throat, stiff neck and immobile jaws, seizures, coronary complications, suffocation from a nonfunctioning diaphragm and swallowing muscles, and, especially in infants, encephalitis, an infection of brain tissue.

bulimia: an eating disorder that pairs binge eating with gagging, purging, and exhaustive exercise to salve guilt, depression, and a neurotic self-accusation of obesity.

cerebral aneurysm: the ballooning of a thin point in a blood vessel to the brain. Rupture and hemorrhage of an arterial wall can cause a collection of fluid blocking brain activity and precipitating pain, double vision, coma, and death. Survivors may experience aphasia, blindness, and/or paralysis on one side of the body.

chemotherapy: the use of toxic drugs or drug combinations to suppress or kill cancerous tissue, to suppress transplant rejection, or to treat autoimmune disease, multiple sclerosis, and rheumatoid arthritis. The degree of toxicity can cause vomiting, diarrhea, anemia, malnutrition, depleted memory, hemorrhaging, and death.

coma: a profound loss of consciousness or long-term vegetative state caused by neurological disease or injury, stroke, intoxication, and loss of oxygen to the brain.

congenital glaucoma: a form of optic neuropathy or nerve damage resulting from internal eye pressure, narrowed visual field, and destruction of the optic nerve.

cross-dresser: an individual who dresses and acts like the opposite gender in public for the purpose of sexual titillation.

delirium tremens (DTs): an acute response to alcohol withdrawal following a period of excessive imbibing or intake of barbiturates and tranquilizers. The DTs can cause increased pulse, hyperventilation, hallucinations, schizophrenia, and a tactile sensation of crawling insects.

dyslexia: a cognitive inability to decode and write words because of faulty brain processing of letter shapes, sounds, and meanings.

edema: the bloating of face or extremities from retained fluids. Swelling is a sign of toxemia during pregnancy and/or delivery that can result in kidney or liver damage, convulsions, coma, and death.

erotomania: a delusion that the sufferer is the love object of a celebrity or prestigious person.

exercise-induced asthma: a noninflammatory breathing deficiency caused by aerobic exercise, stress, and changing environments. During attacks, nose and mouth breathing of cool air expands vessels in the bronchial tract. Edema constricts blood flow and blocks air to the lungs, causing headache, gasping, coughing, wheezing, faintness, and cyanosis or lack of oxygen to the blood.

fetal alcohol syndrome: a physical and mental birth defect resulting from the mother's ingestion of alcohol during pregnancy. Victims suffer stunted growth, facial malformation, damaged nerves, attention deficit, and impulsive behavior.

frostbite: damage to skin and tissue from below-freezing temperature, which constricts blood vessels. Impaired circulation allows tissue farthest from the heart to freeze. Symptoms begin with tingling and burning, numbness, and pain followed by discoloration and nerve damage that may require amputation to prevent death from gangrene.

gender identity disorder: an emotional conflict between an individual's gender and self-identification.

gestational diabetes: an anomaly of the last trimester of pregnancy monitored by glucose screening to prevent miscarriage or an oversized infant requiring a forceps delivery or surgical intervention.

hallucination: a false perception lacking a basis in sensory perception, such as sight, smell, sound, taste, or touch.

hemispherectomy: the disabling or excision of half of the cerebrum to halt seizures or to repair damage caused by trauma or birth defect.

high-altitude pulmonary edema (HAPE): a life-threatening altitude sickness begun by anoxia at elevations over 8,202 feet and resultant swelling from fluid retention, breathlessness, and constriction of arteries and capillaries.

HIV: the human immunodeficiency virus is a retrovirus that spreads through sexual intimacy or contact with infected blood, semen, vaginal and mammary fluid, or other body effluvia.

hydrocephalus: an accumulation of brain and spinal fluid in the cranium that increases intracranial pressure and the risk of mental retardation, cranial bulges and malformation, and convulsions. Within months of birth, victims require surgery to drain excess liquid from the skull.

hysteria: excessive fear or overwhelming emotion or memories beyond the individual's ability to control or tolerate.

identity crisis: a subjective confusion over social, racial, creative, or gender perceptions as they apply to the persona.

liposuction: a surgical excision of fact, liposuction or lipoplasty sculpts a more appealing human shape by withdrawing through a cannula subcutaneous tissue from limbs, abdomen, and buttocks.

Lyme disease: an arthritic syndrome caused by the bacterium *Borrelia burgdorferi* spread by a bite of *Ixodes* tick from a deer or rodent and resulting in chronic neurological disorders.

measles encephalitis: an inflammation of the brain some twenty-one days into a case of measles. The impact of fever, convulsions, and coma can damage the central nervous system and cause death.

metastatic cancer: the spread of malignant primary tumor cells through blood vessels or the lymphatic system to adjacent tissues or organs, especially the adrenal gland, brain, liver, or skeleton.

migraine: a neurological syndrome usually causing debilitating head pain, sensitivity to light and noise, nausea, numbness, and weakness.

myasthenia gravis: a debilitating autoimmune disease marked by neuromuscular weakness, exhaustion, and paralysis of the facial and eye muscles, neck, tongue, and throat. Removal of a malignant thymus gland may restore wellness.

narcissism: obsessive self-love exhibited by conceit, egotism, pride, vanity, superiority, and self-absorption.

non-Hodgkin's lymphoma: invasion of lymph nodes in the groin, neck, or underarm with white blood cells. Symptoms include fever, anemia and weight loss, chronic fatigue and pain, night sweats, patchy skin, and leg swelling.

paranoia: a mental state dominated by anxiety, terror, and delusions of prejudice, stalking, and murder plots.

Parkinson's disease: a degenerative nerve disorder disrupting motor control and increasing debility from garbled speech, swallowing problems, and unilateral palsy, exaggerated gestures, numbness, and rigid limbs.

personality disorder: a mental disorder marked by an inflexible pattern that sets victims apart from normal expectations and behaviors.

phonetic speech disorder: an inability to articulate consonant sounds, such as r and s. Stutterers lose confidence and self-esteem because of frequent taunts and bullying.

posttraumatic stress disorder: a disabling emotional reaction to extreme psychological shock from loss, physical harm, or threat. Unable to cope, victims suffer emotional withdrawal, flashbacks, nightmares, sleeplessness, alienation, and crippling anxiety.

potassium deficiency: the lack of a chemical element that maintains fluid and electrolytic balance. Deficiency threatens the kidneys and triggers cardiac arrhythmia.

preeclampsia: a mysterious and unforeseen gestational hypertension marked by a dangerous rise of proteinuria or protein in the urine. The syndrome jeopardizes the endothelium or lining of the blood vessels in the kidneys and liver of parturient women, especially those carrying multiple fetuses. Toxicity develops through connection to the placenta, which filters the mother's blood before it passes into the fetal circulatory system. The symptoms of preeclampsia appear in high blood pressure readings, seizures, toxemia, and edema in the face and extremities.

proteinuria: the presence of excess proteins in the urine that may precipitate kidney damage or renal failure from impaired filtration of body waste.

psychotherapy: a one-on-one intervention by a medical counselor to enhance the well-being of patients suffering mental and emotional anguish.

ptosis: a congenital defect causing lowered or drooping upper eyelid. The condition results from muscle or tendon weakness and may worsen from fatigue or from the onset of diabetes, brain cancer, or myasthenia gravis.

rheumatoid arthritis: a chronic inflammation and deterioration of the joints, which erodes the skeleton and invades the vessels, muscles, skin, and internal organs to cripple the body.

rhizotomy: the disconnect of nerves from the spinal cord to treat cerebral palsy, multiple sclerosis, or spastic conditions.

sleep apnea: an interruption of several breaths during sleep, apnea subjects the unwary patient to malaise and fatigue as well as interference with the immune system and healing.

solar radiation: invisible radiant energy from the sun and reflected by ice, snow, and shiny surfaces. If unfiltered by protective lenses, the light discolors the skin and endangers eyesight.

survivor guilt: an emotional syndrome called KZ syndrome or concentration camp syndrome that punishes a person for surviving war, epidemic, accidents, or natural disasters. Victims incur depression, flashbacks, malaise, and self-incrimination for being alive and healthy.

thalamotomy: surgery on the thalamus in the brain to remove lesions and electrify defective brain cells causing the spasms of Parkinson's disease.

toxemia: the presence of plant or animal toxins or abnormal protein in the blood, a disorder threatening 7 percent of pregnant women. Poisoning can also result from contact with the venom of spiders, snakes, jellyfish, or scorpions, or from absorption of the castor bean plant.

transsexual: an individual who identifies with the opposite sex or who undergoes hormonal and surgical treatment to suppress the original sex or to change to the opposite sex.

trigeminal neuralgia: sensory malfunction in a cranial nerve that inflicts horrific pain and shock on the jaw, lips, nose, eyes, forehead, and scalp.

ultraviolet radiation: *See* solar radiation

■ Filmography

Additional biographical information is available for the following films and videos:

Mitch Albom
  Tuesdays with Morrie (1999)
Lance Armstrong
  Big Six—Lance Armstrong's Greatest Moments of the Tour De France (2005)
  Lance Armstrong: Racing for His Life (2005)
Roseanne Barr
  Lifetime Salutes Mom (1987)
  Little Rosey (1990)
  Roseanne Barr: Blonde 'N Bitchin' (2001)
Ben Carson
  Gifted Hands: The Ben Carson Story (2004)
Hillary Clinton
  Charlie Rose with Hillary Rodham Clinton (2003)
Pat Conroy
  Charlie Rose with Pat Conroy (1995)
John Bul Dau
  God Grew Tired of Us (2006)
Paula Deen
  Paula Deen Chefography (2006)
  Paula Deen Does Hollywood (2005)
José Feliciano
  Guitarra Mia—Tribute to José Feliciano (2000)
Ernest Gaines
  Ernest J. Gaines: Louisiana Stories (1992)
Elián González
  The Elián González Story (2000)
  60 Minutes: Elián (2005)
Anita Hill
  60 Minutes: The Justice Nobody Knows (2007)
Jeanne Wakatsuki Houston
  Farewell to Manzanar (1976)
Francine Moran Hughes
  The Burning Bed (1984)
Magic Johnson
  Magic Johnson—Above and Beyond (2006)
  Magic Johnson—Always Showtime (2006)
Caroline Kennedy
  Charlie Rose with Caroline Kennedy (2006)
  The Young Kennedy Women (2004)

Jamaica Kincaid
  Charlie Rose with Jamaica Kincaid (1997)
Ron Kovic
  Born on the Fourth of July (1989)
  A Good American: The Ron Kovic Story (1989)
Maya Lin
  Maya Lin: A Clear Strong Vision (1994)
Greg Louganis
  Breaking the Surface: The Greg Louganis Story (1997)
  Looking to the Light (1997)
Jessica Lynch
  Saving Jessica Lynch (2003)
Betty Mahmoody
  Not without My Daughter (1991)
  Without My Daughter (2002)
Toni Morrison
  Charlie Rose with Toni Morrison (1998)
Patricia Neal
  The Patricia Neal Story (1981)
Lorenzo Odone
  Lorenzo's Oil (1992)
Colin Powell
  Charlie Rose with Colin Powell (2003)
  Colin Powell (2004)
Pete Seeger
  A Musical Journey (2006)
  Pete Seeger's Rainbow Quest (2005)
Martha Stewart
  Martha: Behind Bars (2005)
  Martha Stewart: It's a Good Thing (2001)
Piri Thomas
  Every Child Is Born a Poet: The Life & Work of Piri Thomas (2005)
Elie Wiesel
  Elie Wiesel Goes Home (2003)
  First Person Singular—Elie Wiesel (2002)
  Great Souls: Elie Wiesel (2005)
Oprah Winfrey
  Finding Oprah's Roots (2007)
Muhammad Yunus
  Muhammad Yunus Interview with Charlie Rose (2004)

■ General Bibliography

Anderegg, Michael A. *Inventing Vietnam: The War in Film and Television*. Philadelphia: Temple University Press, 1991.

Arena, Christine. *Cause for Success: Companies That Put Profit Second and Come in First*. Novato, CA: New World Library, 2004.

Auslander, Philip. *From Acting to Performance: Essays in Modernism and Postmodernism*. New York: Routledge, 1997.

Baron-Faust, Rita, and Jill P. Buyon. *The Autoimmune Connection: Essential Information for Women on Diagnosis, Treatment, and Getting On with Your Life*. New York: McGraw-Hill Professional, 2004.

Blee, Kathleen M. *No Middle Ground: Women and Radical Protest*. New York: New York University Press, 1998.

Boggs, Carl. *Masters of War: Militarism and Blowback in the Era of American Empire*. New York: Routledge, 2003.

Bostrom, Kathleen Long. *Winning Authors: Profiles of the Newbery Medalists*. Westport, CT: Libraries Unlimited, 2003.

Brakel, Samuel J., and Alexander D. Brooks. *Law and Psychiatry in Criminal Justice*. Buffalo, NY: William S. Hein, 2001.

Brant, Marley. *Happier Days: Paramount Television's Classic Sitcoms, 1974–1984*. New York: Billboard Books, 2006.

Breuer, William B. *War and American Women: Heroism, Deeds, and Controversy*. Westport, CT: Greenwood, 1997.

Buonaventura, Wendy. *Something in the Way She Moves: Dancing Women from Salomé to Madonna*. New York: Da Capo, 2005.

Butler, Jeremy G. *Television: Critical Methods and Applications*. New York: Routledge, 2006.

Caroli, Betty Boyd. *First Ladies: From Martha Washington to Laura Bush*. Oxford: Oxford University Press, 2003.

Carpenito-Moyet, Lynda Juall. "Facing Death." *Nursing Forum* (April–June 2002): 3–4.

Chesler, Phyllis, Esther D. Rothblum, and Ellen Cole. *Feminist Foremothers in Women's Studies, Psychology, and Mental Health*. Binghamton, NY: Haworth Press, 1995.

Cohen, Cathy J. *The Boundaries of Blackness: AIDS and the Breakdown of Black Politics*. Chicago: University of Chicago Press, 1999.

Collopy, Michael. *Architects of Peace: Visions of Hope in Words and Images*. Novato, CA: New World Library, 2000.

Coltelli, Laura. *Winged Words: American Indian Writers Speak*. Lincoln, NE: University of Nebraska Press, 1990.

Crellin, J. K. *Public Expectations and Physicians Responsibilites: Voices of Medical Humanities*. Abingdon, UK: Radcliffe, 2005.

Daniel, Sara. *Voyage to a Stricken Land: Four Years on the Ground Reporting in Iraq. A Woman's Inside Story*. New York: Arcade, 2006.

De Leon, David. *Leaders from the 1960s: A Biographical Sourcebook of American Activism*. Westport, CT: Greenwood, 1994.

Doan, Laura L. *The Lesbian Postmodern*. New York: Columbia University Press, 1994.

Donovan, Kathleen M. *Feminist Readings of Native American Literature: Coming to Voice*. Tucson, AZ: University of Arizona Press, 1998.

Downs, Hugh, ed. *My America: What My Country Means to Me by 150 Americans from All Walks of Life*. New York: Charles Scribner's Sons, 2003.

Fantle, David, and Tom Johnson. *Reel to Real*. Middleton, WI: Badger Books, 2004.

Fetzer, Philip L. *The Ethnic Moment: The Search for Equality in the American Experience.* Armonk, NY: M. E. Sharpe, 1997.

Fineman, Martha, and Martha T. McCluskey. *Feminism, Media, and the Law.* New York: Oxford University Press, 1997.

Foerstel, Karen, and Herbert N. Foerstel, eds. *Climbing the Hill: Gender Conflict in Congress.* New York: Praeger, 1996.

Franck, Frederick, Janis Roze, and Richard Connolly, eds. *What Does It Mean to Be Human?: Reverence for Life Reaffirmed by Responses from Around the World.* New York: St. Martin's Griffin, 2001.

Gabbard, Krin. *Black Magic: White Hollywood and African American Culture.* Piscataway, NJ: Rutgers University Press, 2004.

Gay, Kathlyn. *Leaving Cuba: Operation Pedro.* New York: Twenty-First Century Books, 2000.

Gilman, Sander L. *Making the Body Beautiful: A Cultural History of Aesthetic Surgery.* Princeton, NJ: Princeton University Press, 1999.

Goodwin, Jan. *Price of Honor: Muslim Women Lift the Veil of Silence on the Islamic World.* New York: Penguin, 2003.

Gordon, Phillip H., and Jeremy Shapiro. *Allies at War: America, Europe, and the Crisis over Iraq.* New York: McGraw-Hill, 2004.

Hackett, Jill. *I Gotta Crow: Women, Voice, and Writing.* New York: Watson-Guptill, 2002.

Haddad, Yvonne Yazbeck, Jane I. Smith, and Kathleen M. Moore. *Muslim Women in America: The Challenge of Islamic Identity Today.* New York: Oxford University Press, 2006.

Harper, Phillip Brian. *Are We Not Men?: Masculine Anxiety and the Problem of African-American Identity.* Oxford: Oxford University Press, 1996.

Hecht, Joan. *The Journey of the Lost Boys: A Story of Courage, Faith and the Sheer Determination to Survive by a Group of Young Boys Called "The Lost Boys of Sudan."* Jacksonville, FL: Allswell, 2005.

Henehan, Mary Pat. *Integrating Spirit and Psyche: Using Women's Narratives in Psychotherapy.* Binghamton, NY: Haworth Press, 2002.

Hernandez, Jennifer Browdy de. *Women Writing Resistance: Essays on Latin America and the Caribbean.* Cambridge, MA: South End Press, 2004.

Inada, Lawson Fusao, and the California Historical Society. *Only What We Could Carry: The Japanese American Internment Experience.* Berkeley, CA: Heyday Books, 2000.

Jensen, Joan M. *With These Hands: Women Working on the Land.* New York: Feminist Press, 1981.

Johnson, Chalmers. *The Sorrows of Empire: Militarism, Secrecy, and the End of the Republic.* New York: Henry Holt and Company, 2004.

Kamalipour, Yanya R. *The U. S. Media and the Middle East: Image and Perception.* Westport, CT: Greenwood, 1995.

Kandall, Stephen R. *Substance and Shadow: Women and Addiction in the United States.* Cambridge, MA: Harvard University Press, 1999.

Kennedy, Caroline. *Profiles in Courage for Our Time.* New York: Hyperion, 2002.

Kennedy, Kerry, Eddie Adams, Kerry Kennedy Cuomo, and Nan Richardson. *Speak Truth to Power: Human Rights Defenders Who Are Changing Our World.* New York: Umbrage, 2000.

Kingsolver, Barbara. *Last Stand: America's Virgin Lands.* Washington, DC: National Geographic Society, 2002.

Knightley, Phillip. *The First Casualty: The War Correspondent as Hero and Myth-Maker from the Crimea to Iraq.* Baltimore, MD: Johns Hopkins University Press, 2004.

Kristol, William, and Eric Cohen. *The Future Is Now: American Confronts the New Genetics.* Lanham, MD: Rowan & Littlefield, 2002.

Kubey, Robert William. *Creating Television: Conversations with the People behind 50 Years of American TV.* New York: Lawrence Erlbaum Associates, 2003.

Kutscher, Austin Harrison, John A. Downey, and Georgia Riedel. *Bereavement of Physical Disability: Recommitment to Life, Health, and Function.* Manchester, NH: Ayer, 1982.

Landrum, Gene N. *Empowerment: The Competitive Edge in Sports, Business & Life.* Burlington, ON: Brendan Kelly, 2006.

Land-Weber, Ellen. *To Save a Life: Stories of Holocaust Rescue.* Champaign, IL: University of Illinois Press, 2000.

Lembcke, Jerry. *The Spitting Image: Myth, Memory and the Legacy of Vietnam*. Albany, NY: New York University Press, 1998.

Lincoln, Kenneth. *Native American Renaissance*. Berkeley, CA: University of California Press, 1985.

Luyat, Anne, and Francine Tolron. *Flight from Certainty: The Dilemma of Identity and Exile*. Amsterdam, The Netherlands: Rodopi, 2001.

Mack, Gary, and David Casstevens. *Mind Gym: An Athlete's Guide to Inner Excellence*. New York: McGraw-Hill, 2001.

Mattioni, Gloria. *Reckless: The Outrageous Lives of Nine Kick-Ass Women*. New York: Seal Press, 2005.

Melendez, Miguel. *We Took the Streets: Fighting for Latino Rights with the Young Lords*. New York: St. Martin's Press, 2003.

Meloy, J. Reid. *The Psychology of Stalking: Clinical and Forensic Perspectives*. Burlington, MA: Academic Press, 1998.

Miller, Richard Brian. *Interpretations of Conflict*. Chicago: University of Chicago Press, 1991.

Mitchell, Brian. *Women in the Military: Flirting with Disaster*. Washington, DC: Regnery, 1998.

Morales, Ed. *Living in Spanglish: The Search For Latino Identity in America*. New York: St. Martin's Press, 2003.

Morrison, Toni. "On the Backs of Blacks." *Time* (December 2, 1993).

Mulligan, Michelle Herrera, and Robyn Moreno. *Border-Line Personalities: A New Generation of Latinas Dish on Sex, Sass, & Cultural Shifting*. New York: HarperCollins, 2004.

Newton, Pauline T. *Transcultural Women of Late-Twentieth-Century U.S. American Literature*. Burlington, VT: Ashgate, 2005.

Nicol, Brian. *Stalking*. London: Reaktion Books, 2006.

Pelton, Robert Young. *The World's Most Dangerous Places*. New York: Tembo, 2003.

Riches, William T. *The Civil Rights Movement*. New York: Palgrave, 2004.

Ruiz, Vicki, and Virginia Sanchez Korrol. *Latina Legacies: Identity, Biography, and Community*. Oxford: Oxford University Press, 2005.

Safire, William, ed. *Lend Me Your Ears: Great Speeches in History*. New York: W. W. Norton & Co., 1997.

Saguy, Abigail C. *What Is Sexual Harassment?: From Capitol Hill to the Sorbonne*. Berkeley, CA: University of California Press, 2003.

Seaward, Brian Luke. *Managing Stress: Principles and Strategies of Health and Wellbeing*. Boston: Jones & Bartlett, 2006.

Shreve, Susan Richards. *Dream Me Home Safely: Writers on Growing Up in America*. Boston: Houghton Mifflin, 2003.

Silliman, Jael Miriam, Anannya Bhattacharjee, and Angela Yvonne Davis. *Policing the National Body: Sex, Race, and Criminalization*. Cambridge, MA: South End, 2002.

Sjoberg, Laura. *Gender, Justice, and the Wars in Iraq: A Feminist Reformulation of Just War Theory*. Lanham, MD: Lexington Books, 2006.

Skaine, Rosemarie. *Women at War: Gender Issues of Americans in Combat*. Jefferson, NC: McFarland, 1999.

Solo, Pam, and Gail Pressberg. *The Promise and Politics of Stem Cell Research*. Westport, CT: Greenwood, 2006.

Suss, Elaine. *When Hearing Gets Hard*. New York: Bantam, 1993.

Tasker, Yvonne. *Working Girls: Gender and Sexuality in Popular Cinema*. New York: Routledge, 1998.

Thomas, Marlo. *The Right Words at the Right Time*. New York: Simon & Schuster, 2002.

Turner, Marlene E. *Groups at Work: Theory and Research*. New York: Lawrence Erlbaum Associates, 2000.

Valadez, John, dir. *Beyond Brown*. Oakland, CA: Firelight Media, 2004. Video.

Van Gorp, Hendrik. *Genres as Repositories of Cultural Memory*. Atlanta, GA: Rodopi, 2000.

Wall, Cheryl A. *Worrying the Line: Black Women Writers, Lineage and Literary Tradition*. Chapel Hill, NC: University of North Carolina Press, 2006.

Weiner, Bernard. *Judgments of Responsibility: A Foundation for a Theory of Social Conduct*. New York: Guilford Press, 1995.

Weisser, Susan Ostrov, and Jennifer Fleischner. *Feminist Nightmares: Women at Odds: Feminism and the Problems of Sisterhood*. New York: New York University Press, 1995.

Welch, Michael R. *Flag Burning: Moral Panic and the Criminalization of Protest*. Edison, NJ: Aldine Transaction, 2000.

Werner, Emmy E. *Through the Eyes of Innocents: Children Witness World War II*. New York: Westview Press, 2001.

Wertsch, Mary Edwards. *Military Brats: Legacies of Childhood inside the Fortress*. Bayside, NY: Altheia Productions, 1991.

White, Christie C. *Wives and Warriors: Woman and the Military in the United States and Canada*. Westport, CT: Greenwood, 1997.

Wiggins, David K., and Patrick B. Miller. *The Unlevel Playing Field: A Documentary History of the African American Experience in Sport*. Champaign, IL: University of Illinois Press, 2003.

Wilson, Anna. *Persuasive Fictions: Feminist Narrative and Critical Myth*. Cranbury, NJ: Bucknell University Press, 2001.

Wright, Ronald. *Stolen Continents: 500 Years of Conquest and Resistance in the Americas*. Boston: Mariner, 2005.

■ INDEX

About the Author

MARY ELLEN SNODGRASS is the author of numerous reference works, including *Signs of the Zodiac: A Reference Guide to Historical, Mythological, and Cultural Associations* (Greenwood, 1997).